Dream Reader

DREAM READER

Psychoanalytic Articles on Dreams

Edited by

**Toni M. Alston
Roy C. Calogeras
Heinrich Deserno**

**International Universities Press, Inc.
Madison   Connecticut**

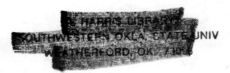

Copyright © 1993, International Universities Press, Inc.

Library of Congress Cataloging-in-Publication Data

Dream reader: psychoanalytic articles on dreams/edited by Toni M.
  Alston, Roy C. Calogeras, Heinrich Deserno.
      p. cm.
    Includes bibliographical references and indexes.
    ISBN 0-8236-1452-2
    1. Dreams. 2. Dream interpretation. 3. Psychoanalysis.
  I. Alston, Toni M. II. Calogeras, Roy C. III. Deserno, Heinrich,
  1945-
RC489.D74D72 1993
154.6′3—dc20   93-17645
                                                                     CIP

Manufactured in the United States of America

To the Memory of Dr. Bertram Lewin

CONTENTS

Section III
TYPICAL AND TRAUMATIC DREAMS

Section IV
COMMUNICATIVE AND INTRAPSYCHIC FUNCTION
OF DREAMS

Section V
DREAMS AND MANIFEST CONTENT

Section VI
SYMBOLIZATION IN DREAMS

Section VII
RESISTANCE, TRANSFERENCE, AND DREAMS

Section VIII
CHILDREN'S DREAMS

Section IX
DREAMS AND RELATED STATES

ACKNOWLEDGMENTS

We express our gratitude and appreciation to the authors of the articles (or the executors of their estates) who gave us permission to reprint their work in the present *Dream Reader*. In granting their permission, many of the authors added personal words of encouragement, noting that the projected dream anthology would fill a definite need because no such omnibus volume has existed. We also owe a debt of appreciation to the editors of the following analytic journals for their kindness in granting us permission to reprint articles: *The Psychoanalytic Quarterly*, *The Journal of the American Psychoanalytic Association*, *The Psychoanalytic Review*, *Psychiatry*, *The Annals of Psychoanalysis*, *The Bulletin of the Menninger Clinic*, and *The Psychoanalytic Study of the Child*. In addition, we owe thanks to our *Ministerium Sekretärin*, Frau Anita Ertz, for her yeoman work in typing the majority of the articles in manuscript form, and to our personal secretary, Mrs. Madeleine Fitzky, for her assistance in the numerous editorial tasks associated with preparing the present volume. We acknowledge a debt of thanks to Mr. Bob Lobou, Librarian at the State University of New York, Stonybrook L.I., and Mrs. Josephine Shapiro, Managing Editor of *Psychoanalytic Quarterly*, for assistance in locating the executors of the estates of deceased authors. Additionally, we are indebted to Dr. Judith Nelsen of Chicago who assisted us in locating the addresses of several hard-to-find retired authors in the Mid-Western United States. The kindness of the secretarial staff and the librarian of the Sigmund-Freud-Institut in Frankfurt-am-Main is also most gratefully acknowledged.

FOREWORD

Rudolf Ekstein, Ph.D.

Before the massive exodus of European analysts to North America and elsewhere just prior to the Second World War, psychoanalysis was always considered to be a depth psychology which had as one of its most important tenets the interpretation of dreams. For most European analysts the dream was truly the "royal road" to seeking enlightenment from the unconscious. However, since World War II and the shifting of the *Zentrum* of psychoanalysis from Europe to the English-speaking world, and particularly to the United States, the interpretation of dreams (at least as Freud conceived of it) has undergone a not so subtle change. In many analytic societies and institutes the dream no longer has the role of a unique phenomenon explicating the unconscious. On the contrary, it has become just another psychic product open for analytic examination. This downgrading of the dream's role is linked, in my view, with the subtle emergence in psychoanalytic theory and practice of a kind of psychoanalytic behaviorism in which behavioral referents quite at a distance from the unconscious are hailed as making psychoanalysis not only more "scientific" but more open to theoretical "progress" because of this now more "balanced approach." Fortunately, there have been islands of resistance to this downgrading of the dream (and hence the unconscious), but as a whole the primary place of the dream and its interpretation has lost ground.

The *Dream Reader*, in my opinion, is an attempt to offer a correction to this position. It records those fortunate islands of resistance by gathering together a sample of the most creative analytic articles on dreams since World War II, and in so doing, points to what we all need to be reminded of—the seminal importance of the dream's role in psychoanalysis. The editors, with their intellectual roots in America, Greece, and Germany, have felicitously divided their volume into nine sections, each with a specific focus. While Section I speaks about the multiple uses of the dream, Section II focuses on the use of dreams in the psychoanalytic situation and highlights Lewin's article on "Dream Psychology and the Analytic Situation." The next sections (III through V) contain papers dealing with such topics as typical and traumatic dreams, the communicative function of the dream, and the dream's manifest content.

Section VI gathers together a well-chosen group of articles on the important area of symbolization in dreams. Section VII presents a discriminating set of articles on transference and countertransference manifestations in dreams.

A section of considerable interest to me is Section VIII, which is occupied with children's dreams—their specific uses during therapy and their differentiation from daydreams and psychoticlike material. Of the papers included in this section, I found the article by Leo Rangell (chapter 42, "A Treatment of Nightmares in a Seven-Year-Old Boy") particularly stimulating. Here he reports a unique therapeutic experience in which he supervised by mail the boy's treatment by his father. The final section, Section IX, addresses the nature of the dream in relation to hypnosis and related states, providing us with some little-known findings regarding dreams induced by hypnosis, sleepwalking, a psychotic experience, and the identity of unconscious sources connecting myths and dreams.

In summation, this dream anthology gives us an excellent selection of articles published after the Second World War. Its references will be of almost encyclopedic value to the reader, open a view to the work done after the pioneer work of Freud and his first collaborators, and encourage us to think of the dream as an area of endless exploration, of stimulation, and of research opportunities. I would want thus to enlarge on Freud's definition of the dream as the royal road to an understanding of the unconscious, and suggest the dream is also the *royal road to finding a new adaptive capacity*.

EDITORS' INTRODUCTION

Aristotle, at the beginning of his *Metaphysics*, states that "all men are possessed by the desire to know." We feel that all analysts have a "desire to know" and remain current about dreams. Our purpose in bringing together the most significant and current psychoanalytic papers on dreams written since World War II is predicated on this need to know that we have recognized for some years. Previously, there has been no omnibus volume of representative psychoanalytic articles on dreams or dreaming to which the analyst, psychologist, psychiatrist or social worker could refer. Nor has there been a work to which the analyst or dream investigator could refer for a succinct current overview of the field.

In the course of making our selection of articles, we have tried to evaluate as carefully and validly as possible every legitimate dream article appearing in English language psychoanalytic or related journals since the end of the Second World War. In making our final judgment as to include or not include a given article, we have been guided by the twin criteria of: (1) determining whether the article makes a contribution toward extending our clinical or theoretical knowledge of the psychoanalytic approach to the dream; and (2) determining whether the article in question contributes in the broader sense to psychoanalytic practice or theory. In several instances, articles which aptly fit these criteria have had to be excluded because of their monograph length (e.g., Erikson's article on "Freud's Dream of Irma's Injection" (1900); or Mack's "Nightmares, Conflict and Ego Development in Childhood" (1965).

We found the final selection of articles to fall quite naturally into nine categories: Dreams and Their Multiple Uses; Dreams and the Psychoanalytic Situation; Typical and Traumatic Dreams; Communicative and Intrapsychic Functions of Dreams; Dreams and Manifest Content; Symbolization and

Dreams; and so on. We have written brief evaluative introductions to each of these sections, highlighting the nature of each article, and commenting on its role in the particular section.

In reviewing and appraising the articles in this *Dream Reader*, we are once again impressed with how much current psychoanalytic dream research, both clinical as well as experimental, stems from Freud's original formulations, hypotheses and discoveries made in his *The Interpretation of Dreams* (1900). And also how comparatively few really new dream advances have been made, despite the many dream investigations conducted in the post-World War II era. One plausible explanation for this may be found in Ralph Greenson's article (see chapter 8), "The Exceptional Position of the Dream in Psychoanalytic Practice" (1970). There he points out that a "goodly number" of analysts in recent years have downgraded the clinical importance of the dream in the extent that they feel that the dream has no special place in treatment, or they use techniques which indicate that they disregard Freud's theory and overall method of understanding and using the dream in clinical practice. Twenty years later, we find that this judgment and evaluation, in general, still seems to hold true, despite the recent surge of interest and research on psychoanalytic technique, and the increased emphasis paid to its nontransference aspects.

Yet, having noted this relative lag in psychoanalytic dream research, we nonetheless find that small a number of analysts have carried on Freud's work by making truly creative contributions. Based upon our appraisal of the distillate of articles finally appearing in the *Dream Reader*, we find that two analysts have made what can be judiciously considered "advances" in understanding the dream and dream formation in the years following World War II. The earliest are the seminal research papers on Bertram Lewin in which he introduces the novel concept of the "dream screen" (1946a,b, 1948) as a special structure or organization which can be distinguished from the rest of the dream. The dream screen for Lewin represents the "idea of sleep," and it is the element of the dream which fulfills the cardinal idea of falling asleep. It also represents the maternal breast, usually flattened out, as the infant might perceive it while falling asleep. In this regard, Lewin shows how the dream screen is very much related to the idea of forgetting one's dream and to the dynamics and developmental fixations intrinsic to orality itself. A second, but no less important aspect of Lewin's dream investigations is to be found in his classical article, "Dream Psychology and the Analytic Situation" (1955), in which he puts forth the thesis that "analysis-formation" is like "dream-formation," since it involves the same memory traces and psychic structure, although usually in different proportions (see chapter 7). For example, Lewin maintains that the analyst continually operates either to wake the patient somewhat or to put him asleep a little, or to soothe or to arouse, and this effect may be quite unconscious for both patient and analyst.

Next among those who have contributed significantly to our analytic understanding of the dream is Mark Kanzer whose work on the "communicative function" of the dream has added a truly new dimension through which to understand the dream. Kanzer's main thesis, first reported in his paper "The Communicative Function of the Dream" (1955), and reported in the *Dream Reader* in chapter 21 in an "Overview" article on "The Communicative Function of the Dream" by one of the editors, holds that the dream serves a communicative function, directly in terms of introjected objects, and indirectly in relation to the external world. That one, in effect, makes a *special* communication to the person to whom one tells the dream, and that such an interpersonal communication can be understood and brought into conjunction with the dream's intrapsychic and narcissistic function and meaning.

One article, included in the *Dream Reader*, Kleeman's "Dreaming for a Dream Course" (chapter 9), seems, by its novel approach to dream analysis and its carefully reasoned discussion, to clarify significantly aspects of psychoanalytic theory and technique. In this unique communication, candidates in a dream course given at a psychoanalytic institute presented and analyzed their dreams as the main requirement of the course. The course (actually a seminar) began with the instructor (Robert Knight) presenting one of his own dreams, along with some suggestions and guidelines regarding the various approaches to dream analyses. This stimulated the candidates (7 in all) to dream especially for the course and to present their dreams—after constructing their individual analyses—for further discussion and analysis in the group. Although the instructor and the candidate analyzed their dreams essentially from Erikson's "comprehensive approach," as presented in his paper "The Dream Specimen of Psychoanalysis" (1954),* their individual analysis, along with class participation, was in considerable depth and quite insightful. All in all, the class's presentation and way of analyzing their dreams proved to be a highly effective teaching technique and led to fuller and deeper understanding of the process of dream psychology and interpretation.

In closing this Introduction to the *Dream Reader*, we wish to note that the final remarks on these articles, plus the most recent trends occurring during this period, will be included in the *Afterword*. We encourage the interested reader who reads this volume to pick first one or two articles from each section for examination, before more systematically going through the *Reader*. In this way a more representative feeling for the breadth and quality of the *Dream Reader* should emerge.

The Editors

*Erikson was originally scheduled to teach the course.

Section I

Dreams and Their Multiple Uses

This section demonstrates the wide range of topical areas to which legitimate dream investigations may be applied. It begins with Marie Bonaparte's article, "A Lion Hunter's Dream" (1949), in which she shows that a big game hunter's recurrent dreams—following a successful killing of a lion who had almost killed him—resulted not in the typical traumatic dream relating to mastery, but in a type of examination dream where he failed. The section ends with an equally stimulating article, " 'All Roads Lead to Rome': The Role of the Nursemaid in Freud's Dreams" (1973), by Kenneth Grigg, in which he explores the role of Freud's early nursemaid in his dreams, supporting the thesis that Freud's fear of going to Rome was a result of incestuous wishes toward his mother, and the specific choice of this city was an unconscious representation of his feelings toward the Roman Catholic nursemaid who took care of him during his first two-and-a-half years of life. Following the dream-interpretation model set by Freud himself, Grigg convincingly reconstructs Freud's oedipal relationship and examines its effects on producing his "travel phobia" and his "Rome neurosis."

In between these two papers, we present such classical and enduring articles as Rudolph Loewenstein's (1949) paper demonstrating how a patient's posttraumatic dream repeats in distorted and symbolic form the original traumatic event, subsequently transforming the original passive response to an active feat in the process of achieving mastery; Martin Grotjahn's (1945) delightful little contribution on how laughter in dreams constitutes only a partial awakening of the ego and how the sleep ego may laugh about things which the fully integrated and wake ego would not find amusing; Sanford Izner's (1959)

1

closely reasoned paper examining how primal scene dream content appears in analysis as a result of the analyst's interpretation of orally dependent transference reactions; and finally Donald Kaplan's (1962) article in which he discusses, through focusing on the manifest dream content, how defensive transformations from denial to projection occurred in a narcissistic patient, adumbrating important therapeutic changes in the process.

Chapter 1

A LION HUNTER'S DREAMS

MARIE BONAPARTE

In the Kruger National Park, or Transvaal Game Reserve, where the African animals, amongst which thousands of lions are kept in their wild state, there is a ranger called Wolhuter. He is the hero of a drama which having taken place years ago, in August 1903, has since been retold many a time and has made him famous all over South Africa. This is how Lieutenant Colonel Stevenson-Hamilton, the warder and founder of Kruger National Park, relates Wolhuter's accident in his book, South African Eden.

> One day, Wolhuter, in the course of his return home from the Olifants River, having broken up his camp at the Ngwanetsi, set out to march to a place called Metsimetsi, where he intended to sleep at the permanent picket established there. He was accompanied by several Native police and some pack donkeys, but the pace of this form of transport being a slow one, and the afternoon already well advanced, he rode on ahead, accompanied only by his dog. While still some eight miles from his destination, the sun went down, the short twilight soon passed, and in the bed of a small dry water course, which he found himself presently crossing, it was nearly dark. Suddenly, the dog barked, and he saw an animal which, from its dimly discerned colors, he took to be a reedbuck, apparently approaching him from his right front. He was just thinking this rather an unusual proceeding on the part of an antelope, when he all at once realized

This paper was first published in the *Psychoanalytic Quarterly* (1947), 16:1–10.

that the animal was, in fact, a lion, and that it was coming
straight at him. He pulled his horse sharply to the left, by
which action he evaded the full force of the rush, but the
assailant's claws caught the horse's quarters, and, as the
latter bounded forward, Wolhuter, unseated was shot
straight into the jaws of a second lion, which had been
coming up behind. This animal unhesitatingly picked him
up by his right shoulder, and dragged him off. He found
his face pressed against its chest, while his legs dragged
underneath its belly. He was thus hauled over rough
ground for some way (I paced the distance a few weeks
later as ninety-four yards), his spurs catching continually,
until they were pulled off. At first, he says, he gave up all
hope, merely reflected rather bitterly what an ignominious
end for an experienced hunter his was likely to be. Then
he remembered his sheath knife, which he was wont to
carry on the back of his waistbelt. On every recent occasion
when his horse had come down with him, this knife had
fallen from its case, and it was with little hope of finding it
still where it ought to be, that, getting his left, and free,
hand behind and under him, as he was being dragged
along, he proceeded to grope for it. To his surprise and
relief it was miraculously still there, and grasping it tightly,
he pulled it out, and got it into a convenient position. He
knew that this knife represented his very last chance of
saving his life, and he held on to it, he says, as a drowning
man grasps a floating plank. Then, with his one available
hand, which it will be noted was the left, he felt very cau-
tiously around the lion's chest, to the point where he
judged its heart ought to be. He had to exercise the greatest
caution in his movements, for his best hope lay in simulat-
ing death, and thus lulling the lion into a sense of security.
The slightest attempt at a struggle, even any noticeable
movement, would have invited a savage worrying from the
animal, and, of course, the end. Presently at the base of a
small tree, the lion stopped, and let go its hold on his shoulder. This was Wolhuter's chance, and he took it. With desperate backhanded strokes, he twice drove his knife, which
luckily happened at the time to be sharp, into its side, and
then a third time upwards into its throat. It sprang back,
deluging him with its blood as it did so. Wolhuter scram-
bled to his feet, and for a few moments man and beast

faced one another a few paces apart, the former anticipating nothing but a fresh attack. Calling to mind the frequently stated influence of the human voice, he desperately shouted every approbrious epithet which occurred to him at his adversary, which to his astonishment and relief, presently turned round and walked slowly away into the darkness. Wolhuter lost no time in scrambling up the small tree by which he was standing, and managed to reach a branch some eight feet above the ground. Hardly was he ensconced in its fork with the trunk, when he became faint, and fearing he might fall to the ground, he loosed his handkerchief[1] and with it tied himself as securely as he could to the tree. While thus employed he heard the lion groaning a short distance away, and for the first time it dawned on him that he might have killed it. Presently the other lion, which had unsuccessfully been pursuing the horse, came trotting back, Wolhuter's plucky dog, which had never left it, and to whose efforts the horse no doubt owed its own escape, still barking at its heels. Having apparently first stopped at the spot where the attack had taken place, this lion followed the spoor of its mate and that of Wolhuter's to the foot of the tree, around which it continued to patrol, making occasional and cleverly avoided rushes at the dog.

At the end of what seemed a long time, voices were heard, and, by shouting, Wolhuter attracted the attention of his "boys" who, greatly perturbed, released him from the tree, and supported him along the path towards camp. It was a terrible walk for the wounded man—appearing to him to be eighty miles, rather than eight—and during the first part of it, the lion, concealed in the bush, but close to the trail, followed the party probably hoping for a chance to get hold of one of the donkeys. Even when camp was at last reached, and he was able to lie down, there were no medical aids available, except some permanganate of potash, with which an attempt was made to wash his injuries, but after a few efforts, Wolhuter says he stopped his attendants from trying any more, on account of the excruciating pain which any handling of his shoulder or arm caused

[1] Or rather his leather belt, which he showed me when I visited him (August 1941) at Pretoriuskop.

him. By the morning he was running a temperature. There
was of course no skilled assistance, nor indeed any white
man anywhere within reach. He was able however to give
directions to the "boys," and on a rough improvised litter
of branches, was carried for a long two days' journey to
Komati Port. Arrived there, and the district surgeon happening to be absent at the moment, he was sent, still without attention, by train to Barberton, where, for the first
time—nearly three days after the accident—his wounds
were properly dressed. The shoulder was badly lacerated,
and blood poisoning of course supervening, his arm became black, and swelled to an immense size. At first the
doctor did not think he could live, and later, was sure he
must inevitably lose the injured limb from the shoulder,
but a wonderful constitution, and the fact that at the time
of the accident he was in the hardest of condition, without
an ounce of superfluous flesh in his body, ultimately pulled
him through, and in a far shorter time than seemed possible under the circumstances, he was discharged from the
hospital as convalescent. But so terrible an experience
could not leave anyone quite scatheless, and his right shoulder became permanently stiff, with consequent inability to
raise that arm higher than the horizontal—quite sufficient
however for the trigger hand of a rifle!

Such was the terrible accident that happened to Wolhuter.
When I saw him, thirty-eight years later, in August 1941, at
Pretoriuskop, where he still works as a ranger, he was almost
sixty-six years old. He looked still fit though no longer young.
I also met his wife, whom he had married several years after
the accident, and his two children. We all had lunch together.
After he had, at my request, told me most vividly of his accident
and escape, I asked him if he could recall some of the dreams
he had had about it since.

He then told me that, while in the hospital, he had dreamt
of the accident over and over again, but that later, and for a
long time now, dreams about the lion had taken another turn.
So it came about that he dictated some of his dreams for me to
record.

> I am out hunting lions, I see a very big lion, with a very big black mane, a sort of a lion a hunter always hopes he will find one day. He stands broadside on and I aim at him just beside the shoulder. I pull the trigger of the rifle and the shot won't go off. I pull and pull and pull and pull, and finally the shot goes off. I can see the bullet traveling. It hits the lion behind the shoulder, but does not penetrate and falls to the ground. And then I wake.

Subsequently I regretted not having asked Wolhuter to give me the wording of the dreams he had had in the hospital. I consequently wrote to him, asking him to write back. In his answer he said he could report nothing "about the dreams that I used to get in the hospital. After so many years it is not so easy to remember them all, but one that stands out in my memory is this:

> I am out hunting lions, find a troop of them and fire at and hit one and it at once charges me. I fire again but the shot does not go off. I run to a tree close by, climb up it, and get out of reach of the lion whereupon a very big bull buffalo appears and starts butting the tree with his head. The tree sways to and fro and I fall. Then I waken to find it is only a dream, for which I am terribly thankful."

It is a pity Wolhuter could not remember the dreams he had had in the hospital immediately following the accident, but these two are interesting from several points of view.

They no doubt are recurrent dreams inspired by the traumatic event, but they are not typical traumatic dreams. In them the traumatic event is not reproduced monotonously unchanged as is generally the case. The Wolhuter dreams diverge principally in that the dreamer fails where, in reality, the man awake had succeeded. He cannot kill the dream lion as he had killed the real one.

In one respect, however, the dream has improved upon reality. The lion does not seize the man, but it is shot at, or an attempt made to shoot it from a distance, a notable alternation of the situation of immediate danger.

In the second dream (probably the earlier of the two, as Wolhuter did not mention it as still occurring as does the first) one actual detail of the traumatic event is nevertheless reproduced in the episode of the tree. As in reality, the dreaming ranger seeks refuge in a tree. But the security he had in fact attained by climbing into the tree is not achieved in the dream: it "sways to and fro" from the assaults of a butting "very big bull buffalo," another fearsome animal into which the lion is now transformed, perhaps better designed to shake one down from a tree. That these strong animals, a bull buffalo and a lion, are, for the unconscious, incarnations of a phallic father need hardly be stated to analysts. And under the efforts of the big bull buffalo the tree shakes so that Wolhuter falls out, a fatal accident which in reality failed to happen. But then the dreamer awakens and finds, in his own words, that "it is only a dream for which I am terribly thankful."

These words help us to find the clue to these dreams. They are not, as we have said, really traumatic dreams. They remind us rather of another type of dream.

In *The Interpretation of Dreams* (1900), Freud writes:

> Everyone who has received his certificate of matriculation after passing his final examination at school complains of the persistence with which he is plagued by anxiety dreams in which he has failed, or must go through his course again, etc. For the holder of a university degree this typical dream is replaced by another, which represents that he has not taken his doctor's degree, to which he vainly objects, while still asleep, that he has already been practising for years, or is already a university lecturer or the senior partner of a firm of lawyers, and so on. These are the ineradicable memories of the punishments we suffered as children for misdeeds which we had committed—memories which were revived in us on the *dies irae, dies illa* of the gruelling examination at the two critical junctures in our careers as students. The "examination anxiety" of neurotics is likewise intensified by this childish fear. When our student days are over it is no longer our parents or teachers who see to our punishment; the inexorable chain of cause and effect of later life has taken over our further education. Now we

dream of our matriculation, or the examination for the doctor's degree—and who has not been faint-hearted on such occasions?—whenever we fear that we may be punished by some unpleasant result because we have done something carelessly or wrongly, because we have not been as thorough as we might have been—in short, whenever we feel the burden of responsibility.

For a further explanation of examination dreams I have to thank a remark made by a colleague who had studied this subject, who once stated, in the course of a scientific discussion, that in his experience the examination dream occurred only to persons who had passed the examination, never to those who had flunked. We have had increasing confirmation of the fact that the anxiety dream of examination occurs when the dreamer is anticipating a responsible task on the following day, with the possibility of disgrace; recourse will then be had to an occasion in the past on which a great anxiety proved to have been without real justification, having, indeed, been refuted by the outcome. Such a dream would be a very striking example of the way in which the dream content is misunderstood by the waking instance. The exclamation which is regarded as a protest against the dream: "But I am already a doctor", etc., would in reality be the consolation offered by the dream, and should, therefore, be worded as follows: "Do not be afraid of the morrow; think of the anxiety which you felt before your matriculation; yet nothing happened to justify it, for now you are a doctor", etc. But the anxiety which we attribute to the dream really has its origin in the residues of the dream-day.

'The tests of this interpretation which I have been able to make in my own case, and in that of others, although by no means exhaustive, were entirely in its favor (see also pp. 334–335). For example, I failed in my examination for the doctor's degree in medical jurisprudence; never once has the matter worried me in my dreams, while I have often enough been examined in botany, zoology, and chemistry, and I sat for the examinations in these subjects with well-justified anxiety, but escaped disaster, through the clemency of fate, or of the examiner. In my dreams of school examinations I am always examined in history, a subject in which I passed brilliantly at the time, but only, I must

admit, because my good-natured professor—my one-eyed
benefactor in another dream did not overlook the fact that
on the examination paper which I returned to him I had
crossed out with my fingernail the second of three questions, as a hint that he should not insist on it. One of my
patients, who withdrew before the matriculation examination, only to pass it later, but failed in the officer's examination, so that he did not become an officer, tells me that he
often dreams of the former examination, but never of the
latter [pp. 273–275].

Well, Wolhuter, in his recurrent dreams, seems to go
through a kind of hunter's examination: he has to kill a dangerous wild beast, and has to succeed or fail. In the second dream
he manages only to wound the lion, not to knock it out, as he
did in reality, when the lion charges him. But in none of the
dreams does Wolhuter manage to kill the lion. In each he is
practically impotent. In the first dream the lion is invulnerable;
in the second the wounded animal is transformed into an overwhelming "very big buffalo."

So Wolhuter, the triumphant lion killer, celebrated
throughout South Africa for his pluck in one of the most dangerous situations in which a hunter could find himself, appears
in his dream life without force against the same mighty wild
beasts of prey. In his hunter's "examination" he has failed.

On waking from his dreams he is enormously relieved;
he is "terribly thankful" that it was only a dream, a consoling
equivalent to the reassuring hypnagogic dream thought to
which Freud alluded: "You are a doctor this minute. . . ."

How can we account for the fact that such a terrible trauma
as that suffered by the young ranger gave rise to a recurrent
examination dream rather than to a typical traumatic nightmare?

First, we must not forget that we have no text of Wolhuter's
early dreams in the hospital, except what he told me at Pretoriuskop: "While in the hospital I had dreamt of the accident over
and over again" before the dream had changed to its later
forms. So it is possible that the psychic work of binding the fear
into anxiety, as Freud described it in "Beyond the Pleasure

Principle" [1920] in discussing traumatic dreams, had been accomplished while the wounded man lay in the hospital, or for sometime afterward. Second, Wolhuter seems to have been and remained a very healthy and hardy man, and to have withstood the traumatic event with as much pluck as he had shown in extricating himself from the lion's grip. After a few months of convalescence and rest he resumed his work as a ranger amid the wild animals of Kruger Park without any evidence of typical dreams or other symptoms of traumatic neurosis. Whatever other disturbances of his psychological–instinctual life there may have been could not be determined in a brief acquaintance and so long after the event. Third, Wolhuter had been severely mauled by the lion. Freud observed in "Beyond the Pleasure Principle" that injuries and wounds sustained in a traumatic event tend to prevent the development of a traumatic neurosis by fixing the anxiety and diverting it from overwhelming the ego. Fourth, Wolhuter had extricated himself from the danger through his own initiative. In most traumatic events, as railway or motor accidents, plane crashes, the explosion of shells, one is usually saved by chance or "good luck"; one gets passively saved rather than actively saving oneself. In Wolhuter's case, it was the reverse: the young ranger owed his life to his active presence of mind, courage and skill. This circumstance may have contributed to no small degree to turning the traumatic anxiety into an examination dream. We may assume that in each circumstance of life where Wolhuter may have doubted his own capacities, the recurrent dream came to reassure him, as do all examination dreams. "See," it says "it is only a dream that you missed the lion! In reality you killed it," a feeling of satisfaction expressed by his reactions to the second dream: "I awaken and find it is only a dream, for which I am terribly thankful."

It would be interesting to investigate, from this point of view, the dreams of people saved from catastrophes at sea, of which there have been so many in these times, and in which the personal courage, skill, and purposeful activity of the survivors have often made possible their survival and rescue. Do such survivors tend to produce, like Wolhuter, recurrent pseudo-traumatic dreams of the examination type? If so, the part played by "activity," in contrast to passively enduring a catastrophe, would seem to determine the reaction of the psyche to anxiety incident to trauma. Excepting catastrophes that permit no choice, one may argue that the ability to be active, under circumstances that paralyzed others with fear, points to a particularly strong and relatively healthy personality which is less overwhelmed by painful realities, and has less need to adopt neurotic compromises than do most others.

Chapter 2

A POSTTRAUMATIC DREAM

RUDOLPH M. LOEWENSTEIN

A patient, analyzed many years previously, returned for a short period of treatment.

Some time before, he had made a canoe trip with his wife and two other couples. In three canoes they paddled down a river which had many rapids in its course, and which had become swollen from twenty-four hours of torrential rain. In a deep, narrow gorge, the patient's canoe capsized. He and his wife clung to their canoe and were able to attract the attention of their friends who came to rescue them. The wife succeeded in grasping one of the other canoes; the man, however, lost his grip on his own canoe and was carried away by the current. When he struggled to the surface he was far away from the others. He saw that his wife was being rescued. Fortunately, his capsized canoe just then floated by. He obtained hold of it and was swept down several miles by the violent current. Soon he heard the thunder of rapids which he was approaching. He took the precaution of disengaging his body from a rope in which he had become entangled. He was careful meanwhile not to lose his grip on the canoe, knowing that a man cannot by his own exertions keep afloat on the surface of foaming water. From then he recalled only that for what seemed to him an infinitely long time he was under water, trying desperately not to lose his grip on the canoe. When suddenly his head rose above the surface of the water, he was only a few yards from his friends. They succeeded in bringing him, completely helpless and exhausted, to a bank of the river. They rested for a

---

This paper was first published in the *Psychoanalytic Quarterly* (1949), 28:449–454.

13

while, but then had to embark again to complete the remaining fifteen miles of the journey by canoe. They spent a joyful evening celebrating the rescue which seemed almost miraculous to all of them. The night after the accident, the patient had the following dream:

> He is shut in the highest room of a tower. An elderly woman is trying to prevent him from escaping. He succeeds in diving through the floors, ceilings, and walls of the different rooms of the tower, one after the other. He arrives below in a yard, shut off by a large porte-cochere. He hesitates to ring for the concierge and dives through the door, turning outside to the right with a feeling of enormous relief. In the far distance he sees vaguely a medieval château with towers.

The analysis of this dream extended over a period of time, using infantile material known from the previous analysis. For clarity, this material will be presented in a summarized form.

The patient was well aware that the dream was to some extent a revival of the traumatic event of the preceding day. Diving down through ceilings, walls, and doors reminded him of the movement he and his canoe had executed when carried through a waterfall at the head of the rapids. Turning to the right corresponded to the right bank to which his friends took him after he emerged from the water. There are, however, important differences between the traumatic event and the dream. In the event, he was rendered completely passive, owing his life partly to his tenacity in clinging to the canoe, but mainly to the skill and courage of the friends who saved him. These circumstances particularly impressed him painfully after the accident: his very happy and successful life might have been ended by a stupid accident; also, he owed his life to two people whom he liked very much but did not admire greatly. The latter was especially humiliating. In the dream, however, the passive role forced on him by the circumstances of the accident and the rescue was transformed into amazing exploits of activity and initiative.

The detail in the dream of the porte-cochere reminded

him of a Mr. S., whom he had once known. As a young man, Mr. S. had had tuberculosis so severely, he was told by his doctors that he had six months to live. A fanatic mountaineer, he went mountain climbing alone in Switzerland for a few years, and lived many decades longer. Some years after his illness, he became one of the leaders of a revolutionary movement. He and several friends were arrested and imprisoned. They knew that the police were awaiting their attempt to escape in order to shoot them. Mr. S. nevertheless prepared to make his escape by filing the bars and letting down a rope smuggled into his cell. He proposed that his cellmate go first. He refused, and, being a skillful mountaineer, Mr. S. easily climbed down the three stories into the yard which was continuously patrolled. When his cellmate started climbing down, the police shot and killed him. Among the scenes of the escape of Mr. S. were a yard and a porte-cochere which were outside of the walls of the prison. Afraid of being recognized, he did not dare to ring the bell to have the door opened; he saved himself by climbing the wall.

It was of this porte-cochere that the patient dreamed, doing even better than Mr. S. by diving through the door. The patient had never been a good mountain climber, and though a rather good swimmer was never a diver. In the dream he transformed his humiliating passivity during the rescue into an active exploit, identifying with the man who had miraculously escaped death twice.

The diving through the walls reminded him, in addition, of *The Invisible Man*, by H. G. Wells, with the difference that the Invisible Man could not be seen but was caught and killed. Although visible, the dreamer could go through walls as do ghosts. For ghosts, he used the French *revenant*, which means one returned from the dead. He added that for some time after the accident he felt himself to be a *revenant*; that he had almost been in the other world from which he had returned; and he had the impression that he lived on borrowed time.

The dream reminded him of a series of nightmares and events of his childhood, which had been previously analyzed. The old woman, who tried to prevent his flight, resembled a laundress who played a particular role in his childhood. In analysis he had recalled in detail sexual activities between the ages of two-and-a-half and four-and-a-half: masturbation and sexual activities with domestics. To stop him from masturbating, his mother threatened him with paralysis and craziness. He would promise not to masturbate but would start again. The laundress was the last person with whom he had indulged in sexual play, after which his mother caught him and reproached him severely. From then his sexual activity ceased throughout the latency period. In the period from the age of three he had numerous nightmares, which analysis revealed to be centered on the primal scene. In dreams he was threatened by ghosts from which he would escape by running down a flight of stairs. In a first phase the threatening figure was recognizable as the father, in the form of a ghost or a devil, etc. In the second phase the threatening person became a woman.

This shift occurred when the patient was almost four, following an explosion and a fire in the apartment above in which many persons died. The patient remembered that all the children ran downstairs. He was the last, excepting his mother who remained to help the children flee. As the patient was running downstairs, a burning woman,[1] a horrible sight, almost overtook him. It was impossible to decide whether he actually saw her or whether this was a screen memory; however, his subsequent nightmares frequently took the form of fleeing downstairs pursued by a horrible, threatening woman ghost. It had been possible to establish in analysis that this threatening figure was a composite of the burning woman, a friend of the family whom he knew to be his father's mistress, and his mother.[2] The series of nightmares stopped when he ceased masturbating at the age of four-and-a-half. When he last had one of these nightmares, he was nineteen; it followed seeing a play in which a

---

[1] The burning woman was the mother of the family in whose apartment the explosion occurred. She actually died from her burns.

[2] This shift from father to mother as a castrating figure is not, in our opinion, due entirely to the accidental factor of seeing the burning woman. It is not due either entirely to the fact that in his childhood it was the mother who prohibited masturbation and threatened him with castration; for even then he feared his father's wrath much more than his mother's. This shift, which we have observed in other cases, might be explainable by the fact that while the little boy is struggling against his instinctual desires, he gradually identifies with the father during the process of superego formation; and this occurs at a time when the mother is still a temptation, thus a threat.

married woman makes her young lover kill her old husband. In that dream the dangerous woman was the patient's former mistress (for whom he had fought with a man) who later betrayed him.

The posttraumatic dream recalled another series of dreams from childhood, which clearly centered on birth and return to the mother's womb. Diving downwards head first and making his way out reminded him of birth.

Among other associations, the château with the towers, which he saw in the dream with relief, reminded him of fairy tales and corresponding childhood fantasies in which the young hero escapes from a house where he had been kept prisoner by a witch or a sorceress, and returns to his family's château. The towers reminded him of breasts.

Summary

This posttraumatic dream repeats the traumatic event and thus serves gradually to overcome its impact (Freud, 1920; Fenichel, 1945). The reported dream, however, also has the structure of an ordinary dream. The traumatic event is not exactly reproduced, and the distortions are clearly the fulfillment of wishes (Freud, 1900). The wish fulfillment coincides with the overcoming of the traumatic event. The latter is repeated in the form which satisfies the wish fulfilling function of the dream as well as the trend toward mastering the threatening reality.[3]

In his childhood the patient renounced sexual activity, and, thanks to that, gained the security resulting from the elimination of the threat of castration. He benefited from this renunciation in the latency period by building up valuable sublimations. In the dream he once more eliminates by wish fulfillment the threat of danger, mainly in three ways:

He identifies himself with the man who escaped death through his courage and physical abilities. He thus transforms his own passivity in the rescue into an active feat.

---

[3] Unlike the repetitive posttraumatic dreams described by Marie Bonaparte (see chapter 1).

He pictures himself as being reborn, adding to it, moreover, an active initiative.

He represents himself in the dream as fleeing from the
tempting but prohibited sexual objects of his childhood (his
mother and the laundress).

Chapter 3

LAUGHTER IN DREAMS

MARTIN GROTJAHN

In a discussion among psychoanalysts it was stated that people rarely laugh in their sleep. No member of the group could recall the dream of a patient in which laughter occurred. This seems strange in that other emotions (fear, anger, sorrow) are frequently expressed in dreams. It is possible that laughter, unlike any other emotion, is a social form of emotional expression. A person who cries wants to be alone. A person usually laughs when he is in company, seldom when he is alone.

Over a period of time it was possible to collect a few examples of laughter in dreams. These observations illustrated the psychodynamics both of laughter and of dreams, and gave insight into the role of the ego in both.

In the psychoanalytic literature Freud (1900), quoting Ferenczi (1916), reported one "laughing dream" of an elderly gentleman, awakened by his wife who grew anxious because of his loud and continued laughter while asleep, and he recalled the following dream. "I was lying in bed. An acquaintance of mine came in and I tried to turn the lights on. I tried it again and again without being able to do it. My wife left her bed to help me but she was self-conscious because of her negligee. She too gave up and went back to bed. All this was so amusing that I had to laugh terribly" (p. 472).

Freud used this dream to illustrate the distortion of an emotion and the transformation into its opposite. The old man was actually thinking of his arteriosclerosis, his impotence, his

This paper was first published in the *Psychoanalytic Quarterly* (1945), 14:221–227.

old age, and approaching death. The dream work turned his
anxiety, grief, and depression into laughter. The "light of life"
which forms the central motive of the dream cannot be turned
on again, a probably correct, if incomplete interpretation. It is
confirmed by the fact that depressed patients frequently have
pleasant dreams, afterwards complaining about them as highly
disturbing, as if the dream sought to make fun of the depression. Freud did not emphasize the expression of hostility in the
laughter of this dreamer who laughs in the face of death. The
conversion of passive suffering into active aggressive laughter
is successful dream work. This dream is the prototype of the
comical situation: a weak, old man threatened by death and
impotence enjoys a triumph by means of narcissistic wish fulfillment (1900).

A married man of thirty-two, in an analysis because of a
mild obsessive and depressive character neurosis, reported the
following dream.

> I went with my wife, my friend, and his wife to the theater.
> After the performance I get my hat back, but it is changed
> in a funny way. It is a big ten-gallon hat, extremely funny
> looking, soft and wrinkled. I laugh and laugh. My friend
> and his wife find it very amusing too. But my wife regrets
> the end of the once-so-good-looking hat.

In telling the dream the patient is keenly aware of the
discrepancy between the intensity of his amusement and the
silliness of the whole idea.

The patient's first association contained the entire interpretation. It was a joke he remembered, told him the evening
preceding the dream. "Two friends, both drunk, come home
and see two girls walking on the other side of the street. One
friend says: 'There goes my wife with my mistress.' The other
says: 'You took the words right out of my mouth.' "

Further associations gave the transition from joke to
dream, and demonstrated clearly that the two were almost identical. The dreamer at that time was entertaining certain fantasies about his friend's wife. The real reason for his laughter
was as well hidden in the dream as it was in the joke. One

laughs about the story of the two friends each of whom betrays his secret and attacks the other without realizing at first what he is saying. This fact is not immediately apparent. If it were, it would be an obscenity and not a witticism. It becomes obvious only through unconscious elaboration, an unconscious understanding. Only after interpreting the intention of the wit does the listener laugh. The true reason for the dreamer's laughter is as well hidden. His unconscious during sleep performs a task of interpretation similar to that of the unconscious of the listener to the story. Neither the dreamer nor his friends laugh about the hat, no matter how funny it may look. They are amused by the thing the funny hat stands for. In the dream picture and in the disguised wish fulfillment of the dreamer's fantasy the friend's wife enjoys the dreamer's potency which his own wife for reasons of her own seems to depreciate.

A young soldier awakens with loud laughter and tells the following dream.

> I was standing on the front part of a ferry—or an assault boat. I wanted to go back to my office where I was working before the war, but it was under water. I had to break the ice to get at it and I could not do it. My friend Morgan tried to help me but I pushed him into the icy water. It was not dangerous but he was mad as hell. I laughed and laughed. He tried to hit me and I had to run because I could not fight from laughing.

This dream is a nice illustration of the thesis of this paper that laughter in dreams follows the same psychodynamic rules as in waking life and as described and analyzed by Freud (1905a) in *Wit and Its Relation to the Unconscious*.[1] There it is stated that laughter occurs when energy is saved. In the case of wit, aggressive energy is freed. At first aggression is activated in both the witticism and the dream. An effort to repress the aggression succeeds in disguising it and giving it a socially acceptable form; therefore, the energy for repression is no longer

---

[1] This work is listed in the references under its *Standard Edition* title: *Jokes and Their Relation to the Unconscious*—EDITORS.

needed and may be laughed off. Behind the scenes the unconscious is aware of the hidden aggression; otherwise the whole
thing would be no fun. In sleep the level of ego functioning is
lowered. Dream censorship is strong enough to disguise the
intended aggression, but not as strong as it is in waking life.
The aggression of this young soldier against his friend Morgan
was very strong. In an infantile naive way the soldier pushes
his helpful friend into the water, plays a practical and dangerous joke on him. Analysis shows that the soldier resents very
much the fact that Morgan not only is not in the armed services,
but also teases his soldier friend about his voluntary enlistment.
In the dream the soldier kills him by pushing him into cold
water and, moreover, under an assault boat. Because it is disguised in the dream the murder can be enjoyed to the fullest
extent.

A highly gifted, artistic, somewhat schizoid woman of thir-
ty-one reports the following strange dream.

> I met two men who were laughing and laughing. I asked
> them why they were laughing. One turned to me and said,
> "I have no face!" I looked at him—and sure enough—he
> didn't have one. He had a kind of hooded face, as if a
> stocking were pulled over it. He thought it amusing. I am
> horrified to think of it now. The other man said, "I have
> the largest family in the world!" I asked him, "How come?"
> He pulled group pictures out of his pockets and showed
> them to me. "Here is a bunch of fifteen kids of mine, here
> a bunch of twenty," and he pulled out more and more.

The character and strangeness in this dream results probably from the contrast of laughter while dreaming, and horror
in reporting the dream. The man who has "lost his face" is
depreciated, is a nobody, or, in terms of the unconscious, is a
castrated person. He is thus ridiculous, like jokes about a man
with impaired potency. Losing one's face is as uncanny as losing
one's own shadow, to say the least. It was especially uncanny to
this patient for whom the loss of the self was far less a theoretical possibility than a potential reality. She had a justifiable fear

of becoming psychotic. That she represents the man as laughing is very important to this dreamer because the man in this way shows that he does not suffer from his disfigurement, thus reducing the guilt feeling of the dreamer. In this manner the dream work makes certain that the hostility expressed in the loss of the face is successfully disguised. There is, however, a hidden joke in the dream. Actually the man did not lose his face: he is masked. The mask also serves to conceal the identity of the man. Who he is is revealed in the second part of the dream. The second man, who by his laughing reveals his identity with the man without a face, is a father figure, and a father with some special merits: he has the biggest family in the world. In terms of the patient's life history this is really a good joke. According to her, her father had more of a family than was good either for himself or for the patient. This painful fact is exaggerated in the dream to an absurd extreme and by such distortion made acceptable as a joke. The disguise, however, is successful only in sleep during which the censorship is on a lower level than in waking life, for in relating the dream the connection with the true unconscious motivation is too keenly felt to be funny and a feeling of uncanniness predominates.

The next variation of the laughing dream is so obvious in its motivation that it may be illustrated by one short example. A married woman of twenty-six, mother of one child, in analysis because of marital difficulties which were the expression of a character neurosis, had the following dream. "I came to your office and you were very drunk and silly. You made fun of me and everything I said made you laugh harder. I got very angry."

In this dream the emphasis is on the transference. Undisguised, the action takes place between dreamer and analyst. There is hardly any symbolism involved, drunkenness standing as an almost unsymbolic representation of what the patient thinks about her analyst. The patient at that period of her analysis feared she might get along too well with her analyst. The dream anticipates the day when she would talk about her "silly" feelings toward the analyst and probably would be laughed at and humiliated. Realizing this she gets very mad and awakens. Such undisguised transference dreams usually occur in the first part of analysis before the patient develops enough confidence in himself and his analyst to discuss his positive feeling toward the analyst as frankly as other kinds of emotions.

To summarize, laughter does appear in dreams and its psychodynamics are the same as in waking life. As Freud described it, when laughter occurs energy is saved. In the case of wit, aggression is freed from repression; humor releases emotion; in the case of the comic, thought. This release of repressed energy is possible by the formulation of the joke which makes repression unnecessary, and the aggression emerges in a form acceptable to the superego by disguising the hostile motive. A witticism is judged as "good" or "bad" solely according to the form in which it is delivered. If disguise is not successfully formulated, the double-edged character of wit becomes evident and the reaction of the listener changes instantly from pleasure to disgust.

Theodor Reik (1935) illustrated in numerous of his contributions to the psychoanalysis of humor that the release of pent up energy must be sudden; it must be somewhat in the form of a shock which is the sudden recognition or rediscovery of an infantile anxiety. The surprise of laughter is the rediscovery of an old but never forgotten infantile pleasure: aggression against adults, authority, logic, law, and order.

When Theodor Reik read Freud's [The] Interpretation of Dreams [1900] he laughed about the dream interpretations as if he were reading jokes, and this may be repeatedly observed in seminars on dreams given to students of psychoanalysis. It led Freud to apply the psychodynamics of dream interpretation to the psychology of wit. The similarities between dreams and wit are manifold (censorship, primary process, secondary elaboration, etc.), but especially similar are their psychic economic values: the dream is essentially the fulfillment of varied wishes; wit is essentially the fulfillment of an aggressive wish. It does not seem to make much difference whether the aggression is released in the form of a witticism in waking life, or in the form of a dream during sleep.

The fact that laughter occurs relatively seldom in dreams despite its similarities to wit may be explained by the highly asocial, individualistic nature of the dream, and the sociable nature of laughter. Aggressive tendencies are repudiated by the ego, repressed, put through a process of secondary elaboration and disguise before they are acceptable to the ego and readmitted into consciousness. The ego senses with sudden surprise the true meaning of wit but freed from the necessity of exerting a repressive effort, the energy so released is vented in laughter.

In sleep the weakened ego functions like an airplane with set automatic controls; the dream censorship takes over a part of the piloting function of the ego. The reality testing function of the ego not being needed, all that has to be accomplished is the continuation of an undisturbed sleep. The disguise of disturbing id tendencies is accomplished by symbolism; there is no ego to laugh about the disguise.

In certain stages of awakening it may be that certain parts of the ego are functioning while others are still "sleeping." During the moments of awakening, the ego is redintegrated (Grotjahn and French, 1938). Laughter in dreams constitutes such partial awakening. Intrapsychic perception—an important ego function—partially restored, the ego recognizes the hidden meaning of the dream disguise, and the condition under which laughter arises obtains. As in the states of alcoholic intoxication, the ego is tolerant and may laugh about things which the fully functioning ego would not consider too amusing.

Chapter 4

ON THE APPEARANCE OF PRIMAL SCENE CONTENT IN DREAMS

Sanford M. Izner

In the course of the process of psychoanalysis or intensive psychotherapy the occurrence of the dream of the primal scene is an expected and usual phenomenon. Although much has been written about primal scene dreams from the standpoint of their content and structure since the early detailed accounts of Freud (1900) to further accounts by Róheim (1920), Fenichel (1945), and others, there has been little effort directed at any explanation of the circumstances leading to the appearance of these dreams.

It is generally recognized and accepted that primal scene content in dreams may occur during almost any phase of the treatment process; for example, the occurrence of dreams of this nature early in treatment has long been recognized to represent a form of resistance to the intense anxiety liberated by the developing transference neurosis. The content, although seeming out of context with the level of material being recognized by the patient in the analysis at that phase, must serve a different function. We must ask, "What is the defensive function of these dreams?"

At much later phases of the treatment process the recollection of dreams of the primal scene is generally considered to be in keeping with the material being liberated during the analysis, as the defensive structures are removed and information concerning impulses on a deeper level are brought forth. So if

This paper was first published in the *Journal of the American Psychoanalytic Association* (1959), 7:317–328.

a dream occurs, the question that then arises is as follows: "What in effect has given rise to this kind of recollection at this time in treatment?" Since dreams of the primal scene seem to serve defensive functions on several levels, this paper deals with the defensive function of these dreams in relation to certain specific elements in the transference. Emphasis will be placed on the regressive element as a defense mechanism in the transference and its relationship to the dream content. It must be borne in mind that although regression to a specific level of libidinal organization occurs, the other levels of libidinal development remain in evidence, with the level to which regression occurs becoming most prominent.

As will subsequently be demonstrated, the evolution of primal scene dreams was noted rather promptly following transference interpretations which were necessitated by interruptions in treatment or by changes in regularly scheduled appointment times. The patients under observation were confronted with their desire for the attention and interest of the therapist, which was obvious from the analytic material. They all seemed to be ready to recognize this fact; they all acknowledged this desire. When the transference character of this desire was interpreted, on the basis of the affects they had related to the analytic situation, primal scene dreams were presented often in a series for several succeeding visits. In some cases, the dreamer himself was in the midst of the primal scene situation in the dream, or at least in the position of having a "front seat at the affair," as will be shown by the following example.

A twenty-nine-year-old man entered analysis some months after he developed severe anxiety when he became aware that he was staring at the genital area of men. He was unable to form any stable or mature kind of love relationship with a woman. The patient always had intense difficulty with authority figures, which had interfered markedly with his professional training, and gave rise to much shifting of school situations. He was the youngest of three sons, and was his mother's favorite.

Upon entering into analysis, his productions at first were characterized by much anxiety related to his staring at men, in which he easily recognized the homosexual components. He developed an intense, passive, feminine, homosexual transference, with corresponding anal-expulsive and anal-retentive behavior. In the process of working through this position he developed an oral dependency in the transference. His masturbatory fantasies revolved around a rescue fantasy. In these fantasies he is a gambler. A beautiful young girl enters town who is a prostitute or who is about to be employed as one, and the patient rescues her from this fate, or in other variations establishes some kind of control over her attempts at promiscuity.

Primal scene dreams did not occur in analysis, although he reported primal scene observations. After eighteen to twenty months of analysis a series of dreams occurred which showed primal scene content. These were directly related to the analyst's impending vacation, and, as described above, were reactions to the transference interpretation concerning his feeling of being left out or abandoned. These dreams seemed to express rather clearly both the wish to be present where he felt unwanted along with the rather strenuous attempt to deny any feeling of deprivation at being left out. In this way he mastered the problem in the dream. It is also of importance to note that just prior to this period in analysis, the reactions of this man to interpretations seemed to have undergone a change. Earlier in analysis most of the interpretations met with rejection, but at this point he had arrived at a more or less passive acceptance of the interpretations given, corresponding to the orally dependent state to which he had regressed. The oral level of his regressive state was obvious from his feelings of nausea when upset, his loss of appetite, and his revulsion at food. At this point he described that the only real feelings of warmth were the ones he felt as a child at being able to climb into mother's bed to rest against her "large soft breasts"; especially when he was frightened at night.

A detailed report of the events in the analysis leading to a characteristic dream response follows. A shift of his regular appointment schedule was necessary. He expressed concern over losing time in analysis and felt left out. The transference aspect of these feelings was interpreted, and the result was a series of primal scene dreams initiated by a discussion on the part of the patient about a young problem boy who had attempted to have intercourse with a three-year-old girl. The patient wondered if the boy "had seen his parents having intercourse." This was followed by a dream in which the two sides of the bed that he and his wife sleep in are different, and his side is inferior. The patient related this dream to his feelings of being "left out" professionally and not receiving training that he was interested in obtaining, in addition to other feelings of inferiority. This was followed by a dream which portrayed him in a "fenced-in" area in the presence of his wife and another couple. They are awaiting a sign from the "chief" so that they may go ahead, and the "chief" gives the sign that he wants the patient's wife. The patient becomes involved in a fight with the "chief" grabbing the man around the neck and placing a knife at his throat. A hoodlum who is present wants to shoot the patient, but the patient hits both the "chief" and the hoodlum on the head with rocks and the patient and his wife run off. In the patient's associations to the dream it became even more evident that he was protecting his wife from father in the dream. His wife is always closely identified with and even resembles his mother. He was able to recognize that the dream referred to his competition with the analyst professionally, as well as with his father in the oedipal situation. In the dream, he entered into the primal scene and mastered the situation. His attempt to deny his exclusion from the fenced-off area is rather clear.

It was observed that similar dreams were produced when an appointment was canceled or when the analyst had to be away, during periods in the analysis when the patient had regressed to an oral dependent state. In this state of oral dependence the patient did not respond with an open negation to the transference interpretation, but accepted the interpretation passively; however, the dream was induced for the expression of the denial which the patient in this passive attitude of his waking state was not capable of. It appears to be a last line of defense with these people, and certainly we can assume that a defense which was impossible at a conscious level had to be removed into the dream. The state of regression to oral dependence in the transference makes all overt objection to the interpretation impossible as in a helpless, dependent child. This corresponds to suggestions by Anna Freud (1936), and Beres (1956), to coordinate certain defensive maneuvers with various planes or levels in the treatment process. It is as if the patient, when his feeling of rejection or of being left out is pointed out to him as a transference from the parental figures, would respond with a dream that says: "You are wrong, I was not left out, I was really there, I even took part in it." In this connection, we must remind ourselves that dreams in analysis take on another function, that of communication, a function that is not originally inherent in the tendencies that make us dream.

The second case is that of a twenty-nine-year-old, recently married male schoolteacher who sought analysis because he suffered from the fear that he might harm his wife or his in-laws. He had the thought that he might stab them with a knife. He described his wife as sexually cold and unloving. The patient was the second oldest of four children, the youngest of whom was a girl. His father was the provider, but a drunkard, and his mother was eventually hospitalized because of a meno-pausal psychosis. The patient described the oldest son as fa-ther's favorite and the youngest son as mother's favorite, so that the patient felt unloved and unrecognized. Early in treat-ment the patient related many memories that he had of hearing sounds in his parents' bedroom and of sitting up nights with the desire of going into the parents' bedroom, turning on the lights and asking them to explain what was going on in there. He also recalled many incidents of "sleep-walking" as a young child of four or five years of age, at a time when his mother was pregnant and later delivered the younger brother.

In treatment he rapidly entered into a passive, homosexual transference and seemed to pass rather quickly through this phase. Most of his dream material soon dealt with feelings of being deprived of food and drink and many of his desires were put in oral terms. His demands in analysis for attention and interest on the part of the analyst were intense. At the same time he suffered from anorexia, considerable weight loss, and insomnia. It was soon evident that this patient had regressed rapidly to an oral dependent state in the transference, and his reactions to the changing of appointment times or cancellation of them necessitated by the analyst's absence made it obvious that he experienced these interruptions as unfair deprivations on an oral level. At this phase of treatment he was responding to interpretations of the transference with a passive, acceptant attitude. The patient seemingly accepted the transference interpretation concerning his feeling of being deprived rather passively, but subsequently began to present a series of dreams with primal scene content, in sequence. In many of these dreams the patient undid and denied directly what had been related to him in the interpretations. The following series of dreams appeared at the time of the analyst's impending vacation.

First the patient dreamed that he was in bed with his mother, father, and older brother. He was unable to sleep and blamed father for not getting another bed. This dream was followed by one in which the patient is at father's house, having entered through the back door. He hears someone down in the basement but it is dark down there. He tries to turn on the lights but is unable to do so. His younger brother is with him and they decide that someone is in the basement and has done something to the fuses. They go down into the basement and find their father is there working on something in the dark. He is surprised and irritated at their interrupting and he does not want to see them.

Upon the return of the analyst from vacation the primal scene content in the dreams continued. He next dreamed of his older brother having intercourse and of his brother-in-law and fiancée in sexual activity. When another shift of appointments became necessary the patient returned the next day with a dream in which he was in his father's house and his wife was in bed upstairs. The patient was in the attached bathroom. Father shouted from downstairs for the patient to get up and did not believe that the patient was out of bed. Father came upstairs and entered the bedroom and noticed the patient's wife in bed, partially undressed, with one breast exposed. At the next appointment the patient presented a dream in which he and his wife arrive at his in-laws unannounced, and his wife's parents are leaving for Niagara Falls. They invite the patient and his wife to go along and they all leave together in the patient's car. While it was obvious from his associations that the patient felt unwelcome, neglected, and left out in the analysis, with his in-laws and with his own parents, in the dream he denies this feeling almost to the point of ridiculing the suggestion that he could ever have been unwelcome. He seems to say: "Unwelcome . . . I am even welcome on their honeymoon trip to Niagara Falls." The fulfillment of the wish to be present at the primal scene in order to deny the transference interpretation is evident.

The reaction of childlike denial so frequently resorted to in response to a shift in a rigidly regular schedule of appointments, or at vacation times in treatment, when the therapist leaves the patient, makes understandable why this type of dream content appears also in connection with the termination of treatment, or if the possibility of termination is discussed with or presented to the patient. It seems particularly interesting in this regard that in the case of the Wolf Man as described by Freud (1918), the dream of the primal scene was presented very early in the analysis, but the recognition of the full significance of the content of the dream as primal scene material occurred only under the threat of termination of analysis, as discussed by Freud and later mentioned by the Wolf Man himself (1957) in a personal communication to Freud.

To further illustrate the development of this phenomenon in reaction to events related to the transference, without the use of an interpretation, the following examples are presented. Both had been in treatment for a long enough period of time to be in a position to contemplate termination. The first, a married woman thirty-eight years of age who was employed as an executive secretary for a large corporation, entered treatment as the result of several severely traumatic experiences. She was a bright and well-read person who had had active tuberculosis at the age of sixteen, at which time she was hospitalized at bed rest for one year. In her thirty-third year it was discovered that she was afflicted with a chronic illness which could be fatal under more acute circumstances. Two years later and just prior to her entry into treatment she had surgery performed which resulted in the early onset of menopause. This surgery was necessary because of her earlier active tuberculosis. The patient became very upset and depressed following the surgery, and sought treatment. She related her depression to the knowledge that she could never produce a child of her own and kept her husband under constant pressure to agree to adopt a child. All of these attempts led to periods of depression and anger due to the frustration involved.

Her early years were characterized by much shifting of her home situation. The patient was the second youngest of twelve children, being two years older than the youngest girl, at whose birth mother had died. The patient spent most of her early years away from the immediate family and only returned home after her father had remarried. This woman formed a very deep dependent kind of relationship in the therapy with many demands of an oral nature being directed almost continually at the therapist. After approximately three-and-a-half years of therapy, at a time when the patient was reacting with feelings as described above, she was informed by the therapist that there might be some revision of the schedule of her appointments. This was found to be unnecessary, but at the time of her next regularly scheduled appointment she presented the following dream: first, that she is in the home of her uncle and aunt where she had resided from the second to sixth years of her life after her mother's death. It seems that she slept in a crib in a bedroom of her uncle and aunt during some of this time, and there are several graves under the kitchen floor, one of which the patient knows is her mother's grave. Next, she is in the bedroom of her uncle and aunt who are in bed and are fighting over the blankets, pulling back and forth from one side to the other. Her feeling expressed in the dream is that it seems very silly to fight this way over the covers—she would never do anything like that. Her immediate associations to the dream were related to having read in Jones's *Life and Work of Sigmund Freud* (1953–1957) that Freud had suspected that according to some of the productions during analysis of the Princess Marie Bonaparte, she must have witnessed intercourse between some of the servants. This observation was later confirmed for him by investigation. The patient then associated what she had dreamed with what she had read; with her own wish to be present in the therapy and also her wish to be with her uncle and aunt where she had really felt excluded. The threat that she might be left out was undone and denied in the dream.

Another patient, a twenty-seven-year-old married woman, entered treatment abruptly following the death of her foster father and at the time when her husband was sent overseas. She had been the youngest of three children and the only one who was turned over to a children's custodial home at the time of her mother's death. The patient was about eighteen months of age at the time. Within six months time she was adopted by her foster parents who had been unable to have any children of their own. When the patient was six years of age a daughter was born to these foster parents. The patient considered her "sister" the favorite of mother and always felt she was closer to father, although she blamed her real father for sending her away. Her depression and intense anxiety related to the separation from both father and husband and was reflected in all of her activities. Her fears of rejection and abandonment were prevalent throughout the course of treatment and her attachment to the therapist an intensely binding one, characterized by demands for all kinds of gratification on an oral level.

After approximately two-and-a-half years of therapy a situation arose wherein the patient could not have her usual appointment because her therapist had to be out of town and was unable to provide a substitute time for her. She arrived extremely early for her next appointment and was able to relate this to her feelings of exclusion and disappointment and deprivation at not obtaining the appointment time desired and the intense anxiety she experienced as a result of this. She then related a dream which she had the night prior to her appointment. In the dream she is standing outside of a boat viewing a man's back; he is fishing. She knows this man is like father. There is another part of the dream that has to do with the queen or Queen Mother. She associated the dream with her father and the therapist and the feeling that she was excluded from the therapy, because the therapist was too busy to see her, just as she felt as a child when she realized that father was too busy with mother to have time for her. She was then able to realize that she was expressing the thought in the dream that although she felt on the outside, she was really present at what was going on. The dream evidently expressed both the wish to be present at the primal scene and the denial of being left out completely—she was really there. In these last two examples, the loss of mother and the feeling of having been abandoned by her early in life is clear and seems pertinent to the primal scene content in the dreams.

In view of the preceding clinical material and from many other examples and observations, it is proposed that primal scene dream material in analysis and intensive psychotherapy may appear as a result of the interpretation of transference resistances of a rather specific nature. This was noted to occur in patients who regress in the course of analysis to an oral dependent state. Their reactions to the interpretations related to feelings of deprivation, rejection, and exclusion in the transference tends, rather characteristically, to reproduce primal scene content in dreams in an effort to accomplish certain ends. First, there is an attempt at mastery of the situation, in expressing the infantile wish to be present at the union of their parents in intercourse, but second, and from the standpoint of this presentation, most importantly, to deny the significance and the appropriateness of the transference interpretation; that is, to deny that the patient ever felt excluded either in the analysis or in relation to the parents, expressed in terms of the primal scene.

That dreams, although their deepest content is a wish fulfillment, can be used for the purpose of denial was already known by Freud and expressed in the dream introducing the seventh chapter of *The Interpretation of Dreams* (1900), wherein the dreamer attempts to deny the death of his child along with the expression of the wish fulfillment in that the child would still be alive. Another example, taken from the same source demonstrates that in the "dream within the dream" the mechanism of denial of a reality event is rather clear. Freud emphasized the fact that "the dream within the dream" was the most certain affirmation that what had occurred in that portion of the dream was an actual reality event portrayed as if to deny that it had ever occurred. Further confirmation of this sort of attempted denial is given by the patient in the representation of primal scene content in dreams when either threatened by a loss, or presented with actual alteration of the regular sequence of therapeutic appointments; it occurs particularly when the analyst has to leave, a situation over which the patient has little control.

All of the observations and conclusions seem to lead to an extremely important question, namely: what is the significance of the oral dependent state of regression in this phenomenon? There seem to be several important dynamic factors at work. The passive state excludes the use of a more adequate means to cope with the interpretation, namely, negation. This necessitates a retreat to what is apparently a last line of defense; an apparent passive acceptance of the interpretation, with a denial in a dream or fantasy. When the patient is involved in an oral dependent state of regression in the transference, his relationship to the analyst repeats the relationship of the infant to the mother. He experiences any loss as a deprivation in oral terms and even the primal scene acquires oral significance. For at this state of libidinal development, the aggressive castrative behavior of father in the primal scene is experienced by the observing child as a threatened destruction of mother. This is equated with a loss of the breast. Fenichel (1945) discusses the "traumatic state" so often produced in children as the result of the observation of the primal scene, due to "flooding the organism with sexual excitation" often beyond the child's capacity of mastery. He states: "Thus such an experience is likely to connect the ideas of sexual excitation to danger. This connection may be further increased by misinterpretations of what is perceived. The most frequent types of misinterpretation are the interpretations of sexual intercourse as a cruel, destructive act, and the interpretation of the female genitals as the result of castration" (p. 214). This explains the coincident depressed mood, symptoms of nausea and anorexia and revulsive attitude toward food along with weight loss during these periods in analysis or therapy. These symptoms could represent defenses against the reexperiencing of the primal scene material. This suggests that the appearance of primal scene material at the time of approaching termination of analysis or when termination dates have been set, as in the case of the Wolf Man (Freud, 1918; Wolf-Man, 1957), might have a similar explanation.

Many questions remain unanswered and are certainly beyond the scope of this paper, but it would seem important that further investigation related to the stratification of or hierarchy of defenses relevant to the transference in analysis be attempted.

Chapter 5

THE EMERGENCE OF PROJECTION IN A SERIES OF DREAMS

DONALD M. KAPLAN

The following is a presentation of a series of dreams illustrating a particular phase in the analytic therapy of a narcissistic female patient. The phase of treatment that will be brought under discussion has to do with the transition in ego behavior from *denial to projection*, which seems to be a typical event in the analytic therapy of female patients presenting narcissistic maladjustments. Indeed, the writer hopes to demonstrate that a clinical and psychological evaluation of this specific combination of ego reactions is a significant guide to the therapy and prognosis of narcissistic female patients.

In a discussion of male narcissistic patients, Annie Reich remarks that while Freud used the term *narcissistic neurosis* to designate psychotic illness exclusively, the last twenty years or so have taught us to "question the usefulness of a too narrowly circumscribed nosology" (1960a, p. 215), and she goes on to remind us of the ubiquitous overlapping of developmental phases and to suggest that even marked narcissistic tendencies may not entirely interrupt object cathexes. The narcissistic conditions to which the following presentation addresses itself are those characterized by developmental overlapping with more highly developed structures sufficient enough to preclude frank, manifest schizophrenic process. Popularly labeled "borderlines" or, even less exact, "ambulatory schizophrenics," narcissistic patients are those who are commonly given to sudden

This paper was first published in the *Psychoanalytic Review* (1962), 49:37–52.

maniclike reactions, acute, severe, though brief, depressive reactions sometimes with suicidal endeavors, promiscuous and
perverse sexual patterns with significant competence in anticipating and accommodating sexual patterns and requirements
of the partner, homoerotic panic, hypochondriacal involve-
ments, and quite frequently "medicational" addictions of one
sort or another. Further reference to this symptom syndrome
will be made later.

That the following presentation will employ only the manifest content of dreams to the comparative disregard of the
latent meaning might require some additional brief remarks
beforehand in the way of reminding the reader of both the
value and danger of focusing attention in some sort of exclusive
manner upon the manifest content of dreams. The manifest
content of the dream is understood to be the final product of
the dream work, a negotiation between the ego, the superego,
and a forbidden infantile wish. This negotiation represents the
efforts of the ego (albeit, at a regressed level of functioning)
and is interesting for what it tells us about the nature of the
ego. Since ego functioning is a prominent diagnostic criterion,
the manifest content of dreams, especially at the outset of treatment, can be regarded diagnostically; since treatment can be
thought of as an attempt to alter the patient's presenting diagnosis, subsequent dream sequences can go on to inform us of
how and to what extent the treatment process is affecting
changes in the patient's psyche. In connection with these issues,
the reader's attention is called to the contributions of Sheppard
and Saul (1958), Erikson (1954), and Lewis (1959) in which
attempts are made to systematize our inquiry into ego function
by means of the manifest dream. This tradition begins with
Chapter VII of Freud's [The] Interpretation of Dreams (1900)
where Freud's concern with the dream shifts temporarily from
interpretation to the construction of a theory of mind.

The danger here is precisely that danger which sophistication always holds out to those perceptions that are better made
in innocence. As therapists, the more we learn, the less we are
apt to think we need to be told by our patients. It is, for example, a common (and often lamented) observation among psychoanalysts that the practice of subjecting dreams to exhaustive

analysis has become the exception rather than the rule it once was. Summarizing a number of reasons for this evolution in practice, Erikson included the inevitable fact that "we have learned (or so we think) to find in other sources what in Freud's early days could be garnered only from dreams" (p. 131). The parenthetical aside here is certainly not intended to invite an attitude of pompous humility or affected ignorance but is rather a caution against our becoming, in our knowledge, overly goal directed and anticipating of the patient's productions, which, in respect to dreams, is bound to lead to an excessive investment of interest in their manifest content.

With these comments in mind, let us turn to the patient whose dreams will be presented.

I

The patient is an intelligent, gifted, energetic, and exceedingly attractive woman who entered treatment at age thirty-three complaining of severe anxiety and of an incapacity to make decisions. She reported having had a series of painful, disappointing, and futile affairs with numerous men over the past twelve years. A marriage at nineteen to a man much older than herself had ended two years later in a divorce initiated by the patient, and it was the recent news of her former husband's intention to remarry that seemed to the patient to contribute a good deal to the anxiety she presented upon coming into treatment. She described a feeling of desperation that her own life would pass without marriage and motherhood.

The life history that unfolded was eventful. The patient's father died when she was three, and the patient shortly thereafter began to be shifted about with an infant sister and older brother to half-a-dozen shelters and foster homes by a mother who, herself, was going through numerous unsuccessful affairs. The mother appeared to have been deeply attached to her children, but this was often expressed by the mother's meddlesome supervision of the various foster homes, so that the patient was mindful of the mother's devotion yet was deprived by it of an opportunity to get into any long-standing relationships with foster parents. From time to time, the children were re-united with the mother for brief periods but not permanently so until the patient was twelve. Throughout childhood the patient's psychosexual development had to accommodate almost incessant sexual traumata involving, among other things, highly erotic bedtime experiences with her siblings and provocations by her mother, whom the patient described on one occasion as an astonishing, seductive beauty. One of the patient's earliest memories, for example, was the mother's bathing one afternoon with the bathroom door open and instructing the patient, who was then four or five, to ask in a delivery man who had just arrived at the apartment with groceries; the patient remembered having stood in the bathroom doorway looking from the delivery man to her smiling mother and overwhelmed with hatred but subsequently never being able to figure out toward which of the adults in the scene the hatred was directed.

Yet, despite the deprivation, uncertainty, and traumata of the patient's early years, she was able to go on to acquire an education, enjoy a high cultural attainment, and eventually make a gratifying vocational adjustment. At the time she entered treatment, she had been living with and, to a great extent, supporting her younger sister whose emotional adjustment was so marginal as to necessitate continuous outpatient psychiatric care and occasional hospitalization. It might be added that the brother managed to achieve a successful art and university-teaching career; married and the father of three children, he was also to assume financial responsibility for his mother, at times his sisters, and he was the family's main confidant and advisor.[1]

Early in the patient's treatment, which was two sessions weekly on the premises of an outpatient psychiatric clinic, a range of symptoms pathognomonic of a severe narcissistic

---

[1] It is interesting to note in passing the varying degrees of pathology in the two sisters and the brother which even these bare facts suggest, that is, basic pathology in the younger sister, narcissistic pathology—as will be detailed below—in the patient, pathology, if any, at predominantly a more advanced developmental level in the brother. In this family, the degrees of pathology in the children appear to correlate with the degrees of "oedipal deficiency" created by the death of the father when the children were at ages one, three, and seven respectively and with the degrees of susceptibility to the severity of separation from the mother.

neurosis was elicited. In addition to the anxiety already mentioned, the patient was susceptible to states verging on confusion, which coincided with promiscuous sexual activity. A complex of behavior reactions aimed at reestablishing a sense of identity led to episodes of physical exhaustion with consequences to her physical resistance and health—she would engage in tedious lovers' quarrels long into the night, having to carry out arduous work responsibilities the following day; she would skip lunch-hour meals to attend to some obsessive detail like writing a long, explanatory letter to an out-of-town lover or returning home at midday in the hope of finding an expected letter; and she would, as she described it, "eat herself up alive" with intense, scheming ruminations, often into the night. Her reported use of barbiturates, tranquilizers, and alcohol had numerous characteristics of dependency, though her allusions to drugs and alcohol were invariably prefaced by a denial of any addictive experience. In the sessions, her behavior was histrionic and evasive. She suppressed and falsified material and often left large gaps in her productions by simply forgetting material. Though she did not break appointments, she attempted to change appointments and make emergency appointments. She would seize upon trivia and various "clues" as pretexts for extreme, brooding despair and would as quickly revert to moods of carefree elation. The transference, as a point of any interest, let alone conscious emotional experience, was consistently disavowed by the patient, and any reference to it by the therapist was met for quite some time with either agitated impatience or blank disinterest. (This, of course, is not to say that a transference did not exist or that it was not influential.) With excruciating determination she sought to cast the therapist in the role of the master mind for her interpersonal resolutions and strategies, and she would describe the behavior and conversation of people with whom she was having conflict and make all effort to get the therapist to "analyze" their motives and intentions and to predict their behavior. She was characteristically lively and seductive, commanded an easy, winning sense of humor, and very shortly became a "sincere" advocate of "psychoanalysis."

While a number of defensive operations could be demonstrated in this patient's functioning—regression and isolation come readily to mind—it is chiefly the failure of *denial* from which is derived the patient's presenting symptoms both as reported by the patient and evident clinically. The connection between denial, employed as a chief rather than subsidiary defense, and the exuberance, evasiveness, instability, and general "borderline" quality of this patient is documented in the literature:

It is not simply a theoretical nicety to distinguish denial as a defense from the defense *mechanisms* (e.g., repression, isolation, projection) for, though denial is capable of warding off ideation, unlike the mechanisms of defense, it has no structural component and cannot transform primary-process energy into secondary-process energy. It is rather, as Anna Freud put it, a "preliminary stage of defense," and very early in the ego's development it comes into conflict with the ego's inclination to perceive and take into account reality. Though functionally somewhat different, categorically denial is more similar to *displacement* than are any of the defense mechanisms. (Displacement, of course, is also not, strictly speaking, of the category defense mechanism.)

Freud defined denial as the removal of the preconscious cathexis from an idea though not from the accompanying affect, and he was, thus, the first to distinguish denial from repression (1927). (It is this distinction that partly accounts for the exuberance that "passes around" this defense. Patients, on the other hand, who chiefly repress are easily agitated but are affectually dull and withdrawn.) Ostow has cited the arbitrary and opportunistic relationship between denial and reality, and has elaborated Freud's further idea that denial is an act of aggression turned inward, adding that it holds out the advantage of not depleting the ego of energy, so that its presence in the clinical picture countersuggests suicidal success (though not necessarily suicidal attempts [Ostow, 1960]). Lewin has discussed the role of denial in mania and related moods (1950). Fenichel has related denial to falsifications of both the intended (lying) and unintended (screen memories, forgetting) kind. According to Fenichel, denial can serve the formula: "If it is possible to make someone believe that untrue things are true, then it is also possible that true things, the memory of which threatens me, are untrue." But, he adds, "only in tendentious forgetting of external events, in 'screen-memories,' and in perversions, does 'denial' seem to be victorious" (1954, p. 129). Its retention, Fenichel goes on, for extensive conscious and near-conscious falsifications of current reality can be severely pathogenic and can lead to psychosis (1939). The prominence of denial in the clinical pictures of narcissistic disorders has been pointed out by Schafer (1954).

Now, it is well known that what the narcissistic character typically denies is the conflict deriving from intensely demanding oral-aggressive and oral-receptive needs. What is at stake in this conflict is a sense, on the one hand, of omnipotence when the patient feels assured of nonending oral supplies and, on the other hand, neediness, helplessness, and abandonment when the supplies are threatened. When this conflict attaches itself to the sexual function, the loved object acquires the unconscious equivalence of food. Moreover, in some significant way, the object must remain unattainable in order that the oral conflict not be laid to rest and with it the opportunity for testing again and again the patient's oral effectuality. The patient being referred to in this paper, for example, would remark with great chagrin that her whole problem was simply that she could not love men who loved her but had to love men whom she somehow could never really possess. The simplicity, predictability, and repetitiousness of the problematic aspects of the interpersonal relationships of these patients are much like current attempts to abreact a discrete, infantile trauma.

Strongly libidinized and repetitive striving in an adult for mother–infant relationships invariably produces painful anxiety and guilt reactions and leads to psychosexual confusion. The homoeroticism, which this leaves the narcissistic patient susceptible to, is, of course, also denied. However, here the denial is not direct but is rather a denial of ideation that has already been subjected to a particular defensive activity by the patient's ego. The specific defense underlying this denial is *projection.*

The combination of denial and projection in narcissistic disorders has been discussed by Schafer (1954), and while this defensive combination can also be demonstrated in other conditions (e.g., manic depression, paranoia, chronic addiction), its presence in the narcissistic conditions of the type being referred to in this paper is characterized by the stability and relief afforded the patient in the uncovering of projection. In these narcissistic conditions, the removal by treatment of the need to deny amounts to a restoration of a serviceable projective defense mechanism.[2] And it is the serviceability of this defense in narcissistic conditions that imparts a distinctive phase to the treatment of narcissists: There is a sudden relief from symptoms, a pronounced sense of mastery and well-being, and a vigorous determination to break off treatment abruptly. This phase can occur after as brief a period as less than a year of treatment or, as with the patient being presented here, after three years of treatment. It has been the writer's experience with several such cases in recent years that this phase of treatment is forecasted by a dream in which the patient experiences a homosexual assault.

Before turning to the patient's dreams depicting the emergence of this well-retained projective defense and to some of the technical problems that arise, an example of its emergence in treatment may be of some interest. It has been mentioned that the patient had been living with a younger sister at the time she entered treatment. At the outset of treatment, the patient was able to regard the sister only as a dependent, helpless child and as a source of guilt. The patient would defer her comfort and privacy around the apartment to her sister's love affairs and would often dispossess herself entirely in favor of her sister's need for privacy, though she would not request

---

[2] In the frank schizophrenias like manic depression and paranoia and in frank addictions like alcoholism, projection emerges in a state of decompensation, which makes the course of treatment altogether different from that which occurs in narcissistic conditions. The key to the understanding of the role of projection in "ideational" schizophrenia was given by Freud in the Schreber case. Freud was quite explicit (though he is notoriously misread) that the quantitative factor is far more significant in schizophrenia than the choice of defense; that is, not projection but decompensating projection is the sine qua non of paranoia. In manic depression, denial is the key factor in the mania and is comparatively restitutional; the factor in the depression is the failure of projection, for it is this failure that leaves the punishing introject entrenched. In narcissism as well, the fleeting instability of projection leaves the patient susceptible to manic depressive reactions (viz., A. Reich), but the comparative strength of this mechanism keeps these reactions diminutive.

similar consideration for herself. The childhood memories that accompanied these reports had to do with the patient's aggressive and usually successful rivalry with the sister for the attention and affection of the mother, the older brother, and foster parents. These memories of competition with the sister were especially painful when they pertained to periods in which the children had been boarded out, for it was at those times that the mother had charged the patient with the responsibility for looking after the younger sister. The patient's subsequent masochistic renunciation of power for the sister's forgiveness was a feature that could be discerned in most of the patient's significant relationships.

As treatment progressed, it became evident that a large amount of homosexual anxiety and agitation was being generated in the patient by her daily exposure to her sister, whom the patient was growing able to perceive and describe as sexy and immodest. The patient was also able to acknowledge feelings of anger attributable to her sister's immodesty—the sister often lounged around the apartment wearing only panties and would often report her sexual thoughts and activities to the patient at great length. It was not possible for the patient to come to an understanding of the unconscious origins of these feelings of anger, feelings that originated in the patient's early relationship to her mother, certain aspects of which were now being reenacted with the sister as mother. But it was possible for the patient to act on these feelings and to begin to put an end to her sister's provocative behavior. She got her sister to wear more clothes around the apartment, and she made herself less available to her sister's sexual reports. The patient felt licensed to do this in part by an understanding of her history with her sister; for example, the patient's current guilt was for childhood crimes, and in part by a projection of the sexual interests and culpabilities entirely onto the sister. Prior to this capacity to project adequately, the sister's sexual behavior could not be acknowledged by the patient but was simply denied. The projection exonerated the patient sufficiently to come to grips with a significant portion of her everyday reality—the sister was indeed behaving in a distressingly immodest manner. Having done something effectual about the matter, the patient showed a marked relief from anxiety and came into a gratifying sense of control, and while this was the result of functioning on the basis of a profound misperception, it was more satisfactory than the previous vague, passively experienced agitation suffered by the patient vis-à-vis her sister. The cement that bound the relationship had not really been cracked; the idea, for example, of taking separate apartments was completely beyond the patient, indeed, veritably unthinkable.

Projection, furthermore, enabled the patient to investigate ideas about and feelings toward the fantasied "other women," the wives and girl friends in the lives of men with whom she became involved. Among other things, jealousy in other women became entirely plausible to her, and she became more effectual in both her fantasies of and actual dealings with women. This effectuality carried over to men as well. In fact, by the end of the third year of treatment the patient had come away from two affairs markedly unwounded and full of decisiveness and had triumphantly sent both men into psychotherapy.

II

As was said at the outset, in the following dreams from the treatment of this patient the reader's attention is being invited only to the manifest content and specifically to the presence and nature of ego functioning. Some of the literature in which particular principles appear for observing ego functioning in dreams has been cited above. Sheppard and Saul (1958) are especially helpful in providing a systematic ego rating scheme based upon considerations of "distancing" between the impulses in the dream and the dreamer's ego. In respect to their system it might be mentioned beforehand that the following dreams taken as a group seem to contain sufficient ego functioning at a high enough level to classify them as dreams of a nonpsychotic ego. (This would lend support to the validity of the diagnostic differentiation insisted upon at the outset between a narcissistic neurosis and a schizophrenia.) The reader does not need to be told, of course, that none of these considerations can lead to the latent meaning of the dream, which is pursued not by an analysis of ego functioning but by an analysis, through the patient's associations, of the *condensations, displacements, and symbolizations*—the language at the border of the unconscious.

For the sake of readability, the relationship to the patient of persons appearing in the following dreams will be identified in parentheses. It goes without saying that what these dreams are currently intended to demonstrate to the reader, that is, the development of a stabilizing projective defense, is quite different from what they were intended to demonstrate to the patient. The first dream was reported a month after treatment began: "Bill (sister's lover) is pulling green vegetable matter out of Barbara's (sister) open mouth. Then my mouth is open with green vegetable matter stuck in my throat. I become nauseous and gag. Then I woke up."

Like most, though by no means all, initial dreams in treatment, this one makes an obvious and straightforward statement of the nature and level of the patient's current conflict. If the expulsion of unwanted oral contents is thought of as the prototype of projection, the status of this defense in the patient's ego functioning is also obvious in this dream—there is an endeavor to mobilize the defense, which is not altogether successful. Though we no longer think of the content of projection as being restricted to unacceptable homosexual wishes, such a wish is much to the point in this dream in that the patient included in her associations her sister's recent suggestion that they switch sexual partners, which is a perversion that employs a heterosexual object to gratify vicariously and yet deny a homosexual wish toward the object's partner.

The following dream is taken from treatment seven months later:

> I dreamed I was in a room. It was indoors, or, at least, an indoor kind of room but it had an outdoor feeling about it. There were many people in it, none of whom I knew. I began looking for a way out, though I don't know what I was afraid of. I was opening doors along a corridor. One door I opened I was face-to-face with Ira (a former lover). He wanted me to come in with him. I didn't want to. He

insisted. I took off along a street, and after what felt like about five minutes, I decided to go back. On the way back I remember having to stop for a moment because a traffic light was against me.

Here it may be worth pausing briefly to illustrate the difference between viewing this dream for its latent meaning and for its indications of the quality of the dreamer's ego functioning. Upon first hearing the dream, a therapist would very likely entertain two possibilities with regard to the latent meaning: The opening—*I dreamed I was in a room . . . There were many people in it, none of whom I knew*—has a promiscuous inference around which the dream revolves. And there may be an incest wish to which a therapist would be alerted by the indoor–outdoor contradiction at the beginning that suggests the importance of opposites in the rest of the dream: Thus, *There were many people, none of whom I knew,* becomes *There were few people, all of whom I knew.* (family), or, perhaps, *There was one person whom I knew.* (mother). Ira in the dream is then an incest figure. However, in point of fact, the dreamer's associations carried the interpretation in the direction of a masturbation conflict. A significant association was to *five minutes*—an electric clock that hummed loudly and interfered with the patient falling asleep. She was aware of being alone in the darkened room. The *five minutes* can rather safely be taken as *five fingers* or *a hand,* and the forbidden wish is to masturbate. *Ira,* as a lover, offers an escape but this would bring the patient into conflict with the therapist (*traffic light*) whose endeavor at the time of the dream was to stop the patient's acting out.

None of this, however, says much about the ego functioning in the dream, which is a matter of the dreamer's resourcefulness, the quality of her participation, her distance in respect to various impulses, the nature of her role assignments, the complication of retained affect. From the point of view of these things, the dream has a rather weak quality. The patient's ego cannot tolerate the aggression involved in turning down the lover. The urgency of the wish in the dream is so harassing that restriction is assigned to an external agent, the traffic light, which, it should be noted, is a highly distanced feature in being inanimate. Moreover, the patient's responses are exclusively primitive; she registers fear, flight, and passivity.

It was shortly after this dream that the patient began "revising" her "opinion" about other women. They were not as passive and reputable as she had thought. On the contrary, they were greedy and aggressive, disguised by fake respectability. By contrast, the patient described herself as sincere and honest, unwittingly victimized by an enemy she had all along underestimated. In retrospect, it is not implausible to regard the traffic light at the end of the dream (*a traffic light was against me* = red-light) as a reflection of the patient's fear that she was, her denials and rationalizations aside, promiscuous, whorish, disreputable.

The following two dreams occurred near the end of the second year of treatment. The first is a nightmare containing a frank homosexual assault. The second is about a married man the patient was involved with at the time of the dream. His wife figured prominently in the patient's fantasies. The second dream contains a successful projection in that the wife is entirely demeaned, her husband is weak and guilty, the patient is shameless and victorious. Here is the first of the two:

> I am in a hotel room, or rather a hotel. There is a convention going on. I am with this girl whose name I don't remember. It's a salesmen's convention. Suddenly, I have to find the ladies' room, and I begin to go through the corridors in search of it. [I wake up and find I really have to go to the bathroom. The earlier part of the dream has come back to me, I think:] I am riding in a coach car of a railroad train when a woman I have never seen before in reality but apparently with whom I am very friendly makes advances at me. [No, this must have been the end of the dream, because I remember I woke up terrified and went to the bathroom.] Somewhere in the dream I am in my apartment, and Barbara (sister) is standing on the other side of the window on the sidewalk. She is nude. She tells me she has just danced nude before thirty-four people. I am shocked, but also shocked that she did this thing from much the same reason that she began talking Seconal.

While the frankness of the assault and the patient's inability to cope with it in the dream account for the nightmare outcome and speak for a defensive failure, the projection of aggression increases throughout the dream. In respect to the sister, the patient is separate and is able to be critical. Now observe the ego stability in the following dream, despite the latent orality, aggressive rivalry and homoeroticism: "Murray (patient's lover) asks me into a cafeteria for coffee, but when I arrive, he's at a table with his maid (= wife) who in the dream is a Negro. When he sees me enter, he tries to brush me off because he is ashamed. I am revolted by his weakness."

The final dream presented here occurred toward the end of the third year of treatment. Its homosexual content originated partly in the fact that the night it was dreamed the patient had slept at the apartment of a new, female acquaintance. The resourcefulness of the patient in the dream is striking. Though the thematic substance remains similar to the preceding dreams and there are indications of an unaltered latent content, projection is well established and the level of ego functioning is comparatively high. "I am sleeping at Louise's (acquaintance) apartment, in the living room. She is in the bedroom. Her door opens and she comes across the room grinning and determined. She lies down next to me and tries to arouse me. I am terrified. I reach behind me and yank open the drapes, exposing the whole room to the public outside. This stops her all right."

It was shortly after this dream that the patient began to press vigorously to terminate treatment on the grounds of her improved symptom picture. Though an attempt was naturally made to help the patient to comprehend the nature of her current adjustment, she nevertheless broke off treatment. Whether this termination could or could not in fact have been avoided is an interesting question,[3] but what is more relevant here (and will bear on the question) is an understanding of this typical crisis that can arise in these cases. Suffice it to say, the

---

[3]A discussion of this question would have to be preceded by a clarification of what is meant by premature termination in psychotherapy, which, in contrast to psychoanalysis, is characterized as having limited goals. Though the preparation for a psychoanalysis is often one of the goals of psychotherapy, it is not routinely so, and this would need to be clarified as well.

door to further treatment, perhaps psychoanalysis, was left open to this patient.

III

Though the concept of projection as a defense mechanism is not a simple one, clinicians appear to have a far better facility with it than they appear to have with the concept of denial, about which a number of propositions were cited earlier. In regard to the above dreams and to the accompanying restitution in the patient, two aspects of the concept of projection should be singled out. First, unlike denial, which involves a withdrawal of perception from reality (more precisely, internal representations of reality), projection uses reality. Second: projection involves externalization (of libidinal and/or aggressive id and superego impulses directly or previously subjected to a number of defensive possibilities, such as reversal or displacement). The restitutional effects of projection are based on two advantages that originate in these two aspects of this defense mechanism: The projector "(a) may now flee from . . . or righteously retaliate against the 'external' threat or enemy; (b) by projectively purifying himself, he avoids the especially intense subjective pain that would accompany the intrusion of the objectionable material into his self-concept." These restitutional effects are evident in the above dreams and were quite clear in the behavior of the patient. (Though already suggested, it might be worth repeating that where projection emerges and opposite—that is, decompensating—effects are evident, the patient is schizophrenic, and this can be predicted clinically beforehand from numerous indicators, one of which is the altogether different direction taken by the patient's dream productions.)

The depletion in the patient of motivation to continue treatment as a result of her experience of comparative competence and comparative loss of suffering has already been observed. But while the technical problem of arousing and sustaining motivation for treatment is quite significant here, it is not as specific as several other problems, for the problem of motivation is basic to all cases at one point or another. The specific problems here seem to relate to certain phases of the countertransference (and it should be said that the writer does not subscribe to the erroneous view that all technical problems can be reduced to a countertransference variable).

To carry a narcissistic patient from a borderline adjustment on the basis of denial to a less shaky adjustment, as temporary and limited as it may be, on the basis of an increased reliance on projection requires the therapist's attention to that anxiety in himself which can be aroused by the emergence of obvious misperception in his patient. Within our current therapeutic model there is the general postulate that neutrality and abstention are the correct responses when the case before us is showing progress, and intervention and support the correct responses when the case is showing retrogression. The transition in a case from nonperception (denial) to misperception (projection) can easily be confused by the therapist's anxiety for retrogression, and the therapist is then likely to apply a correct principle of technique to a mistaken situation. Few responses on the part of the therapist can arrest the development of this transition in narcissistic patients more assuredly than inappropriate supportive intervention. Indeed, inappropriate support arrests the development of any patient, and it is one of the central theses of this discussion that the transition from denial to projection in narcissistic patients is an inevitable phase of development in their personalities.

Another pitfall exists. These are patients whose transference is almost exclusively at a preoedipal mother–child level, and the countertransference susceptibility is to separation anxiety. In addition, this constellation always searches out in male therapists basic castration vulnerabilities, since the therapist, in these cases, is continuously cast in the role of a woman (mother)—erotic arousal in male therapists by narcissistic patients is often an unconscious countertransference assertion against castration in the transference. While this problem may not be the same for female therapists, the patient's masochistic presentation is very apt to arouse basic vulnerabilities to penis envy.[4]

---

[4] To be sure, these do not exhaust the countertransference possibilities. An abundant variety of other possibilities exist; for example, the patient's promiscuity can arouse resentment in male therapists against an orgiastic, unfaithful, oedipal mother. But the

This state of affairs can lead to an enthusiastic anticipation in the therapist of the restitutional effects of projection which promise relief from the special burdens of the countertransference. As the patient shows signs of retaliation against her previously oppressive environment, the therapist celebrates with inappropriate activity and by so doing can drive the patient into a regression. It may then be seen that the therapist has been caught between a wish to get off a countertransference hook and a fear of separation that only hangs him up again.

Dream material has been presented to demonstrate one source of judgment for the therapist in regard to the course and pace of a typical transition in narcissistic patients. Another source is the patient's actual clinical complaint. Originally, the complaint was of an affective disorder. When the complaint alters and becomes comparatively ideational (nonpsychotic in these cases), the transition can be assumed to have occurred to a substantial enough extent for treatment to direct itself to an analysis of the projective defense. Though ideally we should like the transition to be orderly and treatment to pursue it without interruptions, a temporary hiatus may well exist between the affectual and ideational complaints of the patient. In this turn of events, treatment is apt to be interrupted. But if this eventuality is handled properly and with understanding, the patient, more likely than not, will return in the future for further treatment.

---

pertinence of these other possibilities varies from therapist to therapist. Separation anxiety, castration anxiety, and penis envy, however, are experiential données—their pertinence never varies in the countertransference, only their quantities.

Chapter 6

"ALL ROADS LEAD TO ROME": THE ROLE OF THE NURSEMAID IN FREUD'S DREAMS

KENNETH A. GRIGG

The Czechoslovakian, Roman Catholic nursemaid of Sigmund Freud placed an indelible, highly individualistic stamp on the formation of his oedipal complex. Freud's murderous impulses toward his father have been widely elucidated (Jones, 1953–1957; Grinstein, 1968; Schorske, 1974), based on a relatively great quantity of discussion by Freud himself. Significantly, the founder of psychoanalysis included very little directly concerning his mother in his published works. The reasons for Freud's excluding most of this material probably were twofold: his mother lived until 1930, and portions of his oedipal conflicts were unresolved. Some insight into his oedipal constellation, however, may be gained from a study of the figure of the nursemaid and his ambivalence toward her.

Following the model set by Freud himself (1910a, 1911a, 1928, 1929) in studying the dreams of others, I shall attempt to reconstruct Freud's positive oedipal relationship and to study the effects of the conflicts in producing his "travel phobia" and his so-called "Rome neurosis" (Schorske, 1974) through analysis of dreams involving the nursemaid or her substitutes, demonstrating as many *direct* associations to the dreams as possible.

Although Freud greatly loved travel, it is well known that he had a "phobia" about traveling by train, as well as a fear of dying. Freud's avoidance of entering Rome was a manifestation of a true case of anxiety hysteria. He traveled many times to

This paper was first published in the *Journal of the American Psychoanalytic Association* (1973), 21:108–126.

various parts of Italy, on one trip coming within a few miles of his longed-for destination, but coming back. It is my thesis that Freud's fear of going to Rome was a result of incestuous wishes toward his mother, and the specific choice of the city was an unconscious representation of his feelings toward the Roman Catholic nursemaid of his first two-and-a-half years of life.

Freud eloquently described his discovery of the part played by this woman in letters to Fliess. On October 3rd, 1897, he wrote that his self-analysis might be coming to an end and continued:

> I can only say that in my case my father played no active role, though I certainly projected on to him an analogy from myself; that my "primary originator" (of neurosis) was an ugly, elderly but clever woman who told me a great deal about God and hell, and gave me a high opinion of my own capacities; that later (between the ages of two and two-and-a-half)[1] libido towards *matrem* was aroused; the occasion must have been the journey with her from Leipzig to Vienna, during which we spent a night together and I must have had the opportunity of seeing her *nudam* (you have long since drawn the conclusions from this for your own son, as a remark of yours revealed); and that I welcomed my one-year-younger brother (who died within a few months) with ill wishes and real infantile jealousy, and that his death left the germ of guilt in me. . . .
>
> I still have not got to the scenes which lie at the bottom of all this. If they emerge, and I succeed in resolving my hysteria, I shall have to thank the memory of the old woman who provided me at such an early age with the means for living and surviving [E. L. Freud, 1960, pp. 210–220].

On October 4th he continued:

> Last night's dreams produced the following under the most remarkable disguises:

---

[1] Jones (1953–1957) sets the actual age at four. But two-and-a-half was Freud's age when his first sister was born.

She was my instructress in sexual matters, and chided
me for being clumsy and not being able to do anything
(that is always the way with neurotic impotence: anxiety
over incapacity at school gets its sexual reinforcement in
this way). . . . The whole dream was full of the most
wounding references to my present uselessness as a therapist. Perhaps the origin of my tendency to believe in the
incurability of hysteria should be sought here. Also she
washed me in reddish water[2] in which she had previously
washed herself (not very difficult to interpret; I find nothing of the kind in my chain of memories, and so I take it
for a genuine rediscovery); and she encouraged me to steal
"Zehners" (ten-Kreuzer pieces) to give to her. A long chain
of association connects these first silver Zehners to the heap
of paper ten-florin notes which I saw in the dream as Martha's housekeeping money. The dream can be summed up
as "bad treatment." Just as the old woman got money from
me for her bad treatment of me, so do I now get money
for the bad treatment of my patients; a special role in it
was played by Q, who conveyed through you a suggestion
that I ought not to take money from her as the wife of a
colleague (he stipulated that I should) [pp. 220–221].

Still preoccupied with his analysis of the significance of the
"old woman," Freud asked his mother whether she remembered his nurse.

"Of course," she said, "an elderly woman, very shrewd
indeed. She was always taking you to church. When you
came home you used to preach, and tell us all about how
God conducted His affairs. At the time I was in bed when
Anna was being born" (Anna is two-and-a-half years
younger) "she turned out to be a thief, and all the shiny
Kreuzers and Zehners and toys that had been given you
were found among her things. Your brother Philipp went
himself to fetch the policeman, and she got ten months!'
[pp. 221–222].

Freud felt this information confirmed the conclusions he
had drawn from the interpretations of his dream:

---

[2] See "Rome Series" of dreams, below.

I wrote to you that she got me to steal Zehners and give them to her. The dream really means that she stole herself. For the dream-picture was a memory that I took money from a doctor's mother, *i.e.,* wrongfully. The real meaning is that the old woman stood for me, and that the doctor's mother was my mother. . . . My mother told me that the doctor of my infancy had only one eye,[3] and among all my masters Professor K. was the only one with the same disability!

It might be objected that these coincidences are not conclusive, because I might have heard that the nurse was a thief in later childhood and to all appearances forgotten the fact until it emerged in the dream. I think myself that that must have been the case. But I have another unexceptional and amusing piece of evidence. If the woman disappeared so suddenly, I said to myself, some impression of the event must have been left inside me. Where was it now? Then a scene occurred to me which for the last twenty-nine years has been turning up from time to time in my conscious memory without my understanding it. I was crying my heart out, because my mother was nowhere to be found. My brother Philipp (who is twenty years older than I) opened a cupboard for me, and when I found that mother was not there either I cried still more, until she came through the door, looking slim and beautiful. What can that mean? Why should my brother open the cupboard for me when he knew that my mother was not inside it and that opening it therefore could not quieten me? Now I suddenly understand. I must have begged him to open the cupboard. When I could not find my mother, I feared she must have vanished, like my nurse not long before. I must have heard that the old woman had been looked, or rather "boxed" up, because my brother Philipp, who is now sixty-three, was fond of such humorous expressions, and still is to the present day. The fact that I turned to him shows that I was well aware of his part in my nurse's disappearance [pp. 222–223].

Freud concluded in the same letter that love of the mother and jealousy of the father were general phenomena of early

---

[3] See also the dream "My Son, the Myops," below.

childhood, explaining the "gripping power" of *Oedipus Rex* and *Hamlet*.

Freud, then, began this part of his self-analysis by a denial of the role of his father, in the formation of his neurotic symptoms. However, he was able to displace the "blame" to his nurse-maid from his mother, who immediately followed in his associations. The juxtaposition of the memory of seeing his mother nude to thoughts of his nurse as the "primary originator" [of his neurosis] certainly confirms the equation of the two women. He then discovered that the nurse was his "instructress in sexual matters." There is, of course, the possibility that this "memory" was an oedipal phantasy, similar to those by which Freud was misled by his hysterical patients, whose stories of childhood seduction he at first accepted as fact. An association of impotence is followed by a dream whose wish fulfillment is one of "enlightenment."

The confirmation by Amalie Freud that the employee had indeed been a thief only served to strengthen Freud's apparent defense against coming too close to the real object of his oedipal strivings, his mother. In a different context, he directly equated the two women. On February 9th, 1898 (1960, p. 245), he wrote to Fliess: "There is a rumour that we are to be invested with the title of professor at the Emperor's jubilee on December 2nd. I do not believe it, but I had a fascinating dream on the subject, unfortunately it is unpublishable, because its background, its deeper meaning, shuttles to and fro between my nurse (my mother) and my wife. . . ." In this instance Freud used the German word, *Amme*, the specific term for a nurse for very young children, in juxtaposition to *mutter* (mother). The assonance of *Amme* and Amalie is remarkable. At other times Freud employed *Kinderfrau* for "nurse."

Who was robbing whom of what was a question in Freud's mind. Following the principle of multiple function (Waelder, 1936), one must assume the validity of each of Freud's associations. What Freud wanted to steal from his father—power, money, mother—we now consider a natural component of the oedipal conflict. That he felt "stolen from" by the disappearance of his nurse—through discharge—and his mother —through childbirth—is unassailable.

Thoughts of men who had been blinded, like Oedipus, immediately followed, with a return to the theme of maternal abandonment. Reference to the memory that had been recurring "for the last twenty-nine years" may be a parapraxis, since Freud was at this time forty-one years old. Either he had had the memory from time to time since age two, thirty-nine years before, or it surfaced at age twelve with the recrudescence of oedipal conflicts at the onset of puberty. The intensity of the little boy's feelings were described in this memory of the empty cupboard and his having heard that the nurse had been "boxed" up. Freud (1901), in his discussion of symbolism, stated that "cupboards, boxes, carriages or ovens may represent the uterus."

The role of Philipp in these developments is important. Young Sigmund apparently blamed his older stepbrother for the loss of his nurse–mother. Jones (1953–1957, pp. 9–11) concluded that Freud paired off Jakob, Freud's father, with his "Nannie," the two forbidding authorities, and Philipp with Amalie, Freud's mother, because the latter were approximately the same ages. One step further carries us to the conclusion that Freud equated his father and stepbrother in depriving him of his incestuous objects.

Direct Influence of Nurse

The basic structure of Freud's Oedipus complex is apparent. How, then, did the old nurse contribute to its eventual distinctive nature? From 1883 we have a record of the positive side of Freud's feelings. In December he wrote his fiancée, Martha Bernays, concerning his visit to a Dresden museum: "Raphael's[4] Madonna, on the other hand, is a girl, say sixteen years old; she gazes out on the world with such a fresh and innocent expression, half against my will she suggested to me a charming, sympathetic *nursemaid* [my italics], not from the celestial world but from ours" (E. L. Freud, 1960, p. 82). Note that it

---

[4] See reference to another Raphael in association to "The Three Fates Dream," below.

was "half against my will" that Freud made the Madonna–nursemaid equation, accounting no doubt for the reversals in age and physical characteristics, although the latter referred to the wished-for state—the nonpregnancy of the mother in the "cupboard memory" described above. The youthfulness of the Dresden Madonna at the same time corresponds to Freud's actual nurse, his mother, who was only twenty years old at his birth.

This very "Madonna," a peculiarly Christian, Catholic symbol, is the same woman who imbued her young charge with ideas of God and hell, while at the same time acting as his "instructress in sexual matters." No wonder, then, that we find Freud (1887–1902, p. 237) writing to Fliess in December 1897: "Breslau plays a part in my childhood memories. At the age of three I passed through the station when we moved from Freiberg to Leipzig, and the gas jets, which were the first I had seen, reminded me of souls burning in hell. I know something of the context here. The anxiety about travel is also bound up with it." The trip thus described preceded by a year the one on which Freud saw his mother nude, according to Jones (1953, p. 13). Freud's own associations nevertheless placed them at the same age, indicating certainly an association in his own mind of punishment for incestuous wishes—"burning in hell." Such a representation could only derive from the nurse's Christian influence, for the concept of burning in hell is not a Judaic idea. It would appear, then, that Freud was able to trace his travel anxiety to its origin—oedipal wishes toward his mother with resultant fear of the particular punishment threatened by the nurse's religion. Freud's having opened his practice on Easter Sunday, April 25th, 1886 (1953, p. 143), may have been an act of defiance toward this maternal imago and/or an attempt at reunion with her.

The anxiety at departing on a journey was related to an even more constricting symptom, that is, Freud's inability to allow himself to travel to Rome, the "Rome neurosis." That this conflict also had oedipal roots is indicated in the letter to Fliess of November 5th, 1897 (1887–1902, p. 229), in which he chided his correspondent for "having said nothing about my interpretation of *Oedipus Rex* and *Hamlet*." In the very next paragraph appears a direct association to the archaeology of Rome.

The "Rome Series" of Dreams

The wish to enter Rome was of long standing and led to a number of dreams (1900, pp. 193–198), which serve to illustrate further the nursemaid's effect on Freud's choice of neurosis.

Freud pointed out that the dreams had received "powerful reinforcement from memories that stretched far back into childhood" and were "based upon a longing to visit Rome." He gives a series of apparent rationalizations for not having fulfilled his wish, followed by a dream in which he was looking out of a train window at the Tiber River and the Ponte Sant' Angelo. When the train began to move off, he realized that he "had not so much as set foot in the city."

In another dream someone led Freud "to the top of a hill and showed me Rome half-shrouded in mist." Although he felt he could not give all the details, the theme was "the promised land seen from afar." In the third dream he finally got to Rome but was disappointed. *There was a narrow stream of dark water; on one side of it were black cliffs and on the other meadows with big white flowers. I noticed a Herr Zucker . . . and determined to ask him the way to the city"* (p. 194).

Freud's associations to these first three dreams included his "vain attempt to see in my dream a city which I had never seen in waking life," an apparent denial of his having seen his mother nude on the train. There were references to the landscape with white flowers, the "loveliest water-lilies growing in black water," in Ravenna, as well as "the Dark Cliff, so close to the water" that reminded him "vividly of the valley" near Karlsbad.

To Zucker (sugar) he again associated Karlsbad, where patients with diabetes were sent for treatment. Sweets represent sexual favors, and valleys and ravines symbolize the vagina, in the same way that cliffs do the labia. The Ponte Sant' Angelo must be the bridge (penis) that wishfully reached from young Sigmund to the witch-angel, his nurse (mother, Rome), which, alas, in actuality was only "the promised land seen from afar." The "dark water," however, has a specific relation to the nursemaid who, as we have seen, washed Freud "in the reddish water in which she had washed herself." In yet another letter to Fliess in January 1897, Freud (1892–1899) wrote, "So long as the sense of smell (or taste) is dominant, hair, faeces, and the whole surface of the body—and blood as well—have a sexually exciting effect" (p. 241).

Freud was also reminded of two Jewish anecdotes, the first of which was of "an impecunious Jew [who] had stowed himself away without a ticket in the fast train to Karlsbad. He was caught, and each time tickets were inspected he was taken out of the train and treated more and more severely. At one of the stations on his *via dolorosa* he met an acquaintance, who asked him where he was traveling to. 'To Karlsbad' was his reply, 'if my constitution can stand it.' " The second story was of a Jew who had to ask his way in Paris. To Freud, "Asking the way . . . was a direct allusion to *Rome*, since it is well known that all roads lead there" (p. 195).

Indeed they do! The experienced psychoanalyst has only to read Freud's associations to the manifest content of these dreams to arrive at their latent oedipal wishes: the voyeuristic component—"shrouded in mist," but surprisingly clear, and the basis for Freud's travel anxiety—"without a ticket." The entire proceedings are "colored" by the influence of the nurse who set the stage for Freud's particular "*via dolorosa*," a very Christian symbol.

A fourth dream expressed a wish to meet his friend (Fliess) in Rome, rather than Prague, although he felt that the German language might be better tolerated in the Bohemian town. He related that he "must have understood Czech in my earliest childhood, for I was born in a small town in Moravia which has a Slav population. A Czech nursery rhyme [a screen memory for the nurse?], which I heard in my seventeenth year, printed itself on my memory . . ." (p. 196).

Freud further associated to his last journey to Italy, when he saw the Tiber and sadly turned back only fifty miles from Rome. He based his "longing for the eternal city" on some impressions of his youth—Winckelmann, his school vice-principal, and his resemblance to Hannibal, the Carthaginian general who was fated never to see Rome. "To my youthful mind Hannibal and Rome symbolized the conflict between the tenacity of Jewry and the organization of the Catholic Church" (p. 196).

Grinstein (1968, pp. 77 ff.) has elucidated the histories of these two men. Another Winckelmann, about whom Freud must have known, was a German archaeologist and art historian who first studied medicine and later joined the Catholic Church. He eventually went to Rome as librarian to a cardinal and was murdered by a fellow traveler on a train. Hannibal, on the other hand, never reached Rome, and committed suicide after being defeated by the Romans. Grinstein believes that Freud identified with a passive element he found in these men.

In 1911 Freud (1900, p. 398) added a footnote in *The Interpretation of Dreams*: "incidentally, the symbolic interpretation of undisguised Oedipus dreams was not unknown to the ancients. Rank writes: 'Thus Julius Caesar is reported to have had a dream of sexual intercourse with his mother which was explained by the dream-interpreters as a favourable augury for his taking possession of the earth (Mother Earth).'" Freud follows with a "Typical Example of a Disguised Oedipus Dream," actually an illustration of the reverse Oedipus constellation. Strong evidence, then, is present that Sigmund Freud expected death, like his brother Julius, or, alternatively, passivity—a type of death—as a result of his incestuous wishes to enter Rome.

Although little direct mention of the nurse is made in the Rome series, there can be little doubt that her religious influence strongly affected the latent dream contents. Interestingly, Erikson (1954) emphasizes the religious impressions made by the nurse in his reanalysis of the "Irma Dream," in whose manifest content and associations thereto no references to the old woman or to Rome appear. Erikson, however, was able to make a religious (Catholic) interpretation based on "regressive joining."

Dream of "Going Up the Stairs"

In this dream of May 1897, Freud, incompletely dressed, was going upstairs three steps at a time. He saw a maidservant coming down the stairs, felt ashamed, and felt glued to the steps.

Associations to this dream are present in at least three sources:

1. "It is only in our childhood that we are seen in inadequate clothing both by members of our family and by strangers—nurses, maid-servants, and visitors . . ." (1900, p. 244). "And thus the maid-servant . . . acquired the right to be treated in my dream as a reincarnation of the prehistoric old nurse" (p. 248).

2. "Another presentiment tells me . . . that I am about to discover the source of morality. . . . The accompanying emotion was not anxiety but erotic excitement" (Freud, 1887–1902, pp. 206–207).

3. "It seems as though in sons this death-wish is directed against their father and in daughters against their mother. A servant-girl makes a transference from this to the effect that she wishes her mistress to die so that her master can marry her" (pp. 207–208). The editors state that this was the first hint of the Oedipus complex.

Thus, in Freud's earliest realizations of the existence of the Oedipus complex, he connected his wishes to the mother surrogate, the nurse; to incest and perversions; to morality, reincarnation, and shame; to triangularity (three steps); and to inhibition. Again, the Catholic nurse's characteristic imprint is apparent.

Freud (1900, p. 269; Wolf and Wolff, 1943) recorded a dream of late December 1897: "Another time I had a dream that a man I knew on the staff of the University said to me: '*My Son, the Myops.*' " The main part of this dream again referred to Rome. The locale was a gateway with double doors, the Porta Romana in Siena. The dreamer, sitting on the edge of a fountain, was in tears when a nun brought out two boys. The woman, who had a red nose, asked the elder boy to kiss her goodbye. Instead, he said, "Auf Geseres" to her and "Auf Ungeseres" to the others.

Freud (1900) reported these associations: "Siena, like Rome, is famous for its beautiful fountains . . . another member of my household, our excellent nurse, was recognizably portrayed in the female attendant or nun in the dream." He connected the neologisms to Judaism, but at the same time said,

"The children of Israel . . . eat unleavened bread to this day at Easter" (pp. 442–443).

Again, we have an oedipal configuration, heralded by the division into three parts. Rome once more played an important part with displacement to Siena. The pictorial representations of a "gateway," "double doors," "Porta Romana" are all clearly recognizable symbols for the female genitalia. The manifest content, "a female figure—an attendant or nun," refers in the latent content to Freud's Catholic *Amme*. Tears, no doubt, were shed when she was discharged, at which time she had to hand over her charge. That this old woman had also attended Freud's younger brother, Julius, is almost a certainty. The sibling with the Roman name arrived when Sigmund was nineteen months old, and died eight months later, As previously mentioned, the nursemaid was fired when Freud was thirty months old, when his mother had just delivered her next child.

Finally, the rivalry with the father, Jakob, is delineated—condensed in the word, "Myops." Jakob's eye surgery is implicit in the image, and the allusion to Oedipus clear. The religious references to Judaism and Catholicism probably indicate the conflicts between the negative and the positive oedipal strivings. As Jones (1955, p. 17) pointed out, however, there actually is little but supposition to support the view of Velikovsky (1941) that Freud had an unconscious desire to convert to Roman Catholicism in order to further his worldly desires.

Dream of "The Botanical Monograph"

Among the multiple, interweaving associations to the dream of "The Botanical Monograph" (1900, p. 169) were Freud's wife; his father's eye surgery; the plant genus, *Cruciferae*, which he had failed to identify on a botany examination as a boy; and a footnote referring the reader to his paper on "Screen Memories." The equation of wife-mother-nurse has already been made. As Velikovsky (1941) pointed out, Crucifer means "one who carries a cross." Again, the effect of the religion of the nurse made itself felt.

The "Screen Memories" paper (1899), however, is even more specific. Part of the memory itself is "in front of the cottage door two women are standing chatting busily, a peasant-woman with a handkerchief on her head and a children's nurse" (p. 311). This memory of *two* women represents Freud's mother and his mother surrogate, the nurse. Freud's (1910a) great interest in Leonardo may have been due in part to the presence of two mothers, owing to the artist's illegitimacy. One of the associations to the picking of flowers in the screen memory is, naturally, defloration. Finally, "the peasant-woman cuts the loaf [of bread] with a long knife," an obvious reference to the threat of castration for incestuous wishes.

Dream of "Dishonesty"

In this dream of May 1898, Freud (1900, pp. 336–338) was accused of dishonesty, of having appropriated a missing article. Summoned by a manservant for an examination, he went into a hall with machines which reminded him "of an Inferno with its hellish instruments of punishment." He could not find his hat and could not go when told he could do so.

Freud classified this dream as another example of inhibited movement, representing a "conflict of will"—in this instance of both genital and anal origins. "That I could go was a sign of my absolution." The capitalization of "Inferno" not only accentuates its psychic value but suggests the book by Dante.

Other associations were included in a long footnote to the dream: "My not being able to find my hat was an occurrence from waking life which was used in more than one sense. Our housemaid, who was a genius at putting things away had hidden it.—The end of this dream also concealed a rejection of some melancholy thoughts about death: 'I am far from having done my duty, so I must not go yet . . .'" (p. 337m).

It is possible to arrive at latent meanings of the dream to support my thesis. The use of *men*servants likely is a reversal, as well as a condensation, since Freud found that when one reversal is present in a dream, others should be searched for. (In this dream we also find movement/paralysis as well as birth/

death.) In addition, this bit of the dream work probably was
necessary because admission of the original nursemaid in the
present context was too laden with anxiety. Nevertheless, a
housemaid is referred to directly in the footnote. Dishonesty,
of course, was most cogently connected by Freud to the misdeeds of his nurse. In his original memory of the events,
though, *he* was the one who stole for her.

Next, there is the inhibited movement, and the very strong
anal implications may have represented regressive pulls away
from the genital strivings in that Freud was not yet able to go
to Rome. The image of "the hellish instruments of punishment"
immediately follows spoken words in the dream, which Isakower (1954) and Robert Fliess (1953b) have related to the
superego.

The significance of the "detachability" of a hat was discussed by Freud (1915a) in a short paper on the hat as a symbol
of male genitals. The "missing article" in the dream refers to
castration as well as the loss of the nurse. Lastly, the age, one
year, is emphasized. Julius, Freud's brother, was born when
Sigmund was eleven months old and died when Freud was
nineteen months old. Within one year, then, birth and death
had both occurred, accentuated by the loss of the nurse soon
afterward.

Freud's rich associations reveal his various attempts at coping with the fantasied consequences of the oedipal impulses—trial, reprimand, "going to hell," castration, "reversing"
his wish by making the father the object of his affections or by
regression to anal preoccupations, or finally, even death.

The "Count Thun" Dream

This rather lengthy dream, which occurred in August 1868
and which Freud (1900) used as an illustration for "Infantile
Material as a Source of Dreams," involved a crowd to whom a
Count Thun (or Taafe) was speaking. To his putting a dilapidated leaf into his buttonhole and making a contemptuous gesture, Freud "fired up." (A footnote points out that the German
means "to drive" or "to travel" and is used repeatedly in these

senses in the dream.) The dreamer made his way through a series of rooms until he came to a corridor where a "housekeeper was sitting, an elderly, stout woman." A later scene, the third one, was in front of a [train?] station in the company of an elderly gentleman who was either blind or one-eyed. Freud handed him a male glass urinal, classifying himself as a "sick-nurse!"

In his associations Freud alluded to the Revolutionary Year of 1848. "This revolutionary fantasy . . . was like the façade of an Italian church in having no organic relation with the structure lying behind it." He went on to "think of some orchids which I had brought the same day for a woman friend and also of a rose of Jericho. . . ." Strachey's footnote says, "The Resurrection plant, whose dried fronds unfold under moisture."

Freud continued, "But the rooms (*Zimmer*) also meant 'women' [Strachey adds a note here: "*Frauenzimmer*—literally 'women's apartment,' is commonly used in German as a slightly derogatory word for 'woman'."] . . . In the figure of the housekeeper I was showing my lack of gratitude towards a witty elderly lady and ill repaying her hospitality and the many good stories that I heard while I was stopping in her house" (p. 214).

Freud (1900, pp. 431–434) used this dream later as an illustration of absurd dreams, specifically those related to the death of a father. He identified his brother with the cab driver of the dream, saying, "That year I had called off a trip I was going to make with him to Italy" (p. 432). More thoughts of travel by train in this paragraph are superseded in the very next one by a discussion of the "housekeeper."

A further association was to "boastings" reminiscent of "the great Rabelais' incomparable account of the life and deeds of Gargantua and his son Pantagruel." Grinstein (1968, p. 135) included in his summary of this literary allusion the episode of the Oracle of the Holy Bottle: "Another island on which Pantagruel and his group landed was the island of Popefig-gery. . . . Their adventures on a trip to the island of Papimania gave Rabelais the opportunity to satirize the Pope" (p. 138).

To be considered is the fact that this dream occurred on the anniversary of Freud's father's terminal illness, which led to his death on October 23rd, 1896. It certainly was the son's wish to keep secret, through the symptom formation of his travel anxiety and his inhibition of the wish to visit Rome, his competition with his father and his wish to have intercourse with his mother image, the housekeeper–nursemaid. In order to deny the wish to be rid of the "old man" with the eye disease, Freud used reaction formation by becoming his "sick-nurse," an identification with Freud's own "keeper" earlier.

Dream of "The Three Fates"

After his vacation in 1898, Freud (1900, pp. 204–208) dreamed of going into a kitchen where three women were standing. One was the hostess of the inn and appeared to be making dumplings. She said that the dreamer must wait until she was ready. He felt injured and put on a fur-trimmed overcoat that was too long. A second coat had a long strip with a Turkish design.

Thoughts of The Three Fates produced a memory of his mother's rubbing her hands together. He then thought, "Love and hunger . . . meet at a woman's breast. A young man who was a great admirer of feminine beauty was talking once—so the story went—of a good-looking wet-nurse who had suckled him when he was a baby: 'I'm sorry,' he remarked, 'that I didn't make better use of my opportunity'" (p. 204). The overcoats, Freud said, "clearly referred to implements used in sexual technique. A final association was to "a drug from the dispensary which removes hunger." Again Strachey supplies us with significant information—concerning the word for "dispensary"—"In German 'lateinische Küche' (literally, 'Latin kitchen')" (p. 206).

Grinstein (1968, p. 204) summarizes the story of The Three Fates, of whom Miriam, the sister of the hero, is most important for our purposes. She was deeply devoted to her son, Raphael, a name, as we have seen, which already had great significance. Miriam was "primitive and sophisticated, Jewish and Gentile, magical and worldly, intolerant and yet understanding."

Once more the fusion of nurse and mother, Gentile and Jewish, foreign (Turkish, Latin) and domestic becomes obvious. The oral emphases of the dream were less threatening than the phallic, oedipal strivings. Freud concluded,

> For one of the thoughts which my hunger introduced into the dream was this: "One should never neglect an opportunity, but always take what one can even when it involves doing a small wrong. One should never neglect an opportunity, since life is short and death inevitable." Because this lesson of *"carpe diem"*[5] had among other meanings a sexual one, and because the desire it expressed did not stop short of doing wrong, it had reason to dread the censorship and was obliged to conceal itself behind a dream. All kinds of thoughts having a *contrary* sense then found voice: memories of a time when the dreamer was content with *spiritual* food, restraining thoughts of every kind and even threats of the most revolting sexual punishments [all Freud's italics!] [pp. 207–208].

Dream of "The Bird-Beaked Figures"

The one recorded dream in which Freud's mother appeared as herself contains the final confirmation of the equation of the nurse with mother and of the beginning realization of the existence of the oedipal wishes in Freud himself.

> It is dozens of years since I myself had a true anxiety-dream. But I remember one from my seventh or eighth year, which I submitted to interpretation some thirty years later. It was a very vivid one, and in it I saw *my beloved mother, with a peculiarly peaceful, sleeping expression on her features, being carried into the room by two (or three) people with birds' beaks and laid upon the bed.* I awoke in tears and screaming, and interrupted my parents' sleep. The strangely draped and unnaturally tall figures with birds' beaks were

---

[5] Note the use of the Latin.

derived from the illustrations to Philippson's Bible. I fancy
they must have been gods with falcons' heads from an ancient Egyptian funerary relief. Besides this, the analysis
brought to mind an ill-mannered boy, a son of a *concierge*,
who used to play with us on the grass in front of the house
when we were children, and who I am inclined to think
was called Philipp. It seems to me that it was from this boy
that I first heard the vulgar term for sexual intercourse,
instead of which educated people always use a latin word,
"to copulate," and which was clearly enough indicated by
the choice of the falcons' heads. I must have guessed the
sexual significance of the word from the face of my young
instructor, who was well acquainted with the facts of life.
The expression on my mother's features in the dream was
copied from the view I had had of my grandfather a few
days before his death as he lay snoring in a coma. The
interpretation carried out in the dream by the "secondary
revision" must therefore have been that my mother was
dying; the funerary relief fitted in with this. I awoke in
anxiety, which did not cease till I had woken my parents
up. I remember that I suddenly grew calm when I saw my
mother's face, as though I had needed to be reassured that
she was not dead. But this "secondary" interpretation of
the dream had already been made under the influence of
the anxiety which had developed. I was not anxious because I had dreamt that my mother was dying; but I interpreted the dream in that sense in my preconscious revision
of it because I was already under the influence of the anxiety. The anxiety can be traced back, when repression is
taken into account, to an abscure and evidently sexual crav-
ing that had found appropriate expression in the visual
content of the dream [1900, pp. 583–584].

Freud was clearly implying that he considered this dream
one of the primal scene, by which he was both stimulated sexually and moved to fear castration. The theme of death is an
equation with castration and thereby connects his two "phobias," fear of traveling and fear of death. In the associations to
this dream Freud included the illustrations in Philippson's Bible, the son of the concierge, and the Latin word for copulate.
The reference to the Bible stands in juxtaposition to the son of

the concierge, his "younger instructor" (in sexual matters). The nurse had already been referred to as "my instructress in sexual matters," and she, of course, was also his instructress in Latin *religious* matters. The association to "Latin" is a further evidence that the incestuous wishes toward the mother were involved in Freud's fear of entering "la Bella Roma." Finally, "Philippson" refers not only to the son of the concierge; it also refers to Freud's older half-brother, Philipp, son of their common father. This selfsame Philipp was the one who went for the police, resulting in the discharge of young Sigmund's beloved–hated nurse.

Denouement

Freud's self-analysis continued apace, and his attachment to Fliess lessened . markedly. "Then came the great visit to Rome"—in the summer of 1901—"after which he says his pleasure in life had increased and his pleasure in martyrdom diminished" (Jones, 1953–1957, p. 339). A further consequence was Freud's becoming able to take *active* steps of his own to achieve his long wished-for professional maturity, his appointment to the cherished professorship.

In one of the last letters to Fliess, Freud wrote,

> "The public enthusiasm is immense." Congratulations and bouquets are already pouring in as though the role of sexuality had suddenly been realized by His Majesty, the importance of dreams confirmed by the Council of Ministers, and the necessity of treating hysteria by psychoanalytic therapy accepted in Parliament by a two-thirds majority! . . .
>
> In the whole story there is one person who has proved himself to be a real ass and one whom you don't sufficiently appreciate in your letter: that is me. If I had taken these steps three years ago, I would have been appointed three years earlier, and spared myself a great deal. *Other people are just as clever without having to go to Rome first* [italics added; E. L. Freud, 1960, p. 246].

But without the conflicts over the drive to enter Rome, the world probably would have had to wait for "that first journey into the unexplored territory of the unconscious" (Grinstein, 1968) which led to the discovery of the psychoanalytic method.

Summary

Because Freud did not publish many direct references to his mother, the role of his mother surrogate, the Czechoslovakian, Roman Catholic nursemaid of his first two-and-a-half years, is investigated through Freud's dreams and associations. The oedipal bases for the "travel phobia" and "Rome neurosis" were elucidated through the medium of this "primary originator" of Freud's neurosis.

Section II

Dreams and the Psychoanalytic Situation and Process

Articles in this section reflect, in the main, the controversy or concern over the role which the dream plays in psychoanalysis. The articles by Lewin (1955), Greenson (1970), along with the summary article by the editors on M. Masud Khan's work (see chapter 12), especially speak to this point.

The section begins with Bertram Lewin's now classical paper on the "Dream in the Psychoanalytic Situation" (1955), where he presents the thesis that "analysis formation" is really like "dream formation," and that it involves the same memory traces and psychic systems, though usually in different proportions. As an example he maintains that "blank dreams" are approximated by the "blank couch," explaining that sleeping (or falling asleep) on the couch is where the narcissism of sleep—which is actually under the aegis of the dream experience—comes into the open as "couch narcissism." The most salient points of his argument are: (1) "what happens on the couch" is not something like a neurosis, but instead is "something like a dream"; (2) the analyst is an arouser (of the sleeping–dreaming patient) as well as a day residue; and (3) the analyst continually operates either to wake the patient somewhat or to put him to sleep a little, to soothe or arouse—and this effect may be quite unconscious for both patient and analyst.

Defending this position of the importance of the dream in the psychoanalytic situation is the article by Ralph Greenson, "The Exceptional Position of the Dream in Psychoanalytic Practice" (1970). Here in this clinically precise and well-written contribution, he initially delineates his reasons for writing the paper, explaining that it is principally because of the goodly number of analysts in recent years (1945 to 1970) who deny the clinical importance of the dream and feel that it has no special value for psychoanalytic therapy; and also those analysts who use techniques in a way which indicates that they have disregarded Freud's theory and methods of understanding and using the dream in clinical practice. Second, he gives a number of examples of analysts who work with dreams in ways which he considers unproductive, wasteful, and at times even harmful. Greenson then concludes with a number of clinically supported formulations: (1) the dream is an exceptional and unique production of the patient; (2) dream interpretation cannot be taught to therapists who are ill at ease with the form and content of unconscious mental activities; (3) working with dreams makes an extraordinary demand on both patient and analyst—since the dream is the most intimate and elusive creative part of the patient; and (4) he finds (like Freud) that the dream is the royal road to a knowledge of unconscious activities for both patient and analyst, providing the analyst is not seduced into following "narrow bypaths and deadened streets" based on technical or theoretical prejudices.

Finally, completing the trilogy of articles defending the significance of the dream is the summary article on M. Masud Khan's work, "The Good-Dream, Dream-Space and the Dream-Experience Revisited" (1988), by the editors. This article attempts to describe Khan's efforts to bring the concept of the self, or the self-experience, into conjunction with psychoanalytic dream psychology. Beginning with the "good dream," Khan suggests that it is a measure of the psychic capacity of the individual (i.e., the dream-increment of ego strength) and, in this regard, he finds that the patient who cannot have a "good dream" also cannot creatively use the analytic situation. While the "dream space" is a specific intrapsychic structure where the person actualizes certain types of experiences, such experiences are related to Winnicott's transitional space which a child establishes in order to discover aspects of his self and reality. Finally, the "dream experience" is conceptualized as a special type of primary-process self experience which often bears no direct relationship to the dream text (i.e., the reported dream).

The remaining articles further document a number of important specific issues associated with the dream in the psychoanalytic situation. They include the report by Kleeman, "Dreaming for a Dream Course" (1962), in which analytic candidates in a dream seminar present and analyze their dreams as the main requirement of the course. Next appears the interesting clinical paper by Peck, "Dreams and Interruptions in Treatment" (1961), showing the extent to which anticipated interruptions in analytic therapy are sometimes attended by a noticeable decrease in resistance, which permits the recall of vivid, relatively little-disguised dreams—a state which may well continue not only during the interruption, but after the therapy is resumed. This section ends with Cavenar and Nash's "The Dream as a Signal for Termination" (1976) which concerns itself with the hypothesis (controversial in some quarters) that "termination signal dreams" do exist and have a recognizable form which may serve as reliable indicators that a decision to consider termination is appropriate.

Chapter 7

DREAM PSYCHOLOGY AND THE ANALYTIC SITUATION

Bertram D. Lewin

This paper will try to apply some of our knowledge and theory about sleep and the dream to an understanding of the analytic situation, which is here defined, empirically, as the familiar standard hour, or loosely, as "what happens on the couch"; and sometimes the word *couch* will be used metaphorically as synonymous with "analytic situation." Included in the idea of analytic situation are the phenomena of free association, resistance, transference, repetition, and others well known and generally admitted as working concepts.

Genetically, the analytic situation is an altered hypnotic situation, as the analytic hour is an altered hypnotic session. The analytic patient takes his origin from the hypnotic patient, for originally Freud's patients were attracted to therapy by their knowledge of cures due to hypnosis. The development of analysis from hypnosis has been studied and told with much detail and perspicacity by Ernest Jones (1953–1957). It seems that some patients could not be hypnotized, or they "countersuggested" too vigorously; that is, they had a resistance to being hypnotized or, more likely, a fear of being put to sleep. The refractory patient made the following *as if* proposal that the treatment be modified: "Although I cannot, for reasons of my own, let myself be put to sleep,[1] or into a state resembling sleep,

This paper was first published in the *Psychoanalytic Quarterly* (1955), 24:169–199.

[1] The wording of the "patient's proposal" does not mean that hypnosis is necessarily sleep, any more than "to be put to sleep by ether" means that drug anesthesia is absolutely the same thing as natural sleep. No assumption of the sort is necessary. The assumption merely is that the patient regards being hypnotized, as he might regard being anesthetized, as such an action, and that he has the same attitude toward being

nevertheless I promise to relax as if I were in bed and to tell everything that comes to me in this quasi-hypnotic or quasi-hypnagogic state. In return for this conception, I accept more responsibility for what I say."

We may put it that a resistance appeared in therapy even before psychoanalysis was properly born and was of major importance in its subsequent development. It changed the hypnotic situation into an analytic situation. It should be noted that the time of this change coincides with the time in the embryology of psychoanalysis, when hypnosis was being used not to produce suggestive, irrational cures, but to uncover traumatic, repressed memories; so that this purpose is tacitly assumed in the above-stated bargain.

With this modification of the hypnotic session into the analytic hour, the therapist's theoretical interest was diverted from the problems centering about sleeplike states and became more and more focused on the contents of the patient's remarks and behavior. The study of the patient as a quasi-sleeper or quasi-dreamer was completely subordinated to the therapeutic and theoretical study of his symptoms. The theory of the neuroses was developed, and it seems in retrospect inevitable that the writings on technique should have been couched largely in terms of this theory. The patient on the couch was prima facie a neurotic person and only incidentally a dreamer. It is well, however, to question the complete inevitability of this particular choice of formulation and terminology. We may plausibly speculate whether an alternative path could not have been chosen; namely, to regard the analytic material and "what happens on the couch" not as something like a neurosis, but instead, something like a dream, and to introduce dream concepts and dream psychological terminology. If this path had been taken, quite possibly we would have developed a poorer and less useful terminology than we have now, but that is not the issue. We are not raising the question of better or worse, merely of difference.

The relationship between neurosis theory and dream theory seems to have been a slippery one for analysts to hang on

hypnotized as he might have toward going to sleep (see Freud, 1888–1892; Lewin, 1954).

to. Thus, Freud (1950) confessed that he discovered the essential unity of the two, then forgot, and had to rediscover it. Perhaps it is necessary for all of us to repeat this rediscovery. So much of our analytic phylogeny recapitulates Freud's scientific ontogeny that we may not have, even now, thoroughly "worked through" this insight and taken in all its implications. We have no doubt that the dream is the royal road to the unconscious and that dream analysis is an indispensable instrument in therapeutic practice. We know that the dream is a wish fulfillment and a communication, and we bank heavily on this knowledge. But we have paid little attention to the chief function of dreaming, its guardianship of sleep. Attention to the interpretation of contents and to the dream work has distracted us, here too, from the problem of sleep and from a consideration of the analytic subject as a fractional dreamer or sleeper. Again in retrospect, Freud's rejection of Breuer's ideas of hypnoidal states appears consistent with the general turning from an interest in the sleeper as such.

We all know the psychoanalytic dictum that whatever is rejected in the course of conflict-solving may return and find a disguised place in that which is accepted. So, sleep, excluded by agreement from the analytic situation, gained access to it in another form—the method of free association. I developed this idea in a recent paper (1954), where I pointed out that the wish to be put to sleep, which the patient brought to the hypnotic situation, has been supplanted by the wish to associate freely in the analytic situation. The patient lies down, not to sleep, but to associate. The interpretation of free association as the substitute for sleep in the therapeutic situation was based not only on the tacit bargain cited above, but also on one of Freud's definitions of free association, given in *The Interpretation of Dreams* (1900, p. 102), where it is likened to the state of mind that precedes sleep (also to the hypnotic state).

For our present purposes, then, we shall project the metapsychology of sleep and the dream on the analytic situation. We readily note certain coincidences. Thus the narcissism of sleep, an element assumed in dream psychology, coincides with narcissism on the couch, and the rare blank "sleep dreams" are analogous to the rare transient falling asleep on the couch, both phenomena being the unusual near zeroes of their respective domains. The manifest dream text coincides with the manifest analytic material, expressing, in processed form, latent thoughts become preconscious. Dream formation is to be compared with "analytic-situation formation"; it is the *exception*, to use Freud's word, to the basic narcissism. Other analogies suggest themselves, but because there are so many differences of detail and elaboration, due to the opposite paths taken in the psychic apparatus by the dream process and the analytic-situation process (one terminating mainly in visual hallucinations, the other mainly in words), it is well to consider at first only the broader coincidences.

Narcissism

Since we mentioned the concept of *narcissism* as an element of the psychoanalytic theory of sleep and the dream, and suggested its application in the analytic situation, it would be well to come to terms with this word and its meaning. To ignore its origin in sexology, *narcissism* was introduced into psychoanalysis as a definition of an erotic relationship in which the self was the object, that is to say, self love; but the youth gazing at his image in the fountain always had a more abstract and symbolical quality, as a representation of a form of love, than did, for example, the picture conjured up by the word *libido*, with its etymology of sexual desire and its implication of the excited genital and sexual congress as the representation of object relationship. Narcissism has always seemed to be more conceptual, to be something behind the phenomena, and as far as factual existence is concerned, it has some of the shadowy and absent quality of its mythological eponym's forlorn sweetheart, the nymph Echo.

I mean that narcissism is an abstraction, with visible correlates in childhood psychology, in neurosis, in sleep, and in the love life. Narcissism, as a concept, is behind the dream, behind the depression and elation, behind somatic symptoms, and so on. We must carefully distinguish between narcissism the concept and narcissistic phenomena as we distinguish the conceptual points and lines of pure mathematics from the ink dots and strokes that we see and measure (Hartmann, Kris, and Loewenstein's discussion of theory [1953]). But as the dot is the *approximate* concrete representative of the abstract point, so, I believe, we may take a certain type of blank dream as a sort of concrete, approximate, "inkspot" picture of the abstract "point" narcissism. This blank dream (1953), though concrete, approximates the narcissism of sleep, and as a manifestation, epitomizes what *narcissism* can mean not only in dream and sleep psychology but also in the phrase *narcissistic neurosis*, its content signifying an intense, primitive, direct experience of the baby in the nursing situation, inclusive of sleep at the breast.

The relevance of this discussion of narcissism to the theme, the application of dream psychology to the analytic situation, depends on a rather subtle point. Despite our theory, in ordinary dream interpretation, narcissism is left to one side, and to a certain extent this is also true in our ordinary interpretation of the standard analytic situation. However, certain narcissistic phenomena that appear on the couch (some of them related to sleep) will help us to understand the nature and psychology of the standard situation, as the "narcissistic dream" throws light on the psychology of sleep and ordinary dreaming.

Toxic Technique

Before entering into an investigation of the standard analytic hour, it will be profitable to take up another, simpler modification of the older hypnotist's seance. I refer to what might be called the *toxic therapeutic situation*, where one or another drug is used as an adjuvant or an initiator of something like a cathartic situation. Here it is easy to apply dream psychology to interpret the situation, for the drug produces something like a sleep or a half-sleep state, and the fantasies that appear are readily compared to dream formations. For theoretical purposes, however, let us approach the matter indirectly and treat the situation as a toxic neurosis.

In "Mourning and Melancholia" [1917b], Freud states that a "toxic" condition might of itself lead to narcissistic regression

and depression (and presumably also elation) without the intervention of any object loss. But toxins may initiate many other
types of mental states. In psychiatry, it has long been known
that the psychological contents of a drug psychosis may include
not only manifestations of direct impairment of the cerebral
cortex (disorientation, torpor, intellectual inhibition, etc.), but
also others called "psychogenic" and due to individual mental
factors, such as significant life experiences. In other words, a
drug delirium has somewhat the structure of a dream, the drug
being the incentive to a kind of sleep or "state of narcissism,"
the psychogenic symptoms being cast in a form resembling a
dream.

When "narco" drugs are used in combined sleep- and psychotherapy, they produce a comparable state, where the narcissistic regression of anesthesia, like the narcissism of natural
sleep, is made imperfect by an "exception," which is like a
dream. Excluding such heavy methods as the *Dauerschlaf*, which
would be dreamless, the desideratum in the therapies I have
in mind is not deep sleep nor hallucinosis, but a state nearer
"muttering delirium with sense in it"; that is, something not too
far from intelligible or interpretable hypnagogic free association and catharsis.

From our present standpoint of historical reconstruction,
we may say that the therapist acts here to supply a different
answer to the problem raised by the Anna O type of patient, the
type which resists and "cannot be hypnotized." The primitive
resistance to being put to sleep is overcome by pharmacological
aid. The drug promotes the relaxation and submission which
is undertaken voluntarily in the hypnotic or standard analytic
situation.

Fear of Sleep and Death

The wish for a soothing drug, or the fear of it, often comes up
in associations during an analytic hour, among other reasons
because of conflicts centering about sleep. The interpretation
of this wish or fear throws light on the resistance of patients
to hypnotism, which was not interpreted when historically the

bargain of free association was struck. Some of the ambivalence about sleep and anesthesia was discussed in a previous paper (1954), where I recounted some of the fantasies of seduction, or of being disgracefully uninhibited in language and action, and the moral objections that were raised to the introduction of the use of chloroform. In his 1888 paper, Freud tried to allay some of the public's and the medical profession's fear of harm coming from hypnotism by reminding his readers that anesthesia had been feared in the same way, but that this fear had gradually been dispelled through familiarity and reason.

It is true, as Freud says, that common sense and familiarity have overcome some of the irrational alarm over being put to sleep by chloroform, and its social sanctioning (*accouchement à la reine*) has caused some of the anxiety to be ignored. Nevertheless, there still remain certain fears of being anesthetized, and the commonest one is not the fear of being uninhibited and losing self-control but the fear of dying. There is no need here to repeat arguments or furnish evidence for the idea that this fear is symptomatic and covers other latent ones. I shall merely name some of the pregenital varieties of the fear of death, or the fear of being put to sleep which is the same. These are: the fear of being devoured, of being poisoned, of being suffocated; and finally, a variety which is not so much a fear of dying in the sense of losing consciousness (sleeping) as a fear of the afterlife (and bad dreams), a fear rather ignored in our materialistic era. The equivalence of sleep and death and its clinical applicability is demonstrated in the following account, kindly placed at my disposal some years ago by Dr. Maxwell Gitelson.

> The patient was a fifty-six-year-old man, seen in consultation, who had had a coronary attack, and who after recovery from this was suffering from an aversion to food, from feeling that food did not go down, and from breathing difficulties, subjectively experienced as "inability to get enough of what I need." After much emotional distress and subjective torture, at one point he burst out to his wife and daughter, who were standing by, "I am going to stop fighting this thing. I am going to let myself die." Thereupon he collapsed on the pillow, fully believing that he was

going to die, and instead dropped into the first peaceful sleep that he had had in many months. Dr. Gitelson comments: "This resignation to death really represented in his critical emotional state the development of a capacity to accept a profound oral regression with which death and sleep were equated."

A not irrelevant illness in this patient was a peptic ulcer of many years' standing. (Cf. Stone [1947], who describes sleep on the analytic couch in a duodenal ulcer patient.)

It would not be difficult to imagine that Dr. Gitelson's patient might have shown the same behavior if he had tried to accommodate himself to the analytic couch. The resistance to analysis, like the resistance to sleep or to anesthesia, may, particularly at the beginning, be due to a fear of death or its corollaries. Being hypnotized, anesthetized, killed, put to sleep, are equivalents, and all may be represented by lying down on the analytic couch. Many patients have dreamed of their analysis as a surgical operation, the table (the surgical one this time, not the dining table) representing the bed or couch. By extension, and for other reasons that come from medical education, physicians often think of themselves being dissected when they dream of their analysis, and sometimes they even turn the autopsy into a cannibal procedure. In the literature we have a record of a famous dream in which a young physician with strong scientific curiosity sees himself as a cadaver undergoing dissection. The analysand was of course Freud (1900, p. 452), and since it was a self-analysis, appropriately he is also the anatomist. The dream begins: "Old Brücke must have set me some task; strangely enough it related to a dissection of the lower part of my own body, my pelvis and legs, which I saw before me as though in the dissecting room, but without noticing their absence in myself and also without a trace of any gruesome feeling. . . . The pelvis had been eviscerated . . . ," etc. It is significant historically that the founder of psychoanalysis could see himself as a prosector and at the same time as the anatomical preparation, and later we shall have more to say about the identification of an analysand with a physically ill patient or a cadaver.

At this point, however, I should merely like to emphasize once more the natural unconscious equivalence of sleep and death, both of them states of narcissism, psychologically. Also that the exception to the narcissism of sleep, to wit, the dream, is the same as the exception to the narcissism of death, to wit, the afterlife. But more to the present purpose, I wish to indicate by these examples the sort of resistances there might be to lying down on the analytic couch, and how the couch and the analytic situation itself need interpretation. In all its variety, the most obvious interpretation, not necessarily the deepest, is that the couch is a place for sleeping.

Rank's Fallacy

In the above exposition I have tried to tie up some loose ends, many of them historical, which are related to the main theme of this paper, and to offer some justification for applying sleep metapsychology to the analytic situation. I should like now briefly to discuss an important error, which has a position in the history of psychoanalysis, and which involved both the theory of the analytic situation and the matter of sleep. I refer to the theory propounded by Otto Rank, and by him embodied in a technique, that in analysis patients relive their stay in the uterus and with its termination, their birth.

Rank, I believe, always had an unconscious feeling that the analytic situation was somehow a sleep and that the associative material was the equivalent of manifest dreaming. This I infer from an article of his called *Eine Neuroseanalyse in Träumen* (1924a), a tour de force, based on the tacit assumption that an entire analysis and the whole process of the analytic situation could be understood as if it were a dream. A reading of this paper clarifies some of Rank's later erroneous views.

Rank's argument (1924b) that the analytic situation represents an intrauterine state and its termination a rebirth begins with the observation, correct enough, that rebirth fantasies accompany the resolution of the analytic situation, that patients dream of leaving the analyst as a being born. In this Rank saw not a metaphorical expression of separation, but a "so to speak biological" repetition of the act of birth, *"meist in allen seinen Einzelheiten getreu"* (for the most part accurate in all details), so that the time spent on the couch is a true and immediate replica and reliving of that spent in the uterus. This idea Rank got directly from his patients, and he says *"psychologisch hat also der Patient recht,"* a quotation which conceals evident special pleading. It seems that Rank fell into the same sort of error which so distressed Freud when, at a critical moment in psychoanalytic history, he found that he had been misled by hysterical women's fantasies during analysis into believing that they had really been seduced in early childhood by their father or a near male relative. Freud took the hard step, then, of recognizing his error and realizing that he was dealing with the memory of an infantile fantasy. Rank was not aware that he had been deceived in the same way. He did not take into account the comparable alternative to his interpretation of the rebirth fantasy, namely, that it was a fantasy of waking up. For, among the fantastic elaborations of the fact of pleasurable sleep is the idea that one is in utero, or rather, within the mother's body, and this intramaternal fantasy is a later, more complicated, and more highly processed fantasy of the oedipal period, which contains later knowledge and impressions about gestation.

In other words, Rank could equally well have thought that the fetal postures adopted by patients on the couch and other signs and symptoms of the "intramaternal situation" were fantasy attempts to fulfill the wish to sleep; similarly he could have interpreted the "birth trauma" manifestations as the correlated resistance to waking up from the analytic bed. The insight that really resides in Rank's theory, if one analyzes his elaborations and misunderstandings, is expressed in his statement that *"die eigentliche Übertragungsliebe, die wir bei beiden Geschlechtern analytisch aufzulösen haben, die mütterliche ist . . . ,"* which is blurry and an overstatement, but nevertheless contains an intuition of the whole preoedipal development and approximates in a way an interpretation of the position on the couch as a relationship to the mother. This it is, though hardly so directly and "biologically" (whatever that implies) as Rank states. The couch is reminiscent of *sleep* and therefore an important element of the nursing situation. Rank felt the importance of the fact that the patient was lying down, and that somehow this was connected with the preoedipal relationship to the mother, but in his qualification of the statement quoted above, he himself fell into a fantasy in the clause, "*wie sie in der pränatalen physiologischen Bindung zwischen Mutter und Kind gegeben war.*" Here he was believing a fantasy to be a literal statement of genetic facts.

To Rank, in fact, as to Jung, the story of Oedipus seemed only a myth, not a genetic fact. However, the point here is that Rank's analysis of the analytic situation and his failure to see that he was observing symptoms of sleeping and waking, led him to theorize falsely, and along with Ferenczi for a while, to regress in his technique to a quasi catharsis, where the patient relived fantasies on the couch and acted out the script suggested, and this acting out Rank identified with the therapeutic process. His active injunction, the setting of a definite terminal date, provoked the patient into a regressive protest to having his stay on the couch cut short, and the patient then portrayed being "untimely ripp'd" from the analytic couch as an anxious, painful awakening, the traumatic "birth." In the oedipal setting, the regressively expressed formula for this would read: the father is waking and weaning me betimes from my sleep with the mother.

Rank was not saved from his fallacy by his knowledge of the theory of the neuroses, which indeed was shattered when he applied it to the analytic situation; but he might have been saved from his mistake if he had followed and analyzed thoroughly his perception about the "prenatal state," which meant that the analytic situation was some kind of sleep and the associative material some kind of dreamlike production; that is, if he had consistently applied the metapsychology of the dream. Instead, he built his theory of the analytic situation on unanalyzed infantile fantasies about the unborn child and childbirth.

The reason I have dealt here so extensively with Rank's theory may not be immediately evident. But I regard it as an attempt, thwarted by a mistake, to do what I am attempting now, that is, to project upon the couch and the analytic situation the idea that the patient is as if somewhat asleep.

Free Association

From such general expositions of the analytic situation in terms of sleep and dream psychology, we may turn to individual elements in it, and to begin with, the very important one of free association. It is often profitable and instructive to see a familiar fact in a different context—to see the dream, for instance, as something that occurs in nature as well as in an analytic procedure, which as a matter of fact Freud's own dreams gave us a chance to do. We must, in other words, remind ourselves occasionally that God could not care less whether a dream is reported to an analyst or not; and we may well look for the phenomenal elements of the analytic situation in their natural habitats.

Let us, therefore, consider a solitary individual who is contemplating his own thoughts, feelings, memories, and impulses. Let him approximate Freud's idea of free association by having him limit action to a minimum and by letting him put his mental processes into words with no care for style or form. That he should report these words to anyone is, for the time being, irrelevant. In any event, we have as yet no "analysis," not even a self-analysis, for many persons have used very much this method of introspection for many purposes.

Freud tells us that he came upon this method of giving free rein to the contents of consciousness in the writings of the German author, Boerne. In an essay, "The Art of Becoming an Original Writer in Three Days" (E. L. Freud, 1960), Boerne concludes his exposition with the following words: "Take a sheet of paper and for three days in succession write down, without any falsification or hypocrisy, everything that comes into your head. Write what you think of yourself, of your women, of the Turkish War, of Goethe, of the Funk criminal case, of the Last Judgment, of those senior to you in authority—and when the three days are over, you will be amazed at what novel and startling thoughts have welled up in you. This is the art of becoming a writer in three days"(quoted in Jones [1953–1957]; Zilboorg [1952]). Boerne evidently intended to use the scribbling as the raw material for his literary work. He had as his purpose the liberation of the imagination, or as we might prefer to say, the exploration of the preconscious system, for the advancement of literary composition. In *The Interpretation of Dreams* (1900, p. 102), Freud calls attention to Schiller's use of a method very like free association for the same purpose. We see, therefore, that from the start analysts have known that there was involved not merely a way of thinking, but also purposes and intentions that determined its use.

These intentions may be various. If we consider that works of Herbert Silberer (1909, 1912), another solitary associator, we see two evident motives for his recording freely arising ideas and feelings. One of these motives was psychological investigation in the narrower sense; he was interested in examining the why and how of this variety of thinking. His second purpose might be called, loosely, philosophical or mystical. Pursuing his first intention, Silberer noted his associations and the contents of his dreams and hypnagogic reveries, making scientific inferences and assumptions concerning the representation of waking up, the nature of symbols, and the way certain states of the dreamer enter the manifest dream text. His scientific psychological interest lay not in dream interpretation in Freud's sense of unearthing unconscious contents and wishes, but in establishing the nature of certain formal properties in the manifest contents. In addition to this interest, Silberer had another which he called "anagogic." He used the dream thoughts and associations as incentives and directives for philosophic and theologic speculation, and possibly for the evocation of moods and feelings that went with them. In both endeavors, there was, of course, nothing like the "analytic situation" or a "therapeutic intention." Silberer was led from verbal associations—a cardinal requirement in Freud's definition of free association—into visual and symbolic representation, and in reveries, during states of fatigue, he came very near to dreaming.

Jung was much influenced by Silberer, and it is fair to assume that he was describing his own variant of free association when (1911) he spoke of "undirected thinking," which, he says, starts in words but is later replaced by visual images and after that by dreamlike fantasies. The latter he came to regard as the basic or elemental contents of the unconscious, and he held them in a certain awe, much as the ancients had for dreams that emerged through the gates of horn and ivory to bring to mortals the messages of the gods. They suggested to him ethical and religious beliefs and goals, and reminded him of parallels in myth and fable. As Boerne took notes for literary composition, so Jung (and in part, Silberer) used associations and reveries for metaphysical and mythological constructions. In fact, as Glover (1950) noted, Jung's psychological constructions resemble an Olympus, and his allegedly basic concepts are themselves the complex condensations, distortions, and symbols of a sort of manifest dream text.

Given any fantasy which arises during free and solitary ruminations, such as Silberer's while he gazed into his crystal globe, it is clear that one or another feature will be more likely to impress the observer when he retrospectively assesses them, and that he will be guided by his purposes, special interests, and education. One observer will be struck by the similarity of the given fantasy to ideas he held as a child or which possibly he has heard expressed by children. Another person, with little empathy for children but well versed in cultural history or anthropology, will be more aware that the fantasy resembles a certain series of myths. Consequently, the first observer would ultimately try to construct a psychology of the child, while the second might contribute to anthropology or the history of culture. A third observer, departing from the principle of putting the fantasy into words and running into complex reveries and unusual absorbed states, might come to accept these manifest, processed ideas and qualities as the final disiderata of the method. Still another observer could ignore all the frames of reference mentioned; in fact from Zilboorg's account (1952) of Francis Galton's use of the method, an academic psychologist of the old school, interested in the study of the mind according to the old canons of the science, might view the associations simply as novel, static "enlargements of consciousness." Clearly, all such observers have brought to the field their own measures and coordinates.

Freud's self-analytic intentions and purposes can be indicated in a few words. He approached his own associations as he did those of his patients, and he was guided by the same medical and analytic intentions, little concerned, to begin with, as to their nonmedical application. However, when one uses the word *medical* in connection with Freud, it must be in a very broad and enlightened sense, not synonymous with *therapy*, and including all the connotations and implications of science and research. Free association for him was calm self-observation, and the verbal reporting or recording of the associations, which rules out of the method some of the "inexpressibles" to which Jung refers, or at least insists on attempting to verbalize. This verbalization is by no means impossible; witness the brilliant descriptions of mystical experiences by many saints and poets.

We might use as an instance of Freud's attitude toward nonverbalization his pursuit through indirect associations of the forgotten name, *Signorelli*, when he could bring to mind only the visual images of the artist's frescoes. Under the same circumstances, it is conceivable that some other person, say an artist, not particularly interested in the problem of forgetting, might have been sidetracked into aesthetic moods, and he might have lost his interest in the patient's name. Freud's special interest in remembering and forgetting outweighed any tendency toward pleasurable aesthetic memories. From the purely psychoanalytic point of view or according to Freud's rules, many of the reveries and states of mind in question represent resistances to putting thoughts into words and to the hidden implications and associative links to these same thoughts. In his reference to calm self-observation, as well as in the account of resistance and transference which immediately follows this in *The Introductory Lectures* [1916–1917], Freud leaves aside the problem of the relative awakeness of the person who is freely associating.

There are doubtless many other purposes that free association might be made to serve. Those mentioned are: (1) literary creation; (2) psychological science; (3) mystical experience; (4) ethical and philosophical guidance or inspiration; (5) therapy. As a drug is only *materia medica* in itself and variously utilizable for experiment or therapy or pleasure, so are free associations capable of varied employment. They can be elaborated, superseded, used "anagogically" for moral illumination, or permitted to lead to buried memories, according to the interests and intentions, conspicuous or unconscious, of the self-observer. The thoughts and reveries of the relaxed, solitary person may lead off in many directions, guided by the pleasure principle, by impulses to action (Hartmann, 1947), or by intellectual and secondary intentions. Actions may include gestures or fugues or "rational behavior." The spontaneous ideas of the solitary self-observer can belong to various parts of his personality: different ego interests and pleasure strivings can seize upon the newly arisen ideas and feelings, progressively or regressively (Kris, 1950c). They may be turned into practical channels, such as literary production or problem solving, go over into aesthetic or athletic action, or be passively enjoyed or tolerated.

For the purposes of this discussion, it will be noted that the conception of free association is given a very loose construction. But at its core, again for our purposes, stands Freud's special tight definition of a "condition of calm self-observation . . . something which is quite different from reflection without precluding it," an attention to what is on the conscious surface of the mind, with a relinquishing of all objections to what might appear there, no matter from what source, or what the form or content. Around this nuclear, strictly defined norm radiate the states of consciousness of all degrees of awakeness and sleepiness, including the artificial "toxic" states; and there are insensible transitions toward reveries and dreams in one direction, and, in the other, toward directed, secondarily processed, structured mental work.

Indeed, what William James (1890, pp. 325–326) has to say about primitive reasoning may be interesting in this context. "It is," he says:

> [B]y no means easy to decide just what is meant by reason, or how the peculiar thinking process called reasoning differs from other thought sequences which lead to similar results. Much of our thinking consists of trains of images suggested one by another, a sort of spontaneous reverie, of which it seems likely enough that the higher brutes should be capable. This sort of thinking leads nevertheless to rational conclusions, both practical and theoretical. . . .

As a rule in this sort of irresponsible thinking, the terms
which fall to be coupled together are empirical concretes,
not abstractions. A sunset may call up the vessel's deck
from which I saw one last summer, the companions of my
voyage, my arrival into port, etc.; or it may make me think
of solar myths, of Hercules' and Hector's funeral pyres, of
Homer and whether he could write, of the Greek alphabet,
etc. If habitual contiguities predominate, we have a prosaic
mind; if rare contiguities, or similarities, have free play, we
call the person fanciful, poetic, or witty. The upshot of it
may be that we are reminded of some practical duty: we
may write a letter to a friend abroad, or we may take down
the lexicon and study our Greek lessons [1890, pp.
325–326].[2]

Evidently, James was associating pretty freely himself, and
he goes on to say that such actions as he mentioned, although
"rational," are not performed as the result of reasoning (Hartmann, 1947). Later, under the rubric of *resistance*, we shall refer
to a special sort of action that may issue under such circumstances. Here it will suffice to call attention to James's quietly
inspired differentiation of the prosaic and the poetic mind in
free association, which contains *in nuce* premonitions of psychoanalytic formulations. Writing in 1889, James often astonishes
us by what he might have called "poetic" prophesy; for after
trying to sum up thinking, he says, "if we could say in English
'it thinks' as we say 'it rains' or 'it blows', we should be stating
the fact most simply and with the minimum of assumption. As
we cannot, we must simply say that thought goes on" (James,
1890, p. 224).

I might of course have omitted James's remarks and simply
referred to E. Kris's exposition (1950b) of preconscious thinking, which covers this field; yet, James's words seemed worth
quoting for themselves.

---

[2] William James said that if you have a noble emotion such as you might get from
going to The Symphony, you should do something about it, act on it, even go and pay
a call on your great-aunt.

I wish to thank Dr. Carl Binger for this reference, which he rightly calls "the apotheo-
sis of the pragmatic."

We must now ask how this big, loose process of solitary think-ing or associating differs from the association desirable on the analytic couch. We may say, first of all, that there is probably no transference situation; we say *probably*, for there may be an occult one, such as we believe existed in Freud's thinking in relation to Wilhelm Fliess, and we cannot be too sure whether some of the accounts of self-analysis are entirely accurate when their reporter assumes that there was no analyst. I have in mind Pickworth Farrow's account (1945) and Freud's comments thereon. Certainly, if one has been in an analytic situation, subsequent self-analytic procedures will contain elements of the original transference. However, in nature, there would proba-bly be no analyst in a self-analysis in the narrower sense.

On the other hand, there would certainly be resistances, in the Freudian sense. These Freud observed in his own self-analysis, and he constantly alludes to them in his work with his own dreams. Nor is it hard to make them out in Silberer's or in Jung's writings. Indeed, the recognition that there are resistances to free thought ranks as one of Freud's great techni-cal discoveries. Although some of the persons mentioned near the beginning of this discussion, like Boerne and Schiller, had an inkling that they were overcoming some sort of impediment to thinking, and although some mystics write of the "darkness" when no ineffable experiences can be reached, yet it remained for Freud to note that certain paths of thought "led nowhere," or to a halt, or *"ins Unendliche"* ("into the endless," as he says in one place), and in general certainly away from the place that Freud was interested in—from repressed material which is not ego syntonic. In short, in free solitary association, there may be no transference but there is surely resistance. If, for termino-logical reasons, one wishes to reserve the word *resistance* for the situation on the couch,[3] then one would still have to say *repres-sion* or *defense*.

---

[3] One should not take the phrase *on the couch* too physically and literally. Free associa-tion, and an analytic situation too, occur with a person sitting up or in other positions. But this alters only a few obvious details; the person can also daydream, doze, and even sleep in the sitting position, and he can "associate."

Resistance, Sleep, and the Dream

The analytic resistance is a pragmatic concept. After hypnotism was abandoned, Freud found that the patient would not or could not live up completely to his promise to associate freely in a useful way; and it is well to emphasize the word *useful* and to specify the use. Freud had a therapeutic and scientific intention, and the resistance was directed against the instrument of this intention. I follow Freud in calling free association an instrument, for he compares analytic resistance to the resistance a person might offer to the use of dental forceps. The resistance was discovered in the analytic situation; but in his self-analysis also, Freud felt his resistances as he felt those of his neurotic patients. They felt like a counterforce that reminded him of the countersuggestion he knew from his prepsychoanalytic work, which recalcitrants used against being hypnotized. Resistance, therefore, is something that exists in self-analysis too, but, be it noted, in self-analysis which coincides with Freudian intentions. It also exists in free association and rumination that resembles free association, but if this occurs without Freudian intentions, it may not be noted or, if it is, not considered to be of practical importance.

There is no need here to repeat the insight into resistances which came from further experience with the neuroses. I shall merely mention the addenda to "The Problem of Anxiety," Anna Freud's classic account in *The Ego and the Mechanisms of Defense* [1936], and call attention to Loewenstein's recent paper "Defences, Auto-nomous Ego and [Psycho-Analytic] Technique (1954), and to its bibliography.

I wish to go back to nature and the more general field of solitary association outside the analytic situation. Solitary mediators, or whatever we may choose to call them, who do not have the specific Freudian intent have no objection to the appearance of resistances. When they encounter what we call resistances, they do not face them as Freud had to, for they are swayed by other motives. They are not cosigners of the contract with Anna O. They elaborate the resistances, act them out, enjoy them, or use them in some other way, but they do not recognize them.

The intentions and the point of view are crucial. Freudians must call such manifestations *resistance*, but others may be content with manifest, processed material not to be further analyzed. Boerne and Silberer and William James arrive at ends different from Freud.

On the couch, however, the resistance to being hypnotized or put to sleep shown by Anna O has been replaced by the resistance to free association, its substitute. In the resistance to free association, the old agreement about being put to sleep may be placed on the agenda for reconsideration. The patient, in conflict about free association, may suggest that he be hypnotized or be given a drug. Or he may depart from the basic contract by getting into a mystic state of mind, or into some of the sleepy states described by Silberer. I have indicated in a previous paper that the resistive patient may become either too sleepy or too alert for useful free association. His behavior may come to resemble that of the solitary associator with no Freudian intentions.

If you recall William James's hypothetical case of associations to a sunset, one outcome of the undirected thinking was action: the person was led by his associations to take down a Greek lexicon and study his Greek lesson. Such an action, from our standpoint, would not be an end, though it might have been for James's non-Freudian; we should consider it, even in self-analysis, an evasion of the fundamental rule. We should say, this man has quit associating. In a discussion, Rado once compared a certain resistive acting out to sleepwalking, thus correlating phenomena of resistance with those of the dream, and R. Sterba (1946) reported instances where persons have acted out the dream contents of the previous night. More often action in place of association should be considered a waking-up analogue. But Rado's reference to sleepwalking, perhaps the least "rational" of actions, brings out hyperbolically the fact that, to a Freudian, motion is not in itself an end. It may be as disturbing to free association as to sleep. Aphoristically, one might say that the dream is the guardian of sleep, but the analyst is the guardian of free association.

In the cathartic cure and in early psychoanalysis, did the listening doctor relinquish the use of sleep? Perhaps not entirely, on close inspection, for when the patient found communication impeded, he was encouraged to associate freely (even by the laying on of hands), and in effect he was set to work to produce more or less dreamlike fantasies, to approach therefore in quality the mentation of sleep. At the point of resistance, to put it strongly, the patient was soothed a little, encouraged to be "more asleep." In this context, resistance meant too much alertness which thwarted the doctor's intentions. Other resistances were soon encountered, in which, contrariwise, the patient let himself be in too much of a dream and eliminated too much responsibility and reality testing. With the years, after much study of the neuroses and psychoses, a good deal of this behavior was clarified, and the knowledge that accumulated was formulated in terms of a theory, and finally organized in "The Problem of Anxiety" and the literature that stems from this work.

Affects

Affects on the couch or arising during solitary association are like those that appear in dreams. They are part of the manifest content. The Freudian intention is to analyze them, and as in dream analysis determine whether a "happy mood" may not conceal a fear of death, or whether an anxiety is a signal and a repetition. The solitary meditator may take the affect at its face manifest value and go on from there, taking the elated and depressed feelings especially as warranted.

The Analyst

We may approach the matter of the analyst and where he fits into the metapsychology of the dream by a preliminary consideration of the solitary associator. If he is following Freud's rules, that is, if he is a self-analyst, there may be a kind of occult analyst, or at least an occult transference figure, as we learn from the role which Wilhelm Fliess played in Freud's self-analy-sis. Let us assume, however, for the general situation of self-analysis, that it is possible to do what Freud did in his self-study without someone else (real or ideal), therefore, without a transference.

As to the unanalytic free associator, for his unanalytic pur-poses he may wish to confide, so that we may speak of a possible confidant for such solitary meditations who would be the recipi-ent of the ideas that go through his mind. It is needless to list here the possibilities of such a relationship, which might include any kind of human communication from the most primitive to the most sophisticated, nor do I wish to document them. We again encounter the matter of purpose. Hanns Sachs has de-scribed one variety of such communication in his article, "Day-dreams in Common" (1924), where the common ground was originally the sharing of masturbation fantasies, later of more elaborate stories. Supposing Boerne or Schiller had sought a confidant; then the other person could have been called an editor or a collaborator. Silberer might simply have considered such a person an intruder.

It was during the transition from hypnotic treatment to catharsis and analysis that the neurotic patient changed from being a hypnotic subject to being a confider, and the therapist pari passu became a psychoanalyst. Freud's and Breuer's first subjects came to them with the stated purpose of relief from symptoms, and to the end persons continued to go to Freud either to be cured or to learn, by sampling the cure, a therapeu-tic method. But before there was an official psychoanalysis, patients had come to be put under hypnosis, which they knew of as a sort of magical sleep. The idea that sleep is a magical healing method must be very ancient, more ancient than the sleep of the Aesculapian temple, and the general prevalence of this idea in the unconscious may well have attracted patients to hypnotists. "And God put Adam into a deep sleep," the early anesthetists reminded their theologically oriented opponents and their reluctant patients, and certainly sleep has its rational place in therapy even today. In its origins, however, the thera-peutic use of sleep quite possibly depended on fantasy, and the original hypnotic patients may have asked for it with the idea

that after sleep should come a better waking, one into a new
world, a dreamworld or heaven, in short, into a wish-fulfilling
world where the blind see, the mute speak, the lame walk and
are whole. Baudelaire called the drug addict's goal an artificial
paradise, and this it was that the seeker after hypnotic sleep
desired. The hysterical person, having been hypnotized, acted
out many fantasies and miracles of therapy, and we still see
often enough flights into health of the same shaky order.

The magical sleep maker became a confidant, and the analytic situation arrived in history. But the confidant listening to
associations as they appear is a very special kind of listener.
Sometimes the person on the couch is hardly aware of his presence and is even surprised by it at the end of an analytic session;
at other times, the patient can think of nothing but the analyst's
person. We speak of the transference, thinking of the building
up of fantasies about the analyst which are new editions of
older ones in the patient's history. Evidently the analyst is not
a unitary element that can be directly mapped to a unitary spot
in the diagram of the psychic apparatus and into the psychology
of sleep and the dream. In fact, in what follows it will become
clear that the analyst belongs in several places in the diagram,
also "around" the diagram, and that he can be mapped in terms
of dream psychology as a day residue, as an external excitant,
and as an external or "border" soother.

As the focus for infantile transference fantasies, the analyst
was compared by Otto Rank, with Freud's approval (1917a,
footnote), to a day residue, a recent stimulus of the immediate
environment which is processed into manifest material by the
addition of unconscious ideas. In this sense, the analyst is a
perception, he is recent material. Rank's point was made in
refuting some of Silberer's views of "anagogy" and in reference
to dreams about the analyst, but the waking fantasies on the
couch use him in the same way in this context. That the analyst
is a sleep maker or a waker needs more elaboration, and will
receive it in the discussion that follows. Also, it will be necessary
to analyze in dream metapsychology the superego role often
attributed to him.

Let us leave the patient aside for a moment and consider
the analyst as an interpreter, where his wishes and actions are

central. Is the patient still clothed for him in traces of the sleep or part-sleep from his phylogenetic history as a hypnotic and cathartic subject? Or has the concept of the recumbent sleeper and dreamer been repressed? In the latter case we might look for some return of the repressed, and possibly see it when analysts turn to drugs as an adjuvant to cathartic or analytic therapy. However, let us consider two psychoanalytic aphorisms which epitomize the aim of analysis. The first is: "Where id was, there let ego be!" Let us combine this with another familiar remark, that the ego rejoins the id in deep sleep. The inference is that the analyst is a waker. To confirm this inference, we have another aphoristic statement, much quoted, "*Ich verstand, dass ich von jetzt ab zu denen gehörte, die 'am Schlaf der Welt gerührt' haben, nach Hebbels Ausdruck*" (Freud, 1914a). ["I understood that from now on, I belonged among those who 'disturbed the sleep of the world,' as Hebbel says."] Inescapably the analyst is an arouser, as well as a day residue. As an external neutral fact, regardless of his intentions, he may become part of the subject's analytic-situation manifest content, and he is in the structure of the analytic situation as if a dream day residue. But when the analyst's intentions come into play, and he interprets and analyzes, he is often not in the structure but an external waker or disturber of the situation. We shall see later that he may also at times play the role of a soother.

I suggested in a previous paper (1954) that coincidental with all other effects of the analyst's remarks or perhaps even of his presence, there is a deep effect, which I likened to the musical: the analyst continuously operates either to wake the patient somewhat or to put him to sleep a little, to soothe or to arouse; and this effect may be quite unconscious both for subject and analyst.

There are apparently some simple therapeutic situations, comparable to the standard analytic but different nevertheless, in which the aim is more nearly the simple one of arousing or wakening the patient. The idea that a psychosis is a kind of dream is ancient, and many maneuvers used in the treatment of schizophrenia have a rousing intention, as those most experienced in the field have stated or indicated. Zilboorg (1930), for example, as a preliminary to using the classical technique, put his schizophrenic patient through a course of training in reality discrimination, as if to insert into a dream some of the functions of the waking state. K. R. Eissler (1951) insists on dealing directly with "the primary process," which is a concept of dream psychology, so that the maneuver is a concession to the patient's dreaming. In a somewhat different context, Eissler (1943, 1951) states that at one stage of the treatment, the intellectual content of what is told the patient is not as important as the therapist's voice or manner—that one could influence the patient perhaps even by mumbling, surely a "musical" remark. John Rosen says explicitly and generally, "What is the psychosis but an interminable nightmare in which the wishes are so well disguised that the psychotic does not awaken? Why not then awaken him by unmasking the real content of his psychosis? Once the psychosis is stripped of its disguises, will not this dreamer awaken too?" (1953).

Other, less clearly understood, methods of dealing with schizophrenia put the patient to "sleep" by more or less drastic means. Empirically they often wake up different, and often they speak of the experience as a "rebirth." The "rebirth" fantasy is the counterpart of the "intrauterine fantasy"; the latter is an infantile fantasy which takes the child asleep as its model for life before birth, the "birth" fantasy uses the child's waking up, or perhaps its "waking up" into a dream. In any case, the therapist appears to have the intention of fulfilling the sleeper's wish for a healthy paradise, as I suggested in discussing the use of hypnotic sleep as an implementation of this idea in neurotics. We can gain some insight into the sleep-making intention of the physician by considering the ambivalence of physicians toward patients, their vacillation between a preference for a live or a dead patient, which I partly analyzed as due to their double experience in medical school, where they dealt with cadavers as their first patients and later had to transfer some of their conception of the patient as cadaver to live persons (Lewin, 1946a). But as the sleep therapies of schizophrenia are organized, the doctor's wish to put the patient to sleep is subordinated to his wish to waken him and to cure him. As in surgery, the physician's sleep making enters the larger therapeutic activity with its arousing intention, as a "feedback" and regulator or subordinate action.

To return to the topic of arousing, and the analyst's excitant role in this direction, we may again consider a schizophrenic case. I refer to Nunberg's classic analysis (1948) of the patient who had had a catatonic attack. He constantly referred to the attack as "my dream," and he called his desire for recovery a wish to forget this dream completely. Elsewhere (1953a) I have shown how the wish to forget a dream is equivalent to a wish to be completely awake, and in Nunberg's patient the way this was expressed is worth noting. For he set the physician up as a father and ego ideal, endowed him with tremendous power, expressed deep submission, and stated that he wished to be cured by the "power" of his father's words. That is, as I interpret it, he wished the father to awaken him through powerful loud noises. In infancy, words and noises are powerful excitants and arousers, and apparently the same holds in the case of the dream.

Here I rely on Isakower's studies (1939, 1954), according to which manifest words that appear just at the end of dreams during wakening moments represent wakener–superego, and because they have not been caught by the full dream work, they retain their verbal and environmental sense. Reasoning further, to be wakened is to be weaned, and as a variant, to be brought back to this world, which returns us to Rank and his fallacy. It also reminds us of Rank's insight into the preoedipal transference situation, and of his attempted analysis of the "couch" and of the analytic situation per se. The "couch" means sleep, with its maternal implications; and the spoor of the preoedipal father, who is not a dream element but a wakener, is sublimated in the therapy into the analyst who is not an element of the "couch situation," but one who disturbs the sleep of the world and its inhabitants. The "auditory sphere," which borders on the atmosphere where the sound waves travel, catches most of the stimuli (though surely not all) that awaken the child, the dreamer, and the analysand.

That the analyst is on the border of the dream becomes evident, by contrast, in those dreams where he is represented as a soother, and where there is no border. I am referring to those unprojected, blank, "sleep," or "narcissistic" dreams in which the analyst is represented. For example, in the dream reported by Rycroft (1951), where the border of the dreamer is vague, and the dream is not visually projected but is "pure feeling," the analyst is a soothing atmosphere and the homologue of the breast or dream screen. In Rycroft's report, the patient said he felt as if he were being taken under the analyst's wing, but that there was no visual content, and that it was an allegorical way of expressing a feeling which was more like an emotion. I have encountered comparable "transference remarks" in patients who expressed their preoedipal wish to sleep at the breast by fantasies of occupying the same space as the analyst, as if they could walk right into or through him. This is an unusual mapping of the analyst; it puts him in the place of sleep itself.

Nunberg's patient wished to be thoroughly awake and to forget his catatonic "dream." Rycroft's patient, not psychotic, in dreaming portrayed his analyst as the bland "spirit of sleep" and enjoyed the best night's sleep he had ever had. Both patients centered their relationship about the fact of *sleep*, reminding us again of Freud's bargain with Anna O, and suggesting that both of these patients sensed the relationship *as if* in terms of the old prepsychoanalytic days, when the hypnotist put his patient to sleep and awakened him. Their manifest thoughts referred to this latent doctor–patient relationship.

Other clinical examples might be given, but they are readily available in analytic practice. Therefore, I shall be content to summarize some of the results of our mapping of the elements of dream psychology to the couch situation. With ingenuity, it is possible to find the couch situation's counterparts in *The Interpretation of Dreams*. In the sense of "transference figure," the analyst is to be paired with what seemed in dream interpretation a very minor piece of material: he is the opposite number of indifferent precipitates or day residues to which unconscious ideas lend their cathexis. As interpreter, he stands for another minor element—a current external stimulus, which may threaten to arouse the dreamer, like the real fire in Freud's paradigm of the dream in chapter VII, that of the burning child. He is also the opposite number of certain external stimuli which did not interest Freud in connection with the dream—the stimuli which promote sleep. These were taken for granted and did not need to be counteracted by the guardianship function of the dream, for they too assisted the maintenance of sleep and ordinarily were not registered in the dream. We know a great many of these, differing at different ages: lulling and crooning, the full meal, and other satisfactions, all in a way wish-fulfillments too. There are also soporific drugs, and as an interesting psychological example, the memory of the nursing situation, which, when it appears, often coincides with sound and happy sleep. In this context, the analyst's position is that of peripheral stimulus.

It will be noted that the analyst is at both ends and around the diagram of the psychic apparatus; that he is "around" the couch as the external world is around the dream.

The rest of the mapping on the couch of dream psychology is not difficult, for "analysis formation" is like dream formation and involves the same memory traces and psychic systems, though usually in different proportions. Blank dreams are approximated by the "blank couch," that is, sleep on the couch where the narcissism of sleep which is "under" the dream comes out into the open as "couch narcissism." I omit what the analyst does besides lulling and rousing from the present statement; that is, I omit most of analytic technique, the contents of the specific interpretations and other operations, which of course matter very much. To fall back on Freud's old comparison of hypnosis and chloroform anesthesia, it is what one does after the patient is chloroformed that matters most, and this is what we call technique and not situation. As the surgeon cannot always ignore or completely forget the basic situation of anesthesia, so we cannot always ignore the ratio between sleep and waking in the analytic patient.

Chapter 8

THE EXCEPTIONAL POSITION OF THE DREAM IN PSYCHOANALYTIC PRACTICE

RALPH R. GREENSON

Introduction

Freud considered *The Interpretation of Dreams* his major work. He wrote in the third (revised) English edition, published in 1932, "It contains, even according to my present-day judgement, the most valuable of all the discoveries it has been my good fortune to make. Insight such as this falls to one's lot but once in a lifetime" (1900, p. xxxii). At the end of Part E in the seventh chapter Freud said: "*The interpretation of dreams is the royal road to a knowledge of the unconscious activities of the mind*" (p. 608). A further indication of how important Freud considered this work to be is that he revised and amplified the book on dreams on eight different occasions, the last time in 1930 (Strachey, 1953, p. xii).

You may wonder why I chose to present a paper on the exceptional position of the dream since all this would seem to be common knowledge. A careful reading of the psychoanalytic literature in recent years, however, reveals that a number of psychoanalysts believe either that the dream has declined in clinical importance over the last forty years and is of no special value for psychoanalytic therapy or they use techniques which indicate that they have disregarded Freud's theory and methods of understanding and using the dream in clinical practice. I am also impressed that some influential psychoanalysts contend

This paper was first published in the *Psychoanalytic Quarterly* (1970), 39:519–549.

that this downgrading of the significance of the dream in clinical practice has come about because (1) the structural theory was introduced; (2) Freud's great work on dreams has discouraged attempts at emulation or elaboration; and (3) Freud's concept of the topographic theory has become useless (Waldhorn, 1967, pp. 52, 53). These conclusions and more can be found in a monograph titled [*Indications for Psychoanalysis:*] *The Place of the Dream in Clinical Psychoanalysis* (1967) which is the result of a two-year study of dreams by the Kris Study Group under the Chairmanship of Charles Brenner with Herbert Waldhorn serving as Reporter. Most of the members of this group appear to have concluded that (1) the dream is, clinically speaking, a communication in the course of analysis similar to all others; (2) it does not provide access to material otherwise unavailable; (3) it is simply one of many types of material useful for analytic inquiry; (4) it is not particularly useful for the recovery of repressed childhood memories; (5) Freud's theory that the dream work is governed by the interplay between the primary process and the secondary process is not compatible with the structural theory and ought to be discarded.

I disagree with every one of the conclusions stated above. I am happy to point out that I am not alone in my beliefs, for I have discovered that some members of that section of the Kris Study Group, with Leon Altman as their spokesman, opposed many of those opinions. Altman has recently published a book, *The Dream in Psychoanalysis*, in which he suggests other reasons for the decline in clinical use of the dream. He expressed the opinion that since the coming of the trend toward ego psychology, many analysts have not had the experience of having their own dreams properly analyzed and the lack of this type of personal experience has deprived the psychoanalyst of the conviction that the interpretation of dreams is of outstanding importance for psychoanalysis (1969, p. 1).

Besides that section of the Kris Study Group reported in *The Place of the Dream in Clinical Psychoanalysis*, there are prominent analysts of Kleinian persuasion who also work with patients' dreams in ways which are far removed from what Freud, Isakower (1938, 1954), Sharpe (1937), Lewin (1958, 1968), Erikson (1954), and a host of others have described in their writings on this subject. In this paper I shall attempt to contribute

some clinical material and formulations which I hope will demonstrate how those analysts who seem to operate from diver-
gent theoretical and technical convictions differ from analysts
who believe in the exceptional position of the dream.

It is my belief, after many years of psychoanalytic therapy
with private patients and candidates in psychoanalytic training,
that one cannot carry out genuine analysis in sufficient depth
if one does not understand the structure of dream formation
*as well as the patient's and the analyst's contributions to the technique
of dream interpretation.*

Some General Formulations

The dream I believe is a unique form of mental functioning
which is produced during a special phase of sleep. This phase
is unlike any other phase of the sleep cycle and differs also
from the waking state. The psychophysiological research of
Dement and Kleitman (1957a), Charles Fisher (1965, 1966),
and Ernest Hartmann (1965), among others, has made this
emphatically clear. Recent research suggests the likelihood that
dream deprivation may be the cause of severe emotional and
mental disorders. We may well have to add to Freud's dictum
that the dream is the guardian of sleep, that sleep is necessary
in order to safeguard our need to dream.

The altered balance of mental forces in the dream is produced by bursts of psychic activity that seek sensory release
because sleep diminishes contact with the external world and
also cuts off the possibility of voluntary motor action. The
dream state allows for a reduction and regression of conscious
ego activities and of the censorship function of the superego.
It is important to realize, however, that in a sense, one is never
fully awake nor fully asleep. These are relative and not absolute
terms. Kubie (1966), Lewin (chapter 7), and Stein (1965) have
stressed the merits of keeping in mind the sleep–waking ratio
in studying any kind of human behavior. This helps explain
the fact that in the dream the perceiving function of the ego,
being deprived of the external world during sleep, turns its
energy toward internal psychic activity. Freud wrote that when

people go to sleep they undress their minds and lay aside most of their psychical acquisitions (1916–1917, p. 222). Lewin added that the dreamer generally sheds his body. The dream usually appears to us as a picture and is recorded only by an indefinite "psychic" eye (1968, p. 86).

If we follow the notion of a variable sleep–waking ratio, we are immediately reminded of phenomena similar to dreams: free association, parapraxes, jokes, symptom formations, and acting out. But there are crucial differences. No production of the patient occurs so regularly and reveals so much so graphically of the unconscious forces of the mind as the dream. Dream interpretation can uncover in more immediate and convincing ways not only what is hidden, but how it is hidden and why it is hidden. We gain special access to the interplay and the transitions between the unconscious psychic activities governed by the primary process and conscious phenomena which follow the laws of the secondary process. The proportion between input and output, in terms of reported phenomena and obtained knowledge of unconscious material, is in no other type of psychic phenomena as favorable as it is in dreams (Eissler, 1962).

So long as psychoanalytic therapy focuses on the resolution of neurotic conflicts in which the crucial components are unconscious, it makes no sense to consider every production of the patient of equal potential value. Affects, body language, and dreams are all, in most ways, nearer to those almost unreachable depths we search out so persistently in our analytic work. We attempt to present our findings to the patient's conscious and reasonable ego with the hope of providing him with a better understanding of his way of life and an opportunity for change.

These same points can be expressed structurally by stating that the dream reveals with unusual clarity various aspects of the id, the repressed, the unconscious ego and superego, and to a lesser degree certain conscious ego functions, particularly its observing activities. However, limiting the approach to the dream to the structural point of view is an injustice because it neglects the fact that we also have in the dream more open

access to dynamic, genetic, and economic data of basic importance. Small wonder then that the dream experience itself, often without interpretation, leads more directly and intensely to
the patient's affects and drives than any other clinical material.
This makes for a sense of conviction about the reality of unconscious mental activity unequalled by any other clinical experience. This is particularly true of transference dreams.

The dream is in closer proximity to childhood memories
by dint of the fact that both make use essentially of pictorial
representations. Freud (1900, 1923a) and Lewin (1968) have
emphasized that primitive mentation takes place in pictures and
is closer to unconscious processes than verbal representation.
Even after the child learns to speak, his thinking is essentially
dominated by pictorial representations. Things heard get
turned into pictures, as we know from certain screen memories
(Schur, 1966; Lewin, 1968). If an event is to become a memory
in early childhood, it has eventually to become concretized, a
mental representation, a memory trace. Lewin states that then
we search for lost memories as if they can be found somewhere.
This type of memory, the recall of an objectified experience, is
a step which seems to occur at the end of the first or beginning
of the second year of life (Waelder, 1937; Spitz, 1965). There
are more primitive "imprintings" which are derived from infantile body and feeling states that are not capable of being remembered but which may give rise to mental images and sensations
in dreams. Lewin's ideas on blank dreams and the dream screen
and his discussion of related problems are especially worthy of
note (Lewin, 1953b; 1968, pp. 51, 55).

To return briefly to the special importance of the psychic
eye for the dreamer and the interpreter of dreams. The dream
is essentially a visual experience and most adult recollections of
early childhood come to us as pictures or scenes. The analyst
interpreting to his patient is often working upon a fragment of
historical experience which he hopes will lead to a memory.
Such fragments or details may appear in dreams. When the
analyst tries to fill in the gaps between single interpretations,
he is making a construction, he is trying to recreate a series of
interrelated forgotten experiences. Such conjectures may lead
to recollections but, even if they do not, they may lead to a

sense of probability or conviction that the reconstruction is correct. This may then appear in a dream as an event (Freud, 1937b). Lewin describes this as trying to recreate a story in pictures of the patient's forgotten past. By doing so we attempt to get the patient to scan his past along with us; we are engaged in conjoint looking (Lewin, 1968, p. 17). The ultraclarity of some dream details also indicates that there is a special relationship between the cathexis of looking and the search for memories. This wish to see what actually took place, to be "in" on it, adds to the special sense of conviction that the correct interpretation of a dream can convey.

Ernst Kris decried the one-sided emphasis on analyzing defenses and stressed the importance of reconstructing past historical events so that the patient could "recognize" the pictures drawn as familiar (1956a, p. 59). He believed that memory plays a central role in a circular process which, if integrated, makes it possible for the patient to reconstruct his total biographical picture, change his self-representation and his perspective of the important persons in his world. In Kris's paper on the "good analytic hour," it is remarkable how often he chose examples of hours which contained dreams and recovered memories (1956a).

The predominant elements in the psychic activities that occur in dreams are heavily weighted on the side of the id, the repressed memories, the primitive defensive mechanisms of the ego, and the infantile forms and functions of the superego. Occasionally one can observe more mature ego functions but they are rarely dominant. All this testifies to the high degree of regression that occurs in dreaming, but as in all regressive phenomena, the quality and quantity of regression is uneven and selective in the different psychic structures and functions as Freud pointed out as early as 1917 (1917a), Fenichel in 1945, and Arlow and Brenner in 1964. The clearest and most comprehensive description of the unevenness and selectivity of regression can be found, in my opinion, in Anna Freud's book on *Normality and Pathology in Childhood* (1965, pp. 93–107).

Free association is a similar regressive phenomenon; it is an attempt to approximate something between wakefulness and sleep. The use of the reclining position, the absence of external distractions, the patient's attempt to consciously suspend his ordinary censorship, to abandon strict logic and coherence in his communications, all attest to that. However, real spontaneous free associations are rarely achieved by most patients and are then defended against with far greater sophistication. The point I wish to make is that the dream is the freest of free associations. Slips of the tongue may quickly reveal some deep unconscious insights but they occur rarely; insight is localized and the old defenses are very readily reinstituted. Acting out is by definition ego syntonic to the patient and its infantile origins are strongly rationalized away and defended. By contrast, as bizarre and incomprehensible as the dream may appear, the patient recognizes the dream as his, he knows it is his own creation. Although the strange content of the dream may make it seem alien, nevertheless it is irrevocably his, like his symptoms, and he is quite willing to work on his dreams, provided his analyst has demonstrated how working together on dreams is helpful in achieving greater awareness of the patient's unknown self.

A few words before turning to some clinical examples. In 1923 Freud himself recognized that *some* of his ideas subsumed under the topographic point of view conflicted with the descriptive and dynamic attributes of unconscious mental activities and he introduced the structural point of view (1923b). This new division of the psychic apparatus into id, ego, and superego clarified the role of the conscious and unconscious ego and the conscious and unconscious superego in its conflicts with the totally unconscious id. I agree with Fenichel (1945), with Rapaport and Gill (1959), as well as with Arlow and Brenner (1964), who stress the superiority of the structural theory in affording a clearer and more logical explanation for the origin and fate of neurotic conflicts. I do not agree with Arlow and Brenner, however, that Freud's hypotheses concerning the primary process, the secondary process, and the preconscious should be discarded or that they are incompatible with the structural point of view. Even Merton Gill (1963), who believes that the topographic point of view is conceptually not on a par with the other metapsychological points of view, agrees that some topographic conceptions have an important place both clinically and theoretically. I find this to be particularly true in working with dreams. It is equally important in dealing with patients who suffer from defects and deficiencies in ego formation and the parallel difficulty in building constant internal object representations, problems which go below and beyond the conflict theory of the psychoneuroses. I do not wish to dwell on theory—it is not my strong point, but those interested may turn to the writings of Hartmann (1951), Loewenstein (1954), Benjamin (1959), Eissler (1962), Schur (1966b), Loewald (1966), Mahler (1968), and Fisher's remarks in the panel on "The Psychoanalytic Theory of Thinking" (1958), for a more thorough discussion of the subject.

Clinical Examples

Some clinical examples of how different analysts work with dreams illustrate the divergencies in technique and theoretical orientation. I shall begin with clinical material from the publications of psychoanalysts who work with dreams in ways that seem to me to be unproductive, wasteful, and at times even harmful.

A clinical illustration presented in [*Indications for Psychoanalysis:*] *The Place of the Dream in Clinical Psychoanalysis* (Waldhorn, 1967, pp. 59–67) was that of a thirty-year-old writer in the second year of her analysis. Essentially, she seemed to be an as-if character, exceedingly immature and dependent. There was a childhood history of social failure in competition with her younger sister because of the patient's ineptitude and gaucheness. The patient had severe acne of the face, neck, and back in adolescence and had occasional recurrent active lesions. She was also thin and flat-chested. She entered treatment because of mild depressions, poor concentration, and inability to sustain an intimate relationship with a man. The patient had several brief affairs accompanied by a dread of losing the man and was always flooded by remorse and loss of self-esteem when the affair ended. In the weeks prior to the dream reported, the patient had had sexual relations with a man named John, whom she had known only a short time. He had left town for several

weeks and, in spite of knowing better from past disappointments, she found herself imagining that John loved her and
they would be married. During this interval she brought in a
dream. Now I quote verbatim from the monograph.

> She began the hour as follows: "I had a very bad
> dream. I had cancer of the breast. A doctor, a woman, said
> it would have to be removed. She said that there would be
> after-effects which I would feel in my neck. My friend R.
> had this operation. I was scared and panicked, and won-
> dered how I could get away, run away, and not have to
> have this done." She continued with the following associa-
> tions: "I tried to think why I should have such a dream. I
> thought it must be related to my idea that I am not com-
> plete by myself and that I need some sort of union with a
> remarkable man to make myself complete. This might be
> related to my worry that John was gone and maybe this
> was symbolized by my breast being removed. Actually, I
> am very frightened by things like that. Many people do
> have an obsession about such fears. For example, Paul
> does. Some people can face these things with great courage
> and strength, but not me. I am very frightened when I
> think about the danger of the scorpions in Mexico [she was
> planning a trip in a few months] . . ." [pp. 61 ff.].

The patient awoke, fell asleep, and had another dream but
I shall omit it because the presenter and the group did not
touch upon it. After a few innocuous associations, the analyst
finally spoke and I shall quote his first remarks verbatim.

> At this point the analyst intervened, asking "about your
> dream. What do you associate to the business about the
> doctor?" The patient responded: "She was a matronly type
> of woman, stern. She didn't seem to feel sorry for me or
> anything like that, but just said what would have to be
> done. I was thinking, how could a man make love to me
> without one breast? I would be terribly self-conscious. . . ."
> After a pause the analyst asked: "What about the part in
> the dream about the neck?" She responded: "Sometimes I
> make a wrong movement and my neck muscles can hurt.

That area is vulnerable for me because of my complexion problems involving my chin and neck, about which I have always felt so self-conscious. . . ." The analyst then added: "When you speak of self-consciousness about your skin and neck, does it remind you of the self-consciousness you have recently been describing when you told me about how terrible you felt before you had any breast development?" The patient said: "So, do you think that the fact that John did not call me made me re-experience those feelings of inadequacy? They may still be present" [pp. 62 ff.].

The analyst then offered a long intellectual interpretation and the patient responded in kind.

The Study Group's discussion of this presentation included the following excerpt.

The discussion of this report was initiated by the remarks of the analyst presenting the data. He maintained that the clinical material supported the belief that dreams can best be treated in the same way as other associations in the hours, and not necessarily accorded extraordinary of exhaustively detailed procedural attention as some would insist. Here, in the hours described, the analytic work is focussed on the problems highlighted by the repetitive life experience of the patient. . . . Accordingly, some portions of the dream can be neglected in favor of others, and a dream need have no specific attention directed to it if spontaneous associations are meager and the work with the dream (as opposed to other material) seems less likely to be rewarding. The rich amount of symbolically understandable elements in the second half of the first dream was not explored at all, but it was the analyst's clinical judgment that nothing was lost in the process. . . [pp. 64 ff.].

I shall limit myself to a few remarks about the patient's manifest dream, her associations, the analyst's interventions, and the group discussion. In the first dream the patient is terrified upon discovering she has a cancer of the breast. She is told this by a female doctor who warns her there will be aftereffects. The patient's associations sound to me intellectualized and a rote repetition of old interpretations given her by her male analyst. There does not seem to be any attempt on the part of the analyst to point out her intellectualization or to get to her terror of this malignant thing growing inside her. The analyst did not pursue the only spontaneous free association the patient produced, namely her fear of scorpions in Mexico. After the patient reported the second dream and a few innocuous associations, the analyst asked: "About your dream. What do you associate to the business about the doctor?" To me, the way the question was put gives the impression the analyst is either defensive and hostile or even contemptuous, otherwise he would not use a phrase like "what about the business about the doctor." Furthermore, it is all too intellectual. Words like "what do you associate" push the patient in the direction of intellectual compliance; not the best way to get to feelings or really free, free associations. In general, there was no sign that the therapist was trying to reach or establish contact with the patient's affects; he shows no signs of being "tuned in" on her feelings; on the contrary, he seems to play right along with her intellectualized defensiveness.

If you read the second dream, it seems to express in obvious symbolic terms the patient's envy of her sister and her aunt, but it was completely ignored. Apparently the analyst and the group did not discern any possible connections between cancer, breast, mother, and envy. There also was no apparent awareness of how frequently heterosexual promiscuity is used as a defense against helpless childhood dependency needs with the resultant urges and fears of fusing or becoming reunited with the pregenital mother. There was also no mention of a hostile transference to her male analyst or a wish to have a female analyst. The analyst and the group seemed content to maintain a highly intellectual contact with the patient, and were reluctant to open up the patient's fantasy life and follow wherever it might lead. Toward the end of this discussion in the monograph, there are a few sentences that deserve special comment.

> Such axiomatic procedures as the desirability of working with transference elements before nontransference material, or affect-laden before nonaffect-laden material, or the

necessity of drawing the patient's attention to evident omissions or to an addendum, were all mentioned. The consensus was that these were best considered as tactical maneuvers, subordinated to an overall strategy of the conduct of the analysis, which would, of course, change with the progress of the treatment [p. 66].

In my opinion there is no place for "axiomatic procedures" in trying to do psychoanalytic therapy. It is true that some of us follow certain time-tested technical guidelines in beginning the exploration of such oft-recurring clinical constellations as may occur in associating to dreams or in free association in general. These approaches are tools for investigation. I find the concept of an "overall strategy of the conduct of the analysis" an impressive high-sounding phrase but, in reality, with our present state of knowledge, this "overall strategy" is at best loose, subject to frequent changes and revisions, and full of unknowns. Only psychoanalysts with preconceived and rigid theoretical notions are sure of an "overall strategy." And they also have prefabricated interpretations for all types of patients and disregard the fact that each individual human being is unique, as well as the fact that there is still much even the best of us do not know and cannot predict about our patients. Freud had the humility to say that we should let the patient determine the subject matter of the hour (1905c); he attached great importance to following the patient's free associations. In 1950 Eissler severely criticized Alexander and his followers for making decisions about the definitive strategy for treatment of a case. Eissler felt that Alexander was more interested in validating his own hypotheses than in really analyzing his patients (1950).

This leads to another type of distortion in working with dreams which can be found in the writings of some of the Kleinian analysts. Hans Thorner in studying the problem of examination anxiety illustrated his ideas by describing a patient, a dream, and his interpretations. Again, limitations of space permit me to present only the highlights.

A man of early middle age complained of impotence and that all his love relationships came to a premature end. At times he could begin a relationship but as soon as he felt the woman was interested in him, he had to break off. He was impotent in other spheres of his life as well. Although he had reached a high standard of proficiency in music he was unable to play in public or before his friends. It became clear that all these situations approximated an examination situation. When he applied for a new job he was terrified of being interviewed because of what he considered to be his "black record," although realistically there was little black in his record. During one of these intervals he reported a dream which shed new light upon the nature of his black record. In the dream red spiders were crawling in and out of the patient's anus. A doctor examined him and told the patient that he was unable to see anything wrong with him. The patient replied, "Doctor, you may not see anything, but they are there just the same."

Thorner reports his interpretations to the patient as follows:

> Here the patient expresses his conviction that he harbours bad objects (red spiders) and even the doctor's opinion cannot shake this conviction. The associative link between "black record" and "red spiders" shows the anal significance of his "black record." He himself is afraid of these objects against which he, like the man in the dream, asks for help. This help must be based on a recognition of these objects and not on their denial;—in other words he should be helped to control them. It is clear that we are here dealing with a feeling of persecution by bad internal objects [Thorner, 1955, pp. 284 ff.].

I believe this a prime example of interpreting the manifest content of a dream according to the analyst's theoretical convictions. The patient's associations are interpreted in a narrow preconceived way. The patient's reproach to the examining physician, "Doctor, you may not see anything, but they are there all the same," is not recognized as a hostile transference nor is it acknowledged as a possibly justifiable reproach to the analyst that he really may be missing something. I wonder if the red spiders crawling in and out of the patient's anus are not the patient's reaction to his analyst's intrusive and painful interpretations. But now I, too, am guilty of interpreting without associations.

Another example of a similar type can be found in Hanna Segal's book (1964). She describes a patient, his dream, and her interventions as follows.

> Powerful unconscious envy often lies at the root of negative therapeutic reactions and interminable treatments; one can observe this in patients who have a long history of failed previous treatments. It appeared clearly in a patient who came to analysis after many years of varied psychiatric and psychotherapeutic treatments. Each course of treatment would bring about an improvement, but deterioration would set in after its termination. When he began his analysis, it soon appeared that the main problem was the strength of his negative therapeutic reaction. I represented mainly a successful and potent father, and his hatred of and rivalry with this figure was so intense that the analysis, representing my potency as an analyst, was unconsciously attacked and destroyed over and over again. . . . In the first year of his analysis, he dreamt that he put into the boot of his little car tools belonging to my car (bigger than his), but when he arrived at his destination and opened the boot, all the tools were shattered.

Dr. Segal interprets:

> This dream symbolized his type of homosexuality; he wanted to take the paternal penis into his anus and steal it, but in the process of doing so, his hatred of the penis, even when introjected, was such that he would shatter it and be unable to make use of it. In the same way, interpretations which he felt as complete and helpful were immediately torn to pieces and disintegrated, so that it was particularly following good sessions which brought relief that he would start to feel confused and persecuted as the fragmented, distorted, half-remembered interpretations confused and attacked him internally [pp. 29–30].

Here too, I believe one can see how the analyst's conviction about the correctness of her insights and interpretations tempts her to make detailed interpretations without any of the patient's associations for confirmatory clinical evidence. Once again I do not see in this case presentation any evidence of an analyst and patient working together on a dream. I see instead, an analyst forcing a patient to submit to her interpretation. By doing so this analyst is acting in a way which proves she is really like the patient's hated and envied potent father. No wonder he dreams that all his tools are shattered. To quote Freud: "But dream interpretation of such a kind, without reference to the dreamer's associations, would in the most unfavorable case remain a piece of unscientific virtuosity of very doubtful value" (1925b, p. 128). I must add that many analysts of non-Kleinian affiliation also disregard the patient's associations.

At this point, I will present some work with dreams that I believe exemplifies how an analyst who appreciates the exceptional position of the dream utilizes it in his practice. For the sake of clarity and demonstrability, the dreams I have chosen for illustrations are those from my recent clinical experience with which I was able to work fruitfully. They are not everyday examples of my work with dreams. There are many dreams I can understand only vaguely and partially and some I can hardly understand at all. There are also occasions when the dream is not the most productive material of the hour, but this has been rare in my experience. Freud wrote as far back as 1911 that dream interpretation should not be pursued for its own sake, it must be fitted into the treatment, and all of us agree on this obvious point (1911b).

I realize that no clinical demonstration of the value of dream interpretation will change the opinions of those who are predominantly devoted to theory conservation or theoretical innovations. Their theories seem to be more real to them than the memories and reconstructions of their patient's life history. Working with dreams is not only an enlightening experience for the patient, but it may be a source of new clinical and theoretical insights for the analyst, if he has an open mind. Furthermore, there are some analysts who have no ear or eye for dreams, like people who find it hard to hear and visualize the beauty of poetry, or like the tone-deaf who cannot appreciate the special imagery and language of music, or those who have no facility for wit and humor. Such analysts will lower the importance of dream interpretation, no matter what evidence you present. Finally, there are analysts who, for some other reasons, have never had the opportunity to learn how to listen to, understand, and work with dreams.

The two dreams I shall present are from the analysis of the same patient, a thirty-year-old writer, Mr. M., who came for analytic treatment because of a constant sense of underlying depressiveness, frequent anxiety in social and sexual relations, and a feeling of being a failure despite considerable success in his profession and what appeared to be a good relationship to his wife and children. He had a great fear that he would not be able to do free association at all, and that if he did I would find him empty or loathsome and send him away. We worked on these resistances for several weeks and he was then able on occasion to do some relatively spontaneous free association on the couch. One of the major sources of his resistances in the beginning was his experience with several friends who were also currently in psychoanalytic treatment. They talked freely and often in social situations about their Oedipus complexes, their positive and negative transference reactions, their castration anxiety, their superegos, their incestuous desires, and so on, all of which my patient felt was "textbooky," "artificial," and "a load of crap." Mr. M. was afraid that he would not be able to genuinely accept such interpretations, and yet also dreaded that unknowingly he too might turn out to be a "junior psychoanalyst" socially. I want to present the highlights from an hour in the sixth week of his analysis in which he reported his first dream. He had often had the feeling of having dreamed, but until this point could never remember any of his dreams.

One day he began the hour by stating: "I had a dream but it seems unrelated to anything we have been talking about."

I was making a phone call to some guy in a men's clothing store. I had ordered some clothes made to order and they didn't fit. I asked the guy to take them back but he said I had to come in myself. I told him I was not going to pay for the clothes until they fit. I said it seems like you just took them off the rack. I repeated, I won't pay for the

clothes until they fit. As I said that I began to vomit, so I
dropped the phone and ran into the bathroom to wash out
my mouth. I left the receiver dangling and I could hear
the guy saying, "What did you say, what? What?"

I remained silent and the patient spontaneously began to
speak: "The most striking thing to me is the vomiting. I just
can't vomit, I never, never vomit. I can't even remember the
last time I did, probably as a child sometime. It is like a biological thing, it's so strong. Like in yesterday's hour, I couldn't
get myself to talk. [Pause] Free association is like vomiting." I
intervened at this point and said, "Yes, free association becomes
like vomiting when things are trying to come up in your mind
that you would rather keep inside yourself and away from me.
The dream says it has to do with something not fitting you
properly." The patient quickly replied, "Yes, it's about clothes,
but that is too silly. Why clothes? Clothes not fitting? [Pause]
Oh my God, this can't have anything to do with the analysis.
The man saying, what is it, what, what, that could be you.
[Pause] I leave you talking and go to vomit in the bathroom—but why, why do I do that?" I answered, "When I give
you an interpretation that doesn't seem to fit you, you must
resent it and feel that I just took it off my 'psychoanalytic rack,'
like the other 'textbooky' analysts you have heard about." The
patient: "Oh Jesus, I can't believe it, I thought things like this
only happened in books. How funny!"

At this point, the patient began to roar with laughter and
tears streamed down his face. He gathered himself together
and said: "I never thought things like this would happen to me.
You are right. When you say things that don't seem to fit me,
sometimes I do get annoyed, but I keep it in. [Pause] I get
scared here when I feel angry. It's like being afraid of my father
when I was a kid. [Pause] I now suddenly see a vague picture
of me vomiting when I was about three or four years old.
[Pause] It was with my mother, right on her, she must have
been holding me. She was so nice about it, too, she took me to
the bathroom and cleaned me up and herself too. Amazing,
this whole thing." I answered: "Yes, apparently you were not
afraid to vomit up things in front of your mother, but you must

have been very scared of doing that with your father and now you feel the same way here with me. But you see these kinds of things do tend to come out in dreams or in such things like your forgetting to pay me this month." The patient was startled and blurted out: "This is too much. I had your check in my wallet, but in the last minute I decided to change my jacket and left my wallet at home. And I never even thought of it when I was telling you the dream, all about not wanting to pay that man. Something must really be cooking inside of me." The patient paused, sighed, and after a while I asked him just to try to say what was going on. His associations then drifted to his shame about revealing his toilet activities, masturbation, his hemorrhoids, a history of an anal fistula, and other matters.

I believe this clinical example demonstrates how it is possible to work productively with a first dream, which is contrary to the opinions expressed in the monograph *The Place of the Dream in Clinical Psychoanalysis*. Avoidance of dream interpretation by the analyst can frighten the patient, because the patient may sense the analyst's fear of the dream contents. An analyst's timid approach to a dream may add to a patient's suspicion that he, the patient, is especially full of internal evils or may convince him that he has a frightened analyst. On the other hand, deep interpretations given too early will either frighten the patient into leaving the analysis or it will persuade him that the analyst is omniscient and convert the patient into a devout follower and not a working ally. One has to assess carefully with each patient how much and how little one can do with early dreams and early material in general.[1]

Let us scrutinize more carefully what I tried to do with that first dream. Once the patient was spontaneously able to connect his fear of vomiting with his fear of free association, I first confirmed this representation of his resistance by saying out loud what he had already become conscious of—his dread of losing control over the horrible things inside of himself: vomiting is equated to free association and he vomits into the sink and not into the phone, the analysis. I then felt I could lead

---

[1] See Berta Bornstein (1949), Loewenstein (1951), and Greenson (1967) for examples of their method of dealing with this delicate problem.

him in the direction of trying to discover what was making him vomit. The obvious symbolism of the ill-fitting clothes delivered to him ready made and not made to order, symbols which he himself could grasp, encouraged me to point out his suppressed anger at me for my ill-fitting, ready-made interpretations, taken off my psychoanalytic rack. His laughter was a relief from the fear that he lacked an unconscious mind and was a freak, and also that I might be harsh with him for such thoughts. It was confirmation of the correctness of my interpretation and also an early sign of conviction that there is an active but unconscious part of his mind which does contain specific and personal meanings and they are not as terrible as he had imagined.

My referring to myself as the "textbooky guy" who is unable to tailor his interpretations to suit the patient must have given Mr. M. enough trust in my motherliness so that he could recall an early childhood memory of vomiting on his mother. Here vomiting is loving and not hating. He was then able to contrast this with his dread of vomiting up things in the presence of his father. His later association to the toilet, masturbation, and so forth, indicated an increase in his ability to let things come up in free association in my presence, a lessening of his resistances. Apparently my way of communicating to him helped me establish a working alliance with his reasonable, observing ego.

There are many elements in this dream which I did not point out to Mr. M. but which are of interest to us as examples of the function of the dream work and of the interaction of the primary process and the secondary process as well as of the interaction of the id, ego, and superego. The patient's very first sentence before telling the dream: "I had a dream but it seems unrelated to anything we have been talking about," is an attempt to contradict and deny the very essence of the dream, namely, that it concerns his feelings about me and the analysis. The psychoanalytic situation is depicted as a telephone conversation, only a verbal exchange, and even that is held at a distance. The man he speaks to is referred to as a "guy working in a store," not the most awesome or flattering representation of a psychoanalyst. The insights and interpretations I gave him were represented by clothes, and clothes conceal rather than reveal, an example of reversal and the use of opposites. Psychoanalysis does not strip you, it is supposed to clothe you, a reassurance, a wish-fulfillment. His fear of close emotional contact with the analyst is demonstrated by his refusal to come in person to the store. His leaving the phone dangling and hearing the "guy's voice" saying "what is it, what, what," is a beautiful and hostile caricature of my analytic technique. It is as well his revenge against me for leaving him dangling hour after hour; it is not he who keeps asking desperately, but I. The vomiting is not only an expression of his forbidden instinctual impulses but it is also a self-punishment for his hostility. It is as well a rejection of the interpretations I have been forcing him to swallow and also his spiteful obedience: "You want me to bring things up. Okay, here it is." This is an example of the coexistence of opposites in the primary process.

One can see that the vomiting is derived from both the id and the superego. It also serves the resistances, a defensive function of the ego, by breaking off our line of communication. All this and more is in the dream *and* in the patient's associations, facilitated by the interpretations. Only a fraction of this material can be meaningfully conveyed to the patient in a single hour, but it serves a valuable service for the analyst as source material for clues that will be of use in the future.

Mr. M. continued with the theme of clothes and concealment in the next several hours. As a child of impoverished parents he was embarrassed by his shabby, dirty clothing. He was also ashamed of being skinny and had tried to hide this by wearing several sweatshirts and sweaters on top of each other when he was young. When he later became affluent he bought bulky tweed sport coats and often wore turtle-neck sweaters with a leather jacket and boots. During the postdream interval he recalled stealing money from his father to buy a zoot suit, which was fashionable in his youth, because he wanted to make a good impression at a school dance. He also recalled having severe acne which he attributed to masturbation and which he attempted to cover with various facial creams and lotions. He tried to rationalize his stealing from his father by recalling that his father cheated his customers at times. All this material had the meaning: "I have to hide my true self. If anyone sees beneath my surface he will find me ugly and unlovable. I am a fraud, but so is most of the world. How do I know you are genuine and sincere in your treatment of me and will it change once I am stripped of all my superficial disguises?" (I was not merely working with the manifest dream in the following days, but with the latent dream thoughts which the patient's associations and my interventions had uncovered.)

The second dream of Mr. M. occurred about two-and-one-half years later. The patient had to interrupt his analysis for six months because of a professional assignment abroad and returned some three months before the dream. During this three-month interval of analytic work Mr. M. was in a chronic state of quiet, passive depression. I had interpreted this as a reaction to his wife's fourth pregnancy which must have stirred up memories and feelings in regard to his mother's three pregnancies after his birth. It seemed clear to me that he was reexperiencing the loss of the feeling and fantasies of being his mother's favorite, the only child and the favorite child. The patient accepted my interpretations submissively and conceded they had merit, but he could recall nothing about the birth of his three siblings nor his reactions, although he was over six when the youngest was born. My interpretations had no appreciable influence on his mood.

Mr. M. came to the hour I shall now present, sadly and quietly, and in a somewhat mournful tone recounted the following dream:

> I am in a huge store, a department store. There are lots of shiny orange and green plastic raincoats on display. A middle-aged Jewish woman is arranging other articles of clothing. Nearby is a female manikin dressed in a gray flannel dress. I go outside and see a woman who looks very familiar but I can't say specifically who she is. She is waiting expectantly and eagerly for me near a small surrey, putting clothes in it. I feel sorry for the poor horse and then realize the surrey is detached from the horse. I lift up the surrey to connect it and I am surprised how light the surrey is, but I don't know how to hitch it up to the horse. I also realize then that I was silly to feel sorry for the horse.

Mr. M.'s associations were as follows:

The three women in the dream were so different from one another. The older Jewish woman was a motherly type, working, doing, arranging, like my own mother used to before she became bedridden. The manikin reminds me of how I used to think of gentile girls when I was a kid; beautiful, pure, and cold, like my wife. But they taught me different. The best sex I have ever experienced was only with gentile girls. Jewish women just don't turn me on. They never did. Since my wife's pregnancy our sex life is practically nil. She isn't feeling well and I must say I'm in no mood for sex. I would like to be close to her in bed, but I don't want her to think it is a sexual demand so there is no talking even. I'd like to just be close and cuddle. My wife is so quiet of late. I feel she is getting revenge on me for all my past wrongs. I never realized before I had had such a bad temper and that she had been and still is so afraid of me. [Pause] I feel so alone in that big house of ours. I work like a horse to pay for it. Maybe I am the horse in the dream that I felt sorry for.

I intervened. "It might be so. You think he had such a big load to carry, but then you lift up the buggy and you are surprised to discover how light it is." The patient interrupted me. "That buggy is so light, it's a baby buggy, it's a baby carriage. No wonder it was so light, it was so tiny, and the woman was putting clothes on it, like diapers." [Pause] I interrupted. "A baby buggy is very heavy for a little boy, he has to work like a horse to push it." Mr. M. burst in with, "I can remember trying to push my baby sister in her buggy but it was too heavy for me. Now I see my father carrying the baby carriage downstairs as if it were a toy. I can even remember my brother and me together trying to push it." I interpreted and reconstructed: "I believe you have been depressed ever since your wife got pregnant because it stirred up memories of how you reacted when you were a small boy and your mother got pregnant and delivered your brother and sisters. You didn't want to face the fact that your father was hitched up to the coming of the babies.

You wished you could have been the father of the babies. But you weren't—you didn't know how to do it as a little boy and you felt left out in the cold, detached. You have been depressed about this ever since." After a pause, Mr. M. said, "I've always felt I'm not a real man. I act like one, but inside I still feel a real man should be like my father; strong physically, tough, and unafraid. I can fly airplanes but my hands sweat whenever I want to screw my own wife."

In the next hour the meaning of the green and orange raincoats became clear. The patient spontaneously recalled some dirty jokes from early puberty in which the terms *raincoat* and *rubbers* were used to refer to condoms. He then remembered finding condoms in his father's chest of drawers and later stealing some for his own use, just in case an opportunity presented itself, which, he wistfully said, "didn't occur for several years." By that time the "rubbers," the raincoats, had disintegrated in his wallet. It is worth noting how the hidden old shreds of "rubbers" in the patient's associations were changed into the shiny new raincoats on display in the dream. Here you can see the attempt at wish fulfillment in the manifest content of the dream: "I can buy conspicuous sexual potency in a store or in analysis." Later it also became clear that I too was the poor horse who had him as a big load to carry and also I was the "horse's ass" who could not help him make proper sexual connections with his wife or any other woman.

To me the outstanding element in the manifest dream was the surrey which turned out to be so tiny and light. My translation of the word *surrey* into *buggy* was the crucial technical point. I got from surrey to buggy by visualizing a surrey, which I have never seen in actual life but which brought to mind a popular song, "A Surrey with a Fringe on Top." This led me to baby buggies with fringes on top. Not wanting to push the patient into *my* association of baby buggy, I dropped the baby part and said just buggy, to see where it would lead him. (All this flashed through my mind quickly and was not as carefully thought out as it sounds here.) But I believe I was on the right track as it helped the patient pictorialize a baby buggy. And this enabled him to recall early childhood memories that had been repressed. Once his associations became freer, I could see how the dream work had condensed, reversed, and disguised the agony of feeling abandoned, unloved, inept, and depressed, by pictorializing an attractive woman waiting eagerly for him to join her. The tininess and lightness transforms the surrey into a baby buggy and changes the adult Mr. M. into a jealous, rivalrous small boy who cannot make babies as his big father can. The dream work tries to negate the fact that the father is connected with the mother's pregnancies; the surrey and horse are not hitched together—the patient is unable to hitch a male and female together. The familiar but unrecognizable woman is the mother of his childhood years, whom he has tried to ward off in his memories, in his sexual life, and in the analysis. The hugeness of the department store is a plastic representation of him as a little boy in a situation too big for him, as his present big house makes him feel like a tired old horse. He is full of jealousy, envy, and depression, and sorry for himself.

It was not possible to work on all these points in one hour, but the surrey–baby–buggy dream led in the next hours to the conviction that his present depression and the old underlying depression from childhood, which had brought him into the analysis, were directly connected, hitched up, to his mother's pregnancies and deliveries. The repression, isolation, and denial were temporarily broken through by our work with this dream and there were several tearful and angry hours in contrast to the quiet sadness of the previous months. Making available to the patient's conscious ego the memories and affects related to trying to push the baby carriage made it possible to reconstruct a crucial phase of this man's conflicts in early childhood, which were emotionally inaccessible to him until our work on the dream.

I believe this clinical vignette demonstrates the exceptional position of the dream. Months of what I believe to have been good psychoanalytic work on the patient's acting out or reenactment of the childhood depression provided insight and some understanding, but no emotional or behavioral change although I am fairly sure that it prepared the way for the surrey–buggy dream. It was the dream, however, plus the patient's and analyst's work on it, that made possible the breakthrough to the hidden memories and affects. Only then did the patient

develop a conviction and certainty about the reconstruction—and when he clearly understood and felt the connection
between the seemingly strange, remote, and symbolic elements
of the dream and the events in his present and past life. For
me this is convincing evidence of the special proximity between
the dream, childhood memories, and affects. To a great extent
this depends on whether the patient and the analyst can use
their capacity to oscillate between the primary and secondary
processes in helping one another reach the latent dream
thoughts hidden beneath the manifest dream. The patient contributes by his free associations; the analyst contributes by associating as if he were the patient and then translating his findings
in ways that provide links or bridges to the vital and alive psychic activities in the patient which are capable of becoming
conscious at the moment. This is dependent on the analyst's
capacity for empathy, his ability to visualize the verbal productions of his patient, and then to translate his findings at a time
and in a style and form which are real and plausible to the
patient (Greenson 1966, 1967).

Conclusion

The dream is an exceptional and unique production of the
patient. It is his special creation but can only be fully understood if the analyst and the patient work together by means of
the patient's free associations and the analyst's interpretations.
To work effectively with a patient's dream the analyst must
subordinate his own theoretical interests, his own personal curiosity, and attempt to make contact with what is living, accessible,
and dominant in the patient's psychic life at the time. He must
associate empathically with the patient's material, as if he had
lived the patient's life. Then he must translate the pictures he
gets from the patient's verbal rendering of the dream back into
thoughts, ideas, and words. Finally, he must ask himself what
of all of this will be valuable to the patient's conscious and
reasonable ego and how he can say it effectively to the patient.

This can be learned in one's personal analysis and in supervision in clinical work, if the training and supervising analysts

are competent in working with their patients' dreams. It can be learned to a lesser degree in dream seminars and even from books and papers if the writer is a skillful teacher and uses clinical examples from his own experience. Dream interpretation cannot be taught to people who are not at home or are ill at ease with the form and content of unconscious mental activities. Obviously you cannot teach dream interpretation to those who are blind and deaf to the beauty and wit in the blending of dream formation, free association, and interpretation.

Working with dreams makes extraordinary demands on the patient and the analyst. In a sense the dream is the most intimate and elusive creation of the patient; it is so easy to forget! The patient is then asked to associate as freely as possible to the different elements of this strange material, in the presence of his psychoanalyst. He will be torn between the desires to reveal and to conceal the hidden contents which have unexpectedly risen to the surface. The analyst must listen with free-floating attention, oscillating between the patient's and his own primary and secondary processes. Eventually, he will have to formulate his ideas in words which are comprehensible, meaningful, and alive to the patient. Sometimes he may only be able to say, "I do not understand the dream—perhaps we shall sometime later."

Some psychoanalysts deny the exceptional position of the dream because they have a special difficulty in learning the technique of dream interpretation. Others decrease the importance of dream interpretation to enhance certain theoretical convictions or to attack or defend the beliefs of some honored teacher. I believe that the dream is the royal road to a knowledge of unconscious activities for both the patient and the analyst, provided the psychoanalyst is not seduced into narrow bypaths and dead-end streets by technical or theoretical prejudices. My conviction of the exceptional position of the dream has been confirmed by daily work with patients, in particular their clinical responses, both immediate and long range. This conviction has been substantiated by the results of literally hundreds of analysts whose work on dreams are listed in the texts of Fliess (1953b), Altman (1969), the Annual Survey of Psychoanalysis, the Index of Psychoanalytic Writings (Grinstein,

1956–1975), the Psychoanalytic Quarterly Cumulative Index (1932–1966), and the Chicago Psychoanalytic Literature Index.

I shall close with two quotations. Kurt Eissler has graciously permitted me to paraphrase from a personal communication: "With hard work and fortunate circumstances an analysis may stop all neurotic symptomology, all acting out, all neurotic slips and errors, and it may make the former patient the epitome of normalcy. Nevertheless, the person will never stop dreaming irrational, instinct-ridden, bizarre dreams, a perpetual proof of the ceaseless activity of the unconscious mind" (personal communication). And from Freud, who wrote in 1933, "Whenever I began to have doubts of the correctness of my wavering conclusions, the successful transformations of a senseless and muddled dream into a logical and intelligible mental process in the dreamer would renew my confidence of being on the right track" (A. Freud, 1965, p. 7).

Chapter 9

DREAMING FOR A DREAM COURSE

James A. Kleeman

Psychoanalytic education has been the focus of considerable renewed study in recent years. This is reflected in the prominence given the subject at the Fiftieth Anniversary Meeting of the American Psychoanalytic Association in May 1961, and in two major investigations: The Rainbow Commission and the Survey of Psychoanalytic Education. The latter culminated in Lewin and Ross's book, *Psychoanalytic Education in the United States* (1960), which, of necessity, presents a macroscopic view of psychoanalytic education. This paper, a more microscopic study, deals with a single aspect of the education of a particular group of candidates in one institute, the Western New England Institute for Psychoanalysis. The group was a second-year class of seven members; the "single aspect" is a detailed picture of the course, entitled "Theory and Technique of Dream Interpretation."

The course was held in the fall of 1956. At the beginning it was announced that the last three sessions would be devoted to dream examples from the members of the seminar; each dream was to be that of a patient or of the student himself, not too long, interesting, clear, and with some associations. Each was to be presented in writing to the instructor and students, before the time of presentation, in its manifest form and with a brief case history or account of the background of the dreamer.

At the early meetings the first six chapters of Freud's *The Interpretation of Dreams* (1900) were reviewed. At the third meeting of the course the instructor, Robert P. Knight, presented a

This paper was first published in the *Psychoanalytic Quarterly* (1962), 31:203–231.

dream of his own, dreamed the previous night after an evening spent preparing for the course. The presentation was completely unplanned, and the class was stimulated by this frank approach to teaching. Whereas each of the members had been searching for a suitable dream from a patient, most of them now decided to present their own dreams. The content of these dreams was affected by Dr. Knight's action; his dream and his discussion of it must therefore first be described.[1]

Instructor's Dream

I am taking an exam of unknown content. I know I am not prepared, and find myself in a different position from usual. I am startled by the questions. Time is passing. I am told there is not much time and hurry to another exam, and write at the top, NOT COMPLETED.

Second examination could be botany, more likely zoology. There is a typed paper in outline form (exam form). It's an exam for which there is no preparation. I am supposed to know this, yet it is all strange. The thing I am being quizzed on is ENEMICUM (question of S instead of M) MARCORIDAE (question of N instead of D)—a hairy animal. Ed H. has to do with the preparation of the exam. I start to work on it, and the dream fades out.

The instructor encouraged the class to associate to some of the elements of his dream, much as they might begin to do on hearing a patient relate a dream. Many of these associations coincided with his own. He had spent much time analyzing the dream and shared his results with the group. (Personal associations not referring to the course were omitted.)

The word *enemicum* proved to be a condensation of issues with which the instructor was preoccupied. The first association was to enemy and then to the neurology examination of the American Board some years earlier, where a man with the same

---

[1] I am indebted to Dr. Knight and the members of the class for their willingness to permit this personal material to be published. Minor changes in names and facts, not important in the understanding of the dreams, have been made for the sake of anonymity.

last name as Ed H. made it very uncomfortable for the dreamer: Dr. H. is the enemy whereas Ed H. is friendly. A key association to the dream was "meeting a test" (question of adequacy), which led him to a doubt of his capability in analyzing dreams. The association to *hairy* led from Harry Truman, who had recently received a degree at Oxford, to Erik Erikson, who originally was to teach this course, to "he can teach the course best." *Hairy* led to Erikson in another way: at that time he had just grown a beard.

Dae led to "die"; *Marc* was the name of a friend of the instructor; *marc or idae* could mean, "I make a good mark or I cannot stand it." To make a mark on paper brought the association of an artist; Erikson had talent in both art and dreams; in his paper, "The Dream Specimen of Psychoanalysis" (1954), Erikson out-Freuded Freud, and now the instructor had produced and was going to use his own dream to teach the course.

It was a typical examination dream: although he does not do well, the dreamer has already taken the examination and therefore does not have to worry. The dream stimulus was: "Am I really adequate?" The wish was to outdo Erikson and Freud, and to produce an original dream better than Freud's Irma dream, the subject of Erikson's exhaustive paper.

The course then proceeded to a study of papers on the dream by Freud (1923a, 1925b), Isakower (1938, 1939, 1954), and Lewin (1946b, 1948, 1953b, chapter 7 this volume), and of Erikson's paper (1954).

Study Plan and Background

The intent of the instructor was to use the individual dreams to illustrate the various mechanisms of the dream work and to show how to interpret the latent dream from the day residues and other associations. Here the purpose is to examine a problem that lies between group and individual psychology—to ascertain how much the dreams merely expressed individual dynamics and to what extent they revealed the influence of the group situation of students in a psychoanalytic institute. This also afforded the opportunity to analyze dreams in the more encompassing way recommended by Erikson (1954).

The unusual circumstances under which these dreams were dreamed and selected is an interesting point for study and represents, in a sense, an "experiment-in-nature." The seven candidates, who had many similarities, were exposed to a common suggestion: to bring a dream to the course. This "group stimulus" or "group day residue" could be expanded to include Freud's Irma dream and his treatment of it in *The Interpretation of Dreams* (1900), Erikson's handling of it in his paper (1954), and the instructor's presentation of his own dream. The incorporation of these into the manifest and latent dream and the identifications which emerged will be worthy of note. The influence of dreams first presented upon the dreams later presented seemed minimal.

The institute class was unusually homogeneous. It was the second group selected by this new institute. All seven members were psychiatrists, of similar age and professional background, and had either completed or were in the advanced stages of their training analyses. They had been through the first year together and, in general, were good friends (Lewin and Ross, 1960, p. 326). They had a common goal: to become practicing psychoanalysts. Each had been given permission to start supervised analysis of a patient. Some had started, and others were looking for a control case for treatment under supervision. (In this institute it is the candidate's responsibility to find a suitable patient as the institute itself has relatively few to refer [1960, p. 385].) The students met often for breakfast and lunch or to drive the sometimes considerable distance to classes.

The complete manifest dreams follow in the order in which they were taken up in the seminar. Two of the six dreams dreamed for the seminar[2] are examined more thoroughly for these reasons: they showed, respectively, the most and least manifestly related to the different items being studied, and

---

[2] The dream of the seventh member is omitted, although it was presented for the course. This dream of student D had occurred one-and-a-half years before the course and before he had read *The Interpretation of Dreams* and Erikson's "The Dream Specimen of Psychoanalysis." While it might have served as a control to compare with the other six dreams, D preferred that it be excluded.

more extensive background and associations of these two members were available. Except for a little additional data later obtained from A and B, all of the dream material was presented at the seminar.

A's Dream

On November 16th, A presented this dream dreamed on October 24th.

> A greeting card is being delivered to me. My impression is that it is a get-well card and I think of Ellis, to whom I recently sent a humorous get-well card, and I wonder whether this is a reciprocal kind of joke on his part; but the card is signed down below by E. (or C.) Sacks. The verse on the card is a *boring* one, and has a vague "love" theme.
>
> The scene then shifts to one in which I am with Freddie. He looks much older than I remember him, something like Uncle George. A threatening atmosphere persists as he threatens in a rather sadistic way to stamp on my toes. However, I am quick to remove my foot and retaliate by stamping on his toes. Immediately thereafter I am looking into Freddie's gaping, wide-open mouth, and observe that many of his teeth are strangely located further back in his mouth, under his tongue, uprooted, and in a state of decay. Referring to the foot-stamping battle, he says with an attitude of ruefulness that he used to be much better when he was younger. The dream closes as I am telling him how I changed myself for the better, giving as an example of this my having undertaken to file down my central incisor teeth.

A's dream is amazingly like Freud's Irma dream, paralleling it in the dreamer's background and current situation, and in the manifest and latent dream material. A's identification with Freud, Freud's dream, and Erikson, who analyzed the Irma dream in great detail, is striking.

Background and Current Situation

A was a thirty-five-year-old Jewish doctor, a specialist in psychiatry, living in a predominantly Protestant community. His wife had recently been delivered of their third child. A, himself, was the oldest of three; his two younger siblings were girls. After an inner struggle, A had decided against a full-time academic career and to fortify his income had just opened an office for part-time private practice. He was concerned about securing and holding patients, and was looking for a control. His recent professional decisions promised better pecuniary return but left him isolated. A was primus in several ways: his was the first candidate's dream presented to the seminar, and thus the first offered to public scrutiny, and he had been the pioneer in traveling some distance for didactic analysis and supervision. This was the first time he had subjected a dream to such "exhaustive analysis."

Day Residues

The baby awakened A and his wife at 7 A.M. and his wife went to care for her. The dream occurred between this time and 7:30 A.M., when A arose.

Besides the group wish to produce a "good" dream for the seminar, A had had the particular thought that he would like to have a dream that would be good for teaching without revealing too much; his individual reaction to the instructor's use of his own dream was "admiration plus a certain edginess about the big guy revealing himself." The "dream day" evening had been devoted to an intensive study of Erikson's paper (1954); therefore it was a fresher day residue for A's dream than for any of the other dreams reported.

Associated with the dream was a vague sense of apprehension and hypochondriasis of several days' duration, centering around moderate constipation and paresthesia of the left hand. These corresponded in time to the second anniversary of his father-in-law's death, which resulted from a medical accident while he was being studied for obscure neurological symptoms.

That the numbness might represent a somatized self-punitive identification with the deceased man is supported by other facts, typical of which were A's sense of personal obligation and intense though unwarranted guilt associated with this death; he was torn between being a relative and a physician. Also related was the occurrence of three accidents to himself within two months of the death, two of which could be attributed to his state of mind at the time. Here the questions of concern for the health of self and others, and professional conscientiousness made the first of several appearances. The numbness could be related to death, a theme which pervades part of the latent dream. A was mildly preoccupied with feeling older (cf. 1954, p. 73).

In connection with the opening of a private office, A had received from his father a large check as a gift, accompanied by a greeting card. On the "dream day" evening A replied to his parents in a humorous way by sending them a thank-you note on a Hebrew New Year card. Much ambivalence was associated with the receipt of this present. It had meant stepping on the father for A to become a doctor and analyst, and opening his "own business" was a final blow. The amount of the check was disproportionate to the father's means so that the overcompensatory aspect of it helped inflame the negative part of the ambivalence. This, in turn, resulted in guilt feelings which were intensified by his having been overly brusque in a telephone conversation with his father the same day.

At supper there had been no fresh food in the house, so the family had had buckwheat cakes and a rasher of bacon, the final long step in a change from A's original cultural background. Later in the evening A and his wife had a midnight snack of pizza pie at Freddie's, a place about which A had heard earlier in the day from an adolescent homosexual patient. This had released nostalgia for the city where they had lived for some years and where pizza was superb.

There had been a telephone call that night from Dr. H. Sacks, a colleague, and it led to at least three important associations: he had a son, Erik; he was coming down from Vermont, A's birthplace; and his father was a rabbi, a connection with a crucial transference figure—a young Orthodox rabbi who had played a key substitute paternal role in A's childhood, was a model of integrity, and had a son of the same name and age as A.

Additional Associations

The dream personae suggested the following: "Ellis" was identified as a former professional compeer, recently hospitalized for hepatitis, attributed to dietary indiscretion on a trip to Mexico. "Freddie" is a cousin, three years older, with whom A spent several childhood years and by whom A was exposed to daily sadistic taunting during preadolescence. In later years, when A was in medical school, Freddie confided that he was impotent and was receiving hormonal treatment. He married a non-Jewish girl and became a mailman. The threatening atmosphere in the dream was associated with the way Freddie always treated A; Freddie had been both his closest family companion and the bane of his existence.

In sharp contrast were the associations to Freddie's older brother, Milton, always thought of as an ideal, who was now a successful general practitioner; Milton had surmounted several difficulties in his life and came closest to the "kindly older brother" for whom A searched. "Uncle George" had died a week earlier of stomach cancer; A had displaced this downward as bowel cancer in a verbal slip. This uncle was a renegade, a free thinker and the only family member to break sharply with Kosher tradition.

"E" brought to mind Erikson and the S(E)INE dream (1954, pp. 18–19). A dream detail added later—"the greeting card was fancy or embellished at the top where there was also a C or an E"—suggested that the message, "Get well," might have come from Professor Erikson who was many miles away; the distance had resulted in an interruption of A's analysis and a different instructor for the dream seminar. These associations led readily to the transfer onto Erikson of the figure of the paternal rabbi who had been so important in A's childhood. Other associations made it clear that CE was a cryptographic expression of the wish to *see* Erikson. A related verbal chain led in another way to the S(E)INE dream: C= "see" = "*sehen*" (German "to see") = "*zehn*" (Yiddish phonetic pronunciation) = "S(E)INE."

Other associations to the greeting card included the feeling that A was a bigger success than he knew and brought to mind the convalescent cards he had received when he had a leg fracture after a fall some time before.

A few weeks prior to the dream, A's two older children had stamped on his toes. Looking into Freddie's gaping mouth was a vivid part of the dream—it was the part which was spotlighted. The associations "push youth teeth in" and "like a patient–doctor relationship" came to mind. The example in the final sentence of the dream was real: in his youth A had had his front incisor teeth filed down. The feeling tone as the dream closed was one of cockiness.

Configurational Analysis of Manifest Dream

Verbal: The general linguistic quality of this dream is similar to the Irma dream, as well as to the instructor's dream. The indefinite E or C (used twice) is like S(E)INE, as well as the instructor's dream. The use of spoken words and dialogue is comparable; that is, "the patients" in each—Irma and Freddie—say they used to be better than they are now, and both dreamers imply that *they* are all right. Added meanings are suggested by the various plays on words: get well can be a prosaic message to someone with numbness and constipation, or it can be a sharp command to an analysand, who is momentarily regressed and down at the mouth, from a faraway analyst. Sacks, already overdetermined, means containers as well as being a proper name. *Sensory*: Except for a momentary listening this dreamer, like Freud, is "all eyes," and both Freud and A shift from a general visual to an intent, closeup looking. This can be related to the double use and meaning of C. Furthermore, combining three configurations (*interpersonal, sensory*, and *temporal*) we find that A and Freud both belittle would-be attackers by having them look different (Irma, Dr. M., and Freddie—the latter looks much older and like Uncle George). *Somatic*: Besides offering an acute stimulus for dreaming, somatic references are prominent; the mouth and feet are clearly the center of focus.

Combining the *interpersonal, affective, and spatial*, we find several items. Both dreams open with the dreamer receiving: Freud receiving guests, and A, a greeting card; the affect in each would seem to be festive or at least pleasant. A was expecting a greeting from the Draft Board—a card which would remove him from the seminar—whereas this dream was his ticket to get in. A's dream, like Freud's, contains many affects. Also the activities and spatial configurations of the dreamer are very much like those of Freud: the festive receiving gives way to the receiving of an attack (Irma, Freddie); both dreamers deal with this by an intrusive, coercive kind of examination and investigation (Erikson, 1954, p. 30). The intent viewing of the oral cavity is the most striking of all the similarities; each assumes the role of a medical investigator; there are four instances of looking or observing (five in the Irma dream [Erikson, 1954, pp. 28–29]) and each has two references to thinking. The difference is that A observes alone while Freud momentarily joins. Both dreams end on a high note as the dreamers best the belittlers.

Trends in the Dream and Conclusion

The variety of stimuli and associations to A's dream makes it difficult to distinguish its "group stimulus" from its strictly personal themes. However, the main conflict is between activity and passivity. The dream-wish part of the conflict is the desire to be "top dog," to overcome all belittlers (old ones such as Freddie and father, and potential new ones such as the course instructor and seminar colleagues), and to emulate or surpass the master (father, Freud, Erikson, and the instructor) or be primus in relation to classmates (represented in the dream by Ellis, Sacks, and Freddie). Both Freddie and Uncle George were of short stature, "little guys" (cf., "big guy," the instructor).

The superego opposition to this dream wish results in the guilt and death themes. "Threatening atmosphere" could refer not only to the superego but also to the atmosphere of the dream seminar where A has to deliver the goods. The conflict is implicit in his receiving and then remembering having sent a card. Put in another way, the conflict is portrayed by the passive wish being aroused in the first part of the dream; it is stimulated by the baby's calling for food, thus taking the wife from A; physical symptoms and hypochondriasis; need for patients and a suitable dream; the wish to be like Freud, Erikson, and the instructor; and a longing for the former city with its protectiveness and pizza pies as opposed to the new professional venture and its loneliness.

In the second part of the dream is a reaction to the passive wish; that is, the competitiveness and the statement that the dreamer is doing fine, while his old rival is faring badly. A slip of the tongue about cancer of the bowel instead of stomach is a denial of the oral wish. The filing of the teeth could make them sharper for rivalrous aggression or be an effort to mitigate the oral desire. The cockiness of the finale had a double meaning for A: phallic but also anal (cf., Yiddish for feces). This dream is a plea: "It is not I who am down or look older or am being observed" (A remembered being nervous about presenting the dream); that is, "it is not my mouth that is open." A third way of stating the conflict—if you are too overcompensatory (up) for your passive wishes, you fall (down) again—suggests the following: in the data one can find many references to "up" and "down" (displacement from cancer of stomach to bowel, manifest prominence of mouth and feet, C or E at the top, the feeling of having reached a high point in opening the office, etc.). Geographical history can be added to this: A was born up in Vermont, moved down to New Jersey, and has been gradually moving up since (New Jersey to Connecticut to Massachusetts). A's being a little down was a dream stimulus.

All of the transferences and identifications concern men. The evil prototypes (Erikson, 1954, p. 54) are the ones that find their way into the manifest dream (Freddie and Uncle George are "little guys," down, "odd balls" who do not amount to much). Ellis and Sacks as colleagues are not prototypes, whereas the ideal prototypes (Milton, the rabbi, Freud, Erikson, and the instructor—the "big guys" who are authors, epitomes of integrity, top analysts and teachers) come in only by association.

Perhaps A could not safely aspire that high. Finally, in the happy ending of the last sentence, the dream takes on the quality of an examination dream similar to the instructor's in the sense that everything is all right (Freud, 1900, p. 274).

B's Dream

B began his presentation on the same date as A; it was completed two weeks later. He planned to present a pair of dreams, strikingly different in manifest content and in method used for representability, but related in latent content. Both dreams were very brief, which was not B's usual style. They were dreamed two weeks apart, on Sunday nights. The first occurred on the night of October 7th:

> On awakening I was aware of having had a dream in which *there was a man by the name of KNOWLE KNOWLES*, so that the entire dream consisted of a verbal impression the following morning with no clear-cut visual aspect except that the name seemed all in capitals.

The second dream came on October 21st:

> This dream was entirely a picture with no verbal content; it was a vivid visual dream in which *I was putting my head up to that of a fox*. I saw only the head of the fox in the dream, and it was as though I were kissing or nuzzling the fox, a sort of pet fox.

There was no analysis of the fox dream in the seminar but a few comments will be made about it; it proved to be a highly overdetermined fox. As with A, similarities of B's material to Freud's, the Irma dream, and Erikson's discussion are numerous.

Background and Current Situation

B was thirty-four, in his fourteenth year of marriage, and had three boys aged ten, eight, and five. His only sibling was a brother, three-and-a-half years older, who was married, had two children, and worked with his father in the family retail furniture store in a small city in the Midwest. B's father was a successful Jewish businessman, active in community affairs, widely read, who took special pride in B's scholastic role as primus; a notable exception to B's being primus appeared when he applied for analytic training as his original application for admission was "deferred"—a fact the seminar instructor had pointed out to B some months before at the time of his reapplication. The father had been somewhat disappointed that B did not join him in business. Their most intimate hours had been spent in hunting, fishing, and other outdoor activities; the older brother did not share these interests with the father. Succeeding had always been important to B.

Two years earlier, at the age of sixty, B's mother had died from cancer of the breast. It did not occur to B until he was writing down the dreams for the seminar that the anniversary of his mother's death fell midpoint between the two dreams and had been completely repressed, in contrast to the previous year when he had felt very sad at the time. Three details about the mother seemed pertinent: B felt closer to her than to his father; she was a self-sacrificing person, highly esteemed; she was physically quite attractive and her appearance was important to her.

B had been in private practice for three years and each week did some university teaching. His wife was fond of horses and devoted much time to fox hunting, in which B did not participate. As a child, he had had a head injury after a fall from a horse and part of this memory included the excellent nursing care he received. Currently B was looking for a first control patient; his lack of success so far made him somewhat frantic as an institute rule required six months of supervision before embarking on the next year's classes. He had interviewed a number of prospects but they were unsuitable for various reasons; for example, one young woman with a classical hysterical neurosis, who had seemed like an ideal first control, was approved by the supervisor but became pregnant. B's own analysis had been completed six months earlier.

Day Residues

B had seen in the Sunday paper an engagement picture of a former patient whose name rhymed with KNOWLES: she resembled B's mother; her engagement represented turning down B's solution to her problem of relating to men as she had terminated the recommended therapy shortly after beginning it.

When the instructor had presented his own dream a week before, B had thought to himself: "If the instructor can be that frank, I can be even franker" (and proceeded to produce a manifest dream which tells almost nothing!).

Earlier on Sunday another patient with a history of repeated suicide attempts had called to tell of another suicidal gesture, raising a question of rehospitalization and of legal implications. That night B was debating whether to interview a law student who had been sent as a possible control; the student had also been referred to an institute colleague. Although the latter had told B to go ahead with the interview, he felt some concern that he might be "stealing" from the colleague and felt that he should wait. Part of the referral communication told of a dramatic dream in which the patient saw himself as a fox.

Several occurrences that evening had to do with money. B and his wife had paid bills; he had told his wife they could not afford a new horse she wanted; he had given money to a friend to purchase football tickets for the Yale–Cornell game. Cornell was the father's college and that of two institute colleagues; it was also associated with a guilty debate whether to attend an earlier Cornell game shortly after the death of his mother. One of B's fleeting thoughts that night was that he might be able to take on a control at a very low fee if the bills were not so high.

Additional Associations

On awakening B was not sure whether it was a man or a woman
in the dream but then decided it was a man. His first association
to this doubt was his concern about finding a control; he still
did not *know* whether his first case would be a man or a woman.
Nolle (let it not be) came to mind and became associated with
the suicidal woman patient who had called; this, in turn, led to
a series of present and past patients who had done badly. Knolls
offer vantage points for a good view. Knollwood Road reminded B of a conversation with an institute colleague about
evening meetings of the seminar to facilitate visits to the Bowl
(to watch football) and a reluctance to bring this up lest the
instructor think they prefer football to institute study. On a
different Knollwood Road lived another patient to whom B
wished he had said "no" more definitely. Pooh Bear came to
mind:

> And nobody knows
> (Tiddely pom)
> ....
> How cold my toes
> (Tiddely pom)
> Are growing[3]

A series of Latin terms emerged, several of which are also
legal: *Noli me tangere* (touch me not); *Nolo contendere* (I do not
wish to contend); *Nolle prosequi* (unwilling to prosecute the
point, or the whole case). B thought of declining Latin verbs
for a teacher in preparatory school. There followed a series of
plays on the words: I know; no; owl; now—I know now something I did not before—; know less; no more, no less. There was
a sound association from KNOWLES to nose—sinusitis with
penicillin.[4] Bowles—Chester Bowles—suggested that B was the

[3] From A. A. Milne's *The House at Pooh Corner*. (B is getting cold feet.)
[4] B had had a cold of several days' duration which had progressed to sinusitis with
moderate nasal discomfort, for which he was taking oral penicillin. The dogged persistence of this infection may have been, in part, related to forgetting the anniversary of
his mother's death.

only one among his colleagues who planned to vote Republican. The same colleague who might see the law student had joked with B about this the previous day. The first letters of the two words (KNOWLE KNOWLES) were identified with the instructor and brought to mind: the joking colleague, B's wife, the author of "The Dream Specimen of Psychoanalysis (Erikson, 1954), and "K.K.," the sound which doctors ask patients to make while using suction on an infected nasal sinus.

Configurational Analysis of Manifest Dream

Verbal: Besides the play on words, several other aspects of the verbal configuration are worthy of note. Knowing is of prime importance to the dreamer, especially for the activity (seminar) toward which he is headed. The verbal takes over the stage in this brief dream. The *sensory* has very little part in it: looking assumes importance only in the latent thoughts. *Spatial*: There is no motion, no definition of locus; capital letters involve the only use of space (cf., S(E)INE [Erikson, 1954, p. 19]). The *temporal* is poorly defined. The main clue to time is actually expressed verbally; that is, the wording sounds like the beginning of one of Grimm's Fairy Tales, which reaches back to childhood. The *affective* is strikingly absent in contrast to the strong affects in the latent thoughts; the doubt on awakening is the only hint of manifest affect. The extreme sparseness of the configurations requires an explanation, especially when we add that B's usual style of dreaming included varied and extensive interpersonal, sensory, spatial, affective, and temporal configurations. Here we have a good example of how much can be learned from a dream surface, if only by absences (Erikson, 1954, pp. 19, 55). The dream that did result was the ego compromise between the superego wish to keep peace at any price and an id wish to be best (to be franker than the instructor and tell everything; to produce an even briefer—and better—dream than the S(E)INE dream for Professor Erikson). The superego won as the manifest dream told just enough to enable it to be called a dream (no more, no less), but the repetition of the name ruined any chance of being briefer than S(E)INE; in fact, the ending E of KNOWLE eliminated even a tie.

Another part of the verbal configuration, the absurdity of the name, adds a derisive affect to the NO (Freud, 1900, pp. 434–435) and illustrates an additional ulterior motive for dreaming (Erikson, 1954, p. 46). At the seminar meeting prior to the dream there had been a discussion of whether daytime punners pun more than others in their night productions. B had taken the position, not widely supported by the others, that they do; B, an avid daytime punner, tried in this way to prove his point.

Trends in the Dream and Conclusion

The latent thoughts and wishes included B's desires to be a knowledgeable man and analyst, which conflicted with certain family and recreational activities; there was the wish for an ideal patient, concern for the health of self and others, and professional conscientiousness; there was identification with Freud, the instructor, Erikson, and B's father, and competition with them and his seminar colleagues. Besides the wish to have the best dream, there were also passive wishes: for the mother, for the father, to be cared for, and a momentary passive feminine wish (the doubt on awakening) which was resolved in favor of the masculine. Opposing the aggressiveness toward teachers, fathers, and brothers is a superego wish to keep peace; opposing the passive wishes is a superego insistence on being active, being a man. The dominant transference conflicts displace from father to teachers and from mother to wife; many associations and memories of the intensely rivalrous relationship with the brother are transferred to colleagues.

The repetitive life conflict—should B assert himself or avoid trouble (activity versus passivity)—could be traced in many associations. Two memories from childhood gave clues to the associated conflicts in that period. They related to the two main unconscious drives in the dream: to grab something—a patient, money, an honor, or a woman—and the passive wish to receive or get something for nothing. Identification with the father's shrewdness appears in the plan to go beyond the rules and present a second dream (the fox dream) in an effort to be best. The father represents the ideal prototype of a learned man who is at the same time honest but shrewd. On the issue of shrewdness, the superego says, "Don't be absurd; don't be in a hurry" (*Nolle*).

It is important to note the relation of the dream to the moment in B's life when it was dreamed (Erikson, 1954, pp. 7, 50), when he faced questions concerning the institute, marriage, finances, identifications, his mother's death, and values after the end of his analysis. Another aspect of the manifest configurations pertains. At this point in his personal life there was something B did not want to see, which seemed to be related to the essential absence of the visual in the dream. Predominance of the verbal configuration can be related to intellectualization, a prime defense for B (Erikson, 1954, pp. 19, 20). The vivid visual prominence in the fox dream could then be an overcompensation to the first dream, particularly since the second dream seemed in other ways an effort to supplement inadequacies in the first. The importance of looking as a drive and secondarily as a defense comes through: looking for patients, pretty women, ideals, knowledge, a dream, and at surfaces instead of depths.

B seemed involved in matters of generativity (Erikson, 1954, p. 36)—there were other omitted associations having to do with pregnancy and producing—though there was evidence for a continuing struggle between a sense of intimacy and a sense of isolation (lack of dream population suggests aloneness) and already some concern with problems of integrity. From the dream data we may conclude that psychosexual fixation was at an oral incorporative level (Erikson, 1950, p. 69), and a partial arrest, the uneven assertiveness, occurred at the phallic level (Erikson, 1954, p. 51).

The detailed study of the dreams of A and B, even though it means a sacrifice of details of the other five, is justified by the light a careful review throws on our question for study. This gives us a clue to what the other dreams might have revealed had they been examined as intensively.

C's Dream

On December 1st, C presented a dream she had dreamed on October 3rd. The dream was in two parts. The first part had two subdivisions.

> 1. a. Long table—like a conference table—many people seated around the table. There seemed to be a place for me.
>   b. Same table, covered with a white cloth. More people around. No place for me to sit. I stood on the periphery.
> 2. Fitkin I Amphitheater.[5]

Many male students seated. Among them several female students who looked alike and were all knitting red turtleneck sweaters. The completed parts of the sweaters, the necks, were directed upward and therefore very conspicuous.

Summary of Trends and Conclusions

The preconscious conflict was: "Where is my place? Where do I belong? Am I an outsider or in?" The unconscious themes were: femininity versus masculinity, receiving versus giving, and passivity versus activity. C was the only woman in the class. She had just opened her office for private practice; that is, she was entering the man's world of competition. A theme running constantly through the material was her need to combine being a woman and a practitioner, expressed by the question: should she be telling dreams or at home mothering ("sticking to her knitting"), or both? This conflict found its counterpart in her earlier family constellation.

Manifest References to the Group Stimulus

C's dream was definitely dreamed for the course; it was short, clear, and had concise associations. The long table and conference refer, in part, to the seminar. The only *temporal* reference

---

[5] In a local teaching hospital.

is the suggestive regression in the second part to medical school days after she feels excluded. The feeling of being outnumbered by the males is handled by the only absurdity in the dream—all the females look alike (she multiplies herself) and the sweater necks are red and erect. The question, Is there a place for me?, is answered as the dream found her a place in the seminar.

Latent References to the Group Stimulus

The table brought to mind the table around which the seminar was held, another table from her residency training, and her mother's dining room table. The question of her place with her male analyst came up. The Fitkin I Amphitheater brought back, among other things, a memory from 1947; the seminar instructor had given a lecture there and C was on the periphery. A day residue had been a discussion of the place of dreams in analysis. Association after association echoed the same themes.

On December 15th, D (see footnote 2 above), E, F, and G presented their dreams.

E's Dream

Eleven days earlier E had dreamed: "Cy Lustman was asking me for the program of the New York Psychoanalytic meeting and I looked frantically through my briefcase. . . . I believe something else followed but I cannot remember."

"Above is the way I wrote down the dream a short time after awakening. While I was writing it down, I felt like substituting the German word *Aktentasche* for briefcase [literally translated: *Akten* = documents, *Tasche* = pocket]. Only a few days later, on rereading the dream text I was struck by (1) "Cy"—the person's name is Seymour, and (2) "New York Psa. meeting"—I had meant the midwinter meeting of the Am. Psa. Assoc."

Summary of Trends and Conclusions

This is another fine example of how the material with personal connotations blends with that related to the group stimulus. E is the second of three boys; an excitant for the dream was the older brother's intent to follow an occupation somewhat related to E's, which was opposed by E's wish that he would not. Questions expressed in the dream were: how does E stand in relation to his brothers (actual and analytic) and how can he outdo them, by giving or withholding? A latent conflict about being second referred to family and seminar. The predominant affect was anxious fretting about not being able to produce documents (papers, a dream) which would serve as passports to friendship, academic promotion, the seminar, and the instructor's recognition. E was finally able to produce an acceptable dream while his analyst was away (in New York).

Manifest references to the group stimulus included "Psychoanalytic meeting," "looked frantically," mention of two analytic colleagues, "Cy" and "Lustman," and the brevity of the dream. *Latent references* were the theme of feeling envious of and left by brothers and analysts, concern about normality (his own and in relation to brothers), a delivery theme (papers for promotion, his wife's pregnancy, and a good dream to keep "older brother" from getting ahead), and a worry about revealing too much or being found empty (*Akten* also means nude figure). A preoccupation about whether to do things collaboratively or alone was one of a number of similarities to the total content of Freud's Irma dream.

F's Dream

On Saturday afternoon, December 8th, F dreamed:

> A basement of a home that looks like a rug store. A pile of rolled-up rugs of different sizes on the floor, including rolled-up rubber stair treads. I stand there looking at the rugs and am irritated with my wife who is beside me (but is not seen clearly) because the delivery men have brought the rugs here. "They were supposed to bring them to the new house," I complain, blaming her. Then I run up the stairs, out onto the sidewalk, chasing the delivery men. They are driving off in a large van. I call after them, and

am sure that they hear me, but they drive off into heavy traffic, taking no notice of my yelling at them. I stand there at the curb, angry, yelling at the men in the van.

Summary of Trends and Conclusions

The main theme was concerned with F's needs: it involved complaints against those who do not meet them and cannot be depended upon, and concluded that it is best to do things oneself. Manifestly the dream showed F as very active, but the day residues and other associations portrayed for the most part passive wishes and his feeling of being overburdened. The significant affects were anger (at the frustration of needs) and envy. *Manifest references to the group stimulus* were a basement, delivery men, and delivery to the wrong place. Adding latent thoughts, we find this dream is characteristic of the whole series in having extensive condensations. The basement setting described the seminar location, but also the office of F's analyst, the playroom for his "different-sized" children, the locale of his cleaning activities just prior to the dream, and it is associated with his father's place of business.

"Delivery" was highly overdetermined. F had thought he was selecting a nice, clean (he had several associations to filth), innocuous dream about moving (he and his family were moving in one week to their first house). He was eager to get the dream over and delivered, which also applied to his wife's pregnancy. The delivery of another child involved outdoing his father. Delivery men included reference to the seminar instructor and colleagues. Finally, delivery to the wrong place implied a wish that the seminar might not get to him, a question: "Am I in the wrong place?" and some envy of the prospective delivery of the baby to his wife instead of to him.

G's Dream

I am going to a meeting with a friend—to CCNY.
I am going again by myself. I am driving through Central Park although it seems much hillier than it really

is. I am going up a hill—turns left or right, felt unsure. I
saw familiar buildings of Central Park South to the left
through clouds. They seemed frighteningly (?) close. Then
I knew which turn because the meeting was at 64th (?) and
Broadway. I got to the intersection of 60th Street and saw
a street sign after first being lost again and not knowing
which way to go.

I was in a crowd and overheard someone say, "that
must be Monsignor Sheehan," I doubted it since I called
to mind his appearance and he didn't look like this short,
dumpy fellow.

Then there was an indifferent ending with my wife
remarking, "You've been there, have you?"

Summary of Trends and Conclusions

It is difficult to summarize this rich total dream. An example
of its complexity can be seen in the material about looking. It
is of special interest that G made a conscious decision to have
a dream that night (November 16th) but was nevertheless surprised the next morning that he had done so. Day residues
included dissatisfaction with his performance in analyzing A's
dream at the seminar, reluctance to analyze colleagues' dreams,
ambivalence about public disclosures in general, and annoyance
at "having to dream" for the course and at hearing of an "early
psychoanalytic group" who had to bring their dreams to each
other. Opposition to the wish to have a good dream (to show
up well and unlock the secret of the dream) was evident in the
resemblance of this to an examination dream: in writing down
the data G twice dated it December 16th (presentation was
December 15th), and the final spoken words put the meeting
in the past.

Probable *manifest references to the group stimulus* are meeting,
felt unsure, not knowing which way to go, Sheehan, and short,
dumpy fellow. (Bishop Sheen represents a sector of Catholicism
which G does not espouse, one that is antianalytic.) Adding
latent material we learn more. Debating whether to travel to
Stockbridge alone or with a friend introduced the conflict between a sense of intimacy and isolation. His being an only child

molded a formal aspect of the dream: a person wandering, undecided, looking for the familiar. A concern about competing, feeling one against many, was experienced in the seminar because of a different religious background which, in turn, reconstructed his college situation. This blended with a question of where G belonged: he is not sure of direction, has doubts of his competence; should he be assertive and alone (analyst, priest, seminar leader) or conforming in a group (analysis, seminar, religion, sexual role)? The dream pictured the very themes produced by his life; a series of crises related to being examined. He wished for reassurance, and the predominant affect (insecurity shifting to domestic felicity) and his style of dreaming (of problems solved) provided this. "You've been there, have you?" also is connected with a wish to be finished—with the dream presentation, his analysis, training, and insecurity.

Assertive versus conforming is connected with two of several kinds of looking—active and passive. Manifestly, he was looking at hills, buildings, and for direction. Latently, he was looking for a dream, a control patient, and a place for himself (he wishes to establish himself as an accredited member of analysis, church, and family—with the right to look and doubt); he was looking at colleagues' dreams and was finding his direction in analysis by looking; his analytic hour that day was concerned with scientific "curiosity" and its relation to looking. Monsignor is someone to whom he looks up, and he looks down on the short, dumpy fellow. Sheen has penetrating eyes, the kind that look right through you (which involved concern about exposure).

The short, dumpy fellow had a latent transference reference to the instructor and puzzlement about how to please him. A day residue about being a resident's supervisor was associated with the conflict between being a supervisor or supervisee. The interpersonal configuration depicting a crisis and resolution, and essentially reversing the Irma dream sequence of being with his wife, alone, and then with a friend, is one example from the material which was laden with parallels to Freud's total dream.

Discussion and Conclusions

The conditions under which these dreams were dreamed put this study on the borderline between individual and group psychology and between a strictly clinical and an experimental situation. Thus the material takes a place alongside hypnotically induced dreams (Brenman, 1949; Hall, 1956; Rubenstein, Katz, and Newman, 1957) and dreams involving the Pötzl observation (Fisher, 1954, 1956, 1957). However, compared with hypnotic dreams and Pötzl dreams, this series introduces the additional variable of selection of dreams for presentation. Six of the seven candidates actually dreamed and selected a dream for the seminar. D did not offer a dream dreamed for the seminar.

These dreams share the striking findings of Rubenstein et al. (1957) in hypnotic dreams, and of Fisher (1954) in Pötzl observation dreams that the "experimental situation" also figures prominently as one of the determinants in the dreams. The "experimental situation" (or group stimulus) of the dreams of this seminar was the common stimulus of being students in an institute (Lewin and Ross, 1960, p. 187), in a dream seminar with a requirement to bring in a dream and to read specific literature, including Freud and Erikson, and of having the instructor present his own dream. Some part of the group stimulus was present in all dreams dreamed for the course. The "experimental situation" may also be described by differentiating: (1) identifications with and transferences onto Freud, Erikson, and the instructor; (2) details of the actual setting and mechanics of the dream seminar; and (3) other factors of being a student in an institute. Deserving special emphasis is the wish to have a dream, which was a motivating force for Freud's Irma dream as well as for the instructor's and six candidates' dreams (Erikson, 1954, p. 46).

As we should expect, our detailed examinations of two dreams and our more cursory considerations of four dreams show great variation in the way parts of the group stimulus were incorporated into the manifest and latent dreams, and in the degree to which individual factors dominated each dream.

The diagram employed by Lewin and Ross (1960, p. 328), showing the components of the analytic situation as interlocking circles, could be adapted to illustrate relative influences of personal (present and past), school, and analytic factors on these dreams. A recapitulation of a few examples will suffice: A, who is concerned with besting "fathers," has a dream much related to the instructor, Freud, Erikson, the Irma dream, and S(E)INE dream, whereas F, who is more involved with feeling burdened than with identifications, presented a dream which related only slightly to Freud and the instructor's dream (and not to the others) but did include the basement and delivery men, and the theme of delivery to the wrong place. Only A and B had dreams strongly related to Erikson, whereas those of A, B, E, and G had many connections to the Irma dream. Three of the six referred to a meeting; five included competition with colleagues as clear-cut latent themes. There were individual references to the setting of the dream seminar, such as table and basement, and a number of allusions to delivery.

It is interesting to see the number of ways in which the instructor's total dream was related to competition and identification with Freud and Erikson. An additional manifest detail is the use of botany and zoology, two of the three examples Freud himself used in his description of examination dreams read earlier in the course (1900, p. 275). The instructor's dream contains many themes from the Irma dream. Thus it is a link in the complex relations between the Irma dream, Erikson's paper (1954), and the candidates' dreams.

Interest in the dream surface is increasing (Freud, 1900, p. 506n;204;361;384; Erikson, 1954, pp. 16, 17, 18; Hall, 1956; Saul, 1956). One example from this literature is worth reporting. Roth (1958) declared that "acting out of manifest dream content occurs . . . when resistance [as when exposing one's dream to colleagues] prevents the full . . . interpretation of a dream." In January 1958, when some of the data of this paper were discussed in Professor Erikson's Research Uses course, and when Dr. Lewin was visiting for the Survey of Psychoanalytic Education, C, who was not presenting, appeared at the class wearing a red, turtleneck sweater, a garment not worn before or since. She knew the subject for the day, debated what to wear, but otherwise was oblivious to the meaning of her choice.

Erikson (personal communication) has suggested that the study of manifest dream configurations may reveal occupational specificities and differences specific to the two sexes (1951, 1954, p. 31). Lewin and Ross (1960, p. 144), and Greenacre (1961, pp. 34, 44, 46, 52) review qualities which seem desirable in an analyst. Though the sample is very small, these dreams contain a great deal having to do with thinking, examining, searching, observing, looking, curiosity, and passive receptivity (1961, p. 50).

There are fewer data about sexual configurations. Comparing C's manifest dream with the rest, we find it is the one dream with many static people, the only one with color, and it alone has women in it (except for two wives in the other dreams); a circular arrangement is implied by the table and amphitheater; the white tablecloth, knitting, and use of enclosures are noteworthy (Erikson, 1950, 1951, p. 31; Hall, 1956).

The total dream material suggests some additional information about the atmosphere of psychoanalytic institute education. The group reacted to the frankness of the instructor by bringing in personal dreams instead of those of patients, which was the intention before the instructor presented his own dream. However, the hierarchy of teacher–student or analyst–analysand was maintained in that the instructor omitted most personal associations whereas the candidates were less selective.

One of the most interesting findings reflected in the dreams is the degree to which identifications, superego development, and the seeking of models (p. 234) were still going on in this group, although they were between thirty and forty years old. It emphasizes once again how much Freud and institute teachers serve as figures for identification as well as transference.

The presence of strong passive and dependent strivings and the prominence in all the dreams of the conflict between passivity and aggressiveness, rivalry, and ambitiousness are noteworthy (Lewin and Ross, 1960, pp. 74, 265, 266, 327).

Eisendorfer attaches a great deal of value to the passivity: "Perhaps the core of analytic aptitude in the male resides in his psychologically accessible latent femininity and his correlated passivity. It is this component of his personality that contributes to his capacity to perceive his own unconscious and that of others" (Lewin and Ross, 1960, p. 144).

Anxiety about presenting the dreams to the seminar is reflected in the examination-dream quality of some and in the associations of most. Repeatedly emergent was the wish to have a good dream without revealing too much. There were the conflicting motives of wishing to please the instructor and outperform him (and seminar colleagues).

A great deal more might be said about the amount of involvement of the individual's time and energies in the pursuit of becoming an analyst, including the conflict of attending school at an age when heavy commitments have been made in other areas of life. Spouses' objections to the time demands of the institute were latent in several of the dreams (1960, pp. 73–74).

These dreams offer a contribution to the subject of "normal" dreams and to the concept of normality. As Lewin and Ross (1960, p. 235) stated, "the child, the psychotic, and the 'normal' are contributing to a new psychoanalytic psychiatry and a new psychoanalytic psychology. From the student 'material' at the training analysts' disposal there should arise a new psychoanalytic educational psychology and psychopathology."

The group of six whose dreams are presented seem each to fulfill reasonably well Freud's criteria of normality—having the capacity to love and to work. For example, in 1956 all had completed or were in advanced stages of their training analyses; all functioned at a high level in their vocation in institutions of learning or private practice; all were married and had children. A five-year follow-up reveals that their progression in analytic training has proceeded without interruption, and all have been graduated or are close to graduation. Their professional careers have all advanced to higher levels of responsibility. One has been divorced but has remarried happily. Two, including the latter, have had additional short periods of analysis.

Finally, what rather spontaneously happened in the seminar illustrates a remarkably effective teaching method. This procedure offered opportunity for thorough analysis of a dream which served as a prototype for future self-analysis through dreams. In "The Dream Specimen of Psychoanalysis," Erikson said: "As we review in our minds the incidents of dream analysis in our daily practice and in our seminars and courses, it must be strikingly clear that the art and ritual of 'exhaustive' dream analysis has all but vanished" (1954, p. 5). In this seminar, five of the six candidates who dreamed for the course reported later that they had analyzed these dreams more exhaustively than any in their personal analyses. Several estimated that they had spent as much as sixteen to eighteen hours on their dream.

Summary

The unplanned occurrence of the instructor's presentation of his own dream at an institute dream seminar resulted in the candidates' dreaming dreams for the course. A study of these dreams reveals the atmosphere of psychoanalytic education with special emphasis on identifications, a rather widespread passive dependent trend, and opposing ambitiousness and rivalry. One manifest configuration of the dreams suggests an occupational specific. The dreams and associated data offer a contribution to the subject of "normal" dreams and the concept of normality. The situation proved to be a highly effective teaching technique for a full understanding of dreams.

Chapter 10

DREAMS AND INTERRUPTIONS IN THE TREATMENT

JOHN S. PECK

Interruptions in psychoanalysis refer here to such breaks in the continuity as absences of the therapist for vacations or other reasons, vacations of the patient, and premature termination of the analysis.

The analytic relationship during analysis becomes an important part of the patient's life and frequently appears as part of the day's residue in dreams. It has been noted, for example, that dreams early in analysis frequently refer to such themes as "canceling out," "invaded privacy," "nakedness," "someone sitting behind the dreamer," "miracles," and "numbers," the last a reference to analytic fees and hours (Steiner, 1937). In addition to symbolic representation in dreams, the dynamics of the transference are also reflected topically in dreams. The subject of dreams as resistance has been thoroughly documented (Freud, 1911b; Eder, 1930). The patient produces diffuse and voluminous dreams which give little or no clue to their meaning. "In the attempt to find the meaning of such a dream all the latent, as yet untouched resistances will be roused to activity and soon make it impossible to penetrate very far" (Freud, 1911b). For some patients the analysis is a hypnotic relationship similar to sleep, and the patient's dreams protect and prolong the analysis in much the same way that they function as preservers of sleep (see chapter 7). Toward the end of analysis, dreams are frequently designed to convince the

---

This paper was first published in the *Psychoanalytic Quarterly* (1961), 30:209–220.

therapist that the patient is still sick and needs more treatment. Terminal dreams also frequently express a lack of indebtedness to the analyst (Steiner, 1937).

Freud observed that first dreams in analysis are usually much more revealing than dreams produced after the patient learns that the interpretation of his dreams is painfully revealing (Freud, 1911b). Saul has shown that the first ten dreams of a patient in analysis may contain a useful formulation of the essential dynamics of the case (Saul, 1940). Alexander and Wilson carried this technique a little further and classified dreams under ten headings. They tabulated the frequency of each of these types and from this information formulated the nuclear dynamics of certain psychosomatic conditions (Alexander and Wilson, 1935).

Clear and revealing dreams occur at times other than early in analysis. Dreams are frequently especially revealing in psychosomatic conditions just before an exacerbation of the condition (French and Shapiro, 1949). Unusually revealing dreams are an indication of weak ego functioning, as though a deficient ego is incapable of creating adequate defenses against unconscious drives (Mittelmann, 1949). Dreams after the termination of a successful analysis may be especially revealing (Saul, 1958). Freud reported that the setting of a date for terminating an analysis resulted in the disappearance of chronic and fixed resistances, and in the production of much vivid and very important material by the patient (Freud, 1937a).

It is my observation that dreams reported by a patient shortly before an interruption of the treatment may also be vivid and revealing.

Case 1

A sixteen-year-old schoolgirl was referred for treatment because she twice changed official school records to raise the grades of a friend. Psychotherapy had once been recommended for her when she was a child. She seemed, however, to have been making a reasonably good adaptation to her adolescence. She was popular with her classmates, held a class office, and

was an average scholar. Therapy would not have been considered had she not been discovered altering the school records.

She was the only child of a successful lawyer who had died
two years previously at the age of forty-three, leaving her and
her mother financially secure. She described her mother as
lively and active. They had similar interests and "lived like sisters." The mother was popular with the patient's schoolmates
and made friends with the daughter's beaux, who enjoyed talking with her and confiding in her. The patient was something
of a tomboy and liked having boys as friends without romantic
involvement. She had recently, however, developed romantic
feelings about a boy by whom she was being courted. She
wished for more firm direction from her mother, complaining
that she argued and fought with her too much as a contemporary. Her father's death had not changed this relationship; she
and her mother had always treated each other as equals.

After a few hours of analysis the patient began to resist
further treatment. She said she had no complaints, felt that she
was not different from other girls her age, and, except for
occasional friction with her mother, was satisfied with her life.
She reported that her mother too felt she need not continue
therapy.

During the ninth hour, which she knew would be the last,
she reported a dream. She prefaced it by saying that her
mother, who had some superficial sophistication about psychoanalysis, had told her she should not tell me this dream if she
were going to discontinue therapy.

> Linda is killed in front of our house in a smashup
> between our gardener's truck and a big tractor. My mother
> tells me not to look; that she has to gather up the body and
> take it to Linda's mother. I leave and go to Ruthie's house
> and tell her that I have to leave home; that too many people
> are being killed at our house. We change places, and Ruthie
> goes to my house. I am then riding in a fog in a green
> convertible with the top down. A Mexican girl I know is
> riding with me. We see Linda walking on the street, and I
> think, "She's not dead after all."

The night before she had talked with a friend on the telephone about the fact that Linda had defeated her in a school election. The tractor reminded her that a neighbor was having a sewer connected and, in talking with the neighbors, her mother first discovered that the owner had known the patient's father in business. Ruthie is probably her best friend. Ruthie lives with her parents who both work and are so seldom at home it is as though she has no parents. The Mexican girl was now the friend of a Mexican boy who had been a friend of the patient. This entered into the dream because that night she had had on her bed a boy's jacket which smelled of the hair tonic the Mexican boy used. Her only serious quarrel with her father, shortly before he died, had been about this boy, of whom her father disapproved.

The dreamer disposes of a rival, Linda, by having her killed in an accident indirectly associated with the patient's father. The patient then moves into the house of Ruthie who has, for all practical purposes, no parents. She sends Ruthie, her best friend, to live at her house because too many people are being killed there. At the end of the dream she is with another of her successful rivals and she is surprised to observe that Linda has not been killed after all.

In one sense, Linda, who defeats her rivals, is equated in the dream with the patient's mother who had defeated her in the oedipal rivalry. The patient is then without friend or parents and makes restitution by forming an alliance with a successful sexual rival of hers. Her dream also undoes her intent to have Linda killed. The day's residues are very explicit: the boy's jacket on her bed, the telephone call about Linda's victory.

Her father had been a firm mentor who restricted her sexual behavior (unconsciously a source of control for her oedipal incestuous fantasies). Whatever else he represented, the Mexican boy was an exogamous object. The father's prohibition gave him another meaning in the dream. Left only with her mother, she is treated more like an adult sister than a child. The dream condenses the dispatch of her immediate and of her oedipal rivals, a fate which the patient is trying to avert herself. The Mexican boy becomes a symbol of incest and the Mexican girl in the dream is the disguised maternal object with whom rivalry is denied or repressed. The wish for "more firm-ness" from her mother is to replace the sense of instinctual control lost with the death of her father.

It seemed clear that this resistive patient had this dream and reported it only because she anticipated discontinuing the treatment. Such dreams are quite frequent in my experience. It is as though the ego feels it is safe to risk such revelations when the avenue for flight is open. That the dream was dreamed and reported despite the mother's admonition gives rise to the speculation that it may have been motivated by a budding transference of which no outward sign was manifest, unless it was the overwhelming need to flee from it. As no details of the child's relationship with her father are known, it may have been one which kept the oedipal attachment uncom-fortably close to consciousness. Speculatively, her father's strict-ness about her beau may have been more from jealousy than paternal vigilance.

Case 2

A thirty-year-old housewife sought treatment following an ar-rest for petty theft; she had been indulging in petty theft for about one year. A college graduate, she had been married to a successful professional man for ten years. She was sexually frigid, achieving only clitoral orgasm from manual stimulation.

The oldest of six children, she was reared in great poverty. Her mother was a hysterical woman who made frequent sui-cidal gestures during the patient's childhood, and who screamed and pounded her head against the wall. She was ex-tremely ambitious for the patient and made apparent sacrifices to give her dancing lessons; however, when the daughter was fourteen, she had her try out for a nightclub chorus. This mother remained very competitive with her daughter, con-stantly comparing their figures, coiffeurs, and breast develop-ment. The patient was disconcerted when her mother gave birth to a baby at approximately the same time that she did. The father was a vague, stammering, blushing, ineffectual man who was openly despised by the mother. When the patient was twelve, her father made a sexual advance by putting his hand down the front of her nightgown.

She reported her first dream in the fourth hour of analysis. "After our last session, I had a dream of my father with his face all cut and disfigured. It was horrible and woke me up."

During the hour which preceded the one in which she reported this dream, she had described her father's seductive advance; also a serious accident in which he lost all the fingers of one hand. This had happened shortly after he became involved in an adulterous affair. The mother became aware of this affair only two years before the patient's beginning analysis and had since used it as an additional weapon in her vicious attacks on the father. After telling the dream, the patient talked at length about her mother's hysterical behavior and competitive feelings toward the patient. The dream is clearly oedipal, but reveals little else.

A much more revealing dream occurred after ten months of analysis on the day before the analyst's vacation.

It is in a prison or a school, and my former boss is there. I had been bad and was put in the basement. Others do not know this. There are also colored people in the basement. They are crude and wild. It all takes place around food. It is lunch time. The nice people up above get different [better] food. We prisoners have to use special open toilets, and the colored girls are sloppy and dirty. My mother comes, not knowing that I am in prison, although my husband does. She has brought me a gorgeous two-piece knitted outfit with very short shorts; but it is too big. As she leaves, I ask her to exchange it. Then I get up to the top, and the boss asks where I have been. I am evasive, but he asks what I had eaten, and when I tell him, it gives him a clue showing that I am in trouble. I am now to donate my sperm for artificial insemination, so that my sister-in-law and her husband can have a baby. Somehow this will allow me to escape from the basement prison. I am to do it with a hypodermic needle, and am to meet them at a lab. The trouble has then disappeared: the doctor has said they have to be married first. I am secretly relieved that they can't have a baby, and feel that I have done my duty. I am released from the basement, and my mother returns with a smaller, well-fitting outfit, lovely and dressy. The top fits well, but the pants are so short I am almost unable to wear them. My husband says to take it anyway.

He seems to be unhappy with himself or with the world. He gets in an airplane which is attached to a gasoline pump. He cannot fly it, and drags the gas station with him when he tries to take off. The plane crashes and it wrecked, my husband almost burned. Actually he wasn't hurt.

As no associations were forthcoming, I observed that her dream seemed to include elements of almost every possible conflict. She assented by describing a sense of urgency, a feeling that she had to solve all her problems before I went away on vacation.

This dream gives an almost complete summary of the patient's neurosis and symptomatology. The dream opens with the patient, a guilty criminal, sentenced to filth and inferior food. She is visited by her mother, who is blind to the patient's guilt and brings her a sexy outfit, completely inappropriate, which the patient must reject. The mother is thus doing what she did—pushing the patient into a phallic, seductive role and ignoring the child's incestuous, guilt-laden longings, which in the dream force her to reject this role. In real life she willy-nilly went along with her mother's neurosis and danced and performed. In the dream she rejects this role.

It turns out the patient's former boss is also ignorant of her crime, but her guilt is shown by her eating of the inferior food, which could be related to the patient's character trait of considering herself a poor, deprived girl. The patient's sister-in-law is a successful lawyer, narcissistic and seductive, who has become in reality what the patient's mother wished for her daughter and for herself. The patient offers to give her sexuality to the sister-in-law and is suddenly released from her prison. At this point, her mother again brings her an attractive outfit which she can now accept with some urging from her husband. It appears that the patient has undone her incestuous crime by offering up her sexuality to her mother as personified by the sister-in-law. She and her father are castrated for their misdeeds, and the patient can now come closer to achieving femininity.

But now some ambivalence to her husband appears. He is almost killed in a crash when he tries to fly, still firmly attached to his fuel supply. In reality, the husband was almost wrecked by her arrest, and he later required treatment when his tremendous underlying needs for dependency almost overwhelmed him. The patient's arrest came after many years of considerable frustrations and neglect from her very active and successful husband, during which time she accumulated intense and unexpressed needs for more love from him. Her crime threatened his career, forced him to take urgent action on her behalf, and was followed by more open demands for love on her part.

The dream thus includes elements from all psychosexual levels, shows their interconnections, and clearly links her neurosis with her unconscious awareness of her husband's neurosis. Like the dream of the patient who stopped treatment on the ninth day, this dream shows no separation anxiety but, rather, an unusual richness and clarity of manifest content.

The sense of urgency seems to be an effort to present me with the total picture all at once—to get it settled before the vacation. It is as though the patient can now tell everything because there will be no opportunity to interpret it. The dream also aims to give continuity to her transference by giving the analyst something to think about while they are apart. It reminds the analyst that the patient still has plenty of material to present and that she must not be forgotten during the vacation.

One year after this dream, the patient reported a dream in the hour preceding a ten-day interruption.

You and I are to have a five o'clock appointment before you leave town. I come early and find many people upstairs and downstairs. There are many older, well-dressed Jewish women having parties. I meet you in the hall and you say you will see me at five and hurry off. I wander around, and come upon a radio upstairs, with many older men sitting about. I seem to be younger. One of them takes a fancy to me, and there is a public announcement that he wants to meet me. I am pleased, but embarrassed. He is a boy my age. I go to your office, but you are late. The Jewish women are all around your office; like a dinner at the

> temple. I am introduced to a woman and her young daughter who politely invite me to share their table. I wonder where you are. We have weird food: jelly beans, cabanza beans, and chocolate ice cream which gives me pimples. I choose apricot ice cream but wonder if I should, as the others want some. I go to the kitchen to look for you and everything becomes vague. You are going to meet me in your office, but the party is still there, and you seem part of the party, serving as a host.

She said she had a feeling that she might become completely dependent on me and believed the interruption would be painful because she would miss me a great deal. The ice cream in the dream represented her hungry need for love, and it was good that in the dream she had got her own ice cream. This meant to her that she need not depend on me as a parent. The difficulty in getting me in the dream was to keep from becoming too deeply involved with me and increasing the pain of the forthcoming separation. She became tearful when she expressed a wish that I should love her rather than my wife.

Her conflict and anxiety at the separation mask the other meanings of this dream which was not, moreover, the massive outpouring from the unconscious that the preceding vacation dream had been. The intensity of her transference at the time of this dream accounts for the difference.

During the next two months she worked through some of the meaning of her wishes for love in the transference. Another interruption of one week was preceded by another dream. At this time, the patient's husband was temporarily physically incapacitated, and she reported a newly found ability to mother him. She also noted a tendency to overeat during the last few days. In the last hour she reported the following dream.

> I was out of gas on a hill and began pushing my car toward a gas station at the top. There I found a man arguing violently with his wife which I felt gave me a chance to get some gas. I found I only had two dollars, but I refused the man's offer to help get me a credit card. I tried to seduce him and he kissed me on the top of my head. I felt pleased and the dream faded away.

The previous night she had felt relatively at ease in the company of a group of women. She made the interpretation that the dream referred to my forthcoming absence and that she was asserting her independence by pushing the car herself and refusing the offer of a credit card. She felt the dream represented her mother's mistreatment of her father which had permitted her to feel that she could replace her mother with him. She said she was still not sufficiently grown up to realize that they are married. She said she was demanding with men, and unwilling to share me, or her husband, or her father with others.

She then reported two fantasies she remembered before having gone to sleep that night. In one, she was being criticized by women from notes they had taken about her. These women were praising another woman with whom the patient did not feel competitive: "Not the kind my mother would pit me against but older, heavy, and unattractive." This was followed by fantasy in which someone chopped off her left index finger. This was the finger she used in masturbating, and the hand from which her father lost all his fingers in the accident he suffered after having had an extramarital affair.

Her fantasies and the dream show her progress toward a resolution of her neurosis. The castration fantasy is undisguised, she finds a father who ignores her sexual seductiveness and give her a fatherly kiss in complete contrast to her father's response to her during her childhood. She is resolving her competitive anxiety-laden impulses toward other women. Separation anxiety is handled by a counterphobic maneuver: she pushes her car up the hill, refusing assistance.

This is another instance in which the clarity of the manifest dream content is clearly a reaction to an interruption in analysis. The fantasies preceding the dream are similarly undisguised.

Dreams during a vacation from treatment are frequently presented to the analyst as a gift upon his return, as if to show him that the patient did not forget him and continued to do his analytic work. These too may be unusually vivid. A striking example occurred in the form of a group's reaction to the therapist's vacation. The group consisted of six neurotic patients who had missed two sessions because of the therapist's absence and were for that reason given a special session on his return. It was attended by four of the six patients. Each patient, in turn, presented a dream which had been dreamt during the therapist's vacation. While dreams were regularly a part of the psychotherapy and were frequently presented for discussion, it was unprecedented to hear each patient report a dream, and particularly dreams as vivid as these were.

In 1914 Ferenczi published a brief article stating that patients returning to an interrupted analysis usually report material that had previously played little or no part in the analysis. The transference relationship was quickly reestablished and the analysis on resumption usually went much deeper than it had before. Ferenczi said that after brief interruptions, analyses were usually resumed as though the process were continuing from the preceding day (Alexander and French, 1946).

Alexander describes a technique of planned interruptions of analysis. These were indicated largely to remedy an analytic situation in which the transference gratification outweighed the desire for recovery and led to an impasse in which the patient would continue to come without benefit as long as permitted. Alexander's patients—faced with a planned date for termination or interruption—often produced a stream of analyzable material in an effort to prevent or forestall the interruption. When the analysis was resumed, it was almost always more productive and intensive (Alexander and French, 1946).

The dream material here presented tends to confirm these observations that very effective therapeutic work may be stimulated by an interruption in the analysis, and that the automatic self-analysis that continues within the patient during an interruption or after termination may be especially effective because of a relaxation of repression.

Summary

Anticipation of interruptions of the treatment during psychoanalysis are sometimes attended by decrease of resistance which permits the recall of vivid, relatively little disguised dreams. This state may continue during the interruption and characterizes the dreams that are reported when analysis is resumed.

Chapter 11

THE DREAM AS A SIGNAL FOR
TERMINATION

J. O. Cavenar and J. L. Nash

The question of when to terminate a psychoanalysis has been controversial throughout its history as a treatment. A number of writers have considered the issue, beginning with Freud's observations (1913b) that there is in fact a terminal phase whose movements, like a chess game, may be plotted. The problem of determining the appropriate time for termination is, as we know, enormously complex. It encompasses not only valid intrinsic theoretical issues, but also extrinsic issues brought by the patient, such as economic concerns and occupational pressures; extrinsic issues from the analyst's side may also enter into the decision. These considerations typically lead, however, to a premature breaking off of the treatment, and, ideally, should not be of overriding importance. Signs of symptomatic improvement are of course influential in the decision to terminate, but some analysts (Jones, 1936; Freud, 1937a; Nunberg, 1954; Dewald, 1972) have demonstrated the unreliability of this as a measure of successful treatment.

Glover (1955) calls for the need for confirmatory evidence that the analytic goals have been accomplished. He speaks of the need to eliminate any "miscarriages of judgement due to impatience or boredom or optimism on the analyst's part" (p. 157) and for a detailing of clinical standards other than signs of symptomatic improvement in the decision for termination. In an excellent and comprehensive review of the literature

This paper was first published in the *Journal of the American Psychoanalytic Association* (1976), 24:425–436.

on termination of psychoanalysis of adults, Firestein (1974) demonstrates the multifaceted nature of the problem, and the tendency of most investigators to rely on more than one indicator. In addition to symptomatic improvement, most approaches have encompassed the concepts of structural change (of which there is limited concordance as to determination), intuition (perhaps valid, but impossible to document), improved deployment of ego functions, resolution of the transference neurosis (difficult to appraise, especially prior to its termination and subsequent effect), and countertransference considerations (which are frequently an interference). To some extent the futility of attempting to arrive at reliable indicators for the termination decision is indicated by Firestein's summary statement that "there remains an over-all impression that developments of the greatest therapeutic and analytic significance may occur only after the termination of the analysis has been definitely planned" (p. 892).

We believe the use of dreams within the framework of termination has been neglected. Although it is commonplace to hear of "typical termination dreams" in supervisory hours or at clinical case conferences, they are described as dreams that are characteristic of the termination phase; that is, they occur in their characteristic manner *after* the decision to terminate has been made and verbalized to the patient.

Glover (1955) speaks of "review dreams" (p. 157) as occurring during the course of an analytic treatment, the manifest content of which can be interpreted as an assessment of the patient's progress in overcoming his difficulties, but that these changes can be more closely studied when the patient is subject to recurrent dreams. He cites several examples of such changing recurring dreams, and recommends study of the relation between the dreams and analytic situation of the opening phase, as compared with the dreams and analytic situation of the terminal phase. He says: "we are legitimately influenced by dream-material in considering the termination of analysis" (p. 158). According to his questionnaire report, special clinical factors were felt to offer another measure of the advisability of termination. Alterations in the content of and the affective reaction occuring in dreams were felt to be serviceable criteria.

Stereotyped anxiety and terror dreams often showed, not only a reduction in the amount of symbolic expression during the analysis, but a material reduction in the quantity of anxiety. The persistence of such dreams was an indication that analysis was not complete even if the symptoms had disappeared.

Oremland (1973) presented a specific dream during the termination phase of successful psychoanalyses. In each termination case presented, the dream contained a representation of the patient's primary symptoms with significant modifications and the analyst in undisguised form was directly involved with the symptoms. By contrast, a case is presented in which the symptom was unmodified and the analyst disguised; this case was not considered a successful psychoanalysis. Oremland offers the hypothesis that such termination dreams, although not universal phenomena, are additional evidence that an analytical process was initiated and is now being completed.

Saul (1972) discusses dreams that go beyond insight and deal centrally with how to solve a problem. These he calls dreams of resolution, and suggests that they reflect the patient's grasp of the problem, the kind of solution he struggles with, and something of his degree of success in achieving a solution. He suggests that toward the end of a successful analysis, this type of dream tends to reflect the solution more clearly and usually more realistically; there is less disguise and distortion. These dreams of resolution, along with effective progress in dealing with the major emotional forces in the transference and in life, and the increased frankness of material, all indicate that the analyst might think of a trial ending.

Our investigations have confirmed the usefulness of assessing the changing nature of recurring dreams; we also feel there exist *termination signal dreams*, which make their appearance in the course of analysis prior to termination's being discussed by the analyst or analysand. These dreams have a recognizable form and may serve as reliable indicators that a decision to consider termination is appropriate. They differ from the type of dream that Saul has described as a dream of resolution. In order for a termination signal dream to appear, the original conflicts must be resolved to a maximal degree. Our experience indicates that the termination signal dream is the patient's way of telling himself and the analyst that the conflicts have been worked through, and that termination of the psychoanalysis should be considered. In addition, the appearance of this type of dream may be closely connected with another phenomenon frequently seen: the recurrence of symptoms in the terminal phase of a psychoanalysis.

The literature on the subject of symptom exacerbation in the terminal phase of a psychoanalysis is large and opinion on its significance is divided. Kubie (1968) regards the intensification of symptoms in the termination phase as indicative of failure of transference neurosis resolution, pointing to patients who had a second period of analysis with a second analyst and a conclusion without symptom exacerbation. Ticho, in a recent panel on this subject (Robbins, 1975), said that, for patients in the neurotic range, the first move for termination should come from the patient, although the idea of termination should of course be jointly agreed upon. Ticho believed that recurrence of symptoms at the time of termination is an attempt to delay the final leave-taking, but more likely to appear in response to the imposition by the analyst of a termination date rather than to the introduction of the prospect of termination itself. Robbins, at the same panel, felt that symptom recurrence, intensity, and duration, and the duration and intensity of the terminal phase are influenced by many factors, including how termination is introduced and by whom, the patient's character structure, and whether there is the possibility of a postanalytic relationship.

Others (Reich, 1950; Saul, 1958; Kohut, 1971) see the recurrence of symptoms in a more symbolic and primarily positive light. The recurrence is conceptualized from a revenge motive as the analysand recognizes the final futility of his incestuous wishes. Ekstein's (1965) allusion to the theater is expressive of the ego work implicit in the upsurge: "[a] final adaptive act of mastery which is the dress rehearsal for future adaptive behavior" (pp. 57–78).

Miller (1965) considers symptom exacerbation an indicator of insufficient working through. He suggests that the patient is attempting to preserve infantile fantasies of omnipotence and that the termination phase is the only time that this particular fantasy can be worked through. We agree with Miller's explanation; the type of termination signal dream we are describing is closely tied to a lack of recurrence of symptoms in the terminal phase. It is our thesis that, if the conflicts have been worked through sufficiently so that the analysand may permit himself to experience such a termination signal dream, either symptoms will not recur, or any recurrence will be a short-lived reactivation of the neurosis which may be easily worked through prior to the termination of the analysis.

In the four cases to be presented, termination signal dreams appeared spontaneously in the course of the analysis without termination having been discussed by either the analyst or the analysand. In each case, the appearance of these dreams led to the discussion of termination and the eventual setting of a termination date. In only one of the four cases was there a recurrence of symptoms, and, in that case, it was a brief reactivation of the neurosis which was quickly and completely worked through prior to the termination of the analysis.

Case 1

The patient is a twenty-eight-year-old physician who entered psychoanalysis because of free-floating anxiety, sporadic depression, and an awareness of a fear of being too successful. Although he was successful both academically and professionally, he was never satisfied with his performance. There were marked open conflicts with the father: the patient disliked the father, yet was in awe and admiration of him. He had a rigid obsessive–compulsive character structure with isolation of affect, reaction formation, and denial. The initial transference reactions were to the father, with marked ambivalence. These transferences were gradually worked through, and the patient began to deal with angry feelings regarding the mother. The treatment progressed well, with good symptomatic relief, lessening of superego tension, and a working through of the transference neurosis. At the end of five-and-a-half years of treatment, he brought the following dream:

> I was cleaning and straightening the attic storeroom of
> my father's store. I finished the job, and the storeroom
> appeared to be in excellent shape; my father came to look
> and said that he had never seen the storeroom in such
> good condition. My father suggested I take some time off.
> As I looked over to the right side, you [the analyst] were
> there, smiling as though you approved.

The patient's associations were to the task of cleaning and
rearranging the attic storeroom, which had in fact been his job
when he was an adolescent. His father had never been satisfied
with the patient's work, regardless of how good it might have
been. The patient understood this dream to mean that the
"attic" was in good shape at this point, and that the dream was
suggesting that termination be considered. Two days later, he
brought the following dream:

> I was standing outside of your office, in the hall, looking
> up the hallway. Some person walks by and asks me if that
> is you up the hall. I look, but I really can't tell, but I say to
> the person that it doesn't matter anyway. The feeling in
> the dream was that of just being matter of fact, as if it
> didn't matter if it was you.

The patient understood this dream to mean that he was
now treating the analyst as he would anyone else, that the transference elements had been resolved, and that the analyst now
had no special significance to him. These dreams led to a discussion of termination, not heretofore mentioned, and the setting
of the date for termination. Six months later the case was terminated successfully without any recurrence of symptoms in the
termination phase. One year after termination, the patient continues to do well and is asymptomatic.

Case 2

The patient, a twenty-seven-year-old registered nurse, entered
psychoanalysis because of free-floating anxiety, phobic symptoms, and low self-esteem. She was the product of a family

constellation in which the mother was the dominant marital partner, but very insecure in her role as a woman, wife, and mother, while the father was a chronically depressed, passive, emotionally cold man. The patient was married to a professional man two years older than herself, and had a daughter, age four; there was no significant intrafamilial conflict.

The main defense mechanisms used by the patient were displacement, repression, and denial. Defense analysis soon led to frequent affect flooding, and was followed by formation of an intense transference neurosis; working through proceeded smoothly with minimal acting out; and a good resolution of the transference was obtained, along with easing of superego tensions. At the end of four-and-a-half years of analysis, the patient brought the following dream.

> I came into your office, but instead of lying on the couch, I sat down in the chair. We talked about everyday sort of things, and it was very pleasant. Finally, I looked at my watch, commented that I knew you were very busy and had other people waiting to see you. I said, "It really is time for me to go." I walked down the hallway, waving goodbye to you as I went.

Several sessions later, the patient brought the following dream: "I was standing in front of your office, and your wife and children were there with you. I was telling each of you goodbye, and it was very sad in one way, yet a very happy occasion in another way."

The patient had in fact seen the analyst with his wife during the course of the psychoanalysis, and had read newspaper articles concerning both the analyst's children. The full meaning of these dreams escaped the patient; she was aware of a sense of saying farewell in both dreams, but did not understand that these were dreams signaling that the analysis was finished. Many more such dreams were brought over ensuing hours, and eventually the patient understood these dreams as meaning that she was ready to leave. A date for termination was set by the patient, and the analysis proceeded to a very successful conclusion six months after the first dream reported above.

There was no recurrence of symptoms during the termination phase. Nine months after the termination, the patient continues to do well; she is asymptomatic, is able to carry on her self-analysis, and is happy with herself.

Case 3

This patient, a thirty-five-year-old divorced female Ph.D. candidate, entered psychoanalysis because of her inability to sustain a relationship with a man, inability to complete the work for her degree, and a recent homosexual affair which was the only overt homosexual experience she had ever had. She recalled three recurrent dreams from childhood in the first diagnostic hours. In the first, she had lost a tooth and was panic stricken, angry, and anxious. In the second, a man was swimming after her; she secretly wanted the man to overtake her, yet would swim farther and faster than the man and elude him. Her third dream was of having a defective baby—either defective in body parts of one type or another, or a small child no larger than a lima bean. After three years of analysis, the patient began to redream the childhood dreams with significant modifications. She dreamed that she was looking in a mirror and noticed she had lost a tooth, but instead of panic or rage, she laughed and said to herself that she needed to see a dentist. She dreamed that she was swimming after a man, was going to overtake him and confess her feelings for the man. Then she dreamed that she had a baby and it was perfectly normal. The affect in this dream was one of amazement and happiness that after this period of time she could produce a normal child. She then brought the following dream: "I was riding in the elevator with you, and we were going down from your office. You looked over with a feeling of warmth, understanding, caring, and naturalness. You handed me an identity badge, and it seemed I could wear the badge if I wanted. It was a pleasant feeling."

The patient understood the dream to mean that she had come to analysis looking for her confused identity and now had found it. She felt that this dream was saying the analytic work was done; a discussion of termination ensued, and the patient set the termination date. The analysis terminated successfully four months later. There was no recurrence of symptoms during the termination phase of the treatment, or six months later.

Case 4

This patient is a twenty-nine-year-old married educator whose father committed suicide during the fifth month of her first and only pregnancy; she was well, however, until her son was born. At that time she had an onset of dyspareunia, frigidity, backache, urinary frequency and urgency, and generalized weakness and lethargy. There were mild depressive symptoms. She came for analysis with these symptoms when her son was three years old. The analysis progressed nicely, with a careful working through of an intense transference neurosis. After two-and-a-half years of analysis, the patient brought the following dream: "There was a body in a coffin, and I was aware that decomposition and decay had started."

The patient understood this dream to mean that the feelings about her father that had been worked on so extensively were finally being laid to rest, and were starting to decompose. Within weeks, she brought the following dream:

> I was taking a tour of a ship below decks, and I walked down the hall looking into various rooms. In the rooms were people and things that we had talked about and looked at in the analysis. I was alone, but I felt good about being alone; I felt confident. I looked at all the different rooms and areas, then came up to the deck of the ship. I started down the gangplank; you were at the bottom of the gangplank to help me down. You extended your hand to me in a friendly manner, but I felt I didn't need any help. I looked down at myself, and was surprised to see myself beautiful and nonpregnant.

The patient understood this dream to mean that this was a tour of all the areas and conflicts that had been explored in the analysis, and that she felt good about looking at these areas now. She felt that being alone but confident meant that she no longer needed the analysis or the analyst, just as she didn't need the analyst's hand to make the last step. Being nonpregnant meant to her that the fantasy of being continually pregnant to avoid the loss of the father had been worked through. This dream led to a discussion of termination. The patient set the date—Labor Day! There was a recurrence of many of the presenting symptoms, including symptoms of pregnancy. The patient commented on the return of symptoms, and understood that they were reappearing as a result of termination. She remarked that the symptoms that had previously taken months to understand were now reappearing and disappearing in days. It was felt that possible resistance elements in the patient's interpretation of the dreams had not materialized. The analysis proceeded to a successful conclusion some three months later.

Conclusion

Typical termination dreams occur in response to the decision to terminate; dreams may, however, signal that a consideration of termination is appropriate. In order for these dreams to occur, other parameters of termination must have been met: structural change has by necessity taken place; ego functioning has improved; the transference neurosis has been resolved; and marked countertransference difficulties cannot be present. If any of these areas are insufficiently worked through, the dream will not appear.

We believe this type of termination signal dream is negatively correlated with the recurrence of symptoms sometimes seen in the termination phase of analysis. If the conflicts have been worked through to the point that the analysand may permit himself to experience such a dream, we suggest symptoms will not recur, or any recurrence will be a short-lived reactivation of the neurosis, which may easily be worked through prior to the termination of the analysis.

Chapter 12

THE GOOD DREAM, DREAM SPACE, AND THE DREAM EXPERIENCE REVISITED

T. M. ALSTON, R. C. CALOGERAS, AND H. DESERNO

Introduction

Our purpose in this paper is to present a brief commentary on three significant dream conceptualizations—the good dream, the dream space, and the dream experience—which have appeared at different intervals over the last twenty-five years. These formulations, representing the work of M. Masud Khan (1962, 1972, 1976), describe his attempt to bring the concept of the self, or the self experience, into conjunction with psychoanalytic dream psychology. In what follows, we propose to examine the main elements of each of the above dream concepts; and then to examine the controversy generated by them at the 29th International Psychoanalytic Congress in London in 1975.

The Good Dream

Khan first introduced the concept of the "good dream" in his paper, "Dream Psychology and the Evolution of the Psychoanalytic Situation" (1962), at the 22nd Congress of the International Psychoanalytic Association, Edinburgh, 1961. Before presenting his conceptualizing of the good dream, he first traces its roots to Freud's developing of the psychoanalytic situation. That is, from its origins in the hypnotic dream–sleep situation and the cathartic method to its final form in the free association method, with its similarities to the process of awakening. He acknowledges the work of Lewin (1954; chapter 7), who postulates the similarity between "analytic formation" and "dream formation" with the analyst seen as the "awakener" of the patient from the analytic sleep situation; and also to the debt he owes to Kris's concept of the "good analytic hour" (1956a). Following this preamble, Khan then proceeds to conceptualize and define what he means by the good dream. "By a 'good dream,' I mean a dream which incorporates through successful dream-work an unconscious wish and can thus enable sleep to be sustained on the one hand and can be available for psychic experience to the ego when the person awakens" (1962, p. 25).

Khan clarifies the good dream further:

1. Certain intrapsychic functions and ego capacities are necessary for a person to be able to put together a good dream from his sleep experience ([1962], see pp. 24–25 for an extensive listing). These are: "the ego's capacity to sustain the sleep-wish, controlling excessive influx of primary process and appropriate dosage 'day residues' to structuralize the latent dream-wish into a contained manifest dream" (1962, p. 325).

2. The capacity for having a "good dream" though a prerequisite for psychic health is not a guarantee of it. The "good dream" is the dream increment of ego strength (1962, p. 25).

3. Based on his clinical experience, Khan suggests that patients who cannot have a good dream also cannot creatively use the analytic situation (1962, p. 27).

As an example of a good dream, told by a female patient at the end of her treatment as she was about to take up a responsible job,[1] Khan reports the following dream.

> I find myself in the hospital dispensary. I collect a few bottles of sleeping tablets and walk out. Then I get confused and cannot find my way. Eventually I find myself in the occupational therapy room. I see there are paints and brushes and paper lying around. Since there was no one present I arrange the bottles and start making a still-life painting of them. As I am about to finish I become aware someone is watching me, I became terrified and nearly tear

---

[1] Khan notes that this patient had been an alcoholic and was used to petty stealing.

up the drawing. Then realize that it is not the drawing but
the bottles that I should be concerned about. I had stolen
them. I turn around and the man strikes me as odd: he is
short, grey-haired and looks like a Gestapo officer. He had
a kindly permissive face. I leave everything and walk back
to my bedroom [Khan, 1976, p. 326].

Without going into the specifics of the patient's associations
or too much into her background (she was a qualified doctor,
a refugee from central Europe, whose parents had perished in
the Nazi gas chambers), we turn briefly to Khan's analysis of
the dream in terms of his concept of the good dream. First, he
notes the importance of such a dream just as she is about to
launch herself on a "responsible professional career" [medi-
cine?]. That is, the patient "has acquired enough ego resources
to cope with her guilt on the one hand and to sublimate her
deprivation-experiences with an aesthetic effort" by not swallowing the pills but by painting them. (The patient had entered
analysis because she had taken an overdose of sleeping pills and
had attempted to drown herself in a nearby lake.) Second, Khan
refers to the transference representation of him as the benign
Gestapo officer as "showing an intrapsychic shift from regressive dependence on an idealized figure to that of using him as
a decimating but non-censorious internal figure" (pp. 21–31).
(Several times Khan rescued his patient when she got in trouble
with the police for petty stealing; also the Gestapo–analyst symbolization had many guilty associations for the patient vis-à-vis
the fact that she had been sent a sum of money in order to help
bring her family to England, but had allowed her drinks to be
laced with a strong sedative and had consequently lost all the
money.) Third, Khan concludes that the treatment of this patient had revealed to him "most vividly how a person can hide
her 'true self' behind the most bizarre psychopathology, but
given the right holding-environment her untried ego capacities
can begin to function with amazing intactness and efficiency"
(p. 326). For him, this represented a " 'good dream' because *it
integrated into a coherent experiential narrative what had so far been
split-off and denied aspects of the self*" (emphasis added) (p. 326).

Comment. Over the years since its first postulation, Khan's formulation of the good dream seems to have been accepted as a useful and valid formulation in psychoanalytic dream psychology[2]; and in many instances to be associated with Kris's conceptualization of the "good analytic hour." What seems to be rejected by a number of analysts (Colby, 1958) is its explanation of its dream dynamics as associated with Winnicott's self theory, evoking the "false" and "true" self constructs.

Dream Space

Beginning with his article, "The Use and Abuse of the Dream in Psychic Experience" (1971), Khan adds to his concept of the good dream with a second dream construct which he calls the "dream space." He derives this formulation from two principal sources: (1) from Winnicott's observations on how the child uses the "transitional space" of the paper to draw or doodle in his Squiggles Game (Winnicott, 1971); and (2) from his clinical observations on certain patients who could not use the dream—or rather abused the use of the dream—in productive fashion.

Khan offers a number of definitions or conceptualizations of the dream space. First, " 'dream space' is a specific intrapsychic structure where a person actualizes certain types of experiences" in order to dream. This type of actualization is different from the general process of dreaming and from the dream as a symbolic mental product (p. 315). Second, "dream space is the internal psychic equivalent of what Winnicott has conceptualized as the transitional space which a child establishes to discover his self and reality" (p. 314). Third, in contrast to Lewin's dream screen (1946b), dream space is "something *onto* which the dream imagery is projected. Whereas the dream-space is a psychic area in which the dream process is actualized into experiential reality" (p. 314). Fourth, Khan concludes by suggesting that the incapacity to dream is reflected in the patient's

---

[2] This statement is based on the editors' survey of virtually all the known analytic dream articles appearing since World War II in English and German (and to a more limited extent in French and Spanish) analytic journals (Alston, Calogeras, Deserno, unpublished).

incapacity to use the dream space to actualize the experience of the dream process, and this in turn leads to the acting out of the dream's external reality (p. 314).

Comment. The difficulty which many analysts find with the dream space conceptualization is that it evokes the use of a spatial metaphor to describe a psychic process. Thus, in reference to the "space" in intrapsychic functioning, a dream actualization is said to be occurring, which allows the dream per se to be dreamt. What Khan seems to be trying to conceptualize is that of an affect-experience which is so defended against—by dissociation, isolation, and reversal—that the capacity of the person to use the dream process productively is negated.

Dream Experience

Khan's third conceptualization, that of the "dream experience" (1976), got started when he attempted to distinguish between the difference between the dreaming experience of sleep and the remembered dream text. He writes that this distinction first came about when he was treating young drug addicts.

> I was impressed by the repetitive quality of their dreams and the banality of the imagery entailed. This paralleled their account of their "trip" which was in the spoken narrative always repetitious and cumbersomely prosaic, in contrast to their subjective feeling that they had lived through a very intense, vivid and unique experience in the "trip" itself. [Khan then notes:] I began to suspect that the verbal recall failed, as well as screened, even negated at times, the experience in the actual "trip" [Khan, 1976, p. 328].

A clinical confirmation of this occurred when a "gifted and successful young pop-musician in analysis" clarified these distinctions for him. Khan quotes the patient as saying. "Let me try saying it this way: when I hear the right tune in that state I *am* that tune which I am also hearing. This may sound silly to you but it is true to my experience. There are four of us: the tune, me, listening to the tune and me as one. And yet again we are all one. That is the joy of it" (p. 328).

This patient also had a keen awareness, according to Khan, that there was something he experienced in sleep and in his "trips" which he could not grasp in his ordinary conscious. Subsequently, Khan was able to interpret to him that he (the patient) was speaking of the distinction between the dream experience and the dream text; that when he had come to analysis, it was not to seek relief from a definite symptom, but to inquire into his feeling which he states as—"I am with life but not in it. I know others experience living differently and more fully than me. I am an onlooker" (p. 329).

In summating his conceptualization regarding the dream experience, Khan makes the following points (1976, pp. 329–330).

1. *Dream experience and dream text.* There is a dream experience ("an entirety that actualizes the self in an unknowable way") to which the dream text bears no direct relationship. That is, the two are not complementary or antithetical to each other. Thus, in the self experience of a person, they may sometimes be superimposed and at other times they may be completely separate and unrelated.

2. *What is the dream experience?* The dream experience is not symbolic in the way other dream structures are. It is, following Khan's reasoning, a type or aspect of the primary process (in contrast to the classical primary process view) in which a psychic self state is actualized predominately through "primary process" functioning. The implication here is that the dream experience is a kind of primary process self experience. Sometimes it can be "actualized" and other times it is "lost."

3. *Conclusion.* Khan concludes that a person by means of his dream experience can actualize aspects of the self that may never become overtly available to him via his free associations or through the analysis of his dreams. And yet this dream experience, as difficult as it may be to become aware of, may enrich his life and "its lack can impoverish his experience of others, himself, and his sleep" (p. 330).

London Conference Discussion

The first general (i.e., psychoanalytic) discussion of Khan's three dream concepts occurred in the London IPC in 1975 (for a summary see Curtis and Sachs [1976]). It was there that he summarized his two early concepts—the good dream and the dream space and then gave major emphasis to his new formulation of the dream experience. Providing a backdrop for his discussion, particularly of the dream experience, was the contrasting paper of Harold Blum (1976) who presented the mainstream ego psychoanalytic approach in psychoanalytic practice. Khan's discussion of his dream experience concept stirred considerable debate from the audience as well as rejoinders from the other presenters. The resulting discussion may be divided into two broad groups—those that supported the introduction of the self and self theory as an integral part of psychoanalytic dream psychology, and those that felt that it introduced an unscientific, even mystical element into dream psychology.

Typical of the arguments against Khan's dream concepts was Kernberg's comment that "Khan's attention to the patient's inability to recover the actual dream-experience has the net effect of mystifying the dream by taking it out of our understanding of normal development and placing it into a too abstractly theoretical frame of reference. . . . [He] lifts the idea of dream-experience out of its developmental context in order to use it as an abstract construct true of all patients" (p. 348). In a similar vain, Blum (pp. 353–354) notes that Khan utilizes many aspects of existential philosophy in his dream formulations and one "must distinguish between such philosophical and aesthetic understanding and psychoanalytic understanding, [and he felt that] Khan's emphasis on the incommunicable aesthetic and mystical experience of the patient could lead to mysticism, and a return to the abreactive theory of therapy where the concept of cure would be to release strangulated feelings." In rebuttal, Khan evokes the constructs of "two basic stances which analysts take"—those that use the analysis as work space, and those that use the analysis as play space. Khan avers that he uses the analysis in the latter sense (i.e., as play space) "so that he can help a patient tell a dream in a way that does not kill the dream but helps the patient to be astonished in the telling of the dream" (Curtis and Sachs, 1976, p. 354).

Conclusion

In concluding we would like to offer the following remarks concerning Khan's dream concepts.

1. *Affect Experience.* Since the London Conference, a number of related conferences and seminars have suggested that the dream experience—which Khan spoke of as essentially unknowable—could actually be "knowable" or understood as an affect experience. Perforce, it was out of this affect experience which the dream as a structured psychic product can then emerge. The dream experience can thus be understood as a borderline construct being a pure affect (without structure) and a cognitive–ideational product with inchoate structure (Curtis and Sachs, 1976).

2. *Dream Experience as Basic Fault.* It has been suggested in a number of recent dream seminars (which have considered new constructs in dream psychology) since the London Conference that the dream experience can be understood and become knowable as a dream experience component of the "basic fault." Balint's (1968) basic fault concept postulates that something akin to an earthquake-caused geological fault in the ground which has caused a very elemental defect or deficiency in the self ego's structure and functioning. Thus, with this tie-in with the basic fault, the dream experience is now connected with an early development occurrence rendering it less open to criticism that it is only a philosophical construct with no developmental roots.

3. *Unconscious Aspect of the Total Personality.* Several continental European analysts (e.g., Loch, personal communication, 1988) have suggested that the dream experience could well have something to do "with the unconscious which was never preconscious." Understood in this sense, it would be linked with Freud's concepts of primary repression (Kinston and Cohen,

1986), as well as to his concept of *mood* ("Stimmung")—implied by Freud (1900) as an inclination to affect—and thus could be taken as representing the core of the total personality (= the self) which has not yet been "structured" in its various parts.

Section III

Typical and Traumatic Dreams

Presented in this section are those articles which fall under the rubric of "typical" and "traumatic" dream studies. Following Freud's formulation, such dreams are hypothesized as arising out of typical unconscious conflict situations and give the manifest dream content its typical shape. Quantitatively, a dream may be considered "typical" if it occurs in many people with little variation and "stereotypical" if it recurs frequently in the same individual.

This section begins with two short clinical articles. The first by Jacob Arlow entitled, "A Typical Dream" (1961), explores a recurrent dream in a group of patients in which the subject finds himself interrupted during the act of defecation by the intrusion of a person or persons. Arlow's careful analysis of these dreams and their variations reveal that they express a disguised fulfillment of wishes growing out of primal-scene experiences. The second article, Sandor Feldman's "Interpretation of a Typical and Stereotyped Dream Met with only During Psychoanalysis" (1945), presents a number of variations of such a dream (e.g., "While a patient is lying on the couch, the analytic session is disturbed by the presence or movement in and out of the analyst's wife or some other member of his family, etc.") which he finds expresses essentially that the perfect union with the analyst–mother should not be disturbed in any fashion.

Following this, two articles appear dealing with dreams occurring during a traumatic situation. Sidney Tarachow in his article, "The Analysis of a Dream Occurring During a Migraine Attack" (1946), discusses how a dream—following a traumatic encounter with a castrating father-surrogate—represented a patient's inhibited and masochistic solution of his sexual and competitive drives. It was in this state of massive inhibition that the migraine headache appeared, and during the headache state that the patient had the dream. Next Harold Levitan's short article, "A Traumatic Dream" (1955), describes the unusual occurrence of a traumatic event (i.e., the sudden death of a patient's husband) which was succeeded by an equally traumatic dream—to wit, where a miscarriage of the defensive process in the dream allowed the patient to reexperience the traumatic event as a flashing light during sleep.

A group of four articles next appears dealing with types of anxiety dreams which fulfill the criteria as being "typical dreams." First in this group is Harris's article, "Characterological Significance of the Typical Anxiety Dream" (1951), where he investigates the characterological meaning of essentially two types of typical dreams—those associated with the predominant unpleasant affect of "falling" and those with "being attacked." Second appears Pollock and Muslin's ground-breaking study of "Dreams During Surgical Procedures" (1962), where they analyzed the "dreaming ego's work" of a group of patients undergoing radical surgical procedures, finding that dreams occurring during anesthesia sleep are quite different from natural sleep dreams; and that in "surgical dreams" the ego desperately attempts to integrate syntonically traumatic tensions emerging defensively. Third, Allan Roos's article, "Psychoanalytic Study of a Typical Dream" (1960), presents an in-depth analysis of what he postulates as a typical dream found in a variety of patients in analysis ("The patient is either a passenger or the driver in a vehicle—typically a car—in the back seat of which is a corpse, etc.") In analyzing such dreams, Roos found that there was some actual situation which reactivated early infantile memories and the oedipal struggle—their common dream theme being the death of the parent (usually the father) and the accompanying rescue fantasy. Fourth, in a recent summation article by Renik, "Typical Examination Dreams, 'Superego Dreams,' and Traumatic Dreams" (1981), he holds that these types of dreams all have essentially the same underlying psychic structure and function. In effect, they are dreams of mastery in which the ego attempts to master an underlying

traumatic conflict by the wish-fulfilling activity of giving reassurance; thus, a "piece of reality" (the traumatic event or threatening examination) in the dream often represents the fulfillment of a hidden wish, and what may begin as a traumatic
dream often ends by resembling a typical examination dream.

Chapter 13

A TYPICAL DREAM

Jacob A. Arlow

In *The Interpretation of Dreams* Freud (1900) described a group of so-called "typical" dreams. Such dreams have in common a characteristic situation or set of elements as part of their manifest content representing disguised fulfillment of wishes arising out of typical conflict situations. The form which the manifest content takes as a result of the dream work is of particular significance for its recurrent representation gives the typical shape to this kind of dream. Freud described typical dreams of dead relatives, being nude in public places, failing examinations, and missing trains. In recent years a number of authors have described other typical dreams. The widespread occurrence of such dreams is related to the ubiquity of certain preferred dream solutions of conflict or anxiety situations of common occurrence.

In a group of four patients I have observed a recurrent dream of typical manifest representation related to a characteristic latent content. This dream probably deserves to be regarded as a typical dream. In this dream the subject finds himself interrupted during the act of defecation by the intrusion of some person or persons, or by the occurrence of some event which transforms this usually private activity into a more or less public spectacle. The characteristic mood experienced during such dreams is usually embarrassment or anxiety, although in some such dreams the subject is not concerned and instead reports a comforting feeling which is not at all in keeping with

This paper was first published in the *Journal of Hillside Hospital* (1961), 10:154–158.

his actual or anticipated responses under circumstances such as depicted in the dream.

There are many possible variations of the fundamental manifest elements of these dreams. Most often, the individual is in his own bathroom at home when some intruder, usually a stranger, breaks into his privacy. Usually, as the analysis of such patients proceeds and the transference neurosis comes to the fore, the locale of the dream is shifted to the bathroom in the analyst's office and the intruder becomes the analyst himself or some thinly disguised substitute for him. The alternating relationship between the wish to be observed in the act of defecation and the defense against this wish may be represented in the dream by the factor of the lock on the door being bolted or left open. When the lock is bolted, in magical dreamlike fashion, the intruder manages to get into the bathroom nonetheless. The struggle between wish and defense may influence another element in the manifest dream, namely, the patient's attitude toward the intruder, that is, the amount of consciously experienced outrage, anger, etc., although variations in this particular element, as will be demonstrated below, usually arise, more significantly, from other sources.

The element of breach of privacy may be emphasized in a flamboyant fashion. Thus, the patient may find himself defecating in a public toilet with no door to the cubicle or in the open streets; in a department store window; or, as one patient described it, in that hyperbole for lack of privacy—Grand Central Station. Similarly, the audience which appears unexpectedly on the scene may be an individual or several individuals, known or unknown to the patient, or a large indeterminate mass of persons. In contradistinction to those dreams of being nude in public in which other persons present seem to take no notice whatsoever of the dreamer, in these dreams the intruding audience notices and observes the act of defecation, whether the dreamer responds with shame, anxiety, or indifference.

It is clear, therefore, that an exhibitionistic wish is manifestly being gratified in this dream—but why under circumstances relating to the act of defecation, which in our culture is a function relegated to private execution? Fantasies and neurotic symptoms involving the bathroom and bathroom activities are manifold. Most of these involve expressions of wishes to contaminate, wishes to give offense by odor, etc., arising out of conflicts over masturbation, impregnation, or fear of castration. Observations concerning the specific problem of safeguarding privacy during the performance of the act of defecation are, however, rather rare in the literature.

Patients who had the dream of having their privacy interrupted during the act of defecation had varying degrees of preoccupation or disturbance concerning this element in their actual experience. In only one of the patients who reported this dream were preoccupations of this nature so pronounced as to constitute symptoms. For this patient, the analysis of the "typical" dream contained the solution of a number of troublesome symptoms concerning privacy in the bathroom. For the other patients, only fleeting anxieties or fantasies concerning privacy in the bathroom could be observed. The patient who was excessively preoccupied with bathroom privacy showed a disturbance which took many forms. She was afraid of being disturbed during defecation by someone who would see, hear, or smell evidence of her activity, that is, someone who, in one way or another, would become aware that she was defecating. This anxiety spread to include activities before and after defecation. She was inhibited, for example, about leaving a group in order to go to the bathroom. After she had been to the bathroom to move her bowels she had to be sure that the water in the chamber had been flushed and that no odor remained. She was afraid that someone might come in after her and learn that she had been defecating, although she recognized that this was a universal activity which should not occasion this degree of embarrassment. She was reluctant to move her bowels in a strange bathroom, and when she did so she made doubly sure that the locks were securely closed. At the beginning of her treatment, sharing a bathroom in a hotel or in other places where someone might intrude, or where she might be overheard, was almost impossible for her.

That the fear of being disturbed in the act of defecation, which forms the manifest content of this dream, covered an underlying wish became especially clear in the analysis of these patients during the phase of the transference neurosis. Invariably they had fantasies of being intruded upon by the analyst during the act of defecation in the bathroom in the office. Usually they had such fantasies while so occupied and often unconsciously took steps to translate this fantasy into reality while using the bathroom by leaving the door unlocked, and on some occasions even slightly ajar.

Analysis of these dreams revealed that they expressed disguised fulfillment of wishes growing out of primal-scene experiences. All of the patients who dreamed this type of dream had actually observed intercourse. The act of intercourse is regressively represented by the act of defecation. Both activities, defecation and intercourse, constitute instinctual gratification usually carried out in private, capable of being overheard or observed and of arousing the curiosity of the child. The substitution of defecation as a representation for intercourse is well known in psychoanalysis. There is, however, an additional highly significant element which enters into the structure of this dream. That element is the wish-fulfilling transposition of roles. The dreamer, originally the disturber of an act of instinctual gratification, is, in the dream, the victim of such disturbance. The original outsider who watched from the periphery becomes the center of the activity—being observed by others. The dream, therefore, expresses the wish to be indulging in the same kind of activity as were the parents when they were disturbed. The dream says in effect, "I wish to be embarrassed as they were and for the same reason."

In referring to dreams of this sort patients very frequently associate the expression, "being caught with your pants down," a colloquialism which combines the shame connected with being apprehended during the sexual act. The latent idea of an activity which should be kept secret is represented by its opposite in the manifest dream element of something being made public.

The connection between bathroom activity and intercourse which this type of dream exemplifies is facilitated by the fact that in the history of the patient it frequently occurred that they awoke to go to the bathroom and in the course of doing so observed their parents; or having heard noises in their sleep or while awake, they got up to investigate and gave as an excuse the fact that they were going to the bathroom. It is possible that the sounds of intercourse perceived during sleep were registered in consciousness by the defensive substitution of another kind of sleep disturbance, namely, the need to relieve oneself.

The common childhood fantasy that children are born through an act of defecation contributed to the relationship between the representation of intercourse in terms of defecation, and was related to the thoughts of the patient on observing the parents—"so this is how babies are made." One of these patients had the fantasy of anal impregnation as well as of anal delivery.

Individual elements in this typical dream vary, as can be anticipated, with the specific experiences in connection with the primal scene. Thus, one patient repetitively dreamed of being interrupted in twos in the act of defecation; either two people barged in on her, or having expelled one intruder, another person appeared to breach her privacy. This element related specifically to the patient's experience of having observed the primal scene on two occasions.

As in the structure of the hysterical symptom, so in the structure of this dream, the central figure, the patient in the act of defecating, may be acting out symbolically both the maternal and paternal roles, depending upon how the patient reacted to the experience of witnessing parental intercourse. The mood of the dream, furthermore, is related to the feeling originally experienced by the patient or when subsequently working it through in his recollection of the events. The mood consciously experienced in the dream may also reflect a repetition of how the intruder was greeted by the parents on the original occasion. This latter element was particularly prominent in those situations where the wish for repetition of the experience was heavily weighted with the desire to avenge oneself on the disappointing parent. A subsidiary motive of the dream, therefore, becomes, "I wish you to feel what I felt when I saw what was going on," or "I wish you to feel the way you made me feel when I saw what was going on." This mood was particularly prominent in the dreams of one patient who observed his mother in the act of intercourse with another man while the father was away on a trip. In the manifest structure of his dream of being interrupted during the act of defecation the intruder was, with rare exception, a woman.

In the analysis of this typical dream, an element could be observed symbolizing the idea of awakening. Several of the patients dreamed that they got out of a train and then went to the bathroom, etc. The element of getting out of a train ultimately corresponded with the idea of awakening from sleep. In this respect this represents one of the so-called "transitional" symbols, representing a passage from wakefulness to sleep or vice versa. The representation of leaving a train as indicating leaving sleep would serve to confirm Lewin's (1950) idea about the identity of being asleep with being with or inside the mother.

Since these observations were first made, I have been able to confirm from many dreams presented by patients, and by patients of students in supervision, the existence of a regular connection between the manifest content of this type of "disturbed bathroom privacy" dream with a latent vengeful wish associated with primal-scene experiences.

Chapter 14

INTERPRETATION OF A TYPICAL AND STEREOTYPED DREAM MET WITH ONLY DURING PSYCHOANALYSIS

SANDOR S. FELDMAN

According to Freud we consider a dream "typical" if it occurs in many persons with little variation, and "stereotyped if it recurs many times in the same person.

To the writer's knowledge no atention has been paid to a typical and stereotyped dream which appears only during analysis and is related to it. The emotional accompaniment of the dream is a feeling of resentment expressed in the complaint that the analytic session is disturbed by others in the office or in adjoining rooms whose presence robs the patient of the privacy to which he is entitled. In some cases associations are obtained, but in most instances this is so only when the analysis is far advanced and a great deal of resistance has been removed. Its interpretation, as that of all typical and stereotyped dreams, opens the way to the deepest and most strongly repressed wishes of the patient. A remarkably swift flow of associations often ensues after interpretation has been given, and the relief felt by the patient because a resistance has been overcome is immediately noticeable. The writer has observed this kind of dream in many patients and assumes that other analysts have had the same experience.

The variations of this typical and stereotyped dream are as follows:

First Variation. While the patient is lying on the couch in the office, the analytic session is disturbed by the presence, or

This paper was first published in the *Psychoanalytic Quarterly* (1945), 14:511–515.

movement in and out, of the analyst's wife or some other member of his family. It is the dreamer's feeling that he cannot talk freely, that he cannot tell everything as it comes to his mind.

A male patient who had such a dream in the advanced stage of his analysis immediately associated with it the fact that one or two days before, while in the office, he had heard the voice of the analyst's daughter, who was telephoning two rooms away. Then for the first time, though he had had plenty of opportunity to express it before, he talked freely about the favorable impression that she had made on him. After this he was better able to relive his sexual desire for his mother and sister. The latent dream content referred to the transference situation, and through this to the incestuous love objects. The dream expressed his resistance and his disturbance and resentment at having to bring these repressed wishes to consciousness. He recalled that he had been resentful at the disturbance of his privacy when he heard the voice of the analyst's daughter. On the other hand, it transpired that not he, but the analyst, is deprived of privacy: the patient has now become interested in the analyst's daughter and wants to peep into the analyst's rooms. The whole situation is obviously an exact replica of his childhood situation.

It will not surprise us that a deeper layer contains an even more important wish. The patient's main trouble was that he dreaded any kind of human relationship, even on a superficial level, with men or women. He was impotent and had never had sexual relations. He was once called "an Eskimo" by a girl because of his cold, unaffectionate attitude. He complained that for him a relation with another human being was impossible because he was afraid that sooner or later he would disappoint that person. What he would have liked was the impossible: "an absolute relation," a perfect fusion, a relation in which no disagreement, difference of opinion, or disappointment is possible. In a word, what he wanted was a perfect, unbounded fusion with another person, like the fusion of two amebas. He himself said that such a relation is approximated in intrauterine life. He then admitted that his relation to the analyst in the analysis gratified somewhat this desire, and that the only thing he feared in being cured was that he would lose this "fusion" with the analyst.

All of this represented a marked gain in insight. Previously he had often claimed that he had no feeling at all for his analyst, that he came, paid, and left—a purely business relationship, nothing more. Thus in the deeper latent content of the dream the patient complains that his perfect relationship to the analyst as to a mother is being disturbed by his sexual desire for the analyst's daughter, who again represents his mother (analyst). Until late in his childhood his long widowed mother had shown great affection for him, as had his sister. He completely severed his relations with the family because of his fear that contact with them would revive forbidden desires and castration fear. In so doing he was attempting, at least in fantasy, to preserve his primary desire, that of being in perfect fusion with his mother in a relationship without danger, especially that of castration. This castration threat caused him to regress to a kind of mother–child relationship which was impossible in reality, but which could be satisfied in his fantasies. Thus the deep-seated latent dream content expresses his desire that the perfect fusion with the mother–analyst be not disturbed.

Second Variation. In the second variation of this typical and stereotyped dream, instead of the analyst's relatives, those of the patient are present. The feeling is the same: there is no privacy and one cannot talk freely because of the presence of the patient's mother, sister, etc. During the past fifteen years the writer has heard of a great number of such dreams and has come to the conclusion that they express a resistance against the emergence of persistent strong desires for the persons in the dream. The associations prior to the dream, or those following the interpretation of the dream, reveal two latent dream thoughts. One is "I cannot talk freely in the analytic session because if I did, I would have to talk about my forbidden desires, and it disturbs me that such desires invade my mind." The second is "it disturbs me that I have such desires and I feel inclined to transfer the same feelings to the analyst."

Third Variation. In the third variation of this dream strangers are disturbing factors. Strangers are in the waiting room or office during the patient's analytic hour, or they bar the way, making it impossible for him to get in. For example, a male patient:

> I am coming to analysis and when I enter the waiting room I am disturbed by a couple, husband and wife. You prefer them, inviting the husband into the office to analyze him, and I am left with the wife in the waiting room. I take the other patient's wife for a walk and make amorous advances toward her. On returning to the waiting room, soon after the end of the husband's analytic session, both you and the husband come out. I feel that you resent my advances toward the woman and that you think I have encroached on your territory.

There are two outstanding thoughts in this dream. One is that strangers are preferred to the patient, and the other is that the analyst resents the patient's encroachment on the analyst's territory. The patient is in reality much concerned lest someone get ahead of him. He wants to outshine everybody, he covets the woman who belongs to the other man, and wants to take her away from him. Furthermore, he is afraid to assert himself for fear that others might resent it. The latent dream content expresses his concern lest he reveal that it is he who would disturb the privacy of the analyst, as he has wanted since early childhood to disturb the privacy of the parents. This has been the principal motive of the dreamer since he became entangled in the Oedipus situation. The strangers, as Freud advises us, represent the opposite, that is, the close ones, the relatives, and in the dreamer's case, the mother.

Fourth Variation. In the fourth variation the dreamer is disturbed by the presence of *two* analysts. In the manifest dream content one analyst usually plays a mute role, sometimes as the assistant of the other. The latent dream content refers to the transference situation, and through this to a deeper latent dream content which is usually also the core of the neurosis. The writer would like to emphasize the fact that in the present paper a specific type of transference situation is described, a transference which is characteristic of those patients who produce the typical and stereotyped dream discussed. The latent wish expresses the patient's protest at being analyzed. He wants the analyst to be his mother, to love him and not to analyze him. He wants to cling to the analyst as to a mother. In his fantasy he knows *two* analysts, one who analyzes him and one who loves him. But the second one is mute and does not express his love.

Fifth Variation. This same latent dream thought is the instigator of the fifth variation of the dream in which another analyst is substituted for the real one. The new analyst may be either a male or a female. The patient is frustrated by merely being analyzed; he therefore wishes another analyst to do the work and the real one to love him, or he would rather the analyst be a female in the hope that she will love him as a mother.

Sixth Variation. Finally, in the sixth variation of the dream, the analyst is the same but the office is somewhere else, or the furniture is somewhat different, or the couch is in another location. This expresses the patient's desire *to change the situation*, to change his relation to the analyst, to reestablish and relive the deeply craved for mother–child relationship in which he has no fears, no frustrations, no hardships, only protection and love. This is what he wants in the analysis from the analyst, and because he is frustrated he resists and his resistance appears in the dream.

The writer hopes that further contributions by other analysts to the interpretation of this type of dream will deepen our understanding of it.

Chapter 15

THE ANALYSIS OF A DREAM OCCURRING DURING A MIGRAINE ATTACK

SIDNEY TARACHOW

The object of this communication is to discuss a dream which occurred during a migraine attack in a psychoneurotic. The psychosomatic correlations adduced will be considered in the light of certain ideas advanced in previous clinical and theoretical studies (Selinsky, 1939; Bieber and Tarachow, 1941).

The patient was a twenty-five-year-old professional student who had been having migraine attacks since the age of twelve. They occurred about once weekly, were hemicranial, and were accompanied by nausea, photophobia, and an accentuation of the pain on shaking of the head. He came for treatment of an obsessional neurosis, some of the symptoms of which were obsessive fantasies of hostility to his parents and to others. With analysis there was improvement in the neurosis, and at the point of this writing the migraine attacks were occurring about once a month.

The patient had started a course of instruction in a certain subject. The instructor, on learning his name, inquired whether he was related to another individual with a similar surname. He replied they were brothers. During the course of the afternoon he was asked several questions the answers to which were breezily ridiculed by the instructor. After returning home he checked his answers and found that he was correct and his instructor incorrect. Although the questions involved only minor matters and although he knew the instructor had behaved

---

This paper was first published in the *Psychoanalytic Review* (1946), 33:335–340.

naturally in his usual manner, with great confidence and without malice, nevertheless he felt extremely hostile to him. Several days later he was again in session with the same instructor. This session was long and drawn out. During the latter part he developed a migraine headache which lasted the rest of the night. He made several bonehead remarks during the conference.

That night he had the following dream. In it he was entrusted with a collection of phonograph records by a sergeant. It included a lovely Haydn Symphony which he stole. Later in the dream he was walking at night around the Psychology Building at the University of Iowa and saw soldiers training with wooden guns. He decided to enter the building lest he be made to drill also; he had the feeling of being AWOL. In the basement of the building were the nurses' quarters. He went into the hall and saw an attractive nurse in a nightgown who told him half banteringly and half seriously that she thought he had better leave. He followed her around the corner and bumped into another nurse waiting for the elevator. He knew her somewhat and they exchanged lascivious smiles. He went to the head nurse's room where there was a small foot organ and started to fool around. The head nurse came in and told him he'd better leave or else she'd tell her husband: all this time she was slowly undressing. She also said that ordinarily she might like to hear him play, but not now. He said, "Nonsense, it's a rotten organ being played by a rotten player." He then saw her bare her breasts, which had long, black, conical nipples with red striations and the outline of small buttocks resembling his father's. He then left smilingly and went to the elevator where he met Miss W., done up archaically for bedtime, chin-strap and all. They said hello to one another and she remarked that he looked happy and well: he replied that he was filled with ennui and felt confined and that he would love to hit someone, anything for excitement. Shortly after she left he met a young man with whom he was friendly. The friend said the same thing and the patient told him he felt like a staphylococcus in the geometric center at the bottom of a large colony of the same. The friend laughed and the patient stepped into the elevator. As he was awakening but stuporous, he thought he could use this simile in a novel and have the hero say, "Oh Lord, Doc, cure me with penicillin." Still earlier that night he dreamt he bumped into an old flame from high school and was frightened. She was very pleasant in her talk and he looked covertly to see whether her breasts had enlarged. He had a faint recollection of putting his head on her feet.

The sergeant was at once associated with his brother, father, and physician. The phonograph records represented sexual potency or some sort of potent weapon. Actually he was a fanatical record collector, and his collection was put to fiercely competitive uses. The gift of the Haydn Symphony (in the associations of the dream theft was treated as a gift) represented a loan of sexual potency plus permission to use it. His brother and the physician were the only conceivable sources to him of sexual weapons and sexual permission. The only way to be potent was to ape his brother, and he dared not have intercourse without his brother's consent. The Psychology Building represented the physician's lair, his sexual territory. The first associations to soldiers with wooden guns were of fiercely competitive males with stout phalluses, but the physician's suggestion, that they probably represented males castrated for having the temerity to poach on the physician's preserves, was more convincing. His feeling of being AWOL was thus understandable as a desire to join them, chastise himself beforehand to reduce the tension of waiting for the physician to do it, and to appear to the latter as a debased object unworthy of any reprisals on his part, in short, a masochistic desire.

The nurses, especially the head nurse, were symbols of his mother, the playing of the organ sexual advances. The head nurse's refusal to accept him was typical of his perception of his mother's character. The remarks he made to her paraphrased by the patient as, "My penis is a small penis and I am an incompetent lover" further indicate the masochism. This maneuver was necessary for him not only as a means of appeasing the hostility of his mother-image but as a frantic measure to communicate his insignificance to his father–brother amalgam. They revealed their presence in the dream by the adulteration of his mother's image with their characteristics. Subsequent associations indicated that the buttocks of the head nurse resembled his father's and led to a recollection of a time during a childhood illness when he was revolted by his father's trying to warm him by pressing their naked bodies together.

The rest of the dream represented a self-pitying protest over his defeat and maltreatment. The fragment of the dream about an old flame indicated a similar theme. He meets a mother-image and is frightened. However, she soothes him with pleasant talk and quiets his fears. The girl, in actual life, had no discernible breasts. The fact that she was a female, was the opposite of the image of his mother, and was therefore theoretically unattractive to other males, specifically her brother, made her an ideal sexual companion. Incidentally, the patient's wife represented a compromise between traits which suggested his mother and other traits which denied the incestuous character of the relationship. With this old girl friend in the dream he could have the pleasures of sex without its hazards. This was the reason for the dream anxiety about whether her breasts had enlarged: if they had she would have qualified as a mother-image and led to a sense of defeat at the hands of his brother and father. To be content with a girl shorn of his mother's characteristics was a defeat he accepted: there was a dim recollection of putting his head on her feet.

The dream represented a defeated and masochistic solution of all his competitive feelings with his instructor in the real situation and with his father, brother and physician in the neurotic elaboration of the conflict. The conflict was, of course, stimulated by the classroom competition with the instructor, and was heightened by several accidental factors. One was that the instructor knew the patient's brother, thus additionally facilitating the identification of the instructor with the brother; the other was that the instructor had as a technician an attractive woman of thirty-five, an ideal mother-image for the patient. This was again a fantasied recapitulation of the family constellation. Another contributing factor was, that on the day of the headache, the patient was expected for dinner at the home of his brother.

All these factors stimulated his hostility and rivalry with the instructor and with the unconscious fusion of the father–brother–physician image in its further relations to a series of images representing his mother. The dream indicated that all these tensions found a masochistic, defeated solution; his potency was only borrowed or stolen; he really belonged with other castrated males; the mother–nurse figure was rejecting him; his sexuality was disparaged; he was pictured at the bottom of a colony of bacteria; he was reconciled to a girl shorn of the attributes suggesting his mother. In other words there was a massive defeat and inhibition of his sexual and competitive tensions. It was in this state of massive inhibition that the migraine headache appeared, and during the headache that the patient had the dream under discussion.

The headache (cerebral vasodilatation) is an aspect of somatic inhibition which appeared with the psychic inhibition. This vasodilatation is the somatic fragment of the inhibited posture of the neurotic patient. Instead of mobilizing a posture of aggressiveness he was capable only of a bit of vasodilatation. The psychosomatic symptom, in short, served in a fragmentary way as an imaginary adaptation of paralysis rather than the acceptance of an aggressive facing of the neurotic hazards of competition and sexuality. The reader is referred to Case 2, described in the study by Bieber and Tarachow (1941), in which, as a specific accompaniment to inhibition of impulses, there was a syndrome of headache, clouded thinking, and, most interestingly, conjuctival vasodilatation.

In the two earlier studies material was adduced to indicate that, when there is interference with the normal resolution of impulse tensions, one of two pathological results may occur. If the neurotic interferences with the act are overwhelming, there is collapse or inhibition of tension, and this inhibition finds representation somewhere in the body. If there is interference, but not utter defeat, there is anxiety and an overmobilized somatic state. Wolf and Wolff (1943) made a similar correlation in their subject with a gastrostomy. On the basis of the already reported material and additional, as yet unreported, material the author distinguishes syndromes of overmobilization and syndromes of inhibition as psychosomatic phenomena indicative of an attitude toward an impulse. Many investigators have reported certain specific personality types and specific psychological constellations in relation to various psychosomatic syndromes. The evidence which has come to our hand indicates a different order of correlation, not to specific ego or neurotic structures, but rather to the attitude toward action at a given moment of neurotic stress. If the action is free there are no psychosomatic symptoms: if there is neurotic interference the tension will take one of the two indicated pathological directions. Selinsky (1939), though postulating a certain psychological type related to migraine, came to the conclusion that "the need to repress such (i.e., aggressive) impulses repeatedly brings about a state of conditioned inhibited response and this provokes a migrainous attack, i.e., a retreat." Selinsky seems to consider the migraine "retreat" in symbolic rather than physiological terms and neglects to discuss at any length the vasodilatory aspect of the migraine attack. This author's emphasis would be on the somatic evidence of the collapse of tension, which in the migrainous instance, presents itself in the cerebral vessels.

The purpose of this paper is to present the correlation between the cerebral vasodilatation (migraine) and the inhibition (collapse) of the tension of an impulse in a neurotic patient. The author has also observed the appearance of migraine headaches in some patients after the abrupt cessation of states of high tension or after the sudden termination of tense activity. In certain patients migraine characteristically appears during relaxation and often abruptly after, and not during, a period of high tension. In the author's experience, migraine is a disease of relaxation, inhibition, or collapse of tension, and not a disease of high tension.

Summary

The analysis of a dream which occurred during a migraine attack is presented. The dream indicated a massive inhibition of various tensions. This was correlated with the somatic fragment of inhibition of tension in the shape of cerebral vasodilatation (migraine). Other observations were mentioned of migraine occurring after tension states had collapsed and during relaxation. These data were adduced as further evidence to substantiate the theory that psychosomatic phenomena fall either into the syndrome of overmobilization or the syndrome of inhibition depending on whether the neurotic interferences stimulate a hyperactive attitude or lead to an attitude of total defeat.

Chapter 16

A TRAUMATIC DREAM

Harold L. Levitan

This brief case report describes the unusual occurrence of a shocking event which was succeeded by an equally shocking dream. It shows that the dreamer was as unprepared for the denouement in her dream as she had been for the tragic occurrence earlier the same day. In the dream or series of dreams that follow a severe and sudden trauma, as we know from our experience with the traumatic neuroses, the same or analogous events are ordinarily presented with the accompaniment of anxiety so that the dreamer is not surprised a second time. The failure of this mechanism throws some light on the defensive processes in dreams.

The patient, a forty-five-year-old woman, was informed of her husband's death in the following manner: while upstairs in her bedroom she heard her brother-in-law call to her from the downstairs hall. She went to greet him quite unconcernedly even though it was unusual for him to visit in the middle of the day. When she reached the bottom step he took her in his arms and blurted out the awful news that her husband had suddenly died one half hour before. She experienced a sense of great shock, a sharp sinking feeling in the abdomen, and seemed on the verge of fainting but did not lose consciousness. For the rest of the day she was not so much sad as groggy and in a fog.

Toward morning she dreamed.

She was wandering about the first floor of her house when she encountered her mother. She asked her, "Where is

This paper was first published in the *Psychoanalytic Quarterly* (1965), 34:265–267.

my husband?" Her mother rather casually replied, "He is upstairs in the kitchen." Thereupon she climbed the stairs with the full and happy expectation of seeing her husband at the top, but just as she reached the top step and was about to greet him a blinding flash of light occurred which lasted a split second.

Next she knew that she was awake and crying.

Before the denouement the dream is filled with reversals and substitutions of the real situation in the service of wish-fulfillment. For example, her mother is substituted for her brother-in-law as the bearer of the message, and she states that the husband is upstairs and alive rather than dead. Also the dreamer is asking a question rather than being told the upsetting news. However, although the patient has reported no visual reaction in reality, the moment of denouement in the dream which (as in reality) was the moment of her becoming aware, is unmistakably marked by a visual impression.

A flash of light that takes the dreamer by surprise and blots out all images seemed to me very unusual and on further research I could not find reference to it in the literature. There are, however, some reports in which rather mild phenomena of light are incorporated into the manifest content of the dream (Abraham, 1913a; Greenacre, 1947). But in these instances the light had been subject to the dream work and had therefore a different origin. Indeed, strictly speaking the flashing light in this case is not part of the dream. It is rather a component of the shock consequent to her sudden awareness of loss. The phenomenon of visual shock or "seeing stars" is, of course, well known in waking life. Ernst Kris (1950b) and Phyllis Greenacre (1947) have suggested that the edging of light possessed by certain screen memories is a displacement from the light effect of the visual shock that precedes by an instant the formation of the screen memory. It is not unlikely, as both Paul Schilder (1942) and Max Stern (1961) have pointed out, that so-called primary hallucinations which include flashes of light are mediated not through the visual organ directly but through an acute disturbance to the vestibular system which in turn affects the

other sensory systems. Possibly too the near loss of consciousness at the moment of trauma is another effect of sudden
changes in the vestibular system.

The reworking of traumatic experience by the screen
memory by definition precludes the possibility of a renewal in
full of the realization of the traumatic events. In the nightmares
of the traumatic neurosis and in the nightmare generally the
intense anxiety due to the dreadful content causes the dreamer
to awaken before the denouement. Any consideration of the
reasons for the failure of the protective and alerting mechanisms in this instance must include the extensive denial which
was a prominent feature of the patient's personality, but which
was significantly facilitated and altered by the state of sleep.
The denial in the patient's waking state was very important in
the handling of the trauma from the moment of its occurrence.
As noted earlier, she was, throughout the rest of the day, in a
fog so that she did not apprehend the significance of what
had happened. Thomas French (1937) has stressed the pain-
absorbing powers of sleep and its corollary, the increased reality
orientation of the latent thoughts as sleep lightens. The combination of these two factors may shift the balance from a state
of extensive denial into an abrupt and traumatic awareness of
reality. First, because of the lulling of the denial mechanism by
sleep, the patient was able to gain more awareness of her situation during the early part of her dream than had been possible
during her foggy state in daytime. This faint awareness was
shown by her questioning of her mother as to the whereabouts
of her husband. Thereafter, however, in spite of this faint
awareness the denial was still so broad that no manifest anxiety
could develop. Thus she persisted in thinking of her husband
as alive until too late; whereupon she was once again overcome
by the trauma of her real situation. The negative hallucination
which was the unawareness of the shock of her husband's death
could not be maintained as reality testing increased concomitantly with the lightening of sleep. Freud (1940) has stressed
the two levels of awareness that exist in states of denial. As
shown very clearly here, these two levels in dreams may be

described as simultaneous states of positive and negative hallucination which are maintained in dynamic tension under conditions of delicate balance; this balance may, however, under certain circumstances be abruptly upset.

Summary

Full experience of trauma rarely occurs in dreams. This paper presents an instance of miscarriage of the defensive process in a dream which allowed reexperiencing of the traumatic state as manifested by a flashing light during sleep. Some of the reasons for this failure, with special reference to alterations in the process of denial during sleep, are discussed.

Chapter 17

DREAMS DURING SURGICAL PROCEDURES

GEORGE H. POLLOCK AND HYMAN L. MUSLIN

A state of psychological trauma originates when an ego is over-whelmed by events and cannot deal adequately with reality. The study of such a state can provide much information about the degree of preparedness for the traumatic event, about the effect of the trauma, and about the subsequent restitutive devices used to reestablish a state of equilibrium.

An important field for such a study is the dream life of the traumatized. The dream is a technique the ego uses, actually or potentially, to deal with dangerous situations that arise during sleep. Using the residual thoughts of the previous day, the dream work recathects repressed conflicts and expresses them in camouflage in the manifest dream text. If the dream fails to bind anxiety, the sleeper may awaken and call upon waking defenses to attain this end.

With the artificially maintained continuous sleep of anesthesia, waking up cannot be used as a safety valve; the ego must rely on other emergency devices. Our study deals with this matter. Two patients, one in psychoanalysis, the other in psychotherapy, furnished us with dreams that occurred during surgical procedures. A subsequent analysis of the dreams revealed the unconscious meaning of the surgical intervention and the ego's defensive and adaptive activities that were mobilized by the traumatic events. To test a number of hypotheses that suggested themselves concerning the ego's function during such dreams, we undertook a preliminary investigation. In this

This paper was first published in the *Psychoanalytic Quarterly* (1962), 31:175–202.

report, we shall first present the pertinent psychoanalytic data that gave rise to tentative hypotheses; second, our further investigations and preliminary results, and finally, a delineation of the limitations of our study and suggestions as to areas for future research.

Data

The first patient, a man in his midthirties, had an atrophic testicle, the result of an unsuccessful operation for the repair of a unilateral cryptorchidism at the age of eight. As he matured his other healthy testicle hypertrophied and, contrary to his fearful anticipations, he sired several healthy children. Near the end of his analytic treatment, in its fourth year, he decided to have the atrophic testicle removed, in accord with reality, for his physician had informed him that the nonfunctioning gland might possibly undergo malignant degeneration. Previously similar advice had met with much resistance and anxiety on the part of the patient. When he decided on the operation, he was influenced by the fact that he was still in analysis where he thought whatever feelings that arose could be understood and clarified. The remedy of his defect, which had persisted since childhood, he regarded as a necessary outcome of his analysis. Before the operation he discussed his anxieties quite openly and, since the operation did not entail extensive hospitalization, he resumed his analytic hours the day after.

In his first postoperative analytic hour he reported the following dream which occurred under anesthesia while the testicle was being removed.

> I was engaged in a struggle, a tug of war with an older man. He pulled the rope one way. I tried to pull it the other. It was near a body of water. I was very frightened that I would lose. I suddenly awoke and heard the surgeon say "give him more." I was asleep again and dreamt of a large wrecking ball that was so powerful and strong. It swung from an overhead crane and spectators looked at it admiringly.

His spontaneous associations were to the surgeon who had told him that he awakened from the inhalation anesthesia just as the surgeon was pulling on the spermatic cord. The atophied testicle had been fixed in the scrotum only partially and required manipulation to free it for excision. This apparently caused the patient to awaken. The surgeon had in fact said, "give him more" to the anesthetist. The second dream, of the wrecking ball, occurred when the atrophied testicle was being severed and removed. The patient next recalled that when in the Navy during the war, he had been almost swept overboard but had been saved by a lifeline thrown to him. He associated the surgeon to his father, a physician, whose office had always been for him a fearsome place. Laughing, he recalled the many times he had misidentified the analyst and viewed him as the threatening physician–father. This time, however, the analyst was realistically differentiated as a helping person rather than as a mutilator, nor did the patient really feel that the surgeon was a mutilator. Indeed, he was a considerate person who spared the patient unnecessary pain and was technically very skillful. The patient's accurate appraisal was confirmed by his uneventful and rapid recovery. Despite this judgment, and the realistic preparation, he related the first dream to castration anxiety. The patient thought the rope referred to his "trugged" spermatic cord. His association to the body of water was the dangerous experience in the Navy. He also connected it with urinary activity.

The second dream, which occurred during or after the excision, was associated to a comment the surgeon made when he first examined the patient; he compared the patient's functioning testicle to that of a large bull, explaining that it had enlarged to compensate for the atrophy of the other testis. At that time the patient fantasied himself as a snorting bull, charging about. He summarized the second dream as embarrassment at the nurses seeing him castrated and a wish to have them admire his big, healthy testis.

Several points are clear about these two dreams. The "tug of war" corresponds to the manipulation of the testis and cord before amputation. It is portrayed as a struggle with an older man and associated with a previous real, threatening situation.

The dream that occurred when the testicle was being removed no longer manifestly presents struggle as the important action; the major theme is reassurance and overcompensation. At no time was the patient concerned about malignancy in the testicle and the subsequent histological study showed no such pathological alterations.

The second patient, a married woman in her midforties, had been in psychotherapy for a long time. She had a strong defensive masculine identification with markedly aggressive characteristics. She had always been close to her father who had wished very much for a son. Her masculine identification had drawn her close to her father, without anxiety about the oedipal triumph over her mother. Her husband was a passive man who allowed her to assume a parental attitude and to dominate the family economics. The patient had borne several healthy children and seemed a devoted mother. It was obvious, though the patient was not conscious of it, that not only had she reversed the masculine–feminine role with her husband, but she had transferred attitudes and feelings from her own parents onto her several children.

While in psychotherapy, she began to bleed excessively and irregularly from her vagina. At first she denied any significance other than as heralding her menopause which, since she had resented the menses, she seemed to welcome. Her denial was interpreted to her on several occasions in order to persuade her to be examined medically. When finally she consulted a gynecologist, he found a fibroid uterus and recommended hysterectomy, though he told her that, despite her anemia, there was no need to be concerned about malignancy.

The patient agreed to the operation and spoke freely of the procedure. Her attitude toward surgery was counterphobic, concealing her anxiety about the operation and what it represented. Although she had three children, she expressed regrets about not having a larger family. However, the prospect of not menstruating was anticipated with somewhat pleasant relief. Her sexual behavior was an adaptation rather than a sought-for activity. She had no orgasm and was content that her husband felt gratified.

A simple vaginal hysterectomy was performed under inhalation anesthesia and her postoperative course was without complications. Several weeks after leaving the hospital she expressed her relief at not bleeding constantly and was satisfied with the surgical result. In speaking of the operation, she related spontaneously a dream she had while anesthetized during the hysterectomy. It was so "pleasantly vivid" that she made an effort to remember it. "In the dream she was a little girl playing in a large green field of brightly colored and sweet-smelling flowers. She romped and played and was very happy. In the distance she thought a contented cow was lazing in the sun and grass."

She thought this dream an unusual one for someone undergoing surgery. Asked about the setting of the dream, she remembered vaguely a pastoral scene in her childhood. She had always liked bright colors, flowers, and perfume, although she had rarely had occasion to use them. She wondered if the smell referred to the anesthesia: "It was sweet-smelling and not unpleasant." After this comment she laughed and said that perhaps the dream allowed her to be in a place and time doing things actively, which was more satisfying than lying on an operating table and having her womb removed. The somewhat euphoric tone to her account of the dream, her associations to it and to the whole operative procedure, illustrate her main defensive attempts at handling this very trying event. A depression which was masked by her defensive euphoric attitude emerged a few months postoperatively.

In this dream the manifest affect is that of satisfaction, play, and delight. The dream setting, her self-image, and activity in the dream seem to indicate regression in time, space, and activity. The only direct reference to the surgery was her associating the smell of the flowers with the anesthetic. She had often thought her mother was a "contented cow" and, on many occasions, had referred to her as "Pet Milk," remembering from her youth that the label of this milk had a cow's head on it. She did not, however, make this association to the cow in the dream.

In the above two clinical instances, dreams reported during psychoanalysis and psychotherapy and dreamed during surgical operations seemed to indicate different modes of adaptation to a real, current, traumatic procedure. An exploratory investigation was undertaken. Dr. Muslin was not informed of the findings in the above two cases. His prime responsibility initially was the collaborative planning of the procedures for and actual collection of data. After the investigation was completed, the results obtained, and the conclusions drawn, he was informed of the above clinical material. This approach was intended to minimize, if possible, any bias in the results obtained.

Investigations and Results

To study dreams with a definite traumatic precipitant, where sleep was artificially maintained, the authors used dreams of patients under anesthesia and subjected to various surgical procedures. The patients were admitted to the hospital for indicated surgery. In all instances the surgical procedure was elective and, in all but two, the patients were told that their conditions were nonmalignant. No psychiatric consultation had been requested before surgery. No complications were encountered in the anesthesia or surgical procedures.

The procedure followed with all patients consisted of an interview several days before surgery in order to establish a rapport as well as to obtain brief anamnestic information. Immediately after surgery and as soon as communication could be established, Dr. Muslin went to the recovery room to interview the patient. The dreams were obtained at this time and special emphasis was placed on those that occurred during the surgical procedure. In some instances the patient was seen several days postoperatively in order to learn about the recovery phase and to gather any dreams he might have to tell. Before surgery no specific suggestions were made to the patients about dreams.

The author wished to test the hypothesis that the adaptive ego would attempt to establish a state of equilibrium when the organism was under severe stress in a situation such as surgery. Dreams that occurred during the operative and immediate recovery period would presumably show indications of such ego adaptation. They also hoped that, by collecting and comparing dreams of adult patients, both male and female, undergoing elective surgery that involved meaningful body areas, results could be obtained that would allow them to formulate more precise hypotheses for future testing.

During the phase of data collection, Dr. Muslin was the only psychiatrist in contact with the patients. Since the patients had only a brief relationship with him, limited to one or two contacts before the operation, we cannot state the nature of the presurgical transference reactions. In general, a patient undergoing a surgical procedure welcomes the interest and attention of a member of the hospital staff and we assume there was a supportive aspect in the brief encounter. In all, thirty-eight patients were interviewed before and after surgery. Of these, eighteen reported dreams which they said occurred during the surgical procedure, which we defined as the period of anesthesia induction, surgical operation, and reawakening. The dreams reported cannot be localized in time; some may be from the period of actual surgery, others from the time the patient was awakening from the anesthesia. This assumption, however, is untested, and in the future we shall test the effect on dream formation of anesthesia without the threat of surgery.

Since we knew the dream stimulus in general to be the threat of psychic and physical integrity posed by anesthesia and surgery, we felt justified in expecting that the manifest content of the dream would reveal the main defenses and the conflict, if this was not too threatening, and give indications of the level and type of object relations. It would contain, we thought, representations of the body-part image that were involved surgically; and if there were a series of dreams, these might indicate shifts in the adaptive capacities of the ego.

The dreams and associations of patients having similar procedures will be presented exactly as stated by the patients. A brief discussion of the authors' inferences will follow with references to the works of other investigators studying the particular areas in discussion.

Dental Extractions

The anesthetic used was sodium pentothal given intravenously. The operations were dental extractions, in all instances performed by male dentists.

1. Female, aged twenty-nine: "I was playing an old game, 1-2-3-4 O'Leary. Oh! 1-2-3-4 O'Leary."
2. Female, aged thirty: "I was playing checkers with my first husband. He jumped one of my checkers and took it, but I took all the rest of the checkers. It was a happy scene."
3. Female, aged thirty-four: "I was a little girl and I was running and playing in the country. It was very peaceful and wonderful."
4. Female, aged fifty-one: "It seemed like I was back home in Georgia. I was a young girl about ten years old, and I was playing with my sister, Amelia. We were laughing and happy."
5. Male, aged sixty-one: "I was fighting and arguing with a guy. He was holding me down and taking something away."

The discrepancy between the man's dream and those of the women is striking. In the dream he attempts active mastery; he fights and resists the forcible deprivation of a possession. At its core, this reflects presumably castration anxiety or other fears of bodily destruction. Manifestly, it refers to a struggle with the dentist over the extraction of teeth. The dream is strikingly similar to that of the male patient in the first section of this paper. The dreams of all four women emphasize the playing of games and resemble the dream of the woman noted earlier. This playing activity regressively referred to the past: the first patient repeats a childhood game; the third is a little girl running and playing in the country; the fourth is ten years old. In these three instances object and activity are temporally regressive. No reference is made to the actual dental procedure; the game setting denies the reality of this event. The second patient regresses in time, too; her first husband, she said, was a quiet man, with whom she always had her way. In the dream she outplays him and takes his checkers men after his "attack." Her victory shows an identification with the aggressor, the dentist, who "gets hers," but the aggression is in play, in a happy game. In this instance there are elements similar to those in the man's dream, permitting the inference of masculine competitive conflicts. In general, however, the dreams of the women, contrasted with those of the men, show little open conflict.

Federn (1944) reported a dream occurring during a dental extraction and noted in it both geographic and temporal displacements. The operation took place in New York, but Federn saw himself as a military commander and statesman in Europe who was "putting one province after the other in order." Federn's dream ends with "life was a glorious fight." There was fighting but no personal adversary, as in the dream of the fifth patient above. The identification with the aggressor, as noted for the second patient, is clear. The aggression is more discernible in Federn's dream and in the man's dream than in those of the women.

Lewis (1957), in an excellent paper on the unconscious castrative significance of tooth extraction, besides his own findings, gives a thorough review of the pertinent literature. The castration fears in the male are displaced upwards to the teeth. Reviewing female responses to dental extraction, Lewis points out ideas of castration reaction as well as the fear of being raped during surgical procedure. In our patients, the man's response indicates castration anxiety, but only in the second female patient can one infer phallic castrative competition with the male dentist. This does not preclude the castration conflict in the women; it only emphasizes that the dreaming ego handled the anxiety more regressively and less overtly.

Editha Sterba (1949) reported a three-year-old boy's reaction to tonsillectomy under anesthesia which illustrates very early castration anxiety in connection with a surgical procedure. The patient reported postoperatively: "I dreamed of a bad man who hit me on the cheeks so that my teeth fell out." Later, he said: "I dreamed that bad men did something to me. They wanted to cut off my nose and my pee-pee." There was, therefore, a displacement from tonsils to teeth, nose, and penis. This case illustrates the ego's attempt to bind anxiety about the tonsillectomy without utilizing regression. The problem appears solved by submission to a mutilation of external or visible body parts rather than to the less easily perceived and perhaps mysterious internal tonsils.

Mittelmann (1945) had an analytic patient who underwent painful dental surgery under nitrous oxide anesthesia. Her dreams reflected her concern over the loss of her faculties of perception and mastery. Because of her current transference neurosis, the analyst as well as the dentist was involved in the dreams. In one she dreamed that the dentist was making love to her and she awoke laughing—an obvious denial of painful reality and substitution of a pleasanter physical relationship with a man, which illustrates the ego's adaptive activity. Later dreams not under anesthesia and interpreted on the analytic couch showed that the dental surgery activated unconscious fantasies of genital damage.

Amputations

Both patients were men and the amputations were performed under inhalation anesthesia because of damage due to accidents.

1. Male, aged thirty. One digit of his right hand was amputated. He reported his dream as: "Oh boy, wow! Oh man, what a dream. I was in a hotel room with this beautiful blonde, and we were just going at it—intercourse—I had just got it in." He associated to the blonde with "real gorgeous—I don't recall anybody I ever knew like that. I didn't have anything in my mind like that. I don't know why I should dream that."
2. Male, aged twenty-seven. Two digits of his left hand were amputated. His reported dream was: "I was having intercourse with a girl I just met." He associated to the dream by saying, "This girl, she had black hair and was well-built. I guess she kinda looked like my ex-wife. We've been divorced since December 1956. I came back to the States from overseas then and found her running around on me, so I kicked her out. We got married in 1952. That's life I guess. You know, after Korea, I used to dream quite a bit. All the dreams were about me getting bayoneted or shot."

In both dreams sexual intercourse with an attractive woman is substituted for the traumatic reality. The sexual act replaces ideas of castration or body destruction. Both women were unknown which suggests a transference to the male surgeon. Instead of castration by a man, the dream portrays intercourse with an appealing woman. No ejaculation occurred in these dreams; the existence of the "appendage" was more important than the actual orgastic experience. There is no temporal regression in either dream; both patients function as adult males. The second patient, however, in his associations, points to an oedipal triangular conflict wherein he actively "kicks out" his unfaithful ex-wife, an "ex-object," and this regression is substantiated by additional spontaneous associations to earlier dreams. In these he was being bayoneted or shot, which reflected submission to an aggressive male, as in the actual surgical situation. This, however, is not present in the manifest dream text.

The action in the above two dreams is of the same order as the reassuring, overcompensating elements in the dream of the male patient whose testicle was removed, where the remaining testicle was viewed as a wrecking ball, a large, powerful object to be admired.

Other Surgical Procedures in Males

The following three male patients were operated on while under inhalation anesthesia.

> Male, fifty-three years old. Repair of a diaphragmatic hernia. His dream: "I was riding in a car with this guy. He was short, had gray hair, glasses, and stooped a little bit [an exact description of his surgeon]. He wanted the jacket I was wearing and he fought. He lopped my head off and he rolled a little bit on the car seat. We got out and fought some more and I got my head back on. Then I got into another fight with some other guys about my jacket." Associations: "Sure was a funny dream. The only thing I can put my finger on is a fight I once got into when I was a kid out East, with some toughs—that's the last fight I ever got

into. I was only eleven or twelve. That surgery wasn't tough at all. I was out of my head a lot, but when I got up and remembered this dream, I kept saying I've got to tell Dr. Muslin about it. You remember how nervous I was when the surgeon told me I had to have surgery. I kept thinking I might die."

This dream portrays the operation again as a fight between the patient and his nearly realistically described surgeon. The jacket that was in dispute covered the anatomical zone of the operation. The decapitation and its undoing indicate the ego's successful attempt to keep fighting despite mutilation. The associations were to an adolescent period when the patient had to fight as in examination dreams; he managed to reassure himself by appealing to his survival after an earlier ordeal. To this patient, presurgical contact with Dr. Muslin was more meaningful than "rapport establishment" since Dr. Muslin appears in the dream as a day residue. The emotional importance of understanding contacts with hospital personnel before surgery is well known. Apparently, they may serve as day residues that permit transferences from past reassuring figures to the current emergency. This patient denied conscious fear but his statement, "I was out of my head a lot," may indicate fear of ego disintegration which contributed to the dream content, the loss of his head.

Male, twenty-four years old. Hemorrhoidectomy under anesthesia. The dream: "There were two men fighting on a bridge. One of them was me. Suddenly the bridge collapsed and then everything seemed to go black. Then I said, 'This is silly,' and you were here." Associations: "The first thing that comes to mind is how frightened I am of heights. I remember the time I was with my grandfather and we were in the apartment where he used to live and I looked out of the window and I was frightened. I didn't want to jump. You know it is funny that the operation went so well. I don't have any fears at all. I was frightened beforehand. When do you think I'll be able to urinate with this catheter? That's the only thing that's bothering me

now. If I could only urinate I'd be okay. Is it possible for
me to have trouble for a long time?"

Actually he feared urinating even after he was discharged
from the hospital. Reassurance by the medical personnel, however, helped him overcome this evidently functional inhibition.
A fight is again the central scene of the manifest dream and
the patient's anxiety reached such a pitch that the bridge collapsed and everything blacked out—the ego's temporary failure
at the attempted anxiety binding task. The statement "this is
silly" immediately precedes awakening in the recovery room
and indicates a newer state of ego integration. The anxiety
about urination and subsequent actual difficulty point to the
displacement of anxiety from the hemorrhoidectomy to his ure-
thral function. The regressive conflict is alluded to in his associations to boyhood and his grandfather's apartment. The striking failure of the dream to solve the problem confronting the
ego is unique. If this patient's sleep had not been artificially
maintained, he might have awakened when the bridge collapsed. The "everything going black" seems to indicate a deeper
regression to the very early dream screen of Lewin (1953b), an
evidence of ego regression in the dream text itself.

> Male, forty-four years old, married two-and-one-half years.
> Circumcision for a congenital phimosis. He had resisted
> surgery, electing to bear the pain that was continuously
> present. His dream while anesthetized: "My wife came to
> me as I was lying down and said, 'C'mon, honey, let's go.'
> She was dressed very beautifully. I tried to get up and go
> but I couldn't because my left leg wouldn't move." Associa-
> tions: "I don't know why I should dream that. You see this
> thing [pointing to his penis] has been giving me trouble
> and I figured I better have this taken care of. Had this leg
> broken in '54. I don't know if it'll hold me back from get-
> ting a job. It bothers me sometimes."

A strong latent castration anxiety can be readily assumed
in this patient who, all his life, suffered from a mild, though
painful, impediment in the free use of his penis. His ego deals

with castration anxiety by cathecting a sexual wish to be seduced by his wife. The painful real situation in which his penis finds itself and the mobilized castration fear forces his ego to displace to his leg and to solve the conflict by yielding to it. The general passivity of his ego is indicated by the passive form in which the compensatory, reassuring sexual wish appears in the first place.

Nunberg (1949), in "Problems of Bisexuality as Reflected in Circumcision," described a patient who delayed surgery for some time and refused to sign the necessary operation permission forms. "He maintained that, rendered unconscious by the anesthetic, he would have no control over the surgeon who might then cut more than necessary." In the patient we describe, circumcision was also delayed for a long time even though it was indicated. In the dream, the castrative aspect of the procedure is clearly alluded to despite the displacement. In reality this patient could not use his freshly circumcised genital at the time of surgery, so that temporary incapacity was understandable. The anxiety about future malfunctioning, however, comes to light in the associations. The delaying of surgery by this patient and by Nunberg's resembles that seen in the patient described in the first section above.

Hysterectomy

In all but two of these patients the surgery was an elective procedure and there was no indication of malignancy. Unless indicated, the actual surgical procedure was that of a total abdominal hysterectomy under general inhalation anesthesia.

> A twenty-two-year-old unmarried woman, with a six-year-old son, who lived with her parents. The night before surgery she was very apprehensive about dying and wished to have her mother with her. The dream reported after surgery: "I heard a voice saying, 'That's what you get for keeping your big mouth open.' Then I remember seeing a clear picture of someone with a huge mouth and big shiny teeth. I saw myself as a very small person, going into that big mouth."

The patient associated to this dream only her fear before the operation and how much she wanted her mother there. In the past she had acted out a good deal sexually in defiance of her mother's strict disciplinary standards and methods. Her anxieties postoperatively dealt with being unable to please a man in future sexual relations. This dream conceives of the surgery as a punishment for defying her mother. Her representation of herself as a very small person going into a huge mouth with big teeth speaks for a regression to primitive oral sadistic anxiety, but it may also indicate regression to an early ego state where mother was correspondingly large. The wish to be with mother as her little girl also avoids anxiety about her procreative apparatus. Her anxiety about future sexual intercourse is the only allusion to the surgical procedure.

> A twenty-seven-year-old married woman who had two children, aged three and one-and-a-half years. Her mother died of carcinoma of the uterus when the patient was three years old and she went to live with her grandmother. When the patient was seven, her grandmother, while running after the patient, was hit by a truck and killed. Thereafter, she lived with her father. The father never married because of the patient's horror of a stepmother. The patient married her three-year-younger husband when she was eighteen. Her father died when she was twenty-three and this upset her greatly. She became pregnant immediately after his death. The replacement of the lost object as a motivation for this pregnancy seemed quite clear. The anniversary aspect of the patient's association of her uterine difficulties when her child is three with mother's death of carcinoma when she was three was suggested though not consciously verbalized by the patient. This patient had four brief dreams that she reported. (1) "I was sick and couldn't get awake. I then tried to get up and help other people around me." (2) "I wanted to urinate but they wouldn't let me urinate. I wish they'd open me up and let me urinate." (3) "I was in labor. I was bearing down. It was a good feeling. I was going to get my baby. I felt good having a baby." When asked about this dream she stated: "I was an only child and want to give my babies everything. I'm glad

to have a hysterectomy—not that I don't want kids. Maybe I didn't want to have an operation and want to continue having kids. But then my husband and I talked and he said definitely I should have the operation and not have any more kids. We've had enough. My mother died when I was three." (4) "I was home with my babies. They were vague and far off. I wanted to be with them. They were calling and I couldn't get through. I was floating off into space." "The operation was over so sudden," was her only association.

When the dreams are dealt with directly, the ego's role in attempting a state of balance is quite vividly demonstrated. In the first dream, the ego tries to rouse her but is unable to do so. Instead mastery is accomplished by denying her immobilized state and the intent is to help others around her. In the second dream, anxiety about her realistic immobilized state is evident but refers to the wish to urinate. The surgery is alluded to in her statement about opening her up. In the third dream there is clear awareness that something inside her is being removed. However, instead of recognizing that it is the uterus, she changes the situation into one of childbirth. Thus she denies the essential meaning of the hysterectomy and substitutes a life-bearing event which can no longer take place. Her associations indicate ambivalence about her surgical sterility, and they betray her deeper anxiety about dying of uterine malignancy, related to identification with her mother in the anniversary recapitulations. In the last dream, shortly before awakening, she has left the operating room to be with her children. In all dreams, she was adult and attempting to master, control, and aid others. Dynamically, the feelings about her mother, grandmother, and father indicate a deeper and more serious problem. Defensively, however, these do not emerge in the manifest dreams. The ego protectively keeps the deeper anxiety from emerging while it successfully deals with the trauma of the real events.

A thirty-four-year-old childless married patient, who was very apprehensive during anesthesia induction and who

consciously thought she was going to die, dreamed: "I was
being suffocated and someone was killing me." Her associations referred to the anesthesia mask and her difficulty in
breathing. The overt anxiety was connected only with the
fear of suffocation. There were no objects in this dream
and the anxiety seems to refer to a primitive separation
reaction.

A forty-three-year-old childless married patient dreamed,
"My mother was standing alongside of me very clearly."
Associations: "Mother is always around whenever I need
her. She's always around when I need her." There is no
manifest anxiety in this dream such as was found in the
third hysterectomy patient's dream. Regression to the more
secure maternal protective relationship effectively binds
the surgical anxiety and permits a denial of any surgical or
mutilation anxieties.

A forty-three-year-old childless widow, whose mother died
when the patient was six years old and whose older sister
was a mother surrogate, dreamed: "I was with my sister.
There were a lot of people around—a lot of confusion. My
sister was looking after me." Her associations to the dream
were: "I don't know what the dream means. My sister is
the next one older than me. We have a family of thirteen.
She is my best friend. I was scared before surgery."

This patient had a vaginal hysterectomy. Her dream is very
similar to that of the fourth hysterectomy patient. The patient
entrusts the role of protector to her sister, a realistically closer
mother surrogate. The dream reveals the anxiety present in
the references to the confusion, but the security of having sister
"looking after" her successfully handles her tension.

A twenty-eight-year-old married mother of five children
desired a tubal ligation to avoid future pregnancies. For
various medical reasons, a total abdominal hysterectomy
was recommended instead, and the patient accepted this
decision. Prior to surgery she could not "wait to get it out."
However, in anxiety shortly before the operation, she expressed great concern about the anesthetic. "I'm [going to]

die." Her surgical dream was: "I was standing somewhere on a beach or an island, and there was a lot of water with tall waves surrounding me on all sides, and suddenly I saw a boat in the middle of the lake or ocean. It was a small rowboat, and my husband was sitting in there with the oars alongside and looking at me and grinning. I became very frightened but there didn't seem to be any way out."

In associations, the patient recalled a childhood experience when she was ten or eleven years old. She wished to bathe herself and to stand up in the bathtub to wash herself, but her stepmother vigorously pushed her down into the tub and water. This frightened her a great deal—she did not know why—but she felt as if things were closing in on her. She contrasted this treatment to her father's "tender loving care." He would never force her to sit down in the water and would let her wash herself in any position she desired, and he would remain to watch her.

The very traumatic background in this patient's life is related to the anesthesia dream in which the ego fails to bind her anxiety. One may assume considerable oedipal guilt about the thoroughly repressed erotic relationship with her father, illustrated by the (screen?) memory of her cruel stepmother pushing her down into the bathwater (to prevent her from exhibiting herself as she was used to doing to father?) and causing her to become phobic about drowning. The situation on the operating table apparently revived the memory of the exhibitionistic seduction of father with resultant guilt and fear of punishment. Repressed oedipal wishes emerge in the dream as a defense against her current anxiety in the surgical situation. In this instance, the day residue ineffectively assists in the camouflage of deeper conflicts.

A thirty-year-old married patient with two children had had two cervical conizations for malignancy and, at the time of the hysterectomy, cells were found which indicated more drastic procedures. Prior to surgery she expressed anxiety about losing her uterus as this symbolized femininity to her. Her surgical dream was: "My husband and I were riding in an airplane coming from Japan. The doctor said that we could do anything we wanted to. We were happy and excited." In her associations she said: "That's funny that I should dream that. You see we were in Japan in '55 when the doctors told me that I had early cancer of the womb and I should definitely not have any more children, but I became pregnant and they were all upset. I was pregnant already when we came back from Japan to the States."

Without considering the patient's response to the malignancy per se, we can see that she denies her serious illness and her lack of a uterus. She dreams and directly associates to being pregnant. The same mechanism was seen in the second hysterectomy patient. The trauma for this patient is not only the removal of her uterus, but also the undoubtedly advancing malignancy. Avoidance and reversal into the opposite effectively handle both of these anxieties.

A thirty-seven-year-old married mother of seven children had a vaginal hysterectomy performed for an early localized cervical malignancy. She received a general inhalation anesthetic and dreamed: "I saw my husband in his workclothes, very happy, and all my children were looking at me. I was getting up to prepare breakfast and I was very happy about this. They were all watching me." Her associations to this dream were: "Just before going to surgery I became very frightened. I thought about my last baby who died last December. It hurt a lot. I wondered what this was going to be like. Also, I worried about cancer. One of the doctors told me I had early cancer of the womb. I saw every one of the kids and my husband clearly in the dream."

Here again the predominant dream affect is happiness. Instead of a surgical team, her husband and children are observing her. A further denial through active mastery—she is happily getting up to prepare breakfast and care for her family, instead of returning to the recovery room where she will be cared for. Only in her associations does she mention her malignancy. The connection of dead baby and carcinoma represents a displacement of anxiety onto the infant; it is dead and it is not her life that is threatened. These techniques effect an equilibrium in the face of the double traumatic confrontations.

In this series of dreams of women undergoing hysterectomy, as well as in the pilot case cited earlier, several varieties of response appear in the dream constructions. In contrast to the dreams of the male patients, no fighting with the surgeon occurs in them, and there is no overt mutilation material. The regressive return to an earlier ego state with a maternal figure as protector characterized several cases. Various denials were also described and in two instances of known malignancy, this was also dealt with syntonically. Unlike the dreams of dental extraction, dreams in these more serious surgical procedures showed no games. In several instances the surgical procedures served to stimulate and evoke previous guilt and punishment anxieties, which emerged overtly in the dreams or in the associations.

Discussion

The adaptational nature of the dream was discussed in great detail by Freud in *The Interpretation of Dreams* (1900). Recent revived interest in dream formation and the dream work has given rise to many interesting experimental investigations. In the present investigation we have attempted in a limited way to study certain aspects of the dreaming ego's work by utilizing a semiexperimental approach. Various surgical procedures of specific anatomically and emotionally significant areas were chosen as part of the investigation. Though the limitations of this type of research design are evident, the results appear of sufficient interest to warrant further studies.

In *The Interpretation of Dreams* (1900) and in "The Ego and the Id" (1923b), Freud commented on the question of problem solving in dreams, which French later emphasized in his books on *The Integration of Behavior* (1952–1958). Freud's thesis is that the conflict which results in a dream gives rise to the creative aspect of the fantasy as well as the censoring role. The conflict presents a problem for the dream work to solve. This dream work is part of the ego's attempt to maintain a steady state of balance and avoid being overwhelmed by stimuli. Normally, when the ego cannot solve a conflict by means of a dream, the sleeper awakes. With sleep artificially induced and maintained there is, in addition, a total strain on the organism's homeostatic equilibrium. This occurs during a surgical procedure and the type of dream that is produced illustrates the adaptational techniques employed by the ego. One may ask if the "energy" that ordinarily enters into the sleep preservative functions of the natural dream becomes available for "adaptational maneuvers" in a dream where the sleep is artificially induced and maintained. In such pharmacological sleep, the dreamer loses his ability for self-controlled arousal from sleep and part of the adaptation may concern itself with this loss. This may be a significant theoretical consideration in our further understanding of drug-induced dreams. In two of the dreams cited the ego could not solve the conflict presented to it. In the male hemorrhoidectomy patient the dream went "black" after the bridge collapsed and the next thing he recalled was waking up. The analytic patient cited in the first part of this paper also awakened during the procedure and the dream at the moment of awakening reflected his intense fear and anxiety over the struggle manifest in the dream. That the anesthesia lightened might explain its occurrence but not the specific detail and content which, as was later confirmed in analysis, depended on psychic determinants. The tension, manifested in the dream, conceivably might be responsible for the awakening. With an attempt to awaken more anesthesia might be needed and, if the amount of inhalant administered remained the same, actual awakening might occur. The second hysterectomy patient dreamt that she was sick and could not awaken, whereupon she went on to dream of trying to get up and help other people around her. In this example, the ego attempted a dream solution by utilizing the device that Freud (1900), French (1952–1958), and Kardiner and Spiegel (1947) have designated as active mastery.

Victor Rosen (1950) comments on the change from passive receptivity to active mastery in postoperative patients and points out that the parental figure plays an important role in the development of the mechanism of denial and the capacity for mastery. The reassurance of a parental figure originally encourages the immature ego to master various presenting challenges, after which the mastery and denial mechanisms are internalized and beome part of adult ego operations. When patients dream of reassuring figures of the past, they may be referring to an ego organization level where the "it won't hurt" and "everything will be all right" come from their original sources. Without clarification it may not be completely accurate to speak of the mechanism of denial in these patients. Actually the threatening situation is reformulated so that the intensity of the danger is diminished, which permits the ego to handle it integratively. Elements of avoidance, ignoring, and withdrawal combine with the technique of active mastery to cope with the situation.

Anna Freud, in *The Ego and the Mechanisms of Defense* (1936), describes the result achieved by the various ego defensive operations and their relationship to anxiety. One section of her monumental monograph specifically describes denial in fantasy, word, and act. To this one obviously can add denial in the dream. In the present study, where the real threat is known, this technique is clearly seen. The denial may be a temporal–spatial denial (return to a previous time or place), an object denial (e.g., identification with the aggressor, early object relationship), a conflict denial, or an activity denial.

The active mastery of reality was already noted by Freud in "Beyond the Pleasure Principle" (1920) where he discussed the child's active mastery of anxiety through the turning of an unpleasant experience into a game. This playing of a game allows the child not only to control the situation actively, but also to discharge the energy in a more ego-acceptable fashion. In the patients of this study, because of the real surgical situation, the mental apparatus cannot avoid being flooded with large amounts of stimulation and excitation. The mastery and binding of this tension is handled by the ego in various ways. The dream is an indicator of these types of ego activity.

Pfister (1930), studying shock fantasies that occurred in persons in extreme danger of death, while mountain climbing or in battle, for example, interpreted them by Freud's concept of the protective barrier against stimuli. The fantasies were wishful thoughts which displaced reality at the moment of extreme danger of death. In Pfister's study the fantasies solved all life conflicts, making them smooth and pleasant. In our observations the dreams do more than protect sleep as Freud has postulated for the usual dream. The dreams in these surgical patients represent a total attempt at maintaining homeostasis at a time when threats are actualities. The dream under anesthesia seemingly has the same mechanism that is found in the dreams presented by Freud, but when tensions cannot be integrated, there is no possibility of awakening.

Unlike dreams in traumatic neuroses, the dreams of our patients did not deal with the traumatic event that actually occurred and in no instance did they allude more than symbolically to the surgical procedure. In "Beyond the Pleasure Principle" Freud commented that a gross physical injury, simultaneous with a psychic trauma, diminishes the chances for the development of a neurosis. The "mechanical violence of the trauma" of simultaneous physical injury calls for a narcissistic hypercathexis of the injured organ and binds the excess of excitation without a traumatic neurosis. In these patients the dreams differed from those in the traumatic neuroses. Instead, they showed regressive return to earlier ego states, displacement, reversal, symbolization, and other common ego defense mechanisms. In several instances overt anxiety was manifestly present although even here the anxiety seemed to be displaced onto the anesthetic phase of the surgical procedure.

Deutsch in her paper, "Some Psychoanalytic Observations in Surgery" (1942), noted that the surgical procedure has two separate aspects which are reacted to in different ways: (1) the anesthesia, and (2) the actual surgical operation. She further differentiates two types of anxiety. The first she refers to as narcosis anxiety, which represents death unconsciously and separation from the world, and which reflects an early fear of separation from the mother. Her second category refers to castration anxiety—the actual threat to the organ by the surgical procedure. These findings are confirmed by the present study. The anesthesia anxiety is more overt, appearing directly in the anesthesia dreams. The castration anxiety appears in the dreams of male patients. However, the ego attempts, through various stabilizing devices, to bind this anxiety and the dreams often show the defenses. Deutsch also comments that surgical procedures frequently reactivate old problems of relationships with mother which lead to reactions and fantasies of aggression, guilt, and masochism. This was not uniformly present in the dreams of the women studied by us. As noted, the mother figure frequently served as an auxiliary reassuring ego standing by supportively, and this maternal relationship represented a regressive solution to the problem confronting the patient. None of our male patients showed this type of maternal dream.

With elective surgical procedures there is usually time for psychological preparation for the operation. Pleasant and hopeful fantasies may be added to offset the frightening ones. Thus anesthetist and surgeon, by their reassurances, facilitate the reenactment of old mothering-going-to-sleep experiences (Kohut, personal experience). The psychiatrist talking to the patient preoperatively also can help. Dreams containing this element may be related to this phenomenon and may reflect the actual external or psychological preparation for the trauma. The obvious sex distribution of such dreams, however, cannot be explained solely on the basis of the experience immediately prior to surgery. Obviously, when the patient senses anxiety in the operating room personnel, this may reenforce his concern and be reflected in the resultant dreams. No such external situations were encountered in our series of patients, as the anesthesia and surgery were uncomplicated.

Castration anxiety was not manifest in any of our women patients although in the second "dental-extraction patient" this seemed significant. The absence of castration anxiety material in the women raises the issue: is this evidence against castration anxiety or for something else present in women? Only two hysterectomy patients had dreams and associations directly referable to childbearing. The second hysterectomy patient dreamed of actual sensations of labor while her uterus was being removed. This was apparently a wish for the removal of a child rather than of a uterus. As Deutsch also noted, fighting and castation anxiety were present frequently in the dreams of the male patients. However, in the two finger-amputation dreams there was no fighting but instead reassurance against castration with manifest dreams of sexual intercourse. In the dream that occurred during circumcision there also was no fighting, rather a resigned acceptance of the damaged appendage and a hope that its future functioning would not be impaired. Fighting and castration material appeared in the nongenital and nonamputative situations except in the case where the patient actually was unilaterally castrated. Our number of cases is not large and this may be an artifact, but when an actual castrative procedure occurs that involves the penis or a close facsimile, the dream usually appears not to deal directly with fighting and castration.

The dream associations of two patients who had hysterectomies for known malignancies referred directly to the possibility of death, but anxiety was denied completely by one of the patients and was referred to positively by the other who dreamed of being pregnant and having a live child despite her physicians' cautions.

Federn (1944) points out in his report that the ego has no sleep protecting function during anesthesia and that the dreams frequently are simple wish fulfillments. The nature of the wish, however, is the important consideration. It is our thesis that the dream is the indicator of adaptation. In this was the "wish" maybe for equilibrium.

Weiss (1952) has reported a dream of a woman, under anesthesia and undergoing an abortion, which occurred five years before starting analysis. The patient's evident great discomfort came out in certain of the dream contents. Reporting several other dreams of patients while undergoing surgical procedures, Weiss notes as a common element the feeling of flying or circling in space, a depiction of loss of consciousness. He concludes that dreaming under anesthesia does not have the function of perpetuating sleep but that it "reveals the efforts to master unbearable dynamic conditions, whether it succeeds or fails in doing so" (p. 200). We agree with this, though we emphasize that it is not contradictory of the classic idea of the sleep protective dream function. In sleep external reality can be avoided. Sleep itself can represent the defensive ego operation of ignoring existing traumas and threats.

Janis (1958), studying preoperative and postoperative dreams, concludes that "exposure to any signs of potential mutilation or annihilation will tend to reactivate the seemingly outgrown patterns of emotional response which had originally been elicited and re-enforced during the stress episodes of early childhood" (p. 200). This hypothesis is verified by our data. Our prime focus, however, was on the stabilizing and coping aspects of the ego during the actual stress procedure, and as indicators we used the dreams produced at that particular time. "Fight or flight" was, in reality, impossible then but "fight or flight" was possible and occurred in the dream state. Flight, when it occurred, took place in time or space and was a flight to object relationships that previously were reassuring. Fight also was quite clear in the dreams.

The surgical procedures studied in this research involved the mouth, teeth, anus, penis, uterus, fingers, and thoracic areas. Despite the significance of these anatomical zones in psychosexual development, there was a noteworthy absence of manifest regressive material referable to these specific areas. One must consider the possibility that surgical intervention is of such traumatic magnitude that the response is to stress, rather than to the erotogenic zone directly affected.

The studies reported here are preliminary and some conclusions are assumed, rather than verified, constructs. Nevertheless, the methodology may be useful in other investigations of this topical area and some resulting hypotheses deserve further testing. Dreams during anesthesia, of course, cannot be equated with the dreams of natural sleep and their differences need further study. Furthermore, interpretation from the manifest content of dreams with few associations and from patients not in psychotherapy or psychoanalysis is methodologically hazardous. The exact time the dreams were dreamed is unknown, although, in several instances, it could be assumed that they occurred simultaneously with the surgical procedure; others apparently occurred while the patient was awakening from the anesthetic. The data, we believe, demonstrate the defensive function of dreaming. In surgical dreams the ego attempts to integrate emerging tensions syntonically through various techniques. If it does not succeed the dream either disappears or continues substituting a less frightening conflict for the real situation. Our experimental population does not permit pinpointing why a particular patient dreamed a particular dream with particular manifest content. Many unsolved questions have been raised. However, this comparative study, utilizing such broad variables as the patient's sex, the particular organic disease, and the surgical procedure is significant and allows for the formulation of more specific hypotheses that may be tested in the future.

Chapter 18

CHARACTEROLOGICAL SIGNIFICANCE OF THE TYPICAL ANXIETY DREAM

IRVING D. HARRIS

Introduction

The approach of this report, as implied in the title, represents a departure from the customary approach to the study of dreams. Apart from work done on dream symbols, which are supposed to have a more or less common and constant meaning for all individuals, interest in dreams has mainly centered around the current dynamic conflict. It is the practice in listening to a patient's dreams to ask ourselves: *What present wishes are expressed in the dream? What are the defenses against the wishes? What present ego state is reflected in the dream?* All these questions concern themselves with the immediate present; with the meaning of a particular dream for a particular person at a particular time. This is as it should be insofar as the successful treatment of a patient depends upon the manner in which his current affective states are handled. A knowledge of his emotional conflict in childhood, or even conflict present ten analytical hours before, is not as useful in therapy as a knowledge of what is going on during the actual hour.

Because of this necessary orientation to dreams, their possible characterological significance has been neglected. Of all the dreams which could be investigated for the light they might cast on personality, it seems that the typical anxiety dream would be

This paper was first published in *Psychiatry* (1951), 14:279–294.

the best choice. Because in the typical dreams the manifest content is rather fixed and constant for all individuals and because anxiety is the affect against which personality defenses are erected, an investigation of the characterological significance of typical anxiety dreams appears to be profitable. The approach which is presented in this and a preceding communication by the writer can be simply stated in the following question: What does it tell us about the character structure of an individual if we learn that he has predominantly experienced *one* rather than *another* kind of typical anxiety dream?

Perhaps a brief review of the previous report will be helpful in further orienting tthe reader to the objectives of tthis report. In this earlier paper the writer described some observations concerning the typical anxiety dreams which had been experienced by large groups of so-called normal individuals, and also emotionally disturbed patients. These two typical anxiety dreams were: (1) dreams of falling from heights (falling from cliffs, buildings, bridges, and so on); and (2) dreams of being attacked, threatened, or chased by a dangerous environmental object from which the dreamer has some difficulty escaping (attacked by a lion, chased by a robber, caught in a burning house, and so on). All variations of the former type of dream were included under the heading "falling" dream, and all variations of the latter type of dream were included under the heading "attacked" dream. Upon direct questioning of military draft selectees, military patients, and children and mothers at child guidance clinics, it became apparent that there were individual differences in the occurrence of these dreams and also in the comparative unpleasantness of the dreams. It was observed that these individuals differed as to whether they had had both, one or the other, or neither of these two types of dreams. If they had had both types of dreams, they also differed as to which type they considered the more scary or unpleasant.

Having observed these individual differences, the writer became interested in the question of the significance of the differences. Some data on the release or nonrelease of hostility toward a particular parent suggested that the two typical anxiety dreams might reflect the fears of two psychic dangers;

namely: (1) the danger of loss of love or of separation from the loved one, or supporting object; and (2) the danger of castration or, in a more general sense, injury to or mutilation of the body. In other words, the predominant unpleasantness of the falling dream might reflect the predominant fear of loss of love and support, whereas the predominant unpleasantness of the attack dream might reflect the predominant fear of castration in its most general sense. In this earlier communication the question was posed, What does the predominant psychic threat (possibly reflected in the predominant anxiety dream) tell us about the maturation of the personality or ego? It was speculated that since the danger of loss of love or support is feared earlier than the danger of castration, it might be that the predominant fear of loss of support signifies a fixation at an earlier stage of personality development.

It is the purpose of this report to investigate further the possible characterological significance of the falling and attacked dreams. Perhaps the contrast between this approach and the dynamic approach can be described more concretely now: That a certain patient has a dream of being attacked by a lion might mean a present castration anxiety, but may not tell us anything about his character. However, if *most* of the dreams in this patient's life have been of this type and they are the most unpleasant, it is possible that we can discover some characterological difference in this person as compared with the person who has had the falling dream most frequently or most unpleasantly in his life.

In this communication most of the emphasis will be on the falling dream. The writer feels that less is known about the falling dream than is known about the attacked dream. Psychoanalytic inquiry by Freud and later writers has afforded us a good description of the attacked dreams and a rather complete understanding of the psychic danger of castration which might be reflected in this type of dream. Freud did remark of the attacked type of dream, "They are characteristic as manifest dream content of persons suffering from anxiety . . ." (Freud, 1900, p. 585). Since analysts most frequently come in contact with patients who have the attacked type of dream, an additional inquiry here into this dream would not be as valuable as an inquiry into the falling dream. The question might immediately arise: Does the comparative lack of mention of the falling dream in the psychoanalytic literature mean that patients with these dreams are less anxious or less disturbed than are the individuals with predominantly attacked dreams? It will be recalled from the writer's earlier report that an examination of selectees' dreams indicated that about one half of the selectees had considered the falling dream to be their predominant anxiety dream. It is the writer's belief, and this will be stressed more fully later on, that the lack of mention of the falling dream in psychoanalytic literature and the comparative absence of the falling dream in patients undergoing psychoanalytic therapy is not due to the fact that the falling dream signifies less disturbance, but that the falling dream is frequently associated with a personality type that does not seek or continue psychoanalytic treatment.

The methodology of contemporary psychoanalytic research is to derive understanding of psychic phenomena from patients in treatment. Because patients with predominantly falling dreams are not frequently seen in psychoanalytic treatment (and this has been the writer's experience also), only a small part of the subsequent data is derived from observations on patients in psychotherapy and psychoanalysis. Instead, these data are mainly derived (1) from diagnostic studies of military patients, and (2) from diagnostic studies of children and their mothers at a child guidance clinic. Because of the paucity of material in this report derived from actual psychoanalytic treatment, one of the immediate purposes of this communication is to stimulate others who are doing psychoanalytic treatment to investigate the patients who have predominantly falling dreams.

The plan of this report is to present several character traits which are seen more often in patients with predominantly falling dreams. (Patients with predominantly attacked dreams will be used for purposes of comparison.) These traits are: (1) difficulty in defying the mother and the consequent implication regarding lack of emancipation from the mother; (2) emotionality; and (3) defensiveness. It should be emphasized that these several traits do not represent a syndrome in the sense that all are found in one person, but that they may represent possible outcroppings from a common developmental feature. To anticipate somewhat the subsequent observations and discussion, these traits may have a common origin in that stage of ego maturation in which the psychic mechanisms for regulating instinctual life are externalized.

One word about the terminology: For the sake of brevity, the term *falling patients* (or *attacked patients*) will be used instead of "patients for whom the falling (or attacked) dream is predominantly unpleasant." Falling patient will include those patients who have had the falling dream but never the attacked dream, and those patients who have had both types of dreams but consider the falling dream more unpleasant; the category of the attacked patients was set up in the same manner.

Findings

Difficulty in Defying the Mother

This section can be considered an extension of that part of the previous report in which the writer commented on the difficulty of the falling patient in expressing overt angry defiance to the mother. On the basis of actual observation of children and of retrospective accounts from adults, it appeared that temper outbursts were rarely directed toward the mother in the case of falling patients, whereas this was frequently the case with attacked patients.

It seems valuable, for the following reason, to examine more closely this difficulty in defying the mother. A chronic and marked difficulty in defiance of the mother indicates a strong fear that the maternal support and acceptance will be lost if the child unleashes his hostility toward her. While this fear is normally present in moderate degree in small children, a marked fear of this type probably arises from an increased need for the mother—without whom a desolate chaos would result for the child—and from a dim awareness of the marked destructiveness of his hostility. The behavioral effect of these fears is not only a *difficulty* in defying the mother, but also an increased, close dependent relationship to the mother which ensures the continuation of the needed maternal support and which gives reassurance that the mother has not been destroyed.

Thus, in this section an examination of defiance will necessarily touch on the phenomenon of marked dependence on the mother. Such a dependence, if occurring early enough, does have unfavorable consequences so far as ego maturation is concerned. The infantile ego, unable to cope with the integrative tasks accompanying emancipation from the mother, seeks security in the same overdependence which contributed to the infantilism. In the following observations we shall be concerned then not only with the falling patient's difficulty in defying the mother, but also with whatever implications arise concerning overdependence and failure of ego maturation.

The following case excerpt rather strikingly illustrates the difficulties in defiance of the mother and the overdependence on her which seem characteristic of the falling patient.

Two brothers, identical twins of twelve years of age, were referred to the clinic because of reading difficulties. They lived with their mother in a small town in Illinois, their father having deserted four years earlier. The psychiatric interview with Fred, one of these twins, revealed a boy who was spontaneous, outgoing, friendly, and who could tell the examiner when he was annoyed, depressed, or pleased—whether the occasion for these feelings derived from his mother, his school, or his friends. Although he could say that his mother got him angry, he still had good feeling toward her, stating that she punished him only when he deserved it. When asked about anxiety dreams, he recalled that the worst dream he'd ever had was that something was after him and he could not get away. A dream which was less unpleasant was one in which he was falling off a cliff.

Tom, the other twin, was guarded and tense during the interview. He admitted that he felt a little uneasy about the examination and wondered what was going to come out of it. At times he was able to smile warmly and spontaneously, but for the most part he was reluctant to say much about himself. It was very difficult to get him to admit any angry feelings, but finally he confessed that he did feel anger when other kids hit him. He said that at times he got angry with his brother, but this anger did not last long because he always gave in to his brother. There was no anger directed toward anyone else spontaneously, and when I particularly mentioned his mother, he said, "My mother always does what's right, and I never get angry at her." When asked about dreams, Tom said that the most unpleasant ones were of falling off a cliff. He could remember no other dreams spontaneously, but upon direct questioning recalled dreams of crooks after him. The dream of crooks was not so unpleasant as the falling dream. The lack of any hostility directed toward the mother was quite striking.

The mother stated that Fred, the attacked twin, is the more restless and quick tempered. Fred walked earlier, was more active and curious around the age of two years. Tom, the falling twin, is more affectionate and thoughtful and aims to please. He rarely gets angry, but when he does he expresses it in an explosive fashion after which he seems anxious. Tom in late infancy was less active and would run to mother's lap to be held and fondled.

Here we have a rather well-controlled instance, with the father out of the picture, no other siblings, and with no apparent constitutional differences between the two boys. Yet Tom, the twin with predominantly falling dreams, had much more difficulty in openly showing resentment to and independence of the mother. The overdependent and close relationship he had with the mother in late infancy seems to have persisted, relatively unchanged, to the present time. Thus, his present personality structure or ego state appears to be the result of early fixation rather than of a later regression. Unfortunately, information is not available as to why the twins had different emotional developments. Putting that question aside until later in the discussion, we might content ourselves with the observation that the personality features noted in Tom were associated with the predominance of the falling dream.

A difficulty in defying the mother usually has secondary effects such as a passivity in other relationships not only during childhood, but also in adult life. In confirmation of this finding, the writer has noted that defiant, acting-out behavior, not having to do with the mother, was more frequent in attacked than in falling children. Also, attacked adults (parents of clinic children), much more often than falling adults, stated that they usually *released* (instead of held in) their angry feelings when provoked in an interpersonal situation. In spite of this general tendency to passivity on the part of the falling patients we still have to account for the fact that not a few falling persons either are or give a semblance of being rather free with their aggression, defiance, or hostility. If these persons are actually free in this area, one might doubt that they had original difficulty in defying the mother. If, however, their freedom is due to maternal permissiveness, then the freedom is more apparent than real, inasmuch as the mother is still not being defied, and the loss of her support and love is still not being risked.

The next series of observations deals with the questions just posed. They are concerned with the situation and factors in which defiant aggression is absent or present in the falling patients. The first set of observations deals with military neuropsychiatric patients, the second set with children at a guidance clinic.

A study was made of a small group of military patients who had stated that the mother was the real boss of the family. They had also been questioned as to whether they or some other sibling was the mother's favorite. On the basis of their responses, two groups could be studied: (1) one group which was in a maternal setting apparently conducive to conformity—that is, maternal authority plus favoritism of the patient by the mother; and (2) the other group in a maternal setting apparently conducive to rebellion—that is, maternal authority plus favoritism of another sibling by the mother. These two groups were then studied for the incidence of temper tantrums in childhood, the presence of tantrums being taken to indicate overt rebellion—the absence, to indicate conformity. The results disclosed no differences in incidence of temper tantrums (about 27 percent in each group) between the two groups so long as the predominant anxiety dream was not taken into account. However, when the two groups were divided on the basis of falling and attacked dreams, some very interesting trends were seen.

When the attacked patients were in a setting conducive to conformity (they were the favorites of the authoritarian mother), the incidence of temper tantrums was low (1 out of 12, or 8¼ percent). When the attacked patients were in a setting conducive to rebellion (mother was authoritarian but favored a sibling), the incidence of tantrums was considerably higher (5 out of 10, or 50 percent).

In other words, the attacked patients seemed to behave toward the mother in a fairly understandable or direct way. When feeling loved, they accepted the maternal guidance and prohibitions without rebellion; when feeling that a sibling got more than they did, they became resentful in an open way, that is, with a temper tantrum.

Not so, with the falling patient. In a maternal setting apparently conducive to conformity, the incidence of tantrums was higher (6 out of 15, or 40 percent) than in an apparently rebellious situation (2 out of 13, or 15 percent). In other words, the falling patients showed more aggression when feeling accepted by the mother than when feeling rejected by her.

Comparing the falling and attacked patients, the data suggest that with the falling patients maternal acceptance is necessary before aggression can be shown, whereas with the attacked patients aggression is shown whenever maternal acceptance is lacking. Most striking is the infrequency of open aggression in falling patients when confronted by the frustrating situation of mother being the rejecting authority.

Somewhat confirmatory of these observations on military falling patients are some data on the children referred to a child guidance clinic. Here the evaluation of maternal acceptance was gained from actual interviews with the mothers. The relation of maternal acceptance to temper outbursts of children was strikingly seen in children with predominantly falling dreams. With maternal acceptance, temper tantrums in the falling children were frequent (6 out of 10, or 60 percent). With maternal rejection, they were quite low (1 out of 8, or 12½ percent). (In children with attacked dreams the incidence was 44 and 48 percent, respectively.) Thus, of all the children examined by the writer the lowest incidence of overt aggression was seen in those children with falling dreams who were rejected by the mother.

As to further evidence that in the falling patients aggression or acting out depends upon maternal acceptance and maternal permission, we can consider the findings concerning protectiveness in mothers. Of the many cases seen by the writer which had been referred to the clinic by the juvenile court, there were eight cases in which the mothers protested strongly about the referral and said that their boys were not criminals, that they just got into bad company, that the charges were trumped up, or that the boys might have taken something accidentally, but that they did not steal, and so on. In seven out of the eight cases in which the maternal protectiveness was so marked, the boys had predominantly falling dreams. (In many of the cases in which a boy had attacked dreams, the mother was highly irritated with the boy because of his delinquent behavior and frequently was sympathetic with the juvenile court idea of commitment.) Because of the resistance of the boys and their parents, no therapy was attempted, and so no conclusions can be drawn from observations of these boys in treatment. However, the impression was strong in the diagnostic interview that intermixed with the maternal protectiveness was a permissiveness regarding those socially unacceptable acts.

Let us review the preceding observations more systematically. We have seen that the falling and attacked patients differ as to the factors in the mother–child relationship which decide whether hostile aggression is expressed or not. The falling patient tends not to express direct aggression if the mother is rejecting of him and his aggressive tendencies. He does tend to express aggression if the mother is accepting, permissive, or encouraging regarding it. But, as the observations in the writer's earlier communication indicate, rarely is the permitted aggression directed toward the mother. His temper tantrum, as shown in that communication, tends to be directed toward the father rather than toward the mother. It seems, then, that with the falling patient, it is the mother who wields the power of inhibiting or encouraging the overt aggression.

On the other hand, the attacked patient does not seem as responsive to the direct wishes or commands of the mother per se. He feels more free to retaliate openly against the mother for real or fancied slights, although accepting of mother's commands when these commands are coupled with love. His freedom in retaliation was indicated in the previous report which showed that temper outbursts in the attacked patients were more often directed selectively toward the mother rather than the father. In these patients, then, it seems as though the external power for inhibiting aggression resides not in the mother, but rather in the father.

In the following case example the trends just described can be seen more dramatically. In the case of two half-brothers with different predominant anxiety dreams, the effect of the parental attitudes on the display of aggression seems to be quite in evidence.

> Sam, a fourteen-year-old boy, was involved in a conscious hostile relationship with his strict stepfather. The mother, for various reasons, was so identified with, or protective of Sam that on two occasions she left home taking Sam with her and leaving with the father the two children of the second marriage. Recently she had forced the stepfather to leave the home because he wasn't sympathetic enough to Sam. Sam, in the psychiatric interview, was outspoken about his positive and negative feelings. Questioning revealed that he had the *falling* dream predominantly.
>
> Frank, his nine-year-old half brother, who had developed temper tantrums toward mother following father's absence from the home, and who had ceased to show temper upon father's return, showed a strikingly different picture in the diagnostic interview with the male examiner. He was so apprehensive that he came close to panic when he couldn't do a drawing well enough upon the examiner's suggestion, and also when he couldn't close a drawer that he had opened. Frank revealed upon questioning that he had had predominantly the attacked dream.

In this case the free aggression is present in the brother with predominantly falling dreams, and absent or inhibited in the brother with predominantly attacked dreams. Sam's ease in expressing aggression or hostility seems to be directly connected with his mother's encouragement of his aggressivity. His display or nondisplay of aggression seems to depend more on what mother feels than what father feels. On the other hand, the inhibition of Frank's aggression seems to be a consequence of fear of the father figure and not a result of fear of losing mother's love. It was only during the father's absence from the home that he felt free enough to direct overt temper toward his mother for her obvious partiality to Sam.

If, as is generally believed, the relationship the child experiences with the mother is a reflection of his emotional maturation, one can hardly avoid concluding from the observations presented here that the falling patient is less emancipated from the mother than is the attacked patient. The extreme sensitivity to what goes on in the mother, the inability to react as an independent retaliating or pleasing entity to the rejecting or accepting mother—these traits, suggestive of arrested maturation and emancipation, are more frequently found in these particular falling patients.

However, if the conjecture regarding falling patients is true, one should find other evidence in these patients pointing to early developmental fixation. In this connection the writer wishes now to present briefly some observations on two characteristics found frequently in falling patients: emotionality and defensiveness.

Emotionality

The term *emotionality* perhaps needs some definition. The writer will use it to describe a condition in which the emotions, their satisfaction, and vicissitudes, rather than the reasoning faculties, are the presenting parts of a person's overt behavior. While it is true that the emotions or instinctual drives supply the energy for all the behavior of a person, in this condition the emotions are characteristically seen quite nakedly, that is, without the usual defenses. The term *emotionality* was chosen by the writer principally because these persons, when asked to describe themselves, usually stated that they were "emotional" (*excitable* was another descriptive term).

It is somewhat difficult to describe the condition accurately enough so that it is not confused with the marked "impulsivity" of the psychopath or the reckless daring of the person seeking punishment or disaster. There is a strong resemblance between the *emotional* person—as the term is used here—and the impulsive character described by Reich, if the latter condition is thought of in a less pathologic sense. The emotional person seems to have a keen and vivid awareness coupled with a heightened capacity for sensual enjoyment. He tends to participate totally in a pleasurable activity, to lose or abandon himself in pleasure, very similar to the naive, full enjoyment of the small child who squeals with delight. One gets the impression, furthermore, that this tendency is usually not a regressive one because of guilt or anxiety, but rather a fixation in personality development.

Emotionality as so defined and described was found much more frequently in falling than in attacked patients (about 30 percent of the former and 4 percent of the latter). Perhaps a statistical observation on the relationship of color response on the Rorschach to typical anxiety dreams will help to illustrate this finding and also to further define the term *emotionality*. A group of unselected allergic children of ages seven through eleven who were given Rorschach tests were divided into three groups: (1) those whose responses included no color or at most FC; (2) those whose responses included CF, but no pure C; and finally (3) those whose responses included one or more pure C. Thus, the three groups were arranged in increasing ability to perceive pure color. Such an ability is said to be correlated with a freedom of the emotional life from intellectual or ego controls. It was found that the falling children tended to have this freedom more than did the attacked children. Of ten falling children, one (10 percent) was in the first group, three (30 percent) in the second group, and six (60 percent) in the third group. However, of the twenty-four attacked children, twelve (50 percent) were in the first group, eight (33 percent) in the second, and only four (17 percent) in the third group. While a pure color response is more to be expected in children than in adults, because of the lack of ego control in children, it is interesting that in the falling children rather than in the attacked children the vivid affective or emotional life tended to be less under control of the ego function.

It is with the adults, however, that the childlike affective or emotional intensity will stand out as a personality characteristic. The writer has examined several falling adults who, in addition to being subject to emotional storms, have an exquisite sensory appreciation. One was especially sensitive to colors, another to odors. In two cases in which parents of problem children were seen, the emotionality in the falling parents was quite evident. In one case the father admitted that he was quite emotional, threw himself into his work, which was of a community action type, was quite excited over new places, and would follow the emotional whim of the moment. In the other case, the mother was dramatically emotional and said that the examiner's voice pressed through her like a knife. In both instances their mates declared that these particular parents had less common sense than had the children in the family. The impression was gained that these parents and certain other falling persons conceive of the world as a treasure-trove constructed for their pleasure. An adolescent falling boy of thirteen, referred for stealing, told the writer that when he went down the street he had the idea that everything in the store windows belonged to him, and that it was "just natural for me to take it."

The attacked adults created a different impression. Common sense or appreciation of reality limitation formed an integral part of their personality. Sometimes their conflicts prevented a constructive use of their reality testing, but on the whole they seemed to possess the potentiality for appraising the environment realistically. More often, they seemed to have a cautious, overappreciation of what was not possible in reality. In the cases of attacked children referred for stealing, the concepts of retaliation for grievances and of seeking punishment were more usual than the fantasy that everything belonged to them. Their affective or emotional life was not so vivid, but when so, it tended to be channelized in contrast to the generalized vividness of the falling individual.

Defensiveness

The term *defensiveness* will be used to denote a personality trait whereby an individual tries to prevent others and/or himself from learning what he is consciously feeling or thinking. It denotes, then, the resistance to the emergence of *suppressed* rather than repressed thoughts, feelings, or attitudes. Most people and probably all patients exhibit this trait to a mild degree when they, by an act of omission, fail to make known every unpleasant conscious thought. However, we can speak of marked defensiveness if a person will not allow himself to be questioned—that is, by not appearing for an interview or, when questioned in an interview setting, by attempting to conceal his conscious thoughts through denying their existence, asserting the contrary, or fencing with the examiner. If such behavior is manifested by a person being cross-examined while on trial for some criminal offense, we would not consider it unusual. However, if this behavior occurs in relation to a psychiatric interview, we would suspect that the person was markedly insecure as to how someone else would judge him and his thoughts. Most persons presenting themselves for psychiatric help do not exhibit marked defensiveness for the reason that they realize a rather full and honest account of themselves and their feelings is a prerequisite to getting relief. However, when a person is sent or pressed by others to obtain psychiatric treatment, defensive behavior is frequently seen. In child guidance clinics where parents may be unwilling participants in the investigation of themselves and their attitudes, the phenomenon of marked defensiveness can often be noted. This trait may show up in many forms. In young children and adolescents it takes the form of bland denials, I-don't-know's or a general guardedness. In adults more active techniques are seen. Quite often the adult will strive to impress the examiner with his normality without being asked about it. He will say, in response to a general question, "My childhood was perfectly normal," or, "Whatever dreams I have are normal." In this technique there is a noticeable quick anticipation of an embarrassing question. A variation of this reaction is seen when the person answers immediately in the negative, sometimes before the full question has been asked and certainly before the person has had time to reflect or search his memory.

The phenomenon of marked defensiveness was observed by the writer to be present almost exclusively in persons with falling dreams (22 percent), and was rarely noted in attacked persons (3 percent). This trait frequently rendered the diagnostic interview of parents with falling dreams highly unsatisfactory if not impossible. To get these parents to accept treatment was still more difficult. One mother with falling dreams was quite defensive throughout the diagnostic interview, but because of school pressure consented to be seen at weekly interviews by a social worker. After three defensive interviews barren of spontaneous feeling, she stopped coming to the clinic, giving as an excuse that the child did not enjoy her own play therapy. A father with falling dreams was anxiously defensive throughout the diagnostic interview. He first claimed that his daughter had no problem, then that he had no problem. His wife began weekly treatment interviews and after a few months it became apparent that the father would also have to be treated. The initial examiner wrote asking him to come in but there was no response. Persistent pressure by his wife, who applied the threat of divorce, brought him to the point of accepting an appointment, but he canceled the appointment at the last minute.

In addition to defensive parents at a child guidance clinic, the writer has often noted in private practice the same behavior in many adults who appear to have little desire for emotional catharsis and still less for any exploration of their feelings. They seem to want a bothersome symptom relieved or removed and it is quite difficult, at least for the writer, to educate them to an analytically oriented therapy. More will be said later about the difficulties encountered in treating these persons.

The question arises: Of what use is this trait to the person, and what significance does it have in the maturation of the personality? Obviously, defensiveness serves the function of protecting a person against the consequences of an unfavorable evaluation. Not only does he want to avoid having others think ill of him, but also to avoid thinking ill of himself. In such a person the self-esteem would appear to be low, in a precarious state, and maintained by the process of suppression. The markedly defensive person seemingly fears that the external observer has only to look into his eyes to see how bad he is, and so he is rather active in dispelling that opinion.

Now, in other persons this protection against an unfavorable evaluation is accomplished less through suppressive defensiveness and more through the process of guilt and anxiety which have repressed unacceptable impulses. The greater security of these persons, reflected in their comparative ease in a diagnostic or treatment situation, is probably due in part to the fact that the repressed unacceptable impulses are at a greater distance from the conscious ego and the external observer. Thus, the attacked person tends to ward off unwelcome questioning in a different way. Although usually he is cooperative, at times he will be resistive and suspicious. His resistiveness can usually be reduced by warmth and frankness on the part of the examiner. This person tends more to dispute the right of the examiner to question him, but if he comes of his own free will, or if the necessity for the examination has been explained to him, he will usually respond. Another defense used by the less aggressive attacked person is to answer only what is asked of him or to be generally inhibited in speech. Rarely does he take active measures to convince the examiner he is other than he really is.

It would seem that of the two methods which insure protection against loss of esteem, suppressive defensiveness is the more primitive in that it serves principally as a technique of dealing with external prohibitions and fears of external punishment. A serviceable superego with its internalized prohibitions, such as would arise from the process of repression, appears to be deficient in these defensive persons. It is possible that the superego has not yet been fully organized, and the conscious ego is still faced with the energy-draining task of suppressing unacceptable impulses. That the phenomenon of defensiveness was found most frequently in falling persons appears to lend support to the speculation that the predominance of the falling dream may reflect an arrest in the maturation of the personality.

Discussion

The writer has attempted to demonstrate in the preceding material three characteristics more frequently found in falling persons than in attacked persons. These three characteristics are: (1) A comparative lack of ability, most pronounced in the setting of the mother–child relationship, to express hostility or defiance overtly in an interpersonal situation upon reasonable provocation. This lack of ability is associated with a certain overdependence on the mother. (2) A tendency toward open, full, and naive expression of affect relatively unhampered by intellectual or ego controls—a tendency designated "emotionality." (3) A tendency toward marked defensiveness in which the person protects his self-esteem from unfavorable evaluation by guarding his conscious thoughts and feelings from scrutiny by others and himself—a protection mediated through the process of suppression.

During the presentation of the data some efforts were made to discover theoretically a common origin for these seemingly unrelated characteristics. The writer has speculated that they have their source in an early stage of personality maturation and has suggested that the falling persons in whom these characteristics are most frequent tend to be fixated at this level of maturation. In this particular stage, because of the lack of emancipation from the mother, there is an inability on the part of the infant or small child to react as an independent entity–an entity with its own satisfactory mechanisms for dealing with noxious maternal handling, for regulating its impulses, and for protecting its self-esteem. When the small child is not an independent entity, it must look constantly to the mother or the external world to supply approval or to exert controls over its impulses. This stage might also be described as one in which the principal controls of the instinctual life—that is, the ego and superego—lie externally in the mother from whom the infant has not yet individuated itself. In the next stage, after the individuation, the ego and superego reside internally.

In the subsequent discussion, the writer plans to consider more or less systematically the following topics: (1) the causative factors contributing to the arrest in personality maturation; (2) the question of why this maturational arrest should be noted more frequently in falling persons; and (3) the implications of the data, and the hypotheses for psychiatric diagnosis, prognosis, and treatment.

Causative Factors in Arrested Maturation

The reasons for the fixation at the stage of maturation are not clear, and a full discussion of them would be beyond the scope of this paper. However, some speculations can be made on the basis of our present knowledge. It is generally believed that the infantile ego gains its strength and maturity from exposure to and identification with a warm and predictable mother figure. According to Benedek (1938), a predictable maternal warmth gives rise to confidence which enables the infant to postpone immediate gratification of its instinctual needs. The internalization of the outer good serves the purpose of reducing the anxiety over helplessness in the face of internal demands and thus serves to strengthen the ego. With continuing maternal warmth and predictability, a more realistic and less severe superego is built up within the growing infant. If the infant is exposed to a mother whose emotional investment in the child is ambivalent and/or unpredictable, one would not expect these favorable internalizations to take place. Instead, the infantile ego would remain infantile, still searching for a reliable figure with which to identify and still subject to anxiety over unacceptable impulses which might threaten its precarious hold on and approval from the external world.

Important related observations were reported by Spitz (1965). In his study of the autoerotic activity of infants in the first year of life, Spitz noted that rocking movements, which most often begin about the sixth or seventh month, were more frequent in infants who had been exposed to vacillating, unpredictable maternal emotions and attitudes. The developmental quotient of these infants showed retardation. On the other hand, touching of the genitals, which most often began about the tenth month, was more frequent in infants who had been exposed to warm, consistent, and emotionally balanced mothers. The developmental quotient of these infants showed no retardation.

Spitz believed that the very inconsistent maternal climate surrounding the rocking infants did not favor the process of internalization in the infant. While the autoerotic rocking movements indicated some interchange of affect between infant and mother—affect-starved infants in an institutional setup showed no such autoerotic activity—still the movements were not related to the object. The rocking stimulated the infant internally, arousing pleasurable kinesthetic sensations. It had no reference to a particular object. The genital touching, however, was related to an external object, even though the object was part of the infant's body. Fecal play, the third autoerotic activity, was also interpreted as some type of object relationship, a relationship made possible by the fact that the mothers of fecal-play infants, though ambivalent, maintained their emotional attitudes long enough for the mother image to be internalized by the infant. In conclusion, Spitz contended that in infants whose rocking is the exclusive autoerotic activity in the first year of life, "the nature of the object relation was the most primitive, a primary narcissistic relation, or to be more exact, a regression to the primary narcissistic stage. It is caused by a maternal personality which does not permit the formation of any object relationship whatsoever. The form it takes is a nonobjectal activity of the libidinal drive" (1965, p. 245).

The essence of the etiological theory is that vacillating maternal emotional attitudes do not permit the introjection of mother images, whereas consistent predictable attitudes do make for such introjection. This theory, originally proposed by Wilhelm Reich (1925) to explain the formation of the impulsive character, might also account for the impulsive emotionality noted in some falling persons. A similar etiology has been proposed by Hsu (1949) for the predominant cultural use of suppression—suppression being one of the characteristics found in the defensive falling patients. Hsu, who was interested in the differential cultural use of suppression and repression, suggested that in cultures in which there is a plurality of parent figures within the family, the difficulty in identification with one single figure might lead to the use of suppression rather than repression—repression being accomplished by means of a strongly internalized parent figure.

Maturational Arrest in Falling Persons

We may now take up the question of why the arrest in ego maturation should have been noted more frequently in falling persons. It has already been proposed that developmentally the psychic fear of loss of support and love—reflected in the predominance of the falling dream—may precede the psychic fear of castration or injury to the body—reflected in the predominance of the attacked dream. The fear expressed in the falling dream is separation from an external supporting object of which the dreamer is very needful. It is as though the dreamer could not survive independently of the supporting object—a situation similar to that in which the incompletely individuated infant requires the external object to supply love and controls. On the other hand, the danger expressed in the attacked dream is one in which there is a threat to the now fairly independent organism itself—as though the necessary means for its psychic survival resides within the infant rather than in the external object.

It is quite possible that Spitz's observations on the autoerotic activity of rocking have a direct bearing on why falling persons show characteristics of the infantile ego. Rocking and falling both deal with stimulation of the kinesthetic nerve endings and thus engage the proprioceptive sensory system. The system serves to orient the organism in space and is more archaic than the exteroceptive sensory system which enables the organism to discriminate between favorable and unfavorable external objects. Whereas rocking gives a pleasurable sensation, falling, at least as manifested in the dream, is associated with great anxiety. Freud speculated as to the kinesthetic pleasures in the falling dream and connected them with the delight of the small child in being thrown up in the air. Whether pleasure or anxiety is the consequent affect, the common nervous mechanism in question is the proprioceptive system. It is likely that the first sensations received by the fetus from the outside are equilibratory in nature as a result of the swing of the gravid uterus as the mother moves and walks. These sensations could be either pleasurable or anxiety producing. The exteroceptive system prenatally receives much less stimulation, principally because of the many layers—maternal abdomen, uterine wall, amniotic fluid—existing between the external world and the fetus. Thus it might be speculated that upon failure of the exteroceptive system, after birth, to provide a sense of enduring and satisfying reality—perhaps because of the rapid oscillation in the maternal emotional attitudes—the infant regresses to the more archaic proprioceptive system which provided some predictable security. Whether the regression may go still further to the enteroceptive system and thus explain some of the organ preoccupations, especially those seen in psychotic hypochondriasis, is still more speculative.

The writer has not been able to secure much if any data bearing on the reasons for the predominance of the falling dream. However, he did note in his examination of selectees some evidence which is consistent with the etiological theory discussed regarding difficulties in introjection and identification due to changes in maternal images. The evidence pertains to the relationship between the predominant anxiety dream and the age at which the selectee lost his mother. Of 174 selectees who were separated from the mother before the age of six, 66 percent had predominantly falling dreams and 34 percent had predominantly attacked dreams. However, in 206 cases who had lost the mother between the ages of six and thirteen the percentages were about reversed, being 31 percent and 69 percent, respectively. (The age at which the father was lost had no relation to the predominant anxiety dream experienced.) It is probable that with early loss of the mother there were many insecurities associated with shifting placements and different mother figures. The greater frequency of the falling dream in such early loss might be explained on the basis that the ego identifications and introjections before the age of six are less sturdy and/or that the problem of making new and stable identifications with new mother figures is too difficult because of the differences involved and the plurality of figures.

Implications of the Data

The implications of the data and speculations for psychiatric diagnosis, prognosis, and treatment can carry us far afield. Thus the writer will limit himself here both in the number of topics mentioned and in the depth to which these topics are discussed.

First, the question of nosology may be dealt with. Although the clinical examples of falling persons cited here have been concerned with evidence of ego infantilism, still the writer finds it difficult to state flatly that the predominance of the falling dream is pathognomic of such infantilism and its ominous consequences. If we examine an ego out of context and only fasten our gaze upon evidence of internalization or externalization of controls, then perhaps such a flat statement could be made. But if we think of an ego in context—that is, with its psychosocial integrative capacities—it is likely that a somewhat more conservative appraisal of the predominance of the falling dream is necessary.

It might be safest at this stage of investigation to say that the falling-dream predominance may reflect a stage of ego maturation in which the controls tend to be externalized, whereas the attacked-dream predominance may reflect a stage in which the controls are internalized. Whether or not one stage precedes the other may, even if true, be less important for psychic health than the degree of psychosocial integration achieved by means of this ego state. Thus, extreme degrees of externalization or internalization would, because of the implied personality rigidity, make the person vulnerable to insoluble conflicts. Mild or moderate reliance on one's self or upon external objects may not hamper the person's integrative solution. Instead of saying that internalization is superior to externalization of controls, or that complete individuation of the self is superior to incomplete individuation, we might think in terms of optimum degrees of individuation, with the falling persons on one side of the optimum and the attacked persons on the other.

Thus it may be that falling persons experience no greater nor more enduring conflict than attacked persons, although there may be considerable difference in the manner in which the conflict is resolved. The fact that selectees were evenly divided as to their predominant anxiety dream, the fact that the writer has examined many seemingly well-integrated falling persons, and the fact that persons can adjust well in a culture which relies on more primitive and archaic psychic devices—these facts would support the contention that conflict may not be any more frequent in falling than in attacked persons.

The point can, however, be justly made that there are better and worse types of integration. Granting that some responsiveness to and dependence on the opinions of others is necessary for social harmony, one should note that the climate of psychiatric opinion is to the effect that a better psychosocial integration is achieved when, after intrapsychic integration, a feeling of individuality evolves which then contributes in a creative way to import objects and the social scene. In this sense, the falling person may not have as potentially "good" an integration as the attacked person.

As was stated, the methods of adaptation and solution of conflict probably differ between falling and attacked persons. Thus, object relationships may serve differing purposes. With the falling person an object relationship might tend to make him feel not only more whole and more integrated, but in more extreme cases, also more real, as though external objects were used as reference points, similar to the space-orienting stimuli engaging the proprioceptive system. The consequent urgent need to preserve objects may be manifested by excessive devotion or allegiance to a person, a group, a religion, or a symbol. The excessiveness of such feeling is due to a strong emotional urge to believe, as though not to believe strongly in an external something is tantamount to losing the sense of reality. The attacked person perhaps tends to use object relationship in a freer way since his sense of reality depends more on internalized objects. Strong beliefs about omnipotence would be centered around himself rather than the external world.

This difference in object relationships is displayed also in the ability or lack of ability to speak negatively of other people. The attacked person has comparatively little difficulty in this regard, whereas the falling person, especially in telling of his family background, will speak of others in idealistic or noncritical terms: "My mother was just wonderful," "My childhood was very happy," and so on. One falling adult gave a characteristic response when asked about his particular dislikes in people. After hesitating, he finally said, "What good would it do to start picking at people's faults. When you get through, who would you have left?"

Going back for a moment to the manifest content of the two dreams, we might find some clues to the difference in object relationships. We are aware that the hostile, destructive environmental objects in the attacked dream are projections of the person's own hostile destructiveness. Following Melanie Klein's theoretical conception, we might think of this paranoid projection as an attempt to preserve existing internalizations. Thus, the attacked person can, and in extreme cases must, speak negatively of other people in order to preserve his self-esteem. However, in the falling dream the fault is not projected—the "badness" is within the dreamer, his own impulses are the cause of his destructiveness. The environment is comparatively blameless. Thus, just as the attacked person tries to preserve necessary internalizations by a real or delusionally projective criticism of external objects, the falling person attempts to preserve necessary external objects by a realistic or delusional denial of badness in them. The consequent basic attitude of many falling persons regarding their own likability and other attributes is frequently a disparaging or pessimistic one.

The preceding considerations shed some light, in the writer's opinion, upon the question asked earlier in this communication. Why are falling persons seen less often in psychoanalytic practice than attacked persons? We might ask, what sort of patients seek the type of help psychoanalysis offers, and which patients do analysts accept for analysis? It has been the general experience that those most likely to seek and be accepted for analysis—as opposed to supportive therapy or environmental manipulation—are persons who, troubled by an internal conflict, feel that their conflict can be resolved by elimination of a part of themselves which they regard as ego alien. The falling patients would more likely tend to feel that their conflicts could be resolved by obtaining more external acceptance and support. If, in their development, they have not completely individuated or demarcated themselves from the external world, they also would have more difficulty in distinguishing between self and not-self or between ego syntonic and ego alien elements. The attacked person, on the other hand, with a more complete individuation can better appreciate what is self and not-self and tends to be more sensitive to what is externally foreign or alien to himself.

An indication that the falling person tends to solve his lack of integration by restoring from the outside world what is lacking in him, whereas the attacked person tends to solve his lack of integration by ridding himself of foreign objects, is suggested by some observations concerning children's wishes. In eight cases in which one of the three wishes was to get rid of something—no longer have a reading difficulty, no more disease in the world, and so on—all the children had predominantly attacked dreams, whereas in six cases in which the wish was to restore something missing (my dog would come back, I would be at home, my mother would stop work) five of the children had predominantly falling dreams and one had predominantly attacked dreams.

The principal reason advanced so far for the low incidence of falling persons in psychoanalytic practice is that these persons are not attracted by the type of help psychoanalysis has to offer. Other reasons of possible import, but more debatable, are that the falling patients, if fixated at an early stage of ego maturation, do not possess the ego strength or the capacity for genuine object relationship which is necessary for the success of psychoanalytic treatment. Certainly the impulsivelike emotionality and the defensiveness described earlier in this paper would provide serious obstacles to analysis.

Whereas falling persons might be seen less often in psychoanalytic practice, this would not be necessarily true in general psychiatric practice or in related areas. Their particular integrative solution has no more guarantee of success than has the intrapsychic integrative solution of the attacked persons. Thus, falling persons might be seen often in the large emotionally disturbed fraction of medical practice, in the state hospitals, in prisons, in the indigent section of the population, and in deviant fringe groups. The writer has made no systematic observations regarding these incidences, but from examination of military patients and parents of disturbed children, he feels that there is a strong probability of this being true.

This brings us finally to the area of actual treatment, an area which, because of the paucity of falling patients the writer has had in therapy, cannot be explored adequately in this report. Whether the falling patient, in view of his preferred and accustomed type of solution, can be handled in the usual psychoanalytic manner, or whether he has to be educated to analysis, or whether he needs first considerable ego strengthening, are questions that can be posed rather than answered here. It seems to the writer that, in general, different methods may have to be used with the falling patients. In this connection Anna Freud's description of the two types of treatment of children comes to mind (1926–1927a). *With a boy whose compulsive rituals were based on castration anxiety, the more classic psychoanalytic procedure was used. However, with a girl whose neurotic symptoms were derived from a fear of loss of love, an educational procedure was used which involved changing the external prohibitive parental attitudes.* Anna Freud's theoretical explanation of the difference in procedure was to the effect that in the boy the superego was independent (internalized) and could not be influenced by mere external permissiveness, whereas in the girl the superego was still in communication with and influenced by the parent figures.

Here there is an implication that conflicts arising predominantly from castration anxiety are associated with an independent superego and should be handled by a classical analytic procedure, whereas conflicts arising predominantly from fear of loss of love are associated with a dependent superego and are best handled by modification of the environment. This implication would be supportive of what has been set forth here regarding the predominant psychic threats—fear of loss of love, fear of bodily injury—operating in falling and attacked persons, regarding the locus of the mechanisms of control and finally regarding the methods of solution.

In essence, this paper has been a report of personality trends in a large number of persons. The writer has limited himself to the reporting of clinical impressions based mostly on conscious material and to the proposal of a tentative theoretical structure to explain these impressions. From the aspect of data, this type of report stands midway between a penetrating long-term clinical study of less conscious material in a small homogeneous group and a strictly controlled statistical study of conscious data in a large group. Thus, the limitations here as to methodological rigor call for further reports of a more refined nature. From the aspect of the proposed hypotheses, there is the risk of suggesting a typology in which sharp dichotomies exist. Nothing so rigid is intended here for the reason that the human personality is too complex to be accounted for in these terms. What *is* intended is a viewpoint by means of which the predominant typical anxiety dream acquires further meaning for the diagnostician and therapist.

Summary

In an earlier paper, the author attempted to demonstrate the following: (1) that over 80 percent of a large number of persons (selectees, military psychiatric patients, children, and parents at a child guidance clinic) reported that their most unpleasant dream was one of two typical anxiety dreams—(a) dreams of falling from heights, and (b) dreams of being attacked from without (chased, threatened, stabbed, shot at, and so on); (2) that individual differences existed as to the predominant unpleasantness of these two dreams.

In this communication, enquiry is made as to the characterological significance of the predominant unpleasantness of the falling or attacked dream. Attention is centered on some of the personality characteristics of the falling person. The emphasis on the falling person is due to the author's experience that persons for whom the falling dream has been most unpleasant are infrequently seen in psychoanalytic treatment in comparison with the attacked persons.

Three characteristics found more frequently in falling than in attacked persons are described: (1) comparative inability to express overt defiance, especially in the mother–child relationship, but also in later interpersonal settings; (2) a tendency to express feelings in a full, naive, uninhibited manner; (3) a tendency to use defensiveness as a method of protecting self-esteem. In the discussion, the author suggests that these three characteristics are outcroppings of a stage in ego maturation in which the infant has not fully individuated itself from the mother and consequently in which the psychic controls reside externally rather than internally. Thus, there is a tendency in falling persons, because of this particular type of maturation or failure of maturation, to rely on external controls and objects. Attacked persons, because of greater or excessive individuation, tend to rely more on internal controls. Since psychoanalytic treatment has for a large part been derived from an understanding and handling of the internalized psychic controls, the writer believes it would be of further help to understand a large group of patients who tend to be more dependent on external controls.

Chapter 19

PSYCHOANALYTIC STUDY OF A TYPICAL DREAM

Allan Roos

Everyone recognizes motility as an important characteristic of life and living matter—whether it is the act of extension of the pseudopod of a Paramecium or the locomotion of man. This is reflected in the verb *animate*, which has a double meaning: "To make alive, or fill with breath; also, to give motion to or put into action." The dictionary cites as an example of its use, "the breeze animated the leaves." Often we equate death with the absence of motility. Voluntary control of motility is renounced during sleep, a fact which becomes important in certain neurotic sleep disturbances. During sleep the characteristic unconscious content of such disturbances often expresses an inability to flee from certain dangers or nameless dreads. Sleep itself, if it becomes equated with death, arouses great anxiety.

The identification of life with motility does not always exist, as, for small children, this concept is indistinct and is subject to considerable confusion. Piaget (1955) writes of a time "when the child takes cognizance of the difference between life and death." In describing how one child attempted to satisfy his curiosity about death and to discover distinguishing criteria between life and death, Piaget wrote: "Are they dead (those leaves)?—Yes—But they move with the wind." By coincidence both Piaget's little boy and the lexicographer used the identical image: leaves in the wind.

Over a period of years I have observed what appears to be a typical dream in the analyses of a number of patients. A

This paper was first published in the *Psychoanalytic Quarterly* (1960), 29:153–174.

274

typical dream is, in the classical sense, one whose manifest content is stereotyped and one which occurs fairly frequently in a variety of dreamers.

Freud was fascinated by typical dreams, among which he included examination dreams, dreams of nakedness, dreams of falling and flying, of missing a train, and those which refer to the deaths of relatives or other persons who are close to or have been in an intimate relation with the dreamer. Freud (1900) stated that

> [A]s a general rule, each person is at liberty to construct his dream-world according to his individual peculiarities and so to make it unintelligible to other people. It now appears, however, that in complete contrast to this, there are a certain number of dreams which almost everyone has dreamt alike and which we are accustomed to assume must have the same meaning for everyone. A special interest attaches, moreover, to these typical dreams because they presumably arise from the same sources in every case and thus seem particularly well qualified to throw light on the sources of dreams [p. 241].

Freud noted "with great reluctance" that the accepted, usual technique of dream interpretation was disappointing in revealing the latent content of these typical dreams as the dreamer generally failed to produce associations essential to their understanding. "We are not in general in a position to interpret another person's dream unless he is prepared to communicate to us the unconscious thoughts that lie behind its content. The practical applicability of our method of interpreting dreams is in consequence severely restricted" (p. 241). In a footnote, which he added in 1925, Freud made an exception of dreams which employ *symbolic* elements, in the analysis of which he proposed the use of "a secondary and auxiliary method of dream interpretation."

In his study of dreams and myths, Abraham (1909, pp. 151–209) showed that there were certain fantasies which could not be ascribed to any single individual. Such collective fantasies or myths, and also fairy tales, revealed "the fantasy of a nation."

Abraham had as his purpose the demonstration that Freud's doctrines concerning the dream could to a considerable extent be applied to the psychology of myths and thus provide a new basis for their understanding. He believed that typical dreams had their origin in infantile wishes shared by all mankind, and that these same wishes formed the basis of certain ubiquitous myths. Usually, such desires are repressed during the dreamer's earliest years, and Abraham stressed the derivation of myths and typical dreams from such repressed infantile wishes and memories. Highly instructive in this respect are dreams about the deaths of near relatives. Such dreams do not necessarily mean that the dreamer entertains such a wish at the present time but often signify that he once did so, perhaps in his distant past. Such desires, common to most if not all mankind, are also encountered in myths, which thus express the collective wishes and strivings of a nation.

Referring to Freud, Abraham concluded that the legend of Oedipus contains something which arouses kindred feelings in us all. "In the Oedipus tragedy we see our childhood wishes fulfilled, while we ourselves have in the course of our development replaced our sexual attraction to the mother and our rebellion against the father by feelings of love and piety." (In the Yeats translation, Oedipus, in his death throes, says, "No living man has loved as I have loved.") As Freud says:

> [T]he tragedy itself contains an allusion to the typical dream in which the dreamer becomes sexually united with his mother. . . . The analysis of most myths, as of most dreams, is rendered more difficult by the symbolic disguise of the intrinsic content. It is precisely because this complication is absent in the Oedipus legend, and in the typical dreams whose content is related to it that it is particularly suitable to serve as an introduction to the problem which interests us.

Abraham then conjectures that the symbolism to which Freud called our attention is, and has always been, deeply imbedded in everyone.

Dream formation and myth formation display important similarities and internal relationships. The Prometheus myth, for example, shows the psychological relationship between myths and dreams. Behind the manifest content of both lies a latent content, and the latent content of the dream is accessible through the associations of its dreamer, as the latent content of a myth may be understood by the traditions and legends of what might be called the period of infancy in the life of a people. Similarly, condensation, displacement, and repression are common both to the myth and the typical dream. It is because of a tendency to "mass repression" that a people is no longer able to understand the original meaning of its myths, just as we fail through repression to understand our dreams.

Martin Wangh (1954) described similar unconscious sources of a patient's dream and the ubiquitous myths of "little folk." He also showed that the day residue of the dream has a similar counterpart in the formation of a myth.

The well-populated underworld (or afterworld) of the ancient Greeks contained as one of its geographic landmarks the Acheron, the "river of woe" which, according to legend, emptied into Cocytus, "the river of lamentation." There were three other rivers in Greek mythology involved in the passage of the dead to the Elysian fields or to Hades, the last of them being the Styx, called "the river of the unbreakable oath" by which the gods swear (Hamilton, 1940). Charon, an aged boatman, ferried the souls of the newly dead across the water; however, Charon permitted in his boat only the souls of those on whose lips passage money had been placed. This story of Charon, the ferryman of the dead and of the rivers of the underworld, is here described to call attention to the fact that even in ancient Greece, as today, the necessity of some vehicle for the transportation of the souls of the dead was assumed.[1] This is in sharp

---

[1] I am indebted to Dr. Bertram D. Lewin for the following observation which was told by the daughter of a dying man.

In his near terminal delirium, the old man was evidently imagining and sometimes hallucinating that he was on board a boat, in a way reminiscent of the play *Outward Bound*. He would get out of bed saying that he had to get off the boat, and he would sometimes, when not watched, run into the wall or the furniture in his room. He seemed in this way to show that he knew he was on his last journey and was trying to interrupt it. A stubborn man, he had never in his clear periods admitted that he was in any danger of death.

contrast to the ghost of Hamlet's father who was "doom'd for a certain term to walk the night." The coin which was placed on a corpse's lips or tongue became known as "Charon's obol," a silver piece which represented the fee exacted by Charon for the journey to one or other of the realms of the dead. Similar coins, used for like purposes, were prevalent in Japan, the Balkans, and elsewhere. In Brittany the dead are thought to travel in a type of cart. In Mexico certain indigenous Indian tribes have evolved an elaborate journey which is undertaken by the souls of the newly dead, a journey which lasts for seven days and which involves crossing one or more rivers.

Quite recently, in historical terms, a widespread myth became manifest in Europe. It was described by Marie Bonaparte (1947) as "The Myth of the Corpse in the Car." During World War II the story of the corpse in the car assumed "the widespread dignity of a myth" throughout France. "The death . . . of the stray passenger, the death of a man, seems a pledge of far greater potency and appears to set a seal of finality on fate's decrees."

In the autumn of 1938, Rudolph M. Loewenstein related a curious event as told to him by Marie Bonaparte.

> In September 1938, a young man who was expecting his call up was driving his fiancée to Laval, intending to leve her with relatives. Outside Paris he stops for petrol. A middle-aged couple ask where he is going and then beg a lift for the lady who is going in that direction, whereas the man is returning to Paris to join up the following day. As they drive, the fiancée begins to cry and talk about their imminent separation. The stranger, however, assures them that all will be well and tells the girl to stop crying. "You'll never be called up," she says to the man, "because there won't be a war. Anyway Hitler will be dead in six months." This she repeats several times. At Laval, before taking leave of the young man, she asks whether he intends to return to Paris and when. He replies that he is returning immediately. The lady then advises him not to drive back that night because, if he does, he will find a corpse in his car.

The young people however think her "dotty" and drive off without asking either her name or address. Later, before he leaves Laval, the young man's relatives ask him to give a lift to a lad they know who is also expecting an immediate call up. He agrees. En route the passenger says he feels drowsy, stretches out on the back seat, and falls asleep. Back in Paris, the car stops at the passenger's address; the young man opens the door to wake him and finds the lad dead.

The following story was told to Bonaparte's husband, "with similar assurances of authenticity."

A man is called up. With his wife and daughter he drives to Versailles. It is late and he says to his wife: "I shan't have petrol enough to get up the hill." Two or three hundred meters from the top of the rise to St. Cloud, his tank runs dry. He gets out, looks right and left, but to no effect. Then, however, under the trees, he sees some gypsies to whom he calls for help to push the car uphill. One of the gypsies says: "You won't get back tonight without a stiff in your car." He fills up with petrol and is returning to Paris when he is stopped by a policeman who asks him to take an injured man to the hospital. Before they could reach the hospital, the injured man dies in the car.

Bonaparte speculates about the link between these two happenings which she interprets as much deeper "than the mere truth of one prediction vouching for another. . . . If the myth seemed almost universally to crop up, it is doubtless because war, with its anxieties and dangers, must have revivified within us some of humanity's most ancient beliefs; in this case the conviction of the need for a sacrifice, to obtain some great good fortune." Although Bonaparte does not speculate on the specific nature of this sacrifice, it would seem a likely reference to the death of Hitler, and the release from repression of this ubiquitous death wish.

Dreams

I

A dream was reported by a lawyer who was in psychoanalysis because of a sexual perversion.

> I was driving in my new car through snowdrifts when I realized I was off the road and that I would have difficulty swinging her back, but managed to do so. I looked at the car from the outside and noticed it was gray and wrinkled. I drove to a shop and discussed having it repainted. The question arose as to why I was carrying a corpse around in the car. I don't know if it was in a shroud or coffin but there was some legal question as to whether I could park a car with a corpse in it—this was a source of embarrassment to me.

This patient had just acquired a new car and he came to his analytic hour in it each day, driving a considerable distance. This situation created various problems and much anxiety when the weather was snowy. On the night preceding the dream there had been a heavy snowfall.

The patient's father had died when he was an adolescent and since then he had beome more emotionally involved with his mother, a domineering, highly intelligent, erratic alcoholic. His relationship to her was submissive, and he was frequently faced with the conflict of acceding either to his mother's demands or to his duties toward his wife. The snowdrifts in the dream made high piles similar to those left by a snowplow, and it was difficult to drive the car between them. At this point the patient suddenly recalled a recent difficulty he had experienced during coitus. This consisted of an inability to effect vaginal entry each time he determined to attempt intercourse without recourse to the perverse sexual practice which initially caused him to seek psychoanalytic help. The paint of the car was gray, not unlike the color of his father's hair, and the wrinkled appearance of this paint recalled to the patient James Joyce's reference to the "scrotum-tightening sea." Although the corpse looked unfamiliar, there were many associations to the death of his father and to his horrified fascination at seeing him in the casket. As he recalled looking at the body of his dead father he began to cry, realizing the finality of their aloof, cool, strained, and emotionally unfulfilled relationship. At the time he had cast about for some means of reversing what intellectually he knew to be an irreversible state.

II

Another patient was preoccupied by a conflict of whether or not to leave his elderly, enfeebled parents and to accept a very attractive and remunerative post which would have necessitated living in Europe. "I am seated in a room and am suddenly aware of my wife dragging L into it. He seems to be dead drunk. Then I am going along a canal when I see a small ship all decorated in black coming from the other direction. I hear funeral drums and somebody tells me not to be so gay because the ship is carrying L's body."

L, a friend, always reminded the patient of his brother, who was nine years older than the patient. There was a striking physical resemblance between L and this brother and they had certain common mannerisms and mutual interests. At one time they shared the same apartment. During the evening preceding the dream the patient had come across a letter which L had written, recommending him for the European post. A few years before the patient had arranged a pro forma marriage between L and a former girl friend of the patient whose uncertain immigration status he wished to clarify and support. Shortly after this marriage it was found that the girl was "highly unreliable." The patient interceded, this time unsuccessfully, trying to persuade her to grant L a divorce. Although L repeatedly attempted to reassure the patient that he had gone into the marriage with open eyes and did not hold it against him, the patient nonetheless felt bad about it.

For many years L drank excessively and often would return after an absence of days with a black eye and bandaged head. When sober he had a shy, serious, smiling manner and looked like a bookworm; in these attributes he resembled the patient's infirm, aged father, a retired physician.

The dream occurred the night before the resumption of analysis after my summer vacation. The patient had resented this break in the treatment and had speculated about how I would look when next he saw me. The boat in the dream recalled the little ship which as a boy he and his parents took each year to reach their summer home. "It practically belonged to my father, who made the return trip at least once and sometimes twice a day and so got to know the engineer quite well."

In telling the dream the patient emphasized the enormous sense of gaiety with which he greeted the sight of this boat even after he had been told that it was transporting L's dead body. On awakening he had been struck by the apparent inappropriateness of the affect in the dream.

III

The day after the death of Pope Pius XII, a very successful young business executive with strong latent homosexual tendencies told of having a dream.

> My father was lying like the Pope, stretched out on the back seat of a car. My wife was driving. I was being taken along for the ride—somehow I didn't want to go yet I did. I remember being afraid to say anything about not wanting to go and still feeling that I wanted to see what was going on. I was afraid of the driver. My mother was "in on" the disposal of my father. We drove frantically with father's body twisting along on the back seat. It all resembled an Agatha Christie movie: the man on the back seat of the car, and this group of women who had killed him but not by sticking a knife into him. Somehow they had got the best of him and had done away with him.

During intercourse the previous night the patient suddenly recalled having heard of the Pope's death. Immediately this thought became conscious, he lost his erection and had to withdraw. Why thinking of the Pope's death should have produced this effect puzzled him. He remembered that a pope is, in Italian, called *Il Papa*. He expressed vague fears that somehow the dream might be used against him.

His parents were divorced when he was four or five years of age. His mother was then disconsolate and told him that he would now be the man of the household and take care of her; that they would henceforth be inseparable. He became depressed and hostile when, a few months after the divorce, a stranger moved into the house. The stranger married his mother not long afterward. The patient grew increasingly resentful and began to yearn for his father. In further associations to the dream he remembered the bitterness that had characterized his mother's attitude toward his father, and how provocative had been her exhibitionistic behavior toward the patient. Although not Catholic, the patient had been sent to a parochial school for several years of his childhood. During this period he had been fascinated by the Sisters of the Immaculate Conception who were his teachers.

When an adolescent he arrived unannounced to rejoin and live with his father. He went to his father's apartment without notifying him, found the doors unlocked, and discovered his father having intercourse with a strange woman whom he thought must be a prostitute. The father was embarrassed and apologetic, but the patient never completely forgave what seemed at the time so patent a betrayal.

On the following night the patient dreamed what was clearly a continuation of the first dream. "Somebody had died and I was terribly frightened. I was masturbating in a compulsive way a much older fellow with a large, uncircumcised penis. I couldn't help myself and still I hated doing it. I always hated uncircumcised penises."

The patient was glad that he had been circumcised at birth, although at times he expressed a wish that it had not been done. He loathed the sight of an uncircumcised penis, which he regarded as "something horrid and dirty." He immediately thought of his father whose big, uncircumcised penis had been a source of grim fascination for him during the years of adolescence which followed their reunion. He thought of the uncircumcised penis as unclean, comparing it with the vagina with which it shared malodorous and unappetizing characteristics. When a young boy he asked his father, "What is that?," pointing to his father's penis, and was told, "Oh, that's my chocolate bar."

He complained, "If only they wouldn't plaster pictures of his body all over the papers when a pope dies." It was evident that his father had been killed in the dream and was stretched out on the back seat of the car; it seemed as if all the women who had been close to the patient had killed his father and that he had been one with them. He speculated whether the sexual attraction of playing with his father's uncircumcised penis might be related to his sudden impotence the night before: "Obviously I loved my father much more than I ever realized and yet I also hated him for having left me and mother when I was young."

He suddenly recalled an episode which corresponded to the time of the parents' divorce, during his fourth or fifth year, in which his mother displayed her breasts. He also remembered how exciting but upsetting it had been to see her pubic hair. He apologetically expressed fears of boring me with these memories since without doubt I must have heard similar ones often before. He hated the thought of being sexually under the control of his wife, who was now pregnant. It was she who was driving the car in the dream. Her pregnancy imposed on him a considerable degree of sexual frustration. In recent weeks he had experienced an insatiable appetite for chocolate candy bars, remembering again this reference to his father's penis. He noted various differences between the appearance of his father's uncircumcised and his own circumcised penis. When he was three or four years of age his mother had found him masturbating. She warned him that this would cause his penis to be cut or bitten off.

IV

During an interruption of her analysis, a highly intelligent woman in her middle forties began to speculate about where I might have gone and why. Gradually she noticed that she was becoming increasingly depressed and dreamed

> I was at a family funeral. I saw my father's sister standing at the side of a carriage or caisson on which a dead body was resting. I awoke with a start, terribly worried about my parents' health, and felt that I must phone at once to see if anything had happened to my father. Then I fell asleep again and saw my father dressed in an army uniform, seated on a cot in a barracks room. He looked very much as he usually does. Then I dreamt of finding an analyst with a peculiar name—it seemed to be Japanese.

This dream followed by several days my having told her of plans to move to the West Coast. She found this news unwelcome and repeated it to a confidante who then mentioned an acquaintance recently departed for California and now going to an analyst with a Japanese name. She wondered whether my absence might have been related to a trip to California. Heretofore she had always felt diffident in describing her feelings about me. She regretted never having been able to tell her father that she was in psychoanalysis, and she felt it frustrating that for her this subject was taboo. Yet her father, a retired missionary, would not have understood; he was strict and quick to scold. It had never been possible to have uninhibited talk with her parents, whom she had come increasingly to avoid. She tearfully recalled that her father had been in the army during the First World War. There was some vague memory of having missed him, of having resented his absence, and of having thought she would never see him again. Reconstruction placed these feelings in her fourth or fifth year. She wondered whether his military service accounted for the caisson in her dream. Because, she said, she had had a highly religious training, whenever she contemplated her father's death it was with a feeling of sinfulness: "Talking or even thinking about such things makes me feel awful and unworthy; besides I love my father very much."

V

A woman patient dreamed:

> I was with somebody in an old car. It's funny, he seemed
> familiar and yet I could not recognize him. The old, bro-
> ken-down car had square lines similar to one in a comic
> strip. I was driving, and on the right side of the road there
> was a little house with two doors. I got out and knocked at
> the left door. My oldest sister came to the door and I told
> her I was looking for father and she said he was dead and
> showed me some kind of certificate. I took a lot of blankets
> and covered the whole car like a corpse so I could only see
> straight ahead.

The patient's father had recently died in a remote city, and
she was occupied with protracted funeral arrangements. She
added to the dream that the other person in the car was in the
back seat. "I looked again at this person and saw that it was my
father, stretched out in the back very still, as if he were dead
or asleep." Now she could see her father lying naked on top of
the bed with her mother, perhaps following intercourse. The
sister who appeared in the dream had occupied the room next
to hers during her early years, and she often heard this older
sister and her husband making strange noises which she
thought must be sexual. Repeatedly at such times she felt how
nice it would be to be in her sister's place, yet she feared her
unpredictable, violent brother-in-law who "couldn't resist
young girls or young children."

This patient's father had seduced her sexually during her
fourth year, an experience which had been totally repressed
and one to which she returned repeatedly following its emergence during later phases of analysis. She remembered that he
had sworn her to secrecy with threats.

A night or two before the dream the patient feared she
was going to be smothered by the weights of her husband.
Once, when a little girl, she was rescued by her brother-in-
law when she almost drowned while swimming. She knew that
"fascinating" things occurred between her parents as well as

between her brother-in-law and sister; because she was so much younger than her sister the adults of the family felt free to do things in her hearing which otherwise they would not. She visualized her father's appearance, during the first of several sexual contacts, "like a great mass of white flesh. I remember that both my father and my brother-in-law sometimes would touch or play with me when I was nine. I thought this was my 'magical secret'; the way I had of getting them to love me."

VI

An author was in the third year of analysis when his father died suddenly though not unexpectedly. He was married but remained too strongly attached to his mother. His feelings for his father had always been highly ambivalent. A fortnight after the father's death, the patient reported a dream. "Last night I dreamed I was driving a large black car down a country road. Suddenly I became aware that someone else was in the car. I turned around and saw it was my father, slumped over and ashen. I thought he must be asleep or dead, and I awoke shaking with fright."

The country road reminded him of Shakespeare's pun in Hamlet.[2] The road resembled one on which his father had bought a country house some years previously. The patient never learned to drive a car. The big, black car seemed like a hearse. The patient now thought about his father almost constantly in a regretful, ruminative manner. He expressed identical rueful feelings of unfulfillment and regret at the loss of his father, as had the lawyer who reported the initial dream of this series.[3]

---

[2]Hamlet: Lady, shall I lie in your lap?
Ophelia: No, my lord.
Hamlet: I mean, my head upon your lap?
Ophelia: Ay, my lord.
Hamlet: Do you think I meant country matters?
Ophelia: I think nothing, my lord.
Hamlet: That's a fair thought to lie between maid's legs.
[Act III, Scene II.]

[3]In this connection it is instructive to recall a passage from Freud's preface to the second edition of *The Interpretation of Dreams* (1900, p. xxvi). "For this book has a further subjective significance for me personally—a significance which I only grasped after I had completed it. It was, I found, a portion of my own self-analysis, my reaction to my

The evening preceding the dream, the patient had dined alone with his mother for the first time since his father's death: "It was pleasant being alone with her, just the two of us, although she is still quite sad. We spoke of father and of his sudden death on the train on the way south. I'm sorry I wasn't alone with them, especially as they had suggested that I accompany them. In the dream I was shocked at my father's appearance—he certainly seemed to be dead; or maybe dying. I was surprised to be in the driver's seat."

There is a striking similarity in all these dreams. The patient is either a passenger or the driver in some vehicle, typically a car. In the back of the vehicle is a corpse, manifestly the patient's father, or identified as the father or as an older brother in the latent dream content. The dreams were dreamed by both female and male patients. In each instance some actual situation reactivated early infantile memories and the oedipal conflict. These patients without exception had had severe preoedipal disturbance with severe castration anxiety and a tendency toward regression. These neurotic and developmental disturbances are consonant with the findings of Lampl-de Groot (1952).

These dreams of the death of the father represented either an oedipal wish or a counterphobic fantasy in which the father was rescued. Abraham (1922) showed that the son's impulses of defiance against his father find their chief expression in rescue fantasies. Often in such fantasies the son saves his father or a substitute, for example, a king, from death.

Abraham writes: "In the fantasy which I have in mind the patient imagines himself walking in a street. Suddenly he sees a carriage with the king, or some other highly placed person in it, approaching with alarming rapidity. Boldly he sizes the

---

father's death—that is to say, to the most important event, the most poignant loss, of a man's life." Freud's father had died in 1896, and on November 2nd of that year he wrote to Wilhelm Fliess: "By one of the obscure routes behind the official consciousness the old man's death affected me deeply. I valued him highly and understood him very well indeed, and with his peculiar mixture of deep wisdom and imaginative lightheartedness he meant a great deal in my life. By the time he died his life had long been over, but at a death, the whole past stirs within one. I feel now as if I had been torn up by the roots" (E. L. Freud, 1960).

horses' reins and brings the carriage to a standstill, thus saving the king from mortal danger" (1909, pp. 151–209). Abraham notes that the manifest content of this rescue fantasy contravenes the myth of Oedipus. He emphasizes the similarity between the two fantasies, the manifest content of both having a remarkable similarity. "In both the encounter with the king is represented as a chance occurrence. It is particularly striking, moreover, that in both the king rides in a carriage. The symbolic substitution of king for father and rescue for killing indicates the parallel to the Oedipus myth. The transformation of attack into rescue is a product of the censorship of the neurotic" (1909, pp. 151–209). Abraham observes that the horse is "a symbol of masculine potency and of the male sexual organ. We know that the following dream symbols have the same meaning: engine, motorcar, and steamship. They share in common the quality of pushing forward with overwhelming force. If the son successfully stops the runaway horses, he proves by doing so that his masculine potency is superior to that of his father" (1909, pp. 151–209).

Abraham cites a dream of the rescue.

I am sitting on the left side of my mother in a small two-wheeled carriage, a dogcart which is drawn by one horse. To the right of the carriage, close to the wheel, stands my father. His attitude signifies that he is speaking, or has just spoken, to my mother, but no word is to be heard, and certainly my mother does not react in any way. He looks noticeably tired and pale. Now he turns silently away from the carriage and walks off in the opposite direction to that in which the carriage is facing. Whilst I watch him disappear I have the expectation that he will soon come back again and I turn to my mother with the words: "We could meanwhile drive up and down." Mother now makes a slight movement with the reins which she holds in her hands whereupon the horse slowly begins to move. After a few moments I take the reins from her hands, whip up the horse, and we quickly drive away.

Abraham notes the obvious derivation of this dream from the Oedipus complex. The son is in the father's place in the two-seated carriage. The father is disposed of. Incest is here represented by mother and son driving away together and, characteristically, the incest begins at the moment when the father disappears. Abraham felt that this fantasy had as its aim "the tendency to prevent the parents from coming together. The intention to separate the parents belongs to those instinctual manifestations which derive with particular frequency from the oedipus complex" (1909, pp. 151–209).

The elements of rescue in the Oedipus complex are seen with especial clarity in *Hamlet* which, according to the renowned Shakespearean scholar Georg Brandes (1896), was written immediately after the death of Shakespeare's father. Shakespeare was thus "under the immediate impact of his bereavement and, as we may well assume, . . . his childhood feelings about his father had been freshly revived" (Freud, 1900, p. 265). Usually it is evident that the rescue in the oedipal myth is associated with, and a reaction to the primary hostile attitude of the son toward his father. Oedipus is told by the oracle that he will kill his father and marry his mother, acts which he subsequently unwittingly performs.

A vivid description of the subjective elements of the rescue fantasy appears in chapter nine of Mohandas Gandhi's autobiography (1957).

> During Gandhi's sixteenth year his father was bedridden and Gandhi acted as his nurse. Every night Gandhi massaged his father's legs, a service he loved to do and which he could not remember ever having neglected. Gandhi went for an evening stroll or retired only at the insistence of his father, or after the latter had fallen asleep. "This," says Gandhi, "was also the time when my wife was expecting a baby, a circumstance which, as I can see today, meant a double shame for me. For one thing I did not restrain myself as I should have done whilst I was yet a student. And secondly, this carnal lust got the better of what . . . was even a greater duty, my devotion to my parents, Shravana having been my ideal since childhood."

Gandhi's father had bought his young son, Mohandas, a book describing Shravana's unusual devotion to his parents. Says Gandhi, "I read it with intense interest. There came to our place about the same time itinerant showmen. One of the pictures I was shown was of Shravana carrying, by means of slings fitted for his shoulders, his blind parents on a pilgrimage." The book and the picture left an indelible impression on his mind. Another version relates how Shravana's father was accidentally shot one night by a hunter who mistook him for an animal. Shravana never forgave himself for having put his father down on the ground, thus making the accident possible.

Despite the efforts of physicians and local quacks, the condition of Gandhi's father deteriorated. An operation was recommended but then thought inadvisable because of his advanced age. Gandhi's uncle, much devoted to his brother, arrived. "The dreadful night came. . . . It was ten-thirty or eleven P.M. I was giving the massage. My uncle offered to relieve me. I was glad and went straight to the bedroom. My wife, poor thing, was fast asleep. But how could she sleep when I was there? I woke her up. In five or six minutes, however, the servant knocked at the door. . . . "Get up," he said, "Father is very ill." I knew of course that he was very ill, and so I guessed what "very ill" meant at that moment. I sprang out of bed. "What is the matter? Do tell me!" "Father is no more." So all was over! I had but to wring my hands. I felt deeply ashamed and miserable. . . . I saw that, if animal passion had not blinded me, I should have been spared the torture of separation from my father during his last moments. I should have been massaging him, and he would have died in my arms. But now it was my uncle who had had this privilege. He was so deeply devoted to his elder brother that he had earned the honor of doing him the last services! . . . The shame, to which I have referred, . . . was this shame of my carnal desire even at the crucial hour of my father's death, which demanded wakeful service. It is a blot I have never been able to efface or forget, and I have always thought that although my devotion to my parents knew no bounds and I would have given up anything for it, yet it was weighed and found unpardonably wanting because my mind was at the same moment in the grip of lust. I have always regarded myself as a lustful, though a faithful husband. . . . Before I close this chapter of my double shame, I may mention that the poor mite that was born to my wife scarcely breathed for more than three or four days. Nothing else could be expected. Let all those who are married be warned by my example.

Freud thought that the rescue fantasy might be derived from the child's hearing it said that he owed his life to his parents, more specifically that his mother gave him life (Freud, 1910c). The boy desired

> [T]o return this gift to the parents and to repay them with one of equal value . . . [The boy] then forms the fantasy of *rescuing his father from danger and saving his life*; in this way he puts his account square with him. . . . In its application to a boy's father it is the defiant meaning in the idea of rescuing which is by far the most important; where his mother is concerned it is usually its tender meaning. . . . The son shows his gratitude by wishing to have by his mother a son who is like himself: in other words, in the rescue fantasy he is completely identifying himself with his father. . . . Under the laws governing the expression of unconscious thoughts, the meaning of rescuing may vary, depending on whether the author of the fantasy is a man or a woman. . . . At times there is also a tender meaning contained in rescue fantasies directed toward the father. In such cases they aim at expressing the subject's wish to have his father as a son—that is, to have a son who is like his father.

It is clear that normally, in the oedipal phase of development, a son desires to take his father's place, a daughter her mother's. A frequent variant of this is the fantasy in which a son rescues his father from mortal danger and a daughter her mother from the same.

In 1872, Frances Power Cobbe (1872) published a book which she called *Darwinism in Morals, and Other Essays*. A chapter on dreams, from which the following passage is quoted, is contiguous to our subject.

The subject of a dream being . . . suggested to the brain . . . , the next thing to be noted is, How does the brain treat its theme when it has got it? Does it dryly reflect upon it, as we are wont to do awake? Or does it pursue a course wholly foreign to the laws of waking thoughts? It does, I conceive, neither one nor the other, but treats its theme, whenever it is possible to do so, according to a certain very important, though obscure, law of thought, whose action we are too apt to ignore. We have been accustomed to consider the myth-creating power of the human mind as one specially belonging to the earlier stages of growth of society and of the individual. It will throw, I think, a rather curious light on the subject if we discover that this instinct exists in every one of us, and exerts itself with more or less energy through the whole of our lives. In hours of waking consciousness, indeed, it is suppressed, or has only the narrowest range of exercise, as in the tendency, noticeable in all persons not of the very strictest veracity, to supplement an incomplete anecdote with explanatory incidents, or to throw a slightly-known story into the dramatic form, with dialogues constructed out of their own consciousness. But such small play of the myth-making faculty is nothing compared to its achievements during sleep. The instant that daylight and commonsense are excluded, the fairy work begins. At the very least half our dreams (unless I greatly err) are nothing else than myths formed by unconscious cerebration on the same approved principles, whereby Greece and India and Scandinavia gave to us the stories which we were once pleased to set apart as "mythology" proper. Have we not here, then, evidence that there is a real law of the human mind causing us constantly to compose ingenius fables explanatory of the phenomena around us,—a law which only sinks into abeyance in the waking hours of persons in whom the reason has been highly cultivated, but which resumes its sway even over their well-tutored brains when they sleep [pp. 151–209].

The relationship between dreams and the collective fantasies known as myths is thus well known and long established. As the dream reflects in part the infantile wishes of an individual, so does the myth reflect the strivings, taboos, and motivations of a people. Freud and Abraham have commented on the intimate relationship between dream and myth as regards their comprehensibility, contents, motive forces, and pathological structures which, in Rank's words, justify "the interpretation of myth as a dream of the masses of the people" (pp. 151–209). The hostility of a son toward his father is described in the classical myths of Oedipus and others in all of which some royal father is the recipient of the prophesy of a future disaster to which he ultimately succumbs, the victim of his son. In the Oedipus story parricide is combined with incest with the mother; in another version the story of Cronos, Cronos having been warned that he would be slain by one of his children, kills all of them but one, Zeus, to whom he in turn succumbs.

Abraham (1909, p. 161) explained the difficulty in analyzing the typical dream "by the symbolic disguise of the intrinsic content." He drew a detailed and close analogy between myths and dreams, both of which employ a symbolic mode of representation, and other familiar mental mechanisms, both of which have manifest as well as latent contents, and both of which are susceptible not only to repression but also to proper analysis.

Summary

The analysis of a number of instances of the same typical dream, reported by various analysands, is recorded. Their common theme of the death of a parent and the rescue fantasy is discussed. The similarity of typical dreams to folklore and myth is reviewed.

Chapter 20

TYPICAL EXAMINATION DREAMS, "SUPEREGO DREAMS," AND TRAUMATIC DREAMS

Owen Renik

Introduction

Freud's (1900) analysis of the typical examination dream provides us with a simple and lucid paradigm of dream formation that can be used to illuminate dreams of all sorts. Applying it to certain "superego dreams" permits the analyst to identify feelings of entitlement and self-justification expressed in a dream, which are not obvious at first, and to demonstrate these feelings to patients who may be more used to thinking of themselves as completely preoccupied with self-criticism and the need for punishment. The paradigm of the typical examination dream can also be applied to those posttraumatic dreams in which a traumatic event is exactly reenacted with monotonous and faithful regularity. Such traumatic dreams are usually conceptualized as exceptions to the principle that dreams are wish fulfillments. It is possible to see them instead as disguised fulfillments of the dreamer's wish to be reassured. This view can serve as the basis of an effective therapeutic approach to the traumatic dream, which has sometimes been found to be a troubling and recalcitrant posttraumatic symptom.

This paper was first published in *Psychoanalytic Quarterly* (1981), 50:159–189.

The Typical Examination Dream

Psychoanalytic investigation reveals that various unconscious meanings can attach to the experience of preparing for and taking an examination. The examination itself may be regarded as a proof of sexual performance. Mastering the necessary material is sometimes unconsciously equated with gaining forbidden knowledge of the facts of life in childhood, and producing the correct answers with displaying the products of that forbidden knowledge. Passing an examination can stand for receiving or displaying a baby, a penis, or parental love. By the same token, failing an examination can signify impotence, castration, or abandonment. All these meanings and more were documented by E. Blum (1926) in an early and comprehensive survey in which he emphasized the interweaving of oedipal and preoedipal conflict in fantasies that become associated with examinations.

Examinations have been related to initiation rituals, with all their progressive functions and attendant anxieties. Flugel (1939) and Kafka (1979) showed how a current examination can recall traumatic physical examinations of earlier years, and Galenson (1978) suggested that the link between scholastic examinations and physical inspection creates special test anxieties in women.

This partial list could be extended indefinitely, but an exhaustive catalog of the widely varying content of examination fantasies is not necessary to the main point of my presentation. It is enough to establish that in any number of ways an examination in adult life can take on unconscious significance related to the expression of childhood wishes. The experience of preparing for and taking an examination then becomes drawn into unresolved conflicts pertaining to those childhood wishes. As a result, we see examination anxieties of irrational origin: one's concerns about performance on an examination go beyond realistic appraisals of one's adequacy to the task at hand, and the sense of risk is not accounted for by the objective rewards of passing and the dangers of failing the actual examination. A typical examination dream represents an effort on the part of the dreamer to allay his own irrational examination anxieties.

There are a great many different kinds of dreams in which the theme of examination occurs, and while it may be appropriate to refer to all of them as "examination dreams," only a small number conform to the type described by Freud as *typical* examination dreams. In calling certain examination dreams "typical," Freud referred to more than the ubiquity of their occurrence. He suggested we call a dream typical when its content is highly specific and predictable, and when its significance is so universally the same among different dreamers that something important about the dream's function can be inferred from the manifest content alone, without benefit of associations. Indeed, in the case of the typical examination dream, Freud said it was crucial to make an inference from the manifest content alone, since there is little in the associative material which will be of further use in revealing the major and most immediate aim of the dream.

A typical examination dream occurs during the night of a day when the dreamer has been thinking of an examination he will have to take in the near future. In the dream, the dreamer is taking an examination and is unable to pass it. The reasons for his inability may vary. He may be at a loss to recall the necessary information, give the wrong answers, be unable to write or to speak, mistake the place where the examination is held, and so on. The dream is accompanied by anxiety, often mounting anxiety, not uncommonly to the point that the dreamer awakens.

Freud's analysis of the typical examination dream is based on a simple observation: the examination which appears in such a dream is not the same one which the dreamer will shortly take in waking life. Moreover, the examination which does appear in the dream is invariably one which the dreamer has in reality already taken and passed.

This observation permitted Freud to deduce the main thrust of the typical examination dream. Freud's analysis was in keeping with his view that dreams are wish fulfillments, ultimately in the service of the pleasure principle. His interpretation was that a typical examination dream expresses the dreamer's wish to be reassured of success in his forthcoming examination. The wish is expressed by imagining that the examination shortly to be taken can be equated with one which has been successfully managed in the past. Thus, the dreamer attempts to allay his anxiety about an impending challenge by recalling a past "occasion . . . in which great anxiety has turned out to be unjustified . . . and has been contradicted by the event" (1900, p. 274). In other words, a typical examination dream expresses the thought " 'Don't be afraid, no harm will come to you this time either' " (p. 385).

It is implicit in Freud's formulation that the dream offers reassurance not only against the real difficulty of the examination, but against irrational anxieties stemming from unconscious fantasies about the examination. The wish to succeed in the examination has assumed a forbidden meaning which violates the dreamer's principles of conscience. Accordingly, in the dream, in order to satisfy the dictates of his conscience, the dreamer disguises his forbidden wish for success as a wish for failure. A falsification of reality is involved in the disguise, since an examination that had actually been passed is represented in the dream as if it had not been passed.

Freud did not give an explicit explanation for the feeling of anxiety which accompanies a typical examination dream. Perhaps that was because he felt it was self-evident in the light of principles he had already stated. Since, to my knowledge, the explanation has nowhere been spelled out, it seems worth taking up briefly here.

Throughout his writing on dreams, Freud stated that anxiety arises in a dream when the dream expresses a forbidden wish too directly. This explanation holds for anxiety experienced in a typical examination dream. Dreaming of past achievements when one is worried about what will happen in the future is an obvious fulfillment of the wish to be reassured of success. The disguise of portraying as a failure an examination which the dreamer knows full well he had passed is really quite thin. Anxiety mounts, and sometimes the dreamer even has to awaken to avoid recognizing that the examination he dreams of ended in success. On these occasions, the first thought upon awakening is usually something like, "But that's ridiculous, I've already taken this examination and passed it!"

Freud points out that this idea is no more than the forbidden dream thought, escaped in the nick of time by awakening and transformed into an indignant protest.

It is easy to lose sight of the fact that anxiety in a typical examination dream is occasioned by the extent to which the dream fulfills a forbidden wish to be reassured. If, instead, anxiety is regarded as an expression of the dreamer's realistic fear that he will fail the forthcoming examination, it will be difficult to recognize the typical examination dream's reassuring function (Ward, 1961). The same kind of mistake can obscure the reassuring function of traumatic dreams, as we will see below.

Freud recognized that the typical examination dream fulfills other functions besides the wish to be reassured of success. He pointed to the need for punishment satisfied by the dream and to the expression of the dreamer's guilt feeling that his past successes have been undeserved. McLaughlin (1961) pursued these aspects of the typical examination dream, showing that it can serve as a way of managing both competitive and passive urges through masochistic submission. A number of authors have discussed the link between examination dreams and the transference relationship, emphasizing how the analyst–parent enters the dream in the role of examiner. Kafka (1979) mentioned the wish for greater impulse control expressed in a typical examination dream, which Chasseguet-Smirgel (1976) has linked to the narcissistic wish to be perfect.

Even this brief literature review shows that the familiar idea of multiple, interdependent aims determining any psychic product applies to the typical examination dream. My purpose here is to concentrate on only one function of the typical examination dream, the one emphasized by Freud in his original discussion, and to examine its implications for the understanding of other dreams as well.

Some "Superego Dreams"

Freud's analysis of the typical examination dream is important because it is the only example he gave of a particular paradigm of dream formation. To see how that paradigm may have wider application, we can begin by reviewing and enumerating its essential features and considering some implications of each.

1. *The dream is an attempt to deal with the dreamer's anxiety about a forthcoming event.* In the case of the typical examination dream, the forthcoming event is an examination about to be undertaken. However, since many life events can be experienced as tests, it stands to reason that an actual examination need not be the only occasion for a dream of this kind; nor would we expect the content of such a dream necessarily to depict a literal examination. When a dream, even if not explicitly about an examination, has the features of a typical examination dream, we have the right to wonder what in his future the dreamer is concerned about. Conversely, when a dream is reported in the context of the dreamer's concern about his future, there is always the possibility that the dream fulfills in disguised form a wish to be reassured.

2. *The manifest content of the dream ostensibly portrays failure.* In a typical examination dream, the failure portrayed is specifically failure on an examination. However, any dream whose manifest content is dominated by themes of punishment, humiliation, and the like depicts a kind of failure. Such dreams are sometimes termed "superego dreams." Another clinical implication is that when confronted with what appears to be a superego dream, we may question the ostensible dominance of conscientious factors, keeping in mind that pleasurable self-interest may have had a greater influence in instigating the dream than is apparent at first glance.

3. *Fulfillment of the wish to be reassured is represented in the dream's manifest content.* If an examination is invested with unconscious sexual or aggressively satisfying. However, the wish to be reassured of success, while it certainly pertains to gratification of specific instinctual aims, has another dimension. It is a narcissistic attitude, related to feelings of entitlement and self-justification. Often, it is precisely this narcissistic attitude which the dreamer is most at pains to conceal in a certain kind of "superego" dream. This is not to imply a separate line of development for narcissistic wishes. Feelings of entitlement and self-justification, in my view, are derivatives of the earliest experiences of gratification from a seemingly omnipotent object, just

as superego anxiety has its ultimate origin in the earliest losses of that gratification. I refer here to the ego's capacity to make use of libidinal wish fulfillment fantasies to allay superego anxiety. The examples to follow will illustrate that certain superego dreams, while they claim to be saying, "I really ought to fail," betray the underlying sentiment, "I really deserve to succeed."

4. *The wish to be reassured is fulfilled by means of a piece of reality present in the dream's manifest content.* By "a piece of reality," I mean an actual perceptual experience, judged as real and recalled as real. In the case of the typical examination dream, the crucial piece of reality is the memory of an actual examination, successfully completed in the past. We will see that other actual perceptions appearing in a dream's manifest content can act to fulfill the wish to be reassured, inasmuch as this particular mechanism of dream formation occurs more widely than in typical examination dreams.

5. *The crucial piece of reality is falsified in the manifest content as a means of disguising the dream's fulfillment of the wish to be reassured.* The typical examination dream falsifies a crucial piece of reality—the recollection of a successfully completed examination—by portraying it as a failure. In applying Freud's analysis of the typical examination dream to a wider range of dreams, one discovers a variety of ways by which falsification of a crucial piece of reality can be accomplished to afford disguise for the wish to be reassured. In each example I will present, the particular method of falsification and disguise was characteristic for the dreamer and illustrates a long-standing defensive maneuver which operated in waking life as well. Also in each case, the patient's particular manner of disguising feelings of entitlement or self-justification had its origins in a specific genetic situation.

The clinical vignettes to follow describe three instances in which a dream turned out to contain the same kind of wish fulfillment and disguise described by Freud for the typical examination dream—although this was not always immediately obvious. In each instance, elucidation of this particular mechanism of dream formation revealed the feelings of entitlement or self-justification that had previously not been available for analysis. This is not to say that what I will emphasize constitutes the only or even the most important understanding of the material, or that there existed one exclusively correct interpretative approach to any of these three dreams. The point I mean to stress is that when we are able to discover the self-interested as well as the conscientious motivations which have instigated a so-called "superego dream," we obtain a fuller picture of the dreamer's immediate experience and the analytic work is that much further ahead.

Example 1

A graduate student was having trouble writing her dissertation. This conscientious young woman was plagued by an unjustified fear that she would be accused of plagiarism. She would have to copy work already done, she felt, because she was incapable of being sufficiently original. In the midst of this struggle she had a dream in which she stole a bicycle, was caught and humiliated for it. In her associations she had no difficulty connecting the bicycle with her dissertation, which she also felt she could obtain only through theft. The preceding day she had been thinking how much time she wasted riding her bicycle instead of working on her dissertation.

From our preceding work we had a great deal to draw upon in understanding the dream. For example, successful completion of her dissertation meant following in the footsteps of her academically prominent father, an act which the young woman equated with theft because of its connection with her oedipal triumph and competition with her younger brother. Also, we had given much attention to the significance of producing something and to originality. Bicycle riding was, no doubt, an overdetermined metaphor, referring in part to sexual impulses about which she was concerned. These and similar ideas marked well-traveled interpretive paths that were no less valid for their being familiar, but seemed stale and yielded little of value in connection with this dream.

During the course of the hour, I happened to ask the patient for her associations to the particular bicycle portrayed in the dream. She began to relate what few details she could recall—a headlight, a dented fender, a wire basket on the back—and realized that she was describing the bicycle she currently owned.

Thus the patient's actual bicycle had appeared in the manifest content of her dream; and the discovery of this *piece of reality* necessitated that the dream be understood in an entirely new way. Instead of simply expressing a confession of guilt and a need for punishment, the dream now appeared to contain a complaint of being unjustly accused and attacked for a blameless activity: taking possession of her own bicycle. Following the patient's association of the bicycle with her dissertation, the dream expressed her objection that she had a right to complete her degree and go on in her career without feeling guilty of theft.

As a typical examination dream, a piece of reality was the vehicle by which a wish for reassurance was expressed in the manifest content, but falsification of that piece of reality skewed the apparent meaning of the dream by disguising the pleasurable wish fulfillment. My patient's dream contained a fantasy of getting what she wanted and feeling innocent in doing so, but this aspect of the dream was kept out of awareness by what might be termed an error of omission. Knowledge that the bicycle she "stole" in the dream was in reality her own was disavowed and excluded from the dream report.

Since dreams are nocturnal continuations of preconscious waking thoughts from the preceding day, the aptness of a dream interpretation can be confirmed if it permits these thoughts to be recalled. This young woman had already mentioned having wondered the day before why she spent time riding her bicycle instead of working on her dissertation. After we had unveiled the aspect of her dream which was a complaint and a protest of innocence, she remembered a fleeting idea from the day before, something like "I ought to be able to feel as free and enthusiastic working on my dissertation as I feel now riding my bicycle."

It is my impression that in this sort of dream, the piece of reality through which the wish for reassurance is expressed in the manifest content is usually a day residue for the dream and forms the link to important latent dream thoughts. This is not a very surprising observation if we accept that, despite the self-punitive themes that ostensibly predominated, the dream was likely to have been instigated by a pleasurable wish. My patient managed things so that reality entered, so to speak, on the side of success—as in a typical examination dream.

The particular way in which reality was falsified to disguise a pleasurable wish in the dream exemplified a defensive maneuver of the greatest significance for this young woman. At another point in her analysis, she developed curious physical symptoms which proved to have no organic basis. I suspected a hysterical identification and found a way to ask her if what she was experiencing might not be similar to something she had observed in the past. She was puzzled by my question. She felt certain she had told me of her father's illness (she had not) to which her symptoms obviously corresponded closely. This was the same mechanism as in her dream: she had disavowed knowledge of a critical piece of reality—her father's illness—and excluded it from what she reported to me.

The piece of reality that made its way into this patient's dream was a particular perception—the image of her bicycle. Because of the associations it elicited, the memory of this perception both gave pleasure and aroused anxiety. Because it gave pleasure, it was repeated in her dream; and because it raised anxiety, it was defensively falsified. The specific method used to defensively falsify a stimulating conflict-producing perception was characteristic for her. It also had traceable historical roots.

She had been cared for in childhood by a warm and kindly maid, whose attentions the little girl had sometimes interpreted as openly seductive. When her parents went away, she pretended to herself that the maid was her mother. This game would be conveniently put out of the child's mind when the parents returned. It was one childhood version of the disavowal and omission of a feeling or righteous possessiveness that occurred in her dream.

Analysis of this patient's examination-type dream allowed the focus of the analytic work to alter, adding something to her awareness of her guilty need to fail and to criticize herself. Her covert feeling of entitlement and her need to disguise it could be demonstrated and thus could come under investigation.

The same was true in the case of the second patient, whose examination-type dream falsified a crucial piece of reality by different means.

Example 2

An insurance executive derived little joy from his many achievements because of a pervasive tendency toward self-deprecation. In his treatment we had been able to clarify this trait and speak of it from time to time as his need to see himself as "defective merchandise." He reported the following dream: he was doing calisthenics, wearing a shirt upon which was written the number 803.5. Immediately he pointed out that 803.5 referred to a section of the insurance code relating to defective merchandise, which he had recently been thinking of in connection with an upcoming important settlement. In characteristic fashion, he went on to bemoan his ineptitude in his work and his fear that he would mishandle his responsibilities in the settlement. As further evidence of his incompetence, he related the dream to an injury he had clumsily inflicted upon himself some time ago while doing calisthenics.

I was surprised as he was when he began the next session by telling me that he had checked the insurance code and found that section 803.5 did not refer to defective merchandise at all. He had apparently confused two sections he had been looking over. In fact, 803.5 dealt with situations in which a party to a contract is held not responsible if the contract has been offered to him under false pretenses. My patient now had no alternative but to recognize that the dream expressed another attitude, very different from the one he had first insisted upon. It seemed to present the idea not that he was defective merchandise, but that he had been taken advantage of and placed in a false position. As a result of this new perspective, a number of things came to light, including the patient's view that his boss made it impossible for him to do his work effectively, his disillusionment with me and with his treatment, and certain long-standing complaints about his parents.

Again a piece of reality in the dream represented the fulfillment of a hidden wish—to be exonerated and set free. Disguise of the wish was affected not by omission of the crucial piece of reality, as in the first example, but by a misinterpretation of it. What had initially appeared to be a dream of self-deprecation turned out to contain important elements of self-justification and criticism of others. It was helpful to the treatment when these impulses and the need to disguise them were unveiled. In this case, too, the crucial piece of reality, 803.5, was a day residue for the dream and had participated in what eventually emerged as the latent dream thoughts.

Again, the defensive maneuver upon which the examination-type dream hinged had wider implications. Unlike the young woman in the preceding example, this patient did not disavow or omit the crucial piece of reality. On the contrary, it was explicitly and carefully attended to, but it was misinterpreted. When his capacity for misinterpretation was identified, we could see how often it appeared. He had a habit of reporting the current events of his life to me very carefully, but, of course, in a way that emphasized his inadequacy and failure. It began to be clear that he often "misinterpreted" the significance of some fact that turned out to be crucial. For example, after berating himself because his boss told him he was doing "adequate" work, he inquired and learned that the boss was generally very stinting with praise; thus, "adequate" amounted to a laudatory evaluation. "Adequate," like 803.5, was accurately represented, but inaccurately interpreted.

As a child, this patient was often witness to his alcoholic mother's debilitation and self-indulgence. He did not disavow or deny the events themselves, but he restricted himself to a distorted interpretation of their meaning: he seized upon and ostensibly accepted his mother's accusatory, self-pitying explanation that she drank and behaved as she did because she was overburdened by responsibilities. Clinging to this unreasonable interpretation and not questioning it served a number of important functions for the child, not the least of which was to preserve the image of an adequate mother and to legitimize what took place between mother and son.

Example 3

The analysis of an examination dream can sometimes point the way to a line of interpretation that helps elucidate the transference situation. For a variety of reasons, a young man in analysis was exquisitely sensitive to any feelings of attachment to his analyst. His foremost method of denying them was to experience our relationship entirely in terms of rivalry and struggle. It I canceled an hour, he did the same in short order. If he had fantasies of my enjoying myself over a weekend—something he would never disclose but which I could sometimes infer—he began the week by regaling me with tales of his recent adventures. Any suggestion that his competitive view of our relationship might have a defensive function he dismissed as a hackneyed theory of mine. I was trying to brainwash him into becoming a typical, dependent analytic patient.

Not long after I announced the dates of my impending summer vacation, he had a dream in which he was back in college, meeting in the auditorium with a group of students. It was fall, and the professor was reading aloud from a list of names. Those students who were mentioned would not be allowed to enroll again because they had received "incompletes" in certain necessary courses. The patient knew that his name was to be called. He could remember no more about the dream except a vague feeling of discomfort.

Undoubtedly, the dream had something to do with the upcoming vacation and with the question of whether my patient would continue his analysis in the fall, although he volunteered no concern about my terminating the analysis. As a matter of fact, he made it very clear that he was looking forward to the break and that he was nonchalant about beginning again the following month. He had no associations to his feeling of discomfort and was skeptical that this aspect of the dream had anything to do with me or my vacation. He expected me to assume that he was upset because we were not going to be meeting.

Even from this brief resumé, it is possible to identify a number of issues worth pursuing. For example, the dream suggests my patient was entertaining thoughts of discontinuing treatment but was reluctant to say so directly. The professor forcing him to leave could be looked upon as a wishful externalization, referring to the analyst. It occurred to me that the dream might be similar to a typical examination dream, and I proceeded accordingly.

I took it that the "examination" was the first meeting we were to have in the fall—pictured in the dream as the auditorium meeting. Following the idea that in a typical examination dream the manifest content portrays a failure, "failing" would mean that the patient would be prevented from continuing analysis in the fall, despite his apparent unconcern about that prospect. In order to gain more information about what "passing" might signify, I treated the dream's manifest content just as one would in the analysis of a typical examination dream. I assumed that a past success was represented in disguised form and therefore asked the obvious question: Had he ever been prevented from registering at college? And, of course, the answer was no. Had he ever received an incomplete? Again, no. This, then, was the reassuring piece of reality from the past which had been represented and falsified in the dream, but so far not considered: his undisturbed progress at college. Being allowed to begin school again in the fall must at some time have been a special success for him, in some way equivalent to one he wished to be reassured of being able to repeat with me. But the nature of the past success was as yet not clear. I suggested there must have been some reason that being readmitted in the fall had been a concern for him during his college years.

He responded readily. In order to devote a good part of their time to working on the school newspaper, he and a group of his friends had reduced their loads during the regular academic season, making up for it by scheduling courses in the summer session. When summer came, the temptation to play was too strong for some of his friends, who had received incompletes, and, as a result, had not been allowed to continue the next year. My patient himself had been sufficiently disciplined, but just barely, to get by.

This certainly was a success, and one which could easily be understood in terms of the transference relationship and my vacation. My patient's dream indicated his feeling that he had obligations he must mind over the summer if he wished to insure the continuation of his analysis in the fall. He was afraid that the temptation to play might be too strong for him this time.

We discussed the parallel between his college experience and what could be concerning him about the approaching summer interval in the analysis. I reminded him of the glee he usually felt about "one-upping" me and told him I thought he might be afraid that he would do things over the summer he would not be able to talk to me about when we met again. This brought a rueful chuckle. He admitted he expected me to think of him as pining away, whereas he had no such intention. Furthermore, since I was so straight, he could never be sure how I would regard some of the things he liked to do. (The wishful idea, also expressed by his memory, that he would be the sole survivor in my caseload, did not come to light until much later.)

At this point, it may come as no surprise that for some time in his treatment this patient consciously avoided disclosure of his homosexual activity. Conscious withholding—perhaps keeping secrets would be a better way to put it—was a central defensive maneuver. I had the distinct impression that even before I inquired, he was aware of the associations to his dream that eventually pointed the way to his transference fantasy and perhaps was aware of the fantasy itself. But he kept things to himself until he felt safe in revealing them. As a child, he had many secrets to keep, including his knowledge of his mother's extramarital affairs.

Traumatic Dreams

The specific mechanism of dream formation we have been considering involves the appearance of a piece of reality in a dream's manifest content. Therefore, the subject of posttraumatic dreams—in which an actual experience is reenacted—is a natural extension of the discussion so far.

Following a traumatic experience, it is very common to have dreams in which certain features of the experience are wishfully distorted so as to contradict what was an unpleasant reality. Loewenstein (1949), for example, described the dream of a man who had survived a canoeing accident. In the dream the man dove and twisted actively through obstacles, whereas in reality he had been passively dependent upon rescuers to pull him out of the water. In the dream he remained tensely alert, in contrast to an actual period of unconsciousness during the accident. The dream contained slight distortions of the setting of the accident, which turned out to bear reference to early sexual play with a nurse. This was the dreamer's attempt to reverse the homosexual meaning of his gratitude to the men who had saved his life. In another example, Levitan (See chapter 16) carefully compared the circumstances of a woman's discovery of her husband's death with the content of a dream she had the following night. He found a significant discrepancy: in reality, the woman had been badly shocked by an unexpected announcement from her brother that her husband was dead; but in her dream she became worried and searched for her husband, asking her brother where her husband might be. The dream substituted active anticipation for the actual experience of helpless astonishment. Stein (1961) showed how a traumatic event can be elaborated into a masochistic fantasy, so that sexual pleasure serves to deny the fright and pain of the actual experience.

Posttraumatic dreams like these that alter the actual event present no problem for psychoanalytic theory, nor are they especially difficult to work with in the clinical situation. It is possible to identify wish fulfillments in the manifest content of the dream and to relate these to the dreamer's anxieties and conflicts.

On the other hand, thorny issues arise when it comes to those posttraumatic dreams in which a traumatic event is *accurately* repeated in faithful detail by the dream's manifest content. For the sake of clarity, I will call these "traumatic dreams." Garma (1955) took the position that even in such dreams wishful distortions of the actual traumatic experience are always present, though sometimes difficult to identify. Arlow (see Kris Study Group, Waldhorn [1967]; chapter 13) suggested a wishful element in traumatic dreams when he called them "deeply stimulating," and Wisdom (1949) emphasized that traumatic dreams satisfy the dreamer's need for punishment.

Freud (1920), however, reached a different conclusion. He stated that he could find no evidence for wish fulfillment of any kind in traumatic dreams. He was led to the inference that traumatic dreams fail in the aim of serving as wish fulfillments and must be explained on the basis of another function. Freud went on to suggest that dreams are primarily an expression of the repetition compulsion and that the wish fulfillment in dreams that guards sleep is a secondarily acquired function. Following Freud's line of thought, Stewart (1967), Silverberg (1948), and others have conceptualized traumatic dreams as an attempt on the part of the ego to "master" a traumatic event by repetition.

In my view, to simply say that traumatic dreams are efforts at mastery is in itself ambiguous and not sufficient as an explanation. Unless we are satisfied to call upon the repetition compulsion as a deus ex machina, we are left with the question: How does the exact repetition of a traumatic experience in a dream help to "master" it?

By objecting to the use of the repetition compulsion as a deus ex machina, I do not mean to object to the concept of the repetition compulsion itself. To my mind, Freud marshaled convincing evidence that the tendency to repeat is an unborn capacity of the organism and a characteristic of all instinctual expressions. One of the most instructive instances of his thinking occurs in "Group Psychology and the Analysis of the Ego" (1921) in which he pointed out that imitation (simple repetition) is the forerunner on which identification (a complexly motivated activity) is built. I believe that traumatic dreams are complexly motivated psychic products. They are more than simple repetitions, although they may make use of the capacity to repeat. There is always the need to explain the conditions under which repetition of an experience predominates, as well as the functions served by the repetition.

One explanation frequently offered is that the repetition of a traumatic experience "turns passive into active." However, I believe that this idea does not in itself take us very far in the matter of understanding traumatic dreams. The examples reported by Loewenstein, Levitan, and Stein, cited above, show us that when the need to turn passive into active is a major motivation operating in a posttraumatic dream, wishful distortions of the actual details of the traumatic event are introduced by the dream and can be identified. On the contrary, in "traumatic dreams" (in which the real event is *accurately* reenacted) the dreamer's experience is every bit as passive and terrifying as it was in actuality. One is hard put to find evidence of an increased sense of control on the dreamer's part in a traumatic dream. Furthermore, we have to ask, as Sperling does (see Kris Study Group, Waldhorn [1967]), why the ego in a "weakened" sleep state should be able to do the work of mastery better than in a state of waking alertness.

I believe it is possible to reach an understanding of traumatic dreams which resolves these difficulties. To begin with, we must review what is meant by psychological trauma. Events which cause little or no *material* damage can be *psychologically* traumatic, as we well know. People who escape accidents unharmed, or who witness atrocities but are not themselves touched, can be psychologically traumatized. This is because the experiences elicit unmanageable internal states in the traumatized individual. A psychologically traumatic event has its effects because it calls up frightening impulses and anxieties generated by them. The traumatized individual is provided with *actual perceptions that correspond all too closely to dreaded unconscious fantasy*. It is for this reason that the experience of psychological trauma is so often characterized either by an uncanny feeling—which, as Freud (1919) pointed out, marks a dangerous proximity between reality and unconscious fantasy—or by an altered sense of reality, whose purpose is to defend against the uncanny feeling (Renik, 1978).

We are now in a position to understand why a psychologically traumatic event is sometimes faithfully replicated in a traumatic dream; it is because the actual event can be *reassuring* as well as disturbing. While a traumatic event stirs up dread unconscious fantasy, producing a sense of danger, it also gives evidence that the danger has been *in reality* escaped. Thus, the dreamer goes over and over the real circumstances of the traumatic event in painstaking detail in order to confirm that,

"Yes, that was close; but it was not what I feared," or "That was bad, but not as bad as it might have been."

The kind of repetition that takes place in a traumatic dream (and in waking "flashbacks") is indeed an effort at mastery, consisting of the self-administration of repeated doses of reassurance. Exact repetition permits the dreamer to confirm that reality, even if it is eerily reminiscent of a threatening fantasy, ultimately proves to be different from the fantasy and safe. Moreover, this effort at mastery expresses a wish, namely, that a narrow escape from danger signifies safety for the future. The reworking of a traumatic experience in a traumatic dream is similar to repeated handling of a talisman. The dreamer reassures himself in a way similar to that of the soldier who wears "the bullet that missed" on a chain around his neck.

Thus, in its function of providing reassurance, the traumatic dream is at one and the same time an effort at mastery *and* a wish fulfillment. There seems to me to be no need to contrast these two functions or to hold them in opposition (for a different view, see Stewart [1967]).

The mechanism in which a traumatic dream offers reassurance is precisely the one which we have already seen to operate in the typical examination dream. Reassurance of success in the future is sought through recollection of a success in the past.

In order to spell out more fully the identity between typical examination dreams and traumatic dreams, I will make use of another clinical illustration.

Example 4

A married woman in her thirties sought treatment about two months after she had been in a railway accident. She was traveling cross-country with her husband in a sleeper compartment. In the middle of the night the train was derailed at high speed. Some passengers were gravely injured. This woman and her husband were awakened when their car screeched to a halt, simultaneously tilting violently on its side. They were tossed confusedly about the compartment in the dark, but suffered only bruises. They made their way to safety.

The patient complained of nightly, repetitive dreams in which she experienced exactly the details of the accident—being tossed about in the car, groping for the door and through the corridor, and so on. In the course of our meeting, I had a chance to go over these dreams with her in every particular and could find no departure from what she recalled of the actual events.

It soon became clear that at the time of her accident, the uppermost issue in this woman's life had been her dissatisfaction with her marriage. In fact, the cross-country journey had been the couple's return from a vacation intended to give the relationship one last chance. The vacation had been a failure, and they were planning to separate. (The plans were going on, despite the patient's posttraumatic symptoms.)

This woman was venomous toward her husband, but in a concealed way. From her manner of describing her disappointments in him and the difficulties she anticipated attending the separation, it seemed likely to me that the railway accident had come close to fantasies involving wishes that her husband be killed or injured, as well as fears of talion punishment for herself. I thought she might be going over the events in her dreams to reassure herself that she had not magically enacted her angry wishes and that she had narrowly escaped punishment for having such wishes.

I will not try to describe at length the patient's formidable resistances. Suffice it to say that she showed little interest in self-exploration, but an urgent and earnest desire to be rid of her dreams. I interpreted to her that the accident scared her because it came close to a punishment she dreaded. I thought she might be clinging to the dreams to reassure herself that she was indeed safe. A bit later, I added that she might especially need reassurance if the punishment was connected with angry ideas about her husband, since she was still very angry at him.

She thought what I said interesting, but she did not know if any of it were true or not. For several sessions the material shifted to her plans for the future. Incidentally, she reported that her dreams were becoming less troublesome—probably she was getting over the accident. Since our whole contact had been in the form of a slightly extended consultation, she thanked me for my interest, said she was feeling increasingly better, and guessed she really did not need treatment.

Virtually everything that was said earlier of typical examination dreams applies as well to this patient's traumatic dreams. Certainly her dreams served multiple functions, including a need for punishment and the expression of hostile impulses. However, it is also true that an immediate aim of her traumatic dreams was to provide her with reassurance. To compare traumatic dreams with typical examination dreams, we can apply to the traumatic dream those characteristics already enumerated for the typical examination dream:

1. *The dream is an attempt to deal with the dreamer's anxiety about a forthcoming event.* In the case of this patient's traumatic dreams, the forthcoming event was her separation from her husband. She was afraid she would be punished for her hostile wishes toward her husband by having to suffer an abrupt and damaging disruption of her own career. Her hopes for a new life, not to mention her hopes for a vengeful triumph over her husband, might be drastically contradicted.

2. *The manifest content of the dream ostensibly portrays failure.* Each night in her traumatic dreams, this woman was thrown about in the dark, disoriented, and left uncertain of her fate. The circumstances of the railway accident, frightening and discomforting in themselves, also had an obvious metaphoric connection to what she most feared would happen to her when she and her husband separated. The dream portrayed her life's journey interrupted in a most unhappy way.

3. *Fulfillment of the wish to be reassured is represented in the dream's manifest content.* Just as the typical examination dream takes as its subject a test which has in reality been passed by the dreamer, so the railway accident my patient recreated in her traumatic dreams was one which in reality she had emerged from unharmed; and, just as certain "superego dreams" betray a hidden sense of entitlement, so her traumatic dreams expressed the underlying sentiment, "I deserve to come out of this all right."

4. *The wish to be reassured is fulfilled by a piece of reality present in the dream's manifest content.* The railway accident from which my patient emerged unharmed, which she nightly recreated,

was an actual event, accurately represented in the manifest content of her dreams.

5. *The crucial piece of reality is falsified in the manifest content as a means of disguising the dream's fulfillment of the wish to be reassured.* The means of falsification was a simple one. This woman's dreams concerned themselves only with that part of the accident in which she had been jostled, frightened, and threatened. *Her safe exit from the train,* also a part of the experience, *was never included in her dreams.* This form of disguise, in my experience, is characteristic of traumatic dreams. Only the terrifying beginning of the traumatic event, and never the final relief, enters the dream's manifest content. What was actually a success is thus portrayed as a failure. The method of disguise is the same as in a typical examination dream, in which successful completion of the test, which took place in reality, is not included.

I believe that traumatic dreams deserve to be regarded as "typical dreams," in that it is sometimes possible—indeed necessary—to draw certain inferences from the manifest content alone. The dreamer's associations, if any are produced, are unlikely to take analysis of a traumatic dream any further toward unveiling the reassuring function served by the dream.

Let us consider the following hypothesis: *when a traumatic event is replicated accurately in the manifest content of a posttraumatic dream, it can be assumed that the actual outcome of the traumatic event has been reassuring as compared with the dreamer's unconscious punishment fantasies.*

My observation is that people who have undergone truly damaging experiences do not tend to have what I have termed traumatic dreams (in which the traumatic event is accurately reenacted). Instead, they have the kind of posttraumatic dreams referred to initially, in which the traumatic event is wishfully distorted. For instance, amputees dream of having all their limbs intact. People who have lost loved ones have dreams in which the loved one appears, still alive. On the other hand, traumatic dreams, as a rule, occur following experiences which might be termed "harrowing," when the actual circumstances, though awful, have not led to consequences as awful as were feared—sometimes unconsciously feared. People who survive catastrophes, for example, have traumatic dreams. Often, of course, an experience may be both materially *and* psychologically traumatic. Serious surgical procedures can impose real, physical injury, and at the same time invoke castration fantasies. In situations of this sort, one finds that even if there are wishful distortions, to the extent that the traumatic event is accurately portrayed in a dream, it has a reassuring significance.

Balson's work (personal communication) with the dreams of returned Vietnam prisoners of war points in the same direction. While in prison camp, the prisoners had obvious wish-fulfillment dreams that contradicted the actual trauma: they dreamed of being home for Thanksgiving dinner, and the like. After their release, when their prison camp experiences had achieved the status of a harrowing, but ultimately successful concluded traumatic event, they had dreams in which the actual details of prison life were accurately reenacted. Furthermore, some of Balson's subjects reported a feeling of loss when they eventually ceased to have traumatic dreams, which may have to do with the reassuring function of the dreams and their magical talisman significance.

It would be helpful to add to these observations accounts of work with traumatic dreams reported by patients in analysis. Unfortunately, such data is difficult to come by, possibly because traumatic dreams are likely to occur in situations which dispose the dreamer neither to want, nor to tolerate, extensive psychoanalytic exploration.

Stewart (1967) states that traumatic dreams are not generally useful in therapy. I do not find this to be true. To be sure, there is great difficulty in carrying analysis to the deepest layers of impulse and defense; but this is only to be expected, inasmuch as patients suffering from traumatic neurosis are usually struggling with conflicts which were dormant in ordinary circumstances. It is not surprising that these patients are often content with the benefits of relatively superficial analytic work, if it succeeds in reestablishing the pretraumatic state of affairs. As often as not, interpretation of the reassuring function of traumatic dreams in relation to guilty concerns suffices to achieve symptomatic relief. I have found this an extremely effective technique, especially in cases where even the most tactful references to a need for punishment are misheard by the patient as criticism. Obviously, this is especially to be avoided when it seems unlikely that there will be an opportunity to explore and resolve the transference relationship.

Example 5

A young woman was enjoying her evening out to dinner when her date, a doctor, was suddenly called away to an emergency. He asked her if she might find her own way home from the restaurant, and she agreed. While searching for a taxi, she was accosted and robbed. An unsavory couple forced her into an alley and made her give over all her money. They did her no physical harm, but to insure their getaway forced her to strip off her clothes, which they took with them. They also showed her a knife and told her they would find her and cut her pretty face up if she called the policie.

Six months later when I saw her, she was still in the grip of a severe traumatic neurosis. She was irritable, lethargic, and distracted. She was unable to work or conduct a social life. Also, she suffered from dreams in which she reexperienced precisely the events of the robbery. The dreams were accompanied by feelings of intense, mounting anxiety, and they disturbed her sleep. Although she had little capacity for engagement in treatment, by means of direct questions I was able to piece together a picture of her.

Always popular and attractive, a "prom queen" in fact, this young woman was an unconscious flirt who had to maintain to herself a pretense of total innocence. She needed to remain equally oblivious to the knowledge that she had always been her father's obvious and undisputed favorite. It was not hard to detect in her description of her relationship with her mother the patient's feeling that she was the object of considerable jealousy and resentment. As a teenager she was annoyed by her mother's unnecessary warnings that she could get into trouble if she were not careful.

I suggested to her that the exaggerated impact of what had happened six months before came from the close resemblance between the events of the robbery and the warnings her mother had given her. Maybe she dreamed about it again and again because she could hardly believe she had escaped. We touched upon her sense of being preferred by her father and the specter of maternal jealousy that made her uncomfortable as a teenager.

This was not a treatment that developed into psychoanalysis. The young woman obviously took something from my remarks, but showed no inclination to pursue the direction they indicated. Rather, she began to dwell on a new aspect of the traumatic event—her date's irresponsibility in allowing her to go unprotected into the night. As she began more and more to blame him for what had happened, there was a subtle shift in her view of her parents. Her father, who had always been seen by her as a kind of doting squire, now came in for some criticism. Perhaps his insensitivity had been partly responsible for the difficulties between her and her mother. It was not long before the dreams ceased. My patient began to sleep better, went back to work, and took her leave from me.

In this case analytic work proceeded only far enough to give symptomatic relief. The patient balked at going further. It was useful for her to recognize that her posttraumatic symptoms stemmed in part from a need to reassure herself against her continuing fear of punishment, but she could not tolerate exploration of her own guilt and her feeling that she deserved punishment. She defended against unconscious self-criticism by shifting to criticism of others. It appeared that some of the troublesome conflicts underlying her extreme posttraumatic reaction made their way into her relationship with me. Probably the very helpfulness and noncritical nature of my remarks led her to feel that I favored her as her father had done and was siding with her against her mother as well as against the people who robbed her. Unwilling to analyze her transference fantasies, she retreated in the direction of greater criticism of men and greater appreciation of women, and treatment ended on that basis.

This example again suggests that the anxiety experienced in traumatic dreams arises for the same reason that it does in typical examination dreams: because the reassurance provided by the dream constitutes a forbidden wish fulfillment. In this instance, the patient awoke at the point when she was in danger of realizing that she had escaped the disfigurement she so much feared. Weiss (1952) pointed out that a person has to assure himself that he is truly safe before he can allow himself to experience emotions that he perceives as dangerous. Weiss uses the example of "crying at the happy ending" of a romantic film in which boy meets girl, boy loses girl, and boy gets girl back again. It is Weiss's idea that only at the film's end, when the lovers are safely reunited, does the viewer feel reassured enough to allow himself to experience the sadness he felt while the lovers were separated. Following this line of thought, we can see that a person who has a traumatic dream does not feel safe enough with his relief at the happy ending of his experience to include it in his dream.

It would appear that anxiety occurs in the traumatic dream for the same reason as in the typical examination dream—because the wish to be reassured that the dream fulfills is forbidden. When a dreamer awakens from a traumatic dream with a feeling of relief that it was "only a dream," he is expressing the latent dream thought, disguised in the waking state; for his dream did not include the real happy ending. The situation is parallel to awakening from a typical examination dream with the thought, "But I passed that test!"

The natural history of traumatic dreams is very instructive on this point. Over time, as the immediate fears raised by the traumatic event fade, its reassuring function becomes clearer and clearer. But the reassurance still has a forbidden meaning. Therefore, at later points in his life, when the dreamer feels in danger and seeks to reassure himself by wishfully recalling the reassuring traumatic event in his dreams, it becomes necessary for him to increasingly distort it. The distortions are always in the direction of making the traumatic event worse than it actually was—that is, to disguise the past success as a failure. Thus, what begins as a traumatic dream ends by resembling a typical examination dream.

Many psychoanalysts have observed this evolution. Perhaps the best known example was given by Bonaparte in her charming article, "A Lion Hunter's Dream" (chapter 1). She told of a man in East Africa who was mauled by a lion and dragged away to be eaten, but managed to escape with his life by killing the lion with his sheath knife. At first, the hunter dreamed of this remarkable experience as it actually happened. A bit later, he dreamed of being unable to kill the lion, but managing to take refuge in a tree. Many years later, he had dreams in which he would vainly try to stop the lion's charge, and these dreams would end just as he was about to be devoured. I would explain this as follows: as time went on, the more obvious it became to the hunter that the "trauma" he was recalling in his dreams was in fact a triumph, the more he needed to disguise it.

Bonaparte felt that killing the lion had signified to the hunter his ability to vanquish an enraged oedipal father. She did not give us any specific indications of when, later in his life, the hunter would dream of his forbidden triumph again—in increasingly disguised form—but we can assume it was at moments when circumstances in his life led him to feel in danger of oedipal punishment.

The natural evolution of traumatic dreams into typical examination dreams, which has been repeatedly observed, is not really an evolution in form. The basic mechanism by which the dream is constructed remains the same throughout the series. From beginning to end, the dreamer recalls a real past success in order to reassure himself about the future. What we see is an alteration of content, rather than form; and this occurs because, with the passage of time, the reassuring meaning of recalling the traumatic event becomes more obvious, necessitating disguise of the forbidden wish for reassurance by means of increasing distortion of the details of the actual experience.

In conclusion, I would like to say that the particular mechanism Freud showed to be operating in the typical examination dream, which I have extended to apply to certain "superego dreams" and to "traumatic dreams," probably does not represent a unique form of dream work. During the day, forbidden impulses are activated, and along with them, fears of punishment. The wish to be reassured of safety arises, and a preconscious waking thought forms, in which some piece of reality is used as the basis for a reassuring fantasy. The piece of reality, having achieved wishful significance, appears in disguised form in a dream. This sequence of events may well be a feature of all dreams. Typical examination dreams and traumatic dreams merely give us an opportunity to clearly identify the interplay between perceptions of reality and wish fulfillment in the dream's formation, because the appearance of reality in the manifest content is vividly accented, and our attention is called to it. Occasionally, a "superego dream" permits the same kind of link to be observed. It is not hard to imagine that actual perceptions appear all the time in the manifest content of dreams for the purpose of reassuring the dreamer, but that they usually escape our notice. The importance of identifying day residue in the analysis of dreams relates to this point, since waking thoughts from the day preceding a dream mark the link between the dream's content and the dreamer's perceptions of reality.

Section IV

Communicative and Intrapsychic Function of Dreams

This section begins with Alston's article, "The Communicative Function of the Dream: An Overview" (1987), where she provides a critical overview of three seminal articles in this area. In the first, Kanzer's now classical article the "Communicative Function of the Dream" (1955), she discusses the basic conceptualization and clinical data in support of the thesis that the dream serves a communicative function—directly in terms of introjected objects and indirectly in relation to the external world. In the second, the role of Bergmann's article, "The Intrapsychic and Communicative Aspects of the Dream" (1966), is assessed in terms of his thesis that the need to communicate one's dream is part of Western cultural tradition as well as individual development. And in the third, Calogeras's article, "Husband and Wife Exchange of Dreams" (1977), is viewed as a clinical extrapolation of Kanzer's and Bergmann's work, demonstrating the extent to which a marital couple's dream-exchange and interpretation can lead to a quite unique level of preconscious and unconscious communication. Alston concludes her overview by noting the efficacy of recognizing and using the dream's communicative function in the analytic approach to the interpretation of dreams.

Bridging the gap between the communicative and intrapsychic functions of the dream (at least in the instructive or reconstructive sense), is Frank and Trunnell's, "Conscious Dream Synthesis as a Method of Learning about Dreaming: A Pedagogic Experiment" (1978). In this article, they report an absorbing dream experiment, with first-year candidates in a psychoanalytic institute, whose assignment was one of synthesizing an artificial dream. The object was to provide the student–candidates with the challenge of using what they had learned didactically about dream formation in an active manner.

This section closes with the clinical article by Calogeras, "Marital Conflict in Dreams" (1987), in which he examines the novel phenomenon of how marital conflicts are depicted and elaborated upon in a series of dreams occurring in one of the marital partners (the husband) over a year's analytic treatment. Each dream succeeded in highlighting a different aspect of his marital conflict and then adumbrated what was subsequently played out in his marriage.

Chapter 21

THE COMMUNICATIVE FUNCTION OF THE DREAM: AN OVERVIEW

Toni M. Alston

The dream viewed primarily as an intrapsychic phenomenon has been the cornerstone of analytic therapy and dream psychology since Freud's original publication (1900). The dreamer is simultaneously the author, stage director, and actor(s) in the resulting drama; the enactment of the ensuing drama has as its primary purpose that of preserving the most narcissistic of mental states—sleep. However, Freud has given us a number of analytic hints that there is another important function of the dream (e.g., "This I must tell to the analyst" and "I should not dream of that") without directly emphasizing it.

It is this so-named "communicative function" of the dream which I wish to emphasize by providing a brief overview of three seminal articles in this area. In the first of these articles, "The Communicative Function of the Dream" (1955), Kanzer provides the basic definition, conceptualization, and clinical data; in the second, "The Intrapsychic and Communicative Aspects of the Dream" (1966), Bergmann presents the historical–cultural context along with further clinical data; and in the third, "Husband and Wife Exchange of Dreams" (1977), Calogeras demonstrates how a marital couple's dream exchange and interpretation led to a rather unique level of preconscious and unconscious communication. I will turn first to Kanzer's article.

This paper was prepared especially for the *Dream Reader* and based on several lectures given to the Seminar on Dream Interpretation of the Mainz–Wiesbaden Psychoanalytic Group.

"The Communicative Function of the Dream"

This is the classical article on the communicative function of the dream and points to a new direction which dream research might well take. Kanzer begins by noting that the urge to communicate one's dreams was first described by Ferenczi (1913), who pointed out that the listener chosen for this purpose is preferably the actual subject of the dream. Although the dream seems inherently—in appearance at least—a narcissistic phenomenon, Kanzer demonstrates with a number of apt clinical examples that the dream contains communicative elements which have great importance not only for the therapeutic approach, but for the theoretical formulations of dream psychology. Kanzer's main thesis is that the dream serves a communicative function—directly in terms of introjected objects, and indirectly in relation to the external world.

In support of this thesis, Kanzer approaches the communicative function from different perspectives, citing a number of relevant clinical examples in support. I will cite briefly the most pertinent of these examples.

1. *Incompleted dreams and communication.* Giving numerous examples, Kanzer connects the incompleted dream with its communicative function. He cites instances of "numerous writers and artists, literally inspired by their dreams, who have not completed the dream work until they have communicated it to an audience" (p. 260). Then, extrapolating this to the fate neuroses, he notes as an example how the role of the oracle in the oedipal drama played an important part in provoking the very events portented in myth–dream. Extending this to secondary narcissism, he observes that when the dreamer withdraws from the outer world, he can relinquish his objects only by introjecting them in symbolic form. Thus, external relations, including communication, are thereby internalized. As an example, he cites how: "A single dream image may embody a complicated harmony of past and contemporary relationships and communications—viz, the *R. is my uncle* dream of Freud, which condenses an exchange of opinions among several persons and is climaxed by a message to the dreamer himself" (p. 261).

2. *Impending breakdown of resistances.* In reference to the impending breakdown of resistance (often after a long, dreamless period), the communicative function of the dream is often heralded by a series of dreams in advance of the patient's conscious ability to recognize it. Kanzer (1955) gives the example of an agoraphobic woman, in the throes of attempting to deny the recognition of her intensified sexual feelings, who "was impelled to tell her husband toward whom she was ordinarily most reticent about analytic matters—of a dream in which she was dancing with a certain man (the analyst)." This dream communication served two purposes; first, it was a type of sexual teasing toward her husband which also contained a warning and a reproach regarding his increased alertness and attention toward her; and second, it was a communication to the analyst (in contrast to her habit of forgetting her dreams) to similarly tempt him—by the loving embrace of the dancing partner—and bring about wish fulfillment of the dream's intrapsychic communication.

3. *Regressive behavior.* Kanzer notes that regressive behavior (e.g., acting out and somatizations) can best be grasped and drawn into analytic therapy by means of the communicative aspects of the dream. As an example, he cites a patient (subject to asthmatic attacks when defending herself against erotic feelings for the analyst) who uses the dream to elaborate on the meaning of her regressive symptoms and acts: "I dreamed that I am lying on the couch and you are sitting at the other end of the room. I rise up to come to you but find that there is freshly laid concrete between us. This hardens rapidly as I put my feet in it. I am caught in a vice, am terrified and scream." (She awakened with an asthmatic attack.)

In reference to the communicative function, the asthmatic attach represents the last fragment of the dream and involves the patient's wish to rise from the couch, look at and approach the analyst. Kanzer, in his subsequent analysis of the dream, determined that the analytic routine had caught the patient "in a vice; the attack is not only an inhibiting and self-punishing instrument . . . but is designed, like the scream of the nightmare, to secure immediate help—thus forcing the analyst to abandon his neutrality." In addition, based on the results of her free associations, he found that "the patient feels she has 'put her foot in it,' and the analyst must consider whether his own interpretations were 'too freshly laid,' too 'concrete' and posed the threat of holding her 'in a vice'." The asthmatic attack, as the end-portion of the dream, was also traced back to certain recent exchanges between analyst and patient, where it was the analyst who failed to "rise" to the occasion (p. 262).

4. *Similarities in verbal and somatic language.* Often striking expressions of a dreamer's communicative function are to be found in the similarities of conflicts expressed in a patient's verbal and somatic languages. Kanzer (pp. 264–265) gives an example of a lawyer–patient (suffering from latent paranoid trends and in the midst of a growing homosexual transference) who dreamed: "I was sitting in the men's room and crapping. Judge X came in and washed his hands unconcernedly, and then left with the remark, 'Come in and see me when you are through!' I was mortified."

Kanzer first notes that the informality of the scene and his patient's behavior were not in keeping with the patient's reality behavior, only the mortification was. Three strands of the patient's dream communication were unraveled. First, the patient's association pointed to an occasion where both he and Judge X "waited for a witness to appear and only learned finally that the man had killed himself on the way [to the court]." As a result, "The blow was especially severe to the patient as it meant that a great deal of preliminary work to which he had devoted himself with zeal" would be lost; subsequently, this proved to be a turning point in his career and illness, since "his previous rapid rise was now destined to come to a halt" (p. 264). Second, the patient's associations to "Come in and see me when you are through" brought to his mind the recent discussions with his present supervisor, implying a lack of vigor in prosecuting his court assignments. In the analytic transference, the patient had been alternating between the feeling that "nothing is coming out, nothing will happen" and appeals for special time and attention from the analyst (p. 264). At this point, Kanzer suggests an intermediate meaning of the dream, namely, that the dream fulfills a wish that friendly and informal analytic sessions will succeed "the present period of therapeutic 'crap-ping' " (p. 264). Third, in terms of the patient's somatic language, constipation has been a troublesome symptom. In external reality, the patient's need to withhold "mortifying information" which had pervaded both his work and personal habits; while in the psychic reality of the dream, the intrapersonal and interpersonal communication are starkly revealed: to wit, "the judge is the discoverer of his anal misdemeanors (catches him with his pants down) and exemplified reaction formation (washing of the hands; also, like the present supervisor, he washes his hands of the patient himself). . . . Communication is therefore broken off outwardly by the departure of the judge, while it is established all the more firmly within by sphincter control" (p. 265). In summing up the dream's (communicative) meaning, Kanzer finds that it is a "masterpiece of ambivalence: the invitation to 'come in and see me' is both a sexual overture and a threat of dismissal; moreover, in the reverse sense it is the patient who invites the judge to 'come in' and see him."

Summary and Conclusions

Kanzer ends his article by reiterating his main finding (i.e., the dream serves a communicative function on two fronts) directly in terms of introjected objects, and indirectly in relation to the external world. He then draws the following conclusions: (1) the nuclei of dream communication, when the dream is viewed as an archaic and metaphorical language, occurs at the point when the sphincters (censors) first invoke mental mechanisms to regulate intake and output at the ego boundaries; (2) the language of the dream is an expression of the fact that the sleeper shares his slumber with introjected objects; and it is the secondary narcissism of the sleeper which "allows" for the intrapersonal communication to take place; (3) in analytic therapy, the analyst is drawn into the intrapsychic as well as the external communicative system of the dreamer.

"The Intraspsychic and Communicative Aspects of the Dream"

Some ten years later (1966), Bergmann continues the explication of the dream's communicative function by placing it in historical–cultural context. His thesis holds that the need to communicate one's dreams is part of Western cultural tradition as well as individual development; but with the emergence of the superego (according to him developing about 500 B.C.) the need to communicate one's dreams was subject to repression. In the psychoanalytic situation, however, the recovery of the repressed dream (in part) becomes again possible since two forces are mobilized: one being the wish to communicate, the other being the resistance against communicating. Thus, when both forces operate simultaneously, the wish to communicate will bring forth the recall of the dream, but the resistance will render it unintelligible. In what follows, I will briefly discuss Bergmann's thesis under two topics—the historical–cultural background and its role in psychoanalysis and psychotherapy.

Historical and Cultural Background

In tracing the historical background of the dream's communicative function (and contrasting it with the intrapsychic), Bergmann notes that a significant step occurred during the Greek Enlightenment (around 500 B.C.) which recognized the dream as a psychic product rather than an external visitation (p. 356). However, Greek philosophy has handed down to us two contrasting attitudes via the dream: Plato's knowledge of the dream as an expression of the unconscious wishes, and Aristotle's concept of the dream as a mechanism of discharge. It was Freud's insight that combined the two opposite positions into one unified theory of dream analysis and interpretation. Within this historical–cultural context, Bergmann cites numerous (and quite diverse) examples of the dream's evolvement toward being an intrapsychic and communicative phenomenon rather than a magical, prophetic, or religious one. From these examples, I will cite three of the most relevant.

1. *Dreaming and telling of dreams.* Beginning more in the pre-Greek Enlightenment, dreaming and telling of dreams began to serve a therapeutic function. Of special significance were the so-called "sleep temples"—dedicated to Aesculapius (the ancient god of medicine)—where the supplicant–patient went to sleep and became cleansed (and to dream), and then to have his dream interpreted by one of the Aesculapian priest–physicians. The most famous of these temples was at Epidaurus where Aesculapius himself (!) specialized in interpreting incubation dreams which the supplicant–patient had had in the temple (p. 357). Bergmann notes: "Commemoration tablets exhibited cures for the edification of skeptics. The tablets described not only the cure but also the dream which led to the cure" (p. 357).

2. *Oedipus the King.* Bergmann (p. 358) rightly notes the change in attitude toward the dream in regards to the legend and play of *Oedipus the King.* In Homer's telling of the legend, Oedipus continues to reign *after his guilt has been discovered*, and he is buried with royal honors; while in the play by Sophocles (at the height of the Greek Enlightenment), Oedipus has become a blinded outcast, crushed by his burden of guilt. Exemplifying this change is the following dialogue taken from *Oedipus the King.*

Oedipus:	But surely I must needs fear my mother's bed?
Jocasta:	Nay, what should mortal fear, for whom the decrees of Fortune are supreme, and who hath clear foresight of nothing? 'Tis best to live at random, as one may. But fear not though touching wedlock with thy mother. Many men ere now have so fared in dreams also: but he to whom these things are as naught bears his most easily.

Bergmann (along with Freud and others) has observed that Jocasta clearly recognizes that dreams contain incestuous wishes, and she makes no attempt to invoke supernatural powers to explain them, but rather she implies that the source is to be found in the deeper part of the mind.

3. *Intrafamily dream communication.* Bergmann (p. 358) cites an interesting attitude toward dreams taken from Herodotus'

History (Book VII) which stands midway between the archaic and the Greek Enlightenment points of view.

> Xerxes [the Persian King] was urged by a dream to make war on the Greeks. Artibanus (Xerxes' uncle) answers his nephew with an interpretation that was to become characteristic of the Greek Enlightenment point of view.
>
> > "Whatever a man has been during the day, is wont to hover around him in the visions of his dreams at night." (A clear reference to the day's residue.)
>
> Xerxes (who according to Bergmann represented the archaic point of view; but who also could represent Freud's view of suggested dreams [1900, p. 384]) tells his uncle to put on his clothing, sit on his throne and sleep in his bed. Artibanus obeys and his nephew's dream reappears to him; only in this version it threatens to blind him if he persists in his opposition to war. Artibanus yields and the ill-fated war on Greece began.

Bergmann interprets Herodotus to mean that even persistent dreams need not be prophetic. Additionally, we might add: (1) that this is an intrafamily exchange of dreams exemplifying the communicative function par excellence; (2) it also foretells us what Freud has previously pointed out, namely, that many interpretable dreams are based on suggestion. In this instance, we can hypothesize that Artibanus did receive a message from his nephew about how he wanted him to dream; that is, the war with Greece should take place.

The Role in Psychoanalysis and Psychotherapy

Integrating the historical–cultural origins of the dream as being viewed as psychic process (with the views of Freud, Ferenczi, Kanzer, Greenacre, Rapaport, etc.), Bergmann (pp. 362–363) presents his theory on the communicative and intrapsychic aspects of the dream. First, he holds that dreams are remembered and communicated because the telling of the dream completes the discharge function; while other dreams are remembered because they portray a conflict which cannot be expressed in any other way. The latter dreams, upon examination, often contain a hidden communication to the analyst. Second, not only is there a psychic need to communicate dreams which is part cultural as well as individual development, but with the emergence of the superego (about 500 B.C.) the need to communicate dreams succumbed to repression. In analysis or analytic therapy, with its concomitant regression, the reporting of dreams becomes possible again, particularly since it is sanctioned and encouraged in the analytic process. Third, in the analytic situation, two main forces vis-á-vis the dream are mobilized: one is the wish to communicate; the other is the resistance against communicating. As a result, the telling of the dream represents a compromise formation analogous to symptom formation. To illustrate this last point, Bergmann cites a patient who dreamt *that he met Frank Sinatra in the waiting room.* In his associations the following emerged:

> Sinatra is a singer and that "to sing" means in the language of the underworld, to confess. Those who "sing" are often killed. The "underworld" signifies that the patient's mother would punish him for disclosing her secrets to the analyst. From the intrapsychic view, the dream demonstrates that a punitive, paranoid aspect of the maternal object representation has emerged. As a communication, the dream was an appeal to the analyst to counter the danger, since the patient (unlike Frank Sinatra) could neither be "frank" nor "sing." Although the patient would like to form a therapeutic alliance, he is allowed to express this wish only in code. Finally, to inquire what the dream *means* emphasizes its intrapsychic mode; to ask what the dream *tells* often elicits its communicative function [p. 262].

Fourth, in psychotherapy when much of the transference remains unanalyzed, the communicative function of the dream is of particular significance since what cannot be expressed directly is expressed obliquely and symbolically. This would seem to be the main reason why psychotherapy patients often report dreams though they are aware that the therapist refrains from interpreting them (p. 363).

Conclusions

Bergmann concludes his article by noting a number of situations where the communicative function of the dream has a particular significance: (1) the first dream may be regarded as an attempt to communicate the intrapsychic conflict in code; (2) in the transference the communication has a similar significance; and (3) in impending termination, the termination can often be communicated only in code—indicating the residue of the inner conflicts still remains but that the therapeutic alliance also is still operating (p. 365).

"Husband and Wife Exchange of Dreams"

Ten years later (1977), Calogeras—building on the work of Kanzer and Bergmann—demonstrated the extent to which a marital couple's dream exchange and interpretation led to a quite unique level of preconscious and unconscious communication. Not only did their "dream communication" highlight facets of both their marital discord and personal pathology, but it also actuated them to develop an interpretive dream mechanism (specific to the dream's communicative function) which was not unlike that found in the American Indian Iroquois culture, with resulting therapeutic gains. In what follows, I will discuss briefly the three major topical areas which this couple's dream-exchange adumbrated—an example of this couple's dream exchange, parallels with the Iroquois dream technique, and theoretical issues.

Example of the Couple's Dream Exchange

The background for the dream exchange occurred during the analysis of a young married woman when her husband suddenly began telling her his dreams and she, in turn, began to tell him hers (pp. 71–72). A specific example of this couple's dream exchange occurred when the wife began to challenge her husband's continuing close attachment and involvement with his nuclear family, while requiring her to forego any relationship with hers.[1] In the day's residue, the wife had, for the first time, asked her husband (a surgeon) to discontinue his role as his mother's medical adviser. (Following each visit to her family physician, the mother would return with several prescriptions for her son's approval. Inevitably, he would find some fault with these and change them.) The husband tells his first dream to his wife as follows: "I'm helping this person . . . a woman buys things . . . clothes, shoes. She's poor and she has this young man with her. . . . Nothing seems to work or fit them, but then it finally does or I think it does" (p. 72).

The wife's immediate response to her husband's dream is one of "resentment and feeling forced," followed by a somewhat confused and uncomfortable one of feeling "embarrassed and guilty." Although she does not tell her husband directly of her reaction, she feels "he sensed this." Her resentment stems from the "dream message" (she takes the people in the dream to represent her husband's mother and brother at first) that her husband has not given up any of his commitment to his family and he still "babies" them. She deeply resents this attachment to his mother and brother and reflects that her secondary feeling of embarrassment and guilt actually refers to her own family and how she has not remained "loyal" to them as he has to his. Further associations to her husband's dream lead her to the "communication" that, if her husband wants to treat his mother and brother as babies, then she is certainly not going to have a baby by him! (In her analysis at this time, the patient has been focusing on her "unsuccessful efforts" to becoming pregnant.) Finally, she arrives at what she called the "theme [communication] of the dream" as having to do with the conflict between family loyalty and feeling forced to become pregnant (p. 72).

---

[1]The husband played a most fatherly and possessive role with his mother and younger brother (age 23) who remained unemployed. (The father had died when the oldest son was 15.)

Several days later, the wife "reciprocates" by reporting a dream to her husband.

> Brother and myself were in my bedroom—sleeping, shades pulled down. There is a noise of children playing outside. Finally, my brother opened the window and yelled at them to be quiet. All of them went away except for a few in our house (apartment building). Brother then decided to scare them by calling the police: "So and so, this is the police!"

At first, the wife feels that she is communicating counterresentment of sorts toward her husband by telling him that she still has a family of her own which she has not given up. Her husband's reaction was one of feeling quite hurt and he senses (from his side) the message immediately—that she was acting "lovingly" toward her brother and father. Then an argument ensues about the meaning of "police" in the dream. The husband feels that the "police" represent his wife's reinvoking or reestablishing the primacy of her family and particularly the position of her father. Next, the pregnancy issue is raised and the wife tells her husband (with reference to the children in the dream) that she is not ready to become pregnant yet, although she notes that she is willing to "keep trying" (p. 73).

As a result of this dream exchange, the conflict between husband and wife over their respective families is intensified. However, as the result of this particular exchange, the wife notes that she feels less afraid of losing her husband's love and more trusting. Clearly, this initial dream exchange argued well for the subsequent (and deepening) dream exchanges of this husband and wife.

Parallels with the Iroquois Dream Technique

Calogeras points out (pp. 76–77) that the unique aspect of this couple's dream exchange was the interpretive mechanism they developed in telling each other their dreams—which carried along with it the expectation (even a conviction at the end) that a correct unraveling would bring with it beneficial psychic changes in each. In brief, by means of their dream exchange and reciprocal interpretations, they had developed an effective ideographic "dream language" by which they were able to converse; the end effect of this was a marital atmosphere in which their unconscious played a most creative and therapeutic role. This "theory of dream exchange" which this husband and wife evolved is not unlike the cultural theory of dreams of the Iroquois and, as Calogeras suggests (p. 77), it in many ways bears a significant parallel. A brief account of the Iroquois dream theory follows.

> For the Iroquois, the dream was considered to be the core about which the psychological balance of their culture depended. It was considered to be the unconscious repository of all wishes and desires, and if subject to too great frustration, illness would result. The Iroquois knew that such wishes were often expressed in symbolic and distorted form by the dream, and for that reason, the dreamer could not properly interpret his dreams but needed the help of an outside source. For instance, a shaman could be consulted and a procedure astonishingly like the free-association technique used (Wallace, 1958, 1970). Or, at those occasions of tribal rites or ceremonies, the dreamer–patient could go through his village and present the members with a cryptic summary of his dream or dreams, whereupon the people were then required to unravel the meaning of the dream. (There were actual "dream-guessing" rites during mid-winter, or on occasion of serious illnesses, where the dream riddles were considered and fulfilled.) [p. 77].

This patient and her husband seemed clearly to have employed both of the Iroquois' dream techniques (i.e., the shaman–patient and group–patient procedures) with the modification that their dream communications were considered by their immediate marital units and not by a tribal gathering. Just as the Iroquois dream exchanges offer a workable escape valve for repressed wishes (directed mainly against the tribal members), so did the exchange of dreams between this husband and wife; and just as the therapeutic effectiveness that the Iroquois

placed on fulfilling the dreamer's wishes—actually or symbolically—so did the more sophisticated dream communications
and working through process serve a similar function for this
couple.

Theoretical Issues

In terms of this husband and wife dream exchange, Calogeras
notes a number of pertinent theoretical issues.

1. *On the need to communicate dreams.* Basic to this husband
and wife dream exchange was their need to communicate to
one another in unconscious terms by means of the dream. As
they began to share their dreams, both demonstrated an "ego
readiness" which indicated a major shift in their psychic dynamics and social interaction. Calogeras infers that a basic motive
for the wife's participating in dream exchanges was the nature
of her Oedipus complex and its recapitulation both in the analytic transference and in her marriage. Considered from the
wife's side, her husband seemed to have served as a reproduction of her brother with whom she was linked in an intimate
relationship as a child, and also as the child with whom she was
to be made pregnant by the analyst.

2. *The dream per se as a concrete object.* Based on Kanzer's
hypothesis (1955, p. 244) that the dream may, under certain
conditions of recollection, represent a specific part of the body,
the wife's dream may be understood as being a concrete object—"a baby fertilized by her husband's communications and
then delivered to the analyst. In this "solid object" sense, then,
the dream exchange itself has meaning relating to the actual
birth process, that is, the idea of giving birth is only the end-
state, since behind it is the act of coitus, which ultimately results
in their "joint product"—a child.

3. *Dream exchange and introjected objects.* The wife's resistance
to being pregnant lends itself to formulation that during sleep
an ego "splitting" takes place where the "good or preoedipal"
parent introject is reattached to the ego, and the bad eliminated. Applying this hypothesis to our couple's dream exchange, we can infer that the "good parental objects" were

given the occasion to communicate intrapsychically with one another and thereby be more completely understood; upon their eventual conscious emergence they could then be brought into more meaningful interplay when confronting the conflicts (vis-á-vis the bad parental introjects), it could now be understood as being mastered when she psychologically allowed herself to become pregnant as a result of "expelling" or neutralizing these bad introjects (p. 79).

Conclusions

In concluding his article, Calogeras draws a number of inferences regarding this marital dream exchange (pp. 80–81). (1) It would seem reasonable to infer that unconscious communications—of varying degrees of clarity—where being made from the husband (through the mechanism of the wife's therapy and her unconscious) to the analyst. This tripartite dream situation seemed to function with increasing therapeutic insight for all concerned. (2) Much of this couple's dream material (with its emphasis of the communicative function of the dream) gives support to the theory that a relative commonality of the husband's and wife's conflicts are basic selectors in marital choice. (This couple shared such common denominators as: marked similarity of mother figures; apparent weakness or secondary positions of the fathers; two-child families, with ambivalence toward the other sibling.) (3) Regarding the husband's role in this dream exchange, one can infer that he was, at times, "the pregnant mother," "the infant in the womb," and/or "the child castrated for harboring incestuous fantasies towards the mother." Related to this was his unconscious motive for the disclosure of his dreams to his wife—the primary determinant of which was to overcome his exclusion from the "triangular" relationship. (4) The temptation to label this dream exchange as an acting-out transference would seem to reflect an over-extension of the concept, which at one time was so indiscriminately advocated in psychoanalytic literature. Rather, as Calogeras infers, the current dream-exchange material would seem to add support to the trend which moves acting out away from regarding it as exclusively undesirable and as a transference resistance, and views it more as the gradual emergence, in novel fashion, of new material from unconscious sources.

Summary

In this overview of the communicative function of the dream, I have endeavored to highlight the main points in its development by providing a brief (but critical) overview of the three seminal articles in this area. In the first, the now classic "The Communicative Function of the Dream," Kanzer provides the basic definition, conceptualization, and clinical data in support of his thesis that the dream serves a communicative function—directly in terms of introjected objects and indirectly in relations to the external world. While in the second, "The Intrapsychic and Communicative Aspects of the Dream," Bergmann presents the historical-cultural context for his thesis that the need to communicate one's dream is part of Western cultural tradition as well as individual development. In the final article, "Husband and Wife Exchange of Dreams," Calogeras discusses how a marital couple's dream exchange and interpretation led to a quite unique level of preconscious and unconscious communication. In conclusion, this overview demonstrates quite clearly the efficacy in recognizing and using the dream's communicative function in the analytic approach to the interpretation of dreams.

Chapter 22

CONSCIOUS DREAM SYNTHESIS AS A METHOD OF LEARNING ABOUT DREAMING: A PEDAGOGIC EXPERIMENT

ALVIN FRANK AND EUGENE E. TRUNNELL

"Building up dreams by synthesis" was one of the methods of dream interpretation described by Freud (1900, p. 311). He regarded synthesizing dreams as the easiest way of making "clear" and "defending the trustworthiness" (p. 310) of the processes of the dream work. By "synthesis" he meant the reconstruction of a dream after the interpretation and elucidation of the dream thoughts. In the interest of discretion, he declined to make this synthesis in the discussion of his own dreams, but subsequently published syntheses of two of Dora's (1905c) and one of the Wolf Man's (1918) dreams. Further, the intuitive synthesis of dreams by a creative writer was a major theme in the "Gradiva" paper (1907a). Later, he commented several times on the similarities between such artistically inspired dreams and real dreams, including their analyzability (1914a, 1925a).

Stimulated by Freud's comments, we developed the idea of using a third variation of dream synthesis as a teaching device. We assigned students the task of purposefully and consciously composing a wholly artificial "dream" that would meet certain prescribed criteria. By the use of this method we anticipated that the conscious active effort required to duplicate the usually passively experienced processes of dreaming would lead to a deeper understanding and appreciation of the dream work,

---

This paper was first published in the *Psychoanalytic Quarterly* (1978), 47:103–112.

of the dream as a creative product, and of the subtleties and intricacies of the primary process. Because the exercise proved to be a most rewarding one, we wish to share it.

The assignment was made midway in an eighteen-session, first-year course entitled, "Introduction to the Psychology of Dreaming," given to two classes at the St. Louis Psychoanalytic Institute. At this point in the course, candidates had already studied the process of dream formation. The following instructions were given to each student:

> Synthesize a manifest dream using the following material. Your unique dream wish is enclosed separately: all others are different. Do not discuss with classmates, but be prepared to respond in class so we can analyze the dream and determine the wish (i.e., be prepared to present associations leading to latent dream thoughts and what is related to dream from day before, childhood, etc.) Dream should include:
> At least two instances of condensation;
> At least two instances of displacement;
> A reversal or a joke or
> A symbol, neologism, or spoken words;
> An example of calculation and/or absurdity and/or intellectual activity;
> It may include the kitchen sink in addition if you so wish.
> Material: You are a twenty-one-year-old male graduate student living in dorms with a male roommate. Each of you has a girl friend with whom each of you occasionally also shares the room (by prearrangement with roommate). Your parents visit on Saturday, see the sights, and watch your football team upset Ohio State. Parents meet roommate and your girl friend for the first time. They seem to like them. You go out to dinner.
> You are a middle child, conventional background. Sister two years older, brother two years younger. No history psychotherapy. You dream the following Saturday night. We will have to determine to whom you tell the dream on Sunday. P.S. If we

can guess the "infantile wish" from the manifest
content, you've not done it.

The condition that the dreamer not be in psychotherapy
was included to limit the number of variables confronting the
dreamer. As was indicated, each of the students was assigned a
different dream wish. A secretary was given a list of different
"infantile wishes" with directions to include one arbitrarily, with
each set of instructions. Hence, no one, including the instructors, could have advance awareness of what "infantile wish"
might be "motivating" any of the "dreamers." The identification
of the wish was expected to reveal its object, in turn revealed
by the identity of the person with whom the "dream" was presumably shared.

Each of the candidates in the two classes participating in
this experiment has succeeded in producing a synthetic dream.
While the task was not a simple one, it did not prove to be
unduly difficult. The students agreed that it was a stimulating,
challenging, and profitable assignment. The technique used by
most was to create the "dream" piecemeal, at intervals, over an
extended period of time, perhaps two or three days. The majority were successful in combining day residue, latent dream
thoughts, and an infantile wish, and translating them all into a
"manifest dream."

Finished "dreams" were "interpreted" (using the usual psychoanalytic technique) by candidates and instructors together
during subsequent class periods. The class atmosphere was one
of informal camaraderie and constructive competition. From
thirty minutes to an hour was spent on each dream. The
"dreamer" was asked for associations to the "events" of the day
preceding the "dream" and to various elements in his "dream."
Only after the exercise was finished (i.e., when the "dream
wish" had been correctly ascertained by the class as a whole)
would the "dreamer" answer questions about why and how he
had constructed his "manifest dream" and how he had done
his "dream work."

While the synthesized dreams lacked the richness contributed by the overdetermination of genuine dreams, they offered
some distinct advantages as a pedagogic device. For candidates

to submit their genuine dreams to open examination in a class might be emotionally very difficult. In this exercise, however, it was comfortable to assume the role of the dreamer of an assigned dream and to participate actively in having it analyzed. A synthesized dream is, of course, simpler than a genuine one and can be understood with less material than is usually needed to illustrate dream formation in an actual case. Finally, as previously indicated, the active synthesizing of a dream (in contrast to analyzing) offers a unique way of understanding dreams and an opportunity to apply and juggle the mechanisms of the dream work. The requirement that these principles be applied in a conscious, problem-solving, goal-oriented effort necessitates the use of previously learned abstract knowledge in a concrete, practical way. In addition, it requires the synthesis of previously discretely defined mechanisms in such a way as to lead to an integrated end product.

To further illustrate the technique, here is a "manifest dream" created by one of the participants:

> Dreamer, as a little boy, is with roommate's girl at a table in a restaurant. The only available light is from a candle in the center of the table. The light is so dim that dreamer thinks he is with his own girl or maybe with his mother. The girl stands up, and dreamer sees that she is high in the middle and round on the end like his mother but much taller than either his mother or himself. She is carrying a doll which looks like the dreamer or his baby. The girl sits down and begins to nurse the doll. Dreamer picks up the candle and passes it back and forth in front of the girl. She reaches for it but he blows out the flame. As he does so, the dreamer begins to grow physically and age at an incredible pace. From a small boy he quickly reaches twenty-one; in a minute more he is thirty-two years older than that. Since he knows this is absurd, he runs to the mirror where he sees his father's face superimposed on his twenty-one-year-old face. The image is perfectly fused at the points where the dreamer and his father actually look alike. The mirror reflection says: "You are my son!"

The "dream work" of this dream was summarized as follows:

Dream Thoughts: My girl is okay but she doesn't hold a candle to my mother. I would like to sleep with my mother but that is forbidden. Of course I'm very young—being born in 1953—so I have time yet to find someone like my mother. I do want to marry and have a baby. If only I were older, I might have met my mother first, married her, and had a baby with her.

Condensation:
    1. Girl stands for mother and for his own girl;
    2. Image, in mirror stands for himself and for his father.
Displacement:
    1. Baby to doll and nursing of doll instead of self-nursing;
    2. Symbolization of intercourse displaced from mother to girl.
Joke: What is high in the middle—round on ends—Ohio.
Symbol: Candle for penis. Also visual representation of "My girl doesn't hold a candle to my mother."
Spoken word: "You are my son," which dreamer must have heard as a child.
Calculation: Thirty-two years plus twenty-one years = 53—the year dreamer was born (reversal also).

The wish was to have a child with the mother. The dream was accordingly told to her. On review, we cannot identify the "reversal" cited in the last line.

What are the assumptions which led us to believe we could imitate, however imperfectly, the process and results of dream formation? First, of course, is a conscious intellectual appreciation of the nature of the mechanisms of the dream work, an understanding which we had imparted in the preceding weeks of study and which we hoped to utilize and test with this exercise. Second is the capacity to use this material in the characteristically illogical manner analogous to dream formation, while still functioning in a logical, purposeful way. This capacity we know as Kris's "regression in the service of the ego." Finally, there is an accessible reservoir of primitive capacities and processes in each of us to draw upon while in the conscious state. We assume such a reservoir as a part of all creativity. Both

Kubie (1958) and Kris (1952) have described the broad range of both preconscious content and thought processes which would satisfy this requirement. Kris stated that "they (preconscious mental processes) cover continual reaching from purposeful reflection to fantasy, and from logical formulation to dream-like imagery" (p. 305).

We expected psychoanalytic candidates, well into their personal training analyses, to take advantage of their potentiality for regressed, preconscious imitative expression in a consciously directed creative effort, a synthetic dream. While the products of these efforts would not duplicate unconsciously inspired and constructed dreams, we could reasonably expect some circumscribed approximation of the processes and results of the dream work. Was this a unique psychological exercise for our students? To the contrary, we assume that the degree of personal analysis required for matriculation had already involved repeated similar experiences. To allow one's self to purposefully regress in a controlled fashion in order to sample one's own inner nature, then to withdraw in order to savor, appreciate, and understand what had been experienced, is the everyday stuff of psychoanalysis. At a crucial moment in their progress as fledgling analysts our students must substitute another person for themselves; they must learn to apply the capacities described above to the observation, understanding, and treatment of others. These are paradigms of the psychoanalytic educational process: the development of capacities for the alternations between logical Aristotelian thought and an appreciation of the madness we call the unconscious; and the ability to replace ourselves with another as the object of study. The process of accomplishing these ends consists of many small steps rather than a few giant ones. We regard dream synthesis as an appropriate and specific action in this progression.

We could not, however, consider the dreams submitted as purely synthetic. It was immediately obvious that the influence of uniquely unconscious factors was visible or highly suspect in the students' completed assignments. We were repeatedly able to discern, as if in the clinical situation working with "real" dreams, unacknowledged influences which manifested themselves in such ways as unexplained overpreoccupations with a given theme or detail, the student "dreamers'" seemingly irrelevant tangents, patently obvious omissions which could not be explained on an intellectual basis, and the structure (contrasted with content) of some of the synthetic dreams. The regression involved in the composition of these dreams had obviously not been entirely "in the service of the ego."

No student described completing his assignment in an intellectual, purposeful, single sitting. Rather, they had worked on it at intervals, usually also "sleeping on it." We compared the "directions" or "material" upon which the assignment was based to Rorschach or TAT cards or the day residue of a naturally occurring dream. We hypothesized that at times during the composition of these "synthesized" dreams—in sleep, through inattention, under "stress" or whatever—unconscious forces had effected "transferences" in exactly the way described by Freud in Chapter VII of *The Interpretation of Dreams* (1900). Here we found that we had also followed Kris's wit and caricature. He distinguished between the former "where the ego abandons its supremacy and the primary process obtains control" and wit and caricature soon extended to "the vast domain of aesthetic experience in general. . . . This process remains in the service of the ego. . . . The contrast is between an ego overwhelmed by regression and a regression in the service of the ego. . . ." The reason for this difference is economic: "It seems that the ego finds its supremacy curtailed whenever it is overwhelmed by affects, irrespective of whether an excess of affect or the ego's own weakness is to be held responsible for the process" (p. 177).

It would seem that at moments in the composition of these synthetic dreams such conditions did exist: that, ironically, at these moments some of their elements approached an authenticity we could not have prescribed. Considering these conditions, we felt some concern about the emergence of uniquely revealing material in these "dreams," however artificial and well defined were the parameters within which they were created and their impact in the classroom. But the preponderance of conscious determinants and the group focus on the primary process from a secondary process viewpoint tended to minimize this inevitable complication. In no case were we aware of anxiety or embarrassment in any candidate regarding his dream's manifest or latent content. In retrospect, we see that because of our concern, we failed to appreciate the positive aspect of this facet of the experience. Realistically, candidates must learn to tolerate and accept others' awareness of the impact of inevitable residual unconscious conflicts on their work. Such self-acceptance is necessary in order to participate productively in, for example, case conferences and supervision. It is one of the steps leading to the recognition of countertransference and the need for continuing self-analysis.

We judged our experiment impressionistically from several perspectives. First, the candidates stated spontaneously and explicitly that they had found it useful in clarifying and facilitating their mastery of the various elements of the dream work. This result was corroborated by the class discussion. There we found areas of deficiency or confusion which had previously escaped both the students' and the instructors' detection. The two most extreme (indeed startling) examples are as follows.

One candidate designed a convincing artificial dream with an intricate underlying dream work. However, he failed to explicitly link this impressive production with his assigned "infantile wish." Somehow, he understood that the wish should be inferred without a clear, stated connection.

Another created a dream and dream work which were technically correct as far as form and mechanisms were concerned. The content was another matter. The entire latent dream was of contemporary origin; it completely lacked anything of childhood.

Finally, we found this exercise to be of real value in the evaluation of the students' progress and our own teaching efforts. We were assured of the candidates' mastery of previously covered material by their successes, as well as alerted to areas of ambiguity by "rough spots" described or detected in the completed assignments. The appreciation of the strengths and weaknesses demonstrated therein helped direct our continuing efforts in areas of both evaluation and teaching. In contrast to the two extreme examples given above, most of the results were reassuring. In another situation it had been difficult to evaluate a candidate because of his lack of participation in class discussions. It was reassuring that he was able to create a technically correct and rather rich synthetic dream.

We wondered if such a reductive approach to the dream and its processes would tend to distract teachers or students from the complexities and ingenuity of the natural phenomena. It was found, however, that our experiment, with its artificial restriction of variables, its clumsy, self-conscious, frustrating approximations of nature, and its pale imitations of the dreams which we are so prone to take for granted each night did not have this impact. Rather, it resulted in a renewed appreciation of the depth and profundities of the dream as process and experience.

Summary

The assignment of synthesizing an artificial dream was given to analytic candidates in a first-year class in the psychology of dreams. The object was to provide students with the challenge of using what they had learned didactically about dream formation in an active creative manner. The synthesized "dreams" lacked the richness of the real thing; in this experiment the means justified the end. We believe this assignment proved very successful in teaching and learning about dream formation and unconscious aspects of creativity as well as some of the vicissitudes of primary processes and unconscious ego, superego, and id influences. In addition, we viewed it as an appropriate step in the students' progress from analysand to analyst.

Chapter 23

MARITAL CONFLICT IN DREAMS

Roy C. Calogeras

I

The present study deals with how marital conflict in dreams may influence the direction and outcome of a marriage. In the analytic material which follows, I will first present the novel phenomenon of how marital conflicts are depicted and elaborated upon in a series of dreams occurring in one of the marital partners over approximately a year of analytic treatment; and then discuss the closely related phenomenon of how such highly conflictual dream material adumbrated what was subsequently played out in the marriage.

The background to the dream series occurred in rather dramatic fashion when I received a late-night telephone call, approximately one week before my summer holiday, from a man who (speaking in a highly agitated manner) stated that he must see me immediately for a consultation because he had just "unaccountably" gotten himself involved in a "disastrous marriage" and he "simply must do something about it." An emergency appointment was scheduled for the next day.

At the appointed time a well-groomed and personable looking man in his midthirties appeared. In a breathless, apprehensive state, he indicated that he had gotten lost on his way over, but nevertheless had managed to get here on time. Immediately he told me that he had had a previous analysis, of some

---

This paper is based on a series of lectures given to the "Psychology of Dream" course, European Division, University of Maryland.

350

two and a half years' duration, some years before, over his conflicts regarding which profession to enter; and, as a result of his treatment, he had decided to follow in his father's footsteps and enter the legal profession. His subsequent education and career as a lawyer had gone exceedingly well, and approximately three years ago he had accepted a position as a legal officer in an international corporation in Europe. Since coming to Europe, the only real difficulty he had had has been "finding the right woman to love and to marry!" He had gone out with many women over the years but had never seemed to find, as he put it, "the right one" and had never married until several weeks ago. It was the crisis over his recent "disastrous marriage" which he wanted to consult me about. ("To be frank, I want to resume my analysis of some twelve years ago. . . . I should have continued long ago on my problems with women . . . but now it may be too late.") Subsequently, the following story emerged.

About one year ago, he had met a teacher (an exchange teacher) at a social gathering and begun dating her. He liked her and they soon developed a steady relationship. However, he soon realized that he didn't love her and tried to "break off" the relationship but was unable to do so. Yet inexplicably, they continued to see each other, and he found himself being drawn (later he described this as feeling compelled) into asking her to marry him, but was able to resist this impulse. Gradually, she began pressuring him to "make a decision" because she wanted to know what his "intentions were"; she either wanted to get married or continue her career as a teacher back in her own country. Then abruptly, in what he described as a weak moment, "I asked her to marry me, and I realized it was a mistake as soon as it came out!" He was unable to back out of the commitment. ("I was unable to act quickly enough.") Soon arrangements for the marriage were being made: a large church wedding was planned, and invitations were sent out after the final date was set. Several weeks before the scheduled wedding, he suddenly broke down and in a tearful, overwrought state told his fiancée that he couldn't go through with the marriage—that he was uncertain about his feeling for her and that he would like very much to wait. His fiancée's reaction to this was to make an immediate appointment for them to see their local minister for "premarital counseling." The patient experienced this counseling as an entrapment, "The minister was completely on her side and didn't give me a chance to verbalize my side of the situation. He just said, 'Just look at this wonderful woman. . . . She has everything a man could want. . . . You have nothing to worry about in getting married, etc.' " As a result of the pastoral counseling, and added to the fact that he decided that "I couldn't disappoint the people to whom we had sent invitations," he went through with the wedding.

This then was the state of his marriage as his treatment began. He had just gotten married two weeks before, and he and his wife immediately agreed to take separate vacations (she to Canada) and he remaining in Europe. (As a matter of fact, he informed me that she had just left on her vacation several days before and he had thus far not missed her.) Because of the crisis nature of his problem (fortuitously his vacation was scheduled to begin at the same time as mine), we agreed to begin the actual analytic work immediately upon return from our holidays. However, I continued to see him in the two days remaining before the holiday in a face-to-face situation. Since the patient was familiar with the analytic pact, basic rule, principle of abstinence, and so on, as well as having had a frequency of five times a week in his first analysis (I also knew his previous analyst by reputation), much of the preparation for analysis in the form of preliminary interviews was by-passed.

II

In his first analytic sessions, the patient told me straight away that he had not missed his wife at all during the six weeks she had been gone on her separate holiday; in fact, in his associations he emphasized repeatedly how relieved he was to be free of her, but he was completely "appalled to find myself in this mess." Then, following some background material on his family—his closeness to his older and younger brothers—he returned to his marital dilemma and specifically to his wife's personality and previous life. She was five years older than he, and has been married twice before. Both marriages had ended abruptly: in the first, a teenage marriage, his wife told him that she was much too young to get married and they were "unable to communicate"; in the second, occurring in her late twenties, her husband became disinterested and then abusive and was not interested in having children so she left him.

During his holiday in Switzerland, while reflecting on his wife's two earlier marriages, he arrived at the conclusion that he had *actually arranged his own marriage much as if he played the part of his parents.* As if to justify this arrangement, he then asserted that his wife was a good housekeeper and able to "cook well and arrange things"; and he acknowledged that she has many "motherly qualities," and that his mother, after a single meeting with his wife, strongly approved of her. Then as these initial sessions come to a close, he revealed that just before he came to Europe some three years earlier, he was engaged to be married to a fellow attorney, M, with whom he had studied, but his mother had not liked this woman, and with some misgivings, he had terminated their engagement. He acknowledged further that he had entertained the secret hope to "back out" of his engagement like he did with M.

The series of dreams extended over approximately one year. However, before reporting any dreams of his own, he revealed that the night his wife returned from her vacation, she had told him her dream in which *they were at a party and the people there decided to exchange partners and he (patient) became interested in two of their friends—who were very attractive—and started kissing them.* He said that he got his wife's unconscious message right away (even though he said nothing to his wife about her dream), namely, that she knew that their marriage was in trouble and that he would like to break away. In his associations to her dream he felt that she was just as ambivalent about their marriage as he; and he wondered whether she might be giving him unconscious permission to have an affair because of being guilty over trapping him into getting married. Suddenly he reversed himself and wondered whether this could all be a projection on his part. ("I think my former analyst might point out to me too that it could be my 'reading into it what I unconsciously want'.") Following further musing about the dream, he had a fantasy in which he was on a troopship sailing out of New

York City harbor during World War II, and he waved to his friends on the dock and saw the Statue of Liberty, thought of being free, and he imagined himself telling his wife all about this when he returned home.

Can He Be Saved Dream

In the next session, he reported the following dream, which he thought had "something to do with the party dream" which his wife told him. "I fall asleep in the living room and either Kay (wife) or my mother is there—I can't remember or say which. Then I see an announcement on the TV saying, 'Can he be saved. . . . Can he be saved'."

His first association was to feel a pain in his chest and to recall that he had a minor congenital heart problem as a child, and he then began to laugh, saying "Here I am falling asleep with both of them—in their presence—and now I'm wondering if I can save myself from them. . . . It's pretty clear that I see a lot of my mother in Kay and that's a big problem. . . . But all men see their mother in the woman they marry. It's a heart problem, isn't it?"

Comment. The patient began his dream series with a dream where he was asleep in a room where both his wife and mother seemed to be fused; it is there that he then announced the core of his marital problem, "Can he be saved?" The repetition of his phrase seemed to point to both his heightened anxiety over his marital dilemma—which involved both his mother and wife—but he also indicated the compulsive nature of the problem. Does the "Can he be saved" phrase indicate the wish-fulfilling element of "Wanting to be saved"? Also in hindsight might we not infer that falling asleep in the dream indicates his intention of presenting his conflicts in the sleep state, that is, by the means of dreams?

Following several weeks in which he reported many incidents relating to the state of uneasiness in his marriage, he alluded to how he was always glad when he could be separated from his wife—either she is at a teachers' meeting or he is busy with legal problems. He reported a three-part dream occurring over the weekend on three successive nights—Friday, Saturday, and Sunday.

Escape and Support Dream

> *Part I*: I'm attending a club with my brother, a male friend, and M (his former girl friend to whom he was once engaged). My brother and his friend are acting like "book-ends" sitting on either side of us (me and M). (His simultaneous associations were to the fact that Kay was not here and he was enjoying himself; and then many associations and thoughts on how passionate M was and what a fool he was not to have married her.)
>
> *Part II*: I'm at some sort of fork in a road—one way leads to where Kay is or lives and the other way to another woman or women. (His immediate thoughts are that his wife is currently away on a three-day teachers' conference and he doesn't miss her at all.)
>
> *Part III*: I'm back in Canada or California with M and we're making love on a couch. On one side of the couch is a big window which is level with us, and on the other side is a window which is higher up. I feel funny because I think that we are being looked at. (His immediate association is that M is very open about sex and expressing it, while he is often inhibited.)

In summarizing his many associations to the three parts considered as a whole, he characterized it as an "escape dream" and he described it as "my wish to leave this loveless and abortive marriage which I have gotten myself into, and find a passionate love marriage with someone like M." However, then he is quick to recognize that there are problems: "I know I have a lot of inhibitions about breaking through this!" In the first dream (Part I) his associations lead him to conclude that he needs support from males to whom he is close—in this case his "brothers and brothers' friends" seem to refer not only to his brothers to whom he still is quite close, but to his former analyst

and to me: "I want you to be like my brothers in a way supporting me." In Part II, on the following night he indicates his
ambivalence (the bifurcation in the road) but still his very strong
desire to leave Kay (my impression was it could also refer to
his ambivalence about remaining in analysis); and in the third
dream (Part III), his associations suggest to him that he has
found love, but again the strong "deterrent fact," as he puts it,
of his ambivalence in treatment here because he feels that he
will have to "expose himself"; that is, his impulsive and hidden
love behavior will have to be looked at by "authorities." The
fact that he had the dream in three parts on three successive
nights suggested to him how difficult it was for him to face not
only the conscious marital conflict with his wife, but also the
roots of all this in his past. He alluded to the fact that he seems
always to break things up in parts, thereby never quite seeing
the whole of anything. As an aside, he noted that in his former
analysis he found that the number three or three things almost
always seemed to be connected to his family—his mother, father
and brothers.

Comment. With his second dream, described by him as an
escape dream, several new themes regarding the marriage are
introduced. Not only does it concern his wish to escape from
the marriage (a highly ambivalent one as it turns out); but if he
is to do so, he needs the strong "bookend" support of his
brother, his friends, his "two" analysts. His ambivalence is further extended to—going into the past, exposing himself to "authorities" when exploring his sexual inhibitions and his fears of
the erotic woman.

For the next month, he reported no dreams, and his sessions were mainly filled with childhood recollections, current
activities with wife, and some transient thoughts and fantasies
about his previous analysis. Then, following a letter from a
former girl friend, S, announcing her engagement, he recalled
with considerable feeling their strong mutual attraction: "She
was Jewish and went off to art school in Paris, but I always
loved her, thought about her, and we always kept in touch. I
even thought that one day we might get married." At this point

he reported another three-part dream which again occurred over the weekend.

State of Marriage Dream

> *Part I*: I'm on a ski slope with my wife, but I have *no* poles while she has "all the equipment." She skies very conservatively, while I ski without poles and soon slip off the course into mud and gravel where there are other people trying to get out.
>
> *Part II*: I'm in this place—a garden—with P (the wife of one of his colleagues to whom he is strongly attracted), and we are going to get something, perhaps flowers or shrubs for my garden. And then P gets this flower for me and we are both happy at her selection.
>
> *Part III*: There is a sudden scene change and P's husband (R) is conducting a tour of the town where I'm living. R points out a place like a camp where he implies that this could have been a prison for real criminals or a concentration camp.

Part I of the dream reminded him of the state of his marriage, particularly his sexual relations with his wife ("We are not coordinated at all, everything ends up in a state of frustration, like mud and gravel."), and he wondered whether this is a premonition of things to come; sometimes now he had no sexual urges at all. He recalled that once in his previous treatment he became impotent for a month. In Part II, his associations focused on the extent to which he always seemed to find love—or was strongly attracted to—forbidden women. ("I just received a letter from S about her coming marriage, and I really loved her; and then there is P, and she is married.") He noted his "odd feelings" now because everything is out of step for him. "The women like M, S and P who are really right for me, I don't seem ready or mature enough for them." Turning to Part II, he states that Part II is a warning to him what will happen if he should step out of line, and he remarks that he has never gone out with a married woman; his strict conscience would never allow that. He thought also that I would "throw him out" if he did something like that. Ending the session with a short silence, he broke it by wondering whether "the camp" in the dream could have something to do with his family. "My mother still writes me several times a week . . . I love it and hate it."

Comment. This third dream introduced the dream representations of the state of his marriage, by first focusing on the sexual dysfunctional relationship with his wife–mother, and then his fears that this might lead to unbearable castration anxiety (impotency) as it did when these conflicts were touched upon in his previous analysis. His "solution" (wish!) was to approach the "erotic woman"—to whom he was greatly attracted—but this posed additional psychical problems for him since such women are always "oedipalized" in his mind and come in conflict with his superego inhibitions. He ended the three-part dream by verifying his still primary love–hate attachment to his mother.

For the next month-and-a-half he ruminated much on "the fact" that he didn't really love Kay, couldn't stay with her but couldn't leave her either. But what is he to do? In one session he presented what he jokingly called "almost a legal brief about the state of my marriage and love life." In summary he first noted that he was selfish, and didn't want to be lonely, and therefore he would remain temporarily with Kay. But second, he knew he needed to find a "real love object," and he was convinced that this would take time. As of now he could tolerate a nonloving and nonpassionate relationship with Kay, but when he got "too frustrated and miserable" he began to seek out a passionate, loving woman like M.

Current Marital State Dream

As the Christmas season drew near, he revealed that he and his wife had decided to take separate vacations over the holidays—he was traveling to Rome, and his wife to Egypt on a Nile cruise. Shortly after this, he had another three-part dream.

Part I: I'm in a restaurant in West Canada or perhaps in California with my wife and parents. We must be on a vacation. Nothing much is happening and I notice that we are not sitting in the main part of the restaurant but are in a little alcove.

Part II: The scene changes and we are in the main part of the restaurant now, and I'm showing my family (mother, father, and brothers) a videotape of our first meeting in the restaurant with Kay. However, on the video, the scene is not the "little alcove" part of the restaurant; we are sitting in the main part of the restaurant with my family, but Kay is no longer there, but G (my first real love relationship in college) is there in her place.

Part III: The restaurant now changes to a football (soccer) field and I'm one of the players. Toni S, the famous German goalee, calls me over and pulls my jersey out of my shorts and turns my collar up and says, "Now you are okay and ready to play!"

His first thought was that the "little alcove" of Part I of the dream aptly described his marriage. ("It's dull and nothing much is happening. Am I trying to exclude it in some way?") In the second part, he stated that having G there in place of Kay (his wife) was like a memory from the past which made him feel quite sad. He recalled that when he was an exchange student in England during his university days, G used to write him every day and wanted to marry him when he returned, but "When I returned I got cold feet and told her that I wanted to wait six months and she was very hurt and refused to see me any more." Now he recalled that just before he had come to Europe she wrote and told him that she was now engaged to be married but still cared for him. ("It was like an invitation to get back together with her if I still cared for her.") Suddenly he turned to Toni S, the famous goal keeper, with whom he always identified whenever he saw him play, and his first thought was that he wished he could be aggressive and block Kay's shots: "If I were in command like Toni S I would not have let Kay force me into this marriage. . . . I'd grab the ball away from her, but I can't seem to do so!" And when he thought of Toni S telling him that his uniform was too tight, etc., he takes that as an indication he should "loosen up and not be so tight inside." And then after a short silence, he said that it was obvious that "You (analyst) stand for Toni S and that I'm very afraid of her (wife) in some funny fashion."

Comment. He prefaces his fourth dream with the residue that he and his wife will be taking separate Christmas vacations. This dream, again broken up into three parts, suggests the current state of his marriage—a state which is essentially isolated from the rest of his emotional life. Not only has he been unable to consummate and consolidate any of his earlier adolescent love-relationships into a marriage, but he reveals how he has been unable to fulfill his wish to develop a masculine identification sufficient to stand up (resolving his oedipal identifications) to the wife–mother and separate from her. His hope is to gain sufficient strength from the analyst–father to carry this out.

III

In his sessions immediately following his holiday in Rome, he indicated that he was just bursting with things which happened and some of his "insights" which he arrived at while there. In Rome he had met several English-speaking families, also on holiday, and they included him in their social life. As a consequence, he again noted that he didn't miss his wife "at all." While there, he had ample time to reflect on things which had occurred during the past year—his "odd marriage," his great difficulties in finding love, and his approaching his past again by resuming his analysis. One of the first "insights" occurred while he was visiting the Vatican museum: "It was while I was looking at all these magnificent works of art from the past that I realized I got involved with Kay because she was motherly and sure of herself. It was just impossible to resist her. I was fixated on her, as you analysts would say!" Again he observed that this was "somehow" connected with his fear of "passionate women."

Prior to his wife's departure on her holiday, she had given him a note to read while she was away. In this note she confronted him with the fact he "wasn't talking to her," by which she meant that he was "untruthful with her." He readily acknowledged that this was quite true, that he was unable to tell her that he would like a trial separation and that he was afraid to tell her these things because he might hurt her and she "might do something impulsive." But when he was asked for his associations regarding the impulsive things she might do, he said that the only thing that came up was a dream which he had over the holiday. Chuckling, he said that it was in two parts, not three, as before.

Rock Concert and Being Tested Dream

> *Part I:* I was at a rock concert with my wife and we were listening to the first act; however, the second act was delayed and since I had to work the next day, and I didn't want to wait, so I left her there.
>
> *Part II*: I am being tested by one of the senior people in my firm who wants to test me on my physical and sports ability. I told the examiner that I don't want to run or jog but will swim. Then I am being tested on my swimming, but it is on grass and I'm going through the strokes and the examiner tells me that it is not quite right, and he shows me or starts to show me how to do it.

When he analyzed this dream over his holiday on his own, he arrived at the thought that the first act (rock concert) definitely depicted his marriage. He has attended the first act but would leave the second ("I've really seen enough of it. . . . It just doesn't work. . . . I am convinced now that I have to leave and let her go on alone.") To being "tested by a senior person for his sports ability" he noted that the analyst was the examiner, and he was criticizing me for not helping him more. ("I thought that if you introduced me to a real, passionate woman now, I could finally tell her [wife] that it was over with.") Next he recalled some vague and disparate thoughts about writing his father and asking for his advice—something he has not done. And he ended with the thoughts that he was "being tested" for his "sexual ability" and that he couldn't really sustain any real, erotic relations with his wife because he always became afraid—sexually exciting or stimulating relationships (he concludes) are forbidden. (The only comment I made to him at this point was that perhaps in some fashion he was also going through "the motion like he was on grass" here in the analysis, and not really getting to the deeper aspects of what was happening.)

In summarizing the main point which now came out of the examiner/tester dream, was the extent to which he felt his father had failed him. He had designated that he wasn't to be tested on running or jogging but on "swimming," and then had only gone through the motion. This then was what he had been doing in the marriage (as well as in his treatment); that is, going through the motions (emotions); the equation of swimming = marriage. Similarly, he had been doing the same thing with the so-called "passionate women" that he found so attractive and yet so threatening; he had been going through the motions, but not developing any real deep attachments to them.

Comment. The residue of this dream is an actual separation from his wife (i.e., taking of separate Christmas holidays), but the subsequent dream reveals how different the unconscious wish-life can be. He first likens the rock concert, which he leaves early, to the state of his marriage—but it is again a bogus separation. For when he is really tested/examined (Part II), it turns out that he is largely still "going through the motions," trying, on the one hand, to please and propitiate the analyst as well as avoiding any deep attachment to the erotic, nonoedipal woman. He ends by implying (wishing?) that the analyst–father will show him the way out of his marital dilemma. Yet in the final analysis he seems unconvinced and ambivalent.

Just before the patient and his wife went off on a three-day ski weekend, he presented what he called his two models of marriage. The first model he designated as the "love marriage" which is exemplified by his young brother who married a Latin-American woman for love. This marriage was actively opposed by his mother and, as a result, his sister-in-law keeps his mother at a distance and won't allow her to see her grandchildren too often. ("She [sister-in-law] sees my mother as a dominating and controlling person and cuts her to the quick if she tries to offer advice or interferes in her family in any way.") The second model, the neutral–rational model, is exemplified by the marriage of his older brother who established a "rationally planned marriage." ("He married a very practical girl with whom he had lived for several years. Everything they do is always arranged and well thought out and under control.") Of the two models, the patient wished he could have the first one, but "knows" that he had "fallen in" the rational "trap," and he is very much afraid to get involved in a passionate or love-relationship model of marriage.

Traditional House and the Double Dream

While on his ski holiday, the patient had two dreams on consecutive nights which he related as one dream of two parts. He noted that his wife almost missed the ski bus taking them on their holiday. He had arrived early and was waiting for her at the bus station.

> *Part I:* I'm with Kay (wife) in a *traditional type of house* with many rooms, but there is little furniture in the house. There is a garage attached to the house and on the roof is a hobo or a gypsy who is living there. Suddenly, Kay shouts out that this man must leave.
>
> *Part II:* The scene shifts to California or British Columbia and I'm in my apartment with my wife, but actually she is somewhere else. I'm giving a party with Pete (patient's best friend) and three or four of my current colleagues at the firm. The women who are at the party are all girls whom I went out with in college, and Pete is matched with Rose—a very beautiful girl with whom I was once passionately in love.

To the first part, the patient notes: first, that "the traditional house is a symbol of our marriage and it has nothing in it" (i.e., no furniture); second, "the hobo and gypsy represent me, and I'm feeling happy that Kay tells me to leave . . . it would be so much easier for me if she decided to break up the marriage"; and third, after a short silence he reluctantly acknowledged that the hobo and/or gypsy could also represent the analyst and that "my wife is telling you to leave her husband alone." (He has many thoughts at this point that he is not really ready to break up the marriage, yet wants to get out of it in some way.)

To the second part, he averred that Pete, whom he had always thought of as his double, and who was now living somewhere in California, had been searching for years for the ideal or perfect woman to marry. (He recounted a long story of how Pete was once engaged to his "dream woman" and then broke the engagement suddenly when he found that this woman had "hidden a child away at school" from him.) Considering the dream as a whole, he stated that it signified his wish "to turn back the clock" and be like his double (Pete); he would very much like to break his "engagement," a slip which he acknowledged after he quickly changed it to "marriage." In the dream he matched himself up with "the passionate woman I loved so much in college and let slip through my fingers." Then he noted that both he and Pete seem attracted to women who are unavailable—still married and not yet divorced, and/or of different religions and are "too desirable or passionate—which makes it difficult to approach them."

In subsequent sessions (reflecting on these two dreams and his ski holiday), he observed that it was now quite clear to him that he was trying to escape from Kay "because I don't have the guts to tell her yet—I just had the thought—although I got mad at her for almost being late and missing the bus, my dream makes me realize that I secretly hoped that she would miss the bus and then I would be free!"

Comment. The two dreams (considered together) begin again with the state of his marriage (empty "without furniture"), but despite the supposed wish to leave the marriage, it nevertheless contains a warning to the analyst (and to himself) not to go on delving too far—that he is still not ready to break up the marriage. The dream also seems to convey a message that his wife wants him to leave treatment, the implication being that he might do so. While in the second part, he introduces his double (his wished-for self) and this allows him to elaborate on the lost opportunities of his early "lost loves." Magically, he wishes to "turn back the clock" and find the desirable, erotic woman of youth, but then the conflicts and ambivalence toward them and toward the oedipal mother make this still impossible at this point.

For the next month-and-a-half, he reported no new dreams but focused on all the "mistakes" which have occurred in his life because of his inability to make decisions. While ruminating on this at the end of this period, he suddenly said, "This is going to be a decision session. . . . I can't go on living a lie like this; I've made a decision. . . . I will seek a divorce." Nevertheless, he qualified this by holding that he can't go through with it now because of a number of reasons: he doesn't want to hurt her feelings ("It would devastate her"), he would feel terribly guilty, which he couldn't manage at this time, and he would feel like he had used her because they jointly own all their properties. Again he thought about "turning back the clock" and he recalled a movie—*Mary Sue Got Married*[1]—which he and his wife had seen the previous evening.

He took the movie much as a dream and obsessed on how he would do the same thing with Kay, if he could turn back the clock two years; he would never have even gone out with her, and he began to focus on the events—almost as if he were in a fantasy state—which led up to asking Kay to marry him. He then recalled the "entrapment" which occurred, and then reported it much as if it were a dream.

Entrapment Dream

I was given the address of this school teacher (C) and I was supposed to pick it up at the local sports club first and then

---

[1] In this movie (according to the patient's version) Mary Sue goes to her twenty-fifth high school reunion (she and her husband are on the verge of divorce), and she is again elected the Prom Queen. While there she faints and in her unconscious state, she goes back to age seventeen, when she was first dating her husband, and

drive to her house. However, when I got here, the address was missing and Kay was waiting for me instead. She invited me to go home and have a drink with her, and before I knew it, we were kissing and had sex.

In analyzing this "entrapment dream," as he called it, he noted that he got involved much too quickly and he felt obligated ("I felt tied to her right away because we had had coitus on the first night and here I was really interested in going out with a colleague of hers"), and entrapped. He then stated he felt almost like a woman must feel with a man: "I was really tied to her. There really was nothing romantic about it. My groin decided for me and I was seduced." Following this, he described the pattern with Kay in which she would call him at his office and invite him to dinner after which they would have sex. ("After each meeting I would feel more obligated and entrapped and guilty.") Later he made an attempt to date C, and found her a very nice person and even felt romantic about her, but Kay found out about it and was insanely jealous and told C, "to get lost, that she saw me first." (The only intervention I made at this time was to try to elicit further associations from him after he had pointed out that he felt like a woman when Kay was pursuing him and also regarding his identification with Mary Sue in the film. He responded that he felt he was acting like he used to act with his mother and perhaps she (mother) was even treating him like a daughter.)

Comment. In this fantasy production which the patient takes as an "entrapment dream," he describes how he was actually seduced by his wife-to-be (reversing roles in the process) and entrapped into the marriage. The residue of this "dream," the *Mary Sue Got Married* film, reveals how readily he can identify with the female who is caught in an unhappy marriage and how helpless and castrated he feels when confronted with a phallic woman like his mother.

---

there—when she turned back the clock—she tries to change things by insulting her husband-to-be by telling him that he is a nerd and doing everything to break up with him.

Solution Dream

Several weeks after this, and immediately following his return from a hospital examination in which he had his minor congenital heart murmur evaluated, he had the following two-part dream.

> *Part I*: Three executives—all lawyers in the firm where I work—were asked to leave their positions because it was found that they were homosexuals. One man was very concerned about it. He was glad to break up with his wife. The second man, also married, had been a star athlete at one time, and seemed to take it very well but he was yet sad. The third man was Mr. Spock (in the Star-Trek TV series) and he took it very rationally and philosophically and was the most composed.
>
> *Part II*: The scene changes and I'm at a business conference in a Swiss mountain resort of X. While there, I go to bed, awake too late for breakfast and too early for lunch, so I decide to go jogging. Then I find myself running up those steep hills—and I think this must be like San Francisco or Montreal—and I find it hard going. Suddenly I see a group of people riding on horses cutting across just in front of me, and they start laughing at me because of my struggles in running up the hill. They shout out: "Get a horse."

His first association to Part I is that homosexuality would be a good defense in court for breaking up a marriage. Next he associated that "leaving the company" meant for him that he was leaving the marriage and that all three men in the dream represent different ways that one could get out of the marriage: the homosexual way, the depressive way, and the suave rational way of a Mr. Spock. He favored the latter, but doubted that he could carry it out. Returning to the "homosexual theme," he said that if he committed infidelity, Kay would leave him, or, in some way, this would be a good excuse for breaking up the marriage on legal grounds. As for "jogging up the hill," of Part II, his associations led to how difficult it was for him to tell his wife his true feelings. The "horse" symbolized for him the strong emotions—the convictions and purpose—that he would need to tell her how he really felt. He guessed that he did have this "condition," yet was not strong enough. In the session following this dream he reviewed once again why he didn't seem to have the courage or strength to talk to his wife directly and argue it out. He warned himself that he had better do something soon or he would get in "too deep and will never be able to get out."

Comment. In this dream, he was still much concerned with terminating the marriage, but the options seemed to be unrealistic. Thus he reviewed his various "solutions" (the happy-opportunistic, the depressed, and the rational suave) in breaking up the marriage because of being "homosexual" (= emasculated or castrated?); and then in the second part, he seemed to give his "solution," concluding how unready (unassertive, unphallic) he still was in psychologically separating from his wife–mother. Although his wish to separate appeared still to be active, he lacked the motivation and will (courage) to confront her. Implied in the dream were his three conflicts—the feminine way he had of relating to his wife, his depressive position suggesting the loss he would feel if he separated from her, and finally the wished-for rational-strength position which would avail him a reasonable solution.

IV

As the Easter holiday neared, the patient began to speak of his plans for a family get-together over the spring vacation. He and his wife would be traveling to Spain to meet his parents, who would be coming from North America to meet them. He wanted fervently to talk to his parents—particularly his father—about his disastrous marriage.

Upon his return from his Spanish trip, he noted that all his plans had gone awry. His father and wife didn't get along. Whatever his father wished to do (e.g., visiting a museum, castle or going to the beach, etc.) his wife would take exception to and suggest going to some other place. He found his mother treating his father in not so subtle fashion "just as if he was one of her sons—like my brothers or myself. . . . I couldn't believe it. She acted like a mother-rooster. I never recognized this before!" Every time he tried to speak with his father alone, and seek his advice, either his mother or his wife would intervene. He lamented that either his wife or mother was in control during the entire trip. On several occasions, he even tried talking to his wife about his feelings, but she always seemed to avoid it by finding other things to do or see. (It was while the patient was going on and on about how helpless he was that I had the fantasy that he should bring in his wife and I should talk to her.) Subsequently, I was able to point out to him that perhaps he wanted me to speak to his wife for him, and if I did, then this would shift the responsibility for any of the consequences from him to me. His immediate response was that he had hoped his father, "the judge, would be able to intervene for him, but I could never even present my case to him." It seemed to him now that both he and his father seemed to be "weak before women. . . . We're controlled by them." He ended one session by fantasizing that I would be sitting on his shoulder, and this would give him courage to tell Kay that he couldn't go on—and wanted a separation and a divorce.

In the next month's sessions, the patient returned to his two models of marriage, but now he extended this to what he referred to as his "passion-love" side and his "rational-love" side. He admitted that he was very much afraid of the passionate-love side, for each time he got close to an erotic woman and fell in love, he became afraid and ran away. Also he notes that often his passionate-love women are still married or have some other attachment and he wonders where this might have its roots. For him, Kay definitely was a rational-love choice. Then he began a kind of phenomenological discussion of what kind of marriage did he really have, and he concluded after a number of sessions that he had a kind of *Superego Marriage* (he used this term), inferring that he got married because of a sense of responsibility; he didn't want to hurt Kay and he didn't want to disappoint his parents—mainly his mother—who approved of his wife-to-be. He concluded that he would have great difficulties in getting a divorce because of what it would mean in his family ("Once you are married, in my family, you're married for life.") Then at this time, he has a short dream about Disraeli, the British prime minister and statesman of the mid- to late nineteenth century.

English Manor House and Disraeli Dream

> I'm visiting a beautiful woman who lives in an English manor house. She is very wealthy, and suddenly I find myself asking her to marry me. She agrees and I'm very happy, but then I wake up abruptly.

His association immediately turned to the biography of Disraeli who married a wealthy woman some years his senior. In the biography, the wife is quoted as saying that she knows her husband married her for her money, but now if they got married, he would marry because of "love." The patient thinks of the analyst as also standing for Disraeli and having married not for money but for "professional reasons," then later (like Disraeli) finding love in his marriage. Without pausing he thinks of his father who knows now that he didn't marry for "love"; he married "because my mother wanted him to, and that was just the way he was treated on the Spanish trip." All of this makes him feel very sad. Again he recalls how like a "little boy" his wife treated him and his father on the trip, and he muses that his father was never really in love with his mother, "He started out like Disraeli but he never found love."

Comment. Prefacing this dream with comments on his marriage as a "superego marriage" based on a deep sense of responsibility, he reports an "English Manor House" dream in which he characterized himself as a "failed Disraeli"; that is, he married out of a sense of responsibility, but has not been able to turn this into love. He noted also his partial identification with his father, who apparently did the same thing as he, and ended up in the same "Manor House." His father (like he) was never able to raise himself above his conflicts of "feeling like a little boy." He wished he could be like the analyst–father (ideal father) in his marriage.

For the next month-and-a-half, the patient was unable to recall any dreams, only noting that "something is happening deep inside. . . . I seem to be reviewing everything about my life even though I can't seem to remember anything." Now the material in his sessions shifted to his earlier analysis, and he wondered whether he really made the right choice by going into the same profession as his father. He saw himself as being very much like his father now—especially in the "obedient, passive way we relate to our wives"—and he became obsessed with why they were unable to speak (about his marriage) when they were in Spain. Rhetorically, he asked, "Was this a conspiracy of silence? My Dad is usually so active in giving his opinions. I had the feeling he wanted to talk to me but we both were inhibited."

Toward the end of the "dreamless period," as he called it, he and his wife were paid a weekend visit by his friend (a doctor) and the friend's girl friend (a teacher). He described this couple's visit as similar to a traumatic memory from the past; the woman was continually pressing her partner to get married, that she wanted him to set a date; while he was continually telling her that he wasn't ready and wanted to wait. The patient and his wife were drawn into the circumstances of how they got married. ("Kay told them [the couple] that she didn't pressure me at all—that I married her because I was ready. Of course this wasn't true and I got very upset and disputed this, Kay started to cry, and the couple started shouting at each other and they finally ended up leaving early. It was a mess!") However, the patient then said that he felt it had broken the "ice barrier," and he had finally told Kay how he felt in an indirect fashion.

Turning Back the Clock Dream

In the next sessions, after reviewing this episode of the couple's visit several times, he noted that he and his wife were not talking to each other. Despite this, they went to a teachers' party together the previous evening, but he became bored, and his wife stayed and he came home alone. That night he had the following dream.

Part I: I'm in this football/soccer stadium in a large crowd, but this stadium suddenly seems more like a swimming pool because both men and women are in the pool competing.

Part II: Then suddenly the scene changes and I'm in the pool and I met this lovely dark-haired petite attractive girl (she's about 18 or 19) and we are standing close together and start embracing and kissing as if nobody is around us. The stadium and all the people just fade away.

The dream first reminded him of a movie which he had seen on his Spanish holiday, in which the heroine had rejected the advances of a man of her own age, but then later recognizes that she loves the man only after she had gone to talk to the young man's father. (He recognized the parallel that he was doing the same thing by coming to see me.) The dream also reminded him of the romantic atmosphere of Spain where all the young people were going around arm in arm and kissing. While in Spain, he had the fantasy that he would like to go there on a honeymoon—if he had a chance to get married again! The "lovely dark-haired girl" reminded him of his brother's Latin-American wife whom the brother had married for love, and whom he (the patient) liked very much. Suddenly he started to tear, and was unable to talk at first, and then said that he was recalling his love for F (a French-Canadian girl whom he dated during his university days) and how they would go to the swimming meets together, following which they would become very romantic in the pool. Then he said, "Oh, oh, I'm turning back the clock again to this passionate girl," and added that his wish in the dream was to undo what had happenend and marry for love.

Following a short silence, he said that he now rarely had sex with Kay, and when he did, he found it very disturbing because he invariably saw his mother's face.

Comment. Following a dreamless period preceded by a frightening drama of seeing a couple enact the same premarital conflict leading to his marriage, he again had a two-part dream which he characterized in wishful fashion as "a turning back the clock dream." But again, despite the evoking of a romantic encounter with an erotic woman of the past, the specter of his mother's face intervened during coitus with his wife, perhaps a premonition of things to come. (In the session following the dream's analysis, he did tell his wife that he wanted a separation.)

In the next session, the patient said that he had made a "breakthrough after a fashion" in finally talking to his wife. He had come home late from work very tired (his wife was not yet there), and he decided to go straight to bed. Then when his wife came in (and he was still in bed) he began to tell her of his real feelings about the marriage. ("I spoke to her of everything we had discussed in our sessions except I didn't ask her outright for a divorce."); and he reported that Kay started to cry and said why didn't he tell her about this before, and he responded that he had been trying for the past year to do just this, but every time he tried, she (or his mother) would block it. Finally, his wife told him that she "still loves him" and would wait for his "decision" (i.e., about a separation or divorce). All of this made him feel so contrite and ashamed that he couldn't sleep the entire night. As a result, he began to have second thoughts about a separation–divorce. He recalled that his mother used to do the same thing with him and his brothers; that is, crying and then get them to delay making a decision. It always worked in her case. But he was determined that it wouldn't work this time. At the end of the session he informed me that for the next two weeks he would be on company business in Northern Europe, so he would not be making his sessions. As he was leaving and was halfway out the door, he said, "Oh, by the way, Kay has asked to go along on the trip, but I'm not sure I want to take her!"

Upon his return, the patient admitted right off that the trip was "contrived," and that he really didn't have to go at this time, but that Kay convinced him to go and take her with him, and he added in a sheepish way, "You know now that I'm not the strong person in resisting a woman's demands," and that this week and the next were going to be his final sessions! In summarizing these two weeks of sessions (8 sessions): First, he told me that he had decided to resign his position and go to Canada with his wife; that he knew that he was not strong enough psychologically to separate from her even though "I know for certain that I made the wrong decision to get married." He realized, he said, that during the two weeks away with Kay he would feel too guilty leaving her at this time, and also he could not leave her for "political" reasons (i.e., he could not go back home alone) the truth being that he needed her more than ever if he was to set up a private law practice. Second, he revealed that he got "uncontrollably upset and panicky" at the letter he received from M (the woman lawyer he was engaged to before he came to Europe) in which she told him that she had ended her affair of four years, and now realized that she "loves him no matter what" [and] "knows from his younger brother that he is now trying to get a divorce and be free." He stated that he should have married her—perhaps if he started his second analysis then he might have—but he noted "she is too passionate and erotic for me, and I can't handle that." Third, he discussed (in his last two sessions) a dream which he had just before he returned from Northern Europe. In telling this dream to his wife, she responded simply by saying, "This dream is a clincher that we'll be staying together."

Everything Is Locked Up Tightly Dream

"There is a trunk or large suitcase, and I'm having trouble packing everything I need into it and closing it. Then somebody brings me some heavy rope or tape, and I manage to get everything into it and lock and tie it up tightly." Immediately after he had this dream, he told himself, "I knew intuitively what it meant—I wanted to lock everything up tightly and didn't want to go into the unconscious anymore." Then he asserted that he wanted to lock up the relationship with his wife, at least until he settled down. He ended his second analysis by saying that he sounded like he was "copping out" but he couldn't face going back to North America alone, even though he may get a divorce from his wife "in a year or so." He noted, "frankly I need the certainty of this relationship."

Comment. This final dream (the residue of which was his "contrived trip" with his wife to Northern Europe, along with a letter from the erotic woman to whom he was formerly engaged telling him that she still loved him and was available) resulted in the message that "everything is now tightly locked-up" and he won't be leaving his wife. This dream depicts this as his "final solution" to his marital strife. That is, he cannot separate from his phallic mother–wife. Not only do they both need each other, but he needed this marriage as a protective mechanism from the threat of the erotic, sexual woman; and he also needed the marital attachment as emotional support to help him set up his law practice when he returned to Canada.

V

The dream series gives us a fascinating glimpse of the unconscious marital dynamics between this man's marriage—its self-arranged nature, his control by the compulsion to repeat, his deep unresolved attachment to the early mother, and his deep ambivalence about terminating his marriage. Each dream depicted a kind of way station in his attempts to break away from the early maternal object, and his failure to internalize a strong enough male identification with the oedipal father so that he could live his adult life free from oedipal struggle.

The patient began the dream series by telling his wife a dream—namely, that their marriage was in trouble and he was going to try to get out of it; and he ended his analytic treatment approximately one year later with another dream, in which he informed his wife that everything was now "locked up tightly" and he won't be trying to leave her (at least for now!). In between these two dreams, he depicted his unconscious struggle to break away from the marriage—essentially an oedipal triangle but with preoedipal features—which dramatically reenacts his unresolved oedipal struggle in terms of his dream life. In short, each of the eleven dreams in the dream series provided an aspect *in miniature* of how he was struggling (and failing)—in terms of his unconscious dream fantasies—to resolve his marital impasse. That he was unable to carry out his consciously stated wish to terminate his marriage attests to the extent to which a confluence of early fixations (linked with the compulsion to repeat), traumas, and conflicts was operating in his marital choice. The fact that his marriage endures, albeit temporarily, points to the continued mutual fulfillment of strong neurotic needs in their marital interaction and just how "pathologically binding this would be" (see Calogeras [1985], for further discussion).

The transference arena of this dream series was largely oedipal (in the complete sense) and father–son in the more restricted sense. Transferentially, the patient was trying to establish or reestablish contact with his father—which he had tried but failed to complete some twelve years before—and work through his oedipal identification with him so that he could resolve the attachment to his mother sufficiently and thereby be able to make the conflict-free choice of an erotic love object as a wife. Subsequently, he became caught in a premature wife–mother oedipal triangle vis-á-vis his marriage, which sent him into enough of a panic so that he reentered analytic treatment. While in treatment, he made repeated attempts to confront the phallic mother qualities of his wife, but in this endeavor he was unsuccessful. The culmination of this occurred during his Spanish trip; there his wife "defeated" his father, as his mother had similarly done to him (and father) some years before. He saw how his mother "wore the pants" in her marriage exactly as his wife was doing with him, reducing him to the role of the little boy. In the Disraeli dream, he tried once more to see if he could find love with this type of woman by wish fulfillingly emulating Disraeli and the analyst–father, but this lasted only a short while. In the transference, temporary identification with the analyst–father gave him enough strength to have the erotic turn back the clock dream, and subsequently to tell his wife that he wanted a separation. However, she would have none of this; she invited herself on his Northern European trip, taking him away from the analysis just when a critical working through phase was commencing, and weakening the growing transference regression which seemed to be tending toward the beginning of a transference neurosis. Once and for all, she succeeded in blocking him from further examining his marital choice.

The patient's last dream—the final solution dream of "locking everything up tightly"—was clearly an acting out of the transference by leaving treatment instead of acting in the transference and remaining in treatment and in Europe. One could say that the analyst–father had "failed him" in the transference realm—by not being strong enough to oppose his wife—just as his father had "failed" him on the Spanish trip. Nevertheless, he seemed able to use this so-called "defeat" in a self-serving, narcissistic fashion by turning the tables on his wife and using her in helping him set up his law practice on their return to Canada.

My counterfeeling and countertransference reactions when I became aware of them took the form of either wanting to rescue him in some fashion by intervening with his wife, or by pushing him prematurely to make a decision. The feeling invoked in me was like walking on a tightrope and trying not to lean too far in either direction but maintain a delicate balance. Despite this countertransferenced cautiousness in making interventions, I yet became aware of—and was able to interpret to him—how he was using me at times to get "favorable judgments" from his wife; and to convey to him that he was not as innocent as he purported to be when he was allegedly "afraid to talk to her."

VI

In conclusion, a number of question or issues regarding the depicting of his marital conflict in dreams emerge. First is the question of why this patient "chose" psychically to use the dream series in attempting to work through his marital conflicts. Ex hypothesi, he seemed to sense that only through the dream could he approach his miscarried marriage, and the compulsion to repeat the core of his unresolved oedipal struggle, and endeavor to come to terms with it. Had he learned from his previous analysis that the dream, in fact, did bear an "exceptional role in exploring the unconscious?" (see chapter

8). We know, of course, that the dream occurs in a unique psychological state which reveals the most basic unconscious wish life of the individual. The fact that this patient adhered to this exceptional role of the dream to convey the core dynamics throughout "his second period of analysis" (i.e., the current one) gives support to this hypothesis. Second is the issue concerned with representing of marital conflicts in the dream per se; that is, the actual nature of its content. The dream material afforded a rare opportunity to examine how husband and wife interaction and marital conflicts may be represented in considerable detail over a period of analytic treatment. For example, fairly unitary and compact symbols or representations of marriage were: "a playing field," "a swimming pool," "an alcove in a restaurant," "a tightly packed suitcase"; while more elaborated symbolizations were: "sleeping in a room where one's mother and wife were also present," "on a ski slope with wife but skiing without poles," "a player on a soccer team and taking instruction from a famous goalee," "a traditional type of house containing little or no furniture," and "jogging up a hill and being told to get a horse." All the symbolization suggested the varied and ingenious condensations of the dream work, yet they demonstrated the efficacy of understanding the various marriage representations if the relevant symbolization were forthcoming. Third is the role which the communicative function of the dream played (Kanzer, 1955). In a previous communication (1977), I have shown how the psychic mechanism of husband and wife exchange of dreams represented a unique way of unconscious communication between them, provided they are willing to accept the psychic consequences of such an exchange. In the present instance, the communicative function of the dream—in its relations to external objects—was used only in the preliminary dream (which the wife told her husband) and which he acknowledged immediately the unconscious message from her that their marriage was highly problematic and his countermessage to her that he wished to separate from her—a message which he did not convey to her directly until much later. Then at the end of the dream series, another message is communicated to his wife by his dream of "everything is locked up tightly." Between these two dreams the focus was on the intrapsychic nature of the dream with the insights derived from each succeeding dream analysis being played out with the wife. Just prior to the final dream (i.e., with the working out of the "swimming pool" dream), he finally told his wife of his wish for a separation. Her reaction was immediate and severe. She seemed to know that if her third marriage is to be saved, she must get her husband away from further understanding of the unconscious conflicts associated with their marriage. By accompanying him on a "contrived" business trip she, in effect, was able to evoke all the transference potential of the early mother image and block further analytic treatment—a defensive maneuver and transference acting out in which her husband colluded. And fourth was the question of whether this patient's second analysis was actually only a second phase of the third part yet to come. Speculatively, could the frequency of the three-part dreams (or the three dreams on consecutive nights) be a harbinger of the third phase of the analysis which will come about after he has established himself in his law practice? Will sexual impotency connected with always seeing his mother's face when he has coitus with his wife force him to resume analysis? Concomitantly, will he be able to examine his fear of the "erotic woman" which he always seems to juxtapose (and to associate with) his ambivalence toward the phallic–oedipal mother?

To summarize, in the present study I have endeavored to examine the nature of marital conflicts as they were depicted in a series of dreams in a thirty-five year old man occurring over a year's analytic treatment. Each of his dreams succeeded in highlighting a different facet of his marital conflicts and then adumbrated what was subsequently played out in his marriage. A number of questions/issues raised by the study were briefly discussed: (1) the patient's "choice" of the dream as a means of working through his marital conflicts; (2) the representing or symbolizing of marital interaction and conflict in dreams; (3) the role played by the communicative function of the dream in the marital conflicts; and (4) the question of whether this patient's second analysis was only the second phase of a third analysis (a third phase) which is yet to come.

Section V

Dreams and Manifest Content

This section opens with Pulver's "The Manifest Dream in Psychoanalysis: A Clarification" (1987)—an article which provides both a clarification of the manifest dream as well as surveying its clinical usefulness as an entity in itself. Pulver begins his clarification by analyzing the nature of the manifest dream under such topical questions as: (1) what really constitutes the manifest dream (i.e., what is its phenomenology); (2) what constitutes "associations" to the manifest dream (i.e., what are the ways and circumstances by which associations can be understood; and (3) what exactly do we mean by interpreting a dream (i.e., the difference between interpreting—saying something to the patient about the dream—and our understanding of the dream). Pulver ends his "clarification" by speaking to the vexing clinical problem of how one can more validly recognize and interpret to the patient certain traumatic childhood experiences which appear undisguised in the manifest dream.

Particularizing on a number of points made in the previous article is Stewart's "Comments on the Manifest Content of Certain Types of Dreams" (1964), where he extrapolates on the wish-fulfilling function of the dream holding that the original function of the dream was actually the mastery of traumatic stimuli. In reference to the unusual dream's manifest content, he considers the case where actual traumatic childhood experiences appear directly in the manifest content of the dream, elucidating how this phenomenon does not represent a failure of the dream work, but rather a use of unconscious instinctual wishes to defend against the recall of traumatic childhood experiences.

The final article in this section, Roth's "Manifest Dream Content and Acting Out" (1958), deals with a provocative thesis; to wit, if a dream is presented during an analytic session which cannot be analyzed because of resistance, it may confidently be expected that at the next session the patient will report how he has acted out quite literally—and not only in symbolic form but in other distorted forms—portions of the *manifest* content of the unanalyzed dream. In those instances where some insight is gained from partial interpretation, the unanalyzed part of the dream will be acted out in greater or less detail.

In addition to the above papers, we highly recommend to our readers an article by Spanjaard (impossible to include because of its length), "The Manifest Dream Content and Its Significance for the Interpretation of Dreams" (1969), a scholarly work which demonstrates that conflictual elements are contained in the manifest dream content and that these elements can be used interpretively. He shows that if one is to approach the manifest content meaningfully, one must take the position of the dreamer in the dream narrative as one's starting point. Further, he holds that the conflict elements of the dream's manifest content can be localized in the most superficial wish and defense, the latter being comparable with the mechanism of negation.

Chapter 24

THE MANIFEST DREAM IN PSYCHOANALYSIS: A CLARIFICATION

"Unofficially, we often interpret dreams entirely or in parts on the basis of their manifest appearance. Officially, we hurry at every confrontation with a dream to crack its manifest appearance as if it were a useless shell and . . . discard this shell in favor of what seems to be the more worthwhile core" (Erikson, 1954, p. 17).

In recent years, particularly since Erikson's classic paper on the Irma dream, analysts have come to realize that the manifest dream is intimately and understandably related to the latent dream and to the dreamer. A body of information relevant to the manifest dream is scattered throughout the psychoanalytic literature, in panels (Babcock, 1966), papers (Spanjaard, 1969; Sloane, 1975), brief monographs (Bernstein and Fine, 1969), and books (Jones, 1962). In spite of the apparent agreement in this literature that the manifest dream is of clinical value in psychoanalysis, a controversy smoulders. My aim here is to define the issues and to clarify the semantic confusion that has contributed to this controversy. In the course of doing this, I shall arrive at two propositions about the manifest dream, neither of which should prove to be very controversial. It will then become apparent that the manifest dream *does* have a place in psychoanalysis, and I shall illustrate this with a brief discussion of two of its many uses.

This paper was first published in the *Journal of the American Psychoanalytic Association* (1987), 35:99–118.

Is There a Controversy?

Controversy is a strong word, but I use it intentionally, since I believe that many analysts have strong feelings about the place of the manifest dream in psychoanalytic therapy. Some of us feel that it is of great value, while others feel it is quite worthless. Perhaps most of us, as Erikson (1954) so neatly points out, are ambivalent. We decry the interpretation of the manifest dream while belying that position in our clinical behavior. In doing so, we are following the example of Freud who, while frequently emphasizing the senselessness of manifest dreams ("These *latent dream-thoughts* contained the meaning of the dream, while its manifest content was simply a make-believe, a façade, which could serve as a starting-point for the associations but not for the interpretation" [Freud, 1925a, p. 44]), just as frequently referred to their understandability ("These initial dreams [in treatment] may be described as unsophisticated: they betray a great deal to the listener, like the dreams of so-called healthy people" [Freud, 1911b, p. 95]). *The Interpretation of Dreams* (1900) is replete with examples of methods of understanding dreams based in part or wholly on the manifest content.

To be sure, Freud had reason to stress the apparent unintelligibility of the manifest dream. In the course of advancing an entirely new approach to the understanding of dreams, he was fighting the centuries-old dream book approach to their interpretation. Our current caveats against interpreting the manifest dream derive at least partly from this concern. In keeping with this, these warnings are often directed to the neophyte, as indicated by their almost exclusive occurrence in our teaching and our texts (see, for example, Altman [1969, pp. 11–12, 44, 145]), rather than in our general literature.

Our antipathy to wild interpretation of the dream book variety, then, is one reason for the depreciation of manifest dreams. A more important reason, however, is our lack of precision in spelling out our meaning when we describe the problems of interpreting manifest dreams without associations. To clarify this, I shall explore three questions: (1) What is the manifest dream? (2) What do we mean by "interpretation"? (3) What are associations?

What Is the Manifest Dream?

When we speak of the manifest dream, we are referring to the verbal report of the dream as given by the dreamer. We tend to think and to talk about *the* manifest dream, as though we are referring to an unvarying entity. The fact is, of course, that there is no single manifest dream. In actuality, the sleeper experiences a perceptual phenomenon, usually visual, which we shall call the dream experience. This dream experience is never available again, not even to the dreamer, whose memory of it is immediately and continuously subject to secondary revision, repression, and a variety of other defensive processes. What we call the manifest dream is actually the dreamer's report at any particular moment, a report that varies according to the psychic factors operating when the report is given. (More accurately, the report will vary according to the distortions introduced between the dream experience and the time of the report. These factors influence the dreamer's *recollection* of the dream experience, and this recollection is then further distorted by factors operating upon the actual report: cognitive style, wishes, and defenses operating at the time of recall, etc.) Although such reports are all based on some aspect of the dream experience, and thus all have something in common, they may differ markedly. This difference has been well documented (Lipschutz, 1954; Whitman, Kramer, and Baldridge, 1963a; Mahoney, 1977) and is only to be expected in view of the variation in the many factors influencing the report. Take, for example, the many situations in which dreams may be recounted: (1) immediately upon wakening from the dream experience—(a) verbally: usually under experimental conditions in dream laboratories, (b) written: usually by patients, by analysts engaged in self-analysis, or by others interested in exploring their own dreams; (2) upon awakening in the morning (verbal or written); (3) at various times after awakening, outside of the therapeutic situation, and usually during the day following the dream experience; (4) in therapy, usually verbally, within a day or two of the dream experience; (5) in therapy, usually verbally, long after the dream experience (childhood dreams, recurrent dreams, "old" dreams recalled in response to various stimuli in the therapeutic situation; (6) finally, as second-hand reports of dreams told to others, usually therapists or experimenters recounting the dream for purposes of clinical exposition or research. This type of "second-hand" manifest dream is often a far cry from the actual report of the dreamer.

In brief, there is no such thing as *the* manifest dream. When we engage in debates about the manifest dream, we are often vague about which manifest dream we are referring to. This vagueness adds fuel to the controversy, since the degree to which the manifest dream can be understood always depends on our knowledge of the context in which it was reported. As analysts, when we speak of the manifest content of specific dreams, we are usually referring to the patient's report of the dream in analysis, and that is the sense in which I shall use the term here.

What Are Associations?

Traditionally, associations are the thoughts that occur to the patient when we ask him to associate to specific dream elements:

> Our first step in the employment of this procedure teaches us that what we must take as the object of our attention is not the dream as a whole but the separate portions of its content. If I say to a patient who is still a novice: "What occurs to you in connection with this dream?", as a rule his mental horizon becomes a blank. If, however, I put the dream before him cut up into pieces, he will give me a series of associations to each piece, which might be described as the "background thoughts" of that particular part of the dream [1900, pp. 103–104].

In clinical practice, however, we find that dreams are rarely reported as pure descriptions of the dream experience, and they are never reported in a vacuum. Many dream reports are interlaced with associations in the traditional sense; for example, "In the dream there were two different dogs, but one was Cedric and one had practically another name. *I think they were both Cedric. One seemed like Cedric as he is now and one like when I was a kid. . . ."* Many contain comments and affective expressions that, although less clearly responses to specific elements, are clearly associations to the dream; for example, "I had *this strange dream this morning.* It was actually kind of pleasant. *It wasn't a nightmare, it was just odd.* I was in a Chinese subway. [laughs] *Don't ask me what that means. . . ."* Furthermore, something, if only the manner in which the patient enters our office and lies down on the couch, immediately precedes the dream report. Something, if only silence, immediately follows it. We know that both, because of their contiguity to the dream, must be regarded as associations to it.

Brenner (1976) has illustrated how these associations often enable the analyst to understand the dream without requesting formal associations to the dream elements. He has suggested that the entire verbal report be regarded as an association to the dream experience, which he equates with the manifest dream. Other analysts regard the entire content of the session as associations to the dream therein. Both of these views, I think, stretch the concept of "associations" too far. The point I wish to emphasize is that in the clinical situation no analyst encounters a manifest dream devoid of associations. When, in discussing the value of the manifest dream, we speak as though it occurs in a void, we mislead ourselves.

What Do We Mean by Interpretation

A final semantic confusion can be cleared up quickly. Questions about the manifest content are often phrased in terms of its value in interpreting the dream. However, "interpreting a dream" has two quite different meanings. In one sense it may refer to something that we say to the patient. In another sense, it may refer to our own deciphering of the dream. To avoid confusion, I shall use "interpretation" to refer to our interaction with the patient, and "understanding" to refer to our own comprehension. Obviously, we may understand something about a dream without interpreting it.

Resolving the Controversy

With these considerations in mind, we are now in a position to look more clearly at the controversy about the manifest dream. To do so, we shall need to avoid the general questions which are usually asked (Is the manifest dream useful? What is its place in clinical psychoanalysis?) and deal with more specific issues. Let us consider first whether the manifest content alone should ever be interpreted to the patient. This might seem to be a perfectly legitimate question to ask, but two considerations indicate that it is irrelevant. First, as demonstrated above, we never encounter "manifest content alone" in the clinical practice of psychoanalysis. Second, contrary to public impression, in carrying out an analysis we do not interpret *any* dreams, manifest or otherwise. Freud's (1911b) technical recommendation still holds:

> I submit, therefore, that dream-interpretation should not be pursued in analytic treatment as an art for its own sake, but that its handling should be subject to those technical rules that govern the conduct of the treatment as a whole. Occasionally, of course, one can act otherwise and allow a little free play to one's theoretical interest; but one should always be aware of what one is doing [p. 94].

This does not mean that the content of an interpretation will never be the explanation of a dream. It *does* mean that such an interpretation will be made only when it serves the purpose of the analytic process as a whole. It does not make good sense, then, to wonder about whether the manifest dream should be interpreted. Our questions must deal with the use of the manifest dream in formulating interpretations and in understanding the patient. Two questions of this nature suggest themselves.

The first is easily answered: Is the patient's report of a dream useful in formulating an interpretation if no formal associations to the dream elements are given? Remembering that the patient always gives some associations to the dream, and that the analyst always knows a good deal about the patient and frequently about the probable day residue, this question can be answered, "Yes, sometimes." "Yes," because understanding a dream may be useful in formulating an interpretation, and our ability to understand at least some of the meaning of a dream upon hearing the verbal report is a matter of common clinical experience. The specificity of such understanding ranges from a general appreciation of some of the dynamics involved to a detailed recognition of the particular unconscious conflict preoccupying the patient. Beres and Arlow (1974) illustrate just how specific this may be in a vignette in which a patient's manifest dream, reported at the beginning of a session, stimulated an immediate fantasy in the analyst, a fantasy which proved to be the latent content of the patient's dream. An even more dramatic example is given in a series of papers by Schur (1966a); Schorske (1974); and Greenberg and Pearlman (1978) demonstrating that a current conflict involving Freud's feelings about the result of Fliess's operation upon Emma was represented, thinly disguised, in striking detail in the manifest content of the Irma dream. Freud did not recognize the connection, but one feels convinced that his analyst would have immediately upon hearing the manifest content.

The qualifier "sometimes" is necessary for two reasons: first, because even if a dream is understood, the appropriate interpretation may be unrelated to its meaning, as, for example, when the patient's motivation for reporting the dream takes interpretive priority; second, because there certainly are manifest dreams that we simply cannot make any sense of, just as there are dreams with formal associations which puzzle us. Nevertheless, *some* manifest dreams contribute to our understanding of the patient, and we are thus led to a second (and much more complex) question: In what ways does this take place? The approaches to the use of the manifest dream in understanding the dream and the dreamer are so numerous and varied that I will do no more here than illustrate two of them. The Appendix outlines a more comprehensive coverage of the topic.

Decoding Manifest Dream Elements: An Illustration

In the translation of manifest dream elements into the latent
thoughts which they disguise, the dream work must be thoroughly understood. The basic mechanisms of the dream
work—condensation, displacement, the need for perceptual
(usually visual) representation, and secondary revision—often
follow principles, which, because they are consistent, may lead
to transformations which are recognizable from the manifest
dream without the aid of associations. Freud gives many examples of these transformations in his various works on dreams,
as, for example, in Chapter 6 of *The Interpretation of Dreams*,
which is full of practical aids to this kind of translation. Understanding these transformations never reveals the entire meaning of the dream (that is, all of the latent dream thoughts and
the unconscious wishes with which they are associated), but it
may be exceedingly useful clinically.

In discussing visual representations based on linguistic
transformations, Freud (1900) wrote, "It would be a work in
itself to collect these modes of representation and to classify
them according to their underlying principles" (p. 408). It
would be a most useful work, a great help in directly decoding
manifest dream elements. Unfortunately, it would also be a
monumental work, certainly beyond the capacity of this paper.
What follows is an illustration of how it might be done, derived
from Freud and focusing on the mechanism of condensation.
Let us take the following latent dream thoughts: "Johnnie, my
first boyfriend, showed me he loved me by sending me a valentine; I wish my analyst would do the same." This is an instance
of a "just-as" relationship, a type often found in latent dream
thoughts. It can be rephrased as, "I wish my analyst would show
me he loves me *just as* my first boyfriend, Johnnie, did, by
sending me a valentine." The parallel relationship "analyst-
Johnnie" is particularly well suited for representation in the
manifest dream by condensation. The condensation follows
consistent principles, and its products are manifested in several
typical forms:

1. Only one person appears in the manifest dream, but he
appears in a situation characteristic of the second person: "I

was in my high-school home room and Johnnie was there. He was sitting behind me, but in high school he sat across the room."

2. One person appears and is identified, and his representation contains an element or elements common to the second: "I was talking to Johnnie. It was definitely Johnnie, even though he had grown a beard."

3. A single unidentified person appears with characteristics of both: "I was talking to a boy about fourteen years old. He was showing me his horn-rimmed glasses and his digital wristwatch." Here the common characteristics are visual features. They might equally well be gestures, words, character traits, or anything identified with the people in the dream thoughts.

4. Only one person appears, "while the other (and usually the more important one) appears as an attendant figure without any other function" (Freud, 1900, p. 321); for example, "Johnnie was giving me a valentine. You were also there, but you weren't doing anything."[1]

This classification includes only products of condensation that are readily translatable from the manifest dream. Since condensation may occur at various stages of the dream work, it may also be represented in the manifest dream through elements decipherable only through associations: "I had an appointment with someone at 7:45 in the morning." Association: "7:45 is when our first home room period started. I used to meet Johnnie there and we'd go into class together." (Although the patient did not mention it, 7:45 was also the time of one of her analytic sessions.) Or, of course, it may occur only in the dream work and not be represented in the manifest dream at all.

All these mechanisms are described in a *single paragraph* of *The Interpretation of Dreams* (p. 320). They represent only a few of the ways in which transformations of the latent dream thoughts are condensed and represented in the manifest dream. While none of them is translatable with certainty in the absence of other data, their value in helping the analyst form conjectures about the meaning of the dream is obvious.

---

[1] ". . . but you weren't doing anything." More than condensation, and easy to translate! It is also a visual representation of a feeling about the analyst.

Although the above is well known, much in the area of translating manifest dream elements remains to be discovered. Take, for example, the meaning of dream symbols. In view of the concerns of psychoanalysis at the time, it is not surprising that Freud concluded that the majority of dream symbols pertain to sexuality, the human body as a whole, children, siblings, birth, death, and nakedness. However, Freud did not claim that symbols must be limited to these topics, and, although modern semiology is divided about this, we do seem to be continually finding new symbols and new things which they symbolize. Reflect upon mirror dreams. Although their narcissistic implications have been recognized for some time (Eisnitz, 1961), their recent examination in the light of our increasing understanding of self-esteem regulation and its disorders has already led to a better understanding of the mirror as a dream symbol (Meyers, 1976; Carlson, 1977). Much the same is happening with other directly translatable aspects of the manifest dream. The list of typical dreams—seventeen by one tabulation (Ward, Beck, and Rascoe, 1961)—is still being added to, as, for example, by several dreams typical of the narcissistic transference (Kohut, 1971).

These are but a few examples of work on the manifest dream. Since more undoubtedly lies ahead, let me conclude this section with a word of admonition. "Translating" manifest dream elements is a seductive operation, and it is easy to jump to conclusions. We should be careful, therefore, to base our contributions to the meaning of manifest dream elements on the firmest evidence. As an example of the kind of mistake which can all too easily be made, let me review some ideas about the meaning of the spoken word in dreams. Freud discussed this many times. As to their source, he never deviated from his original proposition: "When anything in a dream has the character of direct speech, that is to say, when it is said or heard and not merely thought (and it is easy as a rule to make the distinction with certainty), then it is derived from something actually spoken in waking life[2]—though, to be sure, this something is merely treated as raw material and may be cut up and

---

[2]With one exception, that they may represent the exact content of obsessive thoughts (p. 304n).

slightly altered and, more especially, divorced from its context" (Freud, 1900, pp. 183–184). As to the import of spoken words, examples make it clear that this is as infinitely varied as are the latent dream thoughts. Some seem to have superego meanings, but many do not. Nevertheless, in what is regarded as a very significant paper, Isakower (1954) states that *"speech elements in dreams are a direct contribution from the superego to the manifest content of the dream"* (p. 3). Although this is quite incompatible with many of Freud's examples, Isakower regarded it as apodictic. His certainty seems to have been contagious, and I suspect that most analysts today regard spoken words in dreams as superego indicators—this, in spite of the convincing demonstrations by Fliess (1953b) at the time and by Baudry (1974) and Fisher (1976) twenty years later that Isakower was mistaken. This kind of mistake, fueled by our urge to understand, is particularly easy to make when dealing with direct translations of manifest dream elements.

Early Childhood Trauma and the Manifest Dream

As another illustration of the clinical value of the manifest dream, I shall discuss recovery of memories of childhood experiences. It is well known—indeed, it is elementary dream theory—that unconscious childhood wishes are part of the constellation of wishes which motivate most dreams. It is just as well known, but I suspect not as well attended to, that the memory of unconscious childhood experiences, both traumatic and nontraumatic, participate frequently in the latent dream thoughts. When they appear in the manifest dream, they are "invaluable in themselves but seriously distorted as a rule by all the factors concerned in the formation of dreams" (Freud, 1937a, p. 258). My purpose here is to point up that they may also appear in the manifest dream with very little distortion. Their appearance in manifest dreams, though well established, tends to be neglected in clinical practice.

Because of their therapeutic importance, I shall focus on traumatic childhood experiences. First, however, a word about

memories of childhood experiences which, at least on the surface, were nontraumatic. These may appear in either the manifest or latent content in two ways. At times they are used by the
dream work in a manner analogous to indifferent day residues:
as a means of visually representing a conflict to which they are
attached by an associational link. In such cases the remembered
events themselves are relatively unimportant. More frequently,
they are connected with or expressive of childhood conflicts,
and are of importance either in helping us formulate specific
reconstructions or, in a more general way, in helping us demonstrate to the patient the origin of conflicts with which he is
currently dealing. In contrast, traumatic childhood experiences
are, by definition, never "indifferent." In addition to the impact
of the trauma itself, they always serve as organizers for constellations of wishes and fantasies related to important emotional
conflicts, and their recovery is of particular therapeutic value.
We must very often be content with merely reconstructing
them, but there is no question that when we can, we would
prefer to recover them as actual memories. Even when only
reconstruction is possible, the more detailed the reconstruction,
the more valuable. Dreams give us unique access to the material
necessary for such detailed reconstruction, and the undisguised
appearance of memories of childhood traumatic experiences is
thus worthy of particular note.

Since traumatic experiences of adults regularly appear in
their manifest dreams (for example, in the traumatic neuroses),
it should be no surprise that childhood traumatic experiences
should do so also. What *is* surprising is the relative rarity (judg-
ing from the literature) with which they are detected and utilized. Freud (1900) reports several examples of the undisguised
appearance of childhood memories in the manifest dream, but
none of these were overtly traumatic. Nunberg (1948) reports
an example which I present in detail because it illustrates the
clarity with which such memories may be recalled:

> On the day following a discussion of the analyst's forthcom-
> ing vacation, a young woman patient [whose father had
> left the family when she was three years old] reported this
> dream: "I was frantically running along a road, looking for

someone. When I came to the crossroad I didn't know which way to turn." The dream was extremely unpleasant. There was a frantic, hopeless feeling in it. The houses were strange, and she was unable to recognize the scene. This dream was a recurrent one, although she was unable to recall when it had first appeared. . . . The following day the patient told her mother of her dream. The mother recognized the houses, the road and the crossroads in the dream, as the patient described them to her. This was the road which led out of the small town in which they had lived in Europe. Following the father's departure for the United States, the mother said that the child had been inconsolable and on a number of occasions had run searching for her father on this road [p. 24].

Stewart (cited in Bernstein and Fine, 1969, pp. 81–91) describes several patients in whom thinly disguised memories of early traumatic experiences appeared in the manifest content of dreams during analysis. In one patient, these dreams were unusual in style, contained overt incestuous material, were experienced as peculiarly real, strange, weird, and eerie, and were accompanied by considerable anxiety. Stewart implies that these features are characteristic of such dreams, but this conclusion seems to be based on only one case.

In the few instances I have found in the literature (I have not made an extensive search) in which *early* traumatic experiences appeared undisguised in manifest dreams, their recovery leads to a sense of conviction about the incident rather than to an actual memory. Recovery of childhood traumatic experiences in associations may or may not lead to the recovery of an actual memory. The factors that determine whether the event is actually remembered are not clear, although the age at which the experience occurred certainly plays a role. Dowling (1982), on the basis of a case in which the trauma occurred at the age of two, feels that the stage of cognitive development is the determining factor, and that dreams from the period of prerepresentational thought (before 15–24 months) are nonimagic and primarily affective in nature. However, Hadfield (1954, p. 118) reports the reproduction in a nightmare of a traumatic experience occurring at the age of one-and-a-half years, and that dream plus the case which I am about to describe would seem to contradict Dowling's thesis.

The relative dearth of such dreams may merely reflect the infrequency with which they occur. As dreams go, they *are* infrequent, but, if my own experience is at all representative, I suspect that we are also overlooking them. I first came across such a dream about ten years ago, when one was forcibly called to my attention. Since then I have been on the alert, and undoubtedly as a result, have detected this kind of dream in several other patients.

The dream of the patient who forced me to look at this is worth reporting, since it illustrates some of the qualities of such dreams which may alert us to them. In actuality, the traumatic experience was revived in a dream and a hypnopompic state immediately following. It was reported by a young woman during a brief period of twice-weekly psychotherapy which took place a year prior to the beginning of her analysis. During the previous day she had been reading an article on the history of surgery before the discovery of anesthesia, and was captivated by a long passage describing the subjective experience of several patients who had undergone such an ordeal. That night she dreamed that she was lying on a bed in a sparsely furnished room. Two women who were with her began to leave, through what was either a door or an opening in the wall. Although she could recall no affect, she half-awoke, and, in the hypnopompic state which immediately followed, felt her head turned sharply to the left by an external, viselike grip. She then heard loud music and simultaneously experienced a loud buzzing noise which seemed to fill her head. The noise lasted only a short time, and she then awoke completely. During the entire hypnopompic experience she felt overwhelming anxiety and helplessness.

Although the dream seemed related to the article she had read on the previous day, neither she nor I was able to make anything more of the dream at the time, nor on the several occasions when she recalled it during her subsequent analysis. On other occasions during her analysis (in contexts apparently unrelated to the dream) she related that she had undergone radiation treatments to her throat for thymus enlargement as an infant, probably, she thought, before the age of four months. She had known about this for many years, but had never attached any significance to it. Stimulated by the analysis, she wondered whether these could have had lasting psychological effects. Despite my noncommittal responses (I remember feeling they had probably occurred too early to be of significance) and despite her mother's inability to remember any details at all about the procedures, she persevered, and finally obtained a detailed description of them from the physician who had performed them. She had had six irradiations, all performed in the physician's home office, between the ages of six and fourteen months. During the procedure she was immobilized, wrapped in a sheet. Her father held her head turned firmly to the left, while her mother, unable to stand her distress, waited in an adjoining room and played phonograph music loudly to drown out her cries. All the details of the manifest dream (the women leaving, her indistinct perception of the door, the positioning of her head by an external force, the buzzing noise of the X-ray machine, and the music) were confirmed by this description. It seems reasonable to infer that as an infant she experienced the same feelings of panic and helplessness she felt in the hypnopompic state immediately following the dream.

The recovery of this traumatic experience, while not pivotal, was of therapeutic value. As an example of this, let us look at the vicissitudes of one of her symptoms. For as long as she could remember, the patient felt moderate anxiety accompanied by fantasies of pain and mutilation preceding visits to physicians. Like all symptoms, this one had multiple determinants. Early in the analysis, the anxiety changed in character. Although beginning with its usual moderate intensity and accompanying fantasies, on several occasions it increased to an overwhelming degree, and she felt immobile, helpless, and panicky. When this happened her fantasies of mutilation disappeared, and she had no thoughts of any kind except a frightening awareness that she had no idea of what she was anxious about. Since the recovery of the traumatic experience, this new type of anxiety has stopped, and her usual anxiety before visiting physicians has been much less intense.

Such dreams raise a number of theoretical questions, one of which (the wish-fulfillment versus mastery function of the dream) Stewart has discussed in detail. The most pressing *clinical* question is: "How can the analyst recognize such a dream?" Awareness that such dreams may occur is certainly essential, and the analyst should be particularly alert for them when he knows of a specific traumatic event that has been part of the patient's childhood. As to characteristics of the dreams themselves, we can be reasonably certain only that, like the dreams in traumatic neuroses, they are always accompanied by severe dysphoria, usually anxiety. Other identifying features, frequently but not always present, are: (1) the patient's experience of himself as a child; (2) the patient's role as the actor (as contrasted to the observer) in the dream action; (3) dysphoria of such intensity that the patient awakens; (4) the recurrent nature of the dreams, which begin in childhood. In addition, the features Stewart describes are worth keeping in mind, particularly the unusual nature of the dreams and the relative scarcity of associations to them.

Chapter 25

COMMENTS ON THE MANIFEST CONTENT OF CERTAIN TYPES OF UNUSUAL DREAMS

WALTER A. STEWART

Certain types of dreams do not fit into our usual formulation of the dynamics of dreams. Two of these types are considered here: first, those where the manifest content contains overt references to incestuous, sadistic, or immoral wishes; and second, those where a traumatic childhood scene is portrayed in the manifest content.

Accepted psychology of dream function and formation states that the dream serves as the guardian of sleep via hallucinatory wish-fulfillment of infantile strivings. Since too direct representation of the forbidden wishes would create anxiety and end in wakening, they must be censored and distorted by the dream work. The stimulus to the dream, the day residue, is usually some current experience, often of an innocuous nature. Since this experience has not been worked over in consciousness and is susceptible to cathexis by unconscious wishes, it is particularly useful as the vehicle for these wishes.

As a corollary to this formulation, the manifest content was related to preconscious thoughts and to current events. The day residue was portrayed as the "entrepreneur" of the dream and the manifest content described as a "façade." In contrast, the latent content derived from unconscious sources and infantile experiences and wishes, and was the "capitalist" in dream formation. The unconscious sources utilized the day residue in an effort to reach consciousness; the dream work defended

This paper was first published in the *Psychoanalytic Quarterly* (1967), 36:329–341.

against this via primary process distortions and allowed only derivatives to emerge in the manifest content. The interpretation of the dream required associations which "undid" the dream work and permitted the latent dream wish to emerge. These aspects of dream dynamics can be summarized as follows: (1) *One purpose of the dream* is hallucinatory gratification of forbidden infantile wishes. (2) *The manifest content* is related to: (a) the preconscious; (b) current events (day residue, which functions as the "entrepreneur"). (3) *The latent content* is related to: (a) the unconscious; (b) childhood experience and fantasies (which function as the "capitalist"). (4) *The dream work* functions to disguise the forbidden wish and therefore permits the hallucinatory fulfillment without disturbing the sleeper.

Freud repeatedly stressed these relationships. For example, "every dream was linked in its manifest content with recent experiences and in its latent content with the most ancient experiences" (1900, p. 218). On another occasion Freud comments, "On this view [the role of visual memories from childhood] a dream might be described as a *substitute for an infantile scene modified by being transferred onto a recent experience.* The infantile scene is unable to bring about its own revival, and has to be content with returning in a dream" (p. 546). He writes at another point of his discovery from his own dreams as well as those of his patients that "in the latent content of a dream I come unexpectedly upon a scene from childhood, and that all at once a whole series of my dreams link up with the associations branching out from some experience of my childhood" (p. 203). Two references in which Freud discusses the relationship of the day residue to unconscious infantile impulses (1901a, p. 556; 1913a, p. 274) are also relevant here.

The earliest question raised concerning these dream dynamics was in relation to the wish-fulfilling purpose of the dream. "We have accepted the idea that the reason why dreams are invariably wish-fulfillments is that they are products of the system *Ucs*, whose activity knows no other aim than the fulfillment of wishes and which has at its command no other forces than wishful impulses" (Freud, 1900, p. 568).

Certain dreams seemed to be exceptions to this wish-fulfilling function. They included punishment dreams, which were only apparent exceptions since they assuaged the sense of guilt and served the wish for punishment. The general class of anxiety dreams was easily explained as a failure in the dream work. The opposite to this situation occurred in so-called "dreams from above," where the dream work was totally successful. These were dreams in which no representative of infantile unconscious wishes could be seen in the manifest dream, even via derivatives or in distorted form, nor did it emerge in the associations. The dream work was conceived as having performed its work so well that the essential infantile strivings simply could not be uncovered (Freud, 1923a).

This was the situation until 1920 when Freud, because of his further experience with traumatic dreams and in order to explain the frequent allusions in dreams to painful childhood events, modified his earlier formulation. He wrote, "This would seem to be the place, then, at which to admit for the first time an exception to the proposition that dreams are fulfillments of wishes." Freud continues:

> Thus it would seem that the function of dreams, which consists in setting aside any motives that might interrupt sleep, by fulfilling the wishes of the disturbing impulses, is not their *original* function. It would not be possible for them to perform that function until the whole of mental life had accepted the dominance of the pleasure principle. If there is a "beyond the pleasure principle" it is only consistent to grant there was also a time before the purpose of dreams was the fulfillment of wishes [Freud, 1920, pp. 32–33].

He then describes the function of those dreams, which are genuine exceptions to the rule that dreams are directed toward "wish fulfillment," as serving the effort toward mastery of the stimulus. These "genuine exceptions" to the rule have received surprisingly little attention in the literature, possibly because of their rarity in analysis and the fact the truly traumatic dream is less directly useful in the therapeutic effort.

Later Freud again tried to answer "two serious difficulties . . . against the wish-fulfillment theory of dreams

... people who have experienced a shock ... are regularly taken back in their dreams into a traumatic situation. ... What wishful impulse could be satisfied by harking back ... to ... distressing traumatic experience?" He answers this paradox in two parts. First, he explains the memories of sexual trauma from childhood which are referred to in dreams as occurring because the dream work succeeds most of the time in "denying the unpleasure by means of distortion and to transforming disappointment into attainment." Second, dealing with traumatic neuroses, Freud explains, "In their case the dreams regularly end in the generation of anxiety. We should not, I think, be afraid to admit that here the function of the dream has failed" (1933b, pp. 28–29). In the first explanation, where the traumatic events are from childhood and are represented in the latent dream thoughts, the explanation refers to the success of the dream work. In contrast, the explanation of current traumatic events occurring in the manifest dreams depends on the failure of the dream work.

Although there has been a revival of interest in the manifest content of dreams (Alexander and Wilson, 1935; Saul, 1940; Harris, 1948, chapter 18; Blitzsten, Eissler, and Eissler, 1950; Fliess, 1953b; Jones, 1953–1957; Erikson, 1954; Rangell, 1956; Saul and Sheppard, 1956; Grinstein, 1956; Babcock, 1966) there are few well-analyzed examples in the literature of dreams in which the manifest content refers to current traumatic experiences. Bonaparte, in a fascinating case, described the evolution of a repetitive "examination dream" from a traumatic experience (chapter 1). Loewenstein was able to show the complex relationship of the traumatic experience to the manifest and latent content in a well-analyzed dream (1949). Greenacre commented that the "frequent appearance of dreams which exactly reproduce reality events, but seem at first barren of associations ... are indications of the reality of some experience ... being worked with in the unconscious" (1956, pp. 442–443).

A further complication to the psychology of dreams is posed by the class of dreams where the manifest dream directly represents infantile sexual strivings and is therefore "openly

	Experiences From Childhood	Experiences From Adult Life
Events appearing in manifest content of dream	Incestuous, sadistic, or immoral content: results from failure of dream work; may occur with or without anxiety (Freud, 1925b).	Traumatic dreams having the goal of mastery (Freud, 1933b, pp. 28–29).
Events referred to in latent content	(a) *Allusions* to traumatic experiences from childhood—result from the compulsion to repeat and serve the goal of mastery (Freud, 1933b). (b) No apparent reference to infantile wishes; that is, "dreams from above," explained as result of success of dream work (Freud, 1923a).	"Usual dreams" with innocuous day residue plus infantile wishes (Freud, 1900).

incestuous, sadistic, or immoral." Freud (1925b), when considering this class of dreams, wrote with his usual candor and honesty, "The answer is not easy to come by and may perhaps not seem completely satisfying." He again explains these dreams, which end in anxiety and awakening. In terms of the failure of the dream work, thus fitting the understanding of them into the general explanation of anxiety dreams. Of other, similar dreams which occur without anxiety, he suggests that the ego simply "tolerates" them.

These explanations are questionable in terms of scientific methodology, since by employing the concept of the total success or failure of the dream work no further understanding was required; all possible outcomes could be easily explained or possibly even "explained away."

Some of the varied relationships of manifest content to latent content are summarized in the above chart.

Another class of dreams, apparently rare, is not included in the chart. These are dreams in which the manifest content of the dream portrays large parts or the whole of forgotten and often traumatic events from early childhood. Freud cites a number of dream examples which show the hyperamnesic aspect of dreams, in which a forgotten childhood experience reappears in the manifest content of the dream without modification by the dream work. One example is the dream of a young man who dreamed of seeing his former tutor in bed with his nurse. The young man had no memory of this being an actual event which he had witnessed, but found, on asking his older brother, that the incident had actually occurred as he described it and that he had observed it as a three-year-old (Fliess, 1953b, p. 189). Freud describes this type of dream as "quite unusual" but does not comment further on it.

Another example is reported by Nunberg (1955). He describes the dream of a young woman who dreams she is a child "frantically running along a road looking for someone." The dream, occurring during a threatened separation from the analyst, reproduced the exact setting, recognized by the mother, of the road on which the father left town to come to America when the patient was a child of three. Nunberg describes the dream as a traumatic dream and the function of the dream as an effort toward mastery by reliving the experience over and over. He writes, "The dream represents then the only memory of a forgotten experience, which cannot be remembered in any other way."

These dreams pose a final challenge to the accuracy of relating manifest dream to current events and describing their function as that of the entrepreneur, and of relating the latent content to unconscious infantile sexual strivings and childhood experiences which function as the "capitalist."

An extremely interesting series of dreams illustrating the problem has been described by M. R. Horowitz (personal communication). These were dreams of an adult patient in which the manifest content contained overtly incestuous material and repetitive references to a forgotten childhood experience. At the beginning of treatment the patient reported a dream which had occurred earlier and was one of the causes for seeking treatment. The dream was of her having sexual relations with her father. She awoke in terror and then tried to return to sleep in order to continue the dream. However, she could not sleep because of a frightening fantasy that her mother was outside her room with a gun and would kill her. She had been afraid that the dream meant that she was psychotic.

In other dreams of this patient there were constant references to stairs, not knowing, covering up, the fear of someone knowing, coming home early, being unexpected, hiding things from mother, and so on. The recurring references led to the reconstruction of a childhood event in which the patient came home unexpectedly early and discovered her mother in a compromising sexual situation. There is also a recurring and peculiar structure in the manifest content of the dreams in that there are commentary side phrases in most of them. For example, "but I knew he was there"; "but everything looks all right, so it is clear no one will ask questions."

Two aspects are of particular relevance in this fascinating clinical excerpt. First, the manifest content of the dreams contained frankly sexual and often incestuous elements. Second, it is noteworthy that the patient had few associations to the elements in the manifest content of the dream which dealt with the reconstructed childhood experience, nor could specific day residue be discovered which led to the insertion of these elements into the manifest content of the dream. They seemed to be "foreign bodies" inserted into already "unusual dreams" which, possibly based on the transference motivation to communicate, came into the dream in an effort to recall the childhood traumatic event.

Discussion

Problems presented by this and similar dreams require further understanding since they do not fit into our usual formulation of dream psychology. They suggest that we must reevaluate the role of the dynamic forces which lead to dream formation and the interaction between these forces.

The analogy of entrepreneur and capitalist which Freud used may reflect his bias in favor of the forces of the unconscious, as this was the "new fact" of which he was the discoverer. It is, of course, impossible to know the relative importance of

these two factors, both of which are essential to dream formation. Because of this "bias," Freud tended to limit the function
of the dream work to the role of camouflaging forbidden instinctual wishes and compared the manifest dream to the façade
of an Italian church and dismissed it as an "illusion"
(1916–1917, 1925b). This attitude toward the manifest dream
seems to be a historical remnant from the early days of psychoanalysis and predates the period of ego psychology and the
structural hypothesis. Freud mentions as exceptions to this view
of the manifest dream as being merely a façade, certain "undistorted dreams of young children and occasionally adults" (1900,
1901a, 1916–1917). Freud specifically remarked on those factors which could influence the manifest content of the dream
in a footnote where he described changes in dream structure
when adults were in "unusual external circumstances" (1900).
He illustrates this by a reference to deprived and hungry ex-
plorers who report dreams of food, water, and letters from
home. Freud had also used the manifest content of the dream
as providing a clue to the dreamer's character, in this case the
need to confess (Freud, 1913a).

It is suggested that the clinical material described by Horowitz can first be understood as a need to master the infantile
trauma. There was both a wish and fear of recalling the details
of the childhood traumatic event. The patient had been forbidden to recall it, yet fragments of the experience appear in the
manifest content of the dream. To these fragments the patient
had no associations. Being preconscious and once the subject
of memory, these elements may also have resisted dream distortion. The other aspect of the dream which is overtly sexual and
frequently incestuous may not represent a failure of the dream
work, but may serve a defensive function guarding against the
recall of the original trauma. It is suggested that this infantile
sexual material is allowed to evade censorship because it is being
used as guardian of sleep rather than as waker, such as, "Nothing really happened; I only wished it would." We can understand this as the employment of a wish as a defense against
traumatic reality (Jacobson, 1957).

The role of the unconscious wish-fulfilling motive in dream
formation is well recognized. The question raised here pertains

to the relative importance of another motive which concerns mastery of a trauma. This motive is the one described by Freud as serving the "original function" of the dream (1900). It appears to be more accessible to consciousness and can be related to past as well as present events. In our usual formulation of dream psychology it appears as the day residue dealing with preconscious conflicts of current life and, in its most attenuated form, is represented by the innocuous current experiences often used for this purpose. In the "usual" dream the threat to awakening is represented by instinctual wishes which are then gratified and bound in a distorted hallucinatory fashion.

Clinical experience leads us to call these dreams "usual," since in "civilized society" the availability of food and shelter is generally adequate and immediate threat to life is minimal. However, the frustration of the sexual and aggressive drives, because of taboos and inhibition, is maximal. Therefore, in most dreams the unconscious sexual impulses would be the source of danger and the major potential disturber of sleep. This situation was described by Freud: "Dreaming has taken on the task of bringing back under control of the preconscious the excitation in the Ucs, which has been left free; in so doing it discharges the Ucs excitation, serves it as a safety valve and at the same time preserves the sleep of the preconscious for a small expenditure of waking activity" (1900, p. 579).

In marked contrast to this situation stands the traumatic dream. Here the "original function" of the dream is most apparent. In these dreams the wish-fulfilling function is apparently reduced in dynamic importance and the major function of the dream is a mastery of a past or present traumatic event. It then becomes apparent that these two forces do not for any length of time remain independent of each other. In fact, they are uniquely capable of mutual assistance and soon develop an interdependent, reciprocal relationship.

On the basis of this formulation the relationship between the preconscious dream thoughts and the unconscious latent dream thoughts would not always be as simple as "entrepreneur" and "capitalist." Each source could contribute in an independent but interrelated fashion to the manifest content, depending on their relationship to each other, and which one was better able to reduce anxiety. In addition, this genetic view of the evolution of the dream would parallel the concepts concerning the role of repression from its nonpathological to its pathological state.

As an illustration of this thesis we can propose the following steps in the economics of dream formation. If we follow the vicissitudes of the traumatic dream, the function of which is mastery, we see that the first alteration is from passive to active (as in the examples given by Bonaparte [chapter 1] and Loewenstein [1949]). The next step in mastery is apparently a further reediting of the dream based on wish fulfillment. It is in this context that the innocent wish-fulfilling dreams of children are relevant (Freud, 1900). Soon the wish fulfillment involves the infantile sexuality as a defense against the threat of the reality of the trauma. It is at this point that certain dreams in which the manifest content is openly "incestuous, sadistic, or immoral" might be explained without recourse to the hypothesis of the failure of the dream work.

The use of infantile sexual wishes as a defense against trauma, though intended to reassure, soon miscarries and becomes a new source of anxiety. The threatened appearance of gratification of unconscious sexual elements begins to dominate the dream and sets in motion the need for censorship. We then see the usual dream and the usual function of the dream work. These views serve to relate traumatic dreams at one end of the scale to the "usual" dreams at the other end. This is accomplished by suggesting an interrelationship between the mastery of trauma and the wishes of infantile sexuality. This view of dream dynamics may have a wider applicability than is immediately apparent, by helping us to understand a large number of the dreams of the so-called borderline patient.

I have often been impressed by the difficulty of interpreting the dreams offered by borderline patients. In part this can be understood as a consequence of their attitude toward their dreams (Blitzsten et al., 1950). Another factor may be the existence of an ego defect affecting the operation of the synthetic function which results in a failure of the free associations to cluster around the significant material (Jacobson, 1957). However, I suggest that more of the dreams will be understood if we conceive of them as modeled along the lines of the traumatic dream, in the sense that they serve the original function of mastery. Because of the early points of fixation and the arrest in development, the conflicts in severely ill patients are less completely internalized than in the neurotic patient and are represented in terms of the relation of self to object. For example, one patient reported a dream in which she was walking down the street. Everyone was afraid of her because she was radioactive. Since these patients live in a world conceived of as dangerously destructive, each day is filled with frightening and traumatic events, and each day is marked by a preoccupation with the question of survival. The dream can often be understood in terms of this fear of the outbreak of uncontrolled primitive aggression and the fear of the loss of the sense of identity. The dreams represent an effort to master these primitive fears and, as in the traumatic dream, show a greater dependence on the preconscious component of and the original function of the dream.

Finally, further support to this genetic view of dreaming is suggested by those persons who are grieving over the death of a person they loved. Often these patients express a hope that they will have a dream in which the dead person will appear in the manifest content and are appeased and reassured when this occurs. They seem intuitively to understand the restrictions which the loss and the mental pain have imposed on their freedom to think of the lost object. The dream they wait for, besides giving some magical reassurance, may also be an early signal of this loss of inhibition and the mastery of the painful grief. During the period of mastery, dreams are often forgotten or anxiety provoking. After the appearance in the dream of the dead person dreaming can return to its more usual function and structure.

Summary

A review of Freud's discussion of dream psychology points up his modification of the wish-fulfilling function of the dream.

His modification introduced the concept that the original function of the dream was the mastery of traumatic stimuli.

A question is raised and discussed as to the relationship of preconscious and unconscious elements of the dream. Usually we relate manifest content to preconscious source and current life, and latent content to unconscious source and infantile life. Brief clinical examples question these relationships.

In the unusual dreams considered, actual traumatic childhood experiences appear directly in the manifest content of the dream. These dreams were also often openly incestuous. It is suggested that this does not represent a failure of the dream work, but rather a use of unconscious instinctual wishes to defend against the recall of the traumatic childhood experience. This invites a reevaluation of the role of the forces which lead to dream formation. The preconscious forces represented in the day residue are related to the original function of the dream—that of mastery. A reciprocal relationship between these forces, comparable to the mutual influence between ego and id, is suggested.

Chapter 26

MANIFEST DREAM CONTENT AND ACTING OUT

Nathan Roth

Recent studies of dream psychology lay considerable emphasis on the manifest dream content. Erikson (1954), listing a series of features of manifest dream configurations, "would postulate a *style of representation* which is by no means a mere shell to the kernel, the latent dream; in fact, it is a reflection of the individual ego's peculiar time-space, the frame of reference for all its defenses, compromises, and achievements." He says further, in regard to the variety of dream styles, "we would relate them to the respective cultural, interpersonal, and personality patterns." Saul (1956) says: "the manifest dream alone is . . . of great significance and of great practical value in understanding the patient," and advises, "Look for what the dreamer's ego accepts and acts upon in the dream, for this is a prognostic sign as to what he is capable of acting upon in real life." The writer (Roth, 1954) has discussed the manifest dream as a record of the successes or failures of the dreamer's sublimations.

The purpose of this communication is to describe from clinical observations the acting out of the manifest content of dreams, the conditions under which it occurs, and its dynamic and therapeutic significances. Briefly stated, such acting out of the manifest dream occurs with consistent regularity whenever the resistance of the analysand is too great to permit of the interpretation of a dream. If during any analytic session a

This paper was first published in the *Psychoanalytic Quarterly* (1958), 27:547–554.

dream is presented which cannot be analyzed because of resistance, it may confidently be expected that at the next session the dreamer will report how he has acted out quite literally—and not only in symbolic or other distortions—portions of the manifest content of the unanalyzed dream. In instances where some insight is gained from partial interpretation the unanalyzed part of the dream will be acted out in greater or less detail.

The acting out, which is always disagreeable or painful to the patient, is motivated by unconscious repetitive impulses in the patient's neurosis. It is behavior identical with what is familiarly described as the acting out of the transferences (Roth, 1952). This acting out, within or outside the analytic situation, is first stated in the analytic dream. The striving is then to realize the dream wish in some equivalent, but disguised, behavior in external reality. We are reminded of Lewin's (chapter 7) statement that, "Dream formation is to be compared with 'analytic situation formation,' " also his equation of free association with manifest dream content. Elsewhere Lewin (1946b) says, "The young ego does not separate dreams from waking" (in every neurosis the ego is, in some respects at least, "young"), and he (1954) analyzes the conscious behavior of patients in states of ecstasy, mania, and depression as waking dreams. The thesis proposed is that all neurotic and psychotic behavior consists of the acting out of manifest dream content, without any implication that one or the other is primary from the pathogenetic point of view.

Clinically and technically, to enable the patient to understand the meaning of his dreams as they relate to the pathogenesis of symptoms, it is highly significant that the manifest dream content may be reenacted without distortion or disguise (although, of course, this also occurs). It affords the patient an irrefutable demonstration that dreams and neurotic symptomatology as displayed during waking hours stand in a reciprocally explanatory relationship to each other. The patient's cooperation is then the more readily enlisted for the task of establishing clear and detailed connections between dream thoughts and waking life, which provides the most trustworthy information as to the nature of the neurotic process, and places the therapeutic endeavor upon the firmest and most objective scientific basis.

If one views neurosis as a disorder of adaption—and from the social point of view as a process resulting in imperfectly developed or impaired sublimations—it may be observed that the handicaps to efficient functioning from which a patient suffers are not demonstrated at random nor in haphazard fashion, but always in strict connection in time with the same disorders represented in the concurrent manifest content of his dreams. Sterba (1946) described acting out which occurred just prior to reporting dreams that he interpreted as an acting out equivalent to associations to the dreams. This diurnal—nocturnal concordance is a reliable factor when search is being made in dreams for an explanation of waking behavior otherwise incomprehensible.

Neurotic behavior, when studied in relation to a dream which it either follows or precedes, thus consists of acting out parts of the manifest content of the dream. While the manifest dream content may show a symbolic (or otherwise disguised) representation of a certain activity, what is most important is that portions of the manifest content are acted out in waking hours literally as they appear in the dream. There are circumstances, while listening to a patient's report of a dream, when the analyst can be quite confident that he will find the patient acting out the manifest dream content precisely as portrayed in the dream; conversely, there are times, while listening to the associations of a patient, when the analyst can cull from the mass of material little pieces of behavior which he may reasonably expect to be reproduced in the manifest content of an ensuing dream.

The acting out of the manifest content of dreams has an interesting limitation which is reminiscent of a phenomenon observable in hypnosis. It is well known that, generally speaking, individuals given posthypnotic commands will not carry them out if they run counter to strict superego prohibitions. The same holds true with the acting out of the content of the manifest dream. An entire dream may be acted out with the exception of the parts that are too stongly opposed by the superego. The other details of a dream which may be acted out are extremely extensive and varied, for example, the phenomena pertaining to the dream screen itself (Jackson, 1956).

The patient who is acting out the manifest content of a dream is temporarily suffering from a loss of his adaptive capacities. It does not matter what the composition of the reality situation, nor what would be an effective reaction to it, the patient must behave in the manner outlined by his manifest dream content. He is powerless to alter his behavior, despite the occasional conscious wish to act in accordance with reality. This experience for the patient has a peculiarly painful quality. He describes it as "feeling like an automaton," "being out of control of one's own life," "sleepwalking," and so on. Once the patient is led to understand that this uncontrollable acting out reflects the manifest content of his dreams quite accurately, and is the result of the operation of a resistance which prevents the interpretation of his dreams, he is then provided with a powerful incentive to analyze and gain a comprehension of his dreams. The nature of acting out in general, as opposed to the analysis of an unconscious drive, is most easily explained to the patient when illustrated as the dramatization of his dreams. The analyst may thus have a useful implement for preventing the damaging consequences of acting out.

The following incident in the analysis of a patient will illustrate. The patient was a male in his late thirties who had entered psychoanalysis with complaints of not being able to win and hold friends, an inability to plan and carry out projects, failure to achieve the intellectual profundity of which he believed himself capable, and some phobic symptoms. These disorders were the result of his peculiar defenses against his oedipal strivings, which took the form of putting distance between himself and his father and wanting to know nothing about his father's activities lest he reveal an interest in the latter's sexual life. He had been consciously aware of wanting to learn nothing from or about his father, and of wanting his father to remain aloof from his affairs. His painful isolation from his father revealed itself in the transference as a lament that he could not promote the friendly relationship with the analyst that he desired. He reported with his adolescent son the same aloof and cold state of detachment that he had had with his own father, and he dreaded the possibility of having to discuss with his son some sexual problem the boy might bring to him. While analyzing the distance which he had placed between himself and the analyst, as well as the estrangement between himself and his son, he had the following dream.

> He is playing golf with his twin cousins and drives a ball a tremendously long distance, about four hundred yards. As he drives the ball he thinks he is going to have a good season at golf this year and, as he watches the ball in its flight, he thinks so long a drive is impossible and yet there it is. The ball makes straight for the hole but, just before reaching it, hits the frame of a door which stands upright on the green without a door in it. One of the cousins says, "To bad it hit the door frame," implying that otherwise the patient would have made a hole in one.

The door frame was first associated to the fact that the patient's son, who was very worried about his short stature, continually measured his height against the door frame to see if he was growing taller. In the patient's mind the son's shortness represented the stunting of sexual development, which the patient was inflicting on him—specifically the father's wish that the boy should not have an erection. The door frame also referred to the door to the analyst's office, which was troublesome to the patient because every time it opened he was confronted with his feared desire to become friendly with the analyst. The well-driven golf ball represented, among other things, the hostile desire to prevent the son's sexual development, and the anger toward the analyst who aroused anxiety by his friendliness to the patient.

During the course of the session the patient showed great resistance to the analysis of the transference significances of the dream. He became fearful lest he or any member of his family become ill, since he could not feel confident that he could get the aid of a physician, a projection of his unwillingness to take help from the analyst. The chief affects in the dream—hostility, optimism at the likelihood of being able to analyze the hostility and the good consequences thereof, and regret that he was not going to effect this piece of analysis at this time—made the striking of the door frame the most prominent element for associations to the dream. As the patient talked he gave the analyst the convincing impression that he would strike some part of his body against the door frame as he left the room at the end of the hour. This did not happen, perhaps because his feelings of guilt were not strong enough. While waiting for the patient at the next session, the analyst heard a loud crash at the closed door. On opening it the analyst found that, in hanging up his coat in the waiting room, the patient had overturned the coat rack and sent it falling against the door of the consulting room. Apparently the acting out of the manifest content of the dream had had to be delayed until the ensuing session when the patient could find an implement with which to strike the door, and thus make the reproduction of the dream more accurate. Some of the meanings of this behavior are obvious, but attention is concentrated on the acting out. There were other relevant details of the patient's situation immediately prior to his entry into the waiting room, but the example as given suffices to illustrate an acting out of the manifest content of a dream whose interpretation is prevented by resistance.

These observations provide some additional understanding and illustration of Freud's discovery that the formation of a dream requires a preconscious day residue coming into associative connection with an infantile wish which provides the incentive and energy for the dream formation. Since the neurotic behavior of the adult is a revised version and continuation of the infantile neurosis, a link must be found between the current neurosis and the infantile traumata and conflicts, and this link is found in the day residue. As a consequence, examination usually discloses that the day residue is intimately connected with present neurotic problems, and that it is chosen neither as a matter of chance nor solely because of its associative connection with an infantile wish.

The fact that acting out can be demonstrated to the patient as deriving from his manifest dream may serve as a guide to the analyst in determining which parts of a mass of dream material may be chosen for the intensive effort of reaching an interpretation. It may be most efficacious to single out of each dream or portion of a dream that which most clearly reproduces waking behavior. If a particular symptom appears to contain the nuclear conflicts of a disorder, the manifest dream content which most nearly duplicates the symptom should receive the closest interpretative scrutiny.

That there is a variable and indefinite demarcation between dreams and waking reality is a psychoanalytic truism. As the chief function of the dream is to preserve sleep, the dreamer in the dream is trying to find an acceptable resolution for a condensation of realistic and forbidden wishes, present and past. The dream recapitulates for the dreamer the nature of his deprivation and its determinants. The relatively relaxed privacy of the dream makes it safer to permit self-revelation on nonadaptive, infantile determinants of the dreamer's fantasy. The dreamer can always suppress the dream fantasy if it is too disturbing to remember. He can, however, remember it whenever he is ready to profit from its interpretation in psychoanalysis. Róheim (1952) says, "The dream as such is an attempt [of the dreamer] to re-establish contact with [his] environment, to rebuild . . . [his] world." Rycroft (1951) states that "Dreams showing the dream screen are likely to occur when patients with narcissistic fixations are attempting to re-establish emotional contact with the external world" (pp. 178–184). It appears that the dream contains another example of a force operating "beyond the pleasure principle," for in addition to its wish-fulfilling function it serves the efforts of the psyche in its strivings for fuller living, better adaptation, and greater health.

Summary

The acting out of manifest dream content occurs with consistent regularity when resistance prevents the full, or only partial, interpretation of a dream. This relationship between waking behavior of patients and the manifest content of their dreams lends itself to various technical and therapeutic applications in psychoanalysis. It clarifies the structure of both dream and psychopathology, and the function of the dream.

Section VI

Symbolization in Dreams

This section opens with two concise clinical articles. First in this group is Isakower's classic paper, "Spoken Words in Dreams" (1954), in which he extends Freud's hypothesis (i.e., when a spoken utterance occurs in a dream, it originates from an actual remembered speech) to what he calls its logical conclusion; namely, that speech elements in dreams are a direct contribution from the superego to the manifest content of the dream. Second is Grinstein's article, "The Convertible as a Symbol in Dreams" (1954), in which, building on the two generally agreed analytical meanings associated with the automobile symbol in dreams (i.e., its representation as the analysis itself and its symbolizing the entire body ego), he advances the proposition that the choice of a convertible as a symbol expresses the underlying wish (and conflict) that the dreamer could be converted or transformed into a woman. Such a use of the dream elements illustrates what he calls a "plastic word representation" type of symbolization.

Following this appears Calef's "Color in Dreams" (1954) article which advances the thesis that color in the dream shows itself in two ways: (1) the dream censor makes itself known by removing color in the dream; thus the black and white imagery of most dreams is an indication that resistance has camouflaged the latent dream thoughts and wishes; and (2) color in the dream may reappear in the form of symbolic distortions and images linked with scoptophiliac–exhibitionistic impulses.

Two companion articles relating to time and the dream are next presented. Earliest in point of time is Gross's short paper "Sense of Time in Dreams" (1949), which presents his findings that there are two types of dreams in which time appears in the manifest content: in one type the sense of time represents a distorted expression of a highly charged and conflicted *current* object relationship; the second is an attempt to reduce a traumatic ("tragic") frustration of the *past* to a trivial frustration of the present. Juxtaposed to this is Hartocollis' carefully reasoned article of thirty years later, "Time and the Dream" (1980), where his findings suggested just the opposite of those of Gross. In addition, he determines that when time is understood in terms of "perspective" in the dream, it is typically represented in spatial terms; but when it is understood in terms of "duration," it finds expression in terms of motion or situations involving time-bound affects.

Next appears a short article by Loomis connecting symbolization to transference phenomena, "The Concurrent Presentation of a Rare Detail [Symbolization of a Goat's Genitals] in the Dreams of Two Patients" (1956). Loomis traces the source of this symbolization to the transference announcement that he was about to leave his practice to go into the military service.

This section ends with Kanzer's "Observations on Blank Dreams with Orgasms" (1954), a paper dealing with a unique type of symbolization (i.e., what in some ways may be called a nonrepresentation). Here Kanzer extends Lewin's hypothesis (the forgotten dream is a concrete object which has been as if physically lost or misplaced) to the phenomena of forgotten dreams which are linked to a more advanced level of development; that is, particularly to the blank dream which is accompanied by orgasm. Such dreams he finds are correlated primarily to the traumatic experience of observing the mother's genitals which are warded off by a series of defenses that include the inhibition of the visual function.

Chapter 27

SPOKEN WORDS IN DREAMS: A PRELIMINARY COMMUNICATION

Otto Isakower

In *The Interpretation of Dreams*, Freud stated it as an invariable rule that when a spoken utterance occurs in a dream, it has originated from a remembered speech in the dream material, and that the wording of the speech has either been preserved in its entirety or has been slightly altered in expression.

While Freud made no attempt to integrate this statement with his dream theory, leaving it in a completely descriptive state, his subsequent systematic presentations regarding the structure of the personality afford a tactical advantage to a renewed investigation of this special problem.

In a previous paper (1939) I have traced the psychological correlations of the static apparatus, the organ of equilibrium, and of the auditory apparatus. Certain crustaceans "incorporate" particles of sand to use them as otoliths, that is, to aid their orientation in space. The human being's need for orientation, in the widest sense, is met by speech, which also is based upon material taken in from the outer world, through auditory incorporation. Here it is not only the verbal elements themselves, but also the assimilation and correct combination of verbal images, the development of a grammatical and logical order in the processes of speech and thought. This auditory incorporation then becomes of fundamental importance for the functions of the superego, which later in a similar way serves to orient the individual in the outside world as well as in his inner

---

This paper was first published in the *Psychoanalytic Quarterly* (1954), 23:1–6.

world. "The following formula," I stated, "then suggests itself: just as the nucleus of the ego is the body ego, so the human auditory sphere, as modified in the direction of its capacity for language, is to be regarded as the nucleus of the superego" (pp. 340–348). Proofs for this origin of the superego are found in delusions of observation, and in certain other schizophrenic phenomena. In that paper, I suggested it to be worthwhile to examine the relation of the auditory sphere to dreams. While dreams, in general, are usually visual, outside the realm of language, I pointed to a peculiar exception, a phenomenon which occurs while falling asleep:

> [L]inguistic phenomena connected with going to sleep often show an almost exaggeratedly elaborate grammatical and syntactic structure. The speech flows along in complex phrases, with strongly accentuated sentences of an animated and changing form; but it loses its clarity more and more as it proceeds, and at length there remains only an impression of lively and complicated periods without any verbal elements which can be clearly grasped . . . until at last the periods gradually pass over into a scarcely articulated murmur, which stops, starts again, and finally passes over into sleep. One might say that going to sleep itself is a case of "crossing the frontier of speech." . . . Perhaps all this is only another aspect of the fact that before the "censor" . . . withdraws, he seizes the opportunity of making his voice heard once more very forcibly. What we see here is not so much *content* that is characteristic of the superego but almost exclusively the tone and shape of a well-organized grammatical structure, which is the feature which we believe should be ascribed to the superego. At the moment of waking, the linguistic auditory phenomena present themselves in a much briefer and more succinct form. It often happens in this way that a word or short sentence still reaches a dreamer while he is waking up, like a call, and this call has very often a superego tinge, sometimes threatening, sometimes criticizing—words for which the dreamer, as he wakes up, feels an inexplicable respect, although they are very often a quite unintelligible jargon [pp. 340–348].

In that publication I did not carry the argument to what seems to me the logical conclusion: that *speech elements in dreams are a direct contribution from the superego to the manifest content of the dream.* For heuristic reasons I propose to regard this hypothesis equally as apodictic as Freud appears to have presented his original concept of the provenance of speech elements in dreams. An accumulation of observations has confirmed me in my assumption. It may be said that, from a practical point, this view has proved its usefulness; when used as a key, it very often has made possible the interpretation of otherwise refractory dreams. However, the purpose here is not to recommend the usefulness of a rule of thumb, and I shall refrain from giving more than one example, which has been selected for its somewhat atypical character.

A thirty-year-old man whom I analyzed in Vienna had marital difficulties. His extramarital escapades caused him a lot of trouble. He was very fond of housemaids and Wagner operas. He dreamed:

> I and some party members [he was also a very active socialist] are going along the sidewalk of a street which is unfamiliar to me. I say: "How much this Lohengrin is costing me already!" (It is as if we had been planning to arrange a private performance of Lohengrin, and that I had gone to see it at the State Opera House for the purpose of study.) Then I am enumerating the whole cast of the opera accurately and correctly, and I tell them how wonderful it had been. [He had attended a performance of Lohengrin the night before the night of the dream.] I wake up. While recalling my dream, I somehow half hear, half say to myself the phrase: "Your swinish love life [more literally: love-swinishness] shall yet come into the open!" [*"Deine Liebes-schweinereien werden schon noch herauskommen!"*] Immediately I see that this is *nonsense.*

It will be recalled from the opera that when Lohengrin is alone with Elsa in the bridal chamber, he solemnly bids her never to question him nor otherwise try to find out whence he came, nor what his name and kin. Suffice it to state that, up to

the point of waking, the dream is of the most ordinary structure, as dreams go. It also contains a clear-cut linguistic passage
("How much this Lohengrin . . . "), the meaning of which is
readily understood; it conveys, among other things which do
not interest us at the moment, a rather mild dose of self-criticism. But now a curious thing happens. After waking up, and
while he is engaged in retrieving the dream, a very forceful
pronouncement is made by himself and yet not by himself. A
directed effort did not succeed in tracing the origin of the
sentence about *Liebesschweinereien*. Only when the dream had
been analyzed to some extent was the patient able to see that
the sentence was a very forceful reproach from his conscience,
directly referring to the *latent* content of the dream. Immediately upon hearing it, however, he had tried to dismiss it as
nonsense.

This example was selected for various reasons. It offers,
in one dream, two separate elements of speech, differing in
character, yet both with the same meaning. The first one is
integrated with the rest of the dream, conveys its meaning in
a disguised and, in retrospect, rather witty form. Yielding its
meaning only when analyzed, it clearly had been subjected to
the process of secondary redaction.[1] The second one is undisguised, straightforward, emphatic, blunt, threatening, vindic-
tive. It is, however, sufficiently cryptic to be dismissed first by
the dreamer as entirely unconnected with the dream, and as
nonsensical. Or better perhaps, the dreamer, engaged in re-
crossing the barrier of speech toward wakefulness, succeeded
in playing dumb and thus warding off the abortive attempt
of the superego at a first interpretation of his dream. Under
ordinary circumstances, when the dream work has its way, the
secondary redaction takes care of the superego contributions
also. It is understood that the secondary redaction is largely a
function of the superego anyway. The example presented is
one of a miscarriage of the integrating function of the process
of secondary redaction.

*One might say that focusing the mental eye on the dream during
(and immediately after) the process of waking up assists in reinstating*

---

[1]As used here, "redaction" represents a third attempt to render the German *Bearbei-
tung*, after Brill's "elaboration" and Strachey's "revision."

the regime of waking reality. In this phase of transition the super-ego may assert itself with exaggerated vigor, and may appear giving off an emphatically condemning comment on the whole dream. "Taking over again" by the superego may sometimes manifest itself as noisily as at the time when it steps down (see the reference made above to hypnagogic and hypnopompic speech production).

In the second edition of his *Die Traumdeutung* (1900) Freud adds a footnote to what he presented as an "invariable rule" concerning the origin of spoken utterances in dreams. This footnote, I think, goes very far in the direction of my thesis. It says: "In the case of a young man who was suffering from obsessions, but whose intellectual functions were intact and highly developed, I recently found the only exception to this rule. The speeches which occurred in his dreams did not originate in speeches which he had heard or had made himself, but corresponded to the undistorted verbal expression of his obsessive thoughts, which came to his waking consciousness only in an altered form" (p. 304).

What Freud then called "the only exception" may well have been the first to challenge the rule. The next reference to this topic appears in his paper, "On Narcissism: An Introduction" (1914b). There, introducing the concept of the superego, Freud mentions for the first time explicitly that self-observation, in the sense of the paranoiac's delusion of being watched, plays a part in dream formation. Then he adds: "This part is not invariable; probably I [Freud] overlooked it because it does not appear in my own dreams to any great extent; in persons who are gifted philosophically and therefore accustomed to intro-spection it may become very clear" (p. 97). Freud did not link these two observations together, viz. "the only exception" and the part that self-observation plays in dream formation. It should be particularly noted here that Freud does not just say that self-observation plays a part in dreams, but rather in dream *formation.*

All this may serve to emphasize that vestiges of the present thesis are clearly recognizable in Freud's structural concepts.

It must be left for other occasions to study the ambiguity and obscurity of oracles, the spell of quotations, to name only a few of the phenomena which have an obvious bearing upon this topic. For the present we refer briefly to the well-known fact that speech phenomena in dreams not infrequently have a portentous, awe-inspiring character and tone, peculiarly reminiscent of oracles or quotations, and thus suggesting a common origin.[2]

I am aware that a renewed approach to the structural problems of the dream theory, like the one which is herewith briefly introduced, calls, in turn, for still more far-reaching suppositions regarding the nature of the superego.

---

[2]Very much to the point of our disquisition, and closely adumbrating its conclusions, Wolf von Siebenthal writes in his recent book, *Die Wissenschaft vom Traum* (1953):

> In considering the linguistic elements of the dream one has to bear in mind the enchanting and exorcising function which is an inherent primal character of words. This function asserts itself all the more in the state of the spontaneous dream experiences, which are so entirely rooted in subjectivity. Then we may see more clearly that the exorcising incantation is directed against the dreamer's own affects, and that an encroachment upon the dream is "intended" by way of an "insinuation." This is particularly valid for absurd and nonsensical words [p. 222].

Chapter 28

THE CONVERTIBLE AS A SYMBOL IN DREAMS

ALEXANDER GRINSTEIN

The fact that any element in the manifest content of a dream may have more than one meaning is very well known, having been emphasized by Freud (1900, p. 219). He maintained that, in the consideration of a particular element, one must evaluate it in the light of whether it was to be taken in a positive or negative sense, whether it was to be understood historically (as memory or recollection), whether it was to be taken symbolically, or whether its importance depended upon its *wording* (1900, p. 341).

In this brief paper, I should like to discuss the use of a particular type or model of automobile as a dream element. It must be noted, however, that its use, as with any dream element, is determined by the individual life experiences of the dreamer. Very frequently the automobile, as a vehicle, is used to represent the analytic process itself. In such instances it is important to note whether the progress made is slow or fast, whether the road is smooth or rough, and whether the driver of the car seems competent or has difficulties in negotiating the journey.

Quite often the automobile represents the entire body ego of the dreamer and its various parts. In this connection, Sterba (1946), for instance, reported a case of an adult analysand who dreamed of a little boy who damaged the right front fender of a car. On his way to the analytic hour, he stumbled on the front walk, which he had passed innumerable times, fell, and actually

This paper was first published in the *Journal of the American Psychoanalytic Association* (1954), 2:466–472.

broke his arm. One can readily see how in this dream the car was a representative of the total body ego of the patient, so that the right front fender represented his right arm.

The matter of anatomical representation may be carried further in dreams, so that the automobile may refer to the genitals of the dreamer or their functioning. Such a dream may express this by the high speed or power of the car, or the fact that it does not start properly, stalls, and so on. On some occasions its significance, so often equated with phallic functioning, is to be regarded as feminine; as in those instances, for example, where the dreamer finds himself in the protective *interior* of the car, often associated with fantasies of a return to an intrauterine state. From this standpoint, the automobile is treated as a bisexual symbol.

I should like to present five dreams from the analyses of four different male patients where the automobile which was represented in the manifest dream content was specifically designated as a convertible. In these dreams the choice of a convertible depended on the wording, expressing the idea that the patient could be converted or transformed into a woman. Such use of the dream element is thus an illustration of *plastic word representation.*

The first patient, a young bachelor in the first few months of his analysis who was struggling against his intense feminine impulses, had the following dream: He was standing on a little hill and below it on the road he sees a convertible with the top down. A man [X] and a woman [K], who is the wife of X, are sitting in it.

He talked somewhat reluctantly about X, a colleague of his and also one of my analysands, who in reality does not have a convertible. He described him as being very effeminate and his wife K, to whom he himself was somewhat attracted, as somewhat masculine. After a moment, he returned to the subject of X and, rather tactfully, commented on the latter's progress in his analysis, even in the time that he had known him, indicating that he was less feminine than he had been. Then suddenly, after a short pause, he said, "The next thought is about Christine Jörgensen."

The dream meant that he was afraid that I could convert or transform him into a woman, as Christine was by the psychiatrist in Denmark, or into someone like X, who was quite feminine in appearance and who, like himself, was attracted to K. The parallel was that all three of these men had passive feminine tendencies.

About six months later, he had the following series of dreams in one night:

> He is going to see his analyst, who in the dream is a woman. She asks him into her office where there is a couch. His friend [R] and another woman are there. Inasmuch as some general clean-up work is going on there which is disturbing, the analyst asks him to go upstairs with her.
>
> He then remembered another part of the dream which preceded this, but which he had forgotten. He is going somewhere with another man. There is a red convertible standing there with the door open and the motor running.
>
> In another part of the dream he is hunting some very small deer, of which he is somewhat frightened. Someone, a lady, gets shot in the arm.

He was angry with me during the previous session, but could not verbalize this, because of the fact that the session before had been interrupted because I had to take a telephone call. He was unable to talk freely, moreover, because he felt very guilty about the fact that he drove to his analytic hour with his friend R. He had left him in a neighborhood bar and had arranged to meet him there after his appointment with me, so they could drink together.

In the dream he turned me into a woman, but this was a *reversal* of the actual state of affairs as far as his feelings were concerned, since he feared that I would turn him into a woman as a retaliation or punishment for his anger toward me. In the part of the dream (which was at first repressed) having to do with the convertible, he expressed the situation particularly well. His only association to the convertible was that its color reminded him of "something bloody" about which he had some vague thoughts prior to coming for his analytic hour. In other words, he feared that in his analysis *he* would be converted or changed into a woman, that he would be shot, and the result would indeed be something bloody. The expression "door was open" symbolically indicated a passive receptive wish on his part. The fact that the motor was running indicated sexual excitement, as well as his fear of the entire situation and his desire to run away from it.

One can see here how the choice of the element convertible expresses the theme, seen earlier in his analysis, of the unconscious wish to be converted into a woman, as well as an allusion, by its color, to his horror of the dangers of passivity which threatened him in his analysis.

Another patient, who is an only child, had the following dreams in one night:

> Several dream fragments which he feels have to do with men.
>
> He is with a man of approximately his own age. An older man shows them a convertible car of some kind similar to a green panel truck with a canvas top. There is some discussion as to how it works and he politely inquires if the back seat comes out.

The patient was in an intense homosexual transference at the time of this dream. The "dream car" alluded to a truck owned by his uncle, toward whom he had very tender feelings. The green color was a reference to a pun on my name (Greenstein). There were many references to his attraction to men and examples of anal play with a neighborhood boy during his childhood. The dream was thus a polite allusion to an invitation for anal play, the back seat referring to the buttocks. One would suspect that the question which he asks in the dream as to whether the back seat comes *out* was a reversal referring to whether something can be put *in* the back seat (or backside), just as in the early part of the dream, the man who shows him the car is a reversal of his own wish to show his "car" to the other man. The choice of the element convertible is here used to indicate his wish to be converted into a woman and to engage in passive anal play as he did with the neighborhood boy in his childhood.

The third patient, a physician, who had lost his father under tragic circumstances, had been in analysis about two years at the time of this dream.

> He is being driven by a man in a convertible. In his hand there is a small black box like that of an opthalmoscope case. The box drops out of his hands and falls on the road, which is full of many holes. He has the driver stop the car while he gets out to recover the box. Cars go past and heap dirt and sand on the box. As he tries to reach the box, he finds himself going deeper and deeper into a cavern, the box slipping ever lower. He is still trying to reach it when the dream ends.

His associations to the dream concerned a discussion he had had with his fiancée the day before, who would have liked him to buy a convertible. He had no interest in this, however, as he felt that they were too expensive, not safe, and he saw no particular pleasure in driving with the wind blowing on his face. After a moment's pause, he told about reading an article which appeared in the *Journal of the American Medical Association* about Christine Jörgensen. He was very much interested in the fact that the operation was actually a biological castration of a patient with passive feminine tendencies.

Turning to the subject of the black box, the patient recalled that when he was a medical student, he had to purchase an opthalmoscope. A salesman tried to sell him one with a proctoscope attachment so he could do rectal examinations anywhere he went. However, since he felt this was an office procedure, the patient did not buy it.

In his other comments about the black box, he felt it symbolized a coffin which was buried in dirt. This referred to the sudden death of his father. The patient was away from home at the time and was unable to attend the funeral. A great deal of his analysis had been occupied with material dealing directly with the death of his father and his mourning for him. In this dream, one was able to see how he longed to revive his father, to dig him up. The material expressed earlier in the hour (referring to Christine Jörgensen) represented his defense against repressed aggressive impulses which he felt were responsible for his father's death. He was afraid that he would be converted by me into a woman, as a punishment for these wishes. He would be castrated and would have to die for causing a death.

The fourth patient had the following dream: He is riding in a convertible with the top down. Suddenly the top goes up and he feels a kind of tap on both of his shoulders.

For a while the patient talked about the slowness of the progress of the analysis, the persistence of his symptoms, and the terrible expense involved, it now being near the beginning of the month and time for his usual payment. After a while he told the following joke: "It's about the man," he said, "who was going to a doctor for prostatic massages, but finally in order to save money, asked his wife to give them to him. 'Do it the way the doctor did,' he tells her. 'Put your right hand on my shoulder and use your left hand. . . . No, no,' he corrected, 'Put your left hand on my shoulder and use your right hand. . . . No, no that's not right either. Put both hands on my shoulder and use—why that dirty S.O.B.' "

I pointed out that in the telling of the joke he equated me with the physician who had administered the prostatic massages and who, moreover, had been charging his patient so much that he wanted to save money by getting his wife to give him the treatments. The patient, himself, moreover, is here identified with the patient in his story who submits passively to his physician for anal gratification and in this manner becomes converted into a woman. In the dream the fact that he experiences a tap on both of his shoulders makes the situation similar to that in the joke of the patient who was getting the prostatic "treatments." The top of the convertible going up may be a symbolic reference to an erection.

In all the dreams cited we are thus able to see how the use of the automobile, treated as a bisexual symbol, indicates the ease with which sexual inversion is possible in the unconscious of these patients. The specific use of the convertible, however, is to be understood as an example of *plastic word representation*, whereas these patients' choice of the convertible to express their conflicts is, of course, determined by their life history. These patients all have strong passive tendencies. One may see in the associations to the convertible the intense anxiety in connection with it; the tendency toward passivity and its use as a defense against the emergence of dangerous aggressive impulses. Finally, one sees the tendency toward convertibility used as an aggression directed outward (transferred toward the analyst) or directed inward against oneself as a retaliation for hostile impulses.

Chapter 29

COLOR IN DREAMS

Victor Calef

In the seventh chapter of *The Interpretation of Dreams*, Freud (1900) demonstrated that pictorial representation in dreams is an effect of the resistances opposing the progress of thought on its way to consciousness. He characterized this with the term *regression*. Although he spoke of the recasting of the ideational content into sensory images, he was primarily concerned with the pictorial elements, ascribing the color in the dream picture to a repetition of something in the memory. In other words, new sensory perceptions of color revived memory images of color and were thus represented in the dream. Color in dreams could then be interpreted: (1) as actual reproductions of new and old sensory images; (2) as symbols for old sensory impressions; and (3) as partaking of the resistance and regression inherent in the sensory images of a dream.

About six months after the beginning of his analysis, a patient told me that he recalled a fantasy from childhood which had the quality of a vivid recollection both at the time that he had the fantasy as a child and again as the memory of the fantasy was reawakened. The quality of vividness which he described was similar to accounts of screen memories. The fantasy was the recollection of his mother visiting a neighbor's basement where she undressed and swam in the nude in a medicinal pool.[1] Prior to the reawakening of this fantasy, the analysis had

---

This paper was first published in the *Journal of the American Psychoanalytic Association*, (1954), 2:453–461.
[1]Dr. Mortimer Ostow suggested that the medicinal pool might represent a *mikvah*, the Jewish ritual bath.

concerned itself with his fears about being treated like a "little boy." This theme had entered into the analysis from the first and was richly interwoven with the various aspects of his relationship to his mother.

Concomitant with the recollection of the vivid fantasy, he had a transference dream in which the analyst (disguised as a voice from a loud speaker) is going to help the patient (Dick Tracy) to uncover the criminal. The dream ends in a compromise in which the criminal is not caught although the detective gains sufficient distance to look down upon the happenings.

The hours which followed upon the recollection of the fantasy and the report of the dream were once more filled with the theme of the "little boy," dealing primarily with the ingratiating attitudes which he assumed in relation to authority figures and how he despised himself for it. The fantasy of the mother's medicinal bathing receded. He attempted to understand his intense reaction to older men in authority, and his inability to achieve the role of "big boy" or "grown man." In a subsequent hour he reported the following dream: "There are a group of people, half-schizophrenic and half-neurotic. I'm one of them. We're out in the woods in a cabin. There is a large area of *green* and in the middle of it is a large patch of *brilliant orange*."

The associations to the orange color of the dream were a group of memories which began with the recollections of his interests in exploring nature, especially caves. He recalled his childhood fascination with caves and his fears that they would collapse. He linked this with the seeking and finding of condoms which convinced him that sexual relations had actually taken place. These memories, mentioned for the first time in the analysis, and others about the concern and interest in the differences between the sexes, were associated to the conviction that his mother possessed a penis. The early desires to explore his mother's body were implied, while the associations linked the fears he had about being an ingratiating "little boy" who asks for favors with these desires.

The recent material brought out in the analysis receded into the background for a time. The culmination of his resistance was reflected in another series of dreams. He reported that on one day of the weekend he had had a dream which contained just color. It had *blue* and *green* and *red*, and he believed that *yellow* was also present. All he saw was the color. There was no other form and no other content.

During the hour in which he reported the pure color dream, he struggled to "find associations" to the dream. He convinced himself that the dream was related to food in some way, because he and his wife had attempted to use some artificial coloring in the food which they were preparing on the day before the dream. He attempted to intellectualize this conviction and thereby to extract the meaning of the dream. The effort proved fruitless. Nevertheless, his associations hinted at a game which he had told me about previously. On question, he reported that he and his wife had joined in a game of exploring her pregnant abdomen, for the first time in several weeks, on the evening before the dream. But this piece of evidence made no impression upon him until the following hour in which he attempted to deal with the dream once more. He brought up the fact that he had not had enough time on the previous day to tell me of another dream which occurred on the same night as the color dream. The preceding night he had dreamed again, but could not tell me anything about either dream; they had disappeared from memory. He said vaguely, "There may be something about 'three' in both of the dreams," but he was by no means sure.

He was aware that the forgetting of dreams and the rationalization about not having enough time to tell a dream in the previous hour were evidences of a resistance in operation. I asked him if he was aware that the pure color dream was also evidence of a resistance. He then began to recall the other dream of the weekend, the pair to the dream of the primary colors. In this dream, he had walked through a hole in a fence to gain entry into a lot upon which was a store. The store had large plate glass windows in which some handsome sport model automobiles were displayed. There was a sign in the window which said that they could be purchased at $100 apiece and he wondered that they could be so inexpensive. He followed a young girl in romantic pursuit through some tunnels.

When the reluctant maneuvers he made to escape from the implication of his own associations were clear to him, the analysis of the dream proceeded. It became evident that this last dream was a dream of his scoptophilic and exhibitionistic impulses. In the first place, he recalled that he frequently had a fantasy in which he saw a woman carrying a small child; the woman would look at him, look at her baby, and wish that her own youngster would grow up to be such a fine, handsome young boy. The hole in the fence and the entry through it reminded him of female genitalia. He attempted to extract from this the intellectual notion that he must have been thinking of intercourse. He thought of an old preoccupation about how his mother looked when she was young. The associations to sport cars and to the glass windows in which they were displayed brought up many of his early scoptophilic interests. He became convinced that the dream was essentially related to his explorations of caves, his fears of their collapse, his interests in having knowledge of the female body. Finally, his associations about the cheap price of the car permitted him to focus upon the feeling of surprise which he had experienced. He recognized that this was the same feeling which he had in childhood when he was fascinated, mystified, and surprised at how a baby could be put together, complete with two arms and two legs. He recalled that his wife had confessed to him over the weekend that she had a preference for a male child. She had been thinking of a child with two arms and three legs (a male). This was connected with the blue food and the dream of three primary colors. The old fascination with the fact that an infant could be put together just right, so easily, by intercourse, was identical to the feeling of wonder about the cheap sport cars in the dream. The scoptophilic series was completed when, in the following hour, he reported a dream, the content of which was: "When three tables are served simultaneously, then my father will die." The analysis of this dream brought us not only to an examination of his hostile competition with his father but also directly to primal-scene material, as well as to a return to a consideration of the fantasy of his mother's medicinal baths.

Discussion

On the basis of similar experience of which the clinical fragment cited seems typical, the following tentative remarks are
made.

1. When, in an analysis, the attention of the dreamer is
brought to the color in a dream, his immediate response is
frequently one of resistance and surprise, but he is almost helpless to maintain his resistance because an affective concomitant
usually makes itself known in the waking analytic experience
of the dreamer. It is the affect which was hidden in the dream.
The latent content is frequently material from the scoptophilic–exhibitionistic life of the patient. I believe the case quoted
demonstrates this sequence of events. The patient's affect was
surprise, fascination, and mystification, and the content was the
"marvels of procreation." Needless to say, the affect and the
content were both representations of the same partial instinctual drive (scoptophilia). It was not just a generalized affect
that was hidden behind the reproduction of color imagery in a
dream.[2]

The question arises of why color should be linked specifically with the scoptophilic and exhibitionistic impulses. The
most obvious answer seems to be related to the probability that
maturation of color vision occurs at about the same time that
the exploratory impulses are emerging in full strength. (This
conjecture should be compared with observations of the dreams
of the blind.)

2. It seems self-evident that before the maturation of color
vision visual imagery in early infancy must be in indefinable
blacks and whites. As children seem to report color in dreams
rather frequently (at least to me, especially on inquiry), it does
not seem unlikely that imagery in dreams may include color
with maturation of color vision. However, color in dreams does
not seem to be a predominant finding in the dreams of adults,
although it is more frequent than is usually assumed. It is consistent with analytic thought to believe, therefore, that color in

---

[2]The relation between Rorschach color responses and color in dreams has not been
investigated by this writer.

dreams occurs in childhood until the onset of repression. At that time the dream, in the service of the censor, once more becomes predominantly black and white, except under circumstances when the exhibitionistic and scoptophilic impulses threaten to emerge from repression. The appearance of the color then maintains the impulses in repression as the last line of defense. In other words, when repression is enforced more or less completely, dreams appear in black and white; and when repression begins to lift, color in dreams may appear.

At times repression is not successful from the outset, making a demand upon the ego for other defensive maneuvers. Observing a patient who is fixated in this manner, one has the opportunity to see the resultant structures without the complications produced by regression. I believe that one of my patients, a thirteen-year-old girl, is an example of this kind. She reported that she had always dreamed in color. The first dream in her memory was of floating in a *red* rubber tube over a bridge while she watched the *red* water below. She fixed the dream at about the age of six. The most significant conflicts in this child were related to scoptophilic and exhibitionistic impulses. Violent primal-scene material was recovered early in the analytic work. The mother had a severe mental illness, and a seductive father (who persisted in misapplying his reading of psychoanalytic material) kept her struggles alive. She was never permitted the opportunity of dealing with her early experiences. Her fantasy life ran rampant, while her ego struggled to gain control. The intense penis envy from which she suffered found partial solutions in the patient's oscillation between active scoptophilic and exhibitionistic behavior. The dreams in color reflected the unsuccessful attempts made by this girl to deal with the impulses aroused by being a witness to the primal scene. The color disguised her curiosity.

3. An impression I have repeatedly received during the analysis of color in a dream is that the analytic work becomes easier, more free-flowing, closer to the ideal of free association when the attention of the patient is called to the color in his dream.[3] I am not prepared to say whether this arises merely

---

[3]Color in dreams is reported by patients in many different ways. In this report I am concerned primarily with those patients who mention color in a dream and do not emphasize the color, and for the most part do not recognize that they have mentioned

from the surprise that the patient experiences when the analyst shows interest in the unusual detail of the dream; or whether it arises from the fact that the undistorted affective component is experienced in relation to the "unimportant detail" of the dream. It seems, however, that the censorship forces are released under the circumstances described.[4]

4. The psychoanalytic literature fails to elucidate the meta-psychological structure of color in dreams. Linn's recent paper (1954) on color in dreams is an exception. Many authors have spoken of the symbolic meaning of the dream without further elaboration of the dynamics. Because color in dreams is a part of the visual imagery and therefore partakes of the regressive character of the dream, it will be used as a symbol. It scarcely seems justified to ascribe to the color specific and typical symbols for each color, despite the use of color in symbolic form by the waking ego; for example, green equals jealousy.

Many papers report a color or colors in dreams but do not deal with the subject more specifically. Wherever color has been reported as part of a dream, the analysis revealed the latent

---

color in the dream. The color is an unimportant detail so far as they are concerned. It must be pointed out that at times the color is mentioned by a patient only because in his waking experience he associates a specific color to a specific object and the color did not appear in the dream. An example of this might be "a *blue* lake." The significance of this construction is different from one in which the color is reported as having occurred in the dream. The scope of this paper does not include "technicolor dreams" and persistent color dreams, which are more complicated phenomena.

[4]Some other impressions I have from the analysis of color in dreams deserve only a footnote. When the censorship forces are released, as described, it seems as if the analyst gets a clear picture of the genesis and structure of the resistances and of the ego of the patient. Perhaps the insight permitted the analyst under these circumstances is explainable on the basis that the scoptophilic impulses are among the first that have to be dealt with by the ego; the earliest forms of defense, therefore, are called out by the ego confronted with its scoptophilic impulses. When the color in dreams is brought under scrutiny it must then reveal the resistances and defenses in their earliest form.

When I talked to Dr. Siegfried Bernfeld about my observations and deductions concerning color in dreams, he suggested that perhaps the color in dreams was connected with early childhood memories. It seems to me that the idea that early memories may be hidden in the color in dreams is not incompatible with the thesis that scoptophilic impulses are hidden in the color.

It seems worthwhile to investigate the problem of color further, for it appears that we are dealing with an area in which physiological activity (color perception), and its use in a psychological sense, may be observed at the point where the two converge. It may very well be that color perception belongs to the conflict-free ego sphere, and its study may permit a recognition of how it is or is not drawn into the conflict ego sphere. The use that the waking ego makes of color before, during, and after analysis is, I believe, one source for such studies.

content as belonging to the scoptophilic–exhibitionistic impulses of the dreamer, or the associations reported by the author clearly indicated that the patient was dealing with his curiosity. Tausk's (1924) paper is an example of the first type. A large number of the color dreams reported in the literature exposed primal-scene material when analyzed.

Summary

An attempt is made to describe a portion of the metapsychology of color in dreams which belongs both to the content and the form of the dream.

In the reports of dreams, the censor makes itself known in different ways; the patient forgets, the dreams are hazy, there are conscious and unconscious omissions, dream writing, and so on. Another way that the censor has of making itself known is in the use of color in dreams. The black and white imagery of most dreams is an indication that the resistance has taken over to camouflage the latent dream thoughts and wishes. Color, the differentiating medium of vision, is removed in the service of repression. On the threat of the return of the repressed, color in dreams may reappear (especially if the repressed is linked with the scoptophilic–exhibitionistic impulses) and represents a further regression, calling forth the reproduction of sensory images or symbolic distortions of those images.

Chapter 30

SENSE OF TIME IN DREAMS

Alfred Gross

"The Unconscious is Timeless": this psychoanalytic aphorism has blocked many analysts' interest in temporal relationships in dreams. Perhaps the thought that what is valid for the unconscious is valid for dreams overlooked the fact that not everything in dreams belongs or takes place in the system Ucs. At any rate, references to the sense of time are abundant in dreams and are important to dream theory. They may be classified either according to the stage in the dream process at which they appear (manifest dream, latent dream thoughts, or the day residues), or according to different concepts of time. These differences have different practical meanings and perhaps also different theoretical implications.

I

The familiar fact that references to time frequently occur in the manifest dream is strange in itself for several reasons. As elements of the dream thoughts they would, according to Freud, be reduced by the dream work to more elementary mental categories and would thus appear in the manifest dream as either references to space, as figures, or as references to body elements. This general tendency of the dream work to distort notions of time into timeless mental categories can easily enough be understood as the derivative of an ego activity; for as the ego's wish to sleep is mainly achieved by a withdrawal

---

This paper was first published in the *Psychoanalytic Quarterly* (1949), 18:466–470.

from reality, that withdrawal would be impaired by admission of the passage of time, owing to the close relationship between time and reality (Bonaparte, 1940). The conclusion that references to time have no place whatever in the manifest dream assumes that references to time in the manifest dream could come only from the latent dream thoughts. It omits the possibility that references to time in the manifest dream are the distorted expression of latent thoughts not concerned with time at all, or not *mainly* concerned with the time element within those thoughts. It further omits the possibility that references to time in the manifest dream are incorporations of day residues similar to the incorporation of spoken words with little or no distortion.

Actually, all those possibilities, far from being on the level of working hypotheses, have the validity of constant clinical occurrence. Time elements are used—and appear as such in the manifest dream—for the distorted expression of emotionally highly charged thought processes going on behind the screen.

Whenever data like "6 P.M.", "eight-thirty," or "September twenty-sixth," appear in dreams, they express the distortion of an object relationship highly charged with emotion. In analysis the reference is usually to the transference relationship. Outside analysis, confirmation of this rule is occasionally observed. The ego's wish to sleep compels a compromise with its incapacity to withdraw all cathexis from the highly charged object; the compromise is expressed in terms of time. At first look this may appear farfetched. It becomes credible by analogy with the lover's anticipation: "Tomorrow I shall see her again." The "her" will appear in his dream instead of the impersonal "tomorrow," unless there is a conflict involved in his longing for her. The displacement from the person to time is the result of ambivalence or guilt regarding the id impulse which is connected with the object relationship. A dream will illustrate:

> I am sitting in the car at a gasoline station. The man there should fill the tank. It is twelve-thirty, an hour until he closes. He puts two gallons into the car and then stops. Instead of going on filling the tank, he climbs into the car and sits down in the back seat. I sit in the other back seat

and think the man is a homosexual and is going to attack
me. I feel very angry.

Briefly, the dreamer was in a jumble of adverse feelings
against his wife over the weekend, and was looking forward to
his analytic hour on Monday. That, however, was in conflict
with repressed homosexual undercurrents. It required two sessions of associations, inhibited by resistance, to analyze "twelve-
thirty" and "an hour until he closes."

This dream illustrates the following characteristics. (1)
Time is referred to in the manifest dream by precise figures.
Despite its precision the dreamer represses the pertinent associations. (2) The reference to time is a distorted expression of
an object relationship which is current, is highly charged with
emotion, is the focus of a conflict. (3) In psychoanalytic treatment it alludes invariably to the transference. (4) The distortion
chosen by the dream work seems to be mainly, but not exclusively, the displacement of emphasis from the personal object
to the impersonal element of time.

II

In references to time in the past, the element of time is presented by special actions or experiences which contain an *allusion* to time. These dreams, often repetitive from childhood,
have an element of tragedy. To them belong dreams of missing
trains, running after buses, and they show, apart from their
familiar interpretation, a basic overdetermination which alludes, for instance, to a destiny-laden family constellation. It is
characteristic that such dreams are ignored for a long time by
the analysand, so accustomed is he to their repetitiveness.

An analysand, addicted to racing with time during his daily
life, made complicated arithmetical plans to gain two or three
minutes in his schedule. That habit did not conform to the
character of a calm, well-controlled man. One day he told me
of a recurrent dream of missing trains which surprised me by
its contrast to his daily habit. I hinted that he seemed to punish

himself during the night for his game of gaining minutes during the day. He objected emphatically that it was "just the other way round," but then stopped and did not know how and why that reply had occurred to him with that special emphasis; however, in the course of his associations I traced a leitmotiv which alluded to his position in his family. He was the youngest of five children, and he had enjoyed the presence of both parents for only one-and-three-quarters years when they were divorced and his father left the house. Bitter resentment about the absence of the father, whom the older siblings knew much better than he, remained with him and gave him the feeling of having missed something in life which could not be restored. The dream repeated an unresolved trauma of having arrived too late in the family. The dream in the service of the repetition compulsion is evoked as a defense against anxiety in response to traumatic events. Sleep is preserved as if the ego were protected by conjuring up the old family tragedy and ascribing the responsibility for it to the dreamer.

A dream reported by Freud (1900) belongs in the same category, with a characteristic difference of ego reaction. It is the dream of a lady who sits at a performance of a Wagnerian opera which lasts until the next morning. "Her young sister reaches up from the stalls below and wants to pass her a huge piece of coal with the motivation that she had not known that it would take so very long and, no doubt, would be miserably cold by now" (p. 342). Freud comments, "The dreamer herself and her girl friend had *remained sitting*," a German figure of speech for a girl who has remained unmarried. The younger sister who still has chances for getting married passes her the piece of coal "because she had not known that it will take so long a time" (p. 342). What would take so long a time is not stated in the dream. Freud continues, "in an ordinary tale we should say 'the performance'; in the dream, however, we consider the sentence separately, declare it as equivocal and would add 'until she gets married' " (p. 342). Freud does not pursue that element which arouses our special interest here: "that it would take so long a time." Characteristically, it alludes to a deep grievance which the dreamer had experienced with time (*waiting*). That waiting (for a husband) is an experience of her past, as missing (the father) was an experience of the past of the dreamer of missing trains. That past experience of grievous waiting appears in the manifest dream with the same mechanism of distortion.

In these dreams, (1) the reference to time in the manifest dream is presented by a situation in which the dreamer suffers a frustration through time like the frustration of missing (trains) or waiting (for the performance to end). (2) Those frustrations in time in the manifest dream are the distorted expression of frustrations in object relationships *in the past* (in contrast to the first category where the object relationship belonged to the present). (3) The means of distortion consist of attempts to shorten the length of time of frustration ("the train has just left," "the performance lasts to the next morning"); changing the subject of frustration from a destiny-laden or tragic one to one of absurd triviality (train for "father," end of performance for "husband'); the familiar change of the tense from the past to the present.

Summary

1. The paper studies the sense of time in dreams. Only such references to time are investigated as occur in the manifest dream.

2. The two types of dream which resulted from this study show different characteristics. In the manifest dream the first type refers to time in precise figures of astronomical time; the second type alludes to time by presenting situations of frustration through time.

3. This distinction of two types of dream on account of two different forms of time reference in the manifest dream is, however, not accidental. Interpretation shows that each type of time reference in the manifest dream is correlated to a corresponding type of specific thought content which involves a specific task for the dream work. We find the first type to be a distorted expression of a highly charged and conflictual *current* object relationship; the second type is an (often repeated) attempt to reduce a traumatic ("tragic") frustration *of the past* to a trivial frustration of the present.

Chapter 31

TIME AND THE DREAM

PETER HARTOCOLLIS

In his conversations on Freud, psychoanalysis, and more specifically the idea of "a dream language," the Viennese philosopher Wittgenstein (1966) recalls the following experience:

> I was once looking at an exhibition of paintings by a young
> woman artist in Vienna. There was one painting of a bare
> room, like a cellar. Two men in top hats were sitting on
> chairs. Nothing else. And the title "Besuch" (Visit). When
> I saw this I said at once, "This is a dream." (My sister
> described the picture to Freud, and he said, "Oh yes, that
> is quite a common dream"—connected with virginity.) Note
> that the title is what clinches it as a dream—by which I do
> not mean that anything like this was dreamt by the painter
> while asleep. You would not say of *every* painting "This is
> a dream." And this does show that there is something like
> a dream language [p. 43].

Wittgenstein does not explain how its title—"Visit"—made
him feel that the painting was a dream. Freud's alleged interpretation of the painting as being connected with virginity
seems to be based on the assumption that the "visit" of the two
men in top hats ("phallic symbols," as Wittgenstein is ready to
acknowledge) takes place in a prostitution house. But why
Freud agreed with Wittgenstein that the painting depicted a
dream—actually, just the theme of a dream—we are not told

This paper was first published in the *Journal of the American Psychoanalytic Association*
(1980), 28:861–877.

either. I submit, the explanation is in the way the picture deals with time, the intimation of the experience of waiting for something in a bare room, in a place anywhere, anytime.

The Dreamer's Temporal Orientation

Psychoanalytic theory holds that, inasmuch as they are dominated by the unconscious, dreams are not bound by the constraints of time. As Freud (1900) put it, "[in dreams, as in psychosis] there is a complete lack of sense of time" (p. 91). But as is the case with the unconscious, the timelessness of dreams is a relative matter. Both the experience and the abstract notion of time may be present in a dream, even though often in disguise. And when the notion of time is explicitly present, it means something different from what its manifest content indicates. The idea of timelessness for both the unconscious and the dream as an expression of the unconscious refers more to the immediacy of the experience and the seemingly illogical way time is dealt with, rather than to the elimination of time as either experience or concept from the dream or from the unconscious as such. Above all, the idea of timelessness refers to the fact that the contents of the unconscious and of the dream have their origin in the remote past, representing childhood wishes and conflicts that, in spite of the passage of time, have lost none of their appeal or intensity.

In a dream everything is experienced much more immediately than in awakeful reality. Along with the fluidity that characterizes one's pursuits and beliefs in it, there is a sense of urgency or eagerness, a massive narcissistic involvement, an intense investment in the action, in the people, in the purpose that make up the dream. We explain it on the basis of the intensity of the wish that creates the need to dream, the need to experience an altered state of consciousness, one characterized by a broader perceptual field, a fluidity of self-boundaries.

As is the case with our wishes and affects, which, regardless of their time orientation are always felt in the present, time as an experience in dreams is never attributed to anything but the present, even when the experienced events are based on affects and wishes of a different time. Freud's (1900) celebrated Irma dream—the "dream specimen of psychoanalysis" (Erikson, 1954)—was offered to us in the present tense. Here is the beginning of it, in Erikson's literal translation: "A great hall—a number of guests, whom we are receiving—among them Irma, whom I immediately take aside, as though to answer her letter, and to reproach her for not yet accepting the 'solution.' I say to her, etc." (p. 10). The dreamer's temporal orientation is strictly in the present, and any indication that the dream action represents childhood memories or wishes—that it is motivated by the wishes of the past—is under disguise, to be interpreted from the dreamer's associations. When there is open reference to the past, it may be assumed that there is a disguise in it as well.

We may dream of having feelings that we used to have in the past and, once awake and sufficiently removed from the impact of the dream, we no longer recognize in ourselves; however, it is rare to dream of ourselves as being of a different age. We may possess a different identity in the dream, and that identity may be of a different age; yet the consciousness of age remains that of the present, at least implicitly. As Zilboorg (1952) put it, "In the dream one could appear as a mature person (mostly in a dream), walking in the street and suddenly find oneself lying in a crib which the nurse is pushing along. While one is in that dream there is no surprise. There is no surprise while dreaming because there is no concept of opposites, no conception of time, no conception of continuity" (p. 65). Indeed, the experience of the dreamer is ageless, representing the subject's personality in its enduring traits, a self-concept that is related more to early wishes and identifications than to its current age and social role or professional identity.

Time in the Image of Space

In depending the notion of the unconscious as timeless, Freud (as reported in Nunberg and Federn [1974]) acknowledged: "This does not hold absolutely true of the dream because it is

a process taking its course *between* consciousness and the unconscious. . . . The dimension of time is linked with acts of consciousness . . . (p. 291). Elaborating, Federn pointed out that:
"In remembering a dream, we often do not know what was
earlier and what was later: because the dream reaches consciousness, it must be perceived in the context of time, yet because of the timelessness of the unconscious, the dream may
perhaps have no orientation in time. It is true that in its deepest
layers, the unconscious functions without the dimension of
time" (p. 304). Upon listening to Federn's comments, Freud
concluded that "[the latent content of the dream belongs to] a
system in which the element of time plays no role whatsoever.
On the other hand, this system does display something that
resembles what we call 'spatiality' when we refer to objects" (p.
308).

On a number of other occasions, Freud (1900, 1933b)
pointed out that time in the dream is expressed in terms of
spatial relations, the manifest content of the dream transforming time into space. In Freud's (1933b) own words:

> In general, indeed, where it is possible, the dream-work
> changes temporal relations into spatial ones and represents
> them as such. In a dream, for instance, one may see a scene
> between two people who look very small and a long way
> off, as though one were seeing them through the wrong
> end of a pair of opera-glasses. Here, both the smallness
> and the remoteness in space have the same significance:
> what is meant is remoteness in *time* and we are to under-
> stand that the scene is from the remote past [p. 26].

An elaboration of Freud's idea and specific example appeared
in a dream of a young woman in analysis with a student of
mine.

> *Dream 1.* I walked into a gift shop. There was a display
> counter, and on it were some statuettes. As I walked by,
> something dropped by me. Then the irate store owner
> walked up to me and told me I would have to pay for it
> because it had been chipped. I picked it up and I told him,

"No way this is chipped, I have one at home, and it is exactly like this." As I walked away, mad, I felt that he was following on my steps. I kept saying under my breath "Bastard, dirty son of a bitch." Then I noticed a funny device like a telescope that was stretching slowly—the strange thing was, I was looking through the wrong end, I was seeing the owner's face full of anger changing into my stepfather's face.

In associating to the dream, the patient recalled feeling excited, scared, and defiant when her stepfather beat her as a little girl. The appearance of the telescope in the dream, stretching slowly, brought back the memory of the stepfather's penis and angry face—distant, as if through the wrong end of the telescope.

Why space rather than time? What makes dream language prefer to deal in spatial rather than temporal terms, to represent the concept of time in terms of space? Space and time as intuitive notions or categories of the mind, rather than as operational concepts (mathematical, clock and calendar time, or geometric space identifiable in terms of length and shape) are presumably primary. They define our perceptual reality and, whether they are structural givens of the mind or derive from coenesthetic experiences, they are not reducible to one another. The dream work reduces thought into its most intuitive elements, pictorial and linguistic forms that convey their meaning according to the three principles Freud identified as symbolism, condensation, and displacement. Spatial and temporal concepts follow the same dream rules.

Time, however, is not a simple notion. Time is experienced, and later on conceptualized, either as duration or as perspective. The intuition of time as perspective—time as past or future—is predicated on the separation of self-from object representations, on the awareness of self-boundaries apart from the boundaries of objects—all of which implies the notion of space. But it is a different matter with the experience of time as duration, time as the intuition of being and not being, of feeling that things endure, that time moves along, slowly or fast, with or without the self. What determines the experience of time as duration is the instinctual pressure and the relative vitality of our wishes in the unconscious (Hartocollis, 1975). In dreams, it is manifested in terms of motion rather than space as such, slow or fast movement that may refer to dream events as viewed by the dreamer—the dreamer being an observer—or to the dreamer himself as a subject in situations of entrapment, haste, or emergency, where movement or the lack of movement is somehow time bound, as in the following example:

> *Dream 2.* I was with someone riding in the night, a landscape with a bridge. It was a dark, eerie place, with dead trees along the road, dark, dark trees that were dying. It was dark, and water running high under the bridge. We were going to an antique shop to get a crystal bowl, like the one my daughter broke recently, and we had to cross the bridge. There was some desperation about doing that on time, we were waiting for someone, my husband, but you had to cross the bridge now, otherwise you wouldn't be able to do it again. We went ahead and crossed the bridge, and my husband didn't come.

Of course, motion implies space; and the dream just cited is remarkable for its landscape, which is recalled elaborately but as a background for action, as if designed to bring out the idea of change, of movement, of transition, of becoming now, in the present. The dream above conveys the urgency of a conflict which may have its roots in the past and may have repercussions for the future but is experienced as duration, as the process of decaying ("trees dying"), as emergency or internal pressure ("water running high under the bridge"), as the need to hurry ("you had to cross the bridge now . . . there was some desperation about doing that on time"), as the process of resolution ("we went ahead and crossed the bridge"), rather than as something in perspective, a childhood memory, an unresolved conflict from the past, a secret desire, or some concern about the future.

Time and Object Relations

There are dreams, however, in which the notion of time is quite explicit, as clock or calendar time (objective, mathematical, or abstract time), rather than time implied in images of space and motion (subjective time). It has long been known that the presence of objective time in dreams represents a variety of meanings, usually around past experience with time and its passage—anniversaries, deadlines, contracts, fate, death. Thus, according to Freud (1913c), "[The time of day in dreams] very often stands for the age of the dreamer at some particular period in his childhood. In one dream a quarter past five in the morning meant the age of five years and three months, which was significant, since that was the dreamer's age at the time of the birth of his younger brother" (p. 194). In another instance, again as reported by Freud (1913c), time in terms of age represented emotionally charged moments of the past: "A woman dreamt that she was walking with two little girls whose ages differed by fifteen months. . . . It occurred to her that both the children represented herself and that the dream was reminding her that the two traumatic events of her childhood were separated from each other by fifteen months ($3\frac{1}{2}$ and $4\frac{3}{4}$)" (p. 195).

Dreams conceal one thing or another, defensively, for the purpose of protecting sleep. As Marie Bonaparte (1940) put it, "This flight from the tyranny of time which we are able to review each night seems . . . to represent one of the greatest wish fulfillments accomplished by the dream for the benefit of human beings who remain harnessed to time's chariot while day lasts" (pp. 461–462). Presumably dreams conceal the awareness of time in order to escape the vigilance of the superego and the call to goal- or duty-bound reality. Thus time-related concerns in dreams may appear in disguises as figures involving transactions in terms of currency. For example, in a dream reported by Freud (1900, p. 414), a certain amount of money available to pay for "something" was found to represent the length of time the dreamer could afford to remain in treatment.

Otherwise, when time is explicitly present, it stands for something different from what the manifest dream content indicates. Whether implicit or explicit, both kinds of reference to time stand for conflictual, emotionally charged object relations.

According to Gross (chapter 30), abstract, objective time in dreams has reference to problematic relations in the present; concrete or alluded time to traumatic relations in the past. In my experience, and as the dreams quoted earlier from Freud's work may indicate, a good argument can be made for the opposite case: implicit reference to time in dreams may signify concern about a current relationship while explicit, direct time may signify a conflictual relationship in the past or a traumatic event in the early family and childhood in general—the loss of a love object, sibling or oedipal competition, the threat of castration. Dreams of the latter kind tend to be repetitive, recurring periodically since childhood—another indication that they may refer to a past event or to a situation that has had its roots in the past. During the analytic process, such dreams tend to become incorporated in the transference.

An obsessive–compulsive man in analysis for about three years had a series of dreams, all of which involved a strong sense of time:

> *Dream 3.* "I had an odd dream last night," the patient recalled. "It was as if I was an observer back in the fifties. It was in a small industrial town in Pennsylvania, people were on strike against an order by President Eisenhower, an order invoking the Taft-Hartley Law or something like it. I was supposed to be reporting on the strike and then, somehow, there was talk about a sex scandal, an affair involving a union leader and a widow, a woman in her late thirties or early forties. She was complaining that the union leader was rude and had exploited her and so on."

When asked whether he had the awareness of being in the "fifties" while dreaming, the patient ascertained that that was indeed the case, adding that it was like seeing an old newsreel. Then he recalled watching a TV show about the McCarthy era the previous night. He also recalled that after the show he had the wish to be there, to stand up against McCarthy, feeling that Eisenhower had acted "very shabbily." At this point the patient became restless and declared that he had the sense that the dream was not important, it was like a crossword puzzle that had no meaning really, like an intellectual game he was playing by being concerned about such a dream. "I don't know why I brought it up," he said, "it is not connected with me, I have no real feeling for it. I barely remember it, there is such a distance from it, like something that happened during the night and I don't have the sense of any continuity with my real life. I was acting as an observer, I was not terribly interested in the first place, I didn't know where my loyalties lay, there was something unsavory about the way that man treated the poor woman." I pointed out that it was paradoxical to call the dream unimportant and not related to his concerns when he described its content in some detail and expressed intense feelings about it. Reluctantly, he acknowledged that the dream had more meaning than he wanted to believe. He felt attracted to "shabby" love affairs, and he thought he might himself want to behave in the way the labor union leader did in the dream. "Somehow," he said, "I identified with the old man. And yet all the persons involved in the dream were emotionally quite distant from me. I was a reporter doing a story on either side, neither of them was too appealing, etc." At the end of this new disclaimer of feelings, he confessed that he was currently interested in a young woman, a friend of his wife's, whom he found sexually exciting.

The case illustrates a number of points. To the extent that the reference to time in the dream's manifest content and experience is oblique or vague (a period described in terms of a historical figure or event) it pertains to a current interpersonal conflict—the temptation of an extramarital affair. The reference to the past serves as a disguise for the fact that the problem is current. To the extent that is specifies an age or date, the dream refers to an old conflict—oedipal or early adolescent competition with father, as suggested by the fact that the date in the dream coincided with the patient's later childhood. The patient's awareness of the particular time is that of an observer, someone who is emotionally detached from the latent content of the dream. A day later, the same patient reported the follow-ing dream:

> *Dream 4.* "I was in a strange city, wandering around this one area. It was like a golf course, and I found some balls lying around. I walked through a swampy area, and it turned out to be the middle of a town. The dream had something to do with trains, with schedules, going to some other city, traveling around. What stood out in the dream was walking up some place to be on time, some kind of schedule, something to do with trains, being on a train. This one was more like living it, not stopping to observe what I was doing. There was more action than anything else, I was so engrossed in doing things that I can't tell what I was doing. There was a background of interest, enjoyment I suppose, feeling good afterward."

In this dream the reference to time is indirect, contained in the movements of the dreamer through space, the concern with train schedules, and the sense of traveling. Even though the reported experience is pleasant, this may be more in its secondary elaboration than in the actual dream experience, which carries a certain degree of anxiety implicit in the dreamer's preoccupation with schedules and the vagueness of his destination. The patient did not come up with any meaning-ful associations from childhood, but kept returning to current concerns about his family and the guilt he felt for not spending more time with his wife, his frustration with his employment, his heavy work schedule and preoccupation, which did not allow him to finish a paper he was writing for some time now or to concentrate better in his analysis, where he usually had the feeling that he was "meandering" aimlessly, except for yes-terday when he felt that he had discovered something meaning-ful, which made him happy for a while. But now he could not tell what that was. Some time later, the same patient reported a third dream:

> *Dream 5.* "I was in the middle of some war activities, a World War II battle. I was with a general, standing on top

of a hill overlooking a valley where there was another army, the enemy, under another general, who was supposed to be MacArthur. I had the feeling that my general was very indecisive, very slow. The time went by and nothing happened. It was like a calendar in front of me—the days, the months, the years went by, one by one, without much happening."

The patient brought up a number of associations related to experiences of the weekend and his feeling that he was not engaged enough in life; his wife did not want to entertain guests, preferring to stay home with him alone; he felt awkward with his professional engagements, and so on. I reminded him of the fact that just the previous day he was complaining about the slowness of his analysis and blamed the analyst for not being alert enough or interpretive in the right way, wishing to have a different analyst, one who had impressed him with his sense of organization and knowledge of theory in a current seminar. The patient acknowledged that he was concerned about the slow rate of his progress, but thought that it was not entirely the analyst's fault. He recalled that as an adolescent and later, until he started in analysis, he had the fantasy of being General MacArthur's lieutenant and somehow proving to be as decisive a leader as MacArthur. And, as before, he recalled feeling impatient with his father as a child, having the feeling that his father was just a showman, without inner strength or real effectiveness.

Noteworthy also in this dream is its use of spatial concepts and images (standing on top of a hill overlooking a valley) to suggest the sense of time as perspective—surveying the past, reexperiencing the past from the distance of the present. In both instances, however, time is represented objectively (as the idea of past, future, clock time, calendar time) as well as subjectively, that is, implicitly (as in the idea of distance or in a situation involving frustration, haste, an emergency of sorts).

Indirect references to time in terms of situations of frustration or emergency usually involve the immediate experience of time as duration. Such an experience is often related to conflicts involving the superego, object relations generating intense ambivalence and guilt. Inasmuch as the idea of time remains implicit, such relations are likely to have reference to current conflicts—to conflicts involving contemporary relationships. The experience of time as short (or fast) may signify the wishful search for a love object that is either prohibited or unattainable. That was the case in Dream 2, where the dreamer felt in a hurry to cross a bridge threatened by the rising water. She was dissatisfied with her marriage, entertaining the fantasy of running away with a more glamorous man than her husband, ideally with her analyst, toward whom she nurtured strong erotic feelings at that point in her analysis. Time may be experienced as short (or fast), either explicitly or in situations of frustration involving a missed appointment, a departed train, and so on. When time is experienced as long (or slow), either explicitly or in situations of frustration involving waiting and obstacles of one sort or another, the dream may signify guilt over a love object that is ambivalently held. It may be in response to the aggressive part of the ambivalence that the dream, defensively, keeps the object away, out of reach, to preserve it.

Time and Affects in the Dream

Freud ([1900], and as reported in Nunberg and Federn [1974]) held that dreams involving the idea of departing on a journey and missing the train are motivated by the wish to deny the fear of dying. Referring to Stekel's notion of departure as a symbol of death, he pointed out that the dreamer wishes to reassure himself by saying, "you are not going to die, you are not riding along [on the train]" (Nunberg and Federn, 1974, p. 219). Such an interpretation implies an unconscious reference to time as future. To the extent, however, that the fear of dying derives from the childhood fear of castration or separation from a love object, the true perspective of the dream is with reference to the past. Freud, indeed, compared the missed-train dream to another common recurrent dream, the so-called examination dream, which handles anxiety over some current problem by restaging a problematic situation from the past—a classroom examination—that one has been able to overcome.

A special sense of time that refers to a strange familiarity with a certain landscape or locality, what is known as *déjà vu* experience, when it occurs in a dream has, according to Freud (1900), a special meaning: "These places are invariably the genitals of the dreamer's mother; there is indeed no other place about which one can assert with such conviction that one has been there once before" (p. 399).

To the extent that affects—beyond the elementary affective polarity of pleasure–unpleasure—are time bound and dreams have an interest in neutralizing disturbing affects (typically by displacement of their ideational representation to an indifferent object or event [1900]), one might expect them to become disengaged from the dimension of time. As I have shown elsewhere (1972), certain painful affects, such as anxiety, are predicated on the idea of time as future, contained in the idea of confrontation with some vague or explicit danger to the intergrity of the self; while another category of painful affects, such as depression, are predicated on the idea that something detrimental to the self (a loss or failure important enough to lower one's self-esteem) has happened and lies, irrevocable, in the never-never land of the past. The elimination or displacement, of its component sense of time as future or past, would either neutralize the painful affect or convert it into a present-oriented affect, such as anger or boredom (restlessness, impatience), with which a dream can cope by means of immediate action. The following dream may illustrate the point:

> *Dream 6.* "My father was murdered by some robbers; they held my mom, and she had to watch and they cut him into pieces. They cut his legs and arms off and he died praying. The pieces were nailed to a board. The first couple of days I behaved like nothing happened. Two days after he died it hit me, and I cried and I cried at the funeral."

The dreamer felt nothing while her father was dying in the process of being mutilated and crucified (incidentally, the father was a minister). Devoid of time perspective, his death elicited no affect in his daughter and allowed her sleep to continue. The introduction of the time element as past ("two days after he died") made the father's demise meaningful, and the dreamer experienced appropriate feelings of sadness and guilt. How she was able to witness the father's tortured death without horror (a feeling dominated by the sense of time as present) or action may be explained by assuming that the idea of mutilation was displaced from the father's genital organs to his extremities, and that the blame for the cruel act was projected onto the mother, who was in effect the one watching in the dream.

Ordinarily, time can be felt directly as the sense of duration, time moving slowly, fast, or not at all; or indirectly, as tense or perspective, in the context of some time-bound affect, such as anxiety with its sense of expectancy or anticipation of something dangerous for the integrity of the self. But when the affect becomes too intense, the sense of time as perspective becomes secondary or disappears and is replaced instead by the sense of time as duration, until affect and time blend into one ineffable, unbearable experience, and the person loses consciousness. When that happens in a dream, the person wakes up. This is usually the case with nightmares, which contain both an element of fear or pain and the experience of time as dragging out or standing still, a time sense that is the contrary to the experience of timelessness. Erotic dreams have a similar composition and fate: thick, intense pleasure combined with the feeling that time is running out, as if compressed in a capsule or going so far as to disappear into nowhere. Paradoxically, as the person wakes up from such dreams, he feels as if they have lasted an eternity; and he has a hard time to shake away the affect.

Dreams involving a massive discharge of affect stem in all probability from early childhood experiences referring to the primary object relation with mother or father. They tend to recur. They are in essence screen memories of early object relations, as in the following recurrent dream (borrowed from an article by Smith [Stein, 1965, p. 315]).

Dream 7. I am in this space—a nothingness—with no darkness but a diffuse light as if I am on an infinite plane in a kind of foreverness. In the dream [last night] it was like walking through air where everything is white, but the air has some kind of resistance to it like gelatin. There is a corollary dream of being with my mother in some sort of space but with a sense of rooms and soft carpeting—but all with a colorlessness, whiteness. My mother is only a shape or a presence, and I'm very small. It's like getting away to some place where everything is sufficient.

There is here the suggestion of a longing for a close relationship similar to the one that presumably exists in an early phase of infant development with mother, a symbiotic relationship that is characterized by a spaceless quality ("a nothingness") and timelessness ("a kind of foreverness") that is neither spaceless nor timeless really, but embedded in a world of infinite space and time, a boundless world that is described by adults as a mystical or religious experience—an ineffable experience, as they would point out, because it sounds so contradictory when described in terms of space and time. The same contradiction is evident in the above dream. As mystics do, the dreamer is struggling to get around the paradox of representing space and time as senseless or nonexistent when he feels so positive about them, by invoking the sensory dimensions of sight and touch. He describes space in terms of a "diffuse light" and a "colorlessness" that is "really whiteness," and the experience of time as "walking through air [. . . that] has some kind of resistance to it like gelatin." He also identifies mother in terms of space and time as "only a shape or a presence," and the regressive act of reliving the experience in the dream, the reversal of time, as traveling through space away from the here and now, "getting away to some place where everything is sufficient." The awareness of the self as something "very small" next to the mother's "shape or presence" suggests the remoteness of the experience in time through the visual perspective of appearing small in the distance. The idea of smallness also suggests the beginning of a self–object differentiation, something that is further implied in the identification of the space that mother occupies as one "with a sense of rooms and soft carpeting."

In fact, a dream is the closest thing to a mystical experience that an ordinary individual may claim. The blissful experience we can gain in a dream seems to be predicated on the ability of the self to become oblivious of all sensory input, to either ignore it or dissociate it from its material, objective source in the outside world or within one's own body. Whether a metaphor or psychophysical reality, the idea that the body–ego is decathected and all available instinctual energy is concentrated on the mental images of the internal self–object world describes best, so far as I am concerned, the situation that prevails in the dream. Energylike attention, withdrawn from sensory organs and voluntary muscles, cathects the visceral part of the organism, accounting for the warm relaxation, a melting-away-like feeling, experienced as we are about to fall asleep. When this energylike attention flows, so to speak, away from the mental representation of the viscera and cathects exclusively the mental representations of the internal self–object world, a dream is born: consciousness of the mental representations without awareness of the material, time-bound, objective world.

Summary

Like the unconscious, a dream is not bound by the constraints of time; as with the unconscious, however, the so-called "timelessness" of the dream is only relative. Both the experience and the concept of time may be present, either openly or implicitly, in the manifest content of the dream. Time as perspective is typically represented in spatial terms, time as duration in terms of motion or situations involving time-bound affects. The concept or experience of time in the manifest dream may signify an unconscious conflict. When time is explicit, the conflict is likely to refer to an early event or relationship; when time is disguised or implicit in the dream experience, it may signify a current conflict, one involving a contemporary relationship or an early relationship reactivated in the transference. By eliminating time perspective, the dream work can make painful affects more tolerable and thus prevent awakening.

Chapter 32

THE CONCURRENT PRESENTATION OF A RARE DETAIL IN THE DREAMS OF TWO PATIENTS

EARL A. LOOMIS

One morning a middle-aged unmarried woman brought me a dream containing the following elements: A goat with a prominent scrotum was observed eating grass, and the patient—a woman of fifty-odd years—felt suddenly uncomfortable. She awoke tense and anxious. She had no dream associations from the previous day, but did think the dream reminded her of her rural upbringing. She could not bring herself to recall whether or not she had ever seen the scrotum of a goat as a child. She was sure her family had never kept male goats, and she wondered if she had seen them at neighbors' farms. The scrotum itself suggested, interestingly enough (after the expected phallus), the bosom, and the two testes corresponded to the two *breasts*. The scrotal *sac* next reminded her of her handbag, a new one, whose shape was vaguely suggestive. The latter had been bought because a gift purse had been disappointing. Purse in turn suggested vagina and vagina her own dissatisfactions with her sexless life. Thus the breasts and vagina appeared ultimately to be concealed in the woman's dream of a goat's scrotum.

I was naturally intrigued by this rare detail, since goats and scrotums are both relatively rare manifest dream symbols, and also because the combination of the two was altogether new to me.

This paper was first published in the *Journal of the American Psychoanalytic Association* (1956), 4:53–54.

When, later in the day, a younger woman with almost the converse sexual problems (superficially viewed) announced that she had dreamed of a large animal with pendulous testes and horned head, my interest was further aroused. She could not name it at first, wondering if it was wild or tame, African or American. She finally described it as some kind of goat. Associations led principally to the scrotum, reminding her of two principal themes—her hostile, biting fantasies in connection with the fantasy or act of taking the testes of her lover into her mouth, and the purse she had recently heard about. She seemed to enjoy relating that this purse had been imported and was made of the scrotum of an animal, perhaps a water buffalo. The latter reminded her of her hostile, depreciating attitudes toward men (as well as women) and her need to castrate and paralyze anyone with strength. She gave evidence of this as she mused whether the scrotum had been taken from the buffalo before or after his death—and how, if the former, he had managed without it. Doubtless, she felt, he had been "taken down a peg by losing his balls."

Since, as we know, the unconscious of each individual always uses data in its own private way, it is not surprising that each of these two women demonstrated her personal use of the goat theme. The appearance of this detail led me to a good deal of speculation regarding the possible meaning of its concurrence in the lives of two women of over thirty years' difference in age, with vastly different cultural, social, religious, and ethnic backgrounds, and with no known outside contact, save through the rarest passing in my hallway or waiting room. I am sure they did not even know one another's names.

As I pondered over this material, it came to me that the previous day I had heard a story from another patient that had to do with the castrating of pigs. A fresh and painful association of my own then cropped up: I had heard still another story—many years previously—of a *farmer* who allegedly castrated pigs by biting off their testes. I still could not see the source of the goat material until a further association intruded—again from my own past. This farmer had goats and a cart with which he hauled milk. Later, when he had given the goats to his small sons for their amusement, the male goat became obstreperous. I had a fragmentary recollection, which later was confirmed, to the effect that the he-goat had therefore been castrated.

This group of associations demonstrated that the goat–scrotum theme had been in my own unconscious. However, it suggested in no way how and why the theme was conveyed (if it was) to these two women patients, so different from one another, and to no others, so far as I detected at the time.

Presuming the possibility of a "how" by some means of nonconscious and indirect communication, one can go further in speculating *why* these symbols appeared in the two women and how subtle differences in their associations served to demonstrate some important contrasts in their characterology, transference, and current stage in analysis.

The substitution of "udder" as the intermediary—a condensation of breast and scrotum—may aid in this comparison. For one woman this compromise is unacceptable, and her biting hatred remains focused on the genitals. For the other the sucking need finds fulfillment in the midway point of the udder.

The choice of the goat as the animal puzzled me for a long time. My current hypothesis grew in part from my assumption that since it occurred in both patients, it had to do with something or someone they had in common—and that was *myself*. Then it occurred to me that both women had attended a football game in which the Navy team was a contender, that I had shortly before announced that I would be going into the service again and that it would be the Naval branch. And the Navy team's mascot is, of course, a goat. There was the venerable animal. And I was the goat!

It is noteworthy that the goat associations are all from me—the women never did account for the goats' origins. Perhaps this is because it was material too near the transference and my threatened departure—to which the first woman reacted with associations to nursing and the second to castrating and biting.

Chapter 33

OBSERVATIONS ON BLANK DREAMS
WITH ORGASMS

MARK KANZER

Current interest in blank dreams with orgasms has been initiated by the studies of Bertram D. Lewin (1948, 1950), who traces such dreams to earliest recollections of nursing at the breast followed by sleep. Clinically such dreams are of significance in denoting the onset of hypomanic conditions as well as in other crises within the personality (Rycroft, 1951). Recently Lewin has applied his observation of the blank dream and the related dream screen to illuminate the problem of forgetting dreams. "The forgotten dream is a concrete object, which has been as if physically lost or misplaced," he states. Although of the opinion that the forgetting of dreams must always, or practically always, be interpreted in oral terms, he concedes that "some day some additional interpretation may be discovered and empirically substantiated" (1953a, pp. 191–202).

Clinical evidence is presented which provides additional interpretations that may be attached to the forgetting of dreams, particularly when such forgetting is associated with blank dreams accompanied by orgasm. This forgetting is related to defenses of the ego against anal and phallic sexuality. Perhaps the fact that our analysand was not suffering from a severe disorder permits a clearer demonstration of the dynamics in later stages of personality development.

A thirty-year-old man, with a tendency to premature ejaculation, had the fantasy during intercourse that he was raped by

This paper was first published in the *Psychoanalytic Quarterly* (1954), 23:511–520.

the female and sought to withhold the semen which she actively sucked from him. This surrender of control was regressive, and averted the danger of castration by the father as punishment for aggressive masculinity. An anal determinant of the sexual fantasy was found in occasions in childhood when his mother forced him to submit to enemas. He would retain the fluid as long as possible until it burst forth against his will with physically and emotionally shattering consequences.

In the transference the analyst was to be seduced into becoming a similarly raping mother. A period of teasing and of provocative conduct ushered in the "blank dream with orgasm." The patient reacted to the analysis as unreal and pictured it in dreams as a burlesque or television show. Once he fell asleep on the couch and dreamed that his younger brother was passing a yellow pencil to him. Impulses to flee and to move to other cities revealed the terror beneath these defenses; at the same time, exhibitionistic and pregenital drives combined to develop a positive transference that seemed to be especially dangerous.

These drives began to break through in witty but anxious overtures that bore some resemblance to a mild hypomanic attack. The patient recounted jokes and smutty stories, ostentatiously acted at ease, and at parties attempted to attract attention to his entertaining qualities, for example, by blowing smoke rings. The first of the blank dreams occurred when he was awakened by the ringing of the telephone. He discovered that he had had an ejaculation and, on becoming aware of this, recalled sensations as of urine trickling out. An excessively anxious reaction followed in which he feared that his defenses were breaking down, that he would be unable to control himself, and that he would become entirely impotent through analysis.

A few days later three dreams occurred in one night. In the first, he stood at the edge of a swimming pool watching airplanes racing and making a turn about a tall landmark. One plane was heard to throttle its engine and then crashed into a building, ejecting the pilot who fell into the pool. His body was fished out, stiff as a board and with the left leg severed at the knee. Then came a dream which just "slipped away." In the third dream, the patient in his sleep seemed to be straining to move his bowels but could not do so. The thought came to him to get up and take a laxative, yet at the same time he had the contradictory misgiving that if he continued to strain, a bowel movement would take place in bed.

Associations led to childhood experiences of bed-wetting and also to an involuntary bowel movement in school when the teacher ignored his pleas to leave the room. Our interest attaches particularly to the forgotten middle dream. Taking it as a real object, in the manner suggested by Lewin, it may be equated with the lost leg of the pilot who was killed in the first dream. In its middle position between the other two dreams, it is a phallus replaced by a gaping hole; it is also feces that have slipped away. The first dream warns of a turning point which will result in a crack-up and death by a phallic attack; anal and birth fantasies are contained in the image of the body falling into the water; a stiff penis is equated with a corpse and castration. The crack-up itself proves to be an orgasm which splits the body of the patient just as it splits the dream. This catastrophe is inhibited by awakening, however, and is followed by a regressive substitution of anal sensations in the third dream, which further serves to deny and repress the entire erotic fantasy. The contents of the body have not been lost, according to this formula, but have been returned to the rectum and placed under control.

Freud described the forgotten portion of a dream which the analysand reported as "wiped out"; analysis revealed infantile reminiscences of listening to someone wiping himself after defecation (1900). Conversely, an act of anal defiance broke through the amnestic dream screen of the Wolf Man and restored in disguised form the repressed memory of the primal scene (Kepecs, 1952). During his development our patient had sought to control his oral and genital impulses by invoking anal sphincter mechanisms as a means of defense. As in the formula adopted by the Wolf Man, the shutting of the sphincter was paralleled by a shutting of the eyelids, with corresponding inhibition of voyeuristic impulses. The inability to see, represented sensorially by the blank dream, may thus be an expression of motor paralysis and conflict, just as is the inability to move in other dreams that portray the restraint placed upon voluntary motor processes. Actually, quivering of the eyelids became a disturbing symptom during the "blank dream" phase of our patient's analysis.

Further observation showed that blank dreams with orgasm were likely to follow his sexual relations with his wife and, as in the third of the dream fragments described, had the significance of denying the coital experience and permitting it to merge with the blacked-out components of the seminal emission that occurred during sleep. Progress in the analysis revived an earlier adolescent phase when nocturnal ejaculation had been accompanied by visually perceived images which were remembered. Characteristically, these dreams consisted of foreplay with nude women; at the moment of contact between the genitals, however, ejaculation occurred and the patient believed that he induced this deliberately, even in sleep, to avoid the dangers of penetration. Analysis of these dreams and their associations showed strong fetishistic interest in breasts and legs which were equated with maternal phalli. By contrast, the sight or touch of the female genitals resulted in terror and ejaculation; it is likely that our patient's blank dream itself stemmed from a visual concentration upon the "nothingness" of the vagina (Medusa reaction).

It appears possible then that the equation of dream screen with breast described by Lewin may sometimes be regressive, covering underlying fantasies of a maternal phallus. Correspondingly the "lost dream" as a real object refers to the castrated condition of the mother. In another tripartite dream sequence of our patient it is possible to trace such a reference, as well as the more infantile attachment to the breast.

The first of this series was an anxiety dream in which the sleeper drew from his mouth a whole row of teeth. Associations brought to light habits of sucking on fountain pens and other objects, and of scraping off and swallowing fragments of tartar from the teeth. The tartar suggested semen and milk to the patient; the teeth themselves served correspondingly in his fantasies to represent not only breasts but also part of a dentate vagina which drew nourishment from phalli. The teeth were also words uttered during the analysis which the dreamer wished to revoke and put back into his mouth. Lorand has suggested that the dream of losing teeth ultimately expresses the desire to return to infancy; in the same sense, through the equation of teeth with words, safety might be attained through regression to the preverbal period (1948).

Our analysand's dream of losing teeth was followed by a blank dream with orgasm (the blankness perhaps representing the mouth from which all teeth have been drawn) and then by a third dream in which the equation of legs with teeth permits insight into the completion of the underlying processes of thought. In this last member of the series, the dreamer was lying on a football field while two teams of players, including his brothers, swept back and forth over him. He seemed to have no feelings except of intellectual detachment. Glancing at a scoreboard, however, he noticed that one team was beating the other twenty-seven to twenty-two, and he was surprised that so many points had been made.

This dream, like the concluding portion of the earlier tripartite series, shows a reparation of defenses that have broken down in the first and are followed by an orgastic eruption in the second portion. A state of rest is restored after a catastrophe and the dreamer is able to project the active conflicts away from himself and return to sleep. Using the formula "legs equal teeth," he is being eaten by the two teams of brothers (jaws) that sweep over him alternately. His own body is a breast placed at their disposal; nevertheless he remains unconsumed and free of affect—a triumph of the repressive functions. Nursing at the breast, projected in this way, again becomes a preliminary to welcome sleep, not castration or death.

The numbers of the scoreboard proved, through analysis, to be related to the loss and acquisition of teeth; yet in another context they have symbolic meaning in terms of pregnancy and of competition with the father over the size of the family (as well as grudging tribute to the analyst over the points scored). In terms of the leg symbolism, the patient submits masochistically to being trampled on by his brothers and—in his reclining position—has lost the use of his own legs as well as his teeth. He is castrated and must submit to his brothers in intercourse. Fear of being kicked in the genitals did in reality deter him from playing football at one period of his life.

In both tripartite dreams, it may be noted, the first install-ment deals with upper regions of the body or world, from which there is a fall; the third deals with lower regions; in between and associated with orgasm are obviously the genitals. The interest in the oral zone, which is regularly associated with the complex breast and dream screen, is therefore probably often an upward displacement from the dreaded yet fascinating maternal vulva. The blank dreams, in our case, seem to have their origin in adolescent dreams with seminal emission in which vision and dreaming were both arrested at the moment of penetrating the vagina. In this sense is to be understood the mythological blinding of Oedipus, of Perseus, and of Orestes when, in various symbolic forms, they made their entrance into the darkness of the mother's body.

A similar reaction, more limited in extent and without or-gasm, was reported by Freud (1900) when he translated the comment of a patient, "at this point [in my dream] there was a gap" which meant, "at this point I saw the female genitals" (pp. 232–233). The blank dream seems to represent an extreme instance of visual block which in milder forms merely blurs and partially obscures elements of the dream field. The extent and intensity of the obliteration correspond apparently to the de-gree of shock associated with the sight of the maternal genital, as in the familiar castration fears that give rise to nightmares and other disturbances following the primal scene (Stern, 1951, 1953). Partial blocking out of the dream field has been ob-served, for instance, in which only the heads or faces of dream figures have been thus affected. In Ferenczi's opinion, incestu-ous motives lay concealed behind such phenomena. In one case that he described (1908) the dreamer would awaken in time to prevent sexual union and ejaculation; this patient, with fetishis-tic inclinations and disturbances of potency, showed distinct resemblances to the one here reported. It is not unlikely, more-over, that the typical dream of nakedness, in which the faces of the spectators are dim, has the same meaning; the "faces" represent displaced and visually repressed genitals.

Memories of the maternal genitals—which would disturb sleep—can therefore be warded off by a series of defenses which include inhibition of the visual function and regression to earlier stages of libidinal satisfaction in relation to the mother. Just as the fetishist clings to the recollection of the hair or garment that occupied his attention at the last moment before the shocking sight of the vulva, so in retrospect the eyes fix upon the breasts before repeating their descent to lower regions of the female body, a process that is represented as a lowering (of vision) which encounters only blandness as it passes over the genitals. The ensuing visual isolation of this region is reproduced in the blank middle portion of the tripartite dreams described. The concomitant orgasm, however, is evidence of the repressed voyeuristic impulse and testifies, moreover, to the oedipal basis of these psychic mechanisms; furthermore, by ridding the body of tension, the orgasm supplements the visual block as a defense against the perpetuation of dangerous instinctual excitement.

The severe curtailment of both sensory and motor functions associated with these reactions is indicative of a momentous crisis. What takes place is the confrontation of the oedipal drives at their moment of strongest expression (conjuring up and imaginatively participating in the primal scene) with the most unrelenting threat of castration. An important element in the ensuing symptoms is the bisexuality of the dreamer's identifications. The masculine desire to penetrate is warded off at the crucial moment by feminine components which, by contracting sphincters and eyelids, shut out the penis and its phallic equivalent, light. Both tendencies achieve release in the act of ejaculation.

The balance between sleeping and waking is drawn into the struggle; feminine and masculine interpretations of the wish to sleep vie for dominance. Sleep as an aggressive and masculine activity is delineated in such symbols as the crashing airplane and the triumphant scoring of touchdowns in the dreams of our patient. Metapsychologically, this aspect derives from the defusion of instincts as the ego, pursuing the wish to sleep, moves to rejoin the id. The image of the infant at the mother's breast offers a satisfying point of transformation from the active to the passive disposition that is required for sleep.

Similar imagery permits actual penetration of the vagina during intercourse, as in the case we have reported. By means of foreplay and reversed positions (the female above) coitus is transformed into oral and anal pantomimes which relieve the castration threat and deny the existence of the vagina; the male, when beneath, is the woman's phallus. Of interest is the divided identity thus achieved with the partner. Before the orgasm, the man is the mother feeding the voracious child; afterwards identifications are interchanged and he is the satisfied child. In anal terms, he is forced to yield the contents of his body which, after the ejaculation, are found deposited in his own body through the same reintrojection of the partner.

All active impulses may be thus projected and indirectly satisfied. The suppression of active perceptive and motor functions is most completely attained in the blank dream, which marks the extinction of the ego as it surrenders the capacities that distinguish it from the id. Fantasies of death and rebirth naturally adhere to this event. The orgasm then may represent the last convulsive effort of the ego to cling to life, with the ejaculatory spasm isolated from and a signal for complete reorganization within the remainder of the personality. When, because of such dangerous implications, the ego dares not relinquish sufficient control to permit sleep, the tensions may be carried over into a dreamlike awakening in which the identifications and the instinctual goals remain confused.

As in the Schreber case, and in others reported by Lewin, such states may usher in a psychosis. The orgasm then becomes conducive not to a discharge but to an intensification of anxieties, and the disposition noted by Ferenczi and Lewin to a succession of ejaculations during the night may prove to repeat and take on aspects of the original trauma. Like a manic attack, an orgasm serves to deny the threat of castration; with the failure of this defense, sexual fulfillment and castration become increasingly as one. In milder disturbances, however, the resultant symptoms are much attenuated and may consist only of such relatively innocuous disturbances as a tendency to premature ejaculation, transient feelings of unreality, or euphoric moods.

Summary

Forgotten dreams, particularly blank dreams accompanied by orgasm, are traced in their multiple significance through various levels of personality development. Their relationship to shock at the sight of the mother's genitals is stressed and linked with milder and partial obliterations of the dream field that occur in other disorder. Premature ejaculation, for example, may be the waking equivalent of a blank dream with orgasm.

Section VII

Resistance, Transference, and Dreams

This section presents articles on how resistances, and transference (including countertransference), manifest themselves in dreams. It begins with two seminal articles on the resistance nature of the written dream. The first, Lipschutz's "The Written Dream" (1954), compares a patient's verbal and written versions of a number of dreams and demonstrates the remarkable difference between the verbal and written content of such dreams; the article ends with a series of well-formulated resistances associated with the written dream. The second article, Blum's "Notes on the Written Dream" (1968), presents in part the interesting finding that the written dream can serve an adaptive purpose.

Following this, the phenomenon of the analyst appearing undisguised in the dream is discussed in Yazamajian's article, "First Dreams Directly Representing the Analyst" (1964). Here he shows how the undisguised representation of the analyst was an attempt to treat him as a "real" person and thus avoid investing him with symbolic importance—in effect, a resistance to transference formation. A primary defense used by this patient, both in his dreams and in real life, was a "flight into reality." Later as the regression in the transference took place, the analyst as an undisguised dream-figure disappeared and was replaced by disguised symbolic figures.

The next article, Keith's "Some Aspects of Transference in Dream Research" (1962), reports on a unique clinical experiment in which transference reactions of patient-subjects toward the dream-researcher are assessed in terms of the effect it had on their dream as revealed by the Kleitman–Dement electroencephalographic technique.

Two articles relating countertransference phenomena to dreams are next presented. Ross and Kapp's article, "A Technique for Self Analysis of Countertransference" (1962), reports on a clinical technique in which visual images of the analyst, in response to the patient's description of his dreams, are used by the analyst as the starting point for uncovering previously undiscovered countertransference responses. And Whitman, Kramer, and Baldridge's article, "Dreams about the Patient: An Approach to the Problem of Countertransference" (1969), discusses a multifaceted study involving psychotherapists (of many different stages of training and orientation) dreaming about their patients, holding that such countertransference indicators can be used in a creative, interpretive fashion rather than be seen merely as a resistance.

The section ends with two clinical papers demonstrating the dream's unique role via interpretation and hidden transference reactions. The first paper, "Termination of a Symptom" (Hurwitz, 1966), describes a clinical vignette (occurring during an analysis) in which a patient's amenorrhea suddenly and dramatically ended after a dream's interpretation. While in the second paper, "Dreams and the Latent Negative Transference" (1975), Izner supports the thesis that the phenomenon of reversal in dreams may be related to specific levels in the defensive organization of the ego—which has been structured as a form of distortion—in order to ward off the expression of latent negative feelings in the transference. He observes that dreams of this nature (i.e., containing many reversal elements) might be considered a distinctive clue to the existence of latent hostile feelings and can be validly interpreted on this basis.

Chapter 34

THE WRITTEN DREAM

Louis S. Lipschutz

Fliess (1948) refers to the written dream as a "much overdetermined typical piece of 'acting out' " (pp. 95–96). Freud (1912), in referring to psychoanalysts instructing patients to write down their dreams, stated: "This direction is superfluous in the treatment. . . . Even if the substance of a dream is in this way laboriously rescued from oblivion, it is easy enough to convince oneself that nothing has thereby been achieved for the patient. The associations will not come to the text and the result is the same as if the dream had not been preserved" (pp. 95–96). He later stated (1933b): "A patient may try to combat the forgetting of his dreams by writing them down immediately after he wakes up. We may as well tell him that it is useless to do so, because the resistance from which he may have preserved the text of the dream will then transfer itself to the associations and render the manifest dream inaccessible for the interpretation" (pp. 95–96).

Abraham (1913b) and Sharpe (1937) described the written dream as a transference dream, a highly invested narcissistic product, a symbolic gift, and emphasized its anal aspects.

On the basis of these observations and their own experience, most analysts do not encourage the writing of dreams, or ignore the written dream if it is brought to the analysis. However, we know that psychoanalysis must regard with interest and curiosity every aspect of the patient's behavior. The writing of dreams during analysis is not an unusual occurrence, and the analyst not infrequently is presented with this form of behavior.

This paper was first published in the *Journal of the American Psychoanalytic Association* (1954), 2:473–478.

An opportunity to study this further came when a twenty-three-year-old, single man, toward the end of his first year in analysis, began writing down his dreams and bringing them to the analysis. At this time he was defending himself against a strong positive transference. Formerly seclusive and sexually inhibited, he had recently begun an affair and had experienced coitus for the first time.

The first indication was in the patient's changed manner. This hour he appeared less anxious and tense, spoke more freely and fluently, and did not keep his hands folded behind his head as he usually did. He then described a dream which was richer in detail than previous dreams, had more narrative continuity, and was told more promptly. Inquiry as to the reason for this change in describing the dream disclosed that this dream had been written down immediately upon awaking, and was being carried in his wallet.

When it was learned that he had not looked at the dream since writing it down, he was asked to continue with his associations and, finally, to read the written dream. It was thus possible to compare directly the verbal and written dreams. During the following two weeks, each hour brought a written dream, presented in the same way.

Four of these dreams will be described in their verbal and written forms so that they may be compared.

Dream 1

Verbal: A beverage cooler with clear bottles. One colored red is tilted at an angle. It seems to belong to a vice-president. He wanted to move it but I wouldn't let him because it would spoil the tests I was making.

Written: A beverage cooler which is filled with pop bottles. I find one which is cocked at an angle. I take it out, angry because it was put there by a vice-president and I say it will ruin the test.

The contrast between the verbal and written dreams is obvious. The written dream is more disguised and actually contradicts the verbal dream. By its distortion, the patient angrily removes the red pop bottle, the penis, from the beverage cooler, the vagina. In the verbal dream he insists that it remain, so that the written dream becomes a defense against the patient's passive feminine wishes as expressed in the verbal dream.

Dream 2

Verbal: I am getting dressed in girl's clothes to go somewhere. I don't know how the fellows will take it so I change back, feeling disappointed.

Written: I get all dressed in girl's clothes but I feel it isn't being received well by the fellows so I put on my own clothes and feel relief.

Again the written dream directly contradicts the verbal. In the verbal dream, the feeling is one of disappointment at having to change back because it is doubtful how the fellows (analyst) will take it. In the written dream the feeling is one of relief.

Dream 3

Verbal: I am in a race. A girl is ahead. We run around three pylon stakes. I eventually won.

Written: I am in an endurance race which is being run around two stakes. I am all out of breath but I win. The runner-up seems to be feminine. I remember being breathless.

Again the contrast is obvious, although not as direct as in the previous two dreams. In the verbal dream the girl is ahead, although the patient eventually wins. In the written dream the patient wins and the girl is second (runner-up). And the written dream which emphasizes that masculinity is ahead seems to represent a defense against the verbal dream somewhat like "the girl is ahead. . . . Eventually I will be a man, but at present I still wish to be a girl."

Dream 4

Verbal: You had a hand in taking

Written: GB's equipment, lathes

GB's tools. You are trying to help me. We are trying to help me. We are in our hot room (a laboratory where refrigeration equipment is tested) making dolls.

and other tools, are being hauled out of production quality, and I find out from you that CD (a girl with whom the patient has been identified) is going to make babies under your supervision.

Here the written version is so elaborated that a girl, CD, is making babies, whereas in the verbal version there is no mention of a girl, and the babies (dolls) are made directly with the patient. In the written version GB's equipment, etc., is hauled away in an impersonal manner, whereas in the verbal version his tools are taken away by the analyst.

The remarkable difference between the verbal and written content of these dreams, and the altered manner of the patient in terms of removing his hands from behind his head, displaying less tension and speaking with more assurance and fluidity, impressed me with the need for dealing directly with the written dream as a resistance. This was done midway through the second week of this period by inquiry regarding the manner of writing the dreams, his feelings at this time, and his feeling about having the written dream on his person during the hour. Along with this, the obvious contradictions in dream content were pointed out and interpreted.

The patient said he felt more secure with the written dream on his person, which he usually kept folded in his wallet in his back pocket. "It is as if I have something to fall back on. It disturbs me not to read dreams or bring them. I won't have anything to bring."

The day following the interpretation he described a dream which had not been written down:

There is an ice-cream cabinet with a gap on the bottom. I am talking on the phone to L (a man in the E department who challenged me and whom no one likes). Someone (J) alongside me warned, "You better be careful what you say," and I revised my conversation accordingly.

The ice-cream cabinet with the gap on the bottom is the patient in a feminine role. Talking on the phone to a person one cannot see represents the analysis. L is obviously the analyst, who even has the same initials. The dream confirms the interpretation and reminds one of Freud's comments about corroborating dreams (1911b). It seems to say: "The analyst sees through my deception (in the written dream). He no longer will permit it so that I cannot use this form of deception (writing) any longer and will have to be careful about what I say" (p. 96).

He then described the process of writing down the dream on awaking. It was spasmodic in character. There would be a flow of words, then a pause, a period of increasing tension, then another flow of words accompanied by relief; and the process would continue until the dream was written. He quickly recognized that these feelings were similar to those he had while defecating and while taking examinations where his writing had a similar spasmodic quality, and during which he had once masturbated. He said, "The anxiety is similar to that when I was writing examinations. At first nothing would come, then I would start writing, feel relieved, pause, become tense, start writing again, and so on."

The nature of the patient's handwriting in these written dreams should be mentioned. In contrast to his usual rather neat and even writing, these were sprawling and smeary, uneven, smudged, and written with a soft pencil. The papers were all of the same size, texture, and of thin stock. They came from a desk calendar pad about 4 × 5 inches, torn off at the top, neatly folded, and carried in a wallet in the back pocket.

The following conclusions are suggested:

1. The form in which a dream is presented has specific meaning and should be studied and investigated the same as any other detail of the patient's behavior in analysis. It represents, as Fliess has stated, "a much overdetermined typical piece of 'acting out.'"
2. The writing of dreams can have the following meanings at different levels:

    a. A gift of feces to the mother with whom the analyst was identified, to placate or win approval.

    b. A more disguised expression of the wish to have an anal baby with analyst as father, as in the "doll dream."

    c. A defense against castration fear by producing and retaining an anal penis, as represented by the written dream brought to the analysis.

3. The written dream is always a transference dream produced specifically for the analyst, to deceive, confuse, placate, or please him.

4. Greater distortion is possible in the written dream since writing is genetically a later ego function than talking. The ego mechanisms of defense therefore influence the written dream more than the verbal dream.

5. The written dream should be considered as an expression of resistance and so treated. By doing so with this patient it became possible to "work through" his passive feelings in the transference and uncover the underlying aggressive oedipal feelings.

6. These conclusions may also apply to notes, letters, autobiographies, and other written productions which may be brought to analysis.

Chapter 35

NOTES ON THE WRITTEN DREAM

HAROLD P. BLUM

The late Sidney Tarachow was very fond of the clinical example in which clinical material is used to illustrate and perhaps extend theoretical conceptions. Utilizing such a clinical example, this paper will deal with certain theoretical aspects of the written dream. This phenomenon will be reported as it spontaneously appeared in the psychoanalysis of a married mother in her early forties. Aspects of the resistance and transference meanings of the written dream will be reexamined in regard to the psychoanalytic situation and dream psychology. Its relation to childhood learning symptoms and certain problems in development, maturation, and sublimation will be given new consideration.

The written dream is scrutinized as a symptomatic action, an overdetermined communication which utilizes both more primitive and more complex ego functions than verbalization in free association. The following material is a summarized case history in which particular attention is paid to the pertinent data. This patient was referred for analysis after an unsuccessful two-and-a-quarter years of stalemated treatment with her previous analyst. Frequently silent, sleepy, and obsessionally focused on boring, petty details, she remained remote from her overwhelming and urgent problems. She was an obsessional character, was often depressed and occasionally had suicidal thoughts. She would compulsively overeat and engage in frequently unsuccessful diets. Her appearance was that of a short,

---

This paper was first published in the *Journal of Hillside Hospital* (1968), 17:67–78.

stocky, but not markedly obese woman, with a rather sad coun-
tenance and relatively restricted motility on the couch which
indicated the frozen nature of her feelings and the rigid control
over her inner tensions. She often felt "like a violin string."
She was frequently preoccupied with financial problems and
claimed that she had discontinued her first analysis primarily
because she could not afford the additional funds. She suffered
from spastic colitis with attacks of cramps, diarrhea, and constipation, as well as occasional headaches and feelings of weight-
lessness in her hands and head. She was rigid, relatively unable
to adapt to any change in her life, and constantly feeling imposed upon by her husband and sons. There was frequent
bickering with her family, quarreling with her husband over
his penuriousness, and with her sons over their excessive demands and irresponsibility.

Her early history was difficult to obtain and considerably
traumatic. She had one sibling two-and-a-half years older, but
an older brother had died of pneumonia before the patient was
born. While telling her that she was lucky to have a brother,
her mother described how she had tried to abort her, indicating
that she was a bitterly unwanted child. At age seven she developed a severe case of pertussis, lost considerable time in school,
and then on return to school showed a remarkable learning
block, with some reading disability, resulting in her being left
back. She remained a mediocre student, and although she attempted college she left because she was unable to concentrate.
There was considerable sexual and aggressive overstimulation
in the family—she had been allowed to share a room with her
brother until she was eleven years of age. Of special importance
was her enormous jealousy of both her living and dead brothers, and the intense fantasy life she had concerning the latter.
In her analysis it appeared that these fantasies were probably
communicated by and shared with her mother, serving to protect her from abortion as well as to protect her mother from
her unconscious murderous hate. She would identify with her
dead brother and engage in masochistic activities to win her
mother's love and to ward off retaliation.

She married a rigid, aloof, and aggressively militant pseu-
do-masculine first husband who died of pulmonary cancer two

years after their marriage. She felt no regrets and later met and married another sexually inadequate man who finally entered psychoanalysis because of constant premature ejaculation. Her first analyst was recommended by her husband's analyst, but it is of considerable importance that her husband had been analyzed through a psychoanalytic clinic. During the analysis it developed that the patient had been enraged at her own later rejection by the clinic and the revival of earlier feelings of jealous hatred toward a favored brother. She interpreted her husband's low fee as proof that he was more accepted and desired. Two themes which became apparent were that she had killed off her first analyst at a point where the first husband had died and her brother was "born"; that she began treatment with me when she had a dead husband, dead brother, and then a "dead" analyst. There were frequent references to pulmonary disease and several times she developed hysterical chest pains. There was a constant intensification of symptoms and aggravation of her stubborn silences and petty verbalized meanderings around the beginning of the month which proved to be inescapably related to the presentation of the bill.

It became apparent that one difference in her second analysis was that she was presented with a bill, whereas the first analyst had invited her to simply tally her own sessions and to present a check during the month at her convenience. With frequent associations and analytic observations of patterns of withholding and cheating, she then revealed that her husband had cheated his first analyst by continuing to pay a markedly reduced fee long after his income had risen considerably. He had therefore cheated his first analyst as she unconsciously was doing through identification with her husband. Her husband had urged her not to tell her new analyst their true income and attempted to financially obstruct the analysis. Having cheated his analyst, her husband's premature ejaculation continued after his analysis, probably as a basic form of cheating and withholding from the partner. She was consciously annoyed by her husband's frugality and ejaculatory disturbance, but was unconsciously pleased by her feelings of phallic superiority over him, while unconsciously taking pleasure in the unconscious humiliation of her brothers and father.

The patient rarely brought dreams to her analytic sessions. Although she had briefly kept a childhood diary, she had never before, in all of her analysis, come with any written material. After three years of her second analysis, she walked in and handed the analyst a piece of paper announcing that she had had a sleep disturbance, awoke recalling the dream, and immediately decided to write it down before it would be forgotten. The written dream was as follows:

> Was in house which was attached to other houses almost like apartments. Heard series of blasts—one of which tore down one of my walls. Ran into garage as place of safety. Next running in street—looking for somebody—later thinking in may have been children. I asked policeman what it was all about. Policeman said we were being bombed. Later I didn't recall asking the policeman; I seemed to feel I may have imagined loud noises.

She associated to probably having read an article about bombings or explosions. She originally told the dream in the morning to her children who were under active consideration for psychotherapy, both underachieving in school and manifesting behavioral disturbances. The spastic colitis was active, and after mentioning intestinal symptoms, she then proceeded to "blast" friends for being selfish and indifferent to her difficulties. She had argued with her husband about money at breakfast, and the therapist made the interpretation that she was hiding from her explosive aggression at the analyst. She immediately recalled that she had intended to bring in the check for the analyst but had forgotten, always feeling angry that she had to pay. She thought of the police, not only as protection from projected aggression, but as punishment and arrest for attempted robbery. The analyst pointed out that she had brought him a written dream, handing him this instead of a written check. Associations led to the analyst's handing her a written piece of paper, the bill, resulting in this exchange of notes. The written dream was therefore a mocking, hostile identification with the analyst's rendering the bill. Her writing the dream and forgetting the check preserved the form while reversing or canceling the content.

The patient's behavior repeated earlier patterns of identification with the aggressor and spiteful withholding behavior in her interpersonal relations. She withheld the money while appearing to give a blank check in a masterpiece of negativistic pseudocompliance. Her attack of constipation and diarrhea could be seen in terms of the conflict over withholding and giving, of submission and refusal, pseudocompliance, and disguised defiance. She had the sadomasochistic object relationships typical of the anal phase in which good and bad, black and white, are sharply divided and unintegrated. She was undergoing endless battles to abort or maintain, to destroy or retain the object. While the written dream was an oral narcissistic production, it was also an ambivalent fecal gift in which the anal withholding continued the expression of her insatiable greed and envy. She took refuge in the dream after feeling "blasted" by the bill in reality. In essence, she gave the analyst shit, while hoarding gold. After payment of the bill she was frequently irritable, arguing with her sons over extra cookies, demonstrating crampy diarrhea instead of gracious giving. She became empty and depressed, with one derivative of the suicidal thoughts being "I would rather die than pay," "I'm being castrated and robbed of food and my body contents." Fantasies of being forced to pay were also associated with unconscious guilt feelings related to prostitution fantasies, which were in turn a way of getting back for fee-feces.

The breaking down of the walls and the explosions represented her diarrhea and flatus as well as the failure of her defensive isolation and the emergence of angry affect. Words were also made of air and in the form of invectives and insults were blasts at her family. The communication of the dream to her sons was also an attack on them, because they, by going into treatment, would create financial difficulties and possibly "bomb" her out of her own therapy. Unconsciously she was extremely jealous of her sons' treatment and was attacking them as she wished to attack her brother. The aerial bombardment can be seen to have a very special meaning for this patient with a history of pulmonary disease involving herself, her first husband, and her dead brother. The patient had attacks of choking and coughing during pertussis at age seven, in which she fantasied that the contagion could be spread to destroy her objects, similar to other fantasies of poisonous "shit hitting the fan." The pulmonary death of her first husband had reinforced her omnipotent aggression. However, her learning problem after her pertussis was related to her fantasies of being aborted and destroyed as well as her conviction that because of her aggression and masturbation she would suffer the fate of her oldest brother. Her focus on the dead oldest brother was also a way of disregarding her other brother and treating him as if he, too, were dead. Just as in childhood she destroyed her dolls, destroying her brothers and identifying with an aborting mother, she also presented the analyst with a dead baby who left only paper records of his existence. The content of the dream, the bombing and looking for children, confirms the written message as an ambivalent gift of feces and baby.

The development of her learning problems and reading disability after her pulmonary illness is of considerable significance in understanding the written dream. Not only was this dream a special communication as Kanzer (1955) had noted of reported dreams—to please or appease, smite or spite the analyst—but it was also a very special way of avoiding verbalization, recall, and reflection. From the point of view of resistance, the written dream is an obvious violation of the basic rule, since it is a prepared agenda rather than spontaneous verbalization and recollection. It is an acting out of transference fantasies at home which are then reenacted in the analyst's office where the written communication is brought.

Such descriptions of the transference resistance do not do full justice to the developmental history of this symptomatic action. The transference neurosis repeats symptoms not only from early infancy, such as the anal phase, but also from later developmental periods including latency. Both fantasies and symptoms are shaped and edited by the ego according to growth and experience during succeeding developmental phases. The written dream was a transference repetition of a childhood learning problem. The patient is saying to the analyst "I do not understand it. I cannot read it. You read it and explain it to me." This patient presents therefore a recrudescence of her earlier learning conflict in school, repeated in the analytic situation. The analytic situation has reactivated a school setting in which the patient learns to use and understand language in speaking, reading, and writing. Her silence, her inability to concentrate, her preoccupation with petty trivial details, her pseudostupidity, and her refusal to be educated now reappear in the transference. It is beyond the scope of this paper to discuss the specific problems of learning disability or the general effects of learning disorders of childhood on psychoanalysis or the process of working through in the adult. This patient showed difficulties between active and passive listening and verbalization as well as in fusion and synthesis of the various complex ego activities involved in speaking, reading, and writing. Her overwhelming unneutralized aggression made it difficult to attack problems and turned problem solving into attack. Words were imbued with symbolic instinctualized meanings which invaded the use of language as an autonomous ego function. The inability to read confirmed and extended her pseudostupidity and symbolic castration while gratifying her needs for punishment and failure. In childhood the sadomasochistic struggle with her mother was continued with the teacher from whom she would withhold information and thoughts, and from whom she stubbornly refused to learn. Jarvis (1958), noting identification difficulties in patients with reading disability, observed that the first reader is frequently the mother who presents the child with fairy tales which are highly symbolic of birth, sex, and death. The patient's mother repeatedly regaled her with tales of birth, death, and traumatic attempts at abortion. In addition, the patient was traumatized by the overstimulation of sight and sound in a household of raucous, exhibitionistic turmoil.

In the acquisition of skills leading toward mastery and adaptation, speech is fundamental, and is later followed by the development of reading and writing ability. Writing involving hand, eye, and verbal coordination is a more complex development than spoken language and is a major acquisition for higher education, the transmission of knowledge, and the collection of information. Writing is relatively dependent on reading and a reading disability makes writing incomprehensible and meaningless. As a schoolgirl the patient did her homework in the same way that she submitted the written dream, a pseudocompliance while evading and avoiding the educational process and the schoolteachers' directions.

There is an obvious connection between her reading, her silence, and constipation. She would refuse to give to the teacher as she had earlier withheld from mother in obstinate defiance. She withheld words, feces, money, and feelings, and recalled a game during childhood in which she practiced refusing to think until her mind was actually a total blank. By her silence and constipation she withheld the object and refused external communication. In her learning difficulty she protected herself against incorporation of and penetration by the object. There was major reliance on the primitive defenses of introjection and projection, with many fantasies of incorporation and expulsion, and then renewed defense against sadistic destruction of the object through the incorporation of the expulsion. In refusing to learn she avoided communication from the object, and in refusing to speak she avoided communication to the object. The fantasies of active and passive aggression corresponded to her sadistic and masochistic behavior in the school situation as well as in social relationships.

While the elements of resistance and acting out inherent in this patient's written dream should not in any way be minimized, there is an adaptive effort in her "homework" and attempts to remember for the analyst. Her urge to write includes the injunction to remember and conserve rather than to blast and destroy as in the dream content. The inner command to write the dream serves more than resistance, even though it directly substitutes for writing the check. There is an effort to record and preserve rather than to totally forget and dismiss as she had done in childhood and the first part of her analysis. Writing, as in the educational process itself, may also be viewed here as an attempt to superimpose the secondary process on the primary process of her dream activity and primitive behavior. It is her attempt to reestablish a distant communication with the analyst as though she were sending a letter rather than reporting in person. It is a way of breaking the silence and exercising educational ego skills which had been arrested when she was left back in school at age seven. To put something into writing at times had a greater sense of commitment for this patient than the thin air of speech which could be readily disowned or distorted. Attention to both the written form of this patient's dream, the timing and manner in which it was communicated, and correlation with its content, permitted the decisive emergence of a learning block in the analytic situation as a repetition of a childhood neurotic syndrome.

Discussion

Since Abraham's paper "Shall We Have the Patients Write Down Their Dreams?" (1913b) there has been a general recognition of the resistance to the fundamental rule of analysis in such behavior. Abraham gives examples of the return of the resistance in the attempts to salvage the dream because the writing is either illegible, discarded, or nonproductive of usable associations. Freud (1911b) similarly commented on the written dream, stating: "Even if the substance of a dream is in this way laboriously rescued from oblivion, it is easy enough to convince one's self that nothing has been thereby achieved for the patient. The associations will not come to the test, and the result is the same as if the dream had not been preserved" (p. 96). In effect the efforts to overcome resistance through writing the dream only result in a return of new resistance. Whitman (1963) found these observations not to be universal and suggests that for some patients the recording of dreams is definitely useful in treatment. He theorizes that much dream forgetting is not due as much to resistance as to a functional demand which the ego cannot meet. Upon awakening the confrontation with reality results in shifts to secondary process thinking, to external perception, and to motor activity which is incompatible with the ego state of the dream. According to Whitman, the patient may find it helpful to record a fraction or all of a dream thereby overcoming the tendency to forget and superimposing the secondary process of writing.

While this view may hold for certain patients, it is doubtful that any suggestion by the analyst to write dreams will truly subserve the analytic process. The forgetting of dreams is a phenomenon to be understood both neurophysiologically as well as analytically. In psychoanalysis the suggestion that the patient take notes is a parameter designed to deal with ego disturbance in special situations. This parameter would attempt to support and supplement nondefensive ego functions. When withholding and forgetting due to defense is at such heights that important fantasies and data do not enter free association, and when dreams are not recalled spontaneously, such suggestions are not more likely to remove the resistance than hypnosis or the substitute form of the patient's bringing early letters, diaries, photographs, and so on. Though such procedures may possibly prove helpful, in order for integration and ego reeducation to occur, the patient must have the capacity both to recall and reflect upon dream and memory, fantasy and reality, with affective responses within the analytic situation. The patient is expected to recover memories from recent analytic sessions and childhood, as well as daydreams and dreams. On the other hand, the analyst need make no specific interdiction against writing dreams at the beginning of treatment, and such material, if it arises, can be handled analytically in its spontaneous setting. As noted by Lipschutz (chapter 34), the written dream will then prove to be a richly overdetermined symptomatic action, with a powerful transference significance. Lipschutz had observed that the written dream may be designed to placate or please, confuse or deceive the analyst. This report is also consistent with his observation of the anal meaning of such dreams, as gift or baby, and as defense against castration anxiety through production of an anal penis. It should be emphasized, however, that the dream may signify any object, part object, or body product. Dreaming itself may be psychologically correlated with psychobiological processes such as eating and defecating (Kanzer, 1959). The written dream specifically protects against loss of the dream, and unconsciously against loss of whatever memories and objects the dream represents.

The written dream may represent an effort to reestablish communication while maintaining distance, as in many symptomatic actions there is a concealed identification with the aggressor and the mocking identification with the analyst must be interpreted. The patient can then learn the difference between aggression, assertion, and action. The identification may not only be with the analyst rendering the bill, but with any aspect of analytic writing. I would suggest that the written dream may also refer to the analyst's notes, especially if he takes notes on dreams. The patient may be aware of the analyst's papers and professional interests. This patient's attempt to recapture the lost dream at a time when she felt empty and depressed may be compared to the attempt to guard against loss of supplies and loss of the object. Lewin (1953a) compared the forgetting of the dream to the weaning process, so that the writing of the dream avoids this oral loss. The writing of the dream was consciously designed to avoid loss of the dream. The feeling of the danger of loss was expressed in other terms in the content of the dream, while the writing of the dream may have been a direct substitute for going to the toilet upon wakening. Kanzer (1955) considered the dream itself as occurring in a state of imperfect narcissism, as preserving object relations and the function of communication. The psychological need to maintain object relations is illustrated in many presleep rituals and then continued in dreaming sleep where the dreamer sleeps with the introjected object. The patient's urge to communicate the dream reestablishes object relations with the transference representative of the infantile objects. This patient was preoccupied with overeating and dieting, constipation and diarrhea, with silence and speech, all problems of intake and output. Kanzer further observed that the dream, as an archaic and metaphorical language, appears at the junction points of the ego boundaries where intake and output are regulated. For this patient dreaming was an aggressive defecation and the writing of the dream might be compared to both smearing on paper and wiping—undoing. In school she also attempted to treat the printed and written page as toilet paper to be both valued and discarded. Her written dream subserving both defense and discharge is also a disguised communication to the analyst to take note of the revival of her learning block and the need for education.

The dynamics of this patient's forgotten check and written dream are related to slips of memory and pen. As a symptomatic action, this dream written immediately upon awakening, was analogous to the automatic acts elucidated by Kanzer (1959) as associated with both the recollection and day residue of the dream. The presentation of the bill was a day residue for both the manifest content and writing of the dream. Furthermore, the dream continues the analytic session. Writing her dream, itself both action and verbalization, was an attempt to avoid forgetting and loss of thoughts. It was a compromise action of defense and discharge between the impulse toward "anal bombing" and the hypnotic command to "do her duty" and write the check for the analyst. By the substitute writing, she "took refuge," as in her manifest dream, from the fantasied attack and retaliation of "the battle of the bill," and from mature responsibility. The writing deflected and reflected the infantile aggressive activity represented in the dream and precluded by the motor paralysis of dreaming sleep.

From time immemorial, dreams have been a source of creative inspiration. Kafka was a modern novelist who wrote his dreams and used them directly in his artistic activity. Art work has been compared to dream work, and the manifest content of both novel and dream presents the author's disguised unconscious fantasies. The development of form and style may be compared to the unifying ego trends in the secondary elaboration of the dream.

The writing of a dream may then be related to continuation of the ego activity of secondary elaboration. It is a further attempt at mastery of traumatic chaos in a potential night terror. The writing restores a sense of reality, control, and organization; it externalizes on paper frightening thoughts and emotions. The nightmare is then converted to fiction. In the writer with creative endowment, the dream narrative represents a stage of sublimation. The elaboration and communication in literary art becomes a verbalization, yet unspoken, of forbidden fantasies shared with the reader. Beyond the inhibitions of this patient, the creative writer with the capacity to sublimate turns from bombs to books, from seeking refuge to artistic creation and communication as reparation and restitution for loss.

Summary

The written dream is reviewed and studied as a symptomatic action, representing a complex compromise formation. It is laden with transference significance and expresses both defense and discharge. In the case reported the written dream was a narcissistic production, primarily an ambivalent anal gift, with overtones of preservation and destruction, birth and abortion (death). The writing was related to the day residue, with antithetical elements of both acting out and remembering. The writing of the dream represented an ambivalent identification with the writing analyst, who presents bills, but may also write notes and papers; this is modeled on the earlier identification with the parent–teacher as aggressor. The written dream as "homework" was a revival of a learning disturbance which was a childhood symptom of her unresolved infantile conflicts and sadomasochistic fears of self and object destruction. Writing the dream could also be understood as protecting against loss of the dream as loss of body parts and loss of the object. It had the adaptive purpose of preserving object relations and communication, and mastering night terror by superimposing secondary process on the primary process of the dream. The suggestion to write dreams during psychoanalysis is a parameter, even though the recollection and report of dreams is a complicated demand upon the ego. Incorporating both action and verbalization, the writing of the dream may become a step toward sublimation, and the private nightmare may be converted into communicable fiction.

Chapter 36

FIRST DREAMS DIRECTLY REPRESENTING THE ANALYST

Richard V. Yazmajian

It is an analytic truism that the first dream reported in analysis is uniquely revealing and important. Gitelson (1952), Rappaport (1959), and Savitt (1960) have discussed the special meaning of first dreams in which the analyst is directly represented in an undisguised manner. Papers by Harris (1962) and Feldman (chapter 14) deal with dreams about the analyst, but they report only one first dream. This dearth of papers on the subject is surprising in view of the importance of transference in analytic work.

The cases reported in the literature whose first dreams directly represent the analyst are classified as schizoid personalities and "borderline" cases, or some, as suffering from profound pregenital difficulties associated with gross ego defects and disturbances in object relations. One common characteristic was the tendency to develop rapidly an intensely erotized transference. The authors state that the undisguised representation of the analyst indicated an inability or refusal to differentiate the analyst and important childhood figures, and heralded an early and persistent demand for actual gratification of transference wishes; the patients were said to resemble those described by Nunberg (1951) who were unable to treat the analytic relationship as an "as if" situation. Nunberg states that these patients do not react to the analyst *as if* he were the parent but instead treat him *as* the parent and accordingly demand

---

This paper was first published in the *Psychoanalytic Quarterly* (1964), 33:536–551.

gratifications they received or wished for as children. Interpretation of the basis for their demands tends to bring about little or no change, and their curiously ego-syntonic demands persist. The authors agree that these patients are difficult to manage, their analyses stormy and characterized by much acting out. Some analyses are broken off early, and only a few reach appreciably successful conclusions; in short, prognosis in such cases proves to be generally poor. They emphasize that at times the transference relation to the analyst becomes too "real" because of a contribution to the situation by the analyst himself from his countertransference or from his actual physical resemblance to a parent.

Of these cases only two are described in any detail; the others are described briefly, sometimes in just a few words. Except in the two detailed cases the authors merely offer impressions and broad generalizations based upon little clinical evidence. In this paper the literature is reexamined and reevaluated from the vantage point of the case material presented.

The patient to be considered here had a sister and brother who were two and four years her junior, respectively. She was twenty-six years old when she came for analysis because of growing concern over not being married. She told me she had become involved repeatedly with men unsuitable because of differences in socioeconomic class, nationality, or religion. She also complained of free-floating anxiety, of shyness in social and professional groups, and of occasional depression. Moreover, the patient considered herself naive about sex, could not recall ever masturbating, and had never experienced orgasm in intercourse.

Before seeing me she had gone twice to a consultant. Prior to her first visit to him, she said she felt "as if I were going to meet a lover instead of going to see a doctor for consultation." By the time of the second interview her already intense transference reaction had blossomed and, at the end of the interview, she had the conscious fantasy that he would take her for a walk in the park, return with her to his apartment, and then, quickly, they would have intercourse. These erotic fantasies were not reported to the consultant.

This precocious, highly erotized transference resembles that of patients cited in the literature. Since the literature stresses countertransference problems in such cases, I questioned the consultant about it. He believed that countertransference was not a major factor and that her reactions stemmed basically from within. Both her relation to me and the course of her analysis confirm this.

The patient was given my name and that of another analyst and saw both of us. For various reasons she rejected the other analyst. Her choice of me was unconsciously influenced by her belief that my socioeconomic status rendered me "unsuitable" and the fact that I was young. A young analyst whom she could consider a degraded object was of vital importance to her as a defense against identifying the analyst with her successful, prominent father. Her preoccupation with the social status of her analyst and her consultant had special importance, as will be seen.

In the first interview, she was told that I had time available and could make arrangements for beginning analysis. That evening she had two dreams which she reported the next day. In the first dream she was in the countryside with two men: one, middle-aged and the other, myself. (In this paper we shall often return to this dream which, for convenience, will be designated the "First Dream.") We both spoke with a German accent, but I was represented physically without any modification. Behind a screen she could see the silhouettes of two young, grown boys who were my sons. She felt very happy. In the second dream of the pair she was in an office in a municipal hospital. The office was dark and dreary and had a depressing air about it. I was seated behind a desk. After looking into a huge appointment book, I told the patient that I did not have time to see her. At this she became furious. In this dream also I was represented without any modification but spoke in my normal voice without an accent.

After reporting the dreams, she spontaneously explained their origin. In a matter-of-fact way she said she felt that the "First Dream" was stimulated by her having seen a few doctors about starting analysis. Although all the doctors were American born, she thought the German accents in the dream were prob- ably due to her tendency to think of analysts as Europeans and to the fact that her initial consultant had a German-sounding name. She recalled having seen in the consultant's office a pho- tograph of Freud when he was middle-aged, taken in the com- pany of a young analyst, and felt that this too contributed to the dream. The second dream of the pair, she thought, owed itself to two factors: she had once worked in the same municipal hospital depicted in the dream and had thought the actual physical setting a dreary, depressing one, as it was in the dream. She also found dreary the apartment house in which my office was located and considered my office furnishings and lighting to be rather dark too. Here interest in her dream was abruptly dropped and she went on to discuss other matters.

It seemed at the time that her reporting the dreams, her interest in them, and her attempt to understand them augured well for the analysis. Later experience with the patient indi- cated, however, that she was not attempting to explain these dreams but, rather, to explain them away. She had seized upon a few associations about innocuous realistic matters and had used them, in effect, to dismiss the dreams. She was thus able to deny that they had any unconscious or symbolic meaning. We shall understand these dreams better as we analyze subsequent modifications of them and related vicissitudes of the trans- ference.

Everyone is terrified of his unconscious drives and fantasies but this patient's dread of her unconscious was inordinate. She accordingly reacted to beginning her analysis with great anxiety and much acting out, culminating in her deciding to terminate analysis because it created overwhelming tension. However, re- assurance and interpretation of some of her fears enabled her to continue treatment.

At first she came regularly but chattered endlessly about social activities, her work, and many trivia. She was skimming the surface because of her dread of being overwhelmed by intense affects and fantasies which were reflected in part by dreams of passively being subjected to violence and threats of physical injury related to castration. During this period she would hurriedly go to and from the couch, try not to look at me, and avoid me in a phobic way. On the couch, however, she frequently turned abruptly to look at me. Although this behavior had many unconscious libidinal and aggressive motivations its most compelling reason was to see what I really looked like. She was struggling against her intense inclination to distort her actual image of me in accordance with emerging transference fantasies. Whenever doubts about my physical appearance occurred, she would turn around on the couch to test reality by looking at me. Once she wished to turn and stare at me for several minutes in order to fix in her mind my exact image. She said that if she did not do this her imagination might take over and she would distort greatly her image of me—something she desperately wanted to avoid.

During this early phase, the patient was preoccupied with florid romantic fantasies about her initial consultant whereas I was unceasingly criticized and depreciated. My attire, my speech, and my office furnishings all received their share of scorn. Frequently she commented on how "amusing" I was—even the way I greeted her or bade her good-bye was "amusing." In fact, she declared that lying on the couch and the whole business of analysis was "silly and amusing." Patients who succeeded her envied the smile of amusement with which she passed through the waiting room. This behavior seemed to result from her basically phobic attitude toward me. The depreciations and mockery were intended to create distance and to reduce me to a nonentity not fearsome to her. Her true feelings, however, were reflected occasionally in an outburst of thoughts about my "enormous" intellect, revealing that she considered me a powerful and frightening person. Although she denied emotional interest in me, she admitted to thinking about me a great deal. She wanted to know about my education, marital status, social background, and interests. Her questions were motivated by the same forces that led her to turn around on the couch and fix her mental image of me; her intense need was to know as much as possible about my actual identity and to use this knowledge to reduce my frightening ambiguity, thus avoiding investing me with symbolic importance.

At this point, after a transference allusion to a former lover who had created intense sexual excitement in her, she had three dreams about me in one evening. The first was indirectly typically depreciating of me. In the next two dreams the defenses broke down and her admiration for me was given open expression. I was directly represented in "realistic" professional settings. In the second dream she was in my office, happily advising me on certain matters, but the dream ended with her finding cause to be angry with me. In the third dream she was attending my professional lecture and was aware of feeling deep admiration for me. These dreams occurred when she was profoundly threatened by the danger of unmanageable transference feelings. Although disguised, I was made a contemptible figure in the first dream. The id drives demanded more expression with each dream but could be given expression only by casting our relationship into a realistic one. In the second dream she also used the protection of reversal of roles by helping me with her knowledge, but she still had to close the dream by finding a basis for being angry and withdrawing. In the third dream she openly admired me but only as an auditor at a lecture—a setting recognized by the patient as realistic and impersonal. Of note is her viewing me in an exhibitionistic situation.

As her fears and defenses were gradually interpreted she felt less overwhelmed and more overt sexual ideas began to emerge. A thinly veiled oedipal dream terrified her and she refused to work with it. Her hostile defense against transference feelings was again mobilized as was the need to turn and look at me in order to reestablish her impressions of how I actually looked.

In this emotional state she presented another pair of dreams. In the first she met me in the street while on the way to my office and I said "hello" to her, as had actually occurred on one occasion. The second of the pair depicted my office and patients in a bizarre, mocking manner. Faced with drives that threatened her ego, she again represented our relationship as casual and socially realistic and me as impotent, foolish, castrated, and therefore safe.

A week later this defensive pattern reappeared. Her father had taken her to lunch and had been kind to her. To this she reacted as to a seduction, for so intensely did she fear closeness to her father that she could not let him touch her. She was his favorite child on whom he doted to the point of cruelly ignoring the other children. The sexual yearnings stirred up by her father's interest overwhelmed her and resulted in acting out in life and in the analytic situation, and in another dream of me.

This first of a tripartite dream differed from others about me in that its setting was a shabby, dirty house, the floor covered with mud. Many people were about. She had come for a treatment session and anxiously inquired whether we should be alone. She noted how kind I was as I reassured her that we would be alone. In the second part of the dream a policeman told her that she had done nothing wrong. In the third, she insisted to a girl friend that the friend was wrong to think that some mutual male friend was listed in the social register. In association, she talked of her admiration for me and the beginning of an emotionally personal interest. Her father's kindness and an impending trip he was making with her mother were the other central associations.

In the first dream she attempted to show her relation to me as professional, but the defense failed, and symbols with direct associative threads to the father emerged: I was kind to her as father was; I reassured her that other people would not be allowed to intrude into the relationship as mother was about to do with father. Her guilt was reflected in the second dream, and in the third one she again defensively attempted to dissociate me from her socially prominent father. These transitional dreams, concomitant with the beginnings of conscious transference, heralded an important change in the analysis, now of four months' duration. Instead of typical attacks there appeared seductive attempts to tease and provoke me. As her coquetry mounted and she became irked with what she called my passivity—unconsciously meaning sexual inaction—her dreams changed further. I now appeared only in disguise. At the same time, she expressed wishes for gratification in the analysis like that she experienced at home. The emergence into consciousness of clear and sharp transference feelings made it necessary for the patient to disguise me in her dreams, in which infantile wishes were given even more sway. Although she dreamed often during the remainder of the analytic year, I never again appeared in the dreams without disguise. As her conscious transference fantasies became more direct, bolder, and more preoccupying, she became aware of a sharp diminution in her former daydreams about her consultant who, in fact, now began to appear in her dreams of situations, such as cocktail parties, as a symbolic representation of me. Since I had become a true transference object, the incest taboo prohibited dreaming of me directly.

Eight months after the beginning of analysis she presented, for the first time, what appeared to be a modified version of the "First Dream." In the original dream there were a middle-aged man and myself and two grown boys behind a screen. In the new version, the patient was reading a book and became embarrassed upon seeing photographs of her uncle completely nude. She then found herself in the presence of an unrecognized psychiatrist to whom she directed questions concerning premarital sexual activities which he refused to answer. At that point she was informed that an unmarried relative had become pregnant without having had intercourse and was carrying twins. For the middle-aged man, me, and two grown boys behind a screen of the "First Dream," she had substituted her uncle, an unrecognized psychiatrist, and a virgin carrying twins. The new dream, a more richly symbolic and less disguised form of the earlier one, could be analyzed more fully than her previous dreams. The nude uncle reminded her for the first time of screen memories of often seeing her father nude when she was age three and four. The doctor's refusal of sexual information brought memories of father's refusal to discuss sex with her as a child. He had walked about nude and shaved in her presence. This screen memory and other material pointed up the repetitive exposure to her father's penis and possibly to seeing it in the erect state. She did not then remember noticing her father's penis but vividly recalled how much taller he always seemed than when dressed. These experiences roused her to awe, fascination, and denial of existence of her father's penis. The reworking of the "First Dream" and the analytic accessibility of the reworked dream are reminiscent of the modification that occurs in a screen memory when its defensive aspects are undergoing dissolution during an analysis.

   In the tenth month she recalled, in her associations, the
"First Dream." She felt certain that I had forgotten the dream
after so many months and so described it in detail. Her memory
of it was distorted. She said: "I'm in the country, and there are
a lot of people about. There's an old man with a long, gray
beard. His grown son is behind a screen and I can see his
silhouetted body moving. This old man tells me to lie down and
he will remove the tick embedded in my skin." Of special note
in this memory is the condensation and replacement of the
middle-aged man and me of the original dream by a bearded
figure symbolic of the penis. The "First Dream" had, in effect,
been dismissed by the patient. She now attempted to analyze
her grossly falsified but more symbolic recollection of it. Her
associations consisted of a rich intertwining of thoughts of her
family genealogy, her father's preference for her, and her
thinly disguised fantasies of marriage to me.
   In the case thus far presented, one can see two striking
trends: defensive flight into reality and preoccupation with the
penis. The flight into reality as a defense is seen in her dreams
of the analyst, in her behavior on the couch, and in her life. In
the "First Dream" the patient pictured me with a middle-aged
man in an attempt to deny the transference by separating her
analyst and her father. However, ego control and superego
pressures were not sufficient to prevent some equating of the
two, so both analyst and father speak with accents. Much real
symbolism and its positive affect is evident in the dream because
the dream defenses are weak. Although the dream was interrupted, id drives were in motion and she dreamed again—this
time of being in an office with me and being told that I could
not see her, which made her furious. Threatened ego and
alerted superego seemed to demand that the dream be recast
into more realistic terms and be experienced emotionally in a
negative way in order better to deny the incestuous undertones.
Similarly, on the couch she had to look at me in order to reenforce her true image of me and so stem the distortions effected
by emerging fantasies. All this was combined with a need to
know me as I "really" am and endless talk on the couch about
trivial day-to-day matters.

As these multiple uses of reality as defense broke down, dreams and fantasies emerged. One recurrent central feature of them was awe, fascination, and terror of her father's penis. In her first dream of being in my office the only unrealistic detail was the symbolic representation of my penis by the huge appointment book. In that dream she was angry because I denied her the opportunity to see me; that is, to see my penis. This is a reversal and denial of the fact that I had agreed to see her in analysis and of the dream detail of my having my appointment book in full view of her, as father, in the past, had freely exhibited his penis—her dreams, for example, of seeing me lecture, the reworked version of the "First Dream" when she saw her uncle nude, and her falsified conscious recall of the "First Dream" about the old man with the long beard. It became evident too that her fantasies about my "enormous" intellect, her wish to stare at my face, to know what I was "really" like, had to do with her wish to look at my penis and to know what it was really like.

Transference fantasies of marriage appeared in the second year of her analysis. These were motivated by the wish to identify herself narcissistically with me. I was to serve merely as an appendage to her and become, in effect, her penis. Dreams and fantasies began to indicate powerful wishes to castrate her father and secure his penis. The analysis became stormy with transient breakdowns of the hard-won therapeutic liaison and much acting out. It was at just such times that dreams of the analyst recurred. The dynamics of these dreams followed the same essential patterns as those of earlier ones. However, they became more symbolic and overtly sexual and regularly included members of the family. In one of them, even my face was changed.

Fantasies, dreams, and memories of childhood and adolescence began to make clear how great was the narcissistic injury of being without a penis. Her whole body seemed to her defective, a hurt reenforced by the fact that her sister, two years her junior, had been physically precocious and as big as the patient at age four. In fact, her sister was often supposed to be her twin. To add insult to injury, she was constantly praised for her beauty, making the patient feel like a malformed, ugly dwarf.

Naturally enough, she blamed and hated her mother for her condition.

Her mother had been cold and distant and had relegated much care of the patient to others. Separation anxiety was accordingly great, arising from pathological differentiation of self and mother, and development of her body ego suffered. Hurt, rage, and disappointment in her mother forced her to turn to father who was solicitous, tender, and the possessor of an awesome and magical penis which she hoped to obtain. The wishes he had frustrated were directed toward the analyst with the same desperation. These wishes also mobilized the great castration anxiety that afflicted her on so many levels and was one with primitive separation anxiety. This forced the patient to resort defensively to regressive fantasies and behavior indicative of the prephallic drives behind her relationship to her father. The central theme of these regressive fantasies was to wish to establish a perfect state of fusion with mother.

The fantasy of fusion was gratifying and also served as defense against mobilization of her rage, dangers of retaliation based on projection of her aggression, and anxieties ranging from castration to ego dissolution. One saw these considerations in her sexual activities. In intercourse she wanted to get so physically close to her lover that there would not even exist any air space between them. Although orgastically frigid, she enjoyed intercourse, but when it ended became depressed and hostile. During it she gratified both the fantasy of fusion and the fantasy of intactness of body produced by the penis in her vagina. Termination of intercourse punctured both fantasies, resulting in depression and rage. Her daydreams of sexual intercourse were of a literal melting into her lover's body with no thought or imagery about the penis or vagina. These fantasies were all brought into the transference.

Greenacre (1947) describes the girl's shock at sight of the penis, causing her to see the male as godlike and to seek out masochistic humiliation by men or attempt to inflict humiliation on them. Her patients experienced visual hypersensitivity, headaches, and, what is especially pertinent to us, difficulties in discriminating between the real and the unreal. In my patient all these traits could be seen. Defects in superego formaion evidenced by Greenacre's patients were also similar to those in my patient.

In another paper on screen memories Greenacre (1952) discussed the use of reality to hide reality, a technique my patient used in her struggle to deny the use of reality of the penis. Freud pointed out that the exclamation of patients, "the dream seemed so real!", indicates that its latent content deals with the memory of a real event of childhood. My case suggests that another way of representing a childhood event in a dream is to portray a *present-day reality*. The patient used analyst and analytic situation in her dreams like a screen memory. She often described her dreams as "so ordinary and right out of everyday life" and rejected them as "meaningless." To treat a dream so serves denial when, as infantile memories become more pressing, one would expect the defense to require that the manifest content become ever more permeated with current reality. For example, this happened in the "First Dream," in which I was reresented, but too much infantile material was entering it so it had to be terminated and replaced by a highly "realistic" one. So tenuous were the patient's ego defenses that, as occurs in the formation of day residues, there developed in both her dream life and everyday life a flight into reality in order to ward off unconscious memories by displacement to trivia. Similarly, on the couch she defended herself against acknowledging the reality of my penis by a fetishistic concern with various objects in the office and other "externals" of my life and my "real" identity.

Normally the little girl displaces qualities she ascribes to the penis not only to the actual person of her father but also to other persons, and finally to symbols. To effect displacement to symbols, the ego of the child must be able to establish distance by repression, displacement, and replacing the concrete with the abstract. My patient's attempts to deny the reality of the penis clearly interfered with this process, and this difficulty was reflected in her literal and concrete approach to things. She complained of being excessively materialistic and of being unable to get truly involved in intellectual and abstract matters as others did. In her dreams of the analyst and in her attempts to analyze them, she clung in a concrete manner to perceptions (day residues). She resisted with equal intensity understanding a symbolic element in a dream and seeing the analyst as a symbolic figure.

Keiser (1962) describes similar difficulties encountered in male patients who have been unduly exposed to traumatic and persistent visualization of the genitals of exhibitionistic mothers. His paper stresses the difficulty with which these men internalize the mother and the resultant maldevelopment of the ego function of abstract thinking.

Other writers on the subject of first dreams emphasize that they imply the wish for id gratification and the inability or refusal of the patients to differentiate the analyst and important childhood figures. Rappaport (1959) and Savitt (1960) describe in some detail two men with archaic defects of body ego, severe difficulties in sexual identification, and powerful awe and envy of the fathers' penis. Their initial dreams and behavior in analysis showed that they attempted, as did my patient, to make a mockery of the analysis and the analyst and to resist investing the analyst with symbolic import. In Rappaport's case, he appeared in the first of two dreams. Although portrayed mockingly, he was visualized in an exhibitionistic situation. In the second dream a stranger appeared who was transformed suddenly into the patient's father. Upon the undisguised appearance of the father, the patient awakened. The anxiety caused by the direct appearance of the father would seem to contradict Rappaport's statement that the patient insisted on equating father and analyst. In Savitt's case, the patient dreamed of homosexually seducing the analyst in his office and, in doing so, of scoring another homosexual "conquest" such as he had achieved many times in real life. He insisted he would treat the analyst as he would any "ordinary" man—in short, that he would defend himself against emotionally treating the analyst as a special or symbolic figure. I believe such material essentially reflects ego defense. Both authors immediately interpreted to their patients the resistance to analysis implied in their dreams, but did so in the context of id resistance.

Because the other pertinent analyses cited in the literature were so unfruitful or so quickly terminated, or because the subject of first dreams involving the analyst was only part of a broader subject dealt with by the authors, the conclusions drawn seem impressionistic. For example, in one instance the dream about the analyst is not described. The dreams reported usually involved realistic settings punctuated by direct or symbolic representations of the analyst's penis or by symbolic intrusions of themes of exhibitionism, voyeurism, and castration. It is of interest that, where the history is known, there was often repetitive visual exposure to, or physical contact with, the penises of adults, including the father's. Greenacre (1952) describes a first dream in which she was directly represented. Although Greenacre paid no attention to the unusual form of the dream, she emphasized that her patient insisted that she had never seen a penis until her adulthood. Analysis of the dream subsequently brought up a direct reference to a childhood observation of a cousin masturbating. Greenacre stressed the shocking and traumatizing effect of such a visual exposure and further stated that her patient (like mine) used external reality and ego gratifications as her main defense against instinctual conflicts.

Summary

A case is described in which the first dream reported in analysis contained an undisguised representation of the analyst. Subsequent modifications of this dream, with associated transference vicissitudes and other analytic data, contributed to the elucidation of the first dream. The undisguised representation of the analyst was an attempt to treat him as a real person and thus avoid investing him with symbolic importance: in effect, a resistance to transference formation. A primary defense in the patient's dreams, on the couch, and in her life was a flight into reality. Later, as evidence appeared that the analyst had become a true transference object, he disappeared from dreams and was replaced by disguised symbolic figures. The flight into reality was traced to denial of the reality of her father's penis. This was associated with a fetishistic displacement to concern with the "externals" of life, the analyst's office, and his actual social identity. Concern with present-day realities served to screen childhood events involving her father's exhibitionism.

The previous literature dealing with this subject considers such dreams to reflect id resistances and the inability or refusal of the patients to differentiate the analyst and important childhood figures, but offers little clinical support for such suppositions. Most of the cases cited met with extremely limited analytic results, and the data are sketchy. Reexamination of this literature suggests that the cases presented offer support for the present thesis. In light of these findings, detailed reexamination of this subject seems necessary.

Chapter 37

SOME ASPECTS OF TRANSFERENCE IN DREAM RESEARCH

CHARLES R. KEITH

The dynamics of transference in dreaming have always occupied a prominent place in psychoanalytic dream theory. Clinicians have assumed that the frequency and content of patients' dream reports are closely related to the vicissitudes of the analyst–patient relationship. Fisher (1953) demonstrated the important effect of transference on the results obtained from suggestions to dream. Fisher's suggestions to his subjects to dream underwent many different fates; for example, amnesia for the suggestion, acting out on the part of the subject, and failure to dream, depending on the subject's particular ego structure and the nature of his transference to the physician.

This point of view about dreaming seems at first glance to be at variance with data accumulated in recent years by use of the Kleitman electronic technique for eliciting dreams. Kleitman and his group (Aserinsky and Kleitman, 1955; Dement and Kleitman, 1957a,b; Dement and Wolpert, 1958) found that the concurrence of rapid low-voltage brain waves and rapid eye movements in a sleeping subject indicates the presence of dreaming. Everyone studied so far by them dreamed every night, usually producing a nightly series of four to seven dreams with predictable frequency and duration. Workers in this field have implied that dreaming is a basic biological function, only poorly controlled, if at all, by the individual's ego or environmental factors.

This paper was first published in the *Bulletin of the Menninger Clinic* (1962), 26:248–257.

The following pilot study was designed to study the transference situation between the subject and the researcher and the effect it has on dreams revealed by the Kleitman electroencephalographic technique.

Transference, as used in this paper, is defined as the subject's tendency to distort and to have unrealistic expectations of the researcher resulting from the subject's assigning roles, attitudes, and feelings to the researcher which were originally directed toward important parental figures.

Methods

Three male aides from various Topeka hospitals volunteered after hearing about the project from their nursing supervisors. The only requirement was a high school education. The subjects reported once a week to the research bedroom over a period of eight to ten weeks. Efforts were made to maintain their normal sleeping habits. (Since the subjects were nightworkers, they normally slept during the day.) They were paid eight dollars a day.

Unilateral, orbital, parietal, and occipital electroencephalograph electrodes were fastened to the subject's head by using tape and collodian (Dement and Kleitman, 1957a).

The subjects were then instructed to go to sleep on a bed in the darkened research room. The researcher retired to an adjoining alcove where an Offner Dynagraph was located for continous monitoring of the subject's brain waves and eye movements. The paper was run through the Dynagraph at slow speeds to conserve paper and was speeded up to the usual clinical electroencephalograph rate of three centimeters per second when more detailed examination of the brain waves was necessary.

The following criteria were used for determining the presence of dreaming:

1. Rapid conjugate eye movements
   recorded by the orbital electrode.
   (REM)
   Both occurring after an
2. Rapid low voltage brain wave   initial period of sleep.
   activity without spindling
   recorded by the scalp electrodes.
   (Emerging Stage 1)

The subjects were permitted to dream until a body movement signaled the end of a dream (Dement and Kleitman, 1957b), or until the dream had lasted ten to fifteen minutes. They were then awakened by a buzzer and asked to relate their dreams, if any, to the researcher, who recorded the results for future reference.

After the night's sleep was completed, the subject was asked to tell what he remembered of his dreams that day and then to give associations to his dreams. In addition, the researcher recorded everything the subject said about his personal life and his feelings concerning the research project. A Rorschach test was given to each subject at the end of the project.

Results

Each subject, his responses, and dreams were as foilows:

Subject AR

Mr. AR, a middle-aged, married, hospital aide, grew up in a farm family in which the father set high standards and was intolerant of slackness and poor performance. The subject's mother was a buffer for him against his father's aggression and was his main source of warmth and affection.

The fear of his father and need for maternal support became recurrent themes in all his activities as he grew. Fears of bodily injury, the inability to stand up against authority figures, and the difficulties expressing overt aggression were prominent in his relations with others. Shortly after his marriage, Mr. AR developed a duodenal ulcer, which has remained active up to the present. Also at the time of his marriage, he left farm work, passed up several opportunities to work in factories, and instead became an aide in a hospital, caring for elderly men. He feels "trapped and pushed about" in his job and marriage, but cannot bring himself to change either situation, though he has had many opportunities.

Mr. AR states that he has a rich dream life which helps him to "work off feelings and solve problems."

Transference Effects on Dreaming. Mr. AR's first sleeping day in the research room was restless and no dreams were elicited. On the second day, Mr. AR talked eagerly as the electrodes were being fastened to his head. Spontaneously, he told about difficulties with his children, irritations with his wife, and finally about his active duodenal ulcer. The relation between the fantasies concerning his ulcer and his expectations of the researcher soon became apparent. To Mr. AR, his ulcer represented a bodily injury and an actualization of his castration fears. He frequently compared his ulcer to a maimed foot or amputated hand. His participation in the research project seemed clearly, on one level, to be a search for a new relationship with a father figure which would undo the castration damage and heal his ulcer. With some reluctance, he went to sleep and had one dream, in which a hospital employee (the subject), dressed in white, pulled a piece of metal out of his foot and said, "Now I'll have no more sick leave." The subject's ulcer pains which had bothered him prior to coming to the research room were gone after he awakened.

Mr. AR produced three or four dreams during each of the remaining seven sleeping periods in the research room. He was awakened a total of twenty-six times and was able to recall a dream twenty-five times for a 96 percent average of dream recall. On one occasion, Mr. AR awakened himself and called out that he had a dream to report, since he was afraid that he would not be awakened.

It was postulated earlier that one of Mr. AR's motivations for volunteering as a subject was to seek contact with a physician with whom he could identify himself and obtain relief from certain distressing problems. The prototype for this transference relation was Mr. AR's ambivalence toward his own father, revolving around oedipal conflicts.

The following manifest dreams and association from one "night" of sleep illustrate how the oedipal theme, intertwined with the transference relation, provides an underlying unity:

> 1. "I was trying to find a place to fish on Dad's farm. A bunch of guys were trying to get minnows out of a bucket."
> 2. "Seems to be connected with the first dream. My sister-in-law was on the fishing bank trying to find a latrine. She called the latrine 'Salty.' I pointed to a latrine up the creek, but she said it was too far. I pointed to a closer latrine, but someone had allowed it to fall into the creek. We were trying to fix some food, and some fellow was trying to get change out of a change box."
> 3. "It seemed that I was awake in the dream watching you (the researcher) read a bunch of neurological words and asking me what they meant. Other doctors were there watching the examination. One doctor was fixing up my foot. You asked me about my dreams, and I said my dream was about 'brain'."

Mr. AR produced the following associations about the dreams:

1. "I was a little boy and that's all I remember about it."
2. "Urine salty—kills grass. She called me Swede (sweet)—Dad wanted to know about her—she treats me like a mother. Had to be careful about sexual thoughts toward her. Fellow who destroyed outhouse had ulcers and a gastrectomy (sic). He was happy that he had destroyed outhouse. Sister-in-law wanted to tell Dad. Fellow with ulcers didn't want to. This fellow destroys property of father and expects father to fix up everything."
3. "Brain surgeons remove tumors. Know what is going on inside patient's head. Doctors like to help aides; then the aides help doctors. I change my clothes with doctors. Doctors sometimes let patients die. You were like the brain surgeon and figuring out why I do things and testing me."

The dream sequences and associations obtained on the other nights were essentially similar to the one just described.

Mr. AR reported several interesting changes in his personal life which he attributed to the feeling of strength and well-being imparted to him by the research situation. He began to "interpret" dreams for fellow workers, and advised them about their personal problems. He became more assertive and masculine in dealings with women. Though his ulcer pain was reactivated before each sleeping session, he left at the end of each day feeling "less nervous" and without ulcer pain.

Up to now, the positive side of Mr. AR's ambivalence was most conspicuous. The eruption of predominantly negative transference feelings into the research setting occurred dramatically during the subject's last day in the sleeping room. Mr. AR arrived early and found the researcher trying unsuccessfully to get a window open with a window crank. The subject found a screwdriver and was able to open the window. He then went to sleep, and the first dream was as follows.

> "I was working on father-in-law's lawnmower, trying to fix it for him. He was working with a nut down below, and we were kidding him. A nephew was there who wrinkled up his face—we were going to the nephew's place, but father-in-law didn't want to go."

Mr. AR then went back to sleep.

Approximately 90 minutes later (his usual interval between dreams) the electroencephalogram began to show short bursts of rapid eye movements. After an hour of struggling in this manner, the subject awoke, angrily swore at himself, and asked to get up since he couldn't "turn off his thoughts" and go back to sleep.

The following associations were reported:

"I recalled laughing at my father-in-law, who was trying unsuccessfully to fix the mower. He (the father-in-law) was stupidly trying to use a dinky wrench in the wrong place on the gas tank."

The subject recalled that he started to dream several times before he awakened the second time. Two dream fragments (interrupted by the violent body movements) were reported: In one, he was entering a room with the researcher, and something was about to happen, when he awakened suddenly. In the other, he was looking in a patient's bed and saw something. These dream fragments made him anxious, and he immediately recalled a terrifying nightmare he had the preceding day. In the nightmare, his brother was slowly being sucked into a grinder. As the brother's head was disappearing between the grinding teeth, one of his eyes stood out prominently, and the subject remembered vividly his terror of the eye.

Associations led immediately to death wishes toward his father, and to the fear that his dreams (and death wishes) were prophetic and would come true. Further associations revealed that his ulcer was an internalized source of sudden death for himself and a retribution for his anger toward others. He then compared the researcher with his father and gave vent to many ambivalent feelings about the research situation.

Surely other themes than the oedipal would have emerged if the investigation had continued. But even the small amount of material presented here is sufficient to illustrate the tremendous impact the subject's fantasies, desires, and previous interpersonal relations can have on the ability to produce dreams in a research setting.

Responses to Rorschach cards were numerous, immediate, and productive of many spontaneous associations, often leading into details of the subject's family and married life. These responses paralleled the style and contents of his dream associations.

Subject TL

Mr. TL is a Mennonite college student, who grew up in a moralistic, repressive family environment. His parents were ultraconservative Mennonites who forbade smoking, drinking, movies, and dancing. Any expression of aggression on his part was immediately squelched by physical punishment. The patient's resulting feelings of inadequacy and severe inhibitions made it difficult for him to pursue any definite goal or career. He was fearful that his sexual and aggressive thoughts were equivalent to deeds. Mr. TL felt his dream life was unimportant since he only remembered occasional fleeting dreams involving impersonal, distant objects.

Transference Effects on Dreaming. Mr. TL slept a total of nine days in the research room—approximately sixty hours of sleep. During this entire period, he produced only one clear-cut dream, according to the previously mentioned electroencephalographic criteria for evidence of dreaming. The dream occurred on the sixth day. Before he fell asleep that day, he was given a positive suggestion to dream by the researcher.

The following dream was told when he was awakened by the buzzer: "I was watching a jet airplane flying—it had a big tube in the middle of it which was going up and down. They were testing it."

Associations to the dream included the following: "A new experiment—dangerous—common man doesn't know what dangerous things are going on about him—'high up' people hurt common people."

As the subject talked, he became anxious and had difficulty suppressing his hostility. He was shocked and surprised that the researcher had "probed" him and discovered this dream.

No further dreams were elicited during Mr. TL's remaining three days in the research room. In spite of his fear of dreaming, the subject was able to sleep deeply and restfully as long as seven hours at a time. He entered Stage 1 sleep at regular intervals, but only remained there a few minutes until body movements occurred. After ten to fifteen minutes of restlessness he would then reenter the deeper stages of quiet sleep. Occasionally rapid eye movements occurred in conjunction with the Stage 1 sleep, but they rarely lasted longer than thirty to forty-five seconds. On four occasions the subject was awakened immediately following these brief outbursts of rapid eye movement but was unable to recall a dream. On three occasions the subject, after awakening spontaneously, reported a dream which had not been detected electroencephalographically. All three dreams involved a conversation between two people while the subject passively observed from a distance. These dreams may have occurred during the periods of Stage 1 sleep without eye movements. Dement and Wolpert (1958) have suggested that rapid eye movements may become less pronounced as the dreamer plays a more passive role in his dream.

The subject expressed the following thoughts and feelings about the research project: His greatest fear was dreaming about unclothed women and murder. The electroencephalograph machine could show whether he was having sexual or violent dreams by recording his pulse, breath rate, and actual thoughts. The electrode over his earlobe was placed there to pick up and "overhear" his thoughts. Talking about his dreams might reveal angry feelings toward his parents who would, in some way, find out about these feelings and then be disappointed and angry with him. He was aware of suppressing his dreams while in the research room, so that nothing bad would be revealed about him.

His Rorschach responses tended to be stereotyped, and constricted. On the color cards and on the cards which often give rise to sexual responses, he frequently hesitated several minutes before responding, or would reject the card. The visual imagery stimulated by the Rorschach cards aroused anxiety, correlating well with his fear of producing dream imagery.

The transference situation can be summarized as follows: Mr. TL viewed the researcher as an authoritarian, parental figure who would be able to "read" his mind while he was sleeping, and who would then be able to punish him for his thoughts. This transference was a recapitulation of the intensely ambivalent relations with his parents, particularly the father. The subject resolved the dilemma by massively repressing and denying his sexual and aggressive urges, leading to chronic anxiety, guilt feelings, numerous inhibitions, and a constricted ego structure. This rather tenuous structural balance was continually threatened by the research situation which encouraged expression of unconscious material via dreams while the subject was in a state of reduced ego functioning (sleep). So intense was his apprehension that the subject was somehow able to repress even the formation of hallucinatory dream images, as inferred from the almost total absence of rapid eye movements.

Subject MC

Mr. MC, a twenty-eight-year-old, single aide, was a suspicious, lonely man who was apprehensive about the research project from the beginning. He traced his fear of interpersonal relations back to a period of severe enuresis between ages seven and twelve, for which he was spanked and shamed daily by his parents. He stifled and repressed his counteraggression, particularly toward his distant, awesome father. During these years, stuttering became a severe problem. He "learned to swallow" any emotional expression and gradually withdrew into a lonely, schizoid way of life, which he had maintained to the present. The main source of anxiety during his adult years has been occasional, unavoidable contacts with authority figures, particularly army superiors and doctors. He expressed many vague fears concerning the nature of his brain waves and what they would reveal about his inner thoughts.

His first two sleeping days in the research room were restless, and no dream reports were obtained. On the third day, the following dreams were elicited:

1. "I was sweating and trying to climb a rope, but was not getting anywhere."
2. "I was driving in a car by myself, that's all."
3. "I was having intercourse with a girl friend. That's all."

The subject was unable to associate to the dreams which he related in a factual, affectless manner. He became more suspicious and defensive and produced only one more "EEG" dream in the following three days in the research room.

He then began to nap before coming to the research room and shortly thereafter left the project.

Mr. MC asked the same questions about the Rorschach cards that he asked about the electroencephalograph electrodes. He wondered if the cards would reveal his thoughts and feelings without his control. He produced as many as five to seven rapid responses concerning anatomy and predatory animals to each card. By the tenth card, he had become quite suspicious and again questioned the purpose of the test. Thus both the dream productions and the Rorschach responses were difficult for him to produce and seemed to imply to him that his defensive barriers were being threatened.

Comments

These three varied reactions, ranging from profuse dream production to an almost total absence of dreaming, can be explained to some extent by the transference relationship inherent in the dream research.

This transference between the researcher and the subject was intensified by the following regressive factors which have rarely been taken into account by recent dream researchers.

1. All three subjects in this project expressed the fantasy that the use of the electroencephalograph electrodes would allow the researcher to circumvent their usual defenses and discover unconscious, anxiety-arousing material.

2. The regression involved in sleeping, especially while under observation, stimulated many infantile fantasies.

3. Since the purpose of any dream research is to obtain dreams from subjects by various methods, the subjects interpreted their participation in this project as a demand or suggestion that they dream. Fisher (1953) described several pregenital incorporative and expulsive fantasies stimulated in analytic patients by the analyst's suggestions to dream.

4. The tendency of some subjects participating in any research is to transform the researcher into a parent-surrogate and to transfer onto him ambivalent feelings toward their own parents.

The response of the subject to the research situation, and the effect it has on the frequency of dreaming, have implications for studies of dream deprivation. Dement (1960) recently found that he could "deprive" subjects of their dreams by awakening them as soon as electroencephalographic evidence of dreaming appeared. If his subjects were deprived of their dreams for several consecutive nights, they became anxious and often left the research prematurely. Dement postulates that most people need to discharge accumulated tensions each night through their dreams. If this avenue for discharge is denied them by interrupting their dreams, then their tensions will mount and spill over into daytime symptoms of anxiety and fears of the research itself. Some of the anxiety in the dream deprived subjects may have been due to the arousal of unconscious fantasies about the acceptability of their dream "gifts" to the researcher. A factor contributing to the increased quantity of dreaming during and after the deprivation period may be the unconscious wish to please the researcher–parent surrogate. These factors are not offered as complete explanations of the phenomenon of dream deprivation, but they should be explored if deprived subjects continue to show anxiety and a tendency to leave the research.

Summary

The responses of three subjects to the Kleitman electroencephalographic technique for eliciting dreams differed widely. One subject produced dreams almost 100 percent of the time. Another related only one dream during the entire period of study. A third subject left the project prematurely after having several dreamless nights.

The exploration of transference phenomena and unconscious fantasies of the subjects is recommended in future dream research of this type since it appears that these psychological forces can influence the frequency of dreaming.

Chapter 38

A TECHNIQUE FOR SELF-ANALYSIS OF COUNTERTRANSFERENCE: USE OF THE PSYCHOANALYST'S VISUAL IMAGES IN RESPONSE TO PATIENT'S DREAMS

W. DONALD ROSS AND FREDERIC T. KAPP

Since Freud's original mention of *the countertransference* in 1910 (1910b) there have been many contributions to the literature on the phenomena associated with this term. At that time Freud considered that countertransference arose in the physician "as a result of the patient's influence on his unconscious feelings," and he stressed the need for the analyst to "recognize this counter-transference in himself and overcome it." We propose a method to facilitate the self-analysis of countertransference which, at least to our knowledge, has not been published previously. This method is an innovation in technique in line with Freud's principle that "the interpretation of dreams is the royal road to a knowledge of the unconscious activities of the mind" (1900, p. 608). It consists of self-analysis by the psychoanalyst of his personal visual associations to his patient's dreams, in order to reveal previously unconscious countertransference.

Orr (1954) has made a thorough and thoughtful historical survey of the literature on countertransference up to 1954. His review considers the various definitions and technical methods of handling countertransference. Some contributions which appeared after Orr's survey, and which we do not specifically

This paper was first published in the *Journal of the American Psychoanalytic Association* (1962), 10:643–657.

discuss, are included in our bibliography (Slavson, 1953; Mullan, 1955; Nunberg, 1955; Jackson, 1956; Wolstein, 1959; Harley, 1962). The separate definitions of countertransference have led several authors to use other terms to label some of the related phenomena which do not fit with the more usual specific definitions of countertransference as either the analyst's unconscious reactions to the patient's transference, or the analyst's unconscious transference to the patient. Some of these terms are: *counterresistance* (Racker, 1953; Glover, 1955), *counteridentification* (Fliess, 1953a), *the emotional position of the analyst* (Gitelson, 1952), *R* (the analyst's total response to his patient's needs) (Little, 1957), *normal countertransference* (Orr, 1954), *the experiences of the analyst* (Szasz, 1956), and *the analyst's personal equation* (Azorin, 1957).

Regardless of the different ways of viewing countertransference and related phenomena, the technique described in this paper is applicable to the analysis of unconscious components in the analyst's reaction to the patient or in his reaction to the patient's transference.

Method

A number of methods have been described previously for the recognition of countertransference. For example, Maxwell Gitelson (1952), Mabel Blake Cohen (1952), and Karl Menninger (1958) have described several clues which suggest that a countertransference problem is present. They cover a large number of situations which should alert the analyst to examine his own involvement with the patient.

One of the methods accepted for resolving countertransference problems is self-analysis (Reik, 1952; Weigert, 1954; Little, 1957). There is little written on specific techniques for accomplishing this task, presumably because the analyst uses his own free associations, and at times his dreams, in a manner familiar to him from his own analysis, training, and experience with patients. Annie Reich, in discussing some "acute forms of countertransference," writes: "frequently a bit of self-analysis can reveal what is going on and bring about a complete solution of the conflict" (1951, pp. 25–31). Colby refers to the generally accepted phenomenon that "patients' descriptions produce echo responses in the analyst and often he spends a few moments of each hour silently exploring his personal associations" (1958, pp. 99–100). He suggests a "time-spacing" method of self-analysis.

In this paper we present a technique of self-analysis of the countertransference which seems to provide a further tool of value for the analyst. Essentially it consists of using the analyst's associations to his visual images of his patient's dreams. The technique appears to have the merit of providing a simple spontaneous starting point which can be applied either when a countertransference problem has already been suspected or, routinely, to test for countertransference, even without other clues. Our method was developed as the result of the stimulation provided by a talk given by Kanzer on image formation during free association (1958). This led the authors to pay attention to the visual images which came to mind while listening with "evenly suspended attention" (Freud, 1912) as patients told their dreams.

A number of studies of the dynamics of visual imagery have appeared in the psychoanalytic literature. Breuer and Freud drew conclusions from the visual images of patients such as Anna O and Frau Emma von N in *Studies on Hysteria* (1895). In his 1914 revision of *The Interpretation of Dreams*, Freud inserted some comments about Silberer's observations on the transformation of his own thoughts into pictures which occurred especially when he was in a sleepy or fatigued condition. Freud considered such observations to be a way of studying one factor of dream work in isolation (pp. 344, 503). Felix Deutsch pointed out that visual images of patients in the course of analysis may act both as resistance and as communication (1953). Bertram Lewin referred to aesthetic reveries in his patients as resistance alternatives to the verbalization of ideas (chapter 7). Ekstein and Wallerstein included imagery among the phenomena observed in play therapy of children, in the transition phase between verbalization and action (1954). Kanzer gave several examples of the process of analyzing his patients' visual images (1958). It appears, from these authors, that visual imagery, although a resistance to verbalization as secondary-process communication, and in this sense comparable to acting out, is nevertheless much more available for analysis than is acting out.

Discussions of the imaginative process in patients and analyst during psychoanalysis have recognized the value of creative imagination in aiding empathy (Colby, 1958; Beres, 1960). However, the specific use of the imagery experienced by the analyst in response to his patient's verbal report of a dream has not been described. Our basic suggestion is that such images can be used by the analyst for self-analysis in a manner analogous to the way Kanzer and others have described using their patients' images during the course of free association.

Such images appear to be an instance of the unconscious activity of analyst's mind, caught as a snapshot, in the process of responding to the unconscious activity of the patient's mind. The verbal description of the dream by the patient represents the final result of the patient's dream work including secondary revision. The form in which the analyst conceptualizes it, however, is a new version of the patient's dream to which the unconscious feelings of the analyst have contributed. The analyst's visual images of the verbal representations of his patient's dream portray the mind of the analyst as well as that of the patient.

Visual images experienced by the analyst while awake, rather than while sleepy or fatigued, even when they occur during the state of "evenly suspended attention," are surely not exactly comparable to images formed while dreaming, or fully comparable even to the images of the patient in the special analytic state on the couch. Medlicott (1958), discussing some relations between waking imagery, dream imagery, and hallucinations, pointed out distinctions as well as similarities. Some of the features of the analyst's images arise from the special circumstances. If one considers that the analyst is not free to verbalize his associations as is the patient, let alone act out his feelings toward the patient, it is not surprising that the unconscious mental activity of the analyst can include the changing of "involuntary ideas into visual and acoustic images" (Freud, 1900, p. 102), as a phase in the analyst's response to his patient. Furthermore, in Fisher's reports on his experimental study of the construction of dreams and images, he has indicated that "Images associated with repressed unconscious childhood memory content do not appear in all subjects but only in those who are freer, less inhibited and less resistant" (Fisher, 1957, p. 38). Consequently it seemed that the visual images of the "less resistant" analyst, in response to the patient's dreams might be used for self-analysis of both dynamic and genetic unconscious elements in the analyst's countertransference reaction.

In our experience such images may "pop" into the center of the analyst's awareness while he is listening to the patient's report of a dream. At other times they appear vague and fleeting and at the margin of consciousness, but they can be captured. The scenes may be recognizable as pertaining to recent or past memories of the analyst. Often such images and memories occur in rapid succession.

Free association to these occurrences often reminds the analyst of his own analytic insights which are pertinent to the particular patient. This self-analytic work may be done within the hour in which the dream is presented or at some later time. Obviously, the use of this technique presupposes, on the part of the analyst, his own personal analysis, his psychoanalytic training and experience, and his motivation for a continuing pursuit of insight.

What the analyst does with the increased knowledge obtained by this technique will depend on the individual analysis. In general, this knowledge facilitates the aspect of the analytic process in which that which was unconscious becomes conscious. Specifically, the choice of interpretation by the analyst may be more discriminating after the analyst is more aware of the nature of his own unconscious responses. Occasionally the countertransference insight might be imparted to the patient. Further discussion would be more appropriate after some individual examples have illustrated how our technique has been applied.

Examples

Example 1

A woman patient who had made considerable progress earlier in her analysis had been in the analytic doldrums for several weeks before the dream to be noted. Despite the fact that the analyst had interpreted the conflicts around her erotic transference many times, she could not recognize these feelings. The lack of movement in the analysis and the ineffectiveness of his interpretations were clues to the analyst that there probably was some sort of countertransference resistance.

At this time in the analysis the patient dreamed she was sitting in her dinette with a person whose identity was vague. A woman friend of the patient, who was also in analysis, and who seemed to be living in the same house, came into the room looking ill and said that she was planning to move away. So the dream ended.

While the patient was telling the dream the analyst suddenly visualized a certain dinette from his own recent social experiences. Free association by the analyst to the dinette he had visualized led to a woman the analyst often met socially and whom, frankly, he would have liked to meet much less often because he considered her social behavior to be that of a superficial flirt, a bore, and someone who constantly was demanding various favors from him. He next recalled a woman who had been the housekeeper in the home where he lived as a child. She had been devoted to him but he had gradually come to dislike her because of her stubbornness and her excessive demands on him to reciprocate her love. When she became unhappy in her job and quit, he had been pleased.

Through such associations the analyst began to consider the possibility that subtly and unconsciously he had been encouraging the patient to defend herself against the erotic transference by leaving treatment. It now became clear to him why his previous attempts to interpret the transference had been clumsy and unsuccessful. His unconscious countertransference feeling was one of wanting the patient to leave treatment. Before the analyst recognized these feelings, his interpretations, colored by unconscious feelings of wanting to reject the patient, had been presented in a manner which contributed to the patient feeling that she was being criticized and excluded by her therapist. Once this was clear, the analyst was able to deal with the transference neurosis in a constructive manner and the analysis progressed again. The patient could now accept the nonrejecting clarification of her erotic feelings to the analyst. These feelings and the defenses against them no longer constituted a resistance to analytic movement.

Example 2

A man reported several dreams, the locale of which included the backyard and the driveway of his home during early adolescence.

The analyst found himself visualizing the locale described by the patient in terms of the backyard and driveway of his recent home, a place where his son had often played. He also associated the scene to the backyard of his home during his own adolescence, and to the driveway of the home where he lived when he was four years old. The last scene was associated with an experience when he had not been able to keep an "Irish Mail" handcar bought for him by his father, who decided he was not big enough to operate it. These associations made the analyst aware for the first time that, in part, he had been equating the patient with his son, as well as with himself when he was an adolescent, and with himself when he was struggling with oedipal problems. This insight into previously unconscious countertransference revealed that the analyst was competing to some degree with the patient's father.

Now the analyst could consider more realistically the actual characteristics of the patient's father as contrasted to the distorted picture which the patient had presented of his father and which the analyst had previously accepted. He realized that the patient, out of his oedipal rivalry, had been presenting a somewhat erroneous picture of his father. This clarification paved the way to more effective understanding of the transference and its genetic precursor in the need for the patient to find fault with his father and with himself for doing so. Then the interpretations were made, step by step, of the resistance against recognizing critical feelings about the analyst and, when these critical feelings became conscious, of their competitive nature, paralleling a similar need to find fault with his father in childhood.

Example 3

Early in the analysis of a young, self-assured, and successful businessman who complained of only a few well-delineated neurotic symptoms, the patient dreamed that he was at a restaurant with an older man who offered to treat him. In the dream, the patient told the man that he was not hungry since he had already had dinner at home.

The analyst realized that, in part, this dream pictured the early transference reaction in which the patient was struggling with his feelings about getting more deeply into analysis. The patient was presenting himself as reluctant to accept treatment since he liked things the way they were and had no desire to change.

As the patient described his dream, the analyst visualized a scene in which he had dined at an exclusive club where he had been the guest of an older man. Immediately following this image, he recalled another one of a wedding banquet he had attended when he was five years old. The first image of the club dinner reminded him of his feelings at that time when he was conscious of envy at not being a member of the "Four Hundred"; he recalled how he concealed these feelings by assuming an attitude of nonchalance. The image of the wedding banquet brought back the feelings of happiness and importance at being the cute little boy at the large family party where everybody made a big fuss over him and fed him tidbits. Self-analysis of this material led the analyst to realize that he had made a countertransference identification with his patient. Reminded by this bit of self-analysis that some of his own character defenses were similar to those of the patient, he was able to recognize the patient's feelings behind the facade of self-sufficiency in the dream and to make a much broader and deeper interpretation of the transference which gave recognition to the defensive nature of the patient's superficial attitude to his analysis. The interpretation was confirmed by the patient's expression of feelings of anxiety over competition with the analyst and with his father.

Example 4

A woman patient dreamed that she entered her apartment and found her younger brother eating in her kitchen.

As the patient told the dream, the analyst visualized a particular door and a particular kitchen. He had, of course, never seen his patient's apartment, and the origins of his visualization of her dream were sought in his own associations. The apartment door was recognizable as a condensation of the door to an apartment where he lived early in his marriage, and also of the door to a hotel room which was associated with erotic fantasies stirred up in his own analysis. The kitchen visualized by the analyst was recognizable as pertaining not only to the apartment of his early married life but also to an apartment in which he had lived at the age of six, when he had oral and phallic problems related both to his mother and to his older sister.

These associations led the analyst to become aware of the fact that unconsciously he had been feeling toward the patient as he had toward his wife early in marriage, as he had felt toward his older sister during childhood when he displaced feelings from his mother to her, and as he had felt toward his wife during a period in his analysis when he had displaced feelings to her from his woman analyst. Thus, the analyst was able to gain insight into the countertransference by associating to his visual images of the patient's dream. He was now able to see that not only was the patient transferring feelings to him which she previously had to her younger brother, but also that his countertransference was acting as a resistance and thus blocking analytic progress. He decided that these circumstances warranted a limited interpretation of the countertransference to the patient. He told the patient that not only was she equating the analyst with her younger brother, as he had previously interpreted, but that the analyst had facilitated this by tending to equate her with his sister. This interpretation was followed by new material from the patient indicating greater emotional insight into the brother transference, then by a shift to a father transference, with further movement in the analysis.

Example 5

This example illustrates an instance in which a modification of the suggested technique might have been used to prevent a therapeutic failure. It is taken from the supervision, by an analyst, of a resident doing psychoanalytically oriented psychotherapy.

The patient was an attractive, young, married woman who was unhappy in her marriage and had many phobias. At the time she had the dream to be discussed, the patient was talking to her therapist about quitting treatment because she felt she was getting worse rather than better. The therapist realized the patient was angry at him. He thought that her anger was based on his frustration of her infantile dependent strivings. At this point in treatment, the patient dreamed that she was the bride at a wedding in a Catholic church and was standing next to a tall man whose face she could not see and whom she assumed was the groom. During the dream, the patient felt more and more disturbed because she did not want to marry a man she did not know.

As the patient told the dream, the therapist visualized himself as the groom. Then he visualized his own wedding which had actually taken place not in a church but outdoors and had been in a different faith. He ignored his associations to the patient's dream and went ahead to interpret to the patient his preconceived hypothesis of the transference. He explained to her that she was angry at him because he was not satisfying her excessive needs for attention which were like those of a greedy child. He was disappointed, puzzled, and frustrated when the patient failed to come for the next appointment.

Later, when he discussed this case with his supervisor, the therapist recalled the visual images he had conjured up while the patient was telling her dream. After he told these to the supervisor, it became clear to both of them that the therapist's lack of awareness of his erotic countertransference had blinded him to the implications of even the manifest content of the dream. His inability to see them, and therefore deal with them, had played into the patient's erotic transference and had aroused so much anxiety in her that she broke off treatment.

Discussion

The history of the concept of countertransference in psychoanalytic theory has followed a pathway similar to that of the concept of transference. In the earliest period of psychoanalysis transference was not recognized. Later, after it was recognized, it was considered an unpleasant contaminant and a dangerous resistance that interfered with the treatment process. Still later, the concept of transference came to be recognized as a most important and inevitable aspect of treatment which has to be dealt with constructively in the physician–patient relationship.

A similar development seems to have occurred in the unfolding of the concept of countertransference. Countertransference was at first unrecognized; then it was recognized but considered a contaminant and an impediment to treatment. Only fairly recently have analysts begun to look at countertransference phenomena as inevitable, and even, at times, as useful tools in psychoanalytic treatment (Tausk, 1924; Heimann, 1950; Little, 1951, 1957; Benedek, 1953; Racker, 1953, 1958; Slavson et al., 1953; Tauber, 1954; Orr, 1954; Money-Kyrle, 1956; Tower, 1956; Barchilon, 1958). There is some controversy about the interpretation of the countertransference to the patient, but Margaret Little's discussion of the value of doing so under specific conditions (1951) has been essentially supported by other experienced analysts (Gitelson, 1952; Benedek, 1953).

The example given by Franz Alexander of telling a patient that his behavior was annoying to the analyst can be considered an instance of interpreting the countertransference to the patient. Alexander described the "Corrective emotional experience [as] a consciously planned regulation of the therapist's own emotional responses to the patient's material . . . in such a way as to counteract the harmful effects of the parental attitudes" (Alexander, 1948, p. 287). Leaving aside the controversial aspects about role-playing by the analyst, there is general agreement on the desirability of greater conscious awareness of countertransference.

Lucia Tower has pointed out that earlier attitudes about countertransference tended to keep it concealed (1956). Therese Benedek has expressed the opinion that reluctance to face countertransference has contributed to long and painful transference neuroses (1954). To Levine it seems probable that countertransference accounts for a large percentage of mistakes and failures; Levine feels that the therapist need not be shocked if he has countertransference problems since they are universal (1952). Michael Balint stated that in the Hungarian system of psychoanalytic training, "the interrelation of the transference of the patient and the counter-transference of his analyst is in the focus of attention right from the start and remains there" (1957, p. 299).

The method for self-analysis of countertransference described in this paper provides a further means of making the countertransference conscious so that it can be taken into account. The adult ego of the analyst can then resolve the countertransference in favor of the more mature response. This response can include more discriminating interpretations. Other methods of self-analysis, of course, can achieve the same goal. Furthermore, self-analysis can be applied to visual images which the analyst has in response to material from the patient other than dreams. However, we have found the use of visual images in response to patients' dreams to be a particularly pointed way of assuring that self-analysis is done fairly quickly in a vivid and convincing manner. The use of such fantasies in better understanding the analytic process is an instance of regression in the service of the ego.

Our examples illustrate three applications of this technique. In some it was applied to pinpoint a countertransference problem already suspected from other clues. In others it was used to pick up previously unsuspected countertransference. The last example suggests its possible use in supervision.

We would like to propose a means for assessing the validity of this method. Procedures for validation of insight into previously unconscious countertransference are not well established. We suggest the working hypothesis that the correctness of a countertransference insight is indicated by the same signs that are well known when a correct transference interpretation is made to a patient. These indicators include a sudden change in level of tension, a sudden feeling of the individual understanding himself better, and a subsequent spurt in the progress of the analysis. However, some of these phenomena also occur with inexact interpretations (Glover, 1955). Hence, these criteria are not sufficient.

The most accepted technique for the assessment of countertransference is by supervision with an experienced analyst. Example 5 illustrates how attention to the therapist's images of his patient's dream might have been used to advantage in the supervision of psychoanalytically oriented psychotherapy.

We propose the following plan for the validation of the innovation described in this paper. During the course of analytic supervision there are periods in which the supervisor becomes aware of countertransference problems. At these points, before the supervisor has communicated his impression to the analyst, he might write down his opinion of the countertransference. At the same time, the analyst could take a new dream of his patient and write down his impression of the countertransference derived from his self-analysis of the visual images that occurred to him when the patient told the dream. The two written conclusions from independent material could then be compared.

A discrepancy between the two results would, of course, raise the question as to whether the supervisor or the analyst was closer to the truth: This is a question which arises at times in any case during supervision. Usually the supervisor, with greater experience and less involvement with the patient, is more likely to be correct. Other criteria, such as the subsequent course of the analysis, can be used by both supervisor and analyst to decide the issue.

Such testing of the method during supervision, besides validating or denying the usefulness of the technique, would supplement present methods of supervision. This would provide an additional means by which the analyst in training could increasingly sharpen his ability to recognize his various patterns of countertransference.

Summary

An innovation in technique is presented for the self-analysis of unconscious components in the analyst's reactions to his patient and to his patient's transference. The visual images of the analyst in response to his patient's descriptions of dreams are used by the analyst as the starting point for the uncovering of previously unconscious countertransference.

Pertinent literature on countertransference, self-analysis, and visual imagery is discussed with the explanation of the development of this method.

Four examples of the use of this technique in psychoanalysis are presented; in addition, one example is given from the supervision of psychoanalytically oriented psychotherapy, to illustrate how a modification of this method might have prevented a therapeutic failure.

This technique is consistent with recent emphasis on the inevitability of some countertransference reactions, and even of their being useful when they are recognized, in contrast with earlier tendencies to consider them to be undesirable contaminants.

A suggestion is made for the validation of this technique and for its use in analytical supervision.

Although its use presupposes the skill and motivation of the analyst for the constant pursuit of insight, the method provides a distinct and relatively simple procedure for facilitating the self-analysis of the countertransference.

Chapter 39

DREAMS ABOUT THE PATIENT: AN APPROACH TO THE PROBLEM OF COUNTERTRANSFERENCE

Roy M. Whitman, Milton Kramer, and Bill J. Baldridge

The literature on countertransference is increasing rapidly (Orr, 1954; Wolstein, 1959; chapter 38). Karl Menninger (1958) and Mabel Cohen (1952) both list dreams about the patient as countertransference indicators. Current research into the process of dreaming (Bornstein, 1949; Dement and Wolpert, 1957a,b) has shown that dreams occur much more often than was hitherto suspected (Goodenough, Shapiro, Holden, and Steinschriber, 1959). Such observations, indicating increased quantity of dreaming, when combined with a changing attitude (Little, 1951, 1957; Halpern, 1964) to the purely negative implications of the countertransference, suggest that a reappraisal of the analyst or therapist dreaming about the patient might well be in order. The thesis of this paper is that dreams about patients by the analyst or therapist are occurring more often than is being reported, and, furthermore, that these dreams may be highly productive in providing insight into the transactions of the psychoanalytic or psychotherapeutic process. Because much of our data is from both psychoanalysis and psychotherapy, we shall refer to both processes.

Descriptions of countertransference vary from occasional to invariable (Tower, 1956), from negative to positive (Weigert, 1954), from all-inclusive to partial (Little, 1957; Whitman,

This paper was first published in the *Journal of the American Psychoanalytic Association* (1969), 17:702–727.

1963), and from neurotic to normal (Money-Kyrle, 1956). As an initial approach we propose to classify a dream of a therapist about a patient in the manifest content as a countertransference dream. This provides ease of identification so that we can focus our interest. We recognize that other dreams may be about patients but will be more difficult to identify.

In answer to a possible objection that the presence of a patient in the manifest content of the therapist's dreams means that this is not really the patient, we have two points to make. The first is that which Freud used in discussing dream pairs (1933b), when he commented that the person may appear undisguised in a dream when the behavior is "faintly indicated," the reverse occurring in the second dream. The second is in disagreement with Freud in this same paragraph when he speaks about unrecognizable or "indifferent" persons being substituted for a certain individual. Our position is that the "indifferent substitution" is itself meaningful, and while it may be on the basis of a minor physical characteristic or name similarity, it is much more often on the basis of a significant ego attitude. Thus, there is, in our way of thinking, no "indifferent" manifest content (French, 1952–1958; Savitt, 1960) for the purposes of gaining information about the therapist's attitudes.

It is a striking historical note in psychoanalysis (Erikson, 1954), that the Irma Dream, the first dream ever subjected to intensive scrutiny, can for our purposes also be classified as a countertransference dream. Other than the dreams reported by Freud with his customary courage, there were relatively few instances that we could find of dreams of the analyst about the patient (Gitelson, 1952; Langer, 1952; Orr, 1954; Tauber, 1954; Tower, 1956; chapter 9).

In a previous study of ours (Whitman, Kramer, and Baldridge, 1963a), designed specifically to elicit countertransference dreams by having the therapist report his dreams in a dream laboratory prior to his presentation of a continuous therapy patient at a conference the next day, we were only occasionally successful in recovering such dreams, despite the use of the Kleitman dream awakening technique (Baldridge, Hitman, and Kramer, 1963), and the obvious "Demand" characteristic on the therapist. The cathexis of the therapist was much more toward the approaching conference and less toward the patient than we had hoped. Nevertheless, in the dreams about patients that were reported, we felt that we had opened an avenue of approach to countertransference which could be explored with profit.

In our subsequent supervisory and therapeutic efforts and in our own continuing self-analyses, we paid special attention to dreams about patients. In addition, we asked our colleagues to relate dreams about patients to us when they felt that they could. However, there is an obvious selection process in the dreams we have collected: the dreams are (1) those recalled by the therapist, and (2) those he was willing to share with us.

In summary, our study of countertransference dreams is, therefore, drawn from: (1) Freud's dreams; (2) the findings of our study of therapists' dreams "experimentally" recovered; (3) dreams about patients by psychiatric residents in supervision; (4) dreams of our analytic colleagues as candidates; (5) dreams about patients by psychiatric residents in treatment; (6) dreams about patients by therapists not in treatment or supervision; (7) the literature containing references to therapists' dreams about patients.

Freud's Dreams

Of the fifty dreams of Freud (1900) reported in *The Interpretation of Dreams*, patients appear in the manifest content of three of these dreams. They appear in the latent content as well in seventeen of the fifty dreams (Table 39.1). In a field where quantification is so difficult, this "random" sample of Freud's dreams (random in regard to dreaming about patients) provides a rough quantitative estimation of this type of dream. Thus one can say that 6 percent of the therapists' dreams have patients in the manifest content and 34 percent have patients in the latent content as well. We cite this as a "statistic" since it is roughly in accord with our own self-observations and the reports of our colleagues.

We must reiterate that our operational definition of one type of countertransference dream is the appearance of the patient in the manifest content of the therapist's dream. We recognize fully that this is an oversimplification, that the manifest figure may either be *primarily* the patient or *primarily* another person. In this context, we are interested not in the focal figure but in any aspect of this overdetermined patient figure which leads up to unconscious therapist attitudes potentially relevant to the doctor–patient relationship. Thus, in the first dream that we shall examine, the dream of Irma's injection, Irma is certainly herself, a woman named Emma (Schur, 1966a) whom Freud had seen several months earlier, all patients of Freud, Freud's wife, and several other women via condensation. Further, Irma stands for the mystery of the dream itself, as Erikson (1954) points out.

The Irma Dream

Not only was Freud's dream of Irma's injection the first dream ever subjected to detailed analysis by Freud, but Erikson has elevated it to an even more important place in psychoanalytic history and personality theory by his superb reanalysis of the dream in "The Dream Specimen of Psychoanalysis" (1954). We shall extract those aspects of the dream which are relevant to this paper.

It is a well-known fact that first dreams in an analysis are much more transparent and helpful in formulating the course and development of the transference neurosis than later dreams where defenses of various types have arisen to obscure the dynamics and ego coping mechanisms of the patient. A somewhat similar hypothesis might be used in regard to countertransference dreams before the day-to-day analytic work with that patient has obscured the therapist's initial countertransference orientation to the patient.

Thinking on a longitudinal scale, the Irma dream might then be conceived of as standing in an initiating and foreshadowing relationship to the whole development of the psychoanalytic orientation to patients as conceived of by its originator. Schur (1966a) has demonstrated convincingly in his study that Freud had gone through an exhausting emotional experience with Emma, a patient he had seen several months before the

TABLE 39.1
Freud's Dreams

Total	50
Patients in either latent, or manifest and latent content	17

Latent Only
1. Botanical monograph (pp. 169–176)
2. Closet, open-air (pp. 468–470)
3. 1851 and 1856—Communication from Town Council (pp. 435–439)
4. Famous speakers—Dr. Lecher (pp. 268–269)
5. Funeral oration by young doctor (pp. 178–179)
6. Goethe's attack on Herr M. (pp. 439–441)
7. "Hearsing" (p. 298)
8. "Hollthurn" (pp. 455–459)
9. Riding on a horse-boil (pp. 229–232)
10. Rome in a mist, view of (p. 194)
11. Savonarola's profile (p. 166)
12. Son, news of, from the front (pp. 558–560)
13. Table d'hôte, company at (pp. 636–640)
14. Undressed, running upstairs (pp. 238–240)

Both Manifest and Latent
1. Irma's injection (pp. 106–120)
2. "Autodidasker" (pp. 298–302)
3. Mother and daughter (p. 165)

Irma dream and who had requested nasal operations. In the Irma dream, many of the difficulties experienced by analysts in their work with patients are hinted at, or even explicitly noted, as well as the coping devices used by analysts in their therapeutic and professional lives.

It is also worth commenting that despite the widespread use of the term *countertransference* as a reaction to the patient's transference, or as a reaction to something, countertransference really comes first. There is an analogy with maternal and paternal attitudes to the child which really precede the advent of a child and which greet him upon his birth. As Racker (1953) has pointed out, the patient knows a great deal about the analyst before he sees him (his intellectual and psychological interests, choice of profession, financial status, etc.), whereas the analyst knows much less about the patient. The analyst, therefore, has less data on which to base reality attitudes before the initial

therapeutic encounter and projects his expectations with only
minimal data such as name, referral source, telephone voice,
and so on.

Before we point up this grander conception of the Irma
dream, it is worth quoting once again the dream of Irma's
injection as the first analyzed dream in the history of psychoanalyses and also, according to our definition, the initial countertransference dream:

Dream of July 23rd—24th, 1895

> A large hall—numerous guests, whom we were receiv-
> ing—Among them was Irma. I at once took her on one
> side, as though to answer her letter and to reproach her
> for not having accepted my "solution" yet. I said to her:
> "If you still get pains, it's really only your fault." She re-
> plied: "If you only knew what pains I've got now in my
> throat and stomach and abdomen—it's choking me"—I was
> alarmed and looked at her. She looked pale and puffy. I
> thought to myself that after all I must be missing some
> organic trouble. I took her to the window and looked down
> her throat, and she showed signs of recalcitrance, like
> women with artificial dentures. I thought to myself that
> there was really no need for her to do that—She opened
> her mouth properly and on the right I found a big white
> patch; at another place I saw extensive whitish gray scrabs
> upon some remarkable curly structures which were evi-
> dently modelled on the turbinal bones of the nose.—I at
> once called in Dr. M., and he repeated the examination
> and confirmed it. . . . Dr. M. looked quite different from
> usual; he was very pale, he walked with a limp and his chin
> was clean shaven. . . . My friend Otto was now standing
> beside her as well, and my friend Leopold was percussing
> her through her bodice and saying: "She has a dull area
> low down on the left." He also indicates that a portion of
> the skin on the left shoulder was infiltrated. (I noticed this,
> just as he did, in spite of her dress.) . . . M. said: "There's
> no doubt it's an infection, but no matter; dysentery will
> supervene and the toxin will be eliminated." . . . We were
> directly aware, too, of the origin of the infection. Not long
> before, when she was feeling unwell, my friend Otto had

given her an injection of a preparation of propy, pro-
pysl . . . propionic acid . . . trimethylamin (and I saw before me the formula for this printed in heavy type). . . . Injections of that sort ought not be made so thought-
lessly. . . . And probably the syringe had not been clean [p.
107].

Let us see what we can extract from the dream in terms of
Freud's attitudes toward his patient, Irma.

The initial orientation that we can discern is that the patient comes to him, he does not go to her. The privacy of the
relationship is next stated as Freud takes Irma aside[1] and the
importance of the communication is stressed via his implicit
goal of seemingly answering her letter. We can make our first
countertransference remarks. There is an insistence that the
patient comes to him (how few home visits psychiatrists make!);
and, as though in return almost (Menninger, 1958), the patient
is respected as to her privacy and given individual attention.
The immediate attitude to her involves return communication,
implying that the patient initiates the chain of transactional
communications, and that the analyst promises response. So far
we have listed several positive "countertransference" ingredients (using a very broad definition of countertransference [Lit-
tle, 1957]) which are in the area of respect for both the person
and his privacy.

Are there any negative countertransference operations
hinted at in this sequence? The *great* hall[2] with numbers of
people narrowing to the twosome suggests that the one-to-one
relationship may be a defense against exhibitionistic wishes (of
greatness) which emerge later in the dream and are quite cogently traced back by Erikson to the episode of the chamberpot
and the "little squirt" who will amount to nothing. One also
wonders about the defensive aspects of this twosome in relationship to the wife, who was the other half of the "we" in the
dream, and started out so auspiciously in the dream at the

[1]This is a forerunner perhaps of the widely accepted difficulties inherent in carrying
on a social and professional relationship simultaneously with a patient.

[2]Ross and Brissenden (1961) interestingly use the phrase "hire a hall" for the group
exhibitionistic wishes of the group therapist.

dreamer's side. What he does, looks at, and says should not include her. It is an interesting footnote in the history of psychoanalysis that a wife can enter very much into a treatment relationship; it apparently was the reason why Breuer gave up the treatment of Anna O.

As Erikson interprets this dream, Irma stands for a whole series of women patients. Freud associates "good" and "bad" patients, and an *obstreperous* patient, his wife. Even she is not at ease with him as an ideal patient would be. There are ideal patients, children. They submit easily to examination.

We can now make our second "negative" countertransference observation. Freud is *angry at women patients who will not submit to his interpretation* and prefers children. We are reminded of Lewin's (1946a) cadaver analogy as the ideal patient or the surgical analogy of the anesthetized patient who is passively the object of the doctor's manipulation. Is one of the antecedent motivations of the use of the couch hinted at here?

The next major responses of the dreamer have to do with the starting aspects of what he sees—and sees in the patient's mouth. This is similar to Piaget's observations (1951, pp. 256–257) that young children conceive of thoughts as originating in, as well as emerging from, the mouth. The not yet abandoned practice of washing out the mouth with soap holds the mouth responsible for the words it utters. He is so startled by what he sees in the mouth (therefore, what he hears patients say) that he calls for confirmation from a colleague. He also wants to share this golden treasure of words with others. Halpern's recent article (Halpern, 1969) describes one of Freud's few distortions about classical literature; it is interestingly related to "gold in the mouth."

Does this sequence not sound like the forerunner of the supervisory process now so firmly established as a cornerstone of psychoanalytic education? Dr. M is the authority (Schur [1966b] makes it clear that this is Breuer) who confirms his findings, but whom Freud humiliates via taking away his beard (a sign of status in those times). This twosome enlarges to form a professional group: "We know. . . . " It is at this point, as Erikson has stressed, that Freud abandons his role of the intrusive investigator, looking, weighing, diagnosing, and asking for

confirmation, and turns into, of all things, a joiner. The initial
appeal to authority has turned into an appeal for group conviction and authority, and it is precisely at this point that Freud is
identified with a patient, in a feminine role.

In this dream, the common countertransference reaction
of *too complete identification with the patient* (in the sense of fused
body images) emerges in relation to the supportive and coercive
aspects of the group. Infiltration of the shoulder made him
immediately associate his own rheumatism in his own shoulder.
Polemics which appear sporadically during meetings and even
require response in scientific journals (Radó, Grinker, and Alexander, 1963) can often be traced to a failure on the part of
many analysts to recognize the compelling influence of the
group on their "objective" analytic theories.

The Irma dream, then, not only hints at the discovery of
the meaning of dreams in general (for Freud the dream is the
woman who yields to him), but also points to the future structure of psychoanalytic supervision and group formation as both
an obviously supporting but also coercive fact of life for the
analyst. The difficulty in tolerating the evidence of one's discoveries of the unconscious of patients in isolation from other
observers has led to continuing supervision, continuing study
groups, and the use of societies as validating and guilt-relieving
organizations in addition to forums for the transmission and
sharing of scientific data. Furthermore, the group serves as an
inhibitory influence on the yielding to instinctual impulses. This
dream describes some of the vocational hazards of psychoanalysis (Wheelis, 1958) and the remedy used by this dreamer even
at that time before formal goups had arisen.

Autodidasker Dream

The second dream of Freud in which patients appear in both
the manifest and latent content is the dream of "Autodidasker."

> The first piece was the word "Autodidasker,"[3] which I re-
> called vividly. The second piece was an exact reproduction

---

[3]Some of the recent research differentiating REM and NREM dreams suggests that
this dream is of the NREM variety and, therefore, may have less primary process in it.

of a short and harmless phantasy which I had produced some days before. This phantasy was to the effect that when I next saw Professor N. I must say to him: "The patient about whose condition I consulted you recently is in fact only suffering from a neurosis, just as you suspected" [1900, p. 299].

The essence of Freud's latent dream thoughts dealt with coming to grief over a woman, the two composite names fused in "dasker" being Lasker and Lassalle. They each died due to their relationship with a woman (Lasker died of tabes and Lassalle died in a duel over a woman). Again we see a variant of the theme in the Irma dream of the infected and therefore dangerous woman.

The next set of associations has to do with a man of talent going to the bad in some stories that Freud had given his wife to read. Again we see his fear of coming to grief over his solutions and treatment and *appealing to the authority of the consultant* or "supervision." He is in doubt over his diagnosis of neurosis and therefore fears his treatment may be erroneous. When he learns he is wrong in his fears that the illness might be organic, he resolves to admit this with relief to his consultant at their next meeting.

Mother and Daughter Dream

The third dream was given briefly by Freud for purposes of illustrating the relationship of the day residue to dream formation. "I saw two women in the street, a mother and daughter, the latter of whom was a patient of mine."

The associations deal only with the mother putting up interferences in the way of the daughter's treatment. Again we see the interfering woman blocking successful treatment, although there is no appeal to authority on his part.

The appeal to authority so prominent in the first two dreams chosen for illustration of Freud's dreams about patients brings us to our own research findings on therapists' dreams about patients.

Therapists' Dreams Experimentally Recovered

In a previous study designed to elicit countertransference dreams (Whitman et al., 1963b), we were partially thwarted in this aim by the apparent cathexis that the resident–therapists had toward the experiment and the case conference at which they were presenting the patient. The resident–therapist and his patient each slept in a dream laboratory in two separate buildings, though only the psychiatrist knew of the other's sleeping. At this time we were trying to "force" transference–countertransference reciprocal dreaming for light that it would shed on the transaction of the therapeutic process. The resident–therapist knew only approximately about our area of interest.

Ten residents were awakened thirty-two times when their eye movements indicated dreaming and were able to report twenty-eight dreams. Twelve of these twenty-eight dreams were about the supervisory conference, fifteen about the experimental situation, three had to do with personal concerns, and four were about patients. The experimental situation and the conference overlapped via condensation in some of the dreams, thereby producing a total of more than twenty-eight. It is the four dreams about patients that we propose to examine in detail in this study.

However, first we should look at some of the findings that we reported previously in regard to the resident's concern about being observed in terms of his therapeutic adequacy by both the experimental team and the next day's staff conference. Because these are strikingly reminiscent of the group aspects of the dream of Irma's injection dreamed by Freud sixty-seven years before this study, it is worth commenting upon the content of these dreams, although they are not strictly about the patient. The fearful aspects of the group conference situation which was dreamed of by two residents in terms of a threatening and controlling mob is similar to the coercive and supportive effects of the group that was called in to verify and support Freud's findings in the Irma dream. Again, we return to the intriguing idea that some of the difficulties that have beset the psychoanalytic movement may be traced back not only to the supportive and attractive aspects of group membership, but also to fears in relation to the group, and primitive mechanisms of feminine identification when faced with a threatening group.

Indeed, one of the exact dreams reported by a male resident prior to presenting to a case conference was that of appearing before a crowd as a female. It would appear that one of the defenses against mob violence is a self-castration so that attack is self-inflicted or unnecessary.

In five instances there was a fear of being exposed in what one is doing with subsequent shame about inadequacy. This was expressed by: appearing on TV shows in a negative light, being on weekly news magazine covers, dreaming of a skit by the residents where they are on display before the staff, and, finally, taking projective tests which would reveal "terrible" flaws. Freud's concern about the opinions of his professional colleagues was not unique to him but apparently remains a significant concern for current-day psychiatrists as well, and has often been indicted for the lack of shared research material about the psychoanalytic process. We shall now examine the four dreams of psychiatric residents, experimentally collected, in which the patient appears in the manifest dream content.

Dream 1—Resident BH

> I was dreaming about Mr. J (his patient). He was in a grade school type of classroom. Blackboard and things pinned up on a blackboard so that everybody could see them. He's in the classroom and I'm one of the teachers, and I'm talking to him about his treatment program being changed.

When he was asked to associate to classrooms that night, he associated to a sailboat with a big keel. "Just sailing along without children." Things pinned on the blackboard were his own work as a teacher being looked at by the class or supervisors who would come in. He was very concerned that the conference the next day would be critical of his handling of the patient. Even the patient's productions would be considered inadequate, and as the classroom teacher he was not sure whether his or his patient's productions were on the board. In other words, would the conference be looking at his work or the patient's, or both?

Further associations asked of him were especially important in revealing countertransference attitudes. They concerned his ambivalence about having been a teacher as a young man and his doubts as to whether he had enjoyed this type of activity at all, or done it very well. Was it right to entrust little children to him; or patients for that matter? Maybe children are easier to handle than patients (cf. Freud's associations to the Irma dream), they look up to you more. Thus, we see in this dream both specific (to the patient) as well as general countertransference attitudes, in addition to the anxiety about supervision. He depreciates and infantilizes the patient by making him a grade school pupil and changing the therapist's role to a teacher's role about which he has ambivalence, but much less than about his doctor role. But basically, this is a fairly healthy attitude for a second-year psychiatric resident; the educational situation is one of the most desirable countertransference, as well as transference, models of the psychoanalytic relationship.

Dream 2—Resident RK

> This experiment was over and I asked to have all the tape marks removed so that the patient—that's my continuous case—that was also sleeping tonight would not be aware that I had the tape marks and that they weren't removed. It appeared we were going to see each other that morning as we emerged from the two laboratories. Somebody commented on the marks anyway in the dining hall and the dining hall was in the basement.

He associated to the basement dining hall where all the staff ate at Barnes Hospital. His father had been at Barnes recently and his father had died there under conditions he felt were strongly suspect of not being the best medical care. He had felt that they did not do things right there and that was the reason that his father died of surgical complications. This had been a recent painful loss and he still had a lot of anger about it. He felt it was unfair to use him as an experimental subject. Who would have access to his dreams? Did the patient really have an advantage in being treated in a university hospital, or did they exploit people?

This dream seems to deal with his shame at appearing in the same situation as the patient, the shame being before both the patient and his colleagues. This resident was also in treatment himself, and the dream suggests both his wish to identify with the patient role as well as a wish to keep this hidden. The remainder of the dream seems to deal with the typical experimental subject anxieties and angers as experienced in the laboratory situation (Whitman, 1963). Neither the department, the experimenters, nor the supervisory conference do things right.

Again, however, we see the anxiety in relation to the group situation (the dining hall) with preoccupation about the patient fading to a relatively secondary role in the associations. Nevertheless, there is an identification with the patient as being in a potentially dangerous role of which the least suffering is shame and the most is potential death.

Dream 3—Resident LM

> It had something to do with dream studies and use of the studies. How they could be interpreted and this was the concern as to whether they would be used in relation to the patient. There was a possibility that the patient would be told about his (the therapist's) dreams.

His associations dealt with some feelings that the patient might get some of the information from the dream study. It was sort of a "would it be told to them" concern. At the same time he had a great deal of curiosity about the patient's dreams and wondered if he would be given access to them.

What we see is a manifest concern about the patient and how to help him really hiding a deeper fear that he (the therapist) might be found out about (in supervision or by the research team). Other associations suggested that his finding out about the patient had a guilty quality for which the punishment would be that the patient would find out about him.

Dream 4—Resident TW

> I was doing some work for the Government, probably the Navy, under water, working on something with currents and boat hulls. There was a meeting going on discussing what has been done, and there was supposed to be some big brass connected with this. My continuous case conference patient was describing what was going on and playing the tapes as if he were a TV commentator.

He associated to the apparatus of the dream research. The meeting was actually presided over by his patient in the dream. He was glad that his patient was doing so well (which he actually is) and had gotten a job. The patient was a VA patient, hence the Government. He was uneasy about the big brother aspects of the government.

In the actual presentation this resident was very confused and defensive about his therapy. He was pleased with the patient especially for taking the initiative in getting well away from the psychotherapy. Hiding (underwater) and abdicating therapeutic leadership were especially prominent in the supervision of this resident. But anxiety (about electricity and water) obscured the underlying anxiety about and his orientation toward the patient. The resident would have preferred to keep his therapy as an underground activity and especially did not want the higher ranking member of the department ("big brass") to find out about it. He was pleased that the patient was getting well outside the hospital and very doubtful about the efficacy of his own therapeutic efforts.

These four dreams about patients revealed countertransference attitudes of patient depreciation and infantilization, shameful identification with the patient, fear of therapeutic inadequacy before the groups, reversal of roles with the patient, and abdication of therapeutic leadership. These findings led us to believe that a potentially rich source of insight into countertransference was ready to be tapped. But this hope thus far has not been realized. In only a few instances have supervisees, despite our stated interest in such material given us dream material about the patient they were discussing in supervision. But in those instances the material has been very useful, as we shall illustrate below. Just as in the anxiety revealed in the Dream Laboratory experiment, so do our supervisees carry with them into supervision a great fear of exposure.

Dreams about Patients by Psychiatric Residents in Supervision

Stimulated by the research project, one resident did spontaneously offer one of his dreams about the patient to the continuous case conference.

Dr. RP

> I had a large mansion to dispose of with forty beds. My patient was there, but lost in the shuffle of the forty beds.

He associated his feelings that he was leaving the VA hospital with forty beds on a ward. His intense guilt about abandoning his patient whom he commented as living in one of the rooms in the mansion was discussed actively in the conference and some of his own projected abandonment fears (by the continuous case conference supervisor and the residency training program) were discussed. He later reported that the discussion had made him much more effective in helping the patient face his separation anxiety in subsequent sessions. Previously, because of his own needs to deny his own separation anxiety, he had not allowed the patient to express and work through this problem.

But, by and large, resident–therapists will not tell dreams in their supervisory sessions. One comment from one of the residents who was presenting in a continuous case conference was of interest, "I seem to have dreams about all the other patients that I am treating except the one that I am presenting to you here!"

Apparently the degree of mutual trust and cooperation is not established in a usual ongoing supervisory relationship which is of sufficient depth to permit the exposure of unconscious and preconscious attitudes which would be inherent in the presentation of dream material. This is so, particularly since the dream is so held in awe by the resident who feels the supervisor will see "all" about him via a dream.

We next turn to analytic candidates as a comparison group of more mature individuals who have more extensive supervisory experience and consequently may develop greater trust.

Dreams Reported in Analytic Supervision by Candidates

Thirteen analysts were requested to answer a questionnaire asking information about the following items:

1. The number of dreams about patients in the manifest content reported during their analytic supervision.
2. The general area of the dream (e.g., brother transference, erotic transference, competitive transference, etc.).
3. Details of the dream if the person felt free to share it with an analytic group.

Twelve of the thirteen responded. Five of these reported one or more dreams to their supervisors during their analytic supervision, three of these just reporting one or two dreams. Analyst supervisors corroborated the infrequency of dreams reported to them by candidates and pointed out further that dream material most typically came as confirmatory rather than additional material offering new insight into the therapist–patient relationship.

General comments to this questionnaire are of interest. Several people said that they noticed that the dream material that they reported was not very favorably received so that it tended to discourage further reporting. There was an area of confusion between supervision and treatment: dreams are often felt to be in the exclusive province of therapy. Another analyst reported that he probably still regarded countertransference as a sin rather than as a fact, and therefore did not report such material.

Two examples of such dreams are given:

Dr. FT

> It was something about an attractive female patient who was my sister. We walked down the street together but it was okay because we have a brother–sister relationship and this will not impede the analysis.

The defensive aspects of the sister (counter) transference (defending against an erotic transference) were discussed with the supervisor and examples were looked for and found of buddy–buddy behavior with the patient, which in turn tended to make her more fearful of her own erotic feelings, thus acting as a very real impediment to the analysis. The analyst further recognized that he tended to relate this way to many of his attractive female patients in order to deal with his own erotic feelings. This had the effect of making the patient excessively guilty and ashamed of her own sexual impulses, which was a detriment to the analysis.

Dr. WH

> Halfway through the hour I gave the patient something. I suddenly realized it would no longer be considered an analysis and I became terribly upset.

When he awoke he was glad that it was only a dream. Here we see some of the anxiety stimulated by the requirements of analytic technique and the fear that something would occur to disqualify a "control" case. But again this is in the same vein as our research on supervision. The fear of some inadequacy being exposed is no less in analytic candidates than a resident; maybe it is more. This young analyst's need to give was also a fruitful source of examination and often led to his being more "psychotherapeutic" than "psychoanalytic." The inhibiting force is not, however, incorrect technique, but rather that the supervisor as a representative of the Institute "group" should disqualify him for further psychoanalytic training.

Dreams about Patients by Psychiatrists in Analysis

Two issues block the productive countertransference use of the dreams of therapists who are in treatment at the time they are presenting the dreams. The first is that the identification with the patient role involves more of a transference reaction that the therapist is making to his own therapist[4] rather than the countertransference that he is making to his patient. Again the phenomenon of dreaming "upwards" (Whitman et al., 1963b) rather than downwards is in operation. Very often it seems that certain patients are chosen to present clusters of ego attitudes or id impulses which the patient–therapist is trying to integrate or master within himself.

Thus a patient–therapist dreamed repeatedly about a psychopathic young man whom he was treating. The young man represented ego-alien sexual and hostile impulses clustered about an arrogant ego orientation that the therapist was trying to deal within himself. He had a good deal of anxiety about this attitude in relation to expected criticism for it by his colleagues and his analyst. Nevertheless, his own expectation of derogation by his analyst enabled him to recognize his derogatory attitudes to *his* patient, which then resulted in the patient getting less gratification from his provocativeness.

The second factor is that the dream is dealt with, and properly so, in the context of the transference and the intrapsychic dynamics of the therapist–patient. If the interpersonal aspects of the relationship with the patient are discussed, it is in terms of his own dynamics and not in terms of the actual treatment. Attempts to look at the countertransference aspects of these dreams on the part of the therapist–patient are sometimes a

---

[4]This would be similar to focusing on Freud's relationship to Fliess rather than to Irma.

form of resistance in the analysis. They represent an attempt to turn treatment into supervision (in exact contradistinction to the oft-seen attempt to turn supervision into treatment). But the question would nevertheless arise if these dreams might not be used deliberately in another context, that is, in relationship with an ongoing supervisory relationship, or, indeed, in relationship with the self and the examination of the countertransference on one's own as shown above. Dreams can be used differently in different contexts and for different purposes.

A female therapist reported a dream in which she had put her arms around a young boy she was treating. In her analysis she discussed the wish that her analyst put his arms around her like that. But in her own examination of the treatment of the boy, she recognized that she was giving too much to him because of her own needs to get. She was then able to alter her treatment of him to decrease the impelling vicariousness of her giving.

Thus, we see that the most useful dreams may be those in which there is a recognized communication to the self. The self-communicating function of the dream is not distorted or altered by a therapeutic or supervisory relationship. The dreamer is neither in an analytic nor in a supervisory relationship which makes him defensive. He does not have to hide inadequacies from others, although, of course, there always remains the problem of facing one's own inadequacies.

Dreams about Patients by Therapists Not in Treatment or Supervision

We are now working in the area of the continuous self-examination and scrutiny which should characterize the work of every serious therapist. We are coming closer to one of the central themes of this paper; that is, the use of countertransference dreams to give insight into the unconscious and preconscious attitudes to the patient and only secondarily as a tool for further insight into the therapist's dynamics.

A patient who has had a long and arduous analysis reapplies for treatment. The analyst says that he will reevaluate him in several interviews to see whether more analysis is indicated.

During the course of the evaluation the analyst, Dr. SW, has this dream:

> The patient is in the front seat of the analyst's car. The analyst is sitting in the back seat directly in back of him. (This is a clear spatial description of the analytic relationship.) He asks the analyst whether he should drive and is told to drive if he can. He tries to drive and scrapes the curb guards against the sidewalk, a most unpleasant and grinding sound. They both realize he cannot drive the car.

The analyst recognizes his wish as well as perception that the patient can go no further. The countertransference has to do with the unpleasant nature of the manner of the patient's speech. He has a boring rasping tone. The dream raises the issue of the patient's inability to go further as compared with the analyst's unwillingness to go on with the patient because of some of the patient's unpleasant aspects. The actual decision made was not to resume analysis, a decision governed, of course, by the total clinical picture. But the analyst made allowances for his dislike of the patient as potentially influencing sound clinical judgment.

An analyst has a dream about a sexually inhibited woman who has been in analysis for several years, has worked through some of her inhibitions, but seems unable to establish a lasting relationship with a man. He dreams that he is having intercourse with her in a very giving way. He associates to her sexual deprivation. He recognizes that he is fantasying giving to her what she should properly be finding outside the analysis. He then becomes more alert to cues she is communicating about her relationships with men in which she subtly discourages them. He realizes that the dominant transference is that nobody is as good as the analyst (father) and that he must in some narcissistic way be going along with this. Her depreciation of other men in relation to the analyst becomes a central analytic issue. Working this through on both a current and genetic level then led to the establishment of a relationship with a suitable man and gave her an opportunity to try out her increased sexual freedom with him. The dream clarified the counter-transference bias that the analyst had when he implied agreement with her depreciatory attitudes toward men other than the analyst.

The Literature on Countertransference Dreams

The only examples we could find of the creative use of counter-transference dreams were in papers by Tauber (1954) and Tower (1956). Tauber reported several dreams about patients which he told to them to see if it could help to solve an analytic impasse. He reported very good results with this technique, though he did not neglect to caution against misuse of this method. One cannot disagree with his creative use of data, but there is the uneasy feeling that he is having the patient do work that was properly the work of his own self-analysis.

Having failed to do this self-analysis himself, he is open to additional interpretations of his material above and beyond what he offers in his paper. For example, in one of his illustra-tions he has a dream about a young married woman in analysis in which he is with her on an island in the Mediterranean. There is a romantic quality to the dream. He used this dream which he told to the patient as an entry into some unsatisfactory aspects of her romantic relationship with her husband. He says that he had been avoiding this topic deliberately because the patient had so much distress in her analysis and needed at least to believe that her marriage was sound. What emerges from scrutiny of the dream is that his own romantic attachment and interest in the patient may have made her uneasy in the analysis and even more uneasy about telling him that she was not as happy with her husband as she wished to believe.

Tower (1956) actually describes her startle at a dream of her own in the course of conducting an analysis. The dream led her to some extremely productive insights into the analysis. She dreamed that she was visiting in her patient's home. Only his wife was there who seemed glad to have her, and was most hospitable and gracious. The dream made her realize that the wife was no longer interfering in her husband's treatment. She was able to deal actively with the patient's use of a bad marital situation to play off the analyst and the wife against each other. And the analyst recognized that in her own unconscious lay an overdetermined competition with and fear of another woman in a triangular situation which had permitted the patient to perpetuate the myth of the difficult wife.

Discussion

The definitions of countertransference vary widely (Orr, 1954). It is, therefore, difficult to say what is or what is not a counter-transference dream. One approach is to take a strictly opera-tional definition as we have done in this paper. Our thesis is that countertransference, like transference, is a manifestation of living interaction of one human being with another. It is one of two foci of a transactional process. It would seem that the history of countertransference is running quite parallel with the history of transference. At first an intruding phenomenon, it had to be denied, then it was analyzed to try to minimize it, and then it was used creatively. Finally, it has become one of the very cornerstones of the psychoanalytic method. We there-fore see that such terms as *negative* and *positive* when used in describing countertransference operations have a strong evalu-ative approach and may obscure the creative use of counter-transference.

Convincing writers like Racker (1953), Tower (1956), Tauber (1954), Cohen (1952), and Ross and Kapp (chapter 38) are all moving the study of countertransference phenomena in this direction of usefulness rather than interference. This study is in that spirit.

The appearance of dreams about the patient in the course of supervision and the self-analysis of the therapist have invari-ably been helpful in producing insights into the doctor–patient relationship. It is hoped that this study will stimulate other supervisors and therapists, confident that much more dream material is being produced about patients by therapists, to uti-lize dreams in terms of ego attitudes and orientations to illumi-nate further the therapeutic relationship. When Freud stated that dreams were the royal road to the unconscious, he meant not only the patient's unconscious, but every human being's unconscious. Therapists should use these data not only for purposes of their continuing self-analysis, but also for their continuing examination of their transactions with their patients and their colleagues.

The presence of countertransference dreams offers an operational differentiation between a countertransference attitude and a countertransference neurosis (Gitelson, 1952). The presence of persisting dreams about the patient may strongly suggest that there is a countertransference neurosis: occasional dreams suggest cathexis of a relationship, a basic human attitude which is necessary for the continuation of an ongoing relationship.

Our study on supervision (1963b), as well as Emch's (1955) and Thompson's (1956) studies on social context, and Kleeman's study (chapter 9) on "Dreaming for a Dream Course," all highlight the importance of the therapist's relationships with his colleagues, both on his own and "higher" levels as being a persisting preoccupation which may be greater in psychoanalysis than any other specialty in medicine. Since we are so expressly forbidden to obtain gratifications from our patients, it is not strange that we turn to our colleagues for our work gratifications. How this in turn influences our own lives and our work with patients provides a continuously generating set of data with which we must be ever concerned.

What is the contribution to our understanding of the dreams that we have examined? Apparently, the total set of attitudes to work, patients, colleagues, superiors, and so on, become relevant in the doctor–patient relationship when they impinge on the patient both as an individual figure and as a representative of patients in general, a group of people with whom we spend most of the hours of our professional days. This seems a countertransference orientation common to all our reporting therapists.

The specific thesis that we are offering is that dreams are an extremely useful avenue of approach to transient countertransference attitudes as well. Recent work in ego psychology and the importance of the manifest content in providing information about ego attitudes point up the use of dreams as a way of exploring some aspects of countertransference without disturbing deeper unconscious factors within the therapist.

Dreams may be used by therapists for their own continuing self-analyses as well as for understanding their countertransference attitudes; understanding of the self and understanding of the patient meet in the countertransference dream.

Summary

Current research into the process of dreaming has shown that dreams occur much more often in all human beings than was hitherto suspected. The analyst or therapist is no exception to this finding. Among the dreams of the therapist are dreams about the patient. Dreaming about the patient in the manifest content of a dream is one form of countertransference dream. The percentage of the total dreams of therapists is probably not much different than that which can be deduced from Freud's original book of *The Interpretation of Dreams*; that is, 6 percent of the therapist's dreams have patients in the manifest content and 34 percent have patients in the latent content as well.

The various sources that are examined for dreams about patients by therapists are: (1) Freud's dreams; (2) therapists' dreams about patients experimentally recovered; (3) dreams about patients by psychiatric residents in supervision; (4) dreams about patients of analysts as candidates; (5) dreams about patients by psychiatric residents in treatment; (6) dreams about patients by therapists not in treatment; (7) dreams about patients by therapists not in treatment or supervision; and (8) articles containing references to therapists' dreams about patients.

The scrutiny of dreams about the patient in the course of supervision and analysis has been invariably helpful in producing insights into the doctor–patient relationship. Just as dreams are the royal road to the unconscious of the patient, so are they equally useful in providing a succinct idea of the therapist's attitude to his patient.

Dreams may be used for an investigation of countertransference phenomena. The overall spirit of this study is that
countertransference can be used in a creative way to illuminate
the treatment process. An important differentiation is the difference between countertransference reactions and countertransference neurosis. A countertransference neurosis, a persistent neurotic attitude about a patient, is reflected in persistent
dreams about that patient. Countertransference reactions or
attitudes are seen in occasional dreams about the patient.

Chapter 40

TERMINATION OF A SYMPTOM FOLLOWING INTERPRETATION OF A DREAM

MERVIN H. HURWITZ

A clinical incident is described, in which amenorrhea suddenly and dramatically ended after a dream was interpreted. The patient, aged twenty-six, had been in analysis for three-and-a-half years. She had had sexual intercourse twelve times—of these, eleven after beginning her analysis—and on each occasion, the intercourse was followed by a period of amenorrhea lasting from six to ten weeks. During the amenorrhea, she was extremely upset and anxious, with frequent anxiety dreams. Consciously, she was pregnant until the eventual menstrual flow.

During her analysis, the patient dreamed frequently and associated well to dreams. Her periods of amenorrhea were not exceptional in this regard. Frequent dreams and associations had indicated her desire for pregnancy and for a child, but their interpretation brought about no change in the symptom.

The incident to be described occurred six weeks after a sexual episode, which was followed by amenorrhea with the usual intense anxiety and conscious certainty of pregnancy. On the night prior to the analytic incident, the patient had a "very vague dream." As she recalled it, somehow she was building a mountain, and when it was done, she had a child to keep. At first the dream seemed strange, unrelated to anything in her life, and she tended to dismiss it. Then she began to talk about the man with whom she had had sexual intercourse.

This paper was first published in the *Psychoanalytic Quarterly* (1966), 35:122–124.

"He's a bastard! He's out with someone else and I'm probably pregnant. I hate him! By the time nine months have gone by I will have a mountainous belly. I'm so angry at him I would like to kill him, to tear him apart, to bite him. Oh, I'd even like to bite off his penis. I can almost feel it between my teeth as I chew it." A pause. "Uggh! That's making me feel sick." Another period of silence. "I have to go to the bathroom. I urinated before I came in here, but now I need to defecate. I'm afraid I'll have to get off the couch." Silence. "No, I'm all right now. The thought of chewing his penis made me feel awful, but I feel better now. Somehow I feel stronger. I'm not afraid of him. I'm glad I'm pregnant."

From these associations to the dream and from previous material, it was possible to interpret to her that it was not a baby with which she thought she was pregnant, but a penis; and that in intercourse she believed she had captured the penis and, by her amenorrhea, was retaining it. This was linked with the previous day's resentment at her father for not providing her with a penis. The patient's response to this was very emotional "Really!". Then after a period of silence, she said, "Oh my God, I'm menstruating. I'm pouring." And she rushed off the couch, out of the office, and into the bathroom.

Following this incident, the patient was in analysis for a year-and-a-half, during which time she had intercourse more frequently than before, but without amenorrhea or belief at any time that she was pregnant. Very shortly after the dream interpretation, the patient began to experience vaginal orgasm, which became more frequent with greater sexual experience.

Though menstruation began immediately after an interpretation, this could have been a coincidence. But there has been no amenorrhea for a period of a year-and-a-half following the incident and if the interpretation affected this symptom, it can be assumed that the dream interpretation did affect an immediate flow of menstruum. It should be noted, too, that the patient's menstrual period usually began with a very small flow, described as "spotting," even after a long period of amenorrhea, and in her memory, no period had begun with a sudden copious flow.

Because of the sudden onset of the copious flow one assumes that there was a sudden change in the endometrium. [The mucous membrane lining the uterus. Also called *tunica mucosa uteri*.] Prior to this, the endometrium must have been in the premenstrual stage and very possibly for a long while during the amenorrhea.

Samson Wright (1937) describes the premenstrual stage (eight days before onset of period) as follows: "The endometrium becomes thickened still further; the stroma cells proliferate, enlarge, and become more closely packed and resemble those seen in the early placenta; the glands are markedly distended with mucous, and the epithelium is thrown into folds resembling villi, which project into the lumen, giving the gland wall a saw-edged, tufted appearance; the capillaries become congested (premenstrual congestion) and exudation of clear or blood-stained fluid occurs" (p. 221).

For this premenstrual stage to change into the stage of menstruation, when the actual menstrual flow occurs, blood must begin to pass out of the capillaries, both by diapedesis through intact vessels and through areas where the lining has broken down. The blood, according to Wright, then lies in the stroma, bursts into the lumina of the glands, and accumulates in considerable quantities beneath the superficial epithelium before finally reaching the uterine cavity by stripping off varying amounts of the epithelium.

Thus, for a copious flow of menstruum to begin almost immediately after an interpretation, a great deal would have to occur in a very brief period of time. One would have to assume that the end of the premenstrual stage was at hand, but that for emotional reasons, the progress of the menstrual cycle was suspended at this point. Then the inference would be that as a result of the interpretation, the forces inhibiting the further progress of the menstrual cycle were suddenly removed, allowing the endometrium to break down rapidly and simultaneously in many areas. Such a rapid breakdown seems the only possible explanation, unless the blood was somehow already in the uterine cavity. This latter explanation seems less likely in an otherwise healthy woman.

Summary

A clinical incident is reported in which amenorrhea suddenly and dramatically ended after a dream interpretation. Some speculations are presented pertaining to the physiological endometrial changes which might have occurred in the dramatic termination of the symptom.

Chapter 41

DREAMS AND THE LATENT NEGATIVE TRANSFERENCE

SANFORD M. IZNER

To recognize, understand, and permit working through of the negative aspects of the transference neurosis often poses difficult problems in psychoanalytic treatment. This is especially true for negative elements that remain latent and obscure throughout the course of analysis.

Sterba (1927), among others, has demonstrated very lucidly the difficulties in recognizing and managing the latent negative transference and has emphasized that the progress of analysis may often be impeded by hostile feelings that have not been brought to light and interpreted. Freud (1925a), in summing up the vicissitudes of transference, had this to say: "so long as it is affectionate and moderate, it becomes the agent of the physician's influence and neither more nor less than the mainspring of the joint work of analysis. Later on, when it has become passionate or has been converted into hostility, it becomes the principal tool of the resistance" (p. 42).

Freud (1915b) has also pointed out that the only way we have of recognizing unconscious processes is "under the conditions of dreaming and of neurosis" (p. 187). I shall here confine the discussion to elements of the transference that are principally negative and latent in character and their relation to dreaming.

We will assume that negative or hostile feelings during analysis may be characterized by expressions of direct and overt

This paper was first published in the *Annuals of Psychoanalysis* (1975), 3:165–177.

hostility, avoidance, denial, and negation, some instances of acting out, and overt and conscious breaches of the fundamental rule, along with more subtle forms of expression too numerous and varied to require mention. Many of these forms of expression retain a quality of latency during analysis, in the sense that the feelings associated with them do not obtain direct conscious expression, and even the unconscious derivatives of the affect seem to obtain discharge largely through indirect means. In these situations we recognize most clearly many of the characteristics of primary-process functioning, in which the elements of displacement, condensation, symbolic representation, and other forms of distortion appear to predominate.

Which leads directly to a consideration of the dream as one of the best-defined avenues for expression of ideation and affect. Freud (1900) demonstrated that dreams could be understood only by undoing the dream work, with the help of the patient's associations, so as to discover the latent thoughts responsible for producing the dream. He pointed out that manifest content could only be considered and interpreted in this light. The importance of latent expressions in all analytic work, and particularly in relation to dreams, is well recognized and generally acknowledged. To presume knowledge of what a dream might signify to the dreamer without considering the additional latent associations might be compared with attempting to spend only one surface of a coin—symbolic interpretation notwithstanding (Freud, 1923a, 1925b).

A phenomenon commonly observed in the dreams of patients during analysis is the analyst's recognition that the most significant and pertinent interpretation of a given dream or series of dreams depends on a reversal, or a representation of the situation (or affect) by its opposite in the manifest dream (Freud, 1900).[1] It becomes evident from the latent associations (latent in the sense that the conscious connection between the manifest content and the associations has not been made prior to the verbalization of the expressions) that, in the dream, the patient has actually reversed what he is really experiencing or

---

[1]We are concerned here only with the reversal of manifest dream content and not with chronological reversal in dreams.

might wish to express at that point in the analysis. This seems to be especially true in relation to feelings and events most directly concerned with the transference neurosis. In his discussion of distortion in dreams, Freud described this phenomenon as a wish-fulfillment. He also took up the question of some possible exceptions to the rule.

Freud illustrated that even "counterwish" dreams (which, because of their unpleasant contents or the desire for punishment, might at first glance be considered at odds with the theory) actually comply with the rule of wish-fulfillment. To illustrate this principle further, he utilized dreams that were opposite in manifest content to what was really desired, as determined by the expressions of the patient, stating, "that the non-fulfillment of one wish meant the fulfillment of another" (p. 151). This sort of reversal was most clearly demonstrated in what he termed "contradictory dreams." He noted that the most frequent occurrence of this type of dream followed directly upon his own attempts, during the analysis of some of his patients, to formulate for them the basic expression in the dream: that of a wish-fulfillment. After he had tendered his explanatory remarks to the patient, the dream that frequently followed, when subjected to analysis of the latent content of the associations, expressed the patient's desire to contradict Freud's previous explanation. Among his examples, the following, taken from his analysis of a female patient, is most illustrative:

One day I had been explaining to her that dreams are fulfillments of wishes. Next day she brought me a dream in which she was travelling down with her mother-in-law to the place in the country where they were to spend their holidays together. Now I knew that she had violently rebelled against the idea of spending the summer near her mother-in-law and that a few days earlier she had successfully avoided the propinquity she dreaded by engaging rooms in a far distant resort. And now her dream had undone the solution she had wished for: was not this the sharpest possible contradiction of my theory that in dreams wishes are fulfilled? No doubt; and it was only necessary to follow the dream's logical consequence in order to arrive at its interpretation. The dream showed that I was wrong. *Thus it was her wish that I might be wrong, and her dream showed that wish fulfilled* [1900, p. 151].

Freud added that the contradictory wish represented the dreamer's attempt to deny another inference Freud had made concerning important latent memories which had not yet come clearly to light in the analysis, but which, apparently, were quite true—as if to express the wish that these suspicions were unfounded because the events in question had never occurred at all. The transference character of all this material is clear. Although Freud did not utilize the term *transference* in this instance, there is little reason to question his awareness and understanding of the relation of the patient to the analyst during the therapeutic process, even at this early stage of psychoanalytic development. Freud emphasized the defensive aspect of the contradictory dream as an additional form of dream distortion.

It might be of importance at this point to mention Freud's earliest references to the transference: his discussion in the *Studies on Hysteria* (Breuer and Freud, 1895) of "the transference onto the physician" of distressing ideas, in the sense of making a "false connection." Another very early use of the term *transference* is to be found in his discussion of the Dora case (1905b), where it is used in a sense more closely allied to our present application of the term. In Chapter VII (1900) Freud uses the term in reference to an economic problem. He discusses the energy shift from unconscious wish-fulfillment and the attachment of the disturbing affect to a rather innocuous conscious thought in order to obtain discharge. From the economic standpoint, this sort of energy transfer remains as a component of the mechanism of displacement, which plays such a prominent role in the phenomenon of transference.

But it is in his discussion of "contradictory" dreams that Freud made some of his earliest references to the thought that his patients might desire, in an unconscious way, to express hostile or negative feelings about their relation with him as an analyst. At the same time, he pointed out that the patient's need to oppose what had been communicated by the analyst is actually directed at an intensive warding-off of certain unpleasant memories or experiences that have a latent connection to the material under discussion. This fear that the analyst might infer what has been repressed in association to a relatively innocuous thought coincides with the economic element of the energy transfer mentioned above.

To recapitulate: through an understanding of the latent meaning behind the associations of the patient whose dream was chosen as an illustration, it was made clear that a reversal of the manifest dream content was in order, if one were to grasp what the patient was attempting to convey to the analyst. Freud demonstrated that a reversal of the manifest dream corresponded to what underlay the patient's associations to that dream. It was clear that both the latent material and reversed manifest content pertained to the same idea: that of the wish to prove the analyst wrong. The latent hostile impulse in the phenomenon was directly concerned with the transference neurosis and, in the example given above, seems to represent one of Freud's first expressions regarding latent negative transference feelings.

It is my purpose to demonstrate that the phenomenon of reversal in dreams may be related to specific levels in the defensive organization of the ego, structured as a form of distortion in order to ward off the expression of latent negative feelings in the transference. Dreams of this nature, then, might be considered a distinct clue to the existence of latent hostile feelings and could be interpreted on this basis. At the same time, such an interpretation would provide additional confirmation for the theory that all dreams represent the fulfillment of a wish—and, for the patient in analysis, a wish directly referrable to the transference figure of the analyst as the object choice of that particular level of development and associated with that period of the evolving infantile neurosis. Although reversal or representation by its opposite occurs under many other conditions and, in certain situations, might be utilized to ward off positive feelings, the discussion here will be confined to the use of reversal of manifest dream content as a representation of a regressive form of defensive activity on the part of the ego, in order to provide a distorted presentation of hostility that cannot otherwise be expressed. We might speculate that the dream reversal would be most apt to occur when specific levels of the defensive stratification predominate, especially at times when the patient is anticipating communication of the dream to another, or possibly in situations of self-communication, when he is making an attempt to analyze his own dreams (Beres, 1956; A. Freud, 1965).

As further illustrations of the relation of dream reversal to the latent negative transference, the following situations in analysis may serve to clarify the thesis.

A forty-four-year-old married woman returned to analysis preoccupied with feelings of depression and unworthiness because of her desire to act on sexual impulses that had in the past led to extramarital affairs. She felt she had benefited from her former therapy, in that she had brought many of her disturbing impulses under temporary control, but now sought further help. In addition to her need to depreciate her former analyst for "his excessive talking," she was considerably disillusioned with the analysis because of her impression that the analyst's guidance had led her into divorce proceedings and almost ended her marriage. She had dropped the attempt at divorce when she terminated the analysis, which she felt no longer afforded the protection and control she had sought for her disturbing sexual and aggressive impulses.

The patient, a very bright and competent woman, was employed in a semimanagerial capacity. She worked in order to provide funds for the education of her two daughters, an opportunity she herself had been deprived of because of her mother's feeling that "only boys should go to college"—that girls did not require this background for marriage. Her feeling that her husband was unable to provide the necessary funds seemed to recapitulate many of her attitudes in relation to her parents: she had always experienced her mother as the aggressive and controlling parent, and her father as weak, incompetent, and a poor provider. She described her older brother, an unsuccessful salesman, as similar to her father, whereas her younger brother, whom she had "mothered and taken under her wing," became a physician and a well-trained specialist in his profession.

Soon after her entry into the second analysis, the patient developed a strong positive transference marked by many expressions of her regard for the analyst and colored by numerous dreams that seemed to confirm these feelings. She spoke of her desires to act out some of the libidinal impulses arising out of the transference with men she met at work, but she managed to keep the desire for displacement on a fantasy level. Most of the hostility for both her mother and father in the transference remained latent, except for an occasional reference to her former analyst or a disparaging remark about one of her superiors. While the patient was experiencing fairly intense and overt libidinal feelings in the transference, she decided she would like to increase the number of her analytic visits. Although she repeated this desire on several occasions, her request was not granted. At the same time, she had also felt rejected in her attempt to act out her libidinal impulses with a business acquaintance who did not seem to respond to her interest in him. She became depressed, and, although her overt expressions to the analyst remained positive enough, she presented a dream of the night when her last request had gone ungratified. In the dream, a man is trying to get the patient to go with her, but the patient refuses and wants, instead, to go with her husband, who is nearby.

In associating to the dream, the patient described the intense depression that followed the rejection by her business acquaintance. She was made aware of the reversal of the manifest dream content: that she had really felt rejected by the analyst, who had been so inconsiderate with regard to her request for more analytic time. She realized that she was angry and did not want to be either with the man in the dream or her business acquaintance. In addition, she was expressing in the dream her wish that the rejection in the analysis had never happened at all. Her anger at feeling disregarded was followed by intense hostility to the analyst. The interpretation of her anger was then made in relation to her desire to be cared for and attended to by the analyst as she had once wished to be cared for by her mother. This was clearly a defensive regression from the position of feeling angry with and rejected by the analyst as father in the transference, feelings that had been distorted and mastered by reversal in the dream. In the interval following these interpretations and prior to her next analytic visit, she recalled a dream concerned with a most disturbing repressed memory from early childhood. It involved a primal-scene situation, and the repressed memory recapitulated the patient's depression and anger at being moved out of her mother's bedroom, where she had slept for a considerable part of the first eight years of her life. She recalled being made to sleep in another room at times when her father and mother slept together. She could still remember "those sounds in the night that triggered this fear," accompanied by intense anger and depression. The patient's anger at the analyst, latently present in her associations and manifested by reversal in the dream, seems clear. That this phenomenon is structured to distort and disguise these feelings, enabling the patient to ward off the return to consciousness of the associated repressed and disturbing childhood memory, also seems evident.

Another example taken from the analysis of the same patient further illustrates the thesis of dream reversal. While discussing something in the presence of her family, it occurred to her that her older brother seemed inattentive. She mentioned this to the analyst, and, as usual, there was little comment. At her next appointment she presented a dream: A boy friend of her daughter's is making sexual advances to a girl friend of the patient's. The patient asks, "How can you do this sort of thing?" and he replies, "It's the natural thing to do."

Her associations revealed that her daughter was visited by a boy friend at home that evening and that the patient had gone upstairs to sleep, leaving them alone. She recalled thinking that the boy might make sexual advances to her daughter after the patient had gone to sleep, and then recalled a thought she had had during her previous analytic visit, one she had suppressed. After expressing many positive feelings for the analyst, who gave no evidence of a response, she had had the fleeting thought that he must have fallen asleep. Later, after the visit, she felt very irritable and angry, but was not aware of the reason. When the reversal in the dream was pointed out, the patient became aware that, "it is not the natural thing to do—to react to sexual overtures by going to sleep." This resulted in her feeling quite angry that one should withdraw in this way from her advances, and she related it to the fear that her daughter might be the one who would make sexual advances to her boy friend "in a most natural way," after the patient had gone to sleep: thus the patient had the impulse to make advances to the analyst if she felt he was asleep.

When her latent anger in the transference had been interpreted and expressed, she remembered the older brother's inattentive attitude of a few days before, which brought forth the recall of her intense repressed rage at him. For some time when she was a small child, she had slept in the same bedroom with him. She had often felt angry because of her desire to be involved in sexual play with him and his tendency to ridicule her for these feelings or to ignore her and go directly to sleep. She also recollected a most humiliating thought that had occurred to her at that time—her desire to make sexual advances to her brother (and probably her father too) as he slept. Her latent anger, in defense against reexperiencing the disturbing memories and impulses from childhood, became manifested in the reversal of the dream content. It is of particular interest that latent negative transference feelings of this nature be directed toward the rejecting love object of the oedipal period as the result of the feelings of narcissistic mortification (Eidelberg, 1959) resulting from such experiences.

Another case involved the situation of a twenty-nine-year-old divorced professional man who entered analysis a short time after the disruption of his marriage. At that time he was terribly anxious and depressed, and blamed himself for his wife's breaking up the marriage. In his seven years of marriage, the patient had never been capable of consummating the marriage sexually. His wife had finally decided to go out with other men, which the patient experienced as a devastating injury to his self-esteem. He had been deeply hurt by her leaving. The patient was the only child of a marriage between a successful businesswoman and a man twelve years her junior. The patient's father had been taken into the mother's women's apparel business and was considered by everyone in the family to be her employee.

The patient was very closely attached to his mother, whom he described as a dominant and overprotective woman who argued violently with her rather immature husband. On several occasions she drove him out of the house. The parents were divorced when the patient was twelve years of age, and after that he saw his father on only a very few occasions. For most of his early life, the patient slept in the same room with his mother, even at times when his father was at home. He always felt that his mother was much more closely bound to him than to his father, and he was very dependent on her in return, although he also resented his dependent position.

From the time he began his schooling, the patient was always the best student in his class. His mother took pleasure in his achievement, but he felt her pride resulted from the gratification she experienced from the recognition and admiration of her friends, rather than from a real interest in him. He recalled that in earliest childhood he took considerable interest in women's undergarments and used to wear some of mother's "underthings and corsets" when he masturbated. This masturbation was accompanied by a fantasy of lying in bed dressed as a girl and being masturbated by a fully clothed woman lying alongside of him. His interest in women's undergarments persisted after he entered analysis. Since early childhood he had pilfered or purchased and worn women's "panties."

When he began analysis, he was employed in research work, but was not very productive. He was driven to exposing his genitals at night to women on the street, and his intense anxiety because of these impulses, coupled with his extreme loneliness, led him to seek analysis. Another element of importance seemed related to the patient's realization that he had married shortly before his discovery that his mother was critically ill and might not survive the illness. He had the impression that his mother wanted him to get married, as if she knew she would not be there to take care of him. He realized that after she became ill he no longer had the desire to return home from school to visit her, and avoided seeing her as much as possible.

In any discussion of this patient's productions, it is important to take into account his "sexual reversal" and accompanying feminine identification. His fetishism was present throughout his marriage, and he continued to wear women's underclothes through the early years of analysis. For this patient, almost everything seemed to be "reversed," and for many months all of his dreams were of this nature. In the main, his defenses were characterized by reversing, turning on the self, undoing, isolation, and numerous reaction formations, accompanied by ambivalence in connection with most of his aggressive and sexual impulses. Characterologically, the patient was also immobilized by his parsimoniousness and strong need for self-denial. Although much could be said concerning his productions and symptomatology in relation to the importance of his tendency toward "sexual reversal," we will confine ourselves to the significance of the reversal of manifest dream content as evidence of his latent negative-transference feelings.

The early months of analysis were characterized by compliance and superficial cooperation interspersed with occasional sarcastic or hostile expressions—evidently a reenactment of his early relation with his mother. His dreams, which were all "reversed" in content, expressed this clearly. A rather typical situation in the analysis relevant to the latent negative transference can be described as follows.

The patient had been out of town for a professional meeting and felt guilty for being away from the analysis. On his return, he became aware that he had completely forgotten the material discussed at the meetings. This was uncharacteristic for one with such an excellent memory. After arriving home and before his return to analysis, the patient decided to write a check in payment for his analytic visits for the previous month. He wondered why he felt it was so imperative that he write the check. He experienced difficulty in deciding on the correct total for the check, which also was uncharacteristic for an expert in mathematics who made a practice of calculating things well in advance. He realized that he must have felt "guilty about something." He related the following dream of the night before his return to analysis: He is unable to complete a mathematics examination in time, looks out of the window at the school across the street, and notices a flood in front of the school. He is concerned because he fears the parents will be unable to visit the children there.

It was clear from his associations that the patient felt anxious about returning to analysis, and this feeling, coupled with his intensely ambivalent attitude, was reflected in his strong impulse to write the check and his difficulty with the calculations. When he experienced the impulse to write the check, memories from the meetings returned to consciousness. When the reversed content of the dream was revealed as a fear that, because of anger, "the child could not visit the [analyst] parent," the patient suddenly experienced and expressed his anger about returning to the analysis. Only after he discussed his need to write the check and his guilt about going away was he able to express his anger at the analyst for not struggling with him about his going away as a mother would have been expected to do.

While he was out of town, he had the sudden impulse to "look at women," a desire he had not experienced in years. At the same time he felt a strong impulse to return to dressing in women's undergarments. He recalled how in childhood he used to slip on one of his mother's girdles and masturbate. This brought to mind many of his mother's prohibitions against masturbation and the anxiety and anger they aroused in him. He recalled a dream he'd had, which he dated as having occurred before he was four years old—the earliest dream he could remember. In the dream, he is in bed and his mother is there. She tells him that a friend is coming to visit, and the patient immediately thinks she must mean his father—but then an elephant walks in. The patient felt that this dream must have been related to his childhood desire to "visit his parents" in their bed and his feeling of exclusion and anger when he was not able to do this.

On another occasion, the patient dreamed of being on a train. He was in a dining car, and the waiter brought him five choices of dessert. The patient selected a little brown one and spilled some of it on mother's skirt. He tried hard to wipe it off.

He was immediately aware of the transference reference in the dream, relating the five desserts to the number of analytic visits per week. At the same time, he complained that the times of these visits placed a significant hardship on him and interfered with his recreational activities. He would have chosen other appointment times. The reversed quality of the dream was then interpreted: The patient was angry at not getting his choice of appointment times. In addition, he had evidently experienced this lack of choice as a punitive sort of activity on the part of the analyst, that of getting his "dessert." The patient then expressed his anger at feeling that he did not get what he wanted and was being forced by the analyst to do things on schedule, just as his mother had demanded of him when he was a child. He recalled that she would interrupt his play and insist that he spend a regular time every day on the toilet, attempting to overcome his childhood constipation. As a result, he would be so enraged that with every bowel movement he would make certain that most of the feces would be smeared all over the toilet seat and his clothes. Instead of trying to clean it up as in the dream, he would really rub it in as retaliation for his mother's "rubbing in" his obstinate attitude toward her demands. This was the uncomfortable, repressed memory that his latent hostile feeling in the transference was structured to defend against, in order to assist him in suppressing this impulse in the analysis.

To summarize, an attempt has been made to provide an explanation for the rather frequent clinical experience of the phenomenon of dream reversal and its association to elements of the latent negative transference. The defensive function of reversal in relation to the latent negative transference has been explained, and the connection to repression of unpleasant memories and impulses from the period of the infantile neurosis with the resultant amnesia has been made. The hostile nature of the impulse directed at the love object of the oedipal period had also been described.

In "Instincts and Their Vicissitudes," Freud (1915a) indicated that the defensive phenomenon of reversal must be considered from two separate standpoints: the alteration of the instinctual aim and the change in instinctual content. Alteration of the instinctual aim involves the replacement of active strivings by passivity; alteration of content is limited to the substitution of hatred for love. The situation of dream reversal in relation to the latent negative transference seems to clearly trace this process. A substitution of rage against the frustrating or rejecting love object of the oedipal period develops, along with a regressive return of feelings of childhood helplessness. The accompanying state of passivity results in the need to further distort any activated disturbing impulses by representing them as reversed.

Several questions come to mind. First of all, why, in a dream, does no direct denial of what has been said or done become a major determinant? Second, why, in a person who has been previously capable of expressing overt and direct hostility toward the analyst, do we now find a need to resort to a dream, with the additional distortion of reversal? The explanation offered by Freud (1900) that " 'No' seems not to exist as far as dreams are concerned" (p. 318), an explanation later confirmed by Fliess (1953b), seems to apply. In addition, as analysis proceeds, the state of regressed functioning of the ego results in the utilization of defensive reactions associated with earlier developmental periods. These reactions are directed at warding off feelings associated with experiences of childhood helplessness, feelings that seem to preclude the expression of hostile impulses, especially in response to the control and influence of the transference figure in analysis, who represents the object choice of that developmental period. A stratification of defensive operations is then set into motion, which is directed at the control of anxiety arising in relation to regressive activities utilized in the flight from the threatening negative feelings connected with the oedipal problem in the transference. Anna Freud (A. Freud, 1936, 1965; Beres, 1956) has referred to the existence of anxiety in association with different developmental levels. She has pointed out that the earliest form of anxiety is concerned with the fear of annihilation, which is followed developmentally by the anxiety related to separation from the love object of the preoedipal phase. Castration anxiety arises with the oedipal problem, and she views the appearance of this form of anxiety in the treatment of children in whom it has not existed as evidence of the forward motion of the analytic work. The change in object relations on which this observation is based seems clear. The shift in object choice as a defensive reaction to the transference figure of the analyst seems, in a large measure, to be based on the regressive reversal of this developmental phenomenon. Negative feelings directed at the frustrating or rejecting love object of the oedipal phase and the associated castration anxiety of this period lead to defensive activities that reverse the entire developmental process. As an added result, the anxiety more closely associated with earlier periods of development predominates and constitutes an attempt to totally avoid negative feelings in the transference. The trauma and resultant "scars" of the early object relation contribute to this stratification of defensive operations, which functions to ward off the "narcissistic mortification" so clearly described by Eidelberg (1959).

In the interests of clarity and brevity, no attempt has been made to discuss sexual reversal or reversals of affect in dreams, in connection with latent negative transference. Nor can absurdity in dreams (Freud, 1900) and the connection to latent hostile feelings be taken up here. These topics might provide a basis for further investigation of this problem.

Section VIII

Children's Dreams

In this section are presented those wide-ranging articles pertaining to the role of children's dreams in psychoanalytic theory and therapy. The section begins with Martin Grotjahn's intriguing article, "Dream Observations in a Two-Year-Four-Months-old Baby" (1938). Even though this article was published before the beginning of World War II, it is included here because of the many interesting dream vignettes in so young a child. Two of Grotjahn's main findings were: (1) that the dream experience of his child revealed that the most significant experiences of a child's play may also appear undisguised in his dreams, and (2) that the difference between fantasies and dreams in the child were so slight that the mentations occurring could equally be called playacting, fantasizing, or dreaming. Next is presented Rangell's report of a unique therapeutic experience, "A Treatment of Nightmares in a Seven-year-old Boy" (1950), in which he supervised by mail the boy's treatment by his father. In his discussion Rangell suggests a number of striking parallels and similarities between his patient-at-a-distance and Freud's patient Little Hans.

The next two clinical articles highlight the role of dreams with older children. The first of these, Esman's "The Dream Screen in an Adolescent" (1962), reports on the analysis of a single dream of an adolescent boy which dramatically confirmed Lewin's dream-screen hypothesis in many respects. Second, there appears Harley's closely reasoned clinical article, "The Role of the Dream in the Analysis of a Latency Child" (1962), where she demonstrates how dream material played a dominant role in the analysis of an eight-year-old girl.

This section ends with Ekstein's thought-provoking paper, "Some Thoughts Concerning the Clinical Use of Children's

Dreams" (1981), where he demonstrates the close interplay between children's play and adults' dreams. His findings suggest that equal weight (and no direct preference) should be given the role of the child's dreams versus his play behavior in the therapeutic process.

Although not included in this section because of its length, John Mack's article, "Nightmares, Conflicts and Ego-Development in Childhood" (1965), is well worth a careful study. By means of a careful review of the relevant literature, and closely reasoned analysis of his clinical examples, he admirably supports the thesis that nightmares (which for him include anxiety dreams and night terrors) are more likely to demonstrate developing psychic structure in the child rather than simple wish-fulfillment dreams in which impulses may be met with little or no opposition within the psyche.

Chapter 42

DREAM OBSERVATIONS IN A TWO-YEAR-FOUR-MONTHS-OLD BABY

MARTIN GROTJAHN

Dreams are not the exclusive privilege of man; neither are they the privilege of adults, for observations of babies have shown that dreams occur during the first year of life. Babies suck, smile, or cry during sleep; later they exhibit during sleep signs of more or less violent experiences, especially anxiety and horror.

What happens during a child's sleep may be learned only at a later age when the child is old enough to tell about it. However, after the age of five years, children are not able to report reliably their dream experiences. Children are never much interested in telling the truth, for telling some fantasied adventure is much more fun than to try to give objective information. In a child intelligent enough and willing to remember its dreams, the difference between the report of a real dream and a fantasy is only slight. The healthy child with all its longing for pleasure is attached to the very thrilling present and is directed by the pleasure principle toward the future and therefore seldom spontaneously reports about the past. When it awakens the night is gone, is nothing; the need for a new day and new ventures inhibits every tendency to look back. Interest in the past is a very unchildlike attitude, and is much more characteristic of the adult. The possibility of obtaining reliable dream material by questioning a child is open to doubt because the suggestibility of young children is enhanced by the leading

This paper was first published in the *Psychoanalytic Quarterly* (1938), 7:507–513.

nature of every question, no matter how carefully it may be phrased and the material obtained in such a manner is scarcely trustworthy.

So it happens that nearly all reports of infant dreams come from children five years of age or older. Furthermore such dream reports are obtained in a rather questionable way. They cannot be differentiated from fantasies and have come in the main from neurotic or badly adjusted children. In psychoanalytic literature only Freud (1900) has reported dreams occurring at a very early age, and these will be mentioned later in detail.

Favorable circumstances made it possible to observe the dreams of a boy two years and four months of age. His speech showed the significant features of beginning speech development which, however, were complicated by a bilingual home environment. He used mainly substantives in both English and German and employed them in typical one-word sentences. His preference seemed to be for English. Verbs, mostly English, were seldom employed. A long story was reported by the use of several substantives uttered as exclamations. For instance, when he said, "Sheppy! Poor! Supper! Porch! Spoilt!" he meant "Sheppy, the poor dog, lost his food on the porch and spoiled it." The words were emphasized by vivid facial expressions, gestures of the hands and the entire body. These gestures became especially graphic in instances when words were not available to express his ideas.

At the age of two years and four months the boy had a period in which he apparently developed a need to tell someone, usually his mother, what he had seen, and he began to talk about what might be considered dreams. On going to sleep he always said farewell to his dog, his picture books, and his own image in the mirror and recalled briefly the most thrilling events of the day, stating rather reluctantly that this good time had now passed. Calling the names of some of his friends he added with deep regret, "Mary gone! Sissy gone!" When he had finished this procedure he was ready for sleep.

Approximately three hours after going to sleep the child was regularly taken up by his mother for urination. Often he did not awaken but nevertheless performed his duty so that he must have had some recognition of the situation and of what was expected of him. Sometimes he did awaken but his body seemed to continue in slumber and he was completely hypotonic and without voluntary movements. The awakening was apparent in a very slight and momentary opening of the eyes followed by some clearly pronounced words with which he apparently tried to tell his mother his very recent dream experience.

After a morning during which he had visited the home of another baby whom he did not see, but in whose backyard he found a lonely rabbit which he tried to feed with stones, he repeated this experience at night in his dream, saying, "Rabbit, stones, rabbit, stones, baby where? Baby bed!" It is apparent that the most significant experience of the day was repeated in the dream, and the unsolved problem "Where is the baby?" found its answer in the dream.

Similar repetition of a thrilling situation in dreams occurred several times. After he had seen two puppies having a bitter fight over his mother's gloves, and after he had gone with them for a ride, he said in his half-sleep of the same night, "Wow-wow, ran, gloves, ride car!" But it was not only excitement and thrills that he repeated in his dreams. After he had learned to be careful not to cross the street, and always to watch out for cars he mumbled during sleep "Watch out! Careful! Cars!"

On some occasions the dreams seemed to arouse anxiety as when he said, "Doggies, baby, bites," or on another occasion "Wow-wow bites!" Once he cried fearfully "Monkey!" and awoke spontaneously. He was fearful, tried to leave his bed, but fell asleep again without difficulty. The morning before having this dream he had seen a monkey in the zoo grabbing his mother's gloves.

On another occasion more details were obtained about an apparently terrifying nightmare, also involving monkeys. Again he awoke spontaneously and said words meaning "Monkeys eat up the hair of my head." This statement was closely connected with an experience he had had the previous morning. He had seen a group of monkeys and had watched them with tremendous excitement, mixed feelings of joy, curiosity, and fear.

Completely absorbed he had watched them, slowly retreating from them without losing sight of them, and slowly drawing nearer to the opposite side of the monkey house where other monkeys were sitting in their cages. Finally he stood with the back of his head very near to a monkey which, of course, did not resist the temptation to pull the boy's curls. Panic stricken both of them yelled and ran in opposite directions. Soon the boy laughed about the whole incident but he refused to talk about it during the rest of the day, even when questioned. At night he apparently relived the emotion of shock, working it through by himself and in his own way, indicating an important function of his dream.

The beginning of the Oedipus complex condensed into a short story may be seen in another example of the boy's dreams. One afternoon he refused to take his regular walk to his father's office to accompany the father home. He gave as the explanation of his refusal, "Papa? Does not need! Papa alone!" In these words he stated that he did not wish to see his father who might remain where he was alone. The following night he asked in his sleep "Papa movie? Baby with mother alone!" He meant by this that he hoped his papa would not come home, but would go to a movie so that he might be alone with his mother. The next morning the boy attempted to crawl into bed with his still sleeping mother. He was not taken into bed but to his great consternation was dressed. At noon of the same day he took a beloved doll into his own bed for a moment, then he threw it out of his bed, disappointing it in the same manner his mother had disappointed him in the morning. The following night he wet his bed for the first time in several months. Apparently he was behaving as if to say: "If mother does not love me, why do I need to please her? I prefer to love myself, and so I do what I like." He seemed however to feel somewhat guilty and volunteered an explanation for his bed-wetting. He said that not he, but a dog wet his bed. Hearing his mother say that he was probably guilty of the deed, he tried to prove his innocence by showing her the dog which of course was not to be found in his bed. So he varied his story by saying that the dream dog might have been invisible because it was hidden in the pillows, or "in the shadow." Later he volunteered the information that the dog had bitten him in the buttock.

Food was a favorite theme in his dreams. Usually his dream words were a statement, the meaning of which never became quite clear. He said, "Food noch" which meant in his language either "I have had enough food," or "I wish to have more food." The statement "Have flowers" meant "I want salad," because in his language he called salad flowers. It was an outstanding feature of these little statements that they were spoken in a matter-of-fact tone, very much in contrast to his behavior when awake and expressing a wish. Then he demanded his food in a very distinct way, accompanying his request with motor behavior which no one could misunderstand.

After a period of two months he stopped talking in his sleep because urination was becoming such a completely automatic process that he did not even partially awaken.

It may be doubted that this baby's words were really expressions of dreams. They might also be called memories which had flashed through his mind when he was more or less awake. Such an interpretation is possible, but such memories are accompanied in a child of that age by very vivid visual imaginings. The difference between fantasies and dreams in a child is so slight that it is unnecessary to stress the differences. What happened may equally well be called playacting, fantasies, or dreams.

The very vivid and plastic visual imagination of this child was apparent in his play. On one occasion a bird flew in the open window of the baby's room, and could not find its way out again, very much to the mother's distress and worry. The next day the child repeatedly pointed with his finger to the ceiling, saying "See, see, look, look, peep, peep, there, see?" This was play, but it had in common with dreams the hallucinatory component. Such hallucinatory experiences are everyday instances in every child's life, and were observed many times in this child. He had learned from the child of a neighbor how to kill grasshoppers and found it fun, but when he found none on the rug in his room, he continued to kill them in imagination. His pleasure was nearly the same.

Hallucinations like these which are vivid and visualized recapitulations of memory are at the present time of special interests, because Freud states in his recent paper (1937b) about constructions in psychoanalysis that hallucinations and delusions of schizophrenic patients are reactivated memories, types of dream memory. It seems that these observations of early childhood give some unexpected support to Freud's theory.

The conclusion seems justified that in children, play, fantasies, and dreams are very closely related to each other, and that what in an adult would be called hallucinations may be called vivid visual imaginations, very characteristic of infant thinking, and if such fantasied, hallucinatory form of memory is observed in a sleeping child it may be called a dream.

Freud mentions children's dreams in *The Interpretation of Dreams,* and significantly in the chapter "The Dream As Wish Fulfillment" states that these dreams are "by no means interesting." They are often "simple fulfillment of wishes," and invaluable proof of the wish fulfillment theory of dreams. He mentions mostly dreams of children at the age of five years and more, although he reports two from children less than two years of age. Freud's daughter dreamed about strawberries which she could not have the day before her dream. Freud's little nephew dreamed that he had eaten some cherries which he had in reality given to Freud as a birthday present.

The dream observations reported in this paper contain the element of wish fulfillment, but they are not completely without problems, at least not from the standpoint of the dreamer. To think about meat, salad, and other food may be pleasant for the baby and according to our knowledge may be easily connected with a hallucinatory wish fulfillment; but to dream of rabbits, dogs, monkeys, cars, the other baby, and the father at the movie would indicate that the child was struggling with strong and strange emotions which he could not work through during the excitement and rapidity of reality and which consequently he had to repeat and work through more completely in his dreams.

Wish fulfillment working through the overwhelming emotions of the day, the similarity of the mechanisms in a child's dream hallucinations to those of schizophrenic hallucination are not the only interesting features of dreams at a very early age. Sleep to which the child in very early babyhood devotes most of its time seems to be much more important and preferable to waking life during the first year. The omnipotence of thought, the ability to hallucinate, and the absolute wish fulfillment attained during sleep is continued in a high degree during the waking state at a later time. During very early childhood the waking state seems to be a continuation of getting the same pleasure as in sleep by similar means. Even in the waking state the child in its mental life is still much closer to something that may be similar to the adult dream life than to anything else. There is no superego, not even an ego ideal. There is only an ideal ego, a harmony of instincts, an uninhibited need for satisfaction, and a united, unlimited striving to get it.

Chapter 43

A TREATMENT OF NIGHTMARES IN A
SEVEN-YEAR-OLD BOY

Leo Rangell

The following clinical experience is presented because it seems of interest for several reasons: (1) It shows in rather clear-cut fashion a good part of the psychodynamics' substratum in a typical case of nightmares in a young boy. (2) It made use of psychoanalytic thinking in a unique way. A son was treated by his father through the guidance of an analyst by letters. (3) It presents an almost verbatim, blow-by-blow description of a psychotherapeutic interchange, with causes and effects nakedly outlined. (4) Implications can be drawn relating to the subject of transference in treatment, and also to the general question of the upbringing and education of children.

Some time ago, at my office here in California, I received word from a couple in New York City, close friends of mine for many years, regarding a problem with their seven-year-old son. First I received the following letter from the boy's mother. (Comments appearing in brackets throughout these letters are my own, and have been added for this publication.)

NEW YORK CITY
January 26, 1948

Dear LEO,

Bill and I have decided to write this letter to you because we want to ask your help and advice, and also because we think you'd be interested in the problem we're going to tell you about. It concerns Paul.

This paper was first published in *The Psychoanalytic Study of the Child* (1950), 5:358–390.

At the risk of writing quite a long letter, I'm going to start way back at the beginning, when Paul first started to have nightmares, which was two years ago—just a few months after Anne was born. We spoke to you about it then—you gave us somewhat of an explanation. Somehow, they weren't too bad and as summer came on and he was outdoors a lot they must have disappeared quite a bit because I don't remember his being disturbed by them. However, as last winter approached so did the nightmares come on, and we all had a bad time because of them. Paul would awaken ever night from a dream and would call to me in a voice full of fear. Most of the time Bill or I would go to him and lie down in his bed. If we didn't, he would lie awake whimpering with unhappiness and fear. He had very many colds which I felt were due to his unhappiness at night, and then he became painfully ill with swollen glands which kept him in bed about three weeks. It was during this time that we called John T. [a psychoanalytic colleague in New York] to ask his advice. He was very nice, and when we told him the nature of Paul's dreams at that time, of foxes and wolves pursuing him, he said it was quite a typical case of an Oedipus problem but that it certainly didn't sound bad enough to be treated. He suggested that we try to get from the library a paper by Freud, "The Analysis of a Phobia of a Five-Year-Old," in which the father of the boy with the help of Freud treats his son successfully. Bill made some attempts to get it, but couldn't and let it go. Meanwhile, I had asked John T. what he thought of our moving Paul's bed into our room, and he said that although it might help, we would be making him more dependent on us. However, this was during Paul's illness, and as the nightmares kept him up so much, and he looked so wan I decided to move him into our room, because I felt and still feel that half of his trouble is Anne—he does suffer because of everyone's attentions to her—and that by taking him into our room and leaving her out I was showing him that we love him, that he was still our child. In other words, give him a sense of security which he evidently needed—and lo and behold—the very first night Paul didn't awaken. He was in our room with nary a nightmare for about two months until spring and then we inveigled him back to his own room with Anne. Soon summer came. We went to the country, where we had a two-room bungalow. We all slept in the one bedroom. Paul had a wonderful time all summer. When we came back, it had gotten to the point where I could even shut his bedroom door when he went to sleep and I remember even writing to you about how happy I was that Paul had gotten through that difficult time. I was too hasty in my relief, however, because since then—about two months ago—Paul has awakened every night at least once in a state of fear or anxiety. In the beginning, he asked me to sit on the couch where he could see me until he fell asleep again. This I did. However, some nights when I was particularly groggy or tired, I would foolishly decide to be stern and say that he would have to lie there until he fell asleep again—on those nights he would lie awake hour after hour and call me four or five times on some pretext or other. He would then fall asleep towards morning and would have to go to school overtired and unhappy. This brings up another important point. For the last few months, he has taken a dislike to school, whimpers "must I go?", gets terribly cold, shivers, etc.; in other words, shows manifestations of nervous tension. He happens to be one of the brightest children in the class, gets an honor report card signed by the principal, behaves very well and is very well liked by his teacher. I feel one reason for all this is his dislike of leaving me at home with his sister while he goes off. One indication of this is that he has had two very unhappy severe diarrheas in school in which he did not get to the bathroom in time. Of course the thing is a vicious cycle, for this in itself may be a reason for his disliking school, his fear of not getting to the bathroom in time.

Another very important thing that has happened is that six weeks ago or so, he started to have trouble with his stomach. (He has had for a few years at least a "sensitive" stomach; a lot of foods it seemed would upset him and his diet was always a simple one for fear of his getting a loose stomach. I even remember telling the doctor about his extremely large BMs and he told me at that time if nothing accompanied it that it was nothing.) Every three or four days he would have loose bowel movements, sometimes with cramps, sometimes only a movement of large strings of mucus. We tested his stool for bacteria, etc., and found it negative, and then I used Kaopectate (a medicine intended to put a lining on the BM). Still it didn't help. Then we started working on the theory that it might be an allergy and for four days I kept the poor kid off all wheat—no help. For the past week and a half, I've kept him off all vegetables and juices. Everything was okay until Saturday when he had three bad bowel movements with cramps. I had given him salmon which he may be allergic to, if he does have a food allergy. But, I don't know but that this whole thing is not an emotional problem, and that is why I am writing to you. If it is, I feel something ought to be done. I'll tell you what we've done already. Last week, Bill finally found the paper John referred to. It's not allowed out of the library. Bill is reading it and telling me about it. It has helped somewhat in that we're doing something constructive. We're attempting our own amateur analysis of Paul's emotional life based on the pattern followed by Hans's father. Bill has kept a daily account of the pertinent material which we are enclosing and which we will send to you as our analysis progresses.

We have a specific question however on which we would like your opinion. Should we solve all this sleeplessness at one stroke by the simple device of putting Paul's bed in our room, thus giving him some much needed rest, and maybe helping his stomach by eliminating his fearful dreams? Or, shall we continue our efforts (which don't seem very fruitful as yet) to get at the root of his anxiety while he stays in his own room and continues with his trouble?

As I reread this, it occurs to me that you might get the picture of Paul as being a depressed, morbid, and moody child. On the contrary, he is still the bright, outgoing, social, witty and happy-appearing child in company as you remember him. What I described above, are only the characteristics of his bedtime and pre-bedtime behavior and his appearance during the night.

Bill has been meaning to write to you about this for a long time now, but he has been very busy in his work. We know that you are very busy, but we feel that you will want to know about Paul, and we want to thank you for the time and effort that we are asking you to spend on our problem.

As ever,
Lenore

A day or two later, as promised, a follow-up letter arrived from Paul's father, as follows:

NEW YORK CITY
January 28th, 1948

Dear LEO,

When I talked to John T. about Paul last year, he suggested that I might be able to handle the problem by following the pattern set by Hans' father in Freud's paper "Analysis of a Phobia in a Five-Year-Old." I have been reading the paper in the library, and have been making efforts at analyzing Paul along the lines indicated. Enclosed are the first notes I have made. We don't seem to be getting very far yet, but at least we've gotten Paul to talk to us about his fears and to get them out into the open. I don't feel, however, that he is telling us all he dreams . . . he is still very reluctant, and appears to be holding back. I would appreciate very much your comments and advice. With your help (as Freud helped Hans' father); maybe we can get somewhere. [The flattering analogy did not fail to have its effect!]

   Again, thanks for reading this stuff, and let's hear from you.

                                                         Yours,
                                                         Bill

The following notes were enclosed with the letter:

                                             January 20th, 1948
Paul awoke in the middle of the night, as he has done almost nightly for the past few months, and cried out for us in a voice mingled with fear and entreaty. I went to his bed, in the adjoining room, and found him with that pitifully sad look, his eyes wide and on the verge of tears. He was very morose and reluctant to talk, but indicated he wanted me to stay with him, or at least to sit on the living room couch where he could see me, so that he "could go to sleep better." I asked him what the matter was. No answer. Did he dream something? No answer. Was he afraid? No answer. I explained that I was trying to help and that if he told me about his dreams, or his thoughts, or his fears, I might be able to help him get rid of what was bothering him, so that he would be able to sleep through the night and feel rested for school the next day. At length, he said he had dreamed something: "You know . . . the same thing . . . about animals . . . in the jungle." "What kind of animal?" No answer. "Was it a wolf, or a fox?" "F-O-X," he answered in a whisper, spelling out the word. "What about the fox?" No answer. "What was he doing?" No answer. "What did he look like?" No answer. "Did he look like daddy maybe?" [Paul's father learns fast! This is known as the direct frontal attack.] A wide ear to ear grin replaced the morose look on Paul's face and he lifted his head from the pillow to say, loudly this time, "Are you kiddin!" . . . I: "Why can't you sleep now?"

Paul: "I keep thinking about the dream and it won't let me sleep."

I: "Tell me more about the dream." No answer.

I: "What's in your mind now? What are you thinking about?"

Paul: (In a very low whisper) "An eraser."

I: "What about an eraser?"

Paul: "Nothing. I was just thinking about it."

He was getting very sleepy, and I returned to my bed. He cried out a few minutes later again and Lenore went to him and slept with him the remainder of the night.

The next morning at breakfast Lenore and I explained to him that we were both going to help him get rid of his fear; that there were special doctors, like Leo, who do that sort of thing; but that we were studying from a book and would be able to help him just like a doctor would: that we wanted him to help by telling us all about his fears and dreams and thoughts, which we would be able to understand and explain to him. We said that we both loved him, were not angry because of his fears and insomnia, and would be able to help him sleep through the night without bad dreams if he cooperated. Paul agreed.

I asked again about last night's dream. Paul couldn't remember.

I: "What about the eraser?"

Paul: "Oh, I dreamed that there was a squirrel and an eraser up in a tree, and a fox came along, and the squirrel threw the eraser down on the fox, but that didn't hurt the fox, so the squirrel jumped down from the tree onto the fox to fight him."

[I interpreted this as follows: Paul was the squirrel and with the eraser he tried to "rub out"—or get rid of—the fox, who represents me, his daddy. Not being successful, he jumped down to fight with me himself.]

I suggested this interpretation. Paul laughed, seeming to enjoy it immensely.

I: "What did the fox look like . . . like me maybe . . . did he wear glasses?"

Paul: (sarcastically) "Oh sure, he wore glasses, and a blue suit, and a red tie, and a white shirt, just like you" (describing exactly what I was wearing at the moment).

I explained that Paul might dream of me that way because he thought I might be angry with him; but that I really was not, and, on the contrary, that I loved him very much.

Paul: "Oh, I know you're not angry with me. I know you love me."

Later Paul said that maybe he was the squirrel.

As he left for school, I said: "Goodbye, little squirrel."

He answered: "Goodbye, you great big fat fox!", and left for school in better spirits than we had seen him in a long while, and without expressing concern about his bowel movements (also for the first time in many weeks).

["Fools step in where angels fear to tread." Where a more experienced therapist would wait and exercise caution and restraint, Paul's father, unmindful of the possible consequences and therefore in a sense unfettered by them, jumps in with both feet. It worked. Paul immediately perceives his father in a new role, and unconsciously senses the possibility of a new outlet for dammed-up instinctual energies. His mood lightens, he grins, his spirits lift.]

January 21st, 1948

Paul called out twice in the night, but on each occasion he called once, and on receiving no answer, remained silent and went back to sleep. In the morning, he was very cheerful (unusual) and said: "Wasn't I a good boy? I slept all through the night."

I: "No dreams?"

Paul: "No. I slept all through the night."

January 22nd, 1948

Paul awoke twice during the night, and didn't sleep well until Lenore slept with him. He would not elaborate on what kept him up, except to say that he had the same dream "about the jungle and animals."

January 23rd, 1948

Awoke again. This time I slept with him until he fell asleep again. Nothing from Paul except that the same dreams keep him awake and afraid.

January 24th, 1948

Awoke again. I went to him. Same dream, he said. He also mentions that this time he dreamed of a gorilla who led all the other jungle animals, lions, tigers, foxes, wolves, in their chase after him. The gorilla got closest to him, with his mouth open. "What did the gorilla look like?", I ask. "Like a gorilla," Paul answers, "I suppose you want me to say he looks like you!"

The next day, Paul told me about first thinking of the gorilla after seeing one in a movie in camp this past summer. (In fact, we all saw this film together, last summer in the country—a ridiculous Mack Sennett comedy in which the Our Gang kids chase a gorilla around, and vice versa.)

I: "Did you dream about the gorilla in the country too?"
Paul: "No—because I slept in the same room with you and
             Mommie there."

(We had had a small bungalow in which all our beds were in
the same room.)

Paul then suggested that he would be able to sleep well all
night if we moved his bed into our room. (We had done this last
year for a short time when the same fears had been present.)

I evaded by saying that it would spoil the looks of the apartment, and that Annie, who is a little older now, would not like
being left alone in the other bedroom.

I should also note that Paul is fearful even before his bedtime,
and forewarns us that one of us must sit in the living room where
he can see us from his bed, so that he can fall asleep more easily.
He thinks, he says, of the dreams he has had, and those he is
going to have, and just can't get the animals, the jungle, etc., out
of his mind. [Phobia for sleep itself, and its products.]

                                          January 25th, 1948

Paul awoke again in the middle of the night and I went to
him. At first he was reluctant to talk, denying that he had had
any dream, but after a few minutes said that he had dreamed of
the gorilla again.

Paul: "The gorilla was chasing me through the jungle. I ran
             and just reached the ship in time."
I: "What ship?"
Paul: "The ship to go back to America. It was the Queen
             Elizabeth. Did you hear on the radio that the Queen
             Elizabeth was stuck in the ice yesterday?"
I: "No, I didn't hear. What else did you dream of?"
Paul: "The gorilla jumped after the ship and caught onto the
             back end. But the ship went too fast and he fell into
             the water."

I think it in order at this point to discuss my initial reactions
to these first communications, and to the unusual and uncon-
ventional proposal for treatment which they contained. Clearly,
there was a neurotic symptom present which by its content,
intensity, and duration demanded analytic treatment. Routinely and ideally, referral to a child analyst was in order. This
simple move, however, as is so often the case, was ruled out
promptly for economic reasons. Treatment in a clinic was the

next logical thought, but previous experiences made me dubious about the prospect of securing adequate analytically oriented treatment in this way. This avenue is unfortunately discouraging at the moment. While aware of the dangers inherent in the method proposed by Paul's parents, their request nevertheless intrigued me. There were several important factors in favor of trying it, high among which was the fact that I was strongly and personally motivated by my interest in them. The dangers that I might be working blindly, at a distance, and with insufficient control of the situation, were offset in my opinion by my previous first-hand knowledge of the background and my confidence in the parents. Nor was the temptingly promising beginning already made by Paul's father to be overlooked. Accordingly, it was decided to attempt the treatment in the manner proposed.

Let me interrupt at this point to orient the reader with a few pertinent remarks about the past history as I knew it. At this time Paul was seven years old, a bright, active, and robust youngster. His parents were warm, intelligent, and sincere people, much devoted to and proud of Paul and his sister. His mother had had some chronic anxiety and neurasthenic symptoms of her own, which she tended to displace onto Paul, leading to overprotection and overconcern about what he wore and ate, etc. This had always seemed to be a large factor in the production of the frequent colds, or sniffles or tummy aches which Paul would get at strategic times in his life. The father was an energetic young business man, warm, a loving and "permissive" parent, perhaps somewhat overindulgent. The home atmosphere was harmonious. It is of interest for what follows to state that the parents have had no connection with or background in analysis or medicine except for social relationships with a few analysts and a slight amount of reading in the field. At about one-and-a-half, Paul had a fractured clavicle. At three-and-a-half, a heart murmur was discovered which, although finally diagnosed as functional and of no significance, caused a natural flurry of excitement and concern about him. At four-and-a-half, his only sibling, his sister Anne, was born, with no unusual attendant reaction on Paul's part other than stated in the letters.

My first letter in response to their request follows. These letters were written in an unplanned and spontaneous way, much as one responds in a direct psychotherapeutic situation. They will be reproduced here in the same informality and spontaneity in which they were written, to preserve better the tone of the relationships involved.

BEVERLY HILLS, CALIF.
February 4th, 1948

Dear Bill and Lenore:

Of course, I'll do anything I can to help—. I only hope that my eagerness and concern doesn't impair my judgment. Here is a hurried note to give you some of my preliminary reactions.

1. The whole thing is one problem, the nightmares, diarrhea, stomach trouble, concentration on the bowels, attitude toward school, shaking and quivering, etc. The intestinal symptoms, I am sure, are emotional in origin; the bowel symptoms are what we call regressions due to the phobia. Therefore:

2. I advise stopping completely all emphasis on stomach trouble, diet, bowel movements, etc. Discontinue visits to the M.D. Feed him anything he likes. Be casual about his bowel movements, whether they are one in two days, or three per day. Forget about allergy completely. [With all due respect to allergists, I felt I knew enough about past similar symptoms with Paul, to make this seemingly dogmatic statement with confidence.]

3. The method you propose is very difficult, and has numerous obstacles and drawbacks. For the time being, however, let's try it. From my standpoint, it's 100 percent okay and I'll do all I can. The difficulties are in the distance between us, that it will be hard to keep current, and that I'd have to tell you and explain to you much more than I can ever write. However, your preliminary attitudes on the problem are wholesome. (The last resort, to be kept in reserve, which I would recommend immediately if the money question didn't enter, would be to put the entire thing into the hands of a good child analyst in New York. We'll put that aside for the time being, however, and work this way.)

4. I think the rivalry with Anne is a secondary problem. I think the crux is a parental Oedipus problem.

5. Do not, under any circumstances, yield to the temptation to put his bed in your room. Also, please try very, very hard not to sleep in his bed (either Bill or Lenore). It is all too stimulating to him and

perpetuates the problem. Sit up next to his bed when put to the task, and make repeated attempts to return to your own room. However:

6. Not harshly or critically. Always be reassuring; repeat your love to him. (Don't overdo it though, and make him wonder why you say it so much.)

7. Encourage him to talk and to reveal, as Bill did in the notes. One caution: the interpretations so far were good, but don't make too many seemingly outlandish suggestions. Let him lead the way—you follow. You may have to push and encourage now and then, but mainly let him take the initiative, with you encouraging him. The eraser, and squirrel, and fox—was excellent. (So was his response to it, as you noted.)

8. Answer all his questions about sex truthfully—don't evade—but be simple—and don't tell him more than he asks.

9. The ship dream—the Queen (Elizabeth) was Lenore—he wanted to get on her and be off—you, the gorilla (Bill) came along and jumped on her back (probably his conception of intercourse—the many months in your room play a big part here—he must have many ideas and feelings about this, right and wrong ones):

10. Keep the notes coming. I'll write you as often as I can.

Yours
LEO

A few days later I heard again:

NEW YORK
February 9th, 1948

Dear LEO:

Thank you for your letter, the warm interest you have shown, and the help you have already given us.

Unfortunately, your advice arrived just a few days late, and did not prevent us from making what now appears to have been an error in judgment. Just two days ago, Saturday night, we took the path of least resistance and gave in to Paul's repeated pleas: we moved his bed into our room. He had not had a decent night's sleep in weeks; he looked groggy and tired each morning before school: he was suffering with a cold and seemed unable to shake it off; and Lenore and I were anxious for a night's uninterrupted rest ourselves. So we agreed to Paul's suggestion, with the understanding that this would be temporary and that he himself would ask us to move him back to his own room when he felt ready for it. Since then he has slept better, acted better during the day, and even improved in his bowel movements. He does get up sometimes he says, but "when I see you I feel better and go right back to sleep." Since then, also, I have secured very little material from him—no dreams, no thoughts, no discussion. (The enclosed material was before we moved the bed.)

For some time now Paul has been asking us for a dog. He even thought he might be able to sleep better with his own dog staying in his room. We had not accepted the idea because of our small apartment, the trouble involved, etc.—but now we are using this as a means of retreating from our mistake: Paul has agreed that if I get him a pup he will return to his own room gladly. We shall see.

Meanwhile, I feel that we are almost at a standstill. Since the material that I am enclosing, I have gotten nothing from Paul. As you can see, even before receiving your letter, I was reluctant to force the issue, waiting instead for Paul to lead. Question is, how does one encourage—or do I just wait until he is ready again to give out? [Bill's query can well be identified with by every dynamic psychotherapist who recalls his own development in the field.] About sex: Paul has asked almost nothing at all about sex since last year, when he was given, on his request, pretty detailed information. We had been on the beach, last spring, and met there a young mother with a famous set of quadruplets. On our way home, Paul remarked: "She must have had a lot of seeds," and later, "Her stomach must have stretched a lot when she was pregnant!" That evening he brought the matter up again, and asked Lenore where the seeds come from, how they get into the mother, who puts them there, how, and how do the babies come out. Lenore answered truthfully and without fuss: the seeds are placed by the father; through the vagina; with his penis; and the baby comes through the vagina. Paul laughed and remarked that the penis works "just like a rubber hose." At that time Paul was well and happy, and not having nightmares. Since then, no questions at all on the subject have come up.

Thanks again. Best to all.

BILL AND LENORE

The following notes were enclosed with the letter:

February 4th, 1948

Paul has shown no improvement whatever. In fact, he seems to be worse. He has awakened every single night without exception, fearful, and begging for our company. He denies that he has had any dream, on occasions saying that he just wakes up and is "afraid." If he does dream, he says, it is "the same thing . . . animals and jungles."

Lenore reports that this afternoon (he has been home from school the past few days with a cold), Paul began a conversation by asking about Lenore's parents. When did her father die? How old was he? How old was Lenore at the time? How old was her mother when she died? How old would her father and mother be now? Lenore answered all truthfully, stressing that her parents died when they were very old, that she, Lenore, was a grown-up when they died.

Later on during the same afternoon Lenore noticed Paul looking sad and unhappy. Asked whether anything was the matter, Paul said, "I have a headache. You know, I often have headaches in school. I have to work hard, and I have a headache, when I want to be home with you." [How clearly and unpretentiously Paul describes a conversion symptom.]

Paul was moody and dejected all day at home, and had several crying jags, for no apparent reason.

February 5th, 1948

Paul awoke during the middle of last night and I went to him. He began to cry when I talked to him, would not answer my questions about what was bothering him, and seemed more unhappy than ever. He sighed deeply, his chest heaving, tears welling up into his eyes, and sobs, suppressed, coming up from way down. He had nothing to tell me. I stayed with him until he fell into an uneasy sleep. He awoke again some time later, and Lenore spent the remainder of the night in his bed.

This morning he awoke unhappily, very ill at ease, and crying at the slightest provocation. I tried talking to him again, asking him to confide in us, to tell us his troubles. He only cried more, sobbing as though his chest would burst. This was the most severe unhappiness we had ever seen in Paul. I said: "I think I know what's wrong, Paul. You're worrying about something. You have bad thoughts, maybe, and you're ashamed of them, or guilty about them, and you're too ashamed to tell them to us. But you don't have to be. We love you and we understand that little boys sometimes have these worries. Tell us about them and you'll see that we are not angry or ashamed and that you have nothing to be ashamed, or guilty, of." Paul continued to sob. A few minutes later he calmed down somewhat and I asked when he thought his fears about sleeping alone began.

Paul: "A long time ago, when Anne was in your room, in her
            crib, and I had the other room by myself."
I: "Did you, perhaps, have bad thoughts about Anne at
            that time?"
Paul: Getting tearful again, nods assent.
I: "Did you wish that she would go away?"
Paul: Nods yes.
I: "Or maybe that she should never have come in the first
            place?"
Paul: Nods yes again.
I: "Or maybe that she should die and go away?"
Paul   Nods agreement again, now unable to prevent tears
            once more.
I: "Mommie and I understand why you felt that way,
            Paul, and we are not angry with you because of your
            thoughts. You know, I think that all your bad dreams
            are your own way of punishing yourself for your bad
            wishes about Anne. You feel ashamed and guilty of the
            wishes you had toward her and so you punish yourself
            with frightening dreams about animals. But you don't
            have to punish yourself, because there is no reason to
            feel ashamed or guilty about anything."

Paul calmed down and stopped crying. (I feel sure that Paul's
suppressed hostile wishes are also directed against me, but I don't
know how to proceed to bring this out.)

In the evening, after returning from work, Lenore reports
that Paul had mentioned during the day that he was also worried
that I might die, or might not come home from work some day.
Paul talked with me, in much better spirits and happier than this
morning. He said that he was worried that I might die before I
was an old man, or might not come home from work some day.
I assured him that this was very unlikely, that I was young and
healthy, would always come home from work and wouldn't die
until I was an old man and he a grown-up old man himself. I
asked whether he had ever wished that I would go away and leave
him alone with Mommie. "Oh no," he replied. (Although Hans's
father, in Freud's case, plunges right into this sort of situation
with questions aimed at bringing the child's death wishes toward
his father out into the open, I am afraid to proceed along such
lines, and therefore dropped this questioning on Paul's first negative answer.) [Who can blame him?]

BEVERLY HILLS, CALIF.
February 16th, 1948

Dear BILL and LENORE:

On your second installment concerning Paul, some comments:

1. Can't blame you for giving in and taking him into your room—his entreaties must be pitiful—but do try to undo it and get him back into his room for good. Talk of the whole house as one room, it all belongs to all of you, you're all together, etc. But insist on your sleeping arrangements. Don't evade it as you did in installment one with remarks about the apartment looking better the other way, etc. You've got to be truthful with him—remarks as the above cause you to lose "face" and prestige with him—he'll always take the truth better than anything you can make up. A good way to work out of this would be through:

2. The dog—I am in favor of it, if it is feasible and practical with you and Lenore. It can help—but only if it isn't too much for you in the house.

3. About your being at a standstill—don't worry. In the first place you are not, things are happening. Second, there are stops and starts, and different paces, as he gains courage for new statements and feelers. Just wait, and reassure, and encourage him to talk.

4. About sex—Lenore's answers a year ago were good. There must be more questions though. Watch for them, and answer in the same way—no fuss, no lies, no evasions.

5. His preliminary questions about Lenore's parents (Feb. 4th) were the tentative beginnings of bringing out such thoughts about his own parents.

6. His headaches (as described) are beautifully diagnosed by himself— "When I want to be home with you (Lenore)." I think his frequent colds (and I mean for years, not just now) are similarly used and even possibly originated (with all due respect to the New York winters). Pay little attention to them unless accompanied by fever, etc. Let them disturb his going-out routine as little as possible, not at all if possible.

7. Bill's remarks to him (at his moments of greatest unhappiness, Feb. 5th) about "I know what's wrong, you're worried about something, ashamed and guilty about something, you don't have to worry, we accept and love you anyway, etc.," were very well put. It brings immediate response from Paul. Then came his revelations about Anne, and then about "Bill might die."

8. Bill's direct question then: "Did you ever wish that I would go away?" drew a negative reply. It would have been better, instead of asking, to say some such things as, "Sometimes children

are angry at their daddies and might for some reason wish such a thing"—in a way which makes the thing understandable and not punishable—more will come from him then about it spontaneously.

You're not at all at a standstill. You're on the track; keep him talking, and keep up this general tone with him.

Best regards,

As ever,
LEO

NEW YORK CITY
February 19th, 1948

Dear LEO,

Enclosed find my latest notes on Paul, written after a lengthy conversation with him last night.

At this point, Leo, I must say that I feel unsure of myself and uneasy over developments. The thought plagues me that, on occasion, I do more harm than good, that I may be opening something that I'll be unable to cope with. Take last night's conversation, for example: When we began, Paul was in good spirits; he had had a happy day; he had slept well for many nights; bowels okay; school okay; he was willing to talk. The squirrel–fox dream had caused him no unhappiness or fear, and he related it simply and straightforwardly, smiling as he talked. As we talked about it, however, and after I had outlined the underlying Oedipus pattern, Paul changed, became depressed, reluctant to talk, and finally fearful and in tears. Of course, I reassured him as best I could. But I remain doubtful. Was it correct to explain the dream and its Oedipus pattern to him? Or, in doing so, did I implant, or reinforce, his feeling of guilt, and consequently of fear? The analysis caused him to admit hostile wishes against me, which caused him to cry, and then to fear the fox's punishment. I had the feeling that my assurances were not fully accepted or believed; that Paul was stunned by the realization of the truth of the Oedipus picture, and that, having had hostile wishes against me, he now feared the inevitable punishment. He had a bad night in consequence, and awoke this morning on the unhappy side. Question: Is it proper to explain to Paul the meaning of his dreams, taking the risk of forcing him to unpleasant and emotionally disturbing conclusions? Or should I have waited; Is there value in my just listening to his dream content without analysis?

(Con't-February 20th, 1948)

On arriving home last night, I found your letter, which by indirection answered some of the questions above. I would find it very helpful, however, if you answered them directly in your next reply.

Lenore asked me to tell you that she is following your suggestions: No M.D. visits, no fuss about BMs, no more dieting, no notice of colds, etc. Again, our profound thanks for your wonderful cooperation and help.

Our very best to all of you,
BILL

Enclosed were the following notes:

February 8th, 1948

Moved Paul's bed into our bedroom.

February 18th, 1948

Since Paul has been sleeping in our bedroom, he has slept better, acted happier, and has shown a remarkable improvement in his stomach condition: No cramps or diarrhea, and no worry about too frequent BMs. He doesn't have many dreams, he says. Sometimes he gets up at night, but when he sees us close by, he is not afraid and goes right back to sleep.

A few days ago, he reported this dream: "I was riding on the back of a horse and the horse turned around and kissed me." What did the horse look like? "I think the horse was you, Daddy. He was wearing the same kind of coat that you and Mommie have." (Both Lenore and I recently bought overcoats with fur collars, almost identical in appearance.)

Tonight I was home alone with the children, Lenore having gone off to the movies. Paul appeared in good spirits and I asked if he wanted to talk with me again about his dreams, or his thoughts. Did he think he could try to sleep in his own room by now? He agreed that he would, just as soon as we bought him a dog, as we had promised about a week ago. About dreams, he reported the following, occurring several nights ago: "A squirrel was up in a tree putting his nuts into his hole for the winter time, when one of the nuts fell and hit a fox on his nose. The squirrel jumped down to get the nut and grabbed it in his mouth, whereupon the fox chased him deep into the woods." This reminded Paul, he said, of the other squirrel dream. This time, he said, he thought the fox looked like Mommie. In the first dream, it had looked like Daddy. He thought that he was the squirrel both times. We talked about the dream and what it might mean, and I asked if he remembered what I had said about the last squirrel–fox dream. He said he remembered a little, but wanted me to repeat. I explained, as I had done before, that the animals were symbols representing me and him, that he dreamed of being punished by me (the fox) because he felt guilty of wishes that he may have had toward me at some time in the past; that these wishes sprang from rivalry with me in reference to his mother's love. I assured him that these wishes and thoughts were natural and normal and that both mother and I understood and had no anger toward him and loved him dearly. I suggested that if he understood this clearly and accepted it he probably would not be afraid, or dream of the fox any more. Paul replied that he had bad wishes against Mommie, but not against me. He wished sometimes that Mommie would go away, or not come back, or die, so that we two could be together, like tonight—not the other way around. Then he said that at one time he did have wishes against me, but not now. "You remember," he said, "when I was crying that time and I told you about it." (He was referring to the time when we had talked about Anne.) "I thought you had said it was Anne that time," I said. "Oh yes," he replied, "It was Anne, not you."

I: "Maybe it was about me too."

Paul: "Yes, I think so, I had bad wishes about you too, but long ago, not now."

Paul was reluctant to talk further. He had grown more and more unhappy during this discussion, and was now on the verge of tears. When I asked what was making him cry, he said that it was true that he had had bad wishes against me and that it made him feel like crying. I assured him again that I understood and loved him. He finally fell asleep.

Comment

Paul was probably telling the truth. The horse he was astride this time was the father, who gives him the reassuring and loving kiss. The threatening fox, formerly the father, is now the mother. Both parents wear the same coats. Hostile death wishes toward "Mommie," the wish to be left alone with father, are admitted; and later, more reluctantly, the same "bad" wishes toward the father. Paul is describing his negative Oedipus complex, the boy's tender love for his father, for whom it is his mother who is the rival. This does exist, especially with his "good, permissive, understanding" father, and in fact makes more poignant his conflictual relationship toward his father.

This negative side of the oedipal coin comes out first, and is actually also a sop to the father. Behind it, there comes out of repression, amid tears and anxiety, the "positive" Oedipus, with the painful admission of "bad wishes" toward the father—"but long ago."

What about the father's quite understandable trepidation and anxiety at this point? Was it an indication of things having gotten out of control and should it have led to an abandoning of this treatment? On the contrary, was it not the natural and predictable reaction to the unconscious material which was emerging, the same resistance, in miniature, which one finds in more chronic form in a more prolonged analytic treatment? It was, in fact, a resistance "*à deux*," the cumulative anxiety and subsequent resistance of both father and son to the same material. The reactions of both had to be dealt with.

BEVERLY HILLS, CALIF.
February 24th, 1948

Dear BILL,

Received your letter today. Some comments:

1. You're doing your job well. Take heart. You are in the unfortunate position of dealing with your own son, and therefore wincing with each pain which he feels. Of course, too much anxiety is to be avoided, and is a sign to stop or pull back. But in general, the mobilization of some anxiety during this period cannot be avoided, and even keeps the entire process moving. As a whole, you write of better days and nights, better spirits in Paul, and less physical symptoms. So don't become upset by it. Also, in general, you're doing what it takes a psychiatrist years to learn, and I think doing it well.

2. I acknowledge Lenore's message—good—keep it up and try to be consistent about this—less attention to and fuss about his physical ups and downs.

3. Just listening to the dreams without analysis is sometimes of help in itself—of course if one doesn't understand the meaning there should be no spoken analysis—if one does understand, the interpretation, if given, should be cautious and tentative, and not dropped like dynamite. I don't think you've overdone it. When in doubt, though, just listen, encourage, and reassure.

4. Keep trying to get him back to his room—follow through on your promise of a dog if you can.

5. The horse kissing him—you. Overaffection, and kissing him, and bending over backwards in your concern (which he can sense) can even increase his guilt. He feels that he is so bad, deserves the worst, and gets such kindness; this may worry him. (This is just to be noted and perhaps watched—don't let it confuse you, though, in your attitude toward him.)

6. The squirrel–nuts–fox dream—very interesting. Has to do with his fear of losing or dropping or damaging his nuts (testicles–genitals)—castration fear—probably because of his putting them in the hole (mother's). This information is for you, not for him. He might some day give a better opportunity to bring up the question of fear of damage to his genitals.

7. Don't initiate the discussions now of his hostility to you, proof of which is certainly blatant and undeniable—he might feel you're pressing it and therefore be frightened—but take it up and recognize it and reassure him at any indication he gives about it. He also loves you—very dearly—tell him that too when he shows it—tell him both feelings are there, are mixed and are natural.

8. Have courage—take your time—don't worry. When he becomes upset and tearful, remember that misery and tears have been a regular nightly occurrence for many months, when no attempt was being made to understand them—so an occasional episode like that now is not a heavy price—if it is on the road to progress—which it can very well be.

Yours,
LEO

It was now a full month before the next communication was received:

NEW YORK
March 23rd, 1948

Dear LEO,

I haven't written for this long interval for very happy reasons: I have no notes to send; Paul is a thousand times better in every way; we have had no direct pertinent conversations to be recorded. Let me bring you up to date.

1. We carried out our promise of a dog for Paul with wonderful results. Paul, without the need of any urging from us, carried out his end of the bargain and promptly moved back into his own room. (He had been in our room for just one week.) Since then he has awakened during the night on occasions, but the quality

of his behavior on these occasions has changed: he is no longer overfearful, teary, and sweaty. He simply asks to be covered, or to have the light on, or to have me sit in the parlor where he can see me for a little while. I do what he asks and he generally falls asleep very soon—in a matter of minutes. He says that he has had no dreams, or has forgotten them, or has been awakened by noises, or by the covers falling off, etc. Of late, his awakening at night has become less and less frequent. He never asks me to sleep with him any more. Most important, his entire demeanor is happier and normal upon awakening.

2. His stomach condition has entirely disappeared. There have been no abnormal BMs, no diarrhea, no constipation, no fears along these lines for a long time. Paul is very happy about this and proudly told his M.D. that his stomach was cured. (His pediatrician is a very nice fellow, to whom I described some of the things we've been doing. He agreed and said he'd thought Paul's trouble may have been emotional from the beginning.)

3. Interesting confirmation of your analysis of the ship dream (your letter of 2/4/48). We were having breakfast one morning a few weeks ago, the whole family in a sort of gay mood, and I remarked to Lenore: "You're looking fine this morning, Lenore, very lovely."—to which Paul rejoined, "Aaah, she looks stinky!" "What does she look like, Paul?" I ask. "Like Queen Elizabeth," he replies. "You mean the ship?" asks Lenore. "Naah, crazy, like the Princess, the Queen of England, you know," Paul answers!!!

In general, the sleeping, stomach, school, Paul is a thousand times better. I ask him from time to time if he wants to talk about things, about his former fear, or any questions he might have on his mind, but he answers in the negative. So we've had no more conversations. I don't press the issue, of course, and since he seems to be so much better, and improving steadily, I do nothing but watch, reminding him on occasion that I'm still around to talk about these matters whenever he chooses.

You've been a wonderful help through all this, Leo. In fact, I would never have begun without your guidance and support, and we cannot thank you enough.

Best of everything to all of you from,

BILL and LENORE

P.S.: The family is well: Anne, a wonderful, charming, lovable creature; Lenore is well,—and all of us are looking forward again to the summer. We're going back to the same colony where we had such a good time last year. Our dog is a cute little pup, part

Terrier and part Beagle Hound. We call her George, because we got her on Washington's birthday. Paul and Anne love her; and even I am becoming something of a dog lover myself.

Comment

Some might be inclined at this point to attribute the improved state simply to the acquisition of the dog, following "*post hoc ergo propter hoc*" reasoning. While this may be a temptingly direct way of thinking, it would be an oversimplification of the facts and would indeed do injustice to the basic emotional alterations taking place here. The appearance of the dog on the scene did no more to remove the nightmares than its absence did to produce them. On the other hand, dynamic therapy does not spurn aid from any direction. Paul was ready at this point to shift his attention and libido to this new object and even, to an extent, to "save face" with it.

The dynamic forces and tensions within the various mental agencies, in constant balance, do not realign themselves in one lightning stroke and land with a thump in a new fixed and permanent pattern. Rather they swing in a pendulumlike motion and only gradually do they alter their resultant direction under the pressure of forces applied from without. The new status described by Paul's father was gratifying; however, one could expect some fluctuations to occur before this became a secure and solid position. Newly formed scars need protection and are still vulnerable.

BEVERLY HILLS, CALIF.
March 26th, 1948

Dear BILL and LENORE,

Needless to tell you how glad I was to receive your letter of yesterday, and especially with its contents. I was quite worried about the long silence and hoped it wasn't a sign of some discouraging developments. I was about to write you when your letter came.

The results are even more than I had expected, at least so soon. I wish you would drop me a progress note every couple of weeks or so just to keep me in close contact with the status. What you're doing is right—just a normal attitude now, not pressing, happy at the results, and ready to hear and see if anything more comes up. I'd like a few more months to go by this way before feeling completely that this is now a thing of the past.

The confirmation of the Queen Elizabeth dream certainly is interesting. Also I'm not surprised at the bowels and stomach clearing up along with the fears.

So—keep me posted.

As ever,
LEO

A month later:

NEW YORK CITY
April 26th, 1948

Dear LEO,

Just a progress note to let you know that everything is fairly smooth with Paul. That is not to say that we think that he has resolved completely the problems that disturbed him, but it is evident from his behavior that they no longer rob him of sleep, bring on easy tears, hurt his stomach, and cause him the intense pains that they used to. We have discontinued our regular talks, and he tells me when I ask, that he has nothing further to discuss about his "former troubles." Most nights he sleeps soundly throughout. When he does awaken on occasion, because of a noise or because his covers fall off, he calls and asks me to sit in the living room where he can see me until he falls asleep. I do, staying up for a few minutes only, and Paul goes back to sleep easily and without fuss. He has reported no dreams at all in many weeks.

We do think, however, that his conflicts show more now in his daytime behavior. He is difficult when he doesn't have his own way, even in small matters. He isn't too kind to Anne, socking her around on occasions, fighting over toys, etc. But these manifestations, we feel, are more normal and easier to cope with. In general, we think he has come a long way, and we're very happy with the results.

Despite all this, Paul is a wonderful, enjoyable kid, growing in every direction, interested now in baseball, his two-wheel bike, his newly acquired ability to read, and a million other things. I sometimes get the feeling that, with the one-sided news we've been giving you, you'll get the notion that Paul is nothing but trouble. Far from it. He's still a terrific kid—and still as handsome as the devil.

All of us are well. Summer, at last, is coming, and we're looking forward again to the same colony where we had such a good time last year.

Yours,
BILL

BEVERLY HILLS, CALIF.
May 17th, 1948

Dear BILL and LENORE,

I agree that Paul is much better, and have very little to say on that score in reference to your last letter. I am very pleased with how it sounds. The daytime socking around which he does now, etc., are all normal and certainly can't be labeled "a problem." About the main thing, let's just sit tight; I have nothing to say; just keep on living normally and naturally. Keep your eyes and ears open though for anything which you think may still be references to "it." On the whole, it all sounds good.

Concerning the sleeping arrangements in the summer colony, let's discuss it some more. It is very important not to get him back into your room.

Yours
LEO

NEW YORK, N.Y.
May 21st, 1948

Dear LEO,

There is nothing to report about Paul at this time. Everything is about the same. About this summer, however, it looks as though we will all be sharing the same bedroom, as we did last year. We have a small cottage, with only one bedroom, and any other arrangements are practically impossible. It would, further, be very queer to Paul if we were to insist on crowding him into the very small kitchen (and leave Anne's crib in our bedroom to boot). So it looks as though we'll have to take our chances with the one bedroom setup. Things are smooth now and maybe by summer the danger will be mostly passed, anyhow—what do you think?

Paul awoke one night a few weeks ago and said that he had had a bad dream: He had gone along with me to the office and somehow lost me in the subway. He was panic-stricken upon not being able to find me and awoke in fright. We didn't discuss this as he looked sleepy and eager to go back to sleep. I adjusted his covers and he went right back to sleep. He seldom asks me to stay up to help him go back to sleep anymore. On this occasion I put the light on, at his request, and returned to my room. His mood, almost always, is happy and normal.

Best
BILL

BEVERLY HILLS, CALIF.
June 22nd, 1948

Dear BILL and LENORE,

I note Paul's continued improvement with great satisfaction: That you rarely have to stay up with him now even to help him go back to sleep. The dream about his losing you in the subway is still his concern about the same thing; to get rid of you (that little roué), but he can go back to sleep now with less need for reassurance and with less guilt. He was, as you said, too sleepy to want to hear anything about it, and it was fine to just let him go back to sleep. If he brought it up again later, you might have given him the same interpretations and reassurances as you did in the past on this phase of it.

The main point of this letter now, however, concerns the prospect of the one bedroom again for the family this summer. . . .

What I have to say on this subject might already be to no avail, but I think it will be of help to at least let you know how I feel about it, so that you can be aware of it and ready for what may come. As I said in my last letter, I think it would be very unwise for you all to share one bedroom again, and that every possible effort should be made for some other arrangement. He's a big boy now, and should really be spared the undue stimulation he will unavoidably get if he is in such close physical proximity to your bed. This is the thing he's been struggling with all year, and now it would be like exposing him all over again.

Perhaps the only alternative is the small kitchen you mention. If you could get a cot and crib in there, it should be done. I think both children ought to be in one room by now, instead of Anne with you. Or is it at all possible, because I think this is a "must," to obtain some extra room there, or a porch or anything?

If it's out of the question, then we'll just have to make the best of it. In that event, just use your discretion and judgment, and try to maintain as much privacy for yourselves as possible.

Otherwise, the freedom and outdoor life of the country will no doubt be wonderful for all of you, as well as for Paul. Hope you have a pleasant summer . . .

LEO

P.S.: What I said about the bedroom applies just as well even when you, Bill, won't be there: i.e., when he's alone with Lenore in the room. It isn't the actual sounds that he might hear or what he may see, but what he imagines and feels and thinks and fantasies in such a situation. Another point is that while he may seem to be impervious to it and unaffected at the time, effects of this could show up months later and in many devious ways (as it did in the past).

It seemed as if external conditions just were not going to remain ideal or favorable for healing. Instead, Paul seemed headed, almost as if this were being experimentally controlled, for a repetition of exposure to a traumatic and noxious stimulus. This manner of summer vacation can have a pernicious effect, at this particular point in a boy's life, in several ways. The alternating absence and presence of the father, while the child remains with the mother, represents an alternating unconscious fulfillment and denial of oedipal wishes, a condition which opposes resolution of the complex. This factor was present and played a similar role in the Little Hans case, as will be noted below. Moreover, the physical arrangement in our case is such as to make repeated exposure to primal scene material inevitable; we remember that this had already taken place the entire previous summer.

As it turned out, there was even a further complication, the occurrence of a long-confining physical illness. It was after the summer when I heard again, this time from Paul's mother:

NEW YORK CITY
September 13th, 1948

Dear LEO,

I've asked Bill a few times to report on Paul's progress to you, but he's just been too busy and tired, so I'll try to give you some information.

1. When we got to the country, I separated the bedroom by putting up a curtain on a drawstring and used it every night.

Paul had improved completely at night, but made many remarks during the daytime which showed me that he hadn't gotten over his problem completely. I don't remember all of them but two typical thoughts would be: (1) What if Daddy should have an accident, or die, etc., before coming up. (2) On the subject of penes, how big Daddy's was and how big Grandpa's was, etc.

I felt, however, that things were going well, until Paul became physically sick. He had a very bad time of it in the country, with the village doctor diagnosing it as bronchitis and he grew steadily worse for ten days until we had another doctor look at him. He told us Paul had virus pneumonia, with one lung completely congested. He advised our going home, saying that recovery would be much quicker that way. We took Paul home the very same day. He lay in bed for another three weeks getting stuck with penicillin daily. No small wonder then that he reverted for a brief time to the old Paul with two changes. Whereas before he was quite willing to go to sleep but would have nightmares, now he would refuse altogether to go into his bedroom, would have an outburst of loud crying or yelling, insisting that we stay in his room. This we refused to do, but kept talking to him and reassuring him about things in general. Also, at the same time, I was dismayed to notice that he got diarrhea and made a terrible fuss about cramps and going to the bathroom. This also I'm tickled to say we cured after just a few days by my telling him repeatedly that it was nothing he ate, but some fear or feeling of guilt, or worry, etc. that was causing it. [An indication of a considerably changed and better attitude on the part of the mother, one which bodes well for Paul's future.] His tantrums at bedtime were also very short-lived; he makes no fuss and also sleeps through most nights. I realize now, however, that for Paul the whole idea of a summer away from Bill, with his only coming up for weekends is a bad one. He's lost a lot of weight and looks like a starved child, but I guess he'll pick up soon.

Anne is a happy, independent child, thank God. I've lost quite a few pounds waiting on Paul and gained a few gray hairs—but things are looking up again.

With all our best,
LENORE

Physical illness exerts an effect in several ways. On the one hand it depletes the ego, thereby weakening its defenses and causing regression on that account. In addition it naturally tends toward increased ministration and direct attention from the mother, thus again intensifying the oedipal longings, encouraging fixation, and delaying the onset of the next, the latency period. Confinement in bed, moreover, in itself encourages autoerotic practices with their accompanying fantasies.

BEVERLY HILLS, CALIF.
October 23rd, 1948

Dear BILL and LENORE,

Our correspondence about Paul has sort of slowed down of late, but of course for very good and welcome reasons; i.e., that he was really so much improved and that there was therefore so much less to say about him. However, I would like to make a few comments on your last letter:

1. It certainly is regrettable how that old virus had to come along and give you such a rough time. Now it isn't at all uncommon for an emotional problem like this one to regress; i.e., go backward, during any time of crisis or discomfort, such as a physical illness imposes. Therefore, it is not surprising that you write of the recurrence which took place, both in the bedtime tantrums and in the bowel symptoms. However, I was happy to note that both lasted only a few days and then disappeared. How good it is that you weren't thereby tricked again into dietary measures, overprecautions, and an oversolicitous attitude about the diarrhea. Your present attitude and explanations to him promptly removed the trouble. Try to work hard at keeping this up—it will pay dividends and strong benefits.

2. Some of the daytime comments of his which you quote reveal that he is still working at and adjusting to the same theme, i.e.; his being daddy's rival, which always takes time to resolve and be disposed of. Perhaps it has obtained expression and come more into the open. Just try to retain now the open and understanding attitudes which you've both become so aware of during this whole experience. Let him express his thoughts freely and without fear—this is so healthy compared to keeping it within.

3. The curtain idea was a good compromise during the summer. From now on though, I think he should have his own room always, summer and winter, i.e., separate from you. I guess Anne will of course have to be with him for a while—at least until your next living quarters.

Yours,
LEO

A few days later, a message from the father added his version of this most recent period:

Dear LEO,

About Paul: As Lenore already has written, we returned from the country the first week in August with Paul badly ill. He remained in bed for about four weeks thereafter, in our bedroom, [The mother had neglected to mention this fact in her letter! We must by now wonder whether the ease with which Paul keeps bobbing up in his parents' bedroom may not be an indication of a proclivity on the parents' part to bring this about, perhaps for unconscious reasons of their own.] to keep him away from Anne. Upon this getting well, he put up a little fuss about returning to his own room, and again showed signs of bad bowels—but this lasted for only a few days; we talked about it again, and he returned to his own bed in his own room without much fuss. Since that time things have been fairly smooth. He sleeps well most nights, never asks to have one of us sleep with him, and in general behaves happily and normally. Bowels okay: Nothing much to report in the way of dreams.

Just this week, however, we were sharply reminded that the problem is still there: Paul awoke the other night, fearful and unhappy, and Lenore had to sit on the living room couch (visible from Paul's bed) until he fell asleep. In the morning, after much questioning, he admitted, with obvious guilt, that he had dreamed that "daddy was shot and killed by a cowboy." (He has been seeing a great many bad Western films on the television set of a friend.) Two nights later he awoke again. In the morning he told us that he had dreamed that "daddy fell off the station and was killed by the train." On both these occasions it was difficult to get Paul to tell us the dream. He was very, very guilty and afraid and unhappy. I explained that dreams of this kind are not unnatural, that all little boys have them about their daddies in one way or another, and that I wasn't hurt or insulted or angry in any way—that he had nothing to fear in the way of punishment for these dreams and ought not to feel any guilt about them.

In thinking about these dreams, I have thought that this is much better than last year's gorilla and wolf and fox dreams: Less concealing symbolism; more open reaction to the father rivalry . . . and I see in your letter that you agree.

To Paul, however, I have said nothing this week about why he dreams these dreams—his obvious wish fulfillments re me. I felt that such an explanation might increase his guilt, and make him more unhappy. I simply let it go with assurances that I was not angry, that I understood and still loved him, and that he ought not to feel guilty or afraid. What's your advice on this?

In school, Paul is doing very well—happy, well-adjusted and Phi Beta Kappa. At home, he is always in search of activity, a game, a book, go visit friends, or have friends in his house. Unfortunately, there are not enough nice kids his age on the block and he is often without something to do. We hope to improve this situation soon by getting a piano and beginning his musical education. He is very happy and excited and eager about this. So are we all. Lenore will play again—and even I may take lessons if time permits.

Just a few words about Anne: She is the most charming, delightful, many-sided, enjoyable, lovable imp you ever did see. And that's no exaggeration. . . . Lenore is well, endorses everything I write in this letter, feels just the same way I do about things.

Our best to you,
BILL and LENORE

Should these last two reported dreams, of father being killed by a cowboy, or by the train, obvious father rivalry and death-wish dreams, cause us surprise or disappointment at this point, and should they signalize, as they might at first glance, that we have been deluding ourselves about the existence of a therapeutic process until now? Are these residual dreams analogous to the discovery of malignant glands left behind after the supposed complete excision of a malignant mass—glands which potentially are as ominous and threatening as the original lesion itself? A bit of reflection will reveal the essential differences involved. In the emotional life, the appearance of death-wish dreams in an isolated or occasional way are per se not at all incompatible with so-called complete normality. They are, as a matter of fact, healthy outlets for unacceptable wishes; Theodor Reik's aphorism, "A murderous dream a day keeps the psychiatrist away," derives from this (Reik, 1952).

The present situation is rather to be compared with Paul's previous state. The hostile, jealous conflict with the father is now in the open and undisguised. The father can appear as himself in the dreams and take his punishment; there is no longer a need to create a gorilla, or fox or wolf nor to avoid them in nightly terror. Thus the character of the dreams now and then is qualitatively different; quantitatively too, with regard to frequency: these latest ones are isolated, sporadic, and occasional, while previously the nightmares occurred with methodical regularity, a ghostly form which was visible as soon as the lights were turned off.

The description given of his present general mood and total behavior is also an effective guidepost to the dynamic changes that have taken place. His generally happy and carefree state, his schoolwork, his physical and gastrointestinal health, speak as much as the change in the nightmares. The liberation of energy formerly bound in the internal neurotic conflict is also reflected now in the eager search for new activity, his need and readiness for new objects and new outlets.

With regard to the seemingly monotonous repetition of one theme, the wish to get rid of the father, Freud made the following remarks about the repetition of the same wish in the case of little Hans: "We must not be surprised to find the same wishes constantly reappearing in the course of the analysis. The monotony only arises because the process of interpretation has been completed. For Hans they were not mere repetitions, but steps in a progressive development from timid hinting to fully conscious, undistorted perspicuity" (1907a).

The notes were now becoming further apart:

BEVERLY HILLS, CALIF.
December 25th, 1948

Dear BILL and LENORE,

About Paul: In your last note to us, on October 27th, he seemed quite well and relaxed. You mention two dreams, of father being killed. Yes, I agree with you that there is less concealing symbolism and that this is a sign of the progress he has made. There is a steady progressive development of his acceptance of this idea, from timid hinting at first to more and more real conscious acceptance and digestion of it. You need do no more than you are doing, i.e., steady reassurance without necessarily repeating the interpretations which you have already made.

I hope he is in his own room now for good. I think that even with such provocations as the pneumonia, you ought from now on to do something other than to bring him back to your room. . . .

He seems to be doing fine now as far as sleep, school, bowels, etc. are concerned. His search for new activities is a healthy search for new outlets and sublimations. I hear you already have acquired the piano—how is Paul taking to it?

What is the latest on him? I have a feeling that now this is all becoming a thing of the past. I'd appreciate a note about him, even if (and this is best), it's a negative one.

LEO

The next reply can be considered to mark a satisfactory conclusion to this episode in Paul's life:

NEW YORK CITY
February 8th, 1949

Dear LEO,

The newest thing in our house is our baby grand piano, which has proved to be the happiest investment I've ever made. It has added an additional warmth and joy to the household for all of us. Paul has taken to his lessons like the proverbial duck to water. His teacher, confirming Carl's opinion [a maternal uncle, a talented musician], finds him the most musical kid she's ever met. He absorbs the stuff with ease, practices daily and likes it (so far), and performs before any and all visitors at the drop of a hat. The piano, besides school and other outside interests, has provided Paul with stimulating, engrossing activities, resulting in a tremendous improvement in his total personality—sleep is fine, rarely troubled, bowels okay for as long as we can remember, doing excellently in school (outstanding student), and no discussion at all any more about his former difficulties.

With all our best,
As ever,
BILL, LENORE, PAUL, and ANNE

Only with a proper resolution of the oedipal conflict can instinctual energy really be freed to move on into new directions in the path of emotional development. The vigor with which Paul is now able and eager to follow his natural musical bent and other activities is related to and a sequel of this newly liberated libidinal energy.

Comparison with "Little Hans" Case

There are a number of very striking parallels and similarities in occurrences and background events between this case and Freud's famous Little Hans patient (1909), likenesses which I believe are of more than coincidental significance. First, both were phobics, though Hans's phobia existed all day, while Paul's was more circumscribed, being limited to the specific conditions which prevail during sleep. This is in essence only a quantitative difference. Paul was able to repress the pathogenic conflict during the dynamic conditions of waking life (though to be sure it broke through and showed itself in some ways; for example, the bowel symptoms, general mood, attitude toward school, etc.), but in bed at night conditions changed. The shift of balance in favor of instincts, which occurs then, made other defenses necessary. The dream then attempted to bind together the erupting forces. It failed and anxiety broke through. Phobia was the next step, a phobia directed against the very product of the dream work, the dream itself and its contents. Later the phobia was directed against the conditions under which the dream would appear, the state of going to sleep.

In both cases [i.e., that of Little Hans and Paul] the onset of symptoms occurred at exactly the same age, at four-and-three-quarter years. Both children selected animals as their objects of fear, one the horses of real life, the other the jungle animals of his dream life. The same role is played in both cases by summer vacations and their influences. We recall Hans's summer holidays at Gmunden and the part they played in the unfolding of his story; the intimate closeness there with the mother, while the father was an irregular visitor. The same situation held true in our case. Moreover, in both instances effects did not appear until the return to the city.

Both children can be described as being of superior intelligence, precocious, sensitive, and imaginative. A crucial occurrence to each was the birth of a little sister, to Hans at three-and-a-half, to Paul at four-and-a-half. Not only does this event accentuate and threaten the relationship with the parents, but at the same time, as Freud points out, it revives memory-traces of the child's earliest pleasure experiences, and also in itself causes an outburst of sexual pleasure and curiosity. Physical illness ensued during the course of each treatment, "influenza" in Hans and virus pneumonia in Paul, and each, by the same mechanisms, described above, produced exacerbation of the phobic symptoms.

In each treatment, a most powerful resistance was early removed, and a major impetus given to the ready flow of unconscious material, by prompt enlightenment and interpretation on the subject of jealous and hostile wishes against the father. In both cases, anxiety symptoms are described as existing in the mother, and the dominant role in treatment is spontaneously taken by the father. Both sets of parents are affectionate, permissive, and enlightened in their approach to the children. Strikingly, even the specific sublimation outlets seem to coincide. Freud remarks on Hans's increased interest in music and the development of his inherited musical gift. The very same is now taking place with Paul.

While some of these parallels must no doubt be fortuitous, the general conformity between the two cases must, I believe, lie in the fact that the neuroses of childhood, in contrast to those of adults, are rooted more in universal experiences than in specific individual determinants. This must be more and more true the further back we go, so that the closer we approach the most primitive, original, and least differentiated state, the more does the anxiety-producing stimulus become universal; as ultimately, for example, the birth trauma. That these two cases show such strongly similar trends and events stems from identities in the psychodynamic backgrounds and in the family constellations and attitudes. This would tend to bear out the words with which Freud concludes the Hans case, claiming for it the significance "of being a type and a model," and supposing that "the multiplicity of the phenomena of repression exhibited by neuroses . . . do not prevent their being derived from a very limited number of processes concerned with identical ideational complexes."

Some Remarks on Transference and the Upbringing and Education of Children

I would like to make some remarks about the situation as it was in this case, with the father himself being the one to directly conduct the therapeutic situation rather than, as is usually the case, the intervening analyst. The transference situation, even in the usual setting of a child analysis, is different from that in adult analysis, in that at best the analyst can only in part become the object upon whom the instinctual emotional energies center. This stems from the fact that the original determining figures (i.e., the parents) are still very actively in the picture and the original formative and crucial object relationships are still fluid and not yet solidified. Although this prevents the formation of a typical transference neurosis in child analysis, nevertheless, it is the introduction of a new and different object into the picture—namely, the analyst—which modifies, reverses and rechannelizes the distortions and fixations and displacements which have occurred and are still taking place in the course of instinctual development. At the end of this analytic relationship, the problem always has to be faced of then handing back the now modified and altered child to the very environment in which the traumata responsible for the illness originally took place. It is hoped, of course, and it is one of the necessary goals of treatment, that in the meantime certain changes have also taken place in the central figures of this environment—changes which will thereafter move them in the same current as the analytic process has guided the patient. This often remains as one of the main vexations and drawbacks impeding the end result of child analysis.

In the case here reported, however, as with Little Hans and in several other reported instances, the situation is different in that it is the parent himself who confronts the neurotic process in the child and endeavors to encourage changes. The reversal of the pathologic process, and the redirecting of instinctual energy does not take place via the intervention of a new object, with a new type of relationship which is then transferred back to the parents, but rather by a direct alteration in the attitudes and responses of the very persons who provoked the original repression and displacements. The child is subjected to a new and therapeutic experience in living within the familiar arena of his own life, in situ so to speak, in vivo, rather than to a comparatively artificial and laboratorylike analytic relationship. This is, to be sure, more difficult to achieve in a case in which a neurotic symptom has become fully formed, than it is in the milder and more transient emotional problems of childhood, where the direct enlightenment of the parents is frequently sufficient to produce the desired result. This is no doubt akin to what ordinarily and commonly must take place in the normal, transient fears, anxieties, and phobias of childhood, as these spontaneously dissipate and resolve themselves in response to the proper word or attitude on the part of the loving and understanding parent. Barrett (1937, 1939) recorded two such cases, a little boy and a little girl, in whom transient anxieties and the course of their resolution could be clearly traced in their relation to parental reassurance and explanations. Grotjahn (1938) described parental observations on the dreams of a two-year four-month-old baby and their relation to the transient emotions and anxieties of the previous day (see chapter 42). A case reported by Kubie (1937) shows how a traffic phobia in a six-year-old boy cleared up in response to conversations between the father and son.

When the parents acquire new insight and initiate therapeutic alterations and these then radiate secondarily toward the child, the next problematic step is avoided—that of having the child return for continuing educative influences to a still uncertain environment. Moreover, the way is now open for healthier identification and for a more reasonable superego formation. The still incompletely developed superego, which in its development has begun to show a tendency to excessive demands, is in this case favorably influenced from within. It is not altered by new ingredients added from without, but rather by changing and improving the very ingredients which go to make it up during the process of its being built. When it can be done, this particular way, it seems to me, should have advantages for the child. To insure proper upbringing in statu nascendi is preferable to letting the structure go up and then having to recondition it afterwards by analysis.

Some Further Comments

There are a number of thoughts and questions arising from this case which are worthy of some further remarks and clarification. Some of these were raised at an analytic seminar at which this case was presented, and might serve as a focus for this part of the discussion. One of these issues, for example, is the fact that a number of obviously important topics never came up for discussion and were therefore never interpreted in the interchange between father and son. What about the role of masturbation, for example, which without doubt must have played a large part in bringing on the nocturnal anxiety? This was conspicuously absent in the material; neither was there any specific discussion of anal and other conflicts. Of course, much could be pointed to which did not come up. Paul has not been analyzed. The purpose of the therapy was the application of as much analytic thinking as possible under the limitations imposed, for the understanding and the alleviation of the symptoms. This was achieved, it seems to me, not by an uncovering and making conscious and acceptable all the ramifications of the specific pathogenic conflicts, but rather by the therapeutic emotional experience which Paul underwent in his relationship with his parents. This experience favorably altered the dynamic equilibrium between his instinctual forces on the one hand and on the other the forces of the external world and his nascent and young superego. The prohibiting strength and power of the latter was weakened, first by a new evaluation of and actual change in the nature of the externally threatening castrating figures (parents), and then automatically by a similar change in their internalized representatives within the superego. Instinctual impulses, such as masturbation, with its accompanying oedipal fantasies, could then be more easily and adequately handled.

There are also objections from the opposite direction. Certain people still express reactions of doubt and ambivalence to the basic idea of an approach such as taken in this case, reactions still much the same as those which greeted the Little Hans case and which were countered by Freud forty years ago. Thus since they probably will be duplicated by some readers, we will mention a few minority comments which ran as follows: "All children," it was said, "have nightmares at one time or other; most often these go away by themselves and need no treatment. We should think carefully before interfering with them." Or even more strongly, "Intervention of this sort only serves to stir up and keep active childhood complexes which should be allowed to become dormant and to be resolved by the natural course of growth and development." In reply, it would be well to refer back to the original two letters, in order to recall the pitiful suffering to which Paul was subjected, its intensity, duration, and specific character. Furthermore, all people know what fear is. Yet fears can become phobias of such magnitude as to make intervention not only desirable, but the only humane thing to do. Moreover, symptoms can disappear in different ways, for different reasons, and with different results. A symptom can be frightened or browbeaten away, by either direct or subtle means; but always at high cost to the total character, which pays the price thereafter of having to devote a good portion of its available energy to the forces of repression, with resultant crippling and limitation of the total personality. Or a nucleus is created which later in life can then be reactivated by a trivial stimulus with the formation of full-blown symptoms.

The situation, however, is quite different when, as in this case, the symptom is removed not by increased repression, but rather by undoing the process of repression and replacing it with (1) in part renunciation of instinctual wishes (as the oedipal wish); (2) partial gratification of instincts (as masturbation impulses); and (3) in part discharge through sublimated activity. Far from stirring up and activating pathological complexes and preventing their proper resolution, this process actually tends to prevent and remedy the visible beginnings of maldevelopments in the line of emotional growth. It goes without saying that when the normal course of growth and development is leading to happy results, all this is superfluous.

Finally, and again using as a guide the discussion which this case provoked, it would be well to reaffirm the obvious dangers involved and the need for caution with regard to the method, long-distance correspondence, which of necessity had to be used in this particular clinical instance. It is indeed the rare situation in which circumstances would all conspire, as in this case, to make this even feasible; utter confidence in the parents and thorough familiarity with the local conditions were indispensable prerequisites. In the more usual situations which we meet in our everyday practices, it would be unthinkable to consider carrying on through this thin and insecure line of contact.

August 1950: Paul has remained symptom-free.

Chapter 44

THE DREAM SCREEN IN AN ADOLESCENT

AARON H. ESMAN

The parents of Tommy, a thirteen-and-a-half-year-old Jewish boy who suffered from chronic depression, obesity, recurrent impulsive aggressive outbursts against his parents, and poor school and social adjustments, sought treatment for him after his older sister was returned to a state hospital because of recurrence of severe psychotic symptoms. The boy's mother was a narcissistic, infantile, enormously obese woman who devoted most of her time to playing cards. She saw Tommy alternately as a source of gratification for her unfulfilled needs and as a source of profound narcissistic disappointment. The father was a depressed, bitter man, made almost inarticulate by his barely controlled rage which erupted primarily in repeated verbal threats to kill the boy.

About three months after he began psychotherapy, Tommy reported that he had gone with his father to a baseball game the previous Sunday. They had had little to say to one another, their principal communication consisting of Tommy's request for ice cream and his father's peremptory refusal to buy it for him. That night the child had the following dream.

> I was sitting in a movie theater, or someplace. There was a sort of screen and baseballs were coming out of it toward me. There was a man there who was catching the balls and deflecting them to everyone else, so I couldn't get any.

This paper was first published in the *Psychoanalytic Quarterly* (1962), 31:250.

In a series of papers (1946b, 1948, 1953b) Lewin has presented and discussed the concept of the dream screen; others, including Rycroft (1951), Heilbrunn (1953), Kepecs (1952), and Garma (1955), have confirmed and elaborated Lewin's thesis. The dream screen is conceived of as representing the most primitive infantile precept, the maternal breast—face on which the manifest imagery is projected and at times specifically presented as the object of the dream wish.

The dream reported here appears to exemplify the dream screen concept in all respects. The day residue is an experience of oral deprivation in a profoundly orally fixated boy, in whom depression and overeating represent desperate attempts at restitution for gross early deprivations. The frustrating person in the dream is a direct representation of the reality figure. Aside from its obvious transference implications, the latent content of the dream appears to be: "My father repeatedly deprives me of the breast and milk that I so desperately want. Only by directly representing the breast and its longed-for solace can I remain asleep." Thus, the dream is seen to have oedipal and preoedipal content; it serves the oral regression that is the principal defensive measure at this boy's disposal against the intense rage evoked by the experience of deprivation.

The direct representation of the breast in the form of the dream screen is found in an orally fixated boy with an affective disorder that threatens to develop into a severe and chronic, perhaps, psychotic, illness. This case of a "screen" dream in an early adolescent thus provides further confirmation of Lewin's pioneer observation.

Chapter 45

THE ROLE OF THE DREAM IN THE ANALYSIS OF A LATENCY CHILD

MARJORIE HARLEY

Although not much has been written about the role of dreams in child analysis, it would seem that somewhat opposing views have been noted. There are those who have reported that dreams play an inconsequential role in their treatment of children, and that only incidentally are they told directly to the therapist. Others have been impressed by the frequency and ease with which their child patients are able to communicate their dreams, and even to participate in dream interpretation, attributing this state of affairs to the child's relative closeness to his unconscious and hence to his dream life. Among the latency children who have come my way, some have told their dreams merely occasionally and in general, although not invariably, have tended to veer away from the possibility that any meaning other than what is apparent in the manifest content could have validity; a lesser number have related their dreams rather abundantly, and often have shown zeal and aptitude in unearthing the hidden dream thoughts. Questions concerning these differing attitudes which latency children show toward their dreams are interesting to ask but, for me at least, not easy to answer.

As Bornstein (1951) has reminded us, latency is a time when the child's ego is still actively struggling to establish secondary-process supremacy. Bornstein also has noted how in the latter part of latency, although ego defenses are now more

This paper was first published in the *Journal of the American Psychoanalytic Association* (1962), 10:271–288.

633

consolidated, the child's but recently acquired equilibrium is still, to some extent, precarious. To say this in another way, latency is the time for renunciation of direct instinctual gratification and for emphasis on tangible manifestations of objective reality as distinct from inner fantasy life—on what is "true" as against what is "make-believe"—so that any reminder to the child of his repudiated impulses, or anything which for him contradicts his closely defined principles of logic, may amount to a danger. It may be, therefore, that for some latency children in analysis, dreams are at times too tinged with primary process so that they are forgotten or withheld; or, when they are brought to our hour, any implication that they may contain a meaning other than the manifest one not only threatens an unwelcome disclosure of hidden impulses, but is taken as a violation of the reality constructs which the child must maintain.

In line with this thought and with my own observations, those children whose dream productions tend to be sparse, and who show less inclination to explore the latent dream meaning, are those children whose egos, whether at one time by more appropriate means, or at another by the erection of more inhibitory and constrictive defenses, have been able, for the most part, to protect themselves against too immediate experience with their instinctual strivings. In general, I have found that the relatively infrequent dreams that the greater number of my latency patients have brought to analysis have served purposes other than direct interpretation: either the child's explanation of the occasion for the dream, or the dream's manifest content, have offered a springboard to discussion of everyday events and feelings; or, usually unknown to the child, the dream has helped to clarify or to confirm preceding and subsequent material; or the latter have cast light on the implication of the latent dream thoughts, often too unconscious to permit interpretation; or the dream has stimulated new and valuable play productions or daydreams.

On the other hand, in my experience, those children who have made the most use of dream interpretation have been those under considerable inner pressure, with a corresponding weakness or weakening of the defensive barriers against their excessive excitations. It is for such children that the reported dream has seemed to me not only frequently to serve as a "safety valve" (Freud, 1900; A. Freud, 1926–1927a) for the discharge of instinctual strivings, but also to provide a means of achieving some distance from which they may view their unconscious, as well as some focus for their often intense and diffuse anxiety. Paradoxically, then, while in some instances the dream seemed to bring the child too close to the primary process, in other extremes it seemed to represent a means of obtaining a welcome perspective. It is perhaps superfluous to add that for the latter to occur the child must have sufficient ego control and flexibility to resist the unconscious pulls of the dream, and, at least in some measure, to stand apart from it.

I

In this paper I shall present a few fragments from the first two years of the analysis of an eight-year-old girl, who, at the outset, was burdened by repeated states of ill-contained excitation. When she first came to me, this child was still subordinated to the internal whirl of her infantile sexual and aggressive strivings, and the (psychic) maturational factors of latency had barely come into play. I shall try to point up the relationship between her changing ego–id balances and the transition of her nuclear masturbation theme from acting out, to dream, to verbalized and structured derivative fantasy, to reality-directed imaginative productions. Finally, I shall try to show how, under the impact of the rising tensions of prepuberty, her ego wavered and then reversed its course back to the dream.

This little girl was brought to analysis mainly because of her uncontrolled, provocative behavior and her almost constant high pitch of actual or suspended excitement. She would wear only dungarees, never skirts, and took pride in what she considered her great daring and courage. With her father, however, whom she obviously feared, she was more restrained, provoking him in more subtle ways. Behind this spirited and impish exterior was a lonely child who had been subjected to a series of severe traumata in the preoedipal and oedipal periods, among which were a disturbed infant–mother relationship dating back to the first weeks of life, early states of excessive bodily tension augmented by somatic disorders, and an acutely traumatic tonsillectomy at the height of the phallic phase. In addition, she was still exposed to repeated and excessive stimulation in the home. The parents' relationship was characterized by mutual provocation and rather violent altercations. The father, especially, was subject to severe temper outburst, often followed by expressions of exaggerated contrition, tendencies which he also played out with the child. Until she was well past three, he had openly exposed himself nude before her, frequently taking her into the bathroom with him, and since then had followed this pattern of seduction in more concealed forms. In brief, this child had hardly attained any of the usual latency gains, for apparently she had had little respite from an incessant barrage of heightened inner urgencies, with scant energy free for transformation into ego growth and expansion. Although undoubtedly bright, she showed no interest in learning, she was still unable to read, and her chief preoccupation seemed to be in shocking those around her with her highly sexualized talk.

For some time the child's tantrumlike acting out within the transference situation was so extreme that the minimum margin necessary for analytic work could be achieved after months of ego interpretation, aimed at bringing to the fore the unwelcome affects associated with her unacceptable behavior, and by mobilizing her wish to gain control of her impulses; and, in general, I did not respond either to her attempts to provoke my reactions to her sexual talk or to her exhibitionistic allusions to her masturbation. It became increasingly apparent that the persistent theme in her acting out, although shot through with pregenital destructive elements, especially those of oral–visual incorporation, had drawn its patterning and particular dynamic force from her severe castration complex. Combined in this theme were her castrating impulses, and her identification with the aggressor–father in her enactment of violent primal-scene fantasies, also seeking through this identification to ward off her masochistic strivings; these, nevertheless, attained gratification through the rejections and punishments she provoked.

When she could finally integrate my explanation of the defensive aspects of her outrageous behavior as her wish to possess those qualities which she mistakenly believed to be indicative of masculine courage and strength, her ego was relieved of strain to the extent that she could now begin to substitute some degree of internalization for externalization of her conflicts. It was at this juncture that, very earnestly, she presented me with her first dream, explaining that her mother had told her I would help her understand it: "In the dream I spilled water in your ash tray and you were very angry; and you threw me out, and I woke up crying angry tears."

She was particularly eager to track down the separate dream elements when I exploited her frequently expressed pride in her ability to out-trick others, by my explanation that dreams tried to play all kinds of tricks on the dreamer in order to conceal their true meanings, and that she, in effect, would have to out-trick the dream. *Spilling water* immediately evoked associations to peeping at the boys while they urinated in the school bathroom, and her newly acquired restraint faltered as, with provocating giggling, she told me it was not fair that she could not see her father's penis, which surely would be more exciting than those stupid, tiny penises of the little boys. When I was not too responsive to her seductive overtures, she resumed her more serious and reflective attitude, and volunteered that my *ash tray* reminded her of many fires she had built in it which I had helped her to control; but it seemed to her that in the dream she had been unable to control even the water. She then recalled how she had, the previous year, defiantly stood and urinated on the carpet in her pediatrician's office. She added she now knew she had wanted to show him she was as brave and powerful as he and not afraid to do anything. "That's neat," she suddenly explained, "now I understand the dream. It means I'm still tempted to do those exciting naughty things with you and show I'm as brave as a boy and not afraid, and even make you throw me out; but the dream proves I don't really want to any more because I cried when I had done it. And I must have felt awful because I *never* cry." I heartily concurred with her interpretation, thankful that, at this stage, she had omitted any further references to the phallic implications of the water or the tears. She had understood even more than I knew at the time for she gravely told her father that evening that she was glad she had come to me to be "psychiatrized." There was a fight which she wanted to win from him and I was going to help her understand this so that she would not need to fight any more. When her father asked how she would feel if she won the fight, she says she would feel "good" because then she would be a big, strong man like him; but, on the other hand, she would feel "not so good," because then he would not be her father any more!

II

From this point on the child continued for some time to release her pressure through her frequent use of dream material. These dreams were at first rather nakedly primitive, particularly the second dream which she brought, indicating her willingness to enter into a discussion of its separate elements:

> Mary [her schoolmate] was trying to see if she could ride a wild horse with a squirrel on its back; and the horse reared and ran away but she could ride it; and then she had to ride the horse with a pigeon on its back; and the pigeon pecked at the horse and the horse ran away again; and when it came back Mary was still on it—but her head was off. And then they hung the head in the kitchen.

Horses reminded her of her father; and, following her tendency to dichotomize the creatures of the world into male and female, *squirrels* were boys and *pigeons* were girls because a pigeon was a mother. Therefore, she said, it was safer to ride a horse if you were a boy. She guessed the pigeon was Mom fighting with Dad: though, of course, Mom would *never* bite; but the pigeon also meant that since she, too, was a girl, it would be dangerous for her, also, to fight with Dad. This, she added, would cause disaster, as shown by Mary's loss of her head. Mary, who several times thereafter appeared in her dreams, she later came to associate both with the destructive aspects of herself and with her father, the link between the two being the fact that Mary had bangs, and her father's hair sometimes fell over his forehead like bangs, particularly when he was angry. Thus condensed in Mary was not only her own castration but her father's as well. The *kitchen*, she exclaimed, brought a horrible thought to her mind—that of eating the head. And now she was reminded of two horror stories, one of which reflected a projection of her visual aggressive fantasies. A little boy had shot a rabbit for his supper, and then a man with terrifying eyes stared at him, and the rabbit disappeared into a hole, and the little boy was left with only the hole. "Losing one's head" was also being swept away by one's excitement, and it was this association only that I pursued, using it to show her the pleasure she derived from her terrifying, exciting thoughts, as well as her fearsomely uncomfortable feelings in being so swept away. The exhilaration she enjoyed from her erotization of anxiety could be further demonstrated during the ensuing parchesi game, when toward the end the race was close, and with obvious pleasure she would dramatically exclaim: "I'm so scared—it's so exciting!"

Another dream which reflected the sadomasochistic aspects of the primal scene with its oral–aggressive components, and which appeared a few weeks later was:

> I was at a merry-go-round and grandfather was with us. (Dad wasn't there but I think grandfather was Dad.) And there was a big crowd, and it was time to go, and I started ahead, and all of a sudden there was a big crash, and everyone fell down, and turned around and grandfather's arm was off; and it was awful, and we had to go without him.

The *merry-go-round* made her think of snatching off rings, while *time to go* was bedtime and nighttime and prayertime; and she added, fighting time. *Crowds* were also fighting because people pushed each other in a crowd, while a *big crash* was like a dog fight, and also reminded her of a news item which she had heard on the radio when a woman driver had become "too wild" and had run over a man. *Falling down* led to a memory of a little girl in her kindergarten who had bitten the other children when she was angry and had fallen off her bike and cut her head. My patient supposed this had been a punishment for hurting others. The *amputated arm* resulted in another of her emerging references to a punitive superego figure; she remembered, a long time ago, having seen a little girl in the park without an arm. She had thought then that the little girl had done something bad, so that a policeman had cut off her arm. She knew now that would not happen, but she admitted she was still uneasy when she saw policemen; although she also knew that they were really there to keep people from doing bad things, that was why they punished them. *We had to go without him* was a reversal of the true state of affairs. The dream had occurred on the last night of a short trip with her mother, and the father was at home awaiting their arrival the next day. This trip had been one of those rare occasions when the child could be alone with her mother; and her wish to continue to have the mother to herself was the aspect of this dream chosen for interpretation in order to help her acknowledge her positive longings for her mother's love and protection, which she constantly attempted to ward off.

In general, however, the early dreams with this repetitive primal scene–castration theme were used not only to enable the child to gain increasing insight into her sadomasochistic conception of her parents' love life, her desire to share in this, and the enjoyable excitement she somehow derived from such thoughts, but also to point out the contradiction between the terrorizing, fighting father of her dreams, and her insistent assertions that her father was never angry with *her*. As she came to relinquish her denials she was increasingly able to express her fear of her father, as well as to report and to begin to examine the various occasions on which she provoked him.

Now, for a time dreams entered my patient's analysis far less frequently as she was able to verbalize the theme of her castration complex in manifold accounts of her relatively well-structured night stories (i.e., masturbation fantasies). The essence of these night stories was that with her "little pin" (her clitoris), and the aid of her inseparable imaginary companion, her *seeing-eye* dog, she would fight off and conquer large groups of big boys and men who brandished their huge knives. When she had captured these men and boys she sent them off to the hospital for an operation—a revenge fantasy to her tonsillectomy in the phallic phase, which she recalled with dire assertions that she had felt the doctor was going to do something terrible to her, so terrible she could not imagine what.

My comments that such exciting night stories must also tempt her to exciting things with herself evoked a dream which ultimately led to her confession of masturbation:

> A maid was stacking dishes into a tall stack with her feet and I was knocking them down; and the maid seemed to be me, too; and this man was saying I hurt so-and-so; and then it couldn't have been me any more because I wouldn't want to hurt anyone; and I'm sure that's what woke me up.

Her only association to the maid *stacking the dishes,* which she *knocked down,* was that she was trying to make the maid angry by showing her she should do something better than she, although later material revealed a connection with the object-directed and self-directed destructive tendencies in her masturbation fantasies, as well as her envy of the penis as a superior locus for masturbation. Again, there was a superego reference via *this man* who was saying *she had hurt someone* and who reminded her of a minister and a policeman "who don't want you to do anything wrong," and to her increasing superego internalization, as shown by her earnest declarations that *she "wouldn't want to hurt anyone."* And when, a short time later, she explained the maid's activity with her feet in the dream by reluctantly admitting her masturbation, emphasizing that she had done it long ago and now never, well, hardly ever, and that she would not dream of touching herself with her hand—that was why she pressed her foot against her tinkle-spot—I felt as though her structural development was beginning to resemble that of a latency child.

With some working of her aggressive fantasies and of her concomitant fears of her father, there began to emerge in the analysis signs of positive oedipal material, in which the father appeared more as a tender love object than as a dangerous, contestual figure, although this material was now also used to screen her persisting sadomasochistic fantasies, and the continuing pulls toward identification with her father. Oedipal rivalry for her mother was now flagrantly revealed, and traces of her wishes for an oedipal baby became discernible. One of the few dreams produced in this period showed the attempted transition of the penis wish to the baby wish. In this dream she had found herself in possession of a little boy who was a kind of half-dog, and who liked to be taken care of and fed. He was "brownish, like sun-burned, or like a colored baby, and very tiny, tinier than a real baby." This little dream-baby obviously still bore the earmarks of feces and penis; yet, as she told me the dream, she clasped her hands and said it was the most wonderful dream, and that finding that little boy was like finding something her very own that was living, that she could care for. It was as good as having a dog, and also it was like "having somebody love me and Dad better than he loved Mom."

My patient was now nine. A holiday trip with her eleven-year-old girl cousin, on which the two girls, with a pair of eleven-year-old boys, engaged in dramatic play involving *Liebestod* themes, provoked the repressed sadomasochistic fantasies, and the child returned to her analysis once more in a state of intense anxiety. Her response to my thinking the reappearance of her excitement with the events of this trip was contained in a dream which she could barely remember but which she knew had something to do with a lake. The lake made her think of a swan, which in turn, led to a primal-scene memory (placed at the age of three) of looking at a little glass swan with a key around its neck while her parents were lying in bed, very still—so still that they could not have been doing anything she was not supposed to see. And this dream was followed next day by another:

> I was in the waiting room, waiting for my appointment, and that big teenage boy was before me, and I tried to eavesdrop and you opened the door and roared at me; and your fingernails got longer and longer, and I tried to run away and woke up.

I shall omit her associations save to say that this dream, in a strange way, reminded her of a fairy story that she had "half made up and half taken from a story" that she had once read, the essence of which I gathered was a dream within a dream, in which a child dreamed he was bored, and to escape from his boredom, he was able, within this dream, to dream that he could enter into a beautiful garden and participate in other people's dreams. And one night, when he entered the garden, there was someone there who got bigger and bigger and then vanished into thin air. She hesitated, and then added apprehensively that sometimes she almost remembers having gone into a room and her father coming toward her with his penis getting bigger and bigger. When I remarked it was as if she had felt a big, angry penis was coming at her, she acquiesced and shuddered; sometimes she thought it was like a dream which yet was not a dream, and as though Dad's penis also had disappeared into thin air. Before this session, she had made various references to having seen her father's penis when she was a little girl, but always had insisted it must have been very small, since her parents had married young and her father could not have been more than twelve years old at the time!

III

With this outright acknowledgment of her fear of the "angry penis," the child could express her frightening fantasies of penetration and her own angry envy of this powerful organ; and with the partial working through of her destructive strivings one could observe liberation of energy for deflection into ego-directed activities which could achieve a greater distance from their instinctual sources. For several months my little patient ceased to bring dreams to her analysis, and instead presented me with quite beautiful paintings, at first of dogs and fish almost exclusively, but which gradually evolved into portrayals of human figures and elaborate compositions of family life. Her daydreams were well-defended against any crude intrusion of unconscious contents. Masochistic fantasies were chiefly revealed through her well-written stories in which the leading character, as a result of their deep loyalty to their love objects, usually came to an untimely death. She took a great interest in learning and achievement in her schoolwork, and showed herself to be a quite able child. The hours were now largely filled with discussing her fantasies of her parents' divorce; her tendencies to play one parent against the other; her various triangular intrigues with her friends, and their mutual jealousies. Only very gingerly and in small doses could she openly express her preoedipal longings for love and tenderness from her mother, and her positive oedipal attachment for her father. She was still too threatened by the overwhelming intensity of these feelings and by the dangers of masochistic surrender, and the analysis of her strong sadomasochistic tendencies was by no means complete.

A few months after her tenth birthday, her masturbation temptations, which she had for some time resisted, gained the upper hand; and she began to speak apprehensively of the orgasticlike sensations she experienced. Her fear of the "angry penis," and her aggressive wishes to possess it, again gained the ascendancy. She now tried to defend herself against her need for the sadistic acquisition of the penis, against her masochistic strivings, and against the strong defensive pull toward the protective aspects of a preoedipal bond with her mother, by spinning fantasies of herself as a shy, feminine girl, interested in various older boys in school. She described gentle scenes in which the boys told her how unlike a tomboy she really was, picturing these relationships as the epitome of loving kindness. Yet even in those mild and innocuous daydreams, one could detect a faint echo of her desire to partake of the strength and power of the phallus. Her facade began to crumble as she admitted that in these pleasant ruminations in the ideal girl–boy friendship she inevitably envisaged the boy without a penis; and at this point she confessed she had developed a bus phobia and had been walking to and from her appointments.

In a supreme effort to offset her threatening masturbation fantasies she was able to erect a beautiful, defensive superstructure, containing rich fantasies in the service of ego and superego, which I shall sketch but briefly. For many hours she opened each appointment by sprinkling a patch of stardust on my carpet, over which she led me to the sky, which was the domain of the great King Sun. Of all the children in the world, she alone had been chosen by the king to visit his kingdom and to enter into special communion with him, since she was not too realistic, as were her friends, and more trustworthy than they when it came to keeping secrets. The King Sun was married to the Queen of the East, but they did not spend too much time together, since the Queen was occupied with household affairs of the kingdom, while the King Sun's chief interest was in creating beautiful things. He made, for my patient, special magic pencils and pastels which he prepared from colors he took from the rainbow's children; so when she wrote stories the pencil wrote them for her, and when she made pictures the pastels were of such glorious colors that they turned out the loveliest pictures ever seen. As she elaborated on her fantasy, she referred increasingly to the phallic powers she derived from the Sun; by *gazing* upon him and by his dropping little pieces of his fire on her, she absorbed some of his power and magic. She explained that the Queen did not mind, since he gave her such small pieces, and the Queen still had a big piece left for herself. Her oral strivings forced their way into the fantasy as she spoke of the magic foods the Sun made for her from bits of fire. Then, one day, she decided to transform her sky fantasy into a fairy tale for children which she would illustrate. Before long, however, rifts appeared in this defensive superstructure from which the story was derived; and through slips of the tongue she spoke of *grabbing* off the bits of fire, and, again, of *biting* off bits.

The threatened child now abandoned her story writing, and in her endeavor to escape from the dangers of her aggressive impulses against this King–father, she led me to the other side of the sky, which was night and the domain of the Moon. Most bad thoughts, like the bad dreams of children, existed in the Moon's kingdom. But the Moon was powerful and kind, and tried to prevent these bad thoughts from going down to earth to haunt children, and so captured them and put them in jail. The children needed the protection of the Moon because, although their consciences said: "You'll be sorry if you think bad things," they were not always strong enough to resist the temptation; and then they were punished with bad dreams.

Recently, she added sorrowfully, the Moon had been hit by a satellite, and since then had not been very well and was unable to protect the children on earth; so the children were having bad dreams lately. When I inquired into the status of her bad dreams she answered simply and helplessly: "I haven't had one yet but any night I'm afraid it will strike"; and she told me how she lay in bed each night trying to think the most pleasant thoughts possible in order to ward off the dreaded blow.

That very night the blow fell. The first part of this dream involved the menace of the same Mary who had lost her head in the earlier dream, and who was now relentlessly pursuing the bus on which my terrified patient was riding; while, in the second part, her longing to be passively dependent on her mother and to receive comfort from her was reversed in a scene in which she soothed and reassured her mother. This dream, by way of insight into her wish to be kidnapped by the bus-driver–father, led to the analysis of her bus phobia.

IV

My patient has tried to deal with the heightened instinctual tensions which have announced the prepubertal phase of the analysis by an intense preoccupation with her schoolwork and somewhat frenzied attempts at writing verse. These, however, in large measure have proved ineffectual, because of the intrusions of her destructive tendencies which have imposed too crude and too openly sadistic content upon her productions; hence they have served mainly to intensify her anxiety. And, once again in her analysis, her ego is seeking, through the dream, a means of releasing her excessive urgencies, the bus dream being but the first of a renewed series. While during latency her little verbal offerings of fact and fancy were more like single staccato notes, which nevertheless could be woven onto a latent dream thought, now her dream associations are characterized by a greater richness in range and dimension, and are accompanied by a larger abundance of preconscious material. In closing, I shall reproduce only an abbreviated version of her second prepubertal dream, in which Mary once more made her appearance, and shall not include all her associations which occupied several hours; for she would continually return to this dream, feeling, as she put it, that "it seemed to have just everything in it." It did contain a great deal, but its nuclear castration theme was essentially unchanged from that of her first dream about Mary and her disastrous encounter with the horse.

> I was walking in a bad neighborhood with Mary, like the neighborhood where her riding academy is, and there were drunks all around. We were going by a garage opening and a drunk stood out in front. He leaped toward me and jumped at me and I backed up and got away. Mary's mother was coming up the street—I ran up to her. Then we circled the block because Mary's mother had left something necessary at the garage. The man leaped at me again—he held me by the skirt and I was so terrified I couldn't utter a word. But I got away again and rushed in to Mary and her Mother who told me this drunk was famous all over the world. There was a little, tiny room—painted reddish brown—it was dark, but not completely, because a friendly white candle was burning. Mary's mother had left her thing in this room. She locked Mary and me in there and told us we would be safe, and we lay down close together, very still. Then lots of animals came around and I realized I was wearing a precious jewel necklace I had stolen; and the drunk grabbed me and no one helped me and then the necklace just jumped off me as if it were alive, and jumped on the man, and he was okay and not drunk or dangerous any more.

The day preceding this dream, her father had startled her by entering her room while she was wiping some salve from her hands. Overcome by sudden anxiety related to her masturbation guilt, she *could not utter a word* in response to his query as to what she was doing. She had started to leave the room, but he had *held her by the skirt*. The *garage*, also part of the day residue, recalled an old cripple she had seen at the gas station, and the fact that cripples and very old men frightened and repelled her, symbolizing vengeful castrated figures and her own maimed state; old people also meant death. The uncontrolled drunk *stood out in front* was the angry penis which had come toward her in the dream that yet was not a dream. His being *famous all over the world* she associated with her father's recent completion of a novel, which promised success, and her own great ambition to be famous all over the world, complicated by her recurring guilt over any even minor success, a reaction in part resulting from forbidden phallic attributes which she equated with accomplishment.

Circling the block led to associations of dizziness and the strong sensations she experienced in masturbating. The *reddish-brown* walls of the little room evoked images of rectum and vagina, her confusion between the two, and her fantasy of anal castration as a result of her future husband's error in mistaking her rectum for her vagina, and thus causing it injury and bleeding—a fantasy deriving some of its raw material from her early and rigid toilet training, but finding form and substance in her fusion of the castration implications of her tonsillectomy with the suppository which had preceded it, and which reinforced her oral–anal–vaginal equation. *The reddish-brown* also recalled the menstrual blood on the mother's sheets, which she had previously remembered having first seen when she was three; while the *necessary thing* which Mary's mother had to retrieve was the bloody Kotex which Mary, who had recently begun to menstruate, had shown her, and which had set in motion a whirl of anxieties in regard to menstruation.

The *white candle* and the *stolen necklace* accompanied by *all the animals,* and the necklace which returned itself to the man, thus nullifying his dangerous features, brought to mind her favorite fairy tale, *The White Snake.* In this story a king "who knew everything" had gained his magical powers from his daily consumption of a white snake. His servant stole a piece of snake and scarcely had tasted it when he could hear and understand the language of birds and animals who now kept him, too, informed of everything. This tale reflected not only her obvious wish to incorporate the magical phallus, but her desire to understand the mysteries of birth and death, and of her own body. The *little room* with its candle light where she and Mary *lay so still* she likened to those nights which are sometimes so quiet that one can hear the stillness, like the stillness of her parents when she had looked at the little glass swan. Now, out of this screen memory emerged another screen memory of blue, calm water, and a tall, majestic tree, and a green house where she had lived when she was two. She felt there had been something lovely about the house, and the tree and the water, but that it also concealed some terrible disaster, and since then this green house has persistently woven its way in and out of her dreams and associations, in her endeavor to recapture what she is certain is an important lost memory.

My patient offered her own version of this prepubertal dream wish. When she had spoken of the dream scene in which Mary's mother had assured her the *little room* with its *reddish-brown* walls was *safe,* she was reminded that Mary's mother had hair the same color as mine. Shyly, she suggested that there had been something warm and friendly about the little room, and that meant she wished I would help her make her vagina a safe, friendly place because when she grew up she would need it to love a man and to have a baby. This seemed to me an apt formulation of a major goal in our analytic work to come.

Summary

In this paper I have tried to illustrate, from the analysis of a latency girl who was heavily burdened by the pressures of her inner urgencies, how the dream not only provided a "safety valve" for the discharge of her excessive excitations, but also a means through which to substitute reflective thought for impulsive action. When, especially in the early stages of treatment, her ego could maintain a sufficient margin of distance from her instinctual strivings to enable her to stand apart from herself, as it were, and through the dream medium to glimpse some understanding of what heretofore had been bewildering forces beyond her control, her relief was enormous. I have selected such fragments from her analysis as dealt with her acute castration complex, and have tried to show how, as her ego gained increasing relief from her instinctual urgencies, the dream material gradually faded from the analysis, to reappear with her renewed tensions at prepuberty.

This patient was one among those latency children whose dream material has played a dominant role in the analytic process, and who comprise the minority of those whom I have treated. All of these children experienced considerable pressure from their instinctual strivings, although not always to the same degree as did this little girl, and sometimes only in certain stages of their analyses, as impulses would force their way to the surface, either as a result of stimulation from analytic interpretation, or from experiences encountered outside the analysis. In general, however, it has seemed to me that their use of dream material has tended to coincide with these periods of increased pressure. I would add that within this context of ego–id intimacy, there obviously must be sufficient balance of energies for the ego to experience the processes of the id and yet to maintain that margin of distance which allows for secondary-process functions of observation and reflection; otherwise the result will be either withdrawal and contraction, or too massive and immediate discharge through action.

Perhaps one explanation for the opposing views expressed in regard to the frequency with which children use dream interpretation in their analytic work lies in the differences in technical approaches. While ruminating over this question, I have wondered, for example, whether Anna Freud's statement that "there is nothing easier to make the child grasp than dream interpretation" (1926–1927a) may not be related to that fact that she recorded this observation in 1926, prior to her formulations of the ego's mechanisms of defense. It may be that our current emphasis on defense analysis as our preferred pathway to the id, and our careful avoidance of such id interpretations as may interfere with developing sublimations, result in a greater respect for the latency child's endeavors to meet the maturational demands for supremacy of the secondary process, and conversely help him to circumvent the primary process threat of the dream. To put this in other words, our present-day technique involves a more gradual and a more selective uncovering of id contents, while in the early days of child analysis, the "preparatory period" was the prelude of a more direct exposure of the id. In one sense, then, the earlier methods of child analysis may have come closer, at times, to a seduction of the child's instinctual side and thus may well have led to a generally higher level of tension within the analytic situation.

Chapter 46

SOME THOUGHTS CONCERNING THE CLINICAL USE OF CHILDREN'S DREAMS

RUDOLF EKSTEIN

On May 8th, 1978, Anna Freud gave the annual Freud Lecture in Vienna, and she selected as her topic the importance of child analysis. As I followed her reflections on half a century of child analysis, I played for a few moments with the fantasy that it was child analysis rather than the analysis of adult patients which was developed first. Not the dream but the play of the child would have been considered the royal road to the unconscious, as Erikson (1950) once paraphrased Freud's dictum about the dream.

The direct observation of the child might have led to the development of child analytical techniques. Anna Freud would not have discussed, as she actually did in "Four Lectures on Child Analysis" (1926–1927b), the deviations from and modifications of adult analysis necessary for developing techniques for the analysis of child patients. Rather, if I may follow my fantasy, a later development would have led Sigmund Freud to discuss the deviations from and modifications of child analysis necessary for developing techniques for the analysis of adult patients. Adults, too, have actually expressed much about their inner life through play and games, through acting out, through playacting, and much of what has been learned through the child's play has enhanced the understanding of adult psychic life.

This paper was first published in the *Bulletin of the Menninger Clinic* (1981), 45:115–124.

I am speaking about two roads of the unconscious, two methods, two special forms of dealing with a patient's material. Am I to go the low road or am I to travel the high road? Am I to think of the play of the child as his major form of dreaming? Or am I to think of the dream of the adult as his major form of playing with thoughts, of trying to resolve inner conflict? Melanie Klein (1932) actually suggests in *The Psycho-Analysis of Children* that the play of the child be considered like a dream, be interpreted like a dream. In a contribution of my own (1975) in which I consider the child's play as a form of language, I offer the reverse of this idea and propose that the free associative process of the adult, the analysis of his dreams, be considered a play with language.

Rather than dealing with differing and different schools of thought, I propose that the answer lies with problems of development, the development of language, of systems of communication along developmental lines. Anna Freud (1965) introduces these considerations in *Normality and Pathology in Childhood: Assessments of Development.* In this communication, she speaks about the early difficulty of teaching young analysts the difference between the content of the unconscious and its overt derivatives. It is difficult, she suggests, to differentiate between the latent and the manifest content of a dream, and she could have added that it is also difficult to see the difference between the manifest and the latent content of play. Play thus can be considered the child's free association while the dream is the adult's way of playing, of introducing free association around the manifest dream content. In the same way, to borrow a phrase from Wäelder (1933), the child weaves fantasies around the external object, the toy object, and thus freely associates around and about that object.

My own playful fantasy in which child analysis is developed before adult analysis introduces the idea that the child analyst, having at first been primarily concerned with the play, with the toys of the child, will slowly discover other kinds of material to be observed and considered in the understanding of the child and in the development of adequate therapeutic techniques. My fantasy invents a child analyst who, of course, is also a child observer.

He will also discover that at different ages children use and develop different plays and games which reflect the normal and pathological developmental phases of the child's mind.

In my earlier essay (1975), I refer to the baby's activity at the breast of the mother as the first play. When hunger moves him, he hallucinates the breast, the wish fulfillment, and thus permits delay. The first hallucination about the breast, about the satisfaction to come, is the beginning of the capacity to delay, to anticipate, and to think. This hallucination, a kind of foreplay, leads to the attempt of the child to play with the breast, to scan the horizon for sources of nurture, to grab the breast, and to find fulfillment. After the fulfillment, the child, if encouraged by a responsive mother, will start the afterplay. He scans the environment for the breast, he searches for the nipple, he gets hold of the breast, he tastes once more, he rejects and pushes away. He may play this game several times until he is fully satisfied and falls asleep. Thus he rehearses for the next time, improves his technique, and recalls the moments of frustration. He repeats his conflict and its resolution. He develops the theme of being hungry, of waiting, and of bringing about delay through fantasied wish fulfillment and later through finding, gratifying, and finally remembering the anxious waiting and the happy finding.

This play with the breast then, starting with hallucinations and leading through vigorous activity, builds a bridge between anticipation, conflict, solution, and remembrance. Santayana's (1905–1906) "He who does not remember the past is compelled to repeat it" might as well be a special view of the child's and mother's interplay, leading from anticipation to the act and finally to recollection.

The assumption of hallucinatory gratification leads to the ideas of wish fulfillment in fantasy, a notion that is so important for the understanding of the dream. Freud (1900) advances the idea that behind each dream is a piece of wish fulfillment. The child's first play, indeed a serious play for actual gratification, contains a phase that describes the origin of a dream. May it then be assumed that the first dream is concerned with wish fulfillment, with delay, in order to cope with frustration and to maintain the status quo, the sleep? But this hallucination not only contains the wish to be fulfilled, the activity of nurture, the contact with the mother, the reunion with the breast, but also contains the beginning of methods of delay, the development of defenses, those internal mechanisms that cope with unbearable anxiety, with panic reactions at the moment of slowly awakening and searching for the mother, with the realization that paradise is lost and must be regained.

The child analyst in my fantasy will slowly find his way through the observation of play to the observation of mental activity occurring before physical activity that is directed at external objects, such as the breast first, the toy later. He will then slowly deal with mental content preceding the awakening stage and thus discover the dream. But his first discovery will actually be a precursor of empirical discovery, merely a theoretical construct about the child's dream. He will, therefore, need to look for evidence, and his observation will lead him away from the play to the kind of mental content that can only be observed after the development of language. I do not refer just to verbal language but to the kind of communication systems that exist between mother and baby which are full of meaning. The autistic and symbiotic positions, the attachment and the separation moves would allow the analyst to understand the preverbal fantasy and dream life of the growing child.

The analyst in my fantasy will then discover that the first dreams just as the first daydreams are usually simple wish fulfillments. They seem to be undisguised reflections of the child's wishes. And since they are undisguised, it is usually difficult to differentiate between the dream and the daydream. The younger the child the more difficult it is to establish whether a child is reporting a dream or whether the child is occupied with daydreams.

My daughter Jean Ekstein, a teacher (personal communication), asked second grade boys and girls, between six-and-one-half and seven-and-one-half years of age, to report their dreams. A few examples from the material she collected will illustrate the child's difficulty in differentiating between dream and daydream and will also suggest possibilities for clinical use. I must stress, however, that they were gathered in an educational setting and cannot be related to the usual transference manifestations which occur in child analysis or therapy. In addition, the impressionistic remarks I shall make about these different examples must be considered with caution. They are not meant to reflect the actual activity of a therapist. The remarks I shall append to the manifest productions of the children, be they daydreams, fantasies, or dreams, are my first reactions, a play with symbols, an attempt to put myself into the mind of the child even though I have no more on which to base my conjectures than the material quoted.

> (Lisa:) I dreamt a bear started to eat me. I dreamt I fell off a cliff. I dreamt I was an Indian. I wished I was a mouse. I wished I was a horse. I wished I was a bunny. I wished I was a house. I wished I was a moose. I wished I was a star. I wish I was a tree.

Characteristic of this sequence of wishes is that they start with anxiety-arousing fantasies, perhaps actual dreams, to be eaten by a bear, to fall off a cliff. But slowly the dreamer stops talking about dreaming and turns from dreaming to wishing. The passive, anxiety-ridden fantasy turns into the active preoccupation with positive wish fulfillment.

> (Dennis:) I dreamt that my dad and I were sitting on the patio and a gorilla came and picked the house up and we ran away. He ran after us and he picked me to a planet.

This anxiety fantasy, a splitting of the parental objects, refers to a dangerous situation. Both he and his father are described as helpless, and in some pictures this boy drew, he has himself screaming for help.

> (Stacy:) I dreamt that a monster tried to eat me up but I ran out of the house, but I was in my bed.

This report seems more like a dreamlike fantasy, a terror dream about being devoured; she awakens after the nightmare and is reassured that she does not need to run away but is safe in her bed.

> (John:) I dreamt my friends were walking home from school and they turned the corner and there was a bloody house. They saw my hamster cut in half and they tried to put it together.

This boy expresses a castration fantasy through symbolism, allowing translation of the manifest content, a yearning for help.

> (Bob:) I dreamt that I sleepwalked and I smashed into the wall and then a monster came up and sliced a piece of cheese for me. I dreamt a witch and a pirate were in my house while me and my sister were doing a puzzle and we saw them and they chased us all over the house.

A boy and his sister do puzzles, perhaps forbidden things, together and are chased by a witch and a pirate, poor disguises for threatening parents.

> (Mike:) A vampire tried to eat me at the bus stop. I ran away. I went outside and then I brought a little knife with me and I smashed him. He had more friends but I just killed them all.

Mike sees himself persecuted by the vampire, but proves to himself his omnipotence, suggesting his "little knife" is stronger than a vampire and all the vampire's friends. Counterphobic devices are his way of resolving his anxious dilemma.

> (Susan:) I wish we flew in the sky. I dreamt that an old owl tried to eat me but I ran away. I wish I was a bunny. I dreamt I saw a flying saucer. It tried to eat me but I ran away.

The wish to succeed, to fly to the sky, is countered by the treat from the devouring old owl. The wish to be a little bunny, to be loved, is countered by the fantasy that the huge saucer will try to eat her.

While most of these dreams contain wishes for strength, for being acceptable and loved, they are also fraught with danger and conflict. Almost none of these productions, whether they are dreams or daydreams of momentary inventions, are reported without the mention of overt or underlying conflict. In fact, it is almost statistically predictable what themes will permeate the productions of children of different age groups—oedipal themes, often oral wishes, themes of incorporation and oral threats, castration fears, the desire to attack the other. It is no surprise that these themes follow along developmental lines.

The psychoanalytic literature concerning the dreams of children presents many similar examples and discusses the special technical use of this material in developing adequate therapeutic interventions. Most analysts, I believe, use such dream material to further the psychotherapeutic dialogue. They inquire about the dream, allowing it to become the basis for the dialogue. They are cautious about interpreting symbolic meaning, and their use of this material depends on a variety of factors; on the nature and form of the treatment, on the current transference manifestations, on the nature of the basic conflicts and symptomatology, and on the point that is occupied on the time axis of the treatment program.

Many children, as did the group of children I quoted, combine their verbal representations with drawings and paintings. I had in analysis a twelve-year-old boy who was recovering from psychotic episodes. In a drawing which he prepared for a therapeutic session, he pictured himself as lying in bed, screaming for his father because he felt persecuted by monsters who were about to overwhelm him. He could not really differentiate between a true dream and the constant fantasizing that prevented him from sleeping and caused him to panic. The drawing included the father entering the room and screaming back at his son that monsters did not exist, that it was "all in your mind," and that the boy should go to sleep. When I asked the boy about his picture, he said that since his father had screamed at him, the monsters did not leave and his panic did not subside.

I considered this exchange to be a direct appeal to me. The boy was asking me to prevent his father from frightening him, to force his father out of the fantasy, and to suggest that it was his intrusive father who strengthened the power of the monsters when, indeed, the child wanted his father to come and save him from the monsters. The combination—acting out with his father, producing fantasies, remembering and drawing them, and then bringing the pictures to the hour—illustrated how difficult it was for this boy to differentiate between the waking state and the dream state, between the nightmare and the nightly fantasy that required him to scream for his father and then to ward off his father's intrusion, which the child both wanted and feared. This boy also produced real dreams, but usually they were not available to his memory. He repressed them as soon as he woke up, except that the panic, the fear, and the puzzlement would remain.

A child's degree of illness determines whether he is capabale of differentiating between the dreaming state and the waking state, between delusion and hallucination on the one hand and reality on the other. But what clearly indicated severe mental illness in an adult patient does not have the same implications for a young child. The child does not yet possess the capacity for maintaining reality testing and must regress from time to time to magical thinking and to metaphoric thinking which has a fairy tale quality. This type of thinking, this type of communication, is therefore not only the royal road to the unconscious or rather the derivatives of the unconscious, but it is at the same time also the royal road to reality, to the waking state, to reality testing. This double view of fantasy life, dream life, daydream life, permits the development of therapeutic interventions, technical considerations which have to be considered a two-way street. As the therapist responds to these dreams, he not only moves toward the conflicts of which the child is unaware, but he also moves toward attempts at resolution which may be neurotic in nature but which through the therapist's help allow the child's capacity for adaption to develop.

I often use the dreams of children as if they were fairy tales. Behind every tale there is a bit of psychological truth. The fairy tale is not only magic wish fulfillment, the happy ending, but it is also the representation of inner conflict, of developmental tasks and developmental dilemmas. The fairy tale is more than a cautionary tale. It is not only a warning but also in it is hidden, it seems to me, an adaptive solution.

That child analyst in my fantasy, who starts out with the consideration to play and discovers that the forerunner of play is the dream and the daydream without play action, will then begin to wonder in which way the techniques of child analysis can be modified in order to be used for adults. He will need to write a book on adult analysis, putting down in reverse some of Anna Freud's observations concerning the aspects of adult analysis that are not quite applicable to children. For example, just as children cannot be expected to free associate, adults cannot be expected to sit down with the analyst, look in his play chest, and start to play with toys, to paint, to draw, or to use games. From the play of the child, the analyst in my fantasy will derive a new form of play, the play of the adult, the play with words. As this analyst thinks of the dreams and daydreams of children and of the thoughts they hide, he will suddenly discover that this form of communication is of more use for adults; and thus he will move toward viewing the dream as the royal road to the derivatives of the unconscious. My child analyst will then discover that while motoric activity helps the child to weave his fantasies, his dreams, and his daydreams around external objects, it prevents the adult from observing his mental productions, from freely associating. He will therefore introduce the couch as the stage for the play of the adult patient's dream and free association.

Freud's (1905b) observation of adults led him to discover the mental life of children, their psychosexual and psychoaggressive development. Will the child analyst in my fantasy, merely from the observation of the children, be able to conjecture enough about the mental life of adults? Whether he thinks that "the world is but a dream" or that "all of life is but a play" sooner or later he must move away from generalizations and find that some dreams are better understood as dreams. Both play and the dream have their basis not only in inner life but also in reality. Remembering the poet's words that the child is the father of the man suggests the reverse idea that the father is the son of the child. Just as play turns into the dream will the dream turn into play. Becker (1978) sums up his point of view, shared by me, as follows:

> Although the fundamentals of dream interpretation are the same for all ages, the details of technique vary with the developmental level of the patient, and with other individual traits. The child analyst may have to take active steps to interest his patient in dreams and demonstrate their value.
>
> A child is generally incapable of free association, and frequently cannot associate to elements of his dream. The child analyst, therefore, relies on the flow of material (both verbal expressions and activity) during the session in which the patient reports the dream, his knowledge of current state of the analysis, and the therapist's understanding of symbolism. Thus armed, the analyst can help the patient understand his dreams, and integrate those insights into the analytic work [pp. 373–374].

I only want to add that each specific phase in the development of psychoanalytic technique has led to a belief in the royal road. Around the turn of the century, the dream was considered the royal road. Anna Freud (1965) suggested once that transference was the royal road; Erikson (1950) spoke about play as the royal road. I suggest that the different phases in an individual's development as an analyst, as a psychotherapist, leads him to make such choices. They should not be final choices. An analyst must remain flexible enough to change his point of view when understanding and technique are improved. For this reason I have tried to build a bridge between play and dream without preference for whichever way the child communicates with others and with himself. Studying the differences between and the similarities of these two phenomena will increase the analyst's knowledge about mental development and enrich his technical armamentarium.

Section IX

Dreams and Related States

In this section we present articles pertaining to dreams and such related states as hypnosis, sleepwalking, fairy tales and myths, and reminiscence and daydreams.

Beginning this section are two classical articles exploring the interplay–interrelations between dreams and hypnosis. In her article, "Dreams and Hypnosis" (1949), Brenman finds that there is a wide range of responses to the hypnotic suggestion to dream, but that the so-called average hypnotic dream has a structure which seems intermediate between the spontaneous night dream and the daydream; that is, the primary processes are used more than what is common in the waking ego state, but less than in the typical night dream. Supplementing Brenman's work is Kanzer's enlightening paper "The Therapeutic Use of Dreams Induced by Hypnotic Suggestion" (1945), where he reports the hypnoanalytic treatment of a young soldier suffering from hysterical dyskinesia. The patient was instructed to dream around certain selected topics which had relevance to his hysterical conflicts and passive orientation. Kanzer concludes (in part) that dreams induced in this fashion were of considerable value in helping the patient become aware of a number of unconscious conflicts as well as revealing practical and theoretical aspects of dream psychology.

Next appears Schneck's clinical article, "The Role of a Dream in the Treatment with Hypnosis" (1947), where he illustrates the use of the hypnotic dream in exploring the sources of the conflict underlying a severe tic involving the repetitions, horizontal jerking of the head every few seconds.

Following this appears Jackson's article, "An Episode of Sleepwalking" (1954), where he describes a particular instructive sleepwalking episode which occurred in a patient (in his

663

midtwenties) for the first time only a few days before he became overtly psychotic. Jackson describes the interrelationship between the sleepwalking and the twelve-day psychotic episode, elucidating the commonly held features such as the forbidden incestuous impulses and the defensive maneuver against them.

Finally, the stimulating article by Wangh, "Day Residue in Dream and Myth" (1954), confronts the problem of exploring how the same unconscious forces which go into the production of a dream are also active in the creating of fairy tales and myths. By reference to the dream of a businessman–patient (in which mythlike symbolizations and transformations were prevalent), Wangh was able to demonstrate how those processes involving the day residue participation in the formation of the dream were remarkably similar to how anxiety-arousing cultural phenomena enter into myth formation.

Chapter 47

DREAMS AND HYPNOSIS

MARGARET BRENMAN

Since Schrötter's fragmentary, unfinished investigation in 1911 of so-called "hypnotic dreams," there has been a good deal of glib talk regarding the power of hypnosis to create dreams which, according to most researchers on this problem, are in all ways like spontaneous night dreams. The classic example, often quoted by Freud and by many others since, is that of Schrötter's female subject, presumably an unsophisticated person, who was told while in a deep hypnotic state to dream of having homosexual relations with a lady friend; she promptly reported a "dream" in which the friend appeared, carrying a shabby traveling bag, on which there was a label with the printed words: "For ladies only." This was certainly a provocative outcome but scarcely proof that the response to a hypnotic suggestion to "dream" is a psychological product comparable in all significant qualities to the condensed, delicately wrought content which issues from the dream work during sleep.

It is curious that investigators appear to have taken it for granted that the hypnotic suggestion to "dream" actually issues in a dream (Farber and Fisher, 1943; Wolberg, 1945, 1948). It is as if the belief in the magic power of hypnosis overwhelms the investigator as well as the subject and thus, when the subject responds with a production which often resembles a night dream, it is assumed without further question that there is no difference between the two. The hypnotist might as well assume that were he to command his subject to fly, the resulting activity,

This paper was first published in the *Psychoanalytic Quarterly* (1949), 18:455–466.

whatever its nature, could be called "flight." Assumptions of this sort preclude any fruitful investigation of the true nature of "hypnotic dreams."

We believe, from our observations, that varying depths of hypnosis involve significant and varying changes in ego functioning (Brenman, Gill, and Hacker, 1947); moreover, it is likely that the suggestion to dream produces further alterations. We are not in a position to study the precise nature of these changes, however, so long as we assume that our instruction has an inevitable result.

Before proceeding to a presentation of our preliminary hypothesis regarding the characteristics of the various forms of hypnotic "dreams," we must comment parenthetically on the fact that it is still an open problem as to whether even all night dreams have precisely the same structure, formal qualities, and kinds of distortion. In his chapter, "The Dream Work," Freud says:

> Thus, for example, I remember a dream which on waking seemed so particularly well constructed, flawless and clear that I made up my mind, while I was still in a somnolent state, to admit a new category of dreams—those which had not been subject to the mechanism of condensation and distortion, and which might thus be described as "fantasies during sleep". A closer examination, however, proved that this unusual dream suffered from the same structural flaws and breaches as exist in all other dreams; so I abandoned the idea of a category of "dream-fantasies" [1900, p. 33].

In a footnote added later he comments, "I do not know today whether I was justified in doing so."

Freud's persistent doubt about the uniformity of psychic productions during sleep is further indicated:

> A dream without condensation, distortion, dramatization above all, without wish fulfillment, surely hardly deserves the name. You will remind me that, if so, there are other mental products in sleep to which the right to be called "dreams" would have to be refused. Actual experiences of

the day are known to be simply repeated in sleep; reproductions of traumatic scenes in "dreams" have led us only
lately to revise the theory of dreams. There are dreams
which by certain special qualities are to be distinguished
from the usual type, which are, properly speaking, nothing
but night fantasies, not having undergone additions or alterations of any kind and in all other ways similar to the
well-known daydreams. It would be awkward, certainly,
to exclude these imaginings from the realm of "dreams"
[Freud, 1922a, p. 208].

In still another connection he says: "Indeed the natural
dreams of healthy persons contain a much simpler, more transparent and more characteristic symbolism than those of neurotics, which, owing to the greater strictness of the censorship and
the more extensive dream distortion resulting therefrom, are
frequently troubled and obscured, and are therefore more difficult to translate (1900, pp. 373–374).

We include these comments to suggest that it is probably a
meaningless formulation to ask whether hypnotic dreams are
the same as spontaneous night dreams, as if *all* hypnotic dreams
have certain formal qualities in common which distinguish
them as a group from *all* night dreams. We have observed in
our hypnotic work that there is a great range of psychic production at the instruction: to dream. Perhaps such a range exists
for the spontaneous night dream as well. Papaport is at present
engaged in a study of the problem of night dreams, the preliminary findings of which promise to elucidate this question.

From our preliminary study of the verbatim recordings of
the productions of both normal subjects and patients we have
the following impressions: (1) the response to the suggestion,
"You will now have a dream," ranges from a slightly embellished reminiscence of an actual event to a production which at
least on the surface resembles a classical night dream; (2) by
and large, these productions employ "primary processes" more
than does normal, conscious, waking thought but less than does
the "typical" night dream described by Freud. It might be said
that often the hypnotic dream is a kind of second-rate poetry
in comparison to the tight, complex outcome of the dream

work. Thus, although a wide range of phenomena appears, it may be said, from the point of view of the formal qualities, that the average hypnotic dream takes a position which is intermediate between the conscious waking daydream and the night dream, with considerable overlapping at both ends of the range. In spite of the many similarities to night dreams in the formal structure of some of the hypnotic dreams, it must not be forgotten that while the primary function of the night dream is to guard sleep, the motive power for the hypnotic dream derives from the need to comply, in so far as possible, with the expressed wishes of the hypnotist; thus to guard an interpersonal relationship. We do not yet know what all the implications of this difference are, but we can suppose that it will prove to be an important factor in establishing the differing dynamic roles of the two productions. Although we have not conducted experiments designed to test this problem, we can report that no one of our subjects reported anything remotely resembling a night dream if left to himself. The hypnotic dream, so far as we now know, does not occur spontaneously but only at the explicit or implicit behest of the hypnotist. Another significant difference lies in the fact that whereas one of the prerequisite conditions for night dreaming is the withdrawal of motor cathexes, the maintenance or withdrawal of motor cathexes for the hypnotized "dreamer" is determined by the hypnotist.

With these important differences, there seem to be significant similarities between the hypnotic state and the state of consciousness which gives rise to spontaneous night dreams. In both there are significant alterations in the defensive and in the synthetic functions of the ego. It has been our observation, however, that these alterations in hypnosis are highly variable in different subjects and fluctuate a great deal from moment to moment (perhaps they do in sleep as well); they by no means imply an obliteration of ego functioning (Brenman et al., 1947). Freud has compared the hypnotic state to a state preceding sleep. In his discussion of the necessary conditions for free association, he says: "As will be seen, the point is to induce a psychic state which is in some degree analogous, as regards the distribution of psychic energy (mobile attention), to the state of mind before falling asleep—and also, of course, to the hypnotic state" (1900, p. 102).

Although we are as yet unable to establish a strict continuum in the range of hypnotic dreams we offer a rough classification of these productions which will provide illustrations of their great variety. Before proceeding to these, a technical point of procedure should be clarified. Suggestions to "dream" are given in many different ways. The most frequent techniques described in the literature are: (1) the subject may be told simply, "Now you will have a dream"; (2) he may be posed a specific problem or topic about which to dream; (3) a posthypnotic suggestion may be given to have a night dream on a specific theme; (4) he may be asked to recall a repressed night dream; (5) he may be instructed to continue "dreaming" where a night dream has broken off. We believe that all of these techniques are, in a sense, what Ferenczi called "forced fantasies" brought about in an altered state of consciousness or, better, of ego functioning. We shall indicate in each of our examples which of these techniques was used.

First, an instance of the embellished *reminiscence* was produced by a woman of hysterical character who was being treated for symptoms of anxiety, depression, and multiple somatic complaints. She complained, while in hypnosis, of a pervasive sense of failure and deficiency in the ability to make people like her. She was given the suggestion to dream about this problem and reported: "I saw two of my girl friends on the porch of my home. I was there too. I seemed to be about fifteen years old. They told me they were not going to come back that evening as they had planned, but would come another time." This dull and rather banal response was not typical for this patient, who frequently reported highly condensed hypnotic dreams of a sort to be described later.

Another variety of response is the *static pictorial image*. The following examples are from the records of a middle-aged man with a well-compensated, compulsive character, who was being treated for torticollis. He was not deeply hypnotizable, but at the suggestion to dream in hypnosis he sometimes produced static pictorial images which he found startling. A surprising number of them dealt with his being gazed at intently. In one of the most striking he saw a vivid picture of a figure of indeterminate sex nailed to a cross, with head turned to the right and down, the same position into which the torticollis had twisted his own head. As he watched the figure, the head slowly lifted and the eyes fused into one which gazed at him intently and with great sorrow. The patient had not had, since early childhood, any interest in religion. This image, while it has a dreamlike quality, is relatively static and brief. In another such image he saw an owl watching him intently with great, wide eyes—"as though telling me not to be a fool."

Still another level of production which appears to us distinct both from the reminiscence and the static pictorial image is the *quasi allegory,* a hybrid form, resembling the conscious daydream, but including, in a rather obvious and primitive fashion, some elements of unconscious symbolism. An example of this variety of hypnotic dream is taken from a case, recently reported by McDowell (1948), of a veteran with the presenting symptoms of severe anxiety and ejaculatio praecox. This man was an unsophisticated person who, as far as is known, had no knowledge of the unconscious meaning of symbols. The production we will now describe occurred shortly after the disappearance of his ejaculatio praecox. He was told by the therapist that he would have a dream in hypnosis which would explain the meaning of his previous symptom of "being like a jack rabbit" as he called it. The therapist left the room and when he returned the patient reported the following.

"There were long white stairs going up into the sky, as far as I could see. There were women lined up on both sides of the stairs. They were all reaching out for me as I was running up the stairs as fast as I could run, always running. At the top of the stairs is a beautiful girl with no clothes on, lying on a big, white, soft bed. I reached her, got into bed with her, "came" in a hurry and started running up the stairs again just like before. I looked back and she was still lying there with her arms raised toward me, looking disappointed, but I kept running." This sequence is repeated several times, and he concludes: "I got off the bed the last time and started walking." Now all the other girls were gone, the beautiful woman was waiting and after he had "calmly climbed the stairs, began intercourse calmly—no hurry. We were still doing it when the dream ended."

There is a shallowness and transparency in this response which gives it a rather contrived flavor. At the same time, the presence of the classical symbol of ascending the staircase in this naive man links this production to the regressive archaic night dream.

Still closer to the night dream is a variety of response which we will call the *quasi dream*. Our example is taken from the record of the analysis of a young hysteric. This young woman was possessed of an intense ambition to become a famous writer, having written many elaborate novels while working as a saleswoman. She came for treatment of "spells" during which she became rigid and talked wildly. During the initial interviews she had been told by a young and inexperienced resident physician that if she wanted to be cured of her "spells" she might have to give up her writing. Though dismayed by this prospect, she agreed to come for therapy. She was hypnotized occasionally during the course of the analysis, in periods of great resistance. In one such period, when it seemed that her unconscious competitiveness with the analyst as a defense against her strong passive wishes was fairly close to consciousness, she was hypnotized and told simply, "You're going to have a dream." Her response (in part) follows.

"I'm in a hospital bed . . . I like the room . . . it's not an ordinary hospital . . . it's way up high with a beautiful view . . . the walls are tinted pale green . . . I see the nurse's face or something . . . and it ought to startle me because her fingertips are gone . . . on the first two fingers, down to the second joint . . . and I was going to interrupt and tell the nurse . . . if it is a nurse . . . that part of her fingers are gone . . . but I hate to interrupt when they're talking ["they," unidentified at this point] . . . so I don't say anything . . . they're talking pleasantly and I'm comfortable."

She was asked directly, still in hypnosis, what she thought
the dream meant; she could make nothing of it. Accordingly,
she associated in the usual way, and it then appeared to the
analyst that she was expressing both her wish for and her fear
of the analyst's power over her, the specific threat to her own
power being expressed in the symbol of the missing fingers,
which on one level meant she could no longer type her novels,
and would thus be deprived of her most important weapon.
The dream was not interpreted, and she was given the posthypnotic suggestion to have a night dream which would embody
the same meaning as this hypnotic dream. The next day she
reported a night dream which seemed to state more clearly
her intense defensive strivings for power. This was also not
interpreted and again, on successive days, she was told to
"dream" in hypnosis, with the instruction that these "dreams"
would state even more clearly the same conflict (still not interpreted to her). Finally, she produced the following in hypnosis.

> "I am sitting at a desk . . . a big desk . . . outdoors, looking
> down . . . I'm high up . . . looking down over beautiful sce-
> nery . . . there's a lake, a lot of trees . . . but no other per-
> son . . . just me . . . my desk is smooth and polished and
> large . . . I don't know how it got there."

This seemed a simpler dream than the one about the missing fingers. Her associations in hypnosis made it clear that she
was attempting to usurp the analyst's position. Her wish to be
lofty and godlike, the *defense* against her passive needs and
against her fears of helplessness now obliterated the wishes to
be taken care of.

We have presented this series to illustrate two points: (1)
this is a variety of hypnotic dream which seems fairly close in
quality to night dreams; (2) that in such series there appears to
be a progression either in the direction of accenting the defensive aspect of a conflict or, as we shall see in the next series, in
the direction of exposing more sharply the underlying need or
impulse which is being defended against.

A successful young surgeon, a morphine addict, who was
gradually losing his practice because of his addiction, "dreams"

the following in response to the unstructured suggestion. "You will now have a dream." He is in the operating room, performing an extremely difficult appendectomy and executing it with the utmost delicacy and skill. He describes, largely in the present tense and with relatively little affect, all of the complications and his successful techniques of handling them, lapsing occasionally into the past tense and finally, in response to direct questioning, confirming our impression that he was embroidering an actual experience. This kind of production, while obviously meaningful and perhaps even potentially helpful in therapy, is a far cry from the rebuslike character of the night dream.

In a subsequent session, in response to the same unstructured suggestion to "have a dream," he again produced an actual experience, this time, however, wholly in the present tense and with intense feeling. He reenacted the birth of his son who had not begun to breathe spontaneously. Over and over he shouted, "You've got to make it, Tommy! Breathe, boy! I'm gonna help you! You've just got to!" He went through all the motions of holding the newborn infant up to his mouth and helping him to start respiration. Tears rolled down his face, and finally he announced (still in the present tense) that the baby had begun to breathe and that he knew he had saved him.

On the next occasion, given the same instruction, he reported a production of a different order. The following is an excerpt.

"I am falling asleep now and all of a sudden there is a monster, a terrible monster [voice choking with genuine panic] . . . I can't breathe, it's choking me, it wants to mash me to pieces [breathing with great difficulty] . . . on my chest . . . weighting me down . . . it's horrible, horrible . . . I must fight it . . . it's smothering me, what shall I do? . . . a terrible thing . . . great big body and lots of legs . . ." As he continued this *quasi nightmare*, he began to clench his fists and became frantic. Suddenly, he shouted, "I want to fight it, I have to fight it, can I fight it?" [Therapist: "Yes, you can."] At this point he began to flail his arms in the air, still breathing with great difficulty, and finally

gave a great lurch which landed him on the floor. As he
hit the floor he looked around him in amazement, and
somewhat sheepishly, no longer in hypnosis.

It is evident that these three productions, all in response
to the suggestion to "dream," are significantly different from
each other not only in their manifest content, and in the degree
of uncontrolled affect, but also in the degree to which primary
and secondary processes are employed. It would appear also
that there is a progression from the defensive position taken in
the first hypnotic dream (where he denies his terror of helplessness by performing a delicate operation with utmost skill)
to the second where the defense seems still in evidence, though
somewhat shaky, in saving his child who cannot, at first,
breathe; and finally to the third where there seems no longer
to be any defense against the overwhelming anxiety associated
with his feeling of helplessness and inability to breathe, an anxiety so intense that he breaks out of the hypnotic state altogether.
   In the first of these two series (the hysterical girl), we see
a progressively clearer statement of a defensive position, and
in the second (the surgeon), an increasing disclosure of an underlying terror. Perhaps these progressions are analogous
though not identical with the progression described by Freud
in his discussion of dreams of the same night. He says:

> All dreams of the same night belong in respect of their
> content, to the same whole; their division into several parts,
> their grouping and number, are all full of meaning and
> may be regarded as pieces of information about the latent
> dream thoughts. In the interpretation of dreams consisting
> of several main sections, or of dreams belonging to the
> same night, we must not overlook the possibility that these
> different and successive dreams mean the same thing, ex-
> pressing the same impulses in different material. That one
> of these homologous dreams which comes first in time is
> usually the most distorted and most bashful, while the next
> dream is bolder and more distinct [1900, p. 552].

Freud does not discuss whether the increasing "boldness"
of the night dream refers only to the underlying impulse, or

whether the defense may sometimes be clarified in this way also.

We cannot say from the preliminary survey of our material that this progressive clarification (whether of the underlying need or of the defense) is characteristic for hypnotic dreams in a series.

Summary

We question the assumption that the hypnotic dream is a psychic production which duplicates, either in function or structure, the spontaneous night dream. We suggest instead that there is a wide range of response to the hypnotic suggestion to "dream," the average production having a structure which seems intermediate between the daydream and the spontaneous night dream, in that primary processes are used more than is common in waking thought, but less than in the typical night dream. We add further the tentative suggestion that hypnotic dreams in a series may progressively clarify either the defensive aspect of a conflict or the impulse (or need) which is being defended against.

Chapter 48

THE THERAPEUTIC USE OF DREAMS INDUCED BY HYPNOTIC SUGGESTION

MARK G. KANZER

Hypnosis was the immediate predecessor of psychoanalysis in the study of unconscious mental activity. Freud himself evolved his psychoanalytic theories after he had investigated the phenomena and therapeutic limitations of hypnotic technique. In later years he cited facts of hypnosis to elaborate his theories of the unconscious and particularly stressed the bond between patient and hypnotist as a reproduction of primitive stages in the formation of the superego. In this connection he did not fail to point out elements of hypnosis which underlie the relationship between the patient and the psychoanalyst. Actually, however, Freud made no further direct use of the hypnotic technique after he was once well launched in psychoanalytic therapy. At one point in his writings, he stated that he personally did not feel quite comfortable in the use of hypnotism, and there is, to be sure, a certain incompatibility between hypnosis and psychoanalytic therapy. Hypnosis depends to a great extent on the patient's surrender of conscious control over his memory and impulses to the physician. As hypnosis has usually been practiced, the patient may be relieved of his symptoms but does not understand why he became ill or how he was cured. Striking symptomatic relief is often obtained in this way, but the essential nature of the neurosis is not resolved. It is toward the more fundamental cure of the condition that psychoanalysis is directed. In the course of the latter procedure, the patient is

This paper was first published in the *Psychoanalytic Quarterly* (1965), 14:313–335.

guided to the recollection of forgotten traumatic experiences, gains insight into the nature of his ailment, and plays an active role in the cure. Perhaps the most important dynamic difference between hypnosis and psychoanalysis is their diversity of approach to the problem of "resistances." "Resistances" are dynamic factors, such as shame and anxiety, which lead the patient to submerge in his unconscious certain ideas and drives which, striving for expression, provoke intolerable emotional and cultural problems. In hypnosis, resistances are more or less abruptly submerged, much as consciousness is simply submerged by anaesthesia in the course of an operation. That the hypnotist is able to eliminate resistances so simply is one of the phenomena of the unconscious which has not been completely explained, but it is undoubtedly related to the action of the hypnotist in assuming the role of the omnipotent paternal or materal figure of early childhood. The hypnotic subject reverts temporarily to an earlier dependent uncritical state in which decisions and standards of behavior were determined for him by the parent.

The therapeutic limitations which arise from this situation are (1) the fact that even the hypnotist cannot persuade the patient to sacrifice some of the most vital resistances; indeed, some of the resistances are bound up with the figure of the parent whose role the hypnotist adopts, while other resistances are brought into play at the moment the hypnotist introduces any variation into the procedure which the patient cannot accept as emanating from the illusory parent; (2) a free play of ideas, dependent upon the ready and spontaneous associations to different events and periods of time in the life of the patient, is restricted by the inherently circumscribed mental activity during the hypnotic phase; (3) the conscious ego, not participating in the process, does not derive insight into the nature of the problems involved; and (4) upon emerging from the hypnotic state, the resistances reappear virtually unchanged and perpetuate the essentially undesirable dynamic constellation which has induced previous morbid manifestations.

The aim of psychoanalysis is to alter and break down the resistances themselves to the point where they no longer precipitate a neurosis. Here the analyst likewise takes the role of parental figures but to a degree which permits the consciousness of the patient to enter into the process and to understand, as the treatment proceeds, how his resistances will form and how he may free himself from their influence.

It is not easy to combine psychoanalysis and hypnosis or to alternate between the use of the two procedures. Hypnosis fosters the overevaluation of the parental figure which is so universal in the neuroses. The patient is inclined to expect all help and punishment alike to proceed from the figure of the all-powerful parent just as he did in childhood. He surrenders initiative and becomes extravagant in his love or awe of the hypnotist. If hypnosis is successful, the patient's awe of the hypnotist is increased. If the treatment is not successful, the prestige of the hypnotist is shaken to the point where hypnosis itself can no longer be induced. Psychoanalysis, on the contrary, is inseparable from a critical as well as an adoring attitude toward the analyst and the very trend of the successful analysis is in the direction of weakening the emotional dependence of the patient, increasing his own ability to cope with his problems, and automatically dissolving the patient–analyst relationship. Thus the approach to the patient is very different in the two procedures, and in practice it is commonly held to be inconvenient and without advantage to combine both methods of treatment in dealing with an individual patient.

In recent years, a revival of interest in hypnosis has been noted among psychoanalysts. Part of this interest has been inspired by the unique opportunities which hypnosis affords for the study of the unconscious. The old problem of the long duration and costliness of analysis has also acted as an incentive since the earliest days to search for some simpler and easier method of cure which may be effective, even though not as thorough as the conventional analysis. With the growth of mental health clinics and especially of military neuropsychiatry, this need had become a very urgent problem. Considerable success has been encountered in the adaptation of psychoanalytic knowledge to the immediate needs of the army in dealing with the war neuroses. "Narcoanalysis," a physiological means of inducing a state closely allied to hypnosis, has been found especially useful in gaining direct access to the unconscious and unburdening a soldier of tension and anxiety. Hypnosis, while not suitable for such mass application as narcoanalysis, has a useful place among military psychiatric procedures, especially in recovering lost memories and in providing immediate symptomatic relief in conversion hysteria.

As work with hypnosis proceeds among psychiatrists with a background in psychoanalysis, modifications of the older methods and uses of hypnosis are evolved. Kubie (1945) and Erikson (1950), for instance, have used hypnosis not only to recover early lost memories and to permit the patient to achieve a catharsis of repressed emotions by reliving painful scenes, but have undertaken to modify the superego by presenting successive problems in a series of hypnotic sessions. At the Menninger Clinic (Janis, 1958), progress has been made in drawing data obtained through hypnosis into the scope of consciousness by subsequent discussions with the patient, who is thus encouraged to participate actively in his treatment. Such transitions from the older passive hypnotic technique to active collaboration with the patient in a modified psychoanalysis have been found feasible. As yet the general value and scope of these interesting experiments have not been determined.

Recent psychoanalytic studies of hypnosis include the investigation of dreams which have taken place during or after the hypnotic episode. The observations of Gill and Brenman (1943), and of Farber and Fisher (1943), are of pioneer interest, and give evidence that hypnotic dreams show the same elements of day residues and transference phenomena which are to be found in spontaneous dreams. Material obtained in this fashion can be made the basis for enlightening discussions with the patient. The following case report further indicates some of the possibilities in this direction.

Case Example

Recent History

A twenty-year-old private after thirteen months of service in the army developed generalized jerking movements after a long march during training. The reports of observers indicated that he had been marching at the rear of his group, and after climbing a hill had wandered off in a different direction from the other soldiers. He was found in a deeply somnolent state and after being awakened, displayed bizarre movements and complained of a chilly feeling. He professed amnesia for the events which took place during the climb up the hill and until he was awakened from his sleep.

Observation in army hospitals disclosed almost continuous and rather violent movements of a choreiform type, which seemed semipurposeful in character. His spontaneous gait was suggestive of "jitterbug" dancing. At times the movements of his arms resembled swimming strokes or shadow boxing. The restless agitation continued when the patient was in a horizontal position and did not subside completely even when he was asleep. The violence and constancy of the movements resulted in such helplessness that the patient had to be fed and assisted from place to place. On the other hand, he was never observed to injure himself.

In addition to the jerking movements of the limbs, the most outstanding symptom was a stuttering dysphasic type of speech. His past history indicated that such stuttering had been prevalent during childhood and adolescence, but had subsided for several years prior to its recent reappearance in association with the more generalized motor restlessness.

Physical examinations during hospitalization revealed no somatic disease. Cardiac studies, neuro-status, temperature, sedimentation rate, and blood studies all failed to reveal any evidence of clinical abnormalities. The motor restlessness of the patient did not resemble the typical movements of organic neurological conditions such as chorea, dystonia, or athetosis.

The tentative diagnosis of "Sydenham's chorea" was reached at the Station Hospital where the patient was studied for the first two weeks after the onset of his illness, but was superseded by the diagnosis of "hyskinesia" in the General Hospital where his symptoms were investigated during the following six weeks. The psychiatric observations during the latter period form the basis for the present report.

Past History

The patient was the youngest of six siblings of a Polish Catholic family, born and raised in the vicinity of a large city on the Eastern seaboard. His parents were some forty years older than himself and he was considerably younger than the other siblings, so that he had always held an especially protected position in the family. A special position in the family was further due to the fact that his parents, who had been poor, had reached some degree of financial security in later life and were able to provide this youngest child with privileges which his older siblings had not been given. He was therefore treated with much indulgence by all other members of the family. Outwardly, his development was rather uneventful. He made good adjustments in school and in social life. His general health was usually good. However, at some early period in his life—the exact age could not be established, but was supposedly about seven—the patient suddenly began to stutter immediately after a visit to the dentist. This habit persisted into adolescence.

In school the patient had been an average student but had shown no great interest in any subject and had no definite ambition in regard to his future occupation and position in life. He was quite popular with other boys and was fond of all athletic enterprises, especially swimming and baseball. His earlier years of education were spent at a parochial school where strict moral ideas were inculcated. Sexual development was relatively retarded; he allegedly had never heard of sexual intercourse until the age of sixteen. On two or three occasions after his eighteenth year he visited prostitutes in company with other boys but had little interest in the opposite sex until he entered the army. Then he fell in love with a young woman and considered himself engaged to marry her. Although often in her company, he never attempted to draw her into an intimate relationship.

The military history of the soldier began with a disappointment when he was not assigned to the Coast Guard, a branch of service which had particularly appealed to him because he was acquainted with, and fond of, life by the seashore. He was assigned instead to the infantry and ultimately to airborne

troops. Most of his first year was devoted to training in the use
of guns. During this period he seemd to adjust quite well. It
was at this time that he met and fell in love with his fiancée. A
few weeks before the development of his recent illness, he was
transferred to a new station where his instruction with the airborne troops was begun in earnest. He participated in glider
training and shortly before the hike which precipitated his
symptoms, he was involved in a minor glider accident from
which he escaped without injury but in a slightly shaken condition.

Psychiatric Studies and Treatment During Hospitalization

Preliminary psychiatric interviews revealed a callow, immature
young man who was cheerful, talked readily, and showed little
apparent concern or distress in connection with the continual
and violent movements of his limbs. Attempts to elicit information about possible emotional conflicts were met at every point
by casual and apparently sincere denial that he had any worries
or problems. Even in regard to his obvious physical symptoms
he professed optimism, as a previous medical consultant had
assured him that there was nothing seriously wrong with him
and that he would soon be well. Almost no point of contact for
eliciting or discussing emotional problems could be established.
In particular, he was questioned concerning his dream life and
denied at once that he ever dreamed.

   A few days after admission, narcoanalysis with sodium
amytal was undertaken. Very little additional information could
be obtained from him during the session. Special attempts to
reconstruct events of the amnesic period prior to the development of his involuntary movements met with no success. After a
very small quantity of amytal had been injected, he commented
about "feeling strangely, like a little fellow in a big room—like
Alice in Wonderland."

   On the following day, the first attempt at hypnosis was
made. He proved to be a ready subject. Nevertheless, attempts
to have him relive or recall recent or past traumatic episodes
were not successful. Communication with the patient during

the hypnotic phase was particularly difficult, for his violent movements and stuttering increased markedly as soon as hypnosis began to have an effect and continued until the patient emerged from the hypnotic state. Hypnotic suggestions that the jerkings of his limbs would diminish met with partial success, so that after a few treatments, he had recovered sufficiently to shave himself and write quite legibly.

The failure to establish deeper contact with the patient by hypnosis proved disappointing, especially since amytal injections and daily discussions had failed to provide evidence of the existence of emotional conflict. In an attempt to break through the barrier, dreams were suggested in hypnosis in order to determine whether significant material could be elicited. This proved to be the case, and the results of these hypnotically induced dreams form the basis of the present discussion.

Method

In the hypnotic state, the patient was asked to dream about a certain subject, to remember the dream when he awoke and to communicate the dream to the hypnotist. All other events of the hypnotic session were to be forgotten. Then the patient was permitted to sleep until he awakened spontaneously, usually in about thirty minutes. He was seen shortly after he awakened, and in some thirty sessions, never failed to produce a dream.

> Dream 1: Under hypnosis, the patient was told to dream that he was marching effortlessly. Upon awakening, he reported the following dream: "I was being pulled along in a glider which was at some distance above the ground and which was being drawn by a horse. Something went wrong and I had to jump. However, I remained suspended in the air."

Comment

The topic suggested to the soldier was introduced in the hope of gaining some information as to the hike and the events immediately preceding the development of his symptoms. Since these events were likely to be associated with anxiety and might be deeply repressed, encouragement was given in the form of a suggestion that the march would not be unpleasant. In reality, the last conscious recollections of the hike had been an exceedingly weary and difficult climb up the side of a muddy hill. Actually, the dream proved of value in establishing communication with the patient; he now revealed for the first time that he had recently been involved in a glider accident and had been forced to jump. When asked why he had not described this event previously, especially as he had explicitly denied recent difficulties, problems, or worries, he replied that crash landings were to be expected in training and that he "never worried about such things." It was pointed out to him that in the dream he had likewise experienced no affective response to danger. Curiosity was expressed at this lack of appropriate fear in such a situation. However, the patient was very casual, repeating that he "just did not worry about those things," and concluded with the remark that "dreams do not mean anything anyway."

Dream 2: The second dream occurred spontaneously on the night following the first hypnotically induced dream and appeared to represent another variation of the same theme about "marching without effort."

"Everything was in technicolor. There were blue skies and green grass. I seemed to be repeating an old scene with my father. I was walking along a path with him and we were going uphill. At the top of the hill was a cemetery. As we went along, my father discussed all sorts of subjects with me and told me what the world was really made of."

Comment

Elements in this dream suggested a link to the traumatic situation on the hike. In contrast to the generally pleasant atmosphere of the dream, the path approached a cemetery. In his associations, the patient stated that the scene was a reproduction of actual experiences in his childhood when he walked along this very path, climbed the hill, and had to pass the cemetery.

A second trend in the dream implied that a transference situation had developed, and that the hypnotist was taking the role of a father figure. Again, as in the first dream, there was a hint of impending catastrophe (approaching a cemetery), which aroused no apparent affect.

> Dream 3: It became the practice at this time to hold a daily session with the patient, usually at about the same time each day. The procedure was explained to the patient, not as a matter of hypnosis but as a "relaxing exercise." On the following occasion, the suggestion was made in hypnosis, "Dream that the jerking has stopped!" It was hoped that something might be learned of the unconscious meaning of the jerking.
>
> The patient reported the following dream: "I met my girl friend in town. We went for a walk and took a short cut along the railroad track. We began to count the stars and then the next thing I knew, I was at camp and being awakened by the Sergeant."

Comment

In discussing the dream, the patient said he had walked on the railroad track, and therefore had to maintain a precarious balance. This rigid self-control contrasted with the lack of motor coordination manifested in the patient's symptoms. The theme of "walking" still persisted in the dream and was now associated with a sexual implication, the tryst with the girl. Terminally, there was a violent awakening such as had occurred immediately preceding the onset of his symptoms. The hint of catastrophe at the end of a journey continues as in the first two dreams.

> Dream 4: The theme presented on the following day was more specific: "Dream that the jerking of your legs has stopped!"
>
> "I dreamed that I was on the beach with some friends. We got into a canoe and paddled to Atlantic City. There I was put in line and chosen 'Miss America'! I cried out that

there must be a mistake. Then a man made me hold a cat
while he cut off its tail with an ax."

Comment

The dream inspired by the suggestion that his legs had stopped
jerking revealed fears of femininity (Miss America, selected for
the perfection of her legs) and suggestions of castration anxiety
(removing the tail of the cat). The first part of the dream, where
he was riding in a canoe, also signified a situation in which he
was deprived of the use of his legs. The idea, "Your legs have
stopped jerking," produced only anxiety. The inference may
be drawn that the jerking of the legs was a form of reassurance
that he has not lost them. Such meanings commonly underlie
neurotic symptoms, and if he really feared the loss of his legs,
and if his jerking was his reassurance of still possessing them,
it becomes clear that the hypnotic command to stop the jerking
will only cause tremendous anxiety. It is such facts which reveal
the limitations of hypnosis and direct suggestion and which
establish the value of the subtler and more exact approach of
psychoanalysis.

Incidentally, the theme of the journey terminating in a
catastrophe persisted in this dream. The nature of the catastrophe itself, which has been vaguely associated with ideas of
death, now becomes more specifically a fear of bodily injury—especially, a bodily injury which impairs his masculinity.

> Dream 5: Discussion followed the patient's account of
> each dream, but still little headway could be made in secur-
> ing his active participation in analyzing his conflicts. En-
> couragement was found, however, in the fact that at this
> time he developed bouts of diarrhea which he called
> "runs." Such new developments during the treatment of
> a neurosis usually herald an unconscious response to the
> treatment.
>
> In an effort to formulate the hypnotic dream sugges-
> tion in such a manner as to touch off whatever emotional

reaction might be brewing, a variety of the "free association" technique was introduced into the hypnotic session.
Before a theme for the dream was suggested, the patient
was encouraged to unburden himself, to tell what he desired or feared at the moment. On one such occasion, he
declared that he was upset because he had failed to receive
a letter from his girl friend. He was then told to dream
that he had received such a letter.

"I was on my uncle's farm. I was in an apple tree,
throwing apples to my uncle's daughter who caught them
in her apron. Then we found ourselves in the cellar of the
farmhouse skinning tomatoes. My uncle came in and said
a man was looking for me. I went out and a man drove up
in a truck and dropped a load of letters for me, including
letters from my girl friend and from all the members of
my family."

Comment

It was of interest that a specific dream suggestion ("You will
receive a letter from your girl friend!"), was carried through.
In view of his recent bouts of diarrhea, the marked anal components of the dream were also significant.

Again an intensive attempt was made to establish some
point of contact with the patient in conscious discussions of the
dream material. He proved extremely resistive, and not even
the simple suggestion that the dream represented a fulfillment
of a wish to hear from his girl friend was acceptable to him. He
reiterated that the physician might know about such things but
they were beyond his understanding. The examiner persisted
in emphasizing certain aspects of Dream 4 which indicated sexual curiosity and desire. The patient was brought to the point
of admitting that he "never knew anything about sex until the
age of sixteen." He had not even known that infants were carried prenatally in the body of the mother. Asked how he could
possibly have avoided observing or hearing about such facts,
he insisted sullenly that "such things had never interested him."
Attempts were made to indicate to the patient that there was

something quite remarkable about his sexual ignorance as well as about his failure to experience fear in terrifying situations. The only apparent effect on him was obvious irritation and sulkiness.

> Dream 6: On the night following the previous session, the patient had a spontaneous dream. "I don't remember much about it except that I was digging for a diamond." When asked to associate to the dream, the patient said "When I think of diamonds, I think of a diamond engagement ring for my girl."

A rather successful discussion with the patient ensued. He declared that he was anxious to marry but felt that money stood in the way: he could not afford to buy his girl friend a diamond ring, and he did not feel that he should marry until he was amply provided with funds. His own parents had had a difficult economic struggle in the early years of their marriage and had often warned him against going through similar experiences in his own life. It was apparent that the discussion of the previous day, although outwardly unsatisfactory, had actually struck an emotional response in the patient, for it was followed by a spontaneous dream and by his first really active association and personal communication.

> Dream 7: The theme proposed on this occasion was an encouraging one. "You will have whatever you want. Nothing will interfere."
> The subsequent dream showed the patient shaking hands with Henry Ford, who said something about "a golden pipe."

Comment

It was pointed out to the patient that his dream about diamonds had been followed by a dream about a multimillionaire and gold. In this connection, the patient made the statement that "money really is everything."

Dream 8: The patient was again told to dream that he could have something that he wanted. The intention was to stimulate his fantasies and clarify his goal. It was considered particularly pertinent to determine whether there would be therapeutic value in sending him home on furlough. Neither in dreams nor in his conscious communications did he ever express any such desire.

"I dreamed that I was in camp and that the director selected me from among the other boys to be swimming instructor."

At about this stage in the situation, several hypnotically induced dreams showed similar trends in which, as in the above dream and in the preceding dream of Henry Ford, the patient was given special attention from some powerful and benevolent individual. It was not difficult to trace transference elements in these dreams and to identify the scarcely disguised figure of the hypnotist. Actually, it must have been quite apparent to the patient that he had been selected for special therapeutic attention. His preoccupation with the current situation at the hospital was very striking. For instance, even under hypnosis, when asked what he would like to do if he were well, he stated "I would like to go to the Red Cross and the Post Exchange with the other fellows."

Dream 9: The theme continued to be "You can do anything you want. Nothing will interfere."

"I had a wonderful dream. I was swimming in a river and somehow I drowned. Then I seemed to spin through something—it was very difficult—I came into another world—there were just minds there—I knew everything—*I could do anything I wanted*—I looked down on earth and saw all the silly things that people did. I saw how they tried to keep from dying. I realized that bad people are placed on the earth to trouble the good ones. Around me were bad minds as well as good. Then someone said, 'You have to go back now,' and then I awoke."

Comment

In discussing this dream, the patient maintained that he had never been interested in religion or death and did not believe in life after death. The dream was considered to show the awakening insight on the part of the patient, an emergence from the older pretence that he did not understand things, and in itself seemed to be an allegory of the entire situation in which he underwent hypnosis and then emerged. The hypnotic interval seemed to be an extremely pleasant one. Another interesting point was the use of the very words of the hypnotic command in the dream, namely, "I could do anything I wanted." Extravagant admiration of the hypnotist's powers and knowledge are indicated, and there is a reminder of the father figure in Dream 2, who placed his great knowledge at the patient's disposal.

> Dream 10: A new phase seemed to develop at this time. Hypnotism was supplemented more and more by psychoanalysis because of the insistence of the examiner—now that sufficient material and better contact had been established—in requiring the patient to apply his insight and to participate more actively in the discussion of his problems. Attacks of diarrhea, irritability, and mild depression were more frequently observed. Notes of criticism against the hypnotist began to creep into the dreams. The themes suggested by the hypnotist likewise became deliberately less soothing and more calculated to stir up the emotional problems of the patient. For instance, he was now told to dream that he was marching but had to drag his legs through the mud. This, of course, was aimed at reproducing the traumatic situation, but now without any accompanying reassurance. The patient dreamed that he was crawling through the snow dragging a heavy machine gun behind him.

The associations were illuminating: he declared that the dream reminded him of an episode in the army in which the officer in charge of his platoon had forced him to do unnecessary work and had made him very angry. This officer had the same military rank as the hypnotist. Since transference elements of an antagonistic nature were present in the dream, it is noteworthy that outwardly the patient proved as ready a hypnotic subject as he had done previously, when the dominant feeling was favorable. The disposition of the patient to accept hypnotic commands seemed likewise to have been unaffected by the fact that daily discussions and an increasingly personal relationship had divested the figure of the psychiatrist of much of the illusory quality which gives the hypnotist his influence.

> Dream 11: The elements of anger which had been stirred up in the patient at this stage became manifest again in a spontaneous dream following the preceding hypnotic session in which he was ordered to keep going through the mud even though it was difficult for him.
> "Another soldier and I were in a river up to our waists. In front of us were bushes. Around the bushes came a German. I seized an iron pipe which I was hiding under the water and clubbed the German on the head. The man sank into the water. I and the other soldier crawled up the bank and proceeded to climb a hill which rose before us."

In discussing this dream, the patient was reminded of the hill he had been climbing just before his symptoms developed. Now several recollections about that last hike came back to him. He recalled that while climbing the hill, he had been pulling a machine gun, and felt that he was being "worked like a horse." The corporal kept urging him to keep it up and the patient kept responding "I'm doing the best I can," and his last memories of the incident seemed to be an alternating repetition "keep it up," "I'm doing the best I can," "keep it up," "I'm doing the best I can."

Several elements from preceding dreams could now be combined. In the first dream the horse had been pulling a glider and "something had happened." In Dream 10, he had himself been dragging a machine-gun. Officers had driven him against his will. Now at last he dropped his sullen passive obedience and struck out against his enemies. A healthy transformation was indicated, and the various elements were carefully put together in tentative fashion to explain to the patient the emotional meaning of the situation during the hike up the hill and the ensuing hysterical attack. Outwardly the patient showed no great enthusiasm for these interpretations. On the following day, he had a severe headache and at night had a spontaneous dream (Dream 12), about the Red Cross bringing a piano into his room while he was out. The association to this was that he did not play the piano. The implication seemed to be a protest against the requirements of the hypnotist to fathom and utilize matters beyond his comprehension.

The agitation of the patient continued and manifested itself in restlessness over the prolonged stay in the hospital, which was now of nearly one month's duration. He asked whether there was a possibility that he might be transferred to a Veterans' Hospital. A reassuring note was taken by the examiner. The patient was encouraged and told that he was doing very well. The theme was changed now from "tough assignments" to more pleasant thoughts. The first attempt in this direction was not very successful as the patient was apparently still too much under the influence of his disturbed affect. The theme given on this occasion was a tentative one, "Dream that you are in bed with someone." The sexual implications of the neurosis had not been sufficiently elucidated.

> Dream 13: The patient reported that he had had a nightmare. "I went around looking for work. Everywhere were signs 'Men Wanted.' At one place a watchman said to me, 'You are no man, we do not want you.' I even came to the place where I used to work in civilian life and was told, 'You are shot. You had better go on relief.' Next I went into a bar and the bartender gave me whiskey instead of my usual beer, but my hand shook so that I spilled the drink on the floor."

Comment

The implication of the dream seems to confirm the agitation of the patient and his desire to flee from the unpleasant situation which had developed in the hospital. The "tough assignments" were interpreted as harsh treatment and aroused the misgivings of the patient as to his own masculine capabilities. However, there seemed no refuge available for him and his feeling of helplessness was no doubt accentuated by the sexual connotations of the hypnotic theme, which called upon him to assert his virility.

> Dream 14: Reassuring tactics were continued and again the theme was given to him, "Dream that you are in bed with someone." It may be added parenthetically that the question of latent homosexual trends was not excluded by the wording of this suggestion.
>
> The patient described the following dream in a very cheerful manner. He stated that he had been marching with a knapsack through the desert and had been getting hotter and hotter. He came to a shack. Inside was a girl at a counter. He ordered a drink. The girl went inside into another room and he heard her call him. He went in and found her lying nude on a bed and she said, "If you want me, take me." At this point he awakened.

Comment

Among other things, the dream shows the soldier emerging from the difficult emotional period which he had been passing through (wandering in the desert) and again finding refuge and welcome. It may also be pointed out that despite the various fluctuations in mood and attitude, the patient still proved an excellent hypnotic subject.

> Dream 15: At one stage of the treatment, the endeavor was made to have the patient recall in dreams his childhood visit to the dentist, which had been the occasion for the onset of stuttering.
>
> "I was returning with my aunt from the dentist. I was about four years old. I was crying. All my lower teeth had been pulled. My aunt promised me some candy when we got home."

Comment

We cannot tell whether the dream contains true memories of the traumatic incident. However, the elements in the dream were entirely new and surprising to the patient. Actually, he does not recall the circumstances of his visit to the dentist. He does not know whether his aunt was with him. He does not have information as to the procedure which was carried out in the dentist's office. It is further of interest that the age of the patient in the dream is four, whereas his conscious statement had placed his age at the time as seven years. It is a common experience in psychoanalysis to find that the date of events must be placed further and further back in the patient's life as the treatment really comes to grips with the roots of neurosis.

Dream 16: A by-product of the investigation of hypnotically induced dreams in this case was an attempt to determine the duration of time required for a dream after the hypnotic suggestion is given. Thus the patient would be told to dream about a certain subject and as soon as he had repeated the theme aloud, an interval of time was permitted to elapse. It was found that even fifteen or thirty seconds later, if the patient was awakened, he still described a dream. It was of interest that while the dream reproduced the given theme, there was also an element which showed a reaction to the brevity of the allotted time. The first "quick dream" took place in an interval of five minutes. The suggested theme was "a visit to the occupational therapy department." The ensuing dream showed the patient diving from a board into a pool. The elements of this dream seem to combine a pleasing diversion with the abrupt splash into and out of hypnosis as symbolized by the act of diving. In a previous dream, the hypnotic session had likewise been represented by swimming in water.

Dream 17: The experiment in "quick dreams" proceeded with a dream of thirty seconds duration. "I was climbing a precipice that was almost perpendicular. This precipice was near my home." The theme of the dream had been, "To be nearly home." Something sudden and difficult seemed to be demanded of him.

Again the traumatic dangerous "climb up a hill" appears. The patient's lack of enthusiasm about a visit home has continued. Death is often symbolized in dreams as "home."

Dream 18: Again a "quick dream" was demanded within an interval of thirty seconds, and to complicate the subject, the patient was told to dream that "lots of things had happened." He dreamed that he was taking part in a summer production of Macbeth (which actually had been the case at a summer camp). He and two other boys were playing the parts of the witches. There was a pot which was filled with ice and water to produce vapors, and pasted on the pot was a speech for him to read. (He never could remember his lines, as he was too preoccupied with fears that he would stutter.)

Comment

These three "quick" dreams all showed elements of startling and strenuous experiences.

Psychiatric Studies and Treatment During Hospitalization (concluded)

The therapeutic technique continued to oscillate between stimulating the soldier when he seemed too satisfied with his illness and reassuring and encouraging him when the anxiety was excessive. At the same time, insight and cooperation were constantly sought. Overtly, he showed continual improvement. Stages in his recovery were marked by the first time that he left his room alone, later by his first visit alone to the Red Cross, then by his willingness to go to town with the other soldiers despite the curious glances of strangers. Finally, not only was he able to go to town by himself but hitch-hiked to neighboring cities to see the sights.

There were intervals when he was entirely free of his jerking movements although there were recurrences. Ultimately, after some six weeks of hospitalization, the soldier was discharged from the army and was able to depart for home unattended, in marked contrast to his condition on admission when he had to be moved in a wheelchair and could eat only with assistance. The goal of final therapy in so deep-seated a disorder could not be sought within the framework of military neuropsychiatry.

As to the nature of his neurotic illness, for which the term *hysterical dyskinesia* has been offered, the ailment is probably more closely allied to the category of tics than to that of simple conversion hysteria. As with the related neuroses of tics and stuttering, the nucleus of the symptoms is to be sought in traumatic pregenital fixations of the libido, especially in the anal sphere. A detailed analysis of the psychopathology of this case does not fall within the scope of the present discussion, except to state in summary that this sexually immature individual, under conditions of physical stress and anxiety, regressed to an older neurotic form of behavior characterized by conflicts in the expression of motor impulses. The original nucleus of the neurosis had been confined to a single sphere of motor activity (speech) but recurred in more severe and widespread form in the later attack.

The dynamics of therapy, although utilizing some of the principles of deep analysis, fundamentally involved only the more superficial forces of rest, reassurance and suggestion. It would have been futile to precipitate the patient into a more searching analysis inasmuch as merely a few weeks were available for treatment.

Discussion

As illustrated by the progress of this case, dreams induced in hypnosis may be used, as in psychoanalysis, to reveal emotional problems and past events, to provide quick insight into the patient's character and hidden thoughts, and to afford a basis for therapeutic discussions which will give the patient insight and secure his cooperation in dealing with the neurotic disorder. Typical "day residues" and evidence of transference are to be found in hypnotic as well as in spontaneous dreams. It is of interest to note that even the difficult problem of "negative transference," that is to say, elements of hostility and criticism directed at the hypnotist, may be revealed in the dream and yet not interfere with the cooperation of the patient in the hypnotic process.

Hypnotically induced dreams provide the psychiatrist with unusual opportunities for direct intervention in the unconscious of the patient and offer a field for the experimental study of the dream process. Since the hypnotist is able to provide the topic for the dream, it is possible to secure immediate and relevant data about the meaning of fixed ideas, obsessive practices, fetishes, and other symbolic distortions of the neuroses.

A disadvantage of hypnosis as compared to the usual course of psychoanalysis is the fact that the pace must be forced to a greater extent in hypnosis. For example, it is the hypnotist who determines that the most fruitful subject for a dream may be a certain situation in which he is interested, whereas in psychoanalysis, where the topic is left to the patient, quite surprising but revealing themes appear spontaneously in the dream. Similarly, the course of therapy is more rigid and provides less for spontaneous adjustment in the active hypnotic technique outlined than in psychoanalysis. With these facts in mind, however, even the hypnotist can introduce a considerable measure of free scope for the patient. For instance, in hypnosis, before the topic for the dream is suggested, it is possible to permit the patient a certain amount of free association and to determine the dominant mood or idea of the moment. The topic for the dream can then be suggested to conform with these findings. Moreover, the unconscious drives of the patient are still of great influence in determining the hypnotic dream, as shown by greatly varying dreams which were produced in response to the same theme suggested by the hypnotist, and by the recurrence of certain trends in the dreams despite the different topics presented. Scope for spontaneity in the dream is likewise permitted by offering the patient a very general dream topic. Another advantage provided by hypnosis is the ability to influence the amount of affect released in the dreams by selecting themes which excite or reassure according to the indications of the moment.

An interesting variation to which the hypnotically induced dream may be put is the indirect reproduction of past memories which are too deeply repressed to be otherwise obtained by direct questioning in the hypnotic state.

Therapeutically, the problem of the uncommunicative patient is often one of great difficulty and may provide insuperable resistances to psychoanalysis. In selected cases, preliminary hypnosis or narcoanalysis, or use of such treatment during certain phases of psychoanalysis, may be expedient in curtailing the duration or even permitting the continuance of the treatment. It may be feasible, where the psychoanalyst does not wish to arouse conflict by his own direct intervention, to transfer his case temporarily to a collaborating psychiatrist.

Summary and Conclusion

A twenty-one-year-old soldier with hysterical dyskinesia was treated with the aid of hypnosis. Dreams induced by hypnotic suggestion proved of considerable value in establishing contact with a passive individual and also revealed aspects of dream psychology which are of theoretical and practical value in dealing with the unconscious mind.

Chapter 49

THE ROLE OF A DREAM IN TREATMENT WITH HYPNOSIS

Jerome M. Schneck

The author recently had occasion to treat a patient who was troubled by a repetitious head movement of acute onset and several days duration. Hypnotherapy was employed for relief of this disability. The second hypnotic trance involved the recall of a dream entailing the apparent source of conflict and the main purpose of this paper is to present the data regarding this aspect of the case.

The patient was a twenty-two-year-old soldier who had been in the Army a few years. He had never been in combat. On awakening from sleep one morning he was troubled with a severe, repetitious, horizontal jerking of his head, occurring every few seconds. Evidently no time interval had elapsed between his emergence from sleep and the onset of the head shaking. This motor activity continued virtually unabated for a period of ten days, varying in severity from hour to hour but persisting to some degree nevertheless. Conscious attention on his part to the phenomenon might lessen its severity but the tic returned in force as his thoughts wandered elsewhere.

The patient naturally regarded the situation as acutely disturbing and obviously it was one which demanded as rapid treatment as possible. This was especially necessary for the author in view of the working conditions at this military installation as would be evident to persons familiar with the existing physical setup. (Additional details about the latter have been presented in a paper as yet unpublished.)

This paper was first published in the *Psychoanalytic Review* (1947), 34:485–491.

After a history was obtained and various aspects of the problem and the patient's personality evaluated, hypnotherapy aimed at suppression of the symptom without employing an uncovering technique was decided upon. This method was selected because it was felt at the time that therapy of greater depth could not be planned under the circumstances. The element of time was the main factor involved in this decision.

The patient was placed in a hypnotic trance utilizing visual fixation with suggestions of relaxation and sleep. The trance was moderately deep. Awareness on the part of the patient of disturbing external auditory stimuli was eliminated and hand levitation effected and demonstrated by the patient in the usual manner observed during a hypnotic trance. The patient was offered the opportunity of demonstrating his ability to relax sufficiently in order to produce cessation of the motor phenomenon and encouraged in the belief that this result could well be maintained following his awakening from the trance. His cooperation while in the hypnotic state was apparently complete and when he was awakened from his sleep the tic was no longer evident.

As requested, the patient returned in several days at which time it was learned that some residual motor activity persisted but what remained was insignificant in comparison with the original disability. Another appointment was arranged and the patient appeared again about two-and-a-half weeks after his first visit. Further details elicited were as follows. For all practical purposes the tic had disappeared except on certain occasions. The latter consisted of a few moments at night while he was in bed, just before he would fall asleep, and during walks to the mailroom on the Post. Reasons for the appearance of the symptom at such times were to be explained at the conclusion of this interview following the elicitation of additional information. The patient volunteered further that despite the appearance of the head shaking under these circumstances, the degree to which his head shook was minimal in comparison with its initial severity.

Several reasons prompted reinstitution of a second hypnotic trance. The physician–patient relationship was good and the patient's cooperation apparently sincere. His conscious interest in becoming symptom free was evident. A review of the circumstances surrounding the onset of the symptom warranted the conjecture that attention could be centered specifically on the events of one night in the patient's past, as will be explained. And last but not of least importance was the availability of time for an adequate interview in which an attempt might be made to accomplish the purpose.

In view of the fact that the patient had no symptoms on going to sleep one night but found himself with the disability immediately on awakening the following morning, it was felt that something must have disrupted his psychic equilibrium during the night. Regarding the symptom as essentially psychogenic rather than physiogenic in origin, a dream might conceivably have played an important role. A hypnotic trance was therefore induced to investigate this fact since recall of the dream was not possible at the time during the normal waking state.

The patient went into a trance more rapidly on the second than on the first occasion and without the use of visual fixation. He was returned in the trance state to the aforementioned night with the suggestion to the effect that he was once again asleep just as he had been in the original situation. He proceeded to redream the dream he had had at that time. The dream was long and involved and will not be related in its entirety since much of the material contained therein cannot be used to develop the interesting feature which this paper intends to stress. Suffice it to say that the night's dreaming seemed to consist of a series of scenes, some of which were not apparently related to one another in manifest content. The form of the manifest content revealed the usual results of the dream work utilizing the various functions in the construction of the manifest dream content from latent thoughts.

In part of the dream the patient visualized himself in the presence of his baby daughter who was sitting in a chair and whom he as well as others was attempting to spoon feed. Many hands were outstretched toward the child who proceeded to accept the spoons' contents from all of the outstretched hands except his own. This disturbed the patient a great deal.

The last part of the dream reverted in its manifest content to the baby once again. A scene was depicted wherein the child was surrounded by her mother's relatives and the patient remained an onlooker. The child did not heed him and he felt tempted to take her away from his in-laws. He did not, however, take steps in this direction but turned away from the scene with a feeling of depression and frustration.

After these dream events had been narrated there was a long pause and when the patient was asked what was happening he said he was awakening. Then, still in a trance, he revealed that he had awakened but on inquiry he stated that having awakened his head shaking was noted. Conjecturing that perhaps some dream material or other events of the night had not been revealed the patient was, in the hypnotic state, returned once again to a condition of sleep and asked to relate any further material which might come to mind. He proceeded then to reveal further dream thoughts of which only the last portion again will be mentioned. This consisted once more in its manifest content of an event involving his baby daughter. It was a repetition of the previous scene entailing spoon feeding of his little girl. The baby was sitting in her high-chair and many arms were outstretched toward her and holding spoons containing a delicacy. On this occasion the child, instead of ignoring her father, accepted what he offered. The delight of the patient was evident in his trance. He then identified the other persons in the dream as various in-laws whom he specifically named. Once more the patient related that he was awakening from his sleep and when this was accomplished the patient, still in the hypnotic trance, revealed that his head was not shaking. He was asked whether he had dreamed anything further and responded in the negative. Then he was questioned as to whether this dream was exactly the same as that which he had dreamed several weeks previously just before his symptom appeared. To this he replied that the dream which he had dreamed several weeks previously had ended with the scene wherein he was ignored by his child in favor of in-laws following which he turned to leave the scene with a feeling of depression and frustration. At this point he had awakened and found his head to be shaking. When, however (in his trance), he was asked to continue relating what came to mind, he proceeded to dream anew events which were being dreamed for the first time (while in the hypnotic trance). Interestingly enough he started to relate events of this hypnotically initiated dream from the point where his dream of a few weeks previously had terminated and he carried it through to the description of a similar but previously unsatisfying dream event. Whereas in his former normal sleeping state his dream had terminated unsatisfactorily as far as he was concerned, he was able in the hypnotic state to reorganize the conflict material and terminate his dream to his own satisfaction. As he revealed while under hypnosis, it was only after the latter was accomplished that he was able to awaken symptom free.

The manifest dream content pertaining to the stress situation involving his daughter and his in-laws was substantiated in fact in real life. This conflict was causing him a great deal of distress and often he did his best to suppress thoughts about it, feeling that he was not in a position at the time to deal adequately with the problem. This tendency on his part to suppress conflict material was resorted to frequently as he later revealed. Although the dream work may have functioned adequately for other portions of the dream, the psychic conflict engendered by this troublesome situation had evidently not been dealt with adequately. Despite various distortions to manifest dream content dealing with material at the point of initial awakening had depicted a conflict situation in its true light and consciously unacceptable to the patient.

The question of wish fulfillment arises then in relation to this dream. Brill (1944) has written in a discussion of traumatic neuroses:

> Freud admits here, for the first time, an exception to the rule that a dream represents the realization of a wish, but adds that neither "anxiety" nor "punishment dreams" form this exception. The latter merely presents the appropriate punishment in place of the forbidden wish realization, and thus represents the wish fulfillment of the sense of guilt, which is a reaction to the rejected impulse. But the dreams

of traumatic neurotics, as well as the dreams that reproduce psychic traumas, can no longer be brought under the
category of wish-fulfillment [p. 221].

This patient was not suffering from a "traumatic neurosis"
and so these remarks should not apply to him. One may question also whether this dream could serve as a "punishment
dream" in view of the fact that it was followed immediately by
overt and visible manifestations of psychic conflict during the
waking state. The dream obviously could not have served adequately as punishment but had rather to be followed by a neurotic symptom possibly serving this purpose and manifest in
the waking state. Since this discussion does not purport to deal
with a presentation of the patient's history and personality and
with complete details of the dream events, elaboration of these
points cannot serve a really useful purpose. Nevertheless one
further possibility may be mentioned regarding the problem of
wish fulfillment. One wonders whether it is possible that some
external stimulus or stimuli unknown to the author or to the
patient could have arisen to terminate the patient's sleep at a
most unfavorable point in his dream which may possibly have
continued otherwise to a satisfactory conclusion had it not been
forcibly interrupted.

The relation of the symptom to the dream and its conflict
material was explained by the patient when in the hypnotic
trance. He was specifically asked at the termination of the second (favorably concluded) dream, what the head shaking
meant. To this he responded to his own satisfaction that he was
trying to shake this trouble out of his head. The actual head
shaking, it will be recalled, followed his turning away, in his
dream, from the situation wherein he was ignored by his
daughter in favor of his in-laws, conflict with his in-laws about
the daughter actually existing in real life. When awakening
from the first dream but still in the trance his head was said to
be shaking, but on awakening from the second and satisfactorily
concluded dream ending once again with the same conflict situation now adequately resolved, his head no longer shook. Regardless of the apparent superficiality of this interpretation,
and despite the fact that one may believe this may not be the

only interpretation, the fact remains that following this interview the patient became symptom free. Several weeks later he was heard from again and was at the time quite well. He has continued well to the time of writing.

Reverting to the patient's statement to the effect that his symptom had, following the first hypnotic session, reappeared in mild form at bedtime and when visiting the mailroom, it was learned that just at these times the difficult situation involving his relationship with his daughter and in-laws came to mind. This was always distressing to him. He would think about it shortly before going to sleep and it would disturb him. His head would begin to shake. On visiting the mailroom he would be concerned mainly about receiving a letter from his wife in which she would invariably relate details about the child's activities and welfare and information about the situation existing at home where she lived with her own family. Realization of this relationship between symptom and thought content enhanced the patient's understanding of his problem.

Several psychoanalytic concepts come to mind in reviewing these events, among them the idea of the dream being "the first link in a chain of abnormal psychic structures" comprising among others, hysterical symptoms. Pertinent also is Freud's statement to the effect that: "The hysteric repeats in his attacks and fixates through his symptoms occurrences which have taken place only in his fantasy, though in the last analysis they go back to real events or have been built up from them" (Freud, 1916–1917, p. 284; 1933b).

Returning once again to the dream material of this patient, the data pertinent only to the main purpose of this presentation have been presented. The reminder of the dream events may or may not have been related to the source of conflict. The fact remains that both the original dream and the dream spontaneously evolved by the patient in the hypnotic state terminated in scenes involving his daughter and in-laws, the source of conflict in real life. Should this problem have entered into the remaining dream thoughts although in a more distorted form, it still ought not to be surprising in view of the fact that a latent thought may enter into several manifest elements (Freud, 1900;

Schneck, 1947). The problem of specificity of interpretation has been discussed adequately elsewhere.

The purpose of this paper has been to describe the role of a dream in treatment with hypnosis and not the ultimate results of treatment. The relief of a symptom was effected and the question of "cure" is not raised because no effort was made during therapy to reintegrate totally the personality of this patient. From the facts learned about him it would seem that he would be quite capable of developing similar symptoms in the future. Relief of this symptom may possibly have produced more concrete and lasting results than the immediate simple situation might seem to warrant because, for the first time apparently, this patient was able to observe the peculiar nature of his psychological functioning. This in itself might possibly serve to induce a reorganization and reorientation within the patient's mental life, thus affecting subsequent psychological functioning. Obviously at the present time there is no way of determining the extent to which this reorganization might occur, if it occurs at all. It is very doubtful that the patient would again develop the same symptom as a manifestation of failure in resolving satisfactorily the same problem. From what is known about his personality he might well be expected to develop similar symptoms in relation to other sources of conflict. This has actually occurred in the past although the symptoms subsided spontaneously, but the resemblance in mode of behavior was well recognized by the patient during the discussion following hypnosis (there was recall of events of both hypnotic trances as suggested during the course of the interviews except for posthypnotic suggestions which were always acted upon) and his recall of these past events was spontaneous. Should his anxieties ever be channeled off again into somatic spheres markedly similar to the one just experienced, it would serve ideally to illustrate the naiveté, in choice of symptoms, often ascribed to hysterical patients.

Chapter 50

AN EPISODE OF SLEEPWALKING

Don D. Jackson

There does not appear to be a voluminous literature on somnambulism. Except for a monograph (Sadger, 1920), there are
generally scattered comments on the topic usually included in
discussions of hysterical phenomena. Ferenczi (1913, 1916), for
example, suggests that there are similarities between somnambulism and posthypnotic commands. He uses as an example a
patient whose father used to awaken him with a stern command
of "Get up." Later when he was employed as a tailor by a domineering employer he began having somnabulistic attacks where
he would awaken, remove his nightshirt, and begin sewing motions. Ferenczi speaks of the need to comply which is similar to
posthypnotic commands. He does not discuss preoedipal and
oedipal factors. Sadger (1920), who has written the most complete work on the subject, presents several cases of sleepwalking
and moon walking, but the cases were superficially studied and
he does not discuss dynamics. Fenichel (1945) outlines the dynamics of somnambulism in a fairly satisfactory fashion. He
emphasizes that the sleepwalker is running away from the bed
which is felt as a place of temptation or is walking toward a
place of protection. Fenichel believes that the somnambulistic
state is a mixture of the hypnotic spell and the hysterical dream
state. Abraham (1909), in a discussion of the subject included
in a paper on hysterical states, makes the point that anxiety
attacks stand in close genetic relationship to dream states, and
that his patients with dream states and somnambulism had anxiety attacks but not hysterical motor attacks. In general, then,

This paper was first published in the *Journal of the American Psychoanalytic Association*
(1954), 6:503–508.

psychoanalysts agree on the relation of sleepwalking to hysteria and to phenomena such as posthypnotic suggestion. The infantile prototype of the somnambulistic state may be feigning sleep in order to witness the primal scene, and the need to repress the feelings aroused as well as the attempt to stay asleep. In the clinical material presented in psychoanalytic literature, there is a frequent association of somnambulistic spells and enuresis. In addition to the aggressive and sexual aspects of urination, in some cases it may be the fact the child is picked up and taken to the toilet, often while still asleep, that helps condition the link between urination and the desire to be with the mother, beside the obvious fact that both oedipal wishes and excretory stimuli may be disturbers of sleep. There doesn't appear to be any report of the association of sleepwalking with the onset of a psychosis, although Abraham (1909) mentions the occurrence of hystericlike dream states in schizophrenics.[1]

This episode is presented because it seems to have been the first in the patient's life (although he was in his midtwenties) and because it occurred a few days before he became overtly psychotic. I believe it is possible to make several comparisons between the restitutive and defensive nature of this single act of sleepwalking and the subsequent psychosis.

A young man in his midtwenties had experienced a strong alternating dependency toward his mother and older brother. He shared a room with his brother for his first twelve years. Toward his father he was hostile and contemptuous, but fearful. Throughout his college years there was tremendous pressure from his father, an uncle, and his brother, to enter the family business. The patient did not want to do so, not only because he wished to pursue another vocation, but also because he felt remarkably inferior and inadequate in this work, especially as compared to his brother. At the time of the incident of sleepwalking, he had just returned home from college and was determined to make a stand against being forced into the business. Of great importance, too, was the fact that he had just become engaged to a girl of whom the family strongly

---

[1]Karl Menninger, in *The Human Mind* (3rd ed.) makes the statement: "Sleepwalkers do not, so far as I know, ever become schizophrenic . . ." (p. 241).

disapproved. The patient felt frightened, confused, and in need of support. A few days after his arrival home he had the following experience.

> I thought I dreamed that I got out of bed, went into the kitchen and got a glass of water, put it on the buffet in the dining room and then went back to bed. In the morning when I saw the glass of water where I had placed it on the buffet I realized I must have walked in my sleep.

The patient went on to say that subsequently he had queried his mother, but she had told him he never had been known to sleepwalk. Pursuing a hunch, the therapist asked if the dining room had ever been a bedroom. The patient remarked that the house had been remodeled during his childhood, and the dining room had previously been the parents' bedroom. Incidentally, this is partially verified by a dream, during analysis, in which the patient and his fiancée are lying on shelves in the dining room, as if in bunks, and the father is creeping into the room. He does not see them (perhaps representing the patient's feigning sleep as a child); the patient raises a hammer and awakens in an anxious state. For several days following the sleepwalking incident the patient became increasingly disturbed, and his mother suggested he would sleep more restfully with her. The first night this arrangement was carried out, he lay awake terrified, and with thoughts of murder and suicide. The next morning he was openly delusional, made a suicidal attempt, and was hospitalized.

A few months after this incident was reported in treatment, the patient returned home for a visit. His sister-in-law mentioned to him, during one of their conversations, that his mother had often told of her great affection for the patient, especially as contrasted with her relationship to his brother. The mother stated that the patient had always been considerate of her, and as an example pointed out how even as a small child he would bring her a glass of water when she was bed-ridden with one of her headaches. At this point the patient became quite anxious, and suddenly recalled the episode of sleepwalking which he had reported to the therapist some months earlier. He became curious about its meaning, although originally he had no more than mentioned it.

One of the fascinating things about this somnambulistic incident is its apparent uniqueness in this patient's life. In addition, it occurred later in life than in the majority of recorded instances, and appeared as the harbinger of a psychosis. In attempting to understand the appearance of this episode, it is important to understand the patient's family relationships, as well as the concatenation of preceding events. The overprotecting, seductive manner of the mother has been well documented. It is also clear that this patient was forced to develop the magic cloak of helplessness early in life. He managed to remain especially uninformed in business matters. As he grew older, he identified himself with his brother and was protected by him. This allowed greater freedom from his mother and a certain contemptuousness toward her. It is perhaps pertinent that sleepwalking was not known to occur during the many years he shared a room with his brother nor during several years with college roommates. His first weeks in a Naval barracks were punctuated with enuresis, but sleepwalking was not reported. He had never lived alone. Another possibly related phenomenon that occurred off and on during his life was so-called restless legs. These attacks consisted of painful muscular spasms primarily restricted to the quadriceps, and would generally awaken him. An even more striking involvement of the muscles of locomotion occurred when he was twelve or thirteen. His mother and he had gone on a trip, during one night of which they shared a lower berth. He awakened with a stiff, sore back and paralyzed legs. Observation for three days in a university hospital failed to reveal evidence of poliomyelitis, and he underwent an uneventful recovery. One of his most vivid impressions is of being carried on a stretcher and later his father's arriving with great concern. Somewhere around this time he had an outbreak of overt incestuous dreams. Masturbation began about a year later, and was accompanied by fantasies of being the slave of various female classmates and of being beaten by them across the back and legs. Another incident that seems pertinent here also occurred about his thirteenth year. A chum and he were staying at a summer cottage and arranged with two girls from a nearby camp to have a post-midnight rendezvous. He went to bed greatly excited, but when the chum tried to arouse him for their clandestine appointment he refused to awaken. He recalls having severe abdominal cramps the next morning, and his brother coming to get him and carrying him to the car in his arms.

These happenings suggest a conflict in the patient between his desires for his mother and the dangers of her bed. It seems likely, toward his brother so that while his brother (or substitute) was present, the conflict was less apt to become unmanageable. This is not to say that the protective relationship of the brother did not produce its own peculiar difficulties. The nature of the incestuous mother and brother relationships has been seen during treatment. For example, the relationship with his fiancée so duplicated the intense mutual ties of the mother–son integration that the fiancée had a transitory psychosis when he broke off the engagement—more or less on orders from the brother. The going to sleep period was then beset with fantasies of the fiancée having sexual relations with other men while the patient looked on, helpless and enraged. He would then turn on his stomach and imagine being cuddled up alongside a woman's body while he drifted into a troubled sleep.

In regard to the relationship between the somnambulistic attack and the psychosis, several connections appear in addition to the temporal sequence. In childhood, illness proved to be a *carte blanche* to the mother's bed (as well as arousing affection and concern) and a shield from his father's wrath. Since puberty he was subject to hypomanic attacks which customarily began following some small success or minor triumph. The accompanying fantasy would include ideas of being so great that he would be free of the parents, more important than the brother, and at the same time endear himself to the family, win their respect, and secure the girl of his choice. For the duration of the excitement he would also recognize a definite fear. Elements of these wishes and fears are embodied in both the sleepwalking and the psychosis. Just as the sleepwalking represented going to the mother in an acceptable manner (namely, bringing her water), so did the psychosis in part have the function of a grand renouncing of all dangerous wishes. The elements leading to the sleepwalking occurred under the protective covering of sleep, and these same elements underwent further disguise through regression during the psychosis. The oral features and protective sleep of the somnambulism were maintained during the psychosis in the form of great concern about an adequate number of hours of sleep and an obsessional preoccupation with the proper diet as well as the vital importance of not being left alone. At a time during treatment when the patient was successful in his job and was living alone for the first time, he had a dream that illustrates the restitutive feature of the psychosis. In the dream, he was having an argument with his father and was told he had only twelve or thirteen days in which to do something. The patient tried to pacify the father and remarked, "There was no rush." Twelve days corresponds to the length of stay in the hospital for the psychotic episode. At the time of this dream, helplessness was very much used in the analytic relationship, and sleepiness was a prominent resistance.

One of the questions such a case poses is: Why the advent of a motor phenomenon such as sleepwalking rather than night terrors or anxiety dreams? I believe the answer lies in the strength of the mutual dependent tie with the mother,[2] as well as the fact that she encourages overt activity on the part of the child. This feature corresponds to Ferenczi's (1908, 1913) suggestion of the similarity of somnambulism to the posthypnotic command. I have noted in several cases in the literature that the father traveled or worked at night; hence emphasizing to both mother and child the emptiness of her bed. In this patient's situation there was a remarkable emotional distance between the parents, and the mother took her son on long vacation trips. She exploited his dependency to the extent of making a hypochondriac of him, and in his early life would take him to the bathroom and then to her bed when he awakened with a need to urinate. The patient felt that occasionally he feigned illness to be taken to the parents' bedroom. The advent of genital sexuality increased the dangerous aspects of

---

[2]The patient had two dreams during one night. In the first he is in bed with measles and his mother brings him a glass of water. In the second, she is in bed and he brings her a glass of water.

his relationship to his mother and hence increased the need to be free of her and strengthened the tie to his brother. It seems likely that as the psychosis dawned under the impact of freeing himself from the family and aligning himself with another woman, the early feelings toward the mother were revived. During this period he consciously avoided her, but the passivity inherent in the sleep process made the early dependent impulses difficult to control. The "last straw" for his mental economy seemed to be the night that he actually slept in his mother's bed. The horrifying aspects of his dependency broke through in the psychotic form of "kill" or "be killed."

Summary

A young man had an episode of sleepwalking a few days before the onset of an acute schizophrenic episode. The occurrence of these events coincided with his return home when he experienced marked tension in his relationship to his father and brother and marked seductive smothering from his mother. It is postulated that the somnambulistic episode and the psychosis have certain features in common regarding the forbidden impulses and the defenses against them.

Chapter 51

DAY RESIDUE IN DREAM AND MYTH

MARTIN WANGH

Students of mythology have by now accepted the thesis that human emotion is a dynamic factor in the creation of myth. As the philosopher Cassirer (1944) puts it, in a myth "all objects are benignant or malignant, friendly or inimical, familiar or uncanny, alluring and fascinating or repelling and threatening. . . . The real substratum of myth is not a substratum of thought but of feeling" (p. 75).

Curiously enough, this same author (1944) is of the opinion that Freud's contribution to myth formation is "entirely limited to variations and disguises of one and the same psychological theme—sexuality" (pp. 84–85). This, of course, we cannot accept in view of Freud's profound interest in myth, his repeated discussion of it, and his clear-cut statements with respect to its meaning. He believed that much of mythological thinking is a projection of the psyche onto the outside world (1901b). He even indicated a possible approach to the myth maker's mind.[1]

This paper was first published in the *Journal of the American Psychoanalytic Association* (1954), 2:446–452.

[1]I think we could well assume that in the psyche of the anonymous myth maker the same mechanisms function as in the artist. In his *Psychoanalytic Explorations in Art*, Ernst Kris (1952) points out that:

> During psychoanalytic treatment, it seems comparatively easy to establish connections between preconscious elements in the artist's work and those of which he had always been aware. The contribution desired from the storehouse of memories and the sometimes very numerous clues borrowed from one or the other source in the environment and condensed into a single trait appear in analytic material sometimes without particular effort. But only extended analysis leads to repressed psychic material, to motivation from the id—and only this allows full demonstration of the interaction and interconnection of elements derived from the various stages of awareness [p. 24].

714

In his *New Introductory Lectures* (1933a,b) he wrote: "In the manifest content of dreams there frequently occur images and situations which remind of known motifs in fairy tales, sagas, and myths. The interpretation of such dreams, then, throws a light upon the original interests which have created these motifs."

I myself had the opportunity of observing such imagery in the dream of one of my patients. He was a businessman who owned a house at the edge of a suburban community near a wooded area. The dream was reported in a period of particular emotional stress. He was mourning for his father-in-law. Furthermore, as they had been business partners, there was considerable financial upheaval. The dream was as follows:

> I am at home with my family, yet at the same time it is a mountain inn. We are looking out of the window and see a figure arriving, hiding in or going into a stone entrance. Is it a woman in a red coat? Then it is an older man with a child, then it is a group of dwarfs. The innkeepers indicate that one has to watch out for them. They are liable to steal, eat one out of house and home. . . . We are about to go away from the house when the thought of the dwarfs who might eat everything up holds me back. We are sitting now around the table with the thought that we have prevented it. But among us there is a man with a harelip—one of them.

The dream occurred during an afternoon nap, at the end of a hectic week full of business troubles. Beyond that, the house had been in urgent need of repair work, for which the patient had contracted the week before. On awakening, he heard the gnawing and skittering of squirrels in the attic. On falling asleep he had heard them too, and had thought then, "They are going to eat their way to the pantry." Fully awake, he had listened for the noise of the children at play.

His first association, thus, is to the squirrels. To the red coat of the old woman or man, Santa Claus comes to his mind. The mountain inn reminds him of a horrible night he had spent years ago in a dilapidated inn where rats had scurried through his room all night. The harelip is a reminder of his late, favorite older brother, who had this defect. Hares are rodents too, he thinks. The older man, furthermore, is the children's beloved grandfather who just died. His own late father comes to his mind, and then his grandfather, who, he was told as a child, would watch out for him in heaven. Finally he thinks of his grandmother, who died when he was five years old. She had come with an aunt and a cousin from Europe and had moved in with them into their already overcrowded home on the lower East Side. It was hard to feed three more mouths at the time. Hence the words, "They'll eat you out of house and home." Dwarfs immediately and very intensely are connected with stories about dwarfs or brownies or elves, eagerly read in childhood. The week before he had spoken to the builder about the squirrels in the attic, at which time the builder had laughingly reassured him that in the course of his work they would be chased out. The builder had awakened him from his afternoon nap. The cost of the repairs, on top of his business worries, had oppressed him all week.

The outstanding figures in the manifest content of this dream are, no doubt, the dwarfs or their variations—the old woman or old man with the child. His associations to these figures and their activity and dress lead immediately into two main directions: the squirrels, rats, hare on the one hand, and the dead beloved relatives on the other. The intruder quality is common to both. The squirrels intrude from the day residue, that is, from preconscious thinking. From memory and unconscious thinking, the dead and living rivals are the intruders. The older, the contemporary, and the younger generations are all represented in the associative trend. The manifest dream shows a continuous struggle against the disturbers. It tries to change them as representatives of worries and concern into benevolent creatures. The squirrels become dwarfs, brownies, elves—the little men who in myth do your work while you sleep. The scurrying of the squirrels becomes the hammering and toiling of the elves.

I wish to draw attention to his attempt to master anxiety. Our dreamer's anxiety is primarily connected with the arousal of oral conflicts.[2] The financial and personal loss was perceived by him in terms of threat to his food supplies—the dead relatives, he is warned, will eat him out of house and home. Furthermore, at the end of the dream one of them sits down at the dinner table. No doubt the association to the children is also significant; his worry about providing for them adds to his troubles. The hostility thus liberated toward the beloved objects in such oral terms motivates the dreamer's defense. He asserts affectionately their good and protective qualities. Yet the conflict remaining unsolved arouses anxiety which finally leads to awakening. The intruding figures of the dream are the awakeners in the sense in which Lewin (1952) describes them. From the outside the noise of the squirrels and of the playing children tends toward the same effect. Against the disturbance from within and from without, the defense of denial and transformation into the opposite is used. The myth of the little men comes to the dreamer's service. He tries to sleep on with the comforting thought: "You can rest, you don't need to worry, the little people will protect you and work for you." The squirrels furnish the day residue in the dream in a most prominent manner, yet for the sake of dream formation, unconscious material had to join in to supply the necessary cathexis. This material is represented by the dreamer's dead relatives, rivals in many respects, yet also protectors.

I should like to suggest that a process similar to that which produced my patient's dream also took place in the minds of the creators of the myth of the little people. This worldwide myth, most richly developed in the folklore of the northern and middle European countries, is a myth of poor people—no princes or knights here. The day residue in the dream of our patient is furnished by intruding rodents. We postulate that daily experience with similar enemies operated as a factor in the formation of the myth. Doubtless rodents of one sort or another were a source of anxiety to the people. Doubtless the wooden huts of the poor were infested, and the meager stores of food endangered. The myth turns the hated and feared

---

[2]No doubt genital and anal rivalry with the deceased were also present, but the greatest stress at this time of mourning was felt on the oral plane. This may well be characteristic of mourning in general.

creatures into beneficent little beings—just as in our dream—although their mischievous character is never completely lost in the stories.

Could the myth have been created out of this material alone? Hardly. For the process of myth formation itself is unconscious. In my patient's dream the unconscious source is furnished by his ambivalent relationship to his dead relatives. By linking generation to generation, he denies the phenomenon of death.[3] The same unconscious source, ambivalent relationship to dead relatives, furnishes the power for the creation and persistence of the myth throughout the centuries. As Cassirer (1944) says, "The conception that man is mortal by his nature and essence seems to be entirely alien to the mythical and primitive religious thought. . . . In a certain sense, the whole of mythical thought may be interpreted as a constant and obstinate negation of the phenomenon of death. In Chinese religion, ancestor worship signifies that the ties with the dead are by no means broken and that the dead continue to exercise their authority and protection."

Anthropology tells us that dwarfs, gnomes, and similar little people are chthonic beings, that is, coming from the underworld. The ancestral quality of these little people is equally recognized by all authorities.[4] But the younger generation also, no doubt, entered into the formation of the myth; for gnomes are *little* people. In hungry times the ambivalent feeling toward children must have evoked intense oral conflict, and the myth was an attempt to solve the conflict by turning the children into playful and helpful creatures.

In myths of the little people, the oral aspect is stressed over and over again.[5] Most often elves, gnomes, and the rest have

---

[3]I should like to suggest that such representation of the generations in a dream has the function of denying death; in other words, of allaying the fear of dying.

[4]The Russian *Domovoi*, perhaps, most clearly shows the connection. He is a house spirit, ancestor—usually the founder of the family—who watches over and protects the inhabitants, taking care that all is in order. He lies behind the stove and likes the fire. He is shaggy and has a long beard. His correct name is never used. He is called *He* or *Himself* or *Grandfather (Ded)*. Some of the supper is left out for the *domovoi*, who bustles about in the dark, always busy, guarding against the intrusion of strange, hostile spirits (Leach, 1949).

[5]Phallic elements, however, are not entirely missing: the little man representing the phallus; his noise hinting at the primal scene. Anal material is present, too: the little people often are miners.

to be appeased with food. Oftentimes they steal it,[6] Occasionally they bring it.[7]

Etymological investigation gives us further evidence for our hypothesis regarding the formation of the myth of the little people. One German word for elf is *Kobold*, a species of mischievous and noisy house spirit. He is an ugly dwarf, red from the fire in the hearth.[8] The word *Kobold* is related to the Anglo-Saxon *cofgodas*, meaning household god. Here we see the link to the unconscious source; for household gods have always been associated with ancestor worship.

Brownies in the Scotch saga are goblins who do the housework while the houseowners are asleep. They are usually dwarflike with short brown locks, a brown coat, and a brown hood. They participate in a friendly manner in the fate of the houses in which they live. The Dark Elf of the Edda is described as a wee brown man, a benevolent spirit or goblin of shaggy appearance, supposed to haunt old houses, especially farmhouses in Scotland, and to perform useful household work while the family sleeps. The shagginess of the Dark Elf, like the short brown locks of the brownies, is clearly reminiscent of the furred rodents (Brill, 1944).

To sum up: Our hypothesis is that as the day residue participates in the formation of the dream, so do anxiety-arousing external phenomena enter into myth formation. In themselves these are not effective. They need unconscious cathexis for the production of myth. In the myths of the little people the fear of rodents menacing stores of food furnished the preconscious

---

[6]Dr. Charles Brenner called my attention to the following passage in Heine's "Harzreise," 1. Bergidylle III:

Und das liebe Mädchen spricht:
"Kleines Völkchen, Wichtelmännchen,
Stehlen unser Brod und Speck,
Abends liegt es noch im Kasten,
Und des Morgens ist es weg,
"Kleines Völkchen, unsre Sahne
Nascht es von der Milch und lässt
Unbedeckt die Schüssel stehen,
Und die Katze säuft den Rest."

[7]The Finnish spirit, *Para*, brings money, rye and other goods to his owner, but usually mild cream and butter. In such cases he takes the shape of a cat, a fine example of denial and turning into its opposite (Leach, 1949).

[8]In a personal communication, Dr. Ernst Kris suggested to me that *Kobold* is the representative of the flame itself.

stimulus, while the unconscious material came from the ambivalent relationship toward ancestors and children. The conflict is primarily an oral one. The myth attempts to allay anxiety by denial and transformation, turning the malevolent into the beneficent.

AFTERWORD

In looking back on this selection of the most significant and current psychoanalytic papers on dreams written since World War II, we are able to note the following trends and threads implied by these articles.

First we note that most of the significant advances in the period covered by these articles were accomplished in the '40s, '50s and '60s with the work of Lewin (on the dream screen and the marked similarity of dream-formation with the analytic-formation), and Kanzer's work on the communicative function of the dream. Since that time many interesting clinical articles were published on such topics as: typical and traumatic dreams (e.g., dreams during surgical procedures), symbolization in dreams (e.g., the convertible as a symbol in dreams) and resistance and transference in dreams (e.g., the written dream and the analyst's dream about the patient). However, other than Lewin's and Kanzer's work, no new theoretical advances were made.

Second, the trend in many recent clinical articles, particularly in the '70s and '80s, has been away from searching for the dream's wishful meaning in the latent dream content, but more on making inferences about the patient's psychodynamics directly from the manifest content. (The article "The Manifest Dream in Psychoanalysis: Clarification" by Pulver (1987) seems to adumbrate this trend quite clearly.) In short, a goodly number of analytic papers, in their clinical vignettes, seem to emphasize the interpreting of the dream and its understanding without the patient's associations. It has also been suggested that the interpretation of the dream-without-associations is influenced by the literary criticism doctrine of deconstruction (Luria, 1989). A doctrine which implies that a "text" has been put together like a building or a piece of machinery; and, therefore, it is not subject to a creative analysis and interpretation in the psychoanalytic sense. Self-state dreams, based on self theory, would appear to fit into this category.

A third trend, having its basis in the *Dream Readers'* section on "Dreams and Related States," emanates from Kanzer's hypnosis-and-dream papers of the early post World War II years (e.g., "The Therapeutic Use of Dreams Induced by Hypnotic Suggestion" and "The Metapsychology of the Hypnotic Dream"). From this beginning, a small group of analysts began to use hypnotic techniques to confront certain massive resistance in the psychoanalytic process. One recent paper (Calogeras, 1990) has attempted to develop a workable procedure of hypnotically recovering dreams in a so-called "dreamless" analysis without compromising the basic analytic process.

The fourth trend, introduced by two articles in the present collection (Pollock's and Muslin's "Dreams during Surgical Procedures," and Tarachow's "The Analysis of the Dream Occurring during a Migraine Attack"), suggest the proposition of considering dreams as an "additional" royal road to understanding the somatic illness and problems of the individual. Eissler (1955, pp. 132–138), in a perceptive analysis of a patient's dream, demonstrated how the patient revealed to him that he was having a reoccurrence of a malignancy, necessitating an immediate resumption of his chemotherapy, and other treatment. More recently, Alston (1989) has reported a series of dreams of an AIDS patient in which she was able to show that the course of the patient's physical condition (i.e., his AIDS condition) was closely coordinated with his dream life. In an article published posthumously, Sterba (1990, p. 108) speaks directly to this point when he reports a dream of *a red ribbon stretched out from my abdomen at the level of the gall-bladder*. He notes: "I woke up the next morning with a fever, high white cell count, and 'pleurisy.' But my chest X-ray was normal. It occurred to me that the pain in my back might be from my gallbladder. I told my physician, who made the diagnosis of acute cholecystitis and a surgeon performed an emergency operation and removed my neurotic gall-bladder—in pieces. . . . I was pleased but also puzzled by the unusual transparency of the dream which had allowed me to anticipate my doctors in suspecting cholecystitis."

Finally, there is a significant general trend having to do with a return to studying in detail Freud's *The Interpretation of Dreams* by analysts and analytic candidates. This trend seems to be vitalized to a great extent by recent interest in so-called Freud-Studies, exemplified in this volume by Grigg's article, "All Roads Lead to Rome: the Role of the Nursemaid in Freud's Dreams." An important off-shoot of this is how the analytic candidates' transference to Freud manifests itself in an examination of his dreams in the particular sense, and a renewal of interest in dream analysis and interpretation in the general sense.

In direct line with this we wish to report *ein kleines Experiment* in which the clinical relevance of the 50 or so articles in the *Dream Reader* were evaluated. The subjects (mainly analytic candidates; and psychology and medical students) were instructed, as part of their end-of-course assessment, to evaluate the following specimen dream in terms of the dream articles assigned for reading during their dream courses. A distillate of their answers will be presented after the report of the dream.

The patient, a 35-year-old professional man, married with two children (a boy 3½ and a girl 6), reported the following dream in the second year of his analysis.

I was entering my parents' bedroom and found them lying naked on the bed. I was a child—perhaps 5, 6, or 7. There was a mouse running around and it ran out of their room and hid under the desk in the adjoining room. Then the scene suddenly changes, and I get the feeling that my parents were me and my wife, and we were now lying on the bed! Then my son and I caught the mouse and he said, "Don't hurt it." We took the mouse into the bathroom to wash it off—because it was brown and dirty—and we wrapped it between two towels. (The patient characterizes the dream as a "generational dream" and says that he felt that somebody was looking at him during the second part. As part of the day residue, he noted that his children had been coming into the parental bed for "cuddling" during the night, and he and his wife had become "concerned" about this.)

The subjects' responses—in which there were almost 90 to 95 percent agreement—fell into six categories.

Primal Scene Content. First, the subjects without exception focused on the dream's primal scene content and turned (in their evaluation) to Izner's article "On the Appearance of Primal Scene Content in Dreams" (chapter 4) for enlightenment. Next, they felt that articles on the manifest dream content were most helpful—particularly Stewart's paper on the "Comments on the Manifest Content of Certain Types of Unusual Dreams" (1967) and Roth's article, "Manifest Dream Content and Acting-out" (1958). As regards the latter, they hypothesized that, since the patient has characterized the dream as "generational," acting-out in the family had undoubtedly occurred via the "cuddling" and was now emerging in the dream. They further inferred that the patient was much concerned with the oedipal struggle in his own analysis at this point and that much of it was now coming out in this specimen dream.

Communicative and Intrapsychic Functions. Second, the subjects found the group of articles on the dream's communicative and intrapsychic functions (included in Section IV) as being most relevant in understanding the dream. Specifically, they found that Kanzer's formulations on the dream's communicative function to be most pertinent, and they presented a number of provocative hypotheses vis-à-vis the dream's main communication or message to the analyst. In addition, they noted that Bergmann's ideas (1966) on the cultural-generational aspect of the communicative function of the dream to be significant—especially regarding intrafamily dream communication; and they also determined that Calogeras' "Husband and Wife Exchange of Dreams" (1977) as being quite apropos since they surmised that the patient "must have told the dream to his wife." (An assumption which the patient later confirmed; see also chapter 21.)

Symbolization. Third, the significance of the dream's symbolization was not surprising. Victor Calef's paper, "Color in Dreams" (chapter 29), was cited frequently in understanding the significance of the mouse's color as being "brown and dirty"; and the dream's time-change was found to be very relevant to the articles by Gross (chapter 30) and Hartocollis (chapter 31) on how time is dynamically depicted in dreams. Finally, the subjects' answers pertaining to the son's dream dialogue, "Don't hurt it," was referred to Isakower's article on "Spoken Words in Dreams" (1954); this article spurred much didactic speculation regarding the "true" meaning of spoken words in dreams.

Dream Psychology and the Analytic Situation. Fourth, the subjects found that Lewin's article, "Dream Psychology and the Analytic Situation" (chapter 7), had great bearing on their overall understanding of the dream's construction. They advanced a number of interesting (and often complicated) oedipal reconstructions which they postulated was being carried out simultaneously in both the specimen dream's dream-work formation and the patient's analysis-formation via the transference neurosis.

Transference and Countertransference. Many of the subjects held that the dream was "replete with transference and countertransference nuances" and that most of the articles on this topic (assigned during the course of seminar's duration) were applicable (see Section VII). They concluded that the article by Keith, "Some Aspects of Transference in Dream Research" (1962), and Ross and Kapp's "A Technique for Self-Analysis of Countertransference" (1962) provided most insight in terms of understanding the dream. In addition, they found that Yazamajian's paper, "First Dreams Directly Representing the Analyst" (1964), helped them to understand the patient's statement that, "Somebody was looking at him" during the dream's second part. They inferred that his "somebody" was the analyst-in-the-night and suggested that his inclusion in the dream was the result of his giving the patient some hidden gratification (i.e., a countertransference acting out).

Specific Articles. Finally, approximating half of the subjects gave some attention to specific articles which they found had assisted them in understanding the patient's dream. Among those papers most frequently mentioned were: Masud Khan's good-dream concept (1962; see chapter 12); that is, the subjects felt that the specimen dream fitted the criteria of the good-dream and hence represented a significant therapeutic step forward for the patient; Ralph Greenson's article, "The Exceptional Position of the Dream in Psychoanalysis" (chapter 8); that is, a majority of the subjects felt that the dream demonstrated the unique role which the dream plays in the patient's analysis because of the extraordinary richness of the dream content leading to the patient's unconscious; and Kleeman's article, "Dreaming for a Dream Course" (chapter 9). Many of the subjects felt that the didactic nature of this article enhanced their understanding of their own dream course or seminar.* In short, about twenty-five articles included in the *Dream Reader* were cited by the subjects as being germane to understanding the specimen dream.

The Editors

*The second part of the experiment (the results of which are not included in this report) asked the subjects: (1) to identify temporarily with the patient and give a number of associations to the dream; (2) to describe the dream's principal condensations, displacements, secondary elaborations and symbolizations derived from their associations; and (3) to make several statements about the dream's latent meaning vis-à-vis the patient.

REFERENCES

Abraham, K. (1909), Dreams and myths. In: *Clinical Papers and Essays on Psycho-Analysis*. London: Hogarth Press, 1955, pp. 153–209.

———— (1913a), Restrictions and transformations of scoptophilia in psychoneurotics; with remarks on analogous phenomena in folk-psychology. In: *Selected Papers of Karl Abraham*, with an introductory memoir by E. Jones. London: Hogarth Press, 1949, pp. 169–234.

———— (1913b), Shall we have the patients write down their dreams? In: *The Psycho-Analytic Reader*, ed. R. Fliess. London: Hogarth Press, 1950, pp. 291–293.

———— (1922), The rescue and murder of the father in neurotic phantasy-formation. In: *Clinical Papers and Essays on Psycho-Analysis*. London: Hogarth Press, 1955, pp. 68–75.

Alexander, F. (1948), *Fundamentals of Psychoanalysis*. New York: W. W. Norton.

———— French, T. M. (1946), *Psychoanalytic Therapy: Principles and Application*. New York: Ronald Press, pp. 34–37.

———— Wilson, G. W. (1935), Quantitative dream studies. *Psychoanal. Quart.*, 4:371–407.

Alston, T. M. (1989), The dreams of an AIDS patient: Predicting the course of an illness. Unpublished paper.

———— Calogeras, R. C., & Deserno, H. (unpublished), Bibliography of psychoanalytic dream articles 1945–1988. University of Mainz.

Altman, L. L. (1969), *The Dream in Psychoanalysis*. New York: International Universities Press.

Arlow, J. A., & Brenner, C. (1964), *Psychoanalytic Concepts and the Structural Theory*. New York: International Universities Press.

Aserinsky, E., & Kleitman, N. (1955), Two types of ocular motility occurring in sleep. *J. Appl. Physiol.*, 8:1–10.

Azorin, L. A. (1957), The analyst's personal equation. *Amer. J. Psychoanal.*, 17:34–38.

Babcock, C. G. (1966), Panel report: The manifest content of the dream. *J. Amer. Psychoanal. Assn.*, 14:154–171.

Baldridge, B. J., Hitman, R. M., & Kramer, M. (1963), A simplified method for detecting eye movements during dreaming. *Psychosom. Med.*, 28:78–82.

Balint, M. (1957), *The Doctor, His Patient, and the Illness.* New York: International Universities Press, 1964.

―――― (1968), *The Basic Fault: Therapeutic Aspects of Regression.* London: Tavistock.

Barchilon, J. (1958), On countertransferences "cures." *J. Amer. Psychoanal. Assn.,* 6:222–236.

Barrett, W. (1937), A childhood anxiety. *Psychoanal. Quart.,* 6:530–535.

―――― (1939), Penis envy and urinary control; pregnancy fantasies and constipation; episodes in the life of a little girl. *Psychoanal. Quart.,* 8:211–218.

Baudry, F. (1974), Remarks on spoken words in the dream. *Psychoanal. Quart.,* 43:581–605.

Becker, T. E. (1978), Dream analysis in child analysis. In: *Child Analysis and Therapy,* ed. J. Glenn. New York: Jason Aronson, pp. 355–374.

Benedek, T. (1938), Adaptation to reality in early infancy. *Psychoanal. Quart.,* 7:200–215.

―――― (1953), Dynamics of the countertransference. *Bull. Menninger Clin.,* 17:201–208.

―――― (1954), Countertransference in the training analyst. *Bull. Menninger Clin.,* 18:12–16.

Benjamin, J. D. (1959), Prediction and psychopathological theory. In: *Dynamic Psychotherapy in Childhood,* ed. L. Jessner & E. Pavenstedt. New York: Grune & Stratton, pp. 2–77.

Beres, D. (1956), Ego deviation and the concept of schizophrenia. *The Psychoanalytic Study of the Child,* 11:164–235. New York: International Universities Press.

―――― (1960), The psychoanalytic psychology of imagination. *J. Amer. Psychoanal. Assn.,* 8:252–269.

―――― Arlow, J. A. (1974), Fantasy and identification in empathy. *Psychoanal. Quart.,* 43:26–50.

Berg, C. (1936), The unconscious significance of hair. *Internat. J. Psycho-Anal.,* 17:73–88.

Berge, C. (1949), The symbolism of colors. *Psyché. Rev. Internat. des Sci. de l'Homme et de Psychoanal.,* 4:529–534, 658–662.

Bergmann, M. S. (1966), The intrapsychic and communicative aspects of the dream. *Internat. J. Psycho-Anal.,* 47:356–363.

Bernstein, I., & Fine, B. (1969), The Manifest Content of the Dream. *Monograph Kris Study Group New York Psychoanalytic Institute,* Vol. 3. New York: International Universities Press, pp. 58–113.

Bieber, I., & Tarachow, S. (1941), Autonomic symptoms in psychoneurotics. *Psychosom. Med.,* 3:253–262.

Blitzsten, L. N., Eissler, R. S., & Eissler, K. R. (1950), Emergence of hidden ego tendencies during dream analysis. *Internat. J. Psycho-Anal.*, 31:12–17.

Blum, E. (1926), The psychology of study and examination. *Internat. J. Psycho-Anal.*, 7:457–469.

Blum, H. (1976), The changing use of dreams in psychoanalytic practice: Dreams and free association. *Internat. J. Psycho-Anal.*, 57:315–323.

Bonaparte, M. (1940), Time and the unconscious. *Internat. J. Psycho-Anal.*, 21:427–468.

———— (1947), *Myths of War*. London: Imago Publishing.

Bornstein, B. (1949), The analysis of a phobic child: Some problems of theory and technique in child analysis. In: *The Psychoanalytic Study of the Child*, 3–4:181–226. New York: International Universities Press.

———— (1951), On latency. *The Psychoanalytic Study of the Child*, 6:279–285. New York: International Universities Press.

Brenman, M. (1949), Dreams and hypnosis. *Psychoanal. Quart.*, 18:455–465.

———— Gill, M., & Hacker, F. J. (1947), Alteration in the state of the ego in hypnosis. *Bull. Menninger Clin.*, 11:60–66.

Brenner, C. (1976), *Psychoanalytic Technique and Psychic Conflict*. New York: International Universities Press.

Breuer, J., & Freud, S. (1895), Studies on Hysteria. *Standard Edition*, 2. London: Hogarth Press, 1955.

Brill, A. A. (1944), *Freud's Contribution to Psychiatry*. New York: W. W. Norton.

Bulletin of the Menninger Clinic (1943), Issues on hypnosis, 7/5 & 6.

Calogeras, R. C. (1977), Husband and wife exchange of dreams. *Internat. Rev. Psychoanal.*, 4:71–82.

———— (1985), Early object-relations conflicts in marital interaction. *Psychoanal. Rev.*, 72:31–53.

Carlson, D. A. (1977), Dream mirrors. *Psychoanal. Quart.*, 46:38–70.

Cassirer, E. (1944), *An Essay on Man*. New Haven: Yale University Press.

Cavenar, J. O., & Nash, S. L. (1976), The dream as a signal for termination. *J. Amer. Psychoanal. Assn.*, 24:425–436.

Chasseguet-Smirgel, J. (1976), Some thoughts on the ego ideal. A contribution to the study of the "illness of ideality." *Psychoanal. Quart.*, 45:345–373.

Chicago Psychoanalytic Literature Index 1920–1970. Chicago: Chicago Institute for Psychoanalysis.

Cobbe, F. P. (1872), *Darwinism in Morals, and Other Essays*. London: Williams & Norgate.

Cohen, M. B. (1952), Countertransference and anxiety. *Psychiatry*, 15:231–243.

Colby, K. M. (1958), *A Skeptical Psychoanalyst*. New York: Ronald Press, pp. 99–100.

Colgeras, R. C. (1990), Hypnotically recalling dreams during analysis. Unpublished paper.

Curtis, H. C., & Sachs, D. M. (1976), Dialogue: "The changing use of dreams in psychoanalytic practice." *Internat. J. Psycho-Anal.*, 57:343–354.

Dement, W. C. (1960), The effect of dream deprivation. *Science*, 131:1705–1707.

——— Kleitman, N. (1957a), Cyclic variation in E.E.G. during sleep and their relation to eye movements, body motility, and dreaming. *Electroenceph. Clin. Neurophysiol.*, 9:673–690.

——— ——— (1957b), The relation of eye movements during sleep to dream activity: An objective method for the study of dreaming. *J. Exper. Psychol.*, 53:339–346.

——— Wolpert, E. A. (1958), The relation of eye movements, body motility, and external stimuli to dream content. *J. Exper. Psychol.*, 55:543–553.

Deutsch, F. (1953), Instinctual drives and intersensory perceptions during the analytic procedure. In: *Drives, Affects, Behavior*, ed. R. M. Loewenstein. New York: International Universities Press, pp. 216–228.

Deutsch, H. (1942), Some psychoanalytic observations in surgery. *Psychosom. Med.*, 4:105–115.

Dewald, P. (1972), The clinical assessment of structural change. *J. Amer. Psychoanal. Assn.*, 20:302–324.

Dowling, S. (1982), Dreams and dreaming in relation to trauma in childhood. *Internat. J. Psycho-Anal.*, 63:157–166.

Eder, M. D. (1930), Dreams as resistance. *Internat. J. Psycho-Anal.*, 11: 40–47.

Eidelberg, L. (1959), The concept of narcissistic mortification. *Internat. J. Psycho-Anal.*, 40:163–168.

Eisler, E. R. (1937), Regression in a case of multiple phobia. *Psychoanal. Quart.*, 6:86–95.

Eisnitz, A. J. (1961), Mirror dreams. *J. Amer. Psychoanal. Assn.*, 9:461–479.

Eissler, K. R. (1943), Some psychiatric aspects of anorexia nervosa. *Psychoanal. Rev.*, 30:121–145.

—— (1950), The Chicago Institute of Psychoanalysis and the sixth period of the development of psychoanalytic technique. *J. Genet. Psychol.*, 42:103–157.

—— (1951), Remarks on the psychoanalysis of schizophrenia. *Internat. J. Psycho-Anal.*, 32:139–156.

—— (1955), *The Psychiatrist and the Dying Patient.* New York: International Universities Press.

—— (1962), On the metapsychology of the preconscious. A tentative contribution to psychoanalytic morphology. In: *The Psychoanalytic Study of the Child*, 17:9–41. New York: International Universities Press.

Ekstein, R. (1965), Working through and termination of analysis. *J. Amer. Psychoanal. Assn.*, 13:57–78.

—— (1975), From the language of play to play with language. *Adolesc. Psychiat.*, 4:142–162.

—— (1981), Some thoughts concerning the clinical use of children's dreams. *Bull. Menninger Clin.*, 45:115–124.

—— Wallerstein, J. (1954), Observations on the psychology of borderline and psychotic children. *The Psychoanalytic Study of the Child*, 9:344–369. New York: International Universities Press.

Emch, M. (1955), The social context of supervision. *Internat. J. Psycho-Anal.*, 36:298–306.

Erickson, M. H., & Kubie, L. S. (1940), The translation of the cyptic automatic writing of one hypnotic subject by another in a trance-like dissociated state. *Psychoanal. Quart.*, 9:51–63.

Erikson, E. H. (1950), *Childhood and Society.* New York: W. W. Norton.

—— (1951), Sex differences in the play constructions of preadolescents. *Amer. J. Orthopsychiat.*, 21:667–692.

—— (1954), The dream specimen of psychoanalysis. In: *Psychoanalytic Psychiatry and Psychology*, ed. R. P. Knight. New York: International Universities Press, pp. 131–170.

Esman, A. H. (1962), The dream screen in an adolescent. *Psychoanal. Quart.*, 31:250–251.

Farber, L. H., & Fisher, C. (1943), An experimental approach to dream psychology through the use of hypnosis. *Psychoanal. Quart.*, 12:202–216.

Farrow, E. P. (1945), *Psychoanalyze Yourself.* New York: International Universities Press.

Federn, P. (1944), A dream under general anesthesia. *Psychiatric Quart.*, 18:422–438.

—— (1952), *Ego Psychology and the Psychoses.* New York: Basic Books.

Fenichel, O. (1926), The appearance in a dream of a lost memory. *Internat. J. Psycho-Anal.*, 7:243–247.

―――― (1939), The economics of pseudologia phantastica. In: *The Collected Papers*. Second series. New York: W. W. Norton, pp. 129–140.

―――― (1945), *The Psychoanalytic Theory of Neurosis*. New York: W. W. Norton.

Ferenczi, S. (1908), The analytic interpretation and treatment of psychosexual impotence. In: *Sex in Psycho-Analysis. Contributions of S. Ferenczi*. New York: Dover Publications, pp. 9–29.

―――― (1913), Stages in the development in the sense of reality. In: *Sex in Psycho-Analysis. Contributions of S. Ferenczi*. New York: Dover Publications, pp. 181–203.

―――― (1914), Discontinuous analysis. In: *Further Contributions to the Theory and Technique of Psycho-Analysis*, compiler J. Rickman. London: Hogarth Press, 1951, pp. 233–235.

―――― (1916), Affektvertauschung im Traume. *Internat. Z. Psychoanal.*, 4:112.

Firestein, S. (1974), Termination of psychoanalysis of adults: A review of the literature. *J. Amer. Psychoanal. Assn.*, 22:873–894.

Fisher, C. (1953), Studies on the nature of suggestion: Part I: Experimental induction of dreams by direct suggestion. Part II: The transference meaning of giving suggestions. *J. Amer. Psychoanal. Assn.*, 1:222–255, 406–437.

―――― (1954), Dreams and perception: The role of preconscious and primary modes of perception in dream formation. *J. Amer. Psychoanal. Assn.*, 2:389–445.

―――― (1956), Dreams, images and perception: A study of unconscious-preconscious relationships. *J. Amer. Psychoanal. Assn.*, 4:5–48.

―――― (1957), A study of the preliminary stages of the construction of dreams and images. *J. Amer. Psychoanal. Assn.*, 5:5–60.

―――― (1958), Quoted in: The psychoanalytic theory of thinking. J. A. Arlow, reporter. *J. Amer. Psychoanal. Assn.*, 6:143–153.

―――― (1965), Psychoanalytic implications of recent research on sleep and dreaming. I. Empirical findings. II. Implications for psychoanalytic theory. *J. Amer. Psychoanal. Assn.*, 13:197–270, 271–303.

―――― (1966), Dreaming and sexuality. In: *Psychoanalysis—A General Psychology. Essays in Honor of Heinz Hartmann*, ed. R. M. Loewenstein, L. M. Newman, M. Schur, & A. J. Solnit. New York: International Universities Press, pp. 537–569.

―――― (1976), Spoken words in dreams: A critique of the views of Otto Isakower. *Psychoanal. Quart.*, 45:100–109.

Fliess, R., Ed. (1948), *The Psycho-Analytic Reader*. New York: International Universities Press.

—————— (1953a), Countertransference and counteridentification. *J. Amer. Psychoanal. Assn.*, 1:268–284.

—————— (1953b), *The Revival of Interest in the Dream*. New York: International Universities Press.

Flugel, J. C. (1939), The examination as initiation rite and anxiety situation. *Internat. J. Psycho-Anal.*, 20:275–286.

Fodor, N. (1945), The negative in dreams. *Psychoanal. Quart.*, 14:516–527.

Frank, A., & Trunnell, E. E. (1978), Conscious dream synthesis as a method of learning about dreaming: A pedagogic experiment. *Psychoanal. Quart.*, 47:103–112.

French, T. M. (1937), Reality testing in dreams. *Psychoanal. Quart.*, 6:62–77.

—————— (1952–1958), *The Integration of Behavior*, Vols. 1–3. Chicago: University of Chicago Press.

—————— Shapiro, L. B. (1949), The use of dream analysis in psychosomatic research. *Psychosom. Med.*, 11:110–112.

Freud, A. (1926–1927a), Introduction to the technique of child analysis. In: *The Psycho-Analytical Treatment of Children*. New York: International Universities Press, 1955.

—————— (1926–1927b), Four lectures on child analysis. *The Writings of Anna Freud*, Vol. 1. New York: International Universities Press, 1974, pp. 1–69.

—————— (1936), The Ego and the Mechanisms of Defense. *The Writings of Anna Freud*, Vol. 2. New York: International Universities Press, 1973.

—————— (1965), *Normality and Pathology in Childhood: Assessments of Development*. New York: International Universities Press.

—————— (1978), Die Bedeutung der Kinderanalyse. *S. Freud House Bull.*, 2:8–12.

Freud, E. L., Ed. (1960), *The Letters of Sigmund Freud*. New York: Basic Books.

Freud, S. (1887–1902), *The Origins of Psychoanalysis*. New York: Basic Books, 1954.

—————— (1888–1892), Papers on hypnotism and suggestion. *Standard Edition*, 1:63–128. London: Hogarth Press, 1966.

—————— (1892–1899), Extracts from the Fliess papers. *Standard Edition*, 1:173–280. London: Hogarth Press, 1966.

—————— (1899), Screen memories. *Standard Edition*, 3:299–322. London: Hogarth Press, 1962.

—————— (1900), The Interpretation of Dreams. *Standard Edition*, 4 & 5. London: Hogarth Press, 1953.

———— (1901a), On dreams. *Standard Edition*, 5:629–686. London: Hogarth Press, 1953.

———— (1901b), Zur Psychopathologie des Alltagslebens. *Gesammelte Werke*, 4. London: Imago Publishing, 1941.

———— (1905a), Jokes and Their Relation to the Unconscious. *Standard Edition*, 8. London: Hogarth Press, 1960.

———— (1905b), Three essays on the theory of sexuality. *Standard Edition*, 7:123–245. London: Hogarth Press, 1953.

———— (1905c), Fragment of an analysis of a case of hysteria. *Standard Edition*, 7:1–122. London: Hogarth Press, 1953.

———— (1907a), Delusions and dreams in Jensen's "Gradiva." *Standard Edition*, 9:1–95. London: Hogarth Press, 1959.

———— (1909), Analysis of a phobia in a 5-year-old boy. *Standard Edition*, 10:5–148. London: Hogarth Press, 1955.

———— (1910a), Leonardo da Vinci and a memory of his childhood. *Standard Edition*, 11:57–137. London: Hogarth Press, 1957.

———— (1910b), The future prospects of psycho-analytic therapy. *Standard Edition*, 11:139–151. London: Hogarth Press, 1957.

———— (1910c), A special type of choice of object made by men (Contributions to the psychology of love I). *Standard Edition*, 11:163–175. London: Hogarth Press, 1957.

———— (1911a), Psycho-analytic notes on an autobiographical account of a case of paranoia (dementia paranoides). *Standard Edition*, 12:1–82. London: Hogarth Press, 1958.

———— (1911b), The handling of dream-interpretation in psychoanalysis. *Standard Edition*, 12:89–96. London: Hogarth Press, 1958.

———— (1912), Recommendations to physicians practising psychoanalysis. *Standard Edition*, 12:109–120. London: Hogarth Press, 1958.

———— (1912–1913), Totem and taboo. *Standard Edition*, 13:(VII–XVI)1–162. London: Hogarth Press, 1955.

———— (1913a), An evidential dream. *Standard Edition*, 12:267–277. London: Hogarth Press, 1958.

———— (1913b), On beginning the treatment. *Standard Edition*, 12:121–144. London: Hogarth Press, 1958.

———— (1913c), Observations and examples from analytic practice. *Standard Edition*, 13:191–198. London: Hogarth Press, 1955.

———— (1914a), On the history of the psycho-analytic movement. *Standard Edition*, 14:1–66. London: Hogarth Press, 1957.

———— (1914b), On narcissism: An introduction. *Standard Edition*, 14:73–102. London: Hogarth Press, 1957.

———— (1915a), Instincts and their vicissitudes. *Standard Edition*, 14:109–140. London: Hogarth Press, 1957.

——— (1915b), The unconscious. *Standard Edition*, 14:159–215. London: Hogarth Press, 1957.

——— (1916a), On transience. *Standard Edition*, 14:303–307. London: Hogarth Press, 1957.

——— (1916b), A connection between a symbol and a symptom. *Standard Edition*, 14:339–340. London: Hogarth Press, 1957.

——— (1916–1917), Introductory Lectures on Psycho-Analysis. *Standard Edition*, 15 & 16. London: Hogarth Press, 1963.

——— (1917a), A metapsychological supplement to the theory of dreams. *Standard Edition*, 14:217–235. London: Hogarth Press, 1957.

——— (1917b), Mourning and melancholia. *Standard Edition*, 14:237–258. London: Hogarth Press, 1957.

——— (1918), From the history of an infantile neurosis. *Standard Edition*, 17:1–122. London: Hogarth Press, 1955.

——— (1919), The "uncanny." *Standard Edition*, 17:217–256. London: Hogarth Press, 1955.

——— (1920), Beyond the pleasure principle. *Standard Edition*, 18:7–64. London: Hogarth Press, 1955.

——— (1921), Group psychology and the analysis of the ego. *Standard Edition*, 18:65–143. London: Hogarth Press, 1955.

——— (1922a), Dreams and telepathy. *Standard Edition*, 18:195–220. London: Hogarth Press, 1955.

——— (1923a), Remarks on the theory and practice of dream-interpretation. *Standard Edition*, 19:107–121. London: Hogarth Press, 1961.

——— (1923b), The Ego and the Id. *Standard Edition*, 19. London: Hogarth Press, 1961.

——— (1925a), An autobiographical study. *Standard Edition*, 20:1–74. London: Hogarth Press, 1959.

——— (1925b), Some additional notes on dream-interpretation as a whole. *Standard Edition*, 19:123–138. London: Hogarth Press, 1961.

——— (1926), Inhibitions, symptoms and anxiety. *Standard Edition*, 20:75–175. London: Hogarth Press, 1959.

——— (1927), Fetishism. *Standard Edition*, 21:147–157. London: Hogarth Press, 1961.

——— (1928), Dostoevsky and parricide. *Standard Edition*, 21:173–196. London: Hogarth Press, 1961.

——— (1929), Letter [in French] to Maxime Leroy on some dreams of Descartes. *Standard Edition*, 21:203–204. London: Hogarth Press, 1961.

——— (1933a), Neue Folge der Vorlesungen zur Einführung in die Psychoanalyse. *Gesammelte Werke,* 15. London: Imago Publishing, 1940.

——— (1933b), New Introductory Lectures on Psycho-Analysis. *Standard Edition,* 22:3–182. London: Hogarth Press, 1964.

——— (1937a), Analysis terminable and interminable. *Standard Edition,* 23:209–253. London: Hogarth Press, 1964.

——— (1937b), Constructions in analysis. *Standard Edition,* 23: 255–269. London: Hogarth Press, 1964.

——— (1940), Splitting of the ego in the process of defence. *Standard Edition,* 23:271–278. London: Hogarth Press, 1964.

——— (1950), *Aus den Anfängen der Psychoanalyse.* Frankfurt M.: S. Fischer, 1962.

——— (1954), The Origins of Psycho-Analysis: Letters to Wilhelm Fliess, Drafts & Notes 1887–1902. New York: Basic Books. (Partly, including: A project for a scientific psychology, in *Standard Edition,* 1.)

Frosch, J., & Ross, N., Ed. (1968), *Annual Survey of Psychoanalysis,* 11. New York: International Universities Press.

Galenson, E. (1978), Examination anxiety in women. *Psychoanal. Quart.,* 49:183–184.

Gandhi, M. (1957), *An Autobiography.* Boston: Beacon Press, Chap. 9.

Garma, A. (1946), The traumatic situation in the genesis of dreams. *Internat. J. Psycho-Anal.,* 27:134–139.

Garma, G. (1955), Vicissitudes of the dream screen and the Isakower phenomena. *Psychoanal. Quart.,* 24:369–382.

Gill, M. M. (1963), Topography and Systems in Psychoanalytic Theory. *Psychological Issues,* Monograph 10. New York: International Universities Press.

——— Brenman, M. (1943), Treatment of a case of anxiety hysteria by a hypnotic technique employing psychoanalytic principles. *Bull. Menninger Clin.,* 5:163–171.

Gitelson, M. (1952), The emotional position of the analyst in the psycho-analytic situation. *Internat. J. Psycho-Anal.,* 33:1–10.

Glover, E. (1950), *Freud or Jung.* New York: W. W. Norton.

——— (1955), *The Technique of Psycho-Analysis.* New York: International Universities Press. Including: Counter-resistance and counter-transference, pp. 88–107; The therapeutic effect of inexact interpretation: A contribution to the theory of suggestion, pp. 353–366.

Goodenough, D. R., Shapiro, A., Holden, M., & Steinschriber, L. (1959), Comparison of dreamers and nondreamers. *J. Abnorm. Soc. Psychol.,* 59:295–302.

Greenacre, P. (1947), Vision, headache and the halo. Reactions to stress in the course of superego formation. *Psychoanal. Quart.*, 16:177–194.

—— (1952), The study of screen memories. In: *Trauma, Growth, Personality*. New York: W. W. Norton.

—— (1956), Re-evaluation of the process of working through. *Internat. J. Psycho-Anal.*, 27:439–444.

—— (1961), A critical digest of the literature on selection of candidates for psychoanalytic training. *Psychoanal. Quart.*, 30:28–55.

Greenberg, R., & Pearlman, C. (1978), If Freud only knew: A reconsideration of psychoanalytic dream theory. *Internat. Rev. Psychoanal.*, 5:71–75.

Greenson, R. R. (1960), Empathy and its vicissitudes. *Internat. J. Psycho-Anal.*, 41:418–424.

—— (1966), That "impossible" profession. *J. Amer. Psychoanal. Assn.*, 14:9–27.

—— (1967), *The Technique and Practice of Psychoanalysis*, Vol. 1. New York: International Universities Press.

Griffiths, R. (1935), *A study of Imagination in Early Childhood*. London: Paul Kegan.

Grimberg, L. (1916), On somnambulism. *Psychoanal. Rev.*, 3:386–390.

Grinstein, A. (1956), The dramatic device: A play within a play. *J. Amer. Psychoanal. Assn.*, 4:49–52.

—— (1956–1975), *The Index of Psychoanalytic Writings*. New York: International Universities Press.

—— (1968), *On Sigmund Freud's Dreams*. Detroit: Wayne State University Press.

Grotjahn, M. (1937), The relation of child analysis to education. *Bull. Menninger Clin.*, 1:184–191.

—— (1938), Dream observations in a two-year-four-months-old-baby. *Psychoanal. Quart.*, 7:507–513.

—— (1940), Ferdinand the Bull. *Amer. Imago*, 1:33–41.

—— (1945), Laughter in dreams. *Psychoanal. Quart.*, 14:221–227.

—— French, T. M. (1938), Akinesia after ventriculography. *Psychoanal. Quart.*, 7:319–328.

Group for the Advancement of Psychiatry (GAP). Committee on Research (1959), Some observations on controls in psychiatric research. New York: GAP, GAP Report No. 42.

Haak, N. (1957), Comments on the analytical situation. *Internat. J. Psycho-Anal.*, 38:183–195.

Hadfield, J. A. (1954), *Dreams and Nightmares*. Baltimore, London: Penguin Books.

Hall, C. S. (1956), Current trends in research on dreams. In: *Progress in Clinical Psychology*, 2:239–257.

Halpern, S. (1964), A classical error in Freud's "The Interpretation of Dreams." *Psychoanal. Quart.*, 33:350–356.

Harley, M. (1962), The role of the dream in the analysis of a latency child. *J. Amer. Psychoanal. Assn.*, 10:271–288.

Hamilton, E. (1940), *Mythology*. New York: Mentor Books.

Hárnik, E. J. (1932), Pleasure in disguise, the need for decoration, and the sense of beauty. *Psychoanal. Quart.*, 1:216–264.

Harris, I. D. (1948), Observations concerning typical anxiety dreams. *Psychiatry*, 11:301–309.

———— (1962), Dreams about the analyst. *Internat. J. Psycho-Anal.*, 43:151–158.

Hartmann, E. (1965), The D-state. *New Eng. J. Med.*, 273:30–35, 87–92.

Hartmann, H. (1947), On rational and irrational action. In: *Psycho-analysis and the Social Sciences*, Vol. 1. New York: International Universities Press, pp. 359–392.

———— (1951), Technical implications of ego psychology. *Psychoanal. Quart.*, 20:31–43.

———— Kris, E., & Loewenstein, R. M. (1953), The function of theory in psychoanalysis. In: *Drives, Affects, Behavior*, ed. R. M. Loewenstein. New York: International Universities Press, pp. 13–37.

Hartocollis, P. (1972), Time as a dimension of affects. *J. Amer. Psychoanal. Assn.*, 20:92–108.

———— (1975), Time and affect in psychopathology. *J. Amer. Psychoanal. Assn.*, 23:383–395.

Heilbrunn, G. (1953), Fusion of the Isakower phenomenon with the dream screen. *Psychoanal. Quart.*, 22:200–204.

Heimann, P. (1950), On counter-transference. *Internat. J. Psycho-Anal.*, 31:81–84.

Hsu, F. L. K. (1949), Suppression versus repression. *Psychiatry*, 12:223–242.

Isakower, O. (1938), A contribution to the patho-psychology of phenomena associated with falling asleep. *Internat. J. Psycho-Anal.*, 19:331–345.

———— (1939), On the exceptional position of the auditory sphere. *Internat. J. Psycho-Anal.*, 20:340–348.

———— (1954), Spoken words in dreams. *Psychoanal. Quart.*, 23:1–6.

Jackson, D. D. (1954), An episode of sleepwalking. *J. Amer. Psychoanal. Assn.*, 2:503–508.

——— (1956), Countertransference and psychotherapy. In: *Progress in Psychotherapy*, ed. F. Fromm-Reichmann & J. L. Moreno. New York: Grune & Stratton, pp. 234–238.

Jacobson, E. (1957), Denial and repression. *J. Amer. Psychoanal. Assn.*, 5:61–92.

James, W. (1890), *The Principles of Psychology*. New York: Henry Holt.

Janis, I. L. (1958), *Psychological Stress*. New York: John Wiley & Sons.

Jarvis, V. (1958), Clinical observations on the visual problem in reading disability. *The Psychoanalytic Study of the Child*, 13:451–470. New York: International Universities Press.

Jones, E. (1931), *On the Nightmare*. London: Hogarth Press, 1949.

——— (1936), The criteria of success in treatment. In: *Papers on Psychoanalysis*. London: Maresfield Reprints, 1977, pp. 379–383.

——— (1953–1957), *The Life and Work of Sigmund Freud*, Vols. 1–3. New York: Basic Books.

——— (1955), *The Life and Work of Sigmund Freud*. New York: Basic Books.

Jones, R. M. (1962), *Ego Synthesis in Dreams*. Cambridge, MA: Schenkman.

Jung, C. G. (1911), *The Psychology of the Unconscious*. New York: Moffat, Yard, 1916.

Kafka, E. (1979), On examination dreams. *Psychoanal. Quart.*, 48:426–447.

Kanzer, M. (1955), The communicative function of the dream. *Internat. J. Psycho-Anal.*, 36:260–266.

——— (1958), Image formation during free association. *Psychoanal. Quart.*, 27:465–484.

——— (1959), The recollection of the forgotten dream. *J. Hillside Hosp.*, 8:74–85.

Kardiner, A., & Spiegel, H. (1947), *War Stress and Neurotic Illness*. New York: Hoever.

Keiser, S. (1962), Disturbance of ego functions of speech and abstract thinking. *J. Amer. Psychoanal. Assn.*, 10:50–73.

Kepecs, J. (1952), A waking screen analogous to the dream screen. *Psychoanal. Quart.*, 21:167–171.

Khan, M. M. R. (1962), Dream psychology and the evolution of the psycho-analytic situation. *Internat. J. Psycho-Anal.*, 43:21–31.

——— (1972), The use and abuse of dream in psychic experience. In: *The Privacy of the Self*. New York: International Universities Press, 1974, pp. 306–315.

——— (1976), The changing use of dreams in psychoanalytic practice. In search of the dreaming experience. *Internat. J. Psycho-Anal.*, 57:325–330.

Kinston, W., & Cohen, J. (1986), Primal repression: Clinical and theoretical aspects. *Internat. J. Psycho-Anal.*, 67:337–355.

Klein, M. (1932), *The Psychoanalysis of Children.* London: Hogarth Press, 1975.

Kleitman, N. (1960), Patterns of dreaming. *Sci. Amer.*, 203:82–88.

Kohut, H. (1971), *The Analysis of the Self.* New York: International Universities Press.

Kris, E. (1950a), Introduction. In: *Aus den Anfängen der Psychoanalyse*, by S. Freud. London: Imago Publishing, 1962.

——— (1950b), On preconscious mental process. *Psychoanal. Quart.*, 19:540–560.

——— (1950c), The significance of Freud's earliest discoveries. *Internat. J. Psycho-Anal.*, 31:108–116.

——— (1952), *Psychoanalytic Explorations in Art.* New York: International Universities Press.

——— (1956a), The recovery of childhood memories in psychoanalysis. *The Psychoanalytic Study of the Child*, 11:54–88. New York: International Universities Press.

——— (1956b), On some vicissitudes of insight in psychoanalysis. *Internat. J. Psycho-Anal.*, 37:445–455.

Kubie, L. S. (1937), Resolution of a traffic phobia in conversations between a father and son. *Psychoanal. Quart.*, 6:223–226.

——— (1945), The use of induced hypnagogic reveries in the recovery of repressed amnesic data. *Bull. Menninger Clin.*, 7:172–182.

——— (1958), *Neurotic Distortion of the Creative Process.* Lawrence, KS: University of Kansas Press.

——— (1966), A reconsideration of thinking, the dream process, and "the dream." *Psychoanal. Quart.*, 35:191–198.

——— (1968), Unsolved problems in the resolution of the transference. *Psychoanal. Quart.*, 37:331–352.

Laforgue, R. (1930), On the erotization of anxiety. *Internat. J. Psycho-Anal.*, 11:312–321.

Lampl-de Groot, J. (1952), Re-evaluation of the role of the Oedipus complex. *Internat. J. Psycho-Anal.*, 33:335–342.

Langer, M. (1952), Dos suenos de analistas. (Two dreams of analysts.) *Rev. Psicoanal.*, 9:355–358.

Leach, M. (1949), *Standard Dictionary of Folklore, Mythology, Legend.* New York: Funk & Wagnalls.

Levine, M. (1952), Principles of psychiatric treatment. In: *Dynamic Psychiatry*, ed. F. Alexander & H. Ross. Chicago: University of Chicago Press, 1957, pp. 307–366.

Lewin, B. D. (1946a), Countertransference in medical practice. *Psychosom. Med.*, 8:195–199.

—— (1946b), Sleep, the mouth, and the dream screen. *Psychoanal. Quart.*, 15:419–434.

—— (1948), Inferences from the dream screen. *Internat. J. Psycho-Anal.*, 29:224–231.

—— (1950), *The Psychoanalysis of Elation.* New York: W. W. Norton.

—— (1952), Phobic symptoms and dream interpretation. *Psychoanal. Quart.*, 21:295–322.

—— (1953a), The forgetting of dreams. In: *Drives, Affects, Behavior*, ed. R. M. Loewenstein. New York: International Universities Press, pp. 191–202.

—— (1953b), Reconsideration of the dream screen. *Psychoanal. Quart.*, 22:174–199.

—— (1954), Sleep, narcissistic neurosis and the analytic situation. *Psychoanal. Quart.*, 23:487–510.

—— (1958), *Dreams and the Uses of Regression.* Freud Anniversary Lecture. New York: International Universities Press.

—— (1968), *The Image and the Past.* New York: International Universities Press.

—— Ross, H. (1960), *Psychoanalytic Education in the United States.* New York: W. W. Norton.

Lewis, H. A. (1957), The unconscious castrative significance of tooth extraction. *J. Dent. for Children*, 24:3–16.

Lewis, H. B. (1959), Organization of the self as reflected in manifest dreams. *Psychoanal. Rev.*, 46:21–35.

Linn, L. (1954), Color in dreams. *J. Amer. Psychoanal. Assn.*, 2:462–465.

Lipschutz, L. S. (1954), The written dream. *J. Amer. Psychoanal. Assn.*, 2:473–478.

Little, M. (1951), Counter-transference and the patient's response to it. *Internat. J. Psycho-Anal.*, 32:32–40.

—— (1957), "R"—The analyst's total response to his patient's needs. *Internat. J. Psycho-Anal.*, 38:240–254.

Loewald, H. W. (1966), Review of J. A. Arlow & C. Brenner (1964), *Psychoanalytic Concepts and the Structural Theory. Psychoanal. Quart.*, 35:430–436.

—— (1978), The waning of the Oedipus complex. In: *Papers on Psychoanalysis.* New Haven: Yale University Press, pp. 383–404.

Loewenstein, R. M. (1949), A posttraumatic dream. *Psychoanal. Quart.*, 8:449–454.

—— (1951), The problem of interpretation. *Psychoanal. Quart.*, 20:1–14.

—— (1954), Some remarks on defences, autonomous ego and psycho-analytic technique. *Internat. J. Psycho-Anal.*, 35:188–193.

Lorand, S. (1948), On the meaning of losing teeth in dreams. *Psychoanal. Quart.*, 17:529–530.

Luborsky, L., & Shevrin, H. (1956), Dreams and day-residues: A study of the Poetzl observation. *Bull. Menninger Clin.*, 20:135–148.

Luria, A. (1989), A dictionary for deconstructors. *New York Review of Books*, XXXVI:18, Nov. 28, 1989.

Mack, J. (1965), Nightmares, conflicts and ego development in childhood. *Internat. J. Psycho-Anal.*, 46:403–428.

Mahler, M. S. (1968), *On Human Symbiosis and the Vicissitudes of Individuation*, Vol. 1. New York: International Universities Press.

Mahoney, P. J. (1977), Towards a formalist approach to dreams. *Internat. Rev. Psychoanal.*, 4:83–98.

Marcinowski, J. (1921), Two confinement dreams of a pregnant woman. *Internat. J. Psycho-Anal.*, 2:432–434.

McDowell, M. (1948), An abrupt cessation of a major neurotic symptom following an hypnotically induced artificial conflict. *Bull. Menninger Clin.*, 7:168–177.

McLaughlin, J. T. (1961), The analyst and the hippocratic oath. *J. Amer. Psychoanal. Assn.*, 9:106–123.

Medlicott, R. W. (1958), An inquiry into the significance of hallucinations with special reference to their occurrence in the sane. *Internat. Record of Med.*, 171:664–677.

Menninger, K. (1958), Transference and countertransference. In: *Theory of Psychoanalytic Technique*. New York: Basic Books, pp. 77–98.

Meyers, W. A. (1976), Imaginary companions, fantasy twins, mirror dreams and depersonalization. *Psychoanal. Quart.*, 45:503–524.

Miller, I. (1965), On the return of symptoms in the terminal phase of psycho-analysis. *Internat. J. Psycho-Anal.*, 46:487–501.

Mittelmann, B. (1945), Psychoanalytic observations on dreams and psychosomatic reactions in response to hypnotics and anesthetics. *Psychoanal. Quart.*, 14:498–510.

——— (1949), Ego functions and dreams. *Psychoanal. Quart.*, 18:434–448.

Money-Kyrle, R. E. (1956), Normal counter-transference and some of its deviations. *Internat. J. Psycho-Anal.*, 37:360–366.

Mullan, H. (1955), Transference and countertransference: New horizons. *Internat. J. Group Psychother.*, 5:169–180.

Nacht, S. (1957), Technical remarks on the handling of the transference neurosis. *Internat. J. Psycho-Anal.*, 38:196–203.

Nunberg, H. (1948), *Practice and Theory of Psychoanalysis*. New York: Nervous & Mental Disease Monographs.

———— (1949), *Problems of Bisexuality as Reflected in Circumcision*. London: Imago Publishing.

———— (1951), Transference and reality. *Internat. J. Psycho-Anal.*, 32:1–9.

———— (1954), Evaluation of the results of psycho-analytic treatment. *Internat. J. Psycho-Anal.*, 35:2–7.

———— (1955), *Principles of Psychoanalysis*. New York: International Universities Press.

———— Federn, E., Eds. (1974), *Minutes of the Vienna Psychoanalytic Society*, Vol. 3. New York: International Universities Press.

Oremland, J. (1973), A specific dream during the termination phase of successful psychoanalyses. *J. Amer. Psychoanal. Assn.*, 21:285–302.

Orr, S. W. (1954), Transference and countertransference: A historical survey. *J. Amer. Psychoanal. Assn.*, 2:621–670.

Ostow, M. (1960), The psychic function of depression: A study in energetics. *Psychoanal. Quart.*, 29:355–394.

Peck, J. S. (1961), Dreams and interruptions in the treatment. *Psychoanal. Quart.*, 30:209–220.

Pfister, O. (1930), Schockdenken und Shockphantasien bei höchster Todesgefahr. *Internat. Z. Psychoanal.*, 16:430–455.

Piaget, J. (1951), *Play, Dreams and Imitation in Childhood*. New York: W. W. Norton.

———— (1955), *The Language and Thought of the Child*. New York: Meridian Press.

Plesch, E. (1951), A Rorschach study of rosacea and morbid blushing. *Brit. J. Med. Psychol.*, 24:202–205.

Psychoanalytic Quarterly. Cumulative Index. Vols. 1–35, (1932–1966), New York: The Psychoanalytic Quarterly, Inc., 1969.

Pulver, S. E. (1987), The manifest dream in psychoanalysis: A clarification. *J. Amer. Psychoanal. Assn.*, 35:99–118.

Racker, H. (1953), A contribution to the problem of counter-transference. *Internat. J. Psycho-Anal.*, 34:313–324.

———— (1957), The meanings and uses of countertransference. *Psychoanal. Quart.*, 26:303–357.

———— (1958), Counterresistance and interpretation. *J. Amer. Psychoanal. Assn.*, 6:215–221.

Radó, S., Grinker, R. R., & Alexander, F. (1963), Editorial. American Medical Association (AMA). *Arch. Gen. Psychiat.*, 8:527–529.

Rangell, L. (1956), Panel report. The dream in the practice of psychoanalysis. *J. Amer. Psychoanal. Assn.*, 4:122–137.

Rank, O. (1924a), *Eine Neurosenanalyse in Träumen*. Vienna: Internat. Psychoanal. Verlag.

—— (1924b), *Das Trauma der Geburt.* Vienna: Internat. Psychoanal. Verlag.

Rapaport, D., & Gill, M. M. (1959), The points of view and assumptions of metapsychology. *Internat. J. Psycho-Anal.,* 40:153–162.

Rappaport, E. A. (1959), The first dream in an erotized transference. *Internat. J. Psycho-Anal.,* 40:240–245.

Reich, A. (1950), On the termination of analysis. In: *Psychoanalytic Contributions.* New York: International Universities Press, 1973, pp. 121–135.

—— (1951), On counter-transference. *Internat. J. Psycho-Anal.,* 32:25–31.

—— (1960a), Pathologic forms of self-esteem regulation. *The Psychoanalytic Study of the Child,* 15:215–232. New York: International Universities Press.

—— (1960b), Further remarks on counter-transference. *Internat. J. Psycho-Anal.,* 41:389–395.

Reich, W. (1925), *Der triebhafte Character.* Vienna: Internat. Psychoanal. Verlag.

Reik, T. (1935), *Surprise and the Psychoanalyst.* New York: E. P. Dutton, 1937.

—— (1952), *Listening with the Third Ear.* New York: Farrar Straus.

Renik, O. (1978), The role of attention in depersonalization. *Psychoanal. Quart.,* 47:588–605.

Robbins, W. (1975), Panel report. Termination: Problems and technique. *J. Amer. Psychoanal. Assn.,* 23:166–176.

Róheim, G. (1920), Die Urszene im Traume. *Internat. Z. Psychoanal.,* 6:337–339.

—— (1945), Aphrodite, or the woman with a penis. *Psychoanal. Quart.,* 14:350–390.

—— (1952), *The Gates of the Dream.* New York: International Universities Press.

Rosen, J. N. (1953), *Direct Analysis.* New York: Grune & Stratton.

Rosen, V. H. (1950), The role of denial in acute postoperative affective reactions following removal of body parts. *Psychosom. Med.,* 12:356–361.

—— (1960), Some aspects of the role of imagination in the analytic process. *J. Amer. Psychoanal. Assn.,* 8:229–251.

Ross, W. D., & Brissenden, A. (1961), Some observations on the emotional position of the group psychotherapist. *Psychiat. Quart.,* 35:516–522.

Roth, N. (1952), The acting out of transference. *Psychoanal. Rev.,* 29:69–78.

—— (1954), Sublimation in dreams. *Amer. J. Psychother.*, 8:32–42.

—— (1958), Manifest dream content and acting out. *Psychoanal. Quart.*, 27:547–554.

Rubenstein, R., Katz, J., & Newman, R. (1957), On the sources and determinants of hypnotic dreams. *J. Can. Psychiat. Assn.*, 2:154–161.

Rycroft, C. (1951), A contribution to the study of the dream screen. *Internat. J. Psycho-Anal.*, 32:178–184.

Sachs, H. (1924), The community of daydreams. In: *The Creative Unconscious. Studies in the Psychoanalysis of Art by Hanns Sachs*, ed. A. A. Roback. Cambridge, MA: Sci-Art Publ., 1951, pp. 11–54.

Sadger, J. (1920), *Sleepwalking and Moon Walking.* New York: Nervous & Mental Diseases.

Santayana, G. (1905–1906), *Life of Reason*, Vol. 1. New York: Charles Scribner's Sons, 1922.

Saul, L. J. (1940), Utilization of early current dreams in formulating psychoanalytic cases. *Psychoanal. Quart.*, 9:453–469.

—— (1956), The dream in the practice of psychoanalysis. L. Rangell, reporter. *J. Amer. Psychoanal. Assn.*, 4:122–137.

—— (1958), *Technique and Practice of Psychoanalysis.* Philadelphia: J. B. Lippincott.

—— (1972), *Psychodynamically Based Psychotherapy.* New York: Science House.

—— Sheppard, E. (1956), An attempt to quantify emotional forces using manifest dreams: A preliminary study. *J. Amer. Psychoanal. Assn.*, 4:486–502.

Savitt, R. A. (1960), On the undisguised dream about the analyst. Presented at the midwinter meeting of the American Psychoanalytic Association, New York.

Schafer, R. (1954), *Psychoanalytic Interpretation in Rorschach Testing.* New York: Grune & Stratton.

Schilder, P. (1942), *Mind, Perception and Thought in Their Constructive Aspects.* New York: Columbia University Press.

Schneck, J. M. (1947), The role of the dream in treatment with hypnosis. *Psychoanal. Rev.*, 34:485–491.

Schorske, C. (1974), Politics and patricice in Freud's "The Interpretation of Dreams." *Annual Psychoanal.*, 2:40–60.

Schrötter, K. (1912), Experimentelle Träume. *Zentralblatt f. Psychoanal.*, 2:638–646.

Schur, H. (1966), An observation and comments on the development of memory. *The Psychoanalytic Study of the Child*, 21:468–479. New York: International Universities Press.

Schur, M. (1966a), Some additional "day residues" of "The specimen dream of psychoanalysis." In: *Psychoanalysis—A General Psychology*, ed. R. M. Loewenstein, L. M. Newman, M. Schur, & A. J. Solnit. New York: International Universities Press, pp. 45–85.

——— (1966b), *The Id and the Regulatory Principles of Mental Functioning*. New York: International Universities Press.

Segal, H. (1964), *Introduction to the Work of Melanie Klein*. New York: Basic Books.

Selinsky, H. (1939), Psychological study of the migrainous syndrome. *Bull. NY Acad. Med.*, 5:757.

Sharpe, E. F. (1937), *Dream Analysis*. London: Hogarth Press.

Sheppard, E., & Saul, L. J. (1958), An approach to a systematic study of ego function. *Psychoanal. Quart.*, 27:237–245.

Shevrin, H., & Luborsky, L. (1958), The measurement of preconscious perception in dreams and images: An investigation of the Poetzl phenomenon. *J. Abnorm. Soc. Psychol.*, 56:285–294.

Siebenthal, W. von (1953), *Die Wissenschaft vom Traum*. Berlin: Springer.

Silberer, H. (1909), Bericht über eine Methode gewisse symbolische Halluzinations-Erscheinungen hervorzurufen und zu beobachten. *Jahrb. f. psychopath. u. psychoanal. Forschungen*, 1:513–525.

——— (1912), Symbolik des Erwachens und Schwellensymbolik überhaupt. *Jahrb. f. psychopath. u. psychoanal. Forschungen*, 3:621–660.

Silverberg, W. V. (1948), The concept of transference. *Psychoanal. Quart.*, 17:303–321.

Slavson, S. R., et al. (1953), Symposium on countertransference. *Internat. J. Psychother.*, 3:355–452.

Sloane, P. (1975), The significance of the manifest dream: Its use and misuse. *J. Phil. Assn. Psychoanal.*, 2:57–78.

Smith, S. (1977), The golden fantasy: A regressive reaction to separation anxiety. *Internat. J. Psycho-Anal.*, 58:311–324.

Spanjaard, J. (1969), The manifest dream content and its significance for the interpretation of dreams. *Internat. J. Psycho-Anal.*, 50:221–235.

Spitz, R. A. (1956), Countertransference: Comments on its varying role in the analytic situation. *J. Amer. Psychoanal. Assn.*, 4:256–265.

——— (1965), *The First Year of Life*. New York: International Universities Press.

——— Wolf, K. M. (1949), Autoerotism. Some empirical findings and hypotheses on three of its manifestations in the first year of life. *The Psychoanalytic Study of the Child*, 3–4:85–120. New York: International Universities Press.

Stein, M. H. (1961), Trauma and dream. Paper presented to the meeting of the New York Psychoanalytic Society, February 28th. Abstracted by I. Solomon. *Psychoanal. Quart.*, 30:474–476.

——— (1965), States of consciousness in the analytic situation: Including a note on the traumatic dream. In: *Drives, Affects, Behavior*, Vol. 2, ed. M. Schur. New York: International Universities Press, pp. 60–86.

Steiner, M. (1937), The dream symbolism of the analytic situation. *Internat. J. Psycho-Anal.*, 18:294–305.

Sterba, E. (1949), Analysis of psychogenic constipation in a two-year-old child. *The Psychoanalytic Study of the Child*, 3–4:227–252. New York: International Universities Press.

Sterba, R. (1927), Über latente negative übertragung. *Internat. Z. Psychoanal.*, 13:160–165.

——— (1946), Dreams and acting out. *Psychoanal. Quart.*, 15:175–179.

Sterba, R. F. (1990), Analysis without apparent resistance. *Internat. J. Psycho-Anal.*, 71:107–111.

Stern, A. (1921), Some remarks on a dream. *Internat. J. Psycho-Anal.*, 2:427–429.

Stern, M. M. (1951), Pavor nocturnus. *Internat. J. Psycho-Anal.*, 32:302–309.

——— (1953), Trauma and symptom formation. *Internat. J. Psycho-Anal.*, 34:202–218.

——— (1961), Blank hallucinations: Remarks about trauma and perceptual disturbances. *Internat. J. Psycho-Anal.*, 42:205–215.

Stewart, W. A. (1967), Comments on the manifest content of certain types of unusual dreams. *Psychoanal. Quart.*, 36:329–341.

Stone, L. (1947), Transference sleep in a neurosis with duodenal ulcer. *Internat. J. Psycho-Anal.*, 28:18–32.

Strachey, J. (1953), Editor's introduction to *The Interpretation of Dreams. Standard Edition*, 4. London: Hogarth Press, 1953, pp. 11–12.

Szasz, T. S. (1956), On the experiences of the analyst in the psychoanalytic situation: A contribution to the theory of treatment. *J. Amer. Psychoanal. Assn.*, 4:197–223.

Tarachow, S. (1945), A psychosomatic theory based on the concepts of mastery and resolution of tension. *Psychoanal. Rev.*, 32:163–180.

Tauber, E. S. (1954), Exploring the therapeutic use of countertransference data. *Psychiatry*, 17:331–336.

Tausk, V. (1924), A contribution to the psychology of child-sexuality. *Internat. J. Psycho-Anal.*, 5:343–357.

Thompson, C. M. (1956), The role of the analyst's personality in therapy. *Amer. J. Psychother.*, 10:347–367.

—— (1958), A study of the emotional climate of psychoanalytic institutes. *Psychiatry*, 21:45–51.

Thorner, H. A. (1955), Three defences against inner persecution. In: *New Directions in Psychoanalysis*, ed. M. Klein, P. Heimann, & R. E. Money-Kyrle. London: Tavistock, pp. 282–306.

Tower, L. E. (1956), Countertransference. *J. Amer. Psychoanal. Assn.*, 4:224–255.

Velikovsky, I. (1941), The dreams Freud dreamed. *Psychoanal. Rev.*, 28:487–511.

Waelder, R. (1933), The psychoanalytic theory of play. *Psychoanal. Quart.*, 2:208–224.

—— (1936), The principle of multiple function: Observations on over-determination. *Psychoanal. Quart.*, 5:45–62.

—— (1937), The problem of the genesis of psychical conflict in earliest infancy. *Internat. J. Psycho-Anal.*, 18:406–473.

Waldhorn, H. F., reporter (1967), *Indications for Psychoanalysis: The Place of the Dream in Clinical Psychoanalysis.* Monograph 2 of the Kris Study Group of the New York Psychoanalytic Institute, ed. E. D. Joseph. New York: International Universities Press.

Wallace, A. F. C. (1958), Dreams and wishes of the soul: A type of psychoanalytic theory among the seventeenth century Iroquois. *Amer. Anthrop.*, 60:234–248.

—— (1970), *The Death and Rebirth of the Seneca.* New York: Knopf.

Wangh, M. (1954), Day residue in dream and myth. *J. Amer. Psychoanal. Assn.*, 2:446–452.

Ward, C. H. (1961), Some further thoughts on the examination dream. *Psychiatry*, 24:324–336.

—— Beck, A. T., & Rascoe, E. (1961), Typical dreams: Incidence among psychiatric patients. *Arch. Gen. Psychiat.*, 5:606–615.

Weigert, E. (1954), Counter-transference and self-analysis of the psycho-analyst. *Internat. J. Psycho-Anal.*, 35:242–246.

Weiss, E. (1948), Some dynamic aspects of dreams. In: *The Yearbook of Psychoanalysis*, 5:128–145, ed. S. Lorand. New York: International Universities Press, 1949.

Weiss, J. (1952), Crying at the happy ending. *Psychoanal. Rev.*, 39:338.

Wheelis, A. (1958), *The Quest for Identity.* New York: W. W. Norton.

Whitman, R. M. (1963), Remembering and forgetting dreams in psychoanalysis. *J. Amer. Psychoanal. Assn.*, 11:752–774.

—— Kramer, M., & Baldridge, B. J. (1963a), Which dream does the patient tell? *Arch. Gen. Psychiat.*, 8:277–282.

—— Pierce, C. M., Maas, J. W., & Baldridge, B. J. (1962), The dreams of the experimental subject. *J. Nerv. Ment. Dis.*, 134:431–439.

—— —— —— (1963b), An experimental study of the supervision of psychotherapy. *Arch. Gen. Psychiat.*, 9:529–535.

Winnicott, D. W. (1971), *Therapeutic Consultations in Child Psychiatry*. London: Hogarth Press.

Wisdom, J. O. (1949), A hypothesis to explain trauma-reenactment dreams. *Internat. J. Psycho-Anal.*, 30:13–20.

Wittgenstein, L. (1966), Lectures and conversations on aesthetics. In: *Psychology and Religious Belief*, ed. C. Barrett. Berkeley: University of California Press.

Wolberg, L. R. (1945), *Hypnoanalysis*. New York: Grune & Stratton.

—— (1948), *Medical Hypnosis*, Vols. 1 & 2. New York: Grune & Stratton.

Wolf, S., & Wolff, H. G. (1943), *Human Gastric Function*. London: Oxford University Press.

"Wolf-man" (1957), Letters pertaining to Freud's "History of an infantile neurosis" (1926), trans. B. D. Lewin. *Psychoanal. Quart.*, 26:449–460.

Wolpert, E. A., & Trosman, H. (1958), Studies in the psychophysiology of dreams: 1. Experimental evocation of sequential dream episodes. *AMA Arch. Neurol. Psychiat.*, 79:603–606.

Wolstein, B. (1959), *Countertransference*. New York: Grune & Stratton.

Wright, S. (1937), *Applied Physiology*. New York: Oxford University Press.

Zilboorg, G. (1930), Affective reintegration of schizophrenias. *Arch. Neurol. Psychiat.*, 24:335–345.

—— (1951), Psychoanalytic concepts of sleep and dream. In: *Problems of Consciousness*, ed. H. A. Abramson. New York: Corles, Macy, pp. 62–68.

—— (1952), Some sidelights on free associations. *Internat. J. Psycho-Anal.*, 33:489–495.

NAME INDEX

SUBJECT INDEX

Acoustic images, 526–527
Acting out, 112
  in falling dream patients, 251–252, 254
  manifest dream content and, 381–382, 411–417
  superego and, 413–414
  tantrumlike, 636–637
  in writing dreams, 477, 490
Active mastery, 236–237, 238–239. *See also* Mastery
  in posttraumatic dream, 312
  repetition compulsion in, 312–313
Adaptive capacities, loss of, 413, 414
Addictions, projection in, 45*n*
Aesculapius, sleep temples of, 331
Aesthetic reveries, 525
Affect
  on couch, 98
  flooding, 180
  in hypnotic dream, 673–674
  time and, 458–462
Affect experience, 191
Afterworld, journey in, 277–278
Aggression, in patients with falling vs. attacked dreams, 251–256
Aggressive fantasies, 639–642
Aggressive impulses, defense against, 431–432
Allegory, quasi, 670–671
Amenorrhea, termination of, after dream interpretation, 563–566
Amputation, dreams in, 227–228, 241–242
Anal defiance, 468–469
Anal penis, 492
Analysis-formation, xvii
Analyst. *See also* Therapist-patient relationship
  at border of dream, 103–104
  in dream metapsychology, 98–105

dreams about patients by, 537–562, 555–558
first dream directly representing, 496–510
as interpreter, 100–101
as parent, 496–497
visual imagery of, 525–536
Analytic formation, 185
Anesthesia
  dreams and, 240
  dreams under, 219–244
  ego role in, 242
  sleep induced by, 218–219
Anger, release of, 252
Anna O case, 104
  resistance in, 96–97
Anticipation, sense of, 460
Anxiety
  about future event, 300
  about presenting dreams, 160
  attempt to master, 315, 716–717
  binding of, 230
  with different developmental levels, 580–581
  examination, 296–299. *See also* Examination dream
  over hysterectomy, 232–236
  primal scene dream and, 26–28
  in writing down dreams, 481
Anxiety dream, 8–12. *See also* Examination dream
  causes of arrested maturation and, 263–272
  characterological significance of, 245–273
  defensiveness and, 259–261
  explanation of, 402–403
  of normal vs. disturbed patients, 246
  stereotyped, 176
  teeth in, 469–470
  typical, 196–197

1995